£5

Food Engineering in a Computer Climate

Institution of Chemical Engineers, Rugby, UK

Hemisphere Publishing Corporation
A Member of the Taylor & Francis Group
New York   Philadelphia   London

Food Engineering in a Computer Climate

Members of the Institution of Chemical Engineers
should order as follows:

Worldwide Institution of Chemical Engineers,
Davis Building,
165–171 Railway Terrace, RUGBY,
Warwickshire CV21 3HQ, UK

Non-members' orders should be directed as follows:

UK, Eire and Institution of Chemical Engineers,
Australia Davis Building,
165–171 Railway Terrace, RUGBY,
Warwickshire CV21 3HQ, UK

or Taylor & Francis Ltd, Rankine Road, BASINGSTOKE,
Hampshire RG24 0PR, UK

USA Taylor & Francis Inc., 1900 Frost Road, Suite 101, Bristol,
PA 19007, USA

Rest of the World Taylor & Francis Ltd, Rankine Road, BASINGSTOKE,
Hampshire RG24 0PR, UK

Library of Congress Cataloging-in-Publication Data
Food engineering in a computer climate: a three day symposium organised by the
Institution of Chemical Engineers' Food and Drink Subject Group on behalf of the EFCE
Food Working Party and held at St. John's College, Cambridge, 30 March–1 April 1992.
p. cm. — (Symposium series/Institution of Chemical Engineers; no. 126) (EFCE
publication; no. 88)
"EFCE event no. 452." Includes bibliographical references and index.
ISBN 0–85295–279–1 (Institution of Chemical Engineers). — ISBN 1–56032–255–1
(Hemisphere)
1. Food industry and trade — Data processing — Congresses. I. Institution of Chemical
Engineers (Great Britain). Food and Drink Subject Group. II. EFCE Food Working Party. III.
Series: Symposium series (Institution of Chemical Engineers (Great Britain)); no. 126. IV.
Series: EFCE publication series; no. 88.
TP370.5.F663   1992
664' .00285 — dc20   92–14499
                                                               CIP

Food Engineering in a Computer Climate

A three day symposium organised by the Institution of Chemical Engineers' Food and Drink Subject Group on behalf of the EFCE Food Working Party and held at St John's College, Cambridge 30 March–1 April 1992.

Technical Programme Committee

W. Hamm (Co-Chairman)	Consultant
S.D. Holdsworth (Co-Chairman)	*Formerly* Campden Food and Drink Research Association
P.J. Fryer	University of Cambridge
A. Graßhoff	Bundesanstalt für Milchforschung, Germany
A.P.M. Hasting	Unilever Research
R. Jowitt	King's College, London
D.L. Pyle	University of Reading

Corresponding Members

J.-J. Bimbenet	ENSIA, France
S. Bruin	Unilever Research Laboratorium Vlaardingen, The Netherlands
P. Linko	Helsinki University of Technology, Finland
B.M. McKenna	University College Dublin, Eire

INSTITUTION OF CHEMICAL ENGINEERS

SYMPOSIUM SERIES No. 126
EFCE Event No. 452
EFCE Publication No. 88
ISBN 0 85295 279 1

Printed in Great Britain by BPCC Wheatons Ltd, Exeter

Preface

This conference was organised on behalf of the Food Working Party of the European Federation of Chemical Engineering by the Food and Drink Subject Group of the Institution of Chemical Engineers. The European aspect was considered to be very important in relation to the development of trade within the European Economic Community at this particular time.

The topic for the symposium was chosen because of the importance of the subject to the future development of the food industry. Two particular themes dominate the proceedings, viz the degree of applicability of various computer techniques and possibilities for future developments.

The first section of this book deals with simulation and modelling applications to food processes and shows the success achieved by the various research workers in this important and rapidly expanding area. The next section deals with applications of computers to process design in which the emphasis is on effective design techniques, computer integrated management and automation. An important aspect of the symposium was to highlight the limits of applicability of computers and for this purpose a section on product safety was included. The contributions presented in the final sections are concerned with the application of computers in process control and instrumentation, outlining their role in food safety and the procedures required to achieve continued public confidence in processed foods.

The proceedings of this symposium link developments in research with industrial application, and as can be seen a significant number of papers come from the industrial sector. The organisers have been particularly keen that the contributions should illustrate the application of computers to solving the practical problems of the food industry. The opportunities available to the industry as well as its future requirements are fully documented and it is hoped the contents of the papers presented in this volume will act as a stimulus to future research and development.

Donald Holdsworth
(Co-Chairman)

Contents

Papers
Modelling

Process Design

Product Safety

Process Control

Posters

Modelling

Biotechnology

Process Design

Product Safety

Process Control

Errata

Paper 4 (page 47): Modelling the effect of heated-air drying of grains on their quality for bread baking and for seed (D.M. Bruce and M.E. Nellist).
Equation (9) on page 52 should read:

$$-\frac{dV_r}{dt} = V_r \ \exp \ (140 + 41.4M_s - 427000/(RT_s))$$

Paper 5 (page 57): Modelling and simulation of a glucose-fructose simulated moving-bed adsorber (M.L. Lameloise and V. Viard).
(i) Page 59, line 11, should read 'by fitting the theoretical curve', not 'by fitting the experimental curve'.
(ii) Page 61, line 23, should read 'enables different configurations', not 'unables different configurations'.
(iii) Page 62, line 11, should read 'c_N (1, j+1)', not 'c_N (i, j+1)'.

SIMULATION OF FOOD PROCESSES WITH UNCERTAIN DATA

W R Johns[1]

A simple consistent framework is introduced for simulating complete processes in a flowsheeting environment. An example of the application of the method to the thermal processing of canned food is presented. A quadrature integration procedure is introduced to predict the uncertainty in product quality as a function of the uncertainty in raw material and process characteristics. It is shown that the method gives results equivalent to those obtained by Monte Carlo simulation at least an order of magnitude faster.

1 INTRODUCTION

The food industry is subject to pressures both to provide food that is more "natural" and less processed, and to provide food with even higher levels of safety. There is also continuing pressure to reduce energy usage and effluent production to meet both environmental and economic goals. One of the responses to these challenges is to develop an enhanced simulation capability which can be used both to develop closer on-line control and to design new more effective and economic processes.

Because the food industry is dealing with natural raw materials which exhibit variability in chemical and physical properties, any simulation must also estimate the uncertainty in the predicted output from the process.

Simulation under uncertainty is traditionally approached using discrete dynamic (Monte Carlo) methods. These methods are particulary appropriate when simulating discrete random events. Examples of such events are failure of equipment items or process services, or semi-predictable supplies of raw materials. This methodology has been extensively covered in the Operational Research literature and has been applied in the Food Industry. It will not be covered in this paper. In this paper, we are concerned with the simulation of processes in which there is a continuous functional relationship between inputs and outputs. This relationship may also depend on properties over which there is limited direct control and which may vary randomly. We consider both steady-state and time-varying processes. It should be emphasised that the simulation capability described in this paper is complementary to discrete dynamic simulation and both may be used

---

[1]Intera Information Technologies Ltd, Environmental Division, Henley-on-Thames

together. For example, discrete event simulation may be used to model failure and repair of the feed belt to a hydrostatic cooker where continuous simulation would be used to estimate the effect of such interruptions on product quality.

In Section 2, the approach to simulation of continuous processes without data uncertainty is introduced. As a specific example of the approach, a model for the thermal processing of canned food is developed. As a stand-alone model, it is shown that it is as robust as the best finite difference methods but is a small factor slower. The benefit comes in multi-unit simulation where a general method of extending the gridding of finite difference methods to whole processes is not available. As an elementary step towards the simulation of whole processes, the heat treatment of a can is simulated. The simulation easily handles interfaces between different materials both at the boundary of and within the can.

In Section 3, we introduce a theoretical basis for handling uncertainty by a quadrature integration and a number of formulae are presented for predicting the combined effect of several uncertainties on product characteristics. The procedure differs from Monte Carlo integration in that specific values of the uncertain variables are selected for simulation rather than randomly selected values. The benefit is that many fewer simulations are required. The method is applied to the thermal processing of a canned food to illustrate the simulation of processes with uncertain data.

2 SIMULATION OF FOOD PROCSSES

There are a wide range of simulation systems available for chemical processes. The majority of simulation systems aim to predict "stream vectors", which define the flow rate of each component in each process stream together with the corresponding temperatures, pressures and enthalpy fluxes. Food processes differ from most chemical processes because the streams are not defined by simple lists of components, because there are relatively few process units, and because the simulation of conditions within the units dominates over the problem of determining the conditions between units. For food processes, a simulation system is needed that allows complete flexibility between stream types and solves the equations within units and between units as a single consistent set. Two such systems are Flowpack II [1, 2] and Speed-Up [3]. The former was designed primarily to solve algebraic equations (for steady-state simulation) and the latter to solve differential equations (for dynamic simulation). Both systems are, however, capable of both steady state and dynamic simulation.

This paper describes a method that enables an algebraic equation based system (such as Flowpack II) to be used for dynamic simulation of food processes. The principles developed are, however, equally applicable to a number of other flowsheeting environments [4]. The basis of the method is as follows:

(i) The conditions at time t are defined;

(ii) From the conditions at time t, the derivatives $(\partial X/\partial t)$ with respect to time are calculated;

(iii) An estimate of conditions at time $(t + \delta t)$ is made;

(iv) From (iii), $\partial X/\partial t$ at time $(t + \delta t)$ is calculated;

(v) From (ii) and (iv), a mean rate of change over the time period is estimated $(\delta X/\delta t)$;

(vi) Conditions at time $(t + \delta t)$ are re-estimated from conditions at t plus $(\delta X/\delta t)\delta t$;

(vii) A set of non-linear algebraic equations is set up to match the estimates of steps (iii) and (vi). The flowsheeting environment provides a range of powerful well-validated routines for solving these equations.

In a well mixed vessel X, which may consist of several values, applies to the whole vessel. In a system showing continuous variation, X is measured at a 1, 2 or 3 dimensional array of points and intermediate values interpolated. In order to model the system, it is only necessary to know the conditions at one point and the points immediately adjacent. For well-mixed vessels, the "adjacent points" may be simply the inlet and outlet flows. For a solid object, the adjacent points may be the array of points immediately adjacent. The method allows simple local models of parts of the process can be developed and put together in different ways to set up models of complete processes of arbitrary complexity.

In finite difference and finite element integration procedures, a linearised set of equations is solved at each time step see for example Tucker [8]. In requiring no pre-set geometry and applying no gridding restrictions, we cannot take advantage of such a structure to provide specifically tuned solution procedures. On the other hand, we are able to take advantage of semi-analytical methods to develop local non-linear solutions better than the local polynomial representations on which finite difference methods are based. We may then employ models with larger zones and longer time steps.

Error estimation methods are described which can be used to monitor errors and, in the time dimension, automatically adjust the step length to maintain a pre-set precision.

As an example of the general method, its application to the thermal processing of a foodstuff is described. In Sections 2.1 to 2.3, we describe how the spatial variation in temperature is modelled and in Section 2.4 how this is integrated over time.

2.1 Estimation of heat fluxes for unsteady conduction

The volume is divided into zones bounded by a number of surfaces (which may be flat or curved) and, depending upon symmetry, may also enclose cylinders or spheres.

Consider zone "i" in contact with a number of zones "j", $j = 1, 2, 3$ etc. (the numbering need not be contingous because all relevant zones may not be in contact). The heat flux from zone "j" to zone "i" is given by:

$$q_{ij} = A_{ij}k_i(\partial T/\partial \ell) \tag{1}$$

The net heat flux to zone "i" is then given by:

3

$$q_i = \sum_j q_{ij} \qquad (2)$$

To illustrate the method, we take a conventional polynomial approximation to temperature in the space dimensions but consider alternative temperature vs time relationships.

As an approximation to equation (1), we put

$$\hat{q}_{ij} = A_{ij}\,(T_j - T_i)\,/\,(\delta\ell_{ij}/k_i + \delta\ell_{ji}/k_j) \qquad (3)$$

which, when zones i and j have the same materials, reduces to:

$$q_{ij} = A_{ij}k\,(T_j - T_i)\,/\,(\delta\ell_{ij} + \delta\ell_{ji}) \qquad (4)$$

The error in equations (3) and (4) can be estimated by expressing T_i as a polynominal in ℓ, thus:

$$T_{(i)} = T_i^{(0)} + T_i^{(1)}\ell + T_i^{(2)}\ell^2 + T_i^{(3)}\ell^3 + \cdots \qquad (5)$$

where $T_i^{(k)}$ are functions of time. A similar expression holds for T_j.

At the interface, we have

(i) The temperatures are equal, so that

$$T_i^{(0)} = T_j^{(0)} \qquad (6)$$

(ii) The heat fluxes are equal, ie. $q_{ij} = q_{ji}$, so that

$$k_i\partial T_{(i)}/\partial l = k_j\partial T_{(j)}/\partial\ell$$

giving

$$k_i T_i^{(1)} = k_j T_j^{(1)} = Q, \text{ say} \qquad (7)$$

(iii) The rates of change of temperature are equal, so that

$$\partial T_{(i)}/\partial t = \partial T_{(j)}/\partial t \qquad (8)$$

Note that

$$\frac{\partial T_{(i)}}{\partial t} = -\alpha_i\frac{\partial}{\partial\ell}(A_{ij}\frac{\partial T_{(i)}}{\partial\ell})$$

4

and, sufficiently far from any centre of symmetry, $\partial A_{ij}/\partial \ell$ can be ignored. Hence

$$\alpha_i T_i^{(2)} = \alpha_j T_j^{(2)} = P, \quad \text{say} \tag{9}$$

Substitute equations (6), (7) and (9) into equations (5) and the equivalent equation for $T_{(j)}$. Now substitute $\delta\ell_{ij}$ into the resulting expressions for $T_{(i)}$ and $T_{(j)}$ to obtain T_i and T_j. The expressions for T_i and T_j may be substituted into equation (3) to give:

$$\hat{q}_{ij} = A_{ij}[Q + P(\delta\ell_{ij}^2/\alpha_i - \delta\ell_{ji}^2/\ \alpha_j)/(\delta\ell_{ij}/k_i - \delta\ell_{ji}/k_j) + \ldots] \tag{10}$$

Substituting equation (5) into equation (1) gives:

$$q_{ij} = A_{ij}Q$$

Hence, when

$$\delta\ell_{ij} = \sqrt{\alpha_i/\alpha_j}\,\delta l_{ji} \tag{11}$$

equations (10) and (11) agree up to second order terms and the integration method is second order with respect to distance. If the materials in the two zones are the same, equation (11) reduces to:

$$\delta\ell_{ij} = \delta l_{ji} \tag{12}$$

In other cases the error in using equation (3) can be roughly estimated by calculating $T_i^{(2)}$ from the change in $\partial T/\partial l$ between opposite faces of the zone.

2.2 Unsteady transfer between conductive and convective zones

It can similarly be shown that the following equation is first order for transfer between conductive and convective zones:

$$\hat{q}_{ij} = A_{ij}(T_j - T_i)/(\delta\ell_{ij}/k_i + h_{ij}) \tag{13}$$

A similar equation applies to the simulation of a well-mixed zone adjacent to a conducting zone.

Equation (13) ignores the effect of the thermal inertia of the relatively slow-moving boundary layer in the mixed fluid. This criticism can however be made of any estimate of unsteady heat transfer to any well-mixed or flowing fluid when resistance is measured simply by a heat-transfer coefficient. It is, therefore, consistent with the accuracy of other engineering heat-transfer calculations.

2.3   Unsteady heating of a mixture containing suspended solids

For coarse solids, zones with boundaries matching the individual particles can be set up. For systems with large numbers of small particles which cannot be placed individually, a modified model is needed. We present a simplification which is applicable where the conductivity of the suspended solids is significantly less than that of the suspending material. Each zone contains a number of particles of suspended solids which have the following effects:

(i)   The interfacial areas between zones available for heat transfer are reduced;

(ii)   Heat transfer between the solids is negligible compared to that between fluid and solids (because the points of contact are limited);

(iii)   The suspended solids affect the thermal inertia of each zone as a consequence of heat transfer to and from the suspension. The average temperature profile through the suspended material is similar to that through the bulk material so that the transfer rate to and from the suspension may be modelled by the heat transfer at the point at which T_i is measured.

Equation (3) of Section 2.1 is modified as follows:

$$\hat{q}_{ij} = (1 - \varepsilon) A_{ij} k (T_j - T_i)/(\delta \ell_{ij} + \delta \ell_{ji}) \tag{14}$$

Heat transfer to the suspended material in zone i is given by:

$$q_{si} = V_i a h_s (T_i - S_i) \tag{15}$$

h_s may be obtained from an unsteady-state Nusselt Number which, for conduction, can be calculated from the geometry of the system. For example Johns and Lawn [5] give relationships between Nu and ε for spherical particles. From the outside of the spheres, the transfer coefficient to the surrounding material is approximately $h_o = k[2 + (18/5)\varepsilon^{1/3}]/d$ where d is the diameter of the sphere and k is the conductivity of the surrounding medium. For transfer from the surface of the sphere to its mean internal temperature, the heat transfer coefficient is approximately $h_i = 10k_s/d$. The overall coefficient is then given by $1/h_s = 1/h_o + 1/h_i$.

The interfacial area per unit volume is given by $a = 6\varepsilon/d$. It is not expected that these values will be very sensitive to shape providing that d measures the shortest significant dimension (eg. the side of a cube).

2.4   Integration over time

The analysis presented is for a single uniform material, but it is easily generalised for the other cases.

Heat balance for zone i over period δt is

$$V_i C_{pi} \rho_i \delta T_i = \overline{q}_i \delta t \tag{16}$$

where T_i is assumed to approximate the mean bulk temperature of the zone, and

$$\overline{q}_i = \text{Mean}\{q_{it}, q_{i,t+\delta t}\} \tag{17}$$

The method of calculating the mean determines the characteristics of the integration method. The optimal location for measuring T_i is discussed in Section 2.5.

From equations (2) and (4):

$$q_{it} = \sum_j A_{ij} k(T_j - T_i)/\Delta \ell_{ij} \tag{18}$$

and

$$q_{i,t+\delta t} = \sum_j A_{ij} k(T_j + \delta T_j - T_i - \delta T_i)/\Delta \ell_{ij} \tag{19}$$

Define

$$\tau_i = \alpha \delta t [\sum_j A_{ij}(T_j - T_i)/\Delta \ell_{ij}]/V_i \tag{20}$$

$$\theta_i = \alpha \delta t [\sum_j A_{ij}(T_j + \delta T_j - T_i)/\Delta \ell_{ij}]/V_i \tag{21}$$

and

$$s_i = \alpha \delta t [\sum_j A_{ij}/\Delta \ell_{ij}]/V_i \tag{22}$$

Combining equations (16) to (22) and dividing both sides by $V_i C_{pi} \rho_i$ gives:

$$\delta T_i = \text{Mean}\,[\tau_i, \theta_i \quad s_i \delta T_i]$$

A flowsheeting system can solve the set of non-linear equations so that the δT_j on the RHS cause the correct δT_i to be calculated. For simplicity, we drop the subscript i, giving:

$$\delta T = \text{Mean}\{\tau, \theta - s\delta T\} \tag{23}$$

The integration formulae are then as follows:

Forward Difference. The initial heating rate is considered to be valid for the whole time step so that:

$$\text{Mean}\,\{\tau, \theta - s\delta T\} = \tau$$

giving

$$\delta T = \tau \qquad (24)$$

Backward Difference. The final heating rate is considered to be valid for the whole period so that:

$$\text{Mean}\{\tau, \theta - s\delta T\} = \theta - s\delta T$$

giving from equation (23):

$$\delta T = \theta/(1 + s) \qquad (25)$$

Central Difference. The heating rate is assumed to vary linearly throughout the time period so that the appropriate mean is the arithmetic mean, ie.

$$\text{Mean}\{\tau, \theta - s\delta T\} = (\tau + \theta - s\delta T)/2$$

giving, from equation (23):

$$\delta T = (\tau + \theta)/(2 + s) \qquad (26)$$

Other Difference Formulae. Other means are possible and there are theoretical grounds for applying a logarithmic mean. All means reduce to the arithmetic mean when there is very little change in heat transfer rate over the time-step; ie. when small time-steps are used. For example, taking a geometric mean

$$\text{Mean}\{\tau, \ \theta - s\delta T\} = [\tau(\theta - s\delta T)]^{1/2}$$

we get

$$\delta T = [(s^2\tau^2 + 4\theta\tau)^{1/2} - s\tau]/2 \qquad (27)$$

When $\theta - s\delta T \simeq \tau$, equation (27) reduces to equation (26). For larger differences, it may be noted that the geometric mean does not allow sign changes, so that δT is limited to θ/s. It is thus expected that equation (27) may share some of the stability characteristics of the backward difference formula (equation 25), whilst still having the potential for second order integration.

2.5 Optimal Zone Spacing

Optimal zone spacing minimises truncation errors by ensuring that equation (11) (or 12) applies and that the temperature T_i also corresponds to the mean bulk temperature of each zone. We illustrate the approach to optimal zone spacing by considering the heating of a uniform solid cylinder (can).

As a yardstick, we will first consider annular volumes that are equally spaced radially and axially. For an n zone discretization the zone radii are $(0$ to $r_1)$, $(r_1$ to $2r_1)$, $(2r_1$ to $3r_1)$, up to $((n-1)r_1$ to $nr_1)$. Similarly, for zones equally spaced in the axial direction, heights may be $(0$ to $z_1)$, $(z_1$ to $2z_1)$ up to $((m-1)z_1$ to $mz_1)$ where there are m axial zones. For each zone, the temperature is calculated at the mean values of the ordinates, ie. for zone (i, j)

$$\bar{r}_i = (r_{i-1} + r_i)/2$$

$$\text{and}\quad \bar{z}_j = (z_{j-1} + z_j)/2$$

This discretization gives rise to a first order integration with respect to time, because T_i is not at the mean bulk temperature and second order with respect to the spatial dimension (because $\delta l_{ij} = \delta l_{ji}$).

We now consider optimizing the spacing to minimise integration error.

For the axial dimension, the appropriate mean height is given by:

$$\int_{z_{i-1}}^{z_i} T dz = (z_i - z_{i-1})\, T(\bar{z}) \tag{28}$$

For a quadratic T vs z relationship, equation (28) gives

$$a + b\bar{z}_i + c\bar{z}_i^2 = a + b(z_{i-1} + z_i)/2 + c(z_{i-1}^2 + z_{i-1}z_i + z_i^2)/3$$

For second order integration, terms of up to $\bar{z}_i$ should match, giving:

$$\bar{z}_i = (z_{i-1} + z_i)/2$$

It may be noted however, that near the centre of symmetry, the T vs z profile is dominated by the quadratic term. If z is measured from the centre of symmetry, b will be zero over a significant range. (The analytical solution gives $T = T_0 + cz^2 + ez^4 + .. $).

Improved precision may therefore, be expected by setting:

$$\bar{z}_i^2 = (z_{i-1}^2 + z_{i-1}z_i + z_i^2)/3 \tag{29}$$

For relatively narrow zones, away from the centre of symmetry, $\bar{z}_i$ calculated by equation (29) is very close to $(z_{i-1} + z_i)/2$.

If z_{i-1} and $\bar{z}_{mi}$ are known, equation (29) gives:

$$z_i = [\sqrt{3(4\bar{z}_i^2 - z_{i-1}^2)} - z_{i-1}]/2$$

To maintain 2nd order integration in space, we must have, from equation (12):

$$\bar{z}_{i+1} = 2z_i - \bar{z}_i$$

Hence, starting with $z_0 = 0$ at the centre of symmetry the axial grid spacing should be:

$$
\begin{array}{ll}
— & z_0 = 0 \\
\bar{z}_1 = z & z_1 = \sqrt{3}z \\
\bar{z}_2 = (2\sqrt{3} - 1)z & \text{etc.}
\end{array}
$$

Using the above table, the appropriate spacing can be found for any chosen number of zones.

Similarly, for the radial spacing of zones, we have:

$$\int_{r_{i-1}}^{r_i} Tr\,dr = T(\bar{r})(r_i^2 - r_{i-1}^2)/2 \tag{30}$$

From which

$$a + b\bar{r}_i + c\bar{r}_i^2 = a + b\frac{2(r_{i-1}^2 + r_{i-1}r_i + r_i^2)}{3(r_{i-1} + r_i)} + \frac{c(r_{i-1}^2 + r_i^2)}{2}$$

For second order integration, we should match the coefficient of b, ie. put:

$$\bar{r}_{mi} = 2(r_{i-1}^2 + r_{i-1}r_i + r_i^2)/[3(r_{i-1} + r_i)]$$

As for the axial case, however, it is felt to be more valid to match the coefficients of c, in that in the areas of main interest, b will be zero. We then obtain

$$\bar{r}_i^2 = (r_{i-1}^2 + r_i^2)/2 \tag{31}$$

ie. use the root mean square radius.

The equations give similar results (even for the first zone they differ by less than 6%) but differ considerably from the arithmetic mean (over 33% in first zone).

As for the axial case, successive values of r_i can be calculated started from $\bar{r}_i$. Thus

$$r_i^2 = 2\bar{r}_i^2 - r_{i-1}^2$$

$$\text{and} \quad \bar{r}_{i+1} = 2r_i - \bar{r}_i$$

when, starting with $r_0 = 0$, we have

$$
\begin{array}{ll}
— & r_0 = 0 \\
\bar{r}_1 = r & r_1 = \sqrt{2}r \\
\bar{r}_2 = (2\sqrt{2} - 1)r & \text{etc.}
\end{array}
$$

Both for z and r, the optimally spaced zones get closer as we move away from the centre symmetry.

Interfaces between materials. Material boundaries occur at zone boundaries. The strategy is to divide each of the materials into zones (either uniformly or "optimally"), and arrange the sizes so that, at the interface, equation (11) is approximately met. Thus, for radial spacing, we attempt to ensure that:

$$\bar{r}_{i+1} = r_i + \sqrt{\alpha_2/\alpha_1}(r_i - \bar{r}_i) \tag{32}$$

Since we are restricted to an integer number of zones, equation (32) cannot apply exactly. Consequentley whatever spacing formula is used, the integration is only first order at the boundary. Similar conclusions can be drawn for any number of vertical or radial material boundaries.

Outer boundary. Similarly, whether or not the outer heat transfer coefficient is taken as infinite, the integration becomes first order at the outer boundary. At the outside of the can, some improvement in precision may be achieved by noting that, for uniform heating, the temperature gradient steadily increases from the centre outwards. For example the gradient at the boundary may be estimated from the mean gradient within the can by a formula such as:

$$q_n - 2\bar{q}_n r_n / (r_n + \bar{r}_n)$$

which would be valid for a quadratic temperature gradient.

2.6 Monitoring the accuracy of Integration

Two convenient methods are available for monitoring the accuracy of integration.

Richardson's h^2 method assumes that the order of integration is known. The integration is run twice, the second time with double step-length. For 1st order integration, the estimate of the error of the result with the shortest step length is:

$$\delta Z = (Z_2 - Z_1)$$

where Z_2 is the result with double step length and δZ is proportional to step length.

For 2nd order integration:

$$\delta Z = (Z_2 - Z_1)/3$$

and δZ is proportional to step length squared. In both cases, a more accurate estimate is obtained from $Z = Z_1 - \delta Z$ and the step length may be reduced (or increased) to give an acceptable error.

Aitken's Method is independent of order of integration and requires evaluating the integral for step lengths of $\delta x, 2\delta x$ and $4\delta x$. The order of integration is then given by:

$$N = \log_2[(Z_4 - Z_2)/(Z_2 - Z_1)]$$

and the error is estimated as:

$$\delta Z = (Z_2 - Z_1)^2/(Z_1 - 2Z_2 + Z_4)$$

A more accurate result is again obtained from $(Z_1 - \delta Z)$ and, using the calculated N, step length can be adjusted to achieve a desired accuracy.

For monitoring error (as eg. in the space dimensions), Richardson's method is adequate. For obtaining more accurate values of Z and for adjusting step length, Aitken's method is useful because second-order integration can break down to first order at boundaries. In simulating complete processes, where different parts of the model have been prepared by different authors, Aitken's method can be used to check that routines have been consistently coded to give the desired order of integration.

3 HANDLING UNCERTAINTY

Calculated food process properties depend on the values assumed for uncertain parameters. If there were only one uncertain parameter, it could be described by a mean, standard deviation etc. By substituting possible values of the parameter into the equation predicting the food property, we could obtain a mean and standard deviation for this food property. For multiple uncertain parameters more subtle methods are needed.

Uncertainties may arise in several ways; for example, from batch to batch variations of raw material properties or from our inability to measure accurately a property that has a definite value. In the former case, the product properties may vary randomly batch to batch, whilst in the latter case the properties will be the same but we cannot predict them accurately. Intermediate cases are also, of course, possible. The mathematical treatment for the cases is similar and we will not differentiate between them in the subsequent discussion

A conceptually easy way of estimating the effect of uncertainty is to undertake a Monte Carlo simulation; if 10% of the simulated results fall below a required level there is a 10% chance that the product will not meet that level.

The disadvantage of the Monte Carlo method is that it is time consuming, particularly when high guarantees of achieving a given level of performance are required. For example, if we require that 99.9% of batches meet a given safety standard, it will clearly be insufficient to undertaken 1000 Monte Carlo simulations and obtain only 1 failing case. The difficulties are compounded when we do not know in advance what combinations of uncertain variables are likely to result in extreme values. We have, therefore, developed a means of computing the mean and standard deviation of the product properties from a very limited number of simulations.

The approach adopted is to develop a simple general way of evaluating the expected value $(\bar{f})$ and standard deviation (σ_f) of a function of multiple independent variables, (x_1, x_2, x_3). We wish to evaluate:

$$\bar{f} = \int \int \ldots \int f \varphi_1 \varphi_2 \ldots \varphi_n dx_1 dx_2 \ldots dx_n \qquad (33)$$

$$\text{and} \quad \sigma_f^2 = \int \int \ldots \int f^2 \varphi_1 \varphi_2 \ldots \varphi_m dx_1 dx_2 \ldots dx_n - \bar{f}^2. \qquad (34)$$

Note that, because f^2 is just a different function of $(x_1, x_2 \ldots x_n)$, the method used to integrate equation (33) will also integrate equation (34). Higher moments, I_{3f} etc. can similarly be computed to check that the resulting distribution of f is reasonably normal so that standard probability tables can be used. For processes in which the uncertainties in $x_1, x_2 \ldots$ etc. are not independent (eg. they may be derived from one set of experiments) a set of orthogonal directions are derived in which the variables are independent. It may be noted that this latter problem also invalidates a simple Monte Carlo simulation and the same orthogonalization procedure is required in order to generate the necessary set of pseudo random numbers.

For simplicity, we will first derive the one uncertain variable formulae. The integration is based on the premise that, within a small number of standard deviations of the mean, f can be expanded as a polynominal in x. The method has been adopted by several authors, see eg. references [6] and [7].

Putting $y = (x - \bar{x})/\sigma$ around $x = \bar{x}$ gives:

$$f = f_o + f_1 \sigma y + f_2 \sigma^2 y^2 / 2! + f_3 \sigma^3 y^3 / 3! + \ldots \qquad (35)$$

Substituting equation (35) into equation (33) and integrating gives, for a normal distribution of x:

$$\bar{f} = f_o + f_2 \sigma^2 / 2! + 3 f_4 \sigma^4 / 4! + 1.3.5 f_6 \sigma^6 / 6! + \ldots \qquad (36)$$

$\bar{f}$ is a mean value of f and, for simplicity, we want to obtain $\bar{f}$ by taking a weighted mean of certain values of f, ie:

$$\bar{f} \simeq \sum_i w_i \hat{f}(u_i) \qquad (37)$$

$\bar{f}$ is thus the weighted mean of values of f calculated at various points $(\bar{x} \pm u_i \sigma)$.

Instead of making the w's equal and selecting the u's randomly (as in Monte Carlo), we choose the values to make equations (36) and (37) correspond up to a selected polynomial term.

From equation (35), (see Nomenclature):

$$\hat{f}(0) = f_o$$

and

$$\hat{f}(u) = f_o + u^2 f_2 \sigma^2/2! + u^4 f_4 \sigma^4/4! + \ldots \tag{38}$$

Combining equations (37) and (38) gives:

$$\bar{f} \simeq (w_o + w_1 + w_2 \ldots)f_o \quad + (w_1 u_1^2 + w_2 u_2^2 + \ldots)f_2 \sigma^2/2!$$
$$+ (w_1 u_1^4 + w_2 u_2^4 + \ldots)f_4 \sigma^4/4! + \ldots \tag{39}$$

By matching equations (36) and (39), a set of equations is obtained from which appropriate weightings w_i and evaluation points u_i can be derived to give any desired precision of integration.

There are two approaches to obtaining the values (u_i, w_i). The first is to choose the u_i arbitrarily then the w_i can be obtained from a simple set of linear equations.

For example, if we choose $f(x \pm \sigma)$ and $f(x \pm 2\sigma)$, we get

$$\bar{f} \simeq f(\bar{x}) - 1/2[f(\bar{x} - \sigma) + f(\bar{x} + \sigma)] + 1/2[f(\bar{x} - 2\sigma) + f(\bar{x} + 2\sigma)]$$

which is accurate to σ^5. The second approach is to solve for the u_i and w_i simultaneously, when fewer evaluation points will be needed, but they may be at less convenient intervals. Using this approach the values given in Table 1 are obtained:

Table 1: Quadrature points and weights

Agreement up to:	w_o	w_1	u_1	w_2	u_2
σ	1	—	—	—	—
σ^3	—	1	1	—	—
σ^5	2/3	1/3	$\sqrt{3}$	—	—
σ^7	—	$(3 + \sqrt{6})/6$	$\sqrt{3 - \sqrt{6}}$	$(3 - \sqrt{6})/6$	$\sqrt{3 + \sqrt{6}}$
σ^9	8/15	$(7 + 2\sqrt{10})/30$	$\sqrt{5 - \sqrt{10}}$	$(7 - 2\sqrt{10})/30$	$\sqrt{5 + \sqrt{10}}$

As an example of the use of Table 1, integration accurate to σ^5 can be obtained from the following formula:

$$\bar{f} \simeq 2/3 f(\bar{x}) + 1/6[f(\bar{x} - \sqrt{3}\sigma) + f(\bar{x} + \sqrt{3}\sigma)]$$

In calculating σ_f^2, it must be noted that, in the expansion of $(f - \bar{f})^2$, the first non-zero term is in $y^2\sigma^2$. An integration formula at least valid to σ^2, is therefore required. Similarly higher order integrals are required for evaluating I_{3f} etc.

Note that, for food processes, σ is rarely known with great precision and it is rarely useful to employ more than 2 or 3 points.

For multi-dimensional integration, formulae can be similarly derived. We first define multi-dimensional $\hat{f}$ functions:

$$\hat{f}_1(u_i) = 1/2[f(0,0,..,u_i..,0,0) + f(0,0,...,-u_i,...0,0)]$$

$$\hat{f}_2(u_i,u_j) = 1/4[f(0,0,..,u_i..,u_j..,0,0) + f(0,0,..,u_i..,-u_j,...0,0)]$$

$$+ f(0,0..,-u_i,..,u_j..,0,0) + f(0,0,..,-u_i,..,-u_j...,0,0)] \qquad (40)$$

etc.

until for $\hat{f}_n(u_1,u_2,\ldots,u_n)$ all n parameters are varied over 2^n points.

The simplest formula valid up to σ^3, which has been previously quoted in the literature [6], [7] is:

$$\hat{f} \simeq [\sum \hat{f}(\sqrt{n}\sigma_i)]/n \qquad (41)$$

The disadvantage of equation (41) is that, for large n, it evaluates the functions at an excessive distance from the expected values. Thus, for 9 uncertain variables it calculates f at points $(\bar{x}_i \pm 3\sigma_i)$, beyond which less than 0.2% of values of x lie. It is therefore, not representative of the function in the range of most interest.

A formula giving the same order of integration but with all evaluations at $(\bar{x} \pm \sigma_i)$ is:

$$\bar{f} \simeq \hat{f}_o + \sum(\hat{f}_1(\sigma_i) - \hat{f}_o) \qquad (42)$$

It will be noted that for an n-dimensional function, we still only require $(2n + 1)$, rather than 2^n, points to give agreement up to σ^3.

Families of formulae for agreement to σ^3 and to σ^5 are available which only require of order n^2 function evaluations.

4   APPLICATIONS

The simulation method is illustrated by application to the heating of a cylindrical can and the method of handling uncertainty by application both to a simple analytical function and to the heating of a can. We first show the advantage of employing the general convergence procedures available in a flowsheeting system. We can then explore the benefits of optimal zone spacing and the characteristics of the various procedures for integrating in the time dimension. In Section 4.4, we consider a can containing more than one material. Finally, in Section 4.5 and 4.6 we demonstrate the procedure for handling uncertainties.

4.1 Convergence of time step iterations

In this simple example, the implicit equations are solved at each time step by resubstitution and by a typical convergence routine available in a flowsheeting package (quasi-Newton). The results are compared in Table 2 which shows that the quasi-Newton method reduces the number of iterations dramatically. It is clear that the characteristics of the equations (eg. $\partial T_i / \partial T_j$) change little from time step to time step, so that once a good estimate of the inverse jacobian is available, subsequent steps solve very rapidly. Note however, that, for large time steps, the equations change more, and more iterations are required; without routines such as quasi-Newton, the equations may fail to converge.

The number of iterations per time step gives an indication of the degradation of performance resulting from this implicit iterative procedure. Finite difference methods solve the set of linear difference equations explicitly and, in effect, take one iteration per time step. The number of iterations is thus a measure of the price paid for the flexibility that the "zone model" introduces in enabling simultaneous solution of complete processes.

Table 2: Number of Iterations for convergence at each time step

Number of Zones: 8
Time step: 60 seconds
Convergence Criterion: RMS error 0.0005°C

Time	Resubstitution	Quasi-Newton
120	10	5
240	11	5
840	9	4
900	9	3
1680	8	3
1740	8	2
> 3240	7	2

4.2 Comparison of equal and "optimal" zone spacing

Table 3 gives tables of can centre temperature against time. The "accurate" result was obtained using 64, 32 and 16 zones, 2.5, 5 and 10s time steps in conjunction with Richardson's h^2 method and Aitken's method to ensure that all temperatures are accurate

Table 3: Comparison of equal and "optimal" zone spacing

Time (s)	Temperatures (°C)		
	Accurate	Uniform Spacing	"Optimal" Spacing
0	20.0	20.0	20.0
240	20.1	(21.7)	(27.8)
480	23.3	(26.1)	(20.7)
720	32.9	35.1	30.2
960	45.2	46.3	43.2
1200	57.5	57.6	56.0
1440	68.6	68.2	67.6
1680	78.1	77.6	77.6
1920	86.3	85.7	86.0
2160	93.2	92.6	93.2
2400	99.1	98.5	99.2
2640	104.0	103.5	104.2
2880	108.2	107.7	108.4
3120	111.6	111.3	111.9
3360	114.6	114.2	114.9
3600	117.0	116.8	117.3
Number of zones	64	3	3
Time step	2.5	240	240

to $\pm\, 0.05°$C. For all three columns, the centre temperature was obtained by extrapolation using a 5th order polynominal. From symmetry this polynominal reduces to the quartic $T = a + br^2 + cr^4$ which needs to be fitted through 3 zone temperatures. A 3 zone approximation to the heating curve is thus the minimum that can be used to calculate a centre temperature. With 8 zones and a time step of 120 seconds, computed centre temperatures, on the basis of both zone spacing algorithms are accurate to $\pm\, 0.1°$C.

Applying Aitken's method, it was found that the order of integration for both methods was similar, approximately 1.2. Neither method, therefore, achieves second-order integration in practice (because of first order effects at boundaries). Both, however, are slightly better than first order.

For small times (eg. less than 12 minutes), centre temperatures are predicted inaccurately for both spacing formulae, but more so for the "optimal" zone spacing. These inaccuracies result from errors in the radial profile discussed in section 4.3. These errors are exaggerated for the "optimally" spaced zones because the zone radii are greater than for uniform spacing and a greater extrapolation is needed to estimate the centre temperature.

Further tests have confirmed that computed centre temperatures are not sensitive to changes in zone spacing. This finding encourages confidence that more complex shapes can be simulated with relatively few zones and that the results obtained will not depend critically on arbitrary choices made for the zone shapes.

4.3 Comparison of Difference Formulae

Table 4 shows the outer three zones of a computed radial temperature profile at a number of times. As anticipated in Section 2.4.4, the Geometric Mean Difference formulae is successful in damping instabilities in the computed temperature profile in both the radial and time dimensions. Note, however, that, after sufficient time, the computed instabilities in the central difference computation became self-cancelling and an accurate temperature profile is computed. The Geometric Mean Difference formula always, however, underestimates the heat transfer rate as compared to the Central Difference formula. [It is clear that $(q_1 + q_2)/2$ is always greater $\sqrt{q_1 q_2}$].

Further tests have shown that the Geometric Mean Difference formula always underestimates the true heat transfer rate. The greater stability is, therefore, achieved at the expense of a loss of precision. At the same time it has been shown, using Aitken's method, that, for small time steps, both formulae give better than first order integration. The error in the Central Difference formula is, however, up to an order of magnitude less and it has, accordingly, been used in the remainder of this study.

Even much smaller radial instabilities than those in Table 4 give rise to significant errors when used to extrapolate to the temperature at the axis of the cylinder. This effect is, however, only significant for the first few time steps and has negligible effect when temperatures significant in computing lethality are reached. The initial instability is also illustrated in the first few temperatures shown in Table 3.

Table 4: Calculated temperatures for 16 uniformly-spaced zone model with 40 second time increments

Time	Temperature (°C)					
(s)	Zone 16		Zone 15		Zone 14	
	A	B	A	B	A	B
40	127.0	103.0	54.1	39.1	30.9	24.4
80	105.3	106.3	93.3	69.7	51.8	41.8
120	119.2	114.1	86.5	82.2	64.6	57.0
160	117.1	116.9	95.0	90.4	71.9	67.1
200	120.2	118.8	98.0	95.6	78.5	74.4
240	120.6	120.1	101.6	99.4	83.0	80.0
240*	120.5		101.2		82.8	

Notes:

A — Central Difference Formula.

B — Geometric Mean Difference Formula in range $0.16 < q_{t+\delta t}/q_t < 6.25$. Weighted arithmetic mean outside this range.

* — Correct temperatures obtained from small time increments with either Central Difference or Geometric Mean Difference Formulae.

4.4 Heating two different materials

Table 5 compares the heating rate of a cylinder containing two materials with that of a cylinder containing one uniform material. The mixtures are arranged so that the composite thermal diffusivities are equal, giving a final asymptotic heating rate, $d\ell n(130 - T)/dt$, of 5.25×10^{-4} s^{-1} in both cases.

It will be noted that the initial heating rate for the can containing two materials is considerably higher than that for the single material. Once the asymptotic heating rate is reached, the two material can reaches a given temperature approximately 180 seconds before the uniform can.

Two conclusions can be drawn from these findings. The first conclusion is that the initial heating rate of cans containing mixed materials differs from that of uniform materials having the same experimentally determined thermal diffusivity. Most food processes heat mixed materials so that some of the effects previously attributed to convection may in part be attributed to nonuniformity of material properties. The second conclusion is that a two-material conduction model could be used to simulate convection in a heated can. The effect of convection (particularly fluid movement generated by shaking or rotating a can) is to mix the material thus giving effectively a higher conductivity. This higher conductivity will not apply at the outside of the can which acts as a boundary layer. Using this model, it is possible to fit experimental heating data either by adjusting the diameter of the "convective" zone to match the critical heating rate or by adjusting the "conductivity" that applies under mixing.

Table 5: Heating mixed materials

Time (s)	Uniform Material Temperature (°C)	Two Materials Temperature (°C)
0	20.0	20.0
240	20.1	21.0
480	21.1	27.8
720	25.1	38.6
960	32.0	49.2
1200	40.6	58.7
1440	49.5	67.1
1680	58.2	74.6
1920	66.2	81.1
2160	73.5	86.9
2400	80.1	92.0
2640	85.9	96.5
2880	91.1	100.5
3120	95.7	104.0
3360	99.8	107.0
3600	103.3	109.8

Can diameter 0.0365 m. Inner material diameter 0.02555m.

Initial temperature 20°C. Heating Medium 130°C.

Physical Properties	Uniform	Inner Material	Outer Material
k $(KJm^{-1}s^{-1}\,°C^{-1})$	0.3615	2.00	0.25
C_p $(KJKg^{-1}\,°C^{-1})$	2740.2	2740.2	2740.2
ρ (Kgm^{-3})	1090.0	1090.0	1090.0

4.5 Simulation under uncertainty: multi-variable algebraic function

The function $f = \exp\left(a_1 x_1 + a_2 x_2 + a_3 x_3\right)$ was used to illustrate the quadrature technique developed because it gives an exact analytical solution which can be used as a yardstick against which to judge the numerical methods. Using a 9-point formula, a closer approximation to the analytical solution was achieved than could be obtained with over 1000

Monte Carlo simulations. Using 125 points, a result virtually indistinguishable from the analytical solution was achieved. It could not be matched with over 100,000 Monte Carlo points. The quadrature formulae have the further benefit of giving smooth predictions of confidence limits etc. independent of particular pseudo random number strings.

4.6 Simulation under uncertainty: thermal processing

The mean and standard deviation of the thermal diffusivity of baked beans in tomato sauce obtained from 147 experimental points is 0.00147 cm^2 s^{-1} and 0.00016 cm^2 s^{-1} respectively. By employing the quadrature method described above, we can calculate the expected value of a can centre temperature after any given time. For a UT can (D = 73 mm, H = 115 mm) initially at 20°C heated for 60 minutes at 128.5°C, we obtain an expected can centre temperature of 122°C with a standard deviation of 4.8°C. Thus there is approximately an 84% chance that a can will be heated to above 117.2°C (122 - 4.8) and 16% chance that it will fail to reach that temperature. Note that this calculation did not take account of the initial higher rate of heating achieved with the baked beans than with uniform material of the same composite thermal diffusivity. To take that effect into account a more detailed model with at least one additional uncertain parameter would have been required. We would then have got higher expected temperatures with a greater Standard Deviation.

Direct calculation of probability levels (which is possible for one uncertain parameter) gives closely similar results. We can, therefore, be confident that the quadrature procedure is capable of giving useful results for practical multiple uncertain parameter problems. This example was exceptional in the number and quality of experimental measurements available. In practice, less extensive data would have given almost as much value and similar results could have been obtained using fewer experimental points and only a 2-point quadrature formula. Quadrature integration thus gives an economical way of deriving useful statistical information on food process performance.

In practice, it would also be necessary to compute integrated lethality at any point in a can. The same quadrature points used to calculate lethality statistics also give temperature statistics and statistics of any other desired food property.

5 CONCLUSIONS

A procedure is presented that enables steady state or dynamic models of food processes to be built up in a modular way. The procedure is shown to be flexible and robust. It easily handles discontinuities in food properties which have been difficult to handle with existing methods. The procedure is presented for use in a Flowpack II environment but is directly applicable to any flowsheeting system that handles information flow within and between units in a consistent way. The flexibility is gained at some loss of efficiency in simulating stand-alone units as compared to specially tuned methods.

Handling uncertainty requires a second level of integration in which integration of an objective function is undertaken with respect to the probability functions describing the uncertain variables. This integration is traditionally handled using Monte Carlo techniques. It is shown, however, that substantial economies can be made by using quadrature formulae presented in this paper.

The quadrature formulae can be used in conjunction with the simulation procedure to provide a widely applicable facility to simulate food processing under uncertainty.

ACKNOWLEDGEMENTS

Campden Food and Drink Research Association (G S Tucker) provided the experimental data referred to. P Edevbie analysed the data and undertook tests of the quadrature procedure at South Bank Polytechnic. H Kassim (of South Bank Polytechnic) evaluated the implicit integration procedure against efficient finite difference methods. The work was supported by a consortium of food companies coordinated by CFDRA under the DTI LINK programme and based at South Bank and Chipping Campden.

References

[1] Henton J E and W R Johns. "An extented FORTRAN language for solving sets of simultaneous equations in order to balance chemical process flowsheets", IFAC Symposium "The digital simulation of continuous processes". Gyor (Hungary), September 1971.

[2] Flowpack II, Users Documentation, Imperial Chemical Industries Ltd, Northwich, Cheshire.

[3] Speed-Up. Aspen Technology (UK) Ltd, Cambridge.

[4] Ponton J W. "Dynamic Process Simulation using Flowsheet Structure". Computers Chem Eng, $\underline{7}$, No. 1, pp 13–17 (1983).

[5] Johns W R and Lawn S J. "Unsteady state transfer between a sphere and surrounding stationary medium with application to arrays of spheres" Int. J. Heat Mass Transfer $\underline{28}$, No. 5, pp 1047 – 1053. (1985).

[6] Stroud A H and Secrest D. "Approximate Integration Formulas for Certain Spherically Symmetrical Regions" Math. Comp. $\underline{16}$, 105 – 135, 1962.

[7] Johns W R. "Assessing the effect of uncertainty on the probable performance of chemical processes". NATO Symposium on uncertain systems. Cambridge, April 1971.

[8] Tucker G S. "Development and use of numerical techniques for improved thermal process calculations and control". Food Control, $\underline{2}$, 15–20, 1991.

Nomenclature

a	surface area of suspended solids per unit volume of suspension (m^{-1})
A_{ij}	area of face between zones i and j (m^2)
C_{pi}	heat capacity of material i (KJ kg^{-1} $^{\circ}C^{-1}$)
d	particle diameter (m)
f	output food property (function of uncertain variable x)
f_j	$\partial^j f/\partial x^j$
$\bar{f}$	mean value of f eg. $\int f\varphi dx$
$\hat{f}(u)$	$[f(\bar{x}-u\sigma)+f(\bar{x}+u\sigma)]/2$
$\hat{f}_i$	see equation (47)
g	exponent in equation (29) (s^{-1})
$g_1, g_2...$	exponent in equation (28) (s^{-1})
h_i	heat transfer coefficient from surface to particle to mean bulk temperature within particle (KJ m^{-2} s $^{-1}$ $^{\circ}C^{-1}$)
h_o	heat transfer coefficient from surface of particle of bulk surrounding material (KJ m^{-2} s $^{-1}$ $^{\circ}C^{-1}$)
h_s	heat transfer coefficient between fluid and suspended solids (KJ m^{-2} s $^{-1}$ $^{\circ}C^{-1}$)
h_{ij}	heat transfer coefficient between interface (i, j) and bulk of zone j (KJ m^{-2} s $^{-1}$ $^{\circ}C^{-1}$)
I_j	$[\int(x-\bar{x})^j\varphi dx]/\sigma^j$
I_{jf}	$[\int(f-\bar{f})^j\varphi dx]/\sigma_f^j$
k_i	thermal conductivity of material in zone i (KJ m^{-1} s $^{-1}$ $^{\circ}C^{-1}$)
ℓ	normal distance from interface between zones in direction zone i to zone j (m)
$\delta\ell_{ij}$	normal distance, from point at which T_i is measured, to surface A_{ij} (m)
$\Delta\ell_{ij}$	$\delta\ell_{ij}+\delta\ell_{ji}$ (m)
q_{ij}	heat flux from zone j to zone i (KJ s^{-1})
q_i	net heat flux into zone i (KJ s^{-1})
q_{si}	heat flux to suspended solids in zone $i (KJs^{-1})$
q_{it}	value of q_i at time t (KJ s^{-1})
q_o	coefficient in equation (29) (KJ s^{-1})
$q_{(1)}, q_{(2)}...$	coefficients in equation (28) (KJ s^{-1})
$\bar{q}_i$	mean value of q_i averaged over time interval δt (KJ s^{-1})
$\hat{q}_{ij}$	an approximation to q_{ij}
r	radial distance (m)
r_i	outer radius of zone i (m)
$\bar{r}_i$	mean radius of zone i (m)
s_i	see equation (22)
S_i	mean temperature of suspended solids in zone i ($^{\circ}$ C)
t	time. (s)

T temperature (°C)

T_i temperature at a defined point within zone i (°C)

$T_{(i)}$ temperature within zone i (as a function of ℓ) (°C)

$T_i^{(k)}$ $k!\partial^k T/\partial \ell^k$ in zone i at interface i/j (°C m^{-k})

δT_i change in T_i in increment of time δt. (°C).

u see $\hat{f}(u)$

V_i volume of zone i (m^3)

X any parameter having a point value (eg. temperature)

x an uncertain parameter

$\bar{x}$ mean value of x, eg. $\int x\varphi dn$

y $(x - \bar{x})/\sigma$

z axial distance (m)

z_i distance of outer face of zone i from centre of symmetry (m)

$\bar{z}_i$ mean distance of zone i from centre of symmetry (m)

Z a calculated result (eg. Temperature, lethality)

δZ error in estimating Z

α $k/(C_p \rho)$ thermal diffusivity (m^2 s^{-1})

ε fraction of suspended solids

θ see equation (21) (°C)

ρ_i density of material in zone i (kg m^{-3})

τ see equation (20) (°C)

σ standard deviation of x, eg. $\int (x - \bar{x})^2 \varphi dx$

σ_f standard deviation of f

φ distribution function of x $\int \varphi dx = 1$

COMPUTATIONAL FLUID DYNAMICS APPLIED TO FOOD ENGINEERING AND STORAGE

G. L. QUARINI*

A brief description of Computational Fluid Dynamics (CFD) is given. A number of processes relevant to the Food Industry are studied using CFD techniques.
Keywords: Fluid flow, Heat transfer, Mass Transfer, Food Processing, Storage

Introduction

Computational Fluid Dynamics, (CFD), is the term given to the use of computers to solve fluid flow problems. The usefulness of CFD can be enhanced by extending the solution procedure to include heat transfer, mass transfer and chemical reations. Since fluid flow is an all pervasive phenomenon, the potential application areas for CFD are vast. CFD has penetrated into many industries, where it is used as both a research and product development tool. Beneficiaries include aerospace, automotive, chemical and metallurgical engineers, oceanographers, meteorologists and hydrologists among others.

There are, however, a number of applicataion areas in which CFD is not yet playing a major role. One of these areas is food processing and storage. Since many of the problems associated with food manufacture and storage are similar to those found in a number of other industries (eg the process industry), where CFD is already a useful tool, the time is now right to 'graft' as much of the CFD experience as appropriate. This will bring significant benefits for a relatively low investment.

It would be incorrect to suggest that CFD will be able to answer all (or many) of the problems encountered in the food industry accurately, quickly and inexpensively. Present CFD methods suffer from a number of deficiences including:

> achieving converged solutions
> identifying or developing appropriate models
> turbulence modelling
> need for fast computers with large memories
> need for requiring skilled personel

Nonetheless, the few examples presented in this paper clearly indicate the power and potential value of CFD as a tool for food technologists, and designers of equipment used in food manufacture and storage.

* CFDS, Harwell Laboratory, Oxon

CFD Technique

Associated with CFD are a number of inherent problems. Some are connected with the numerical/computational techniques employed, while others are related to our lack of knowledge and ablility to represent the physical phenomena controlling fluid flow, heat and mass transfer.

Physical Modelling

This includes choosing the simplest mathematical model and boundary conditions which adequately represents the true problem. For example, the following questions must be answered before we can proceed: is a time independent (steady state) solution adequate?, do we need to carry out a three-dimensional (rather than two-dimensional) calculation?, is the flow turbulent and, if so, what turbulence model should be used?. Boundary conditions need to be established, sometimes this can be a surprisingly difficult task.
Particular difficulties associated with the food processing industry include:

> identification of suitable heat and mass transfer coefficients. This is important in drying, cooking and refrigeration,

> development of 'clever' models to represent heat and mass transfer in solids. This is particularly important when a complex process needs to be represented, eg a change of state (removal of water, chemical change),

> choosing appropriate values of emissivity, and knowing how these may change with variations of temperature and time.

Once the boundary conditions and phsical models have been chosen, the problem is reduced to a set of complex, coupled, non-linear transport equations. This will typically include three momentum equations, one of conservation, a number of equations to model the turbulence phenomenon, an energy (or temperature) equation, and transport equations to represent different chemical species. The relevant equations are given in the Appendix.

Numerical Modelling

Here we include the mesh or co-ordinate system required to represent the geometry to be modelled, the discretization scheme used to approximate the differential operators present in the equations and the numerical solution algorithm adopted.

Essentially CFD entails the division of the computational domain into a number of smaller control volumes. What happens in each control volume is dependent on what is going on in its adjacent neighbours. The coupling between the control volumes is in fact controlled by the fluxes of mass, momentum and energy across the control volume faces. This coupling is described by the equations of:

> mass conservation,
> momentum (Navier-Stokes),
> energy.

The discretization of these equations results in a set of algebraic equations. The discretization process introduces errors, the magnitude of these depends on the order of the approximation used. In general, these errors decrease as the control volumes are made smaller.

There are a number of possible methods of solving the algebraic equations. A robust and reasonably common technique is to solve for each variable (eg velocity components, temperature, turbulence quantities) for the whole computational domain, assuming that the other variables are fixed. This iterative technique requires some special treatment for the pressure which appears in the momentum equation. This usually takes the form of some iterative method in which the pressure distribution is determined from the conservation equation. The errors associated with the specific solution techniques include computer round-off, and convergence limits.

Examples of the use of CFD in the Food Process Industry

CFD can provide benefit to the food processing industry in the following areas, and in some cases is already doing so:

> drying
> mixing
> cooking (baking)
> refrigeration
> clean room conditions

In the drying area we consider the analysis of the performance of spray dryers; for mixing, we look at batch mixing vessels; in the baking area, we briefly view the modelling of the phase change problem; and we present a preliminary study on the performance of a cold display cabin for the refrigeration topic.

Drying

Spray dryers are widely used in the food process industry for the production of commodities such as instant powdered coffee and powdered milk. The size of these dryers can vary enormously, from a meter or so to many tens of meter in diameter. Essentially they work by attempting to hold droplets of fluid in a warm dry gas stream for long enough for the droplet to evaporate leaving the solid product. Nearly all of these types of dryers impart a circular motion on both the droplets and the gas stream.

The CFDS code FLOW3D has been used to investigated the performance of these units with considerable success. The models and physics within them have progressed to a point where :

> the droplet trajectory is computed in a Lagrangian framework

> the evaporation from the drop is computed as a function of local conditions including temperature, vapour pressure, and velocity

Figures 1 to 3 show the grid used to represent the geometry and some particle (droplet) tracks within the dryer. There are significant lessons to be learnt, including:

> the trajectory of small particles (droplets) are different from those of the larger ones

> recirculation zones exist within the units

> residence time varies for different particle

Mixing

Mixing must be one of the most common operations used in the food processing industry, however, it is difficult to do well in an optimized way (ie with minimum energy input and in the shortest possible time). Batch reactors are frequently used in the chemical and food processing industries. These invariably have some form of stirrer or paddle, and perhaps some baffles and some heat transfer surfaces.

The CFDS codes FLOW3D and ASTEC have been used to study the mixing process in such equipment. Figure 4 present the grid used to represent the geometry and some of the results from the CFD calulations. Here the worthwhile lessons are:

> the amount of stochastic enrgy (turbulence) being fed into the vessel is not uniformly distributed,

> the position of the stirrer affects the quality of the mixing.

Phase Change (Baking)

Here the problem addressed is the temperature-time characteristic of a material containing a volatile component which is placed in a hot environment. Such problems occur when bread dough is placed in an oven. They also occur when structural cement is exposed to very hot fire contitions!. In both cases the material heats up, however its temperature is moderated by the effect of the 'boiling off' process of the volatile component. In the case of bread and cement, the volatile component is water.

Figure 5 refer to the temperature-time history of a hypothetical cylinder of material. Heat gained by the cylinder is set by a heat transfer coefficient as well as an enhancement from radiation. The important thing to note is that as the temperature of the cylinder increases, the quantity of heat absorbed decreases, since the driving temperature difference decreases.

One can also see the effect of the volatile component on the temperature-time distribution; the rate of temperature rise being severely reduced as the bulk temperatures approach the boiling point of the volatile component.

Refrigeration

Refrigeration is one of the most important methods of food storage used in industrialized countries. It is used to store meat for long periods of time a relatively low temperatures, it is also used as a method of extending the shelf life of foods such as dairy products, while still enabling customers to pick what they want.

Here the interesting problems are:

mass transfer by evaporation/dehydration

buoyancy induced flows, this is especially important when the driving temperature differences are large and the forced cooling flows are small.

Figure 6 shows the mesh used, and some very interesting phenomena. The CFDS code, FLOW3D has been used for this very preliminary work.

Clean room conditions

The provision of adequate standards of cleanliness and appropriate levels of ventillation is of vital importance to the food process industry. CFD can be used to study the flow of air within food production halls, by adopting particle tracking techniques, the movement of particulate matter can be predicted. These techniques can be used as tools by designers to optimise the ventillation within a working environment. They can be extended to help select the the optimal position of ventillation ducts, working areas and machines.

Figures 7 and 8 show some flow predictions obtained with FLOW3D in a room containing a number of obstructions (machines). Particle tracking has been used to help visualise the flows. Further work was undertaken to 'optimise' the location and height of the ventillation inlet ducts so as to minimise recirculation zones within the room. If required, the analysis could be used to minimise the residence time for air within pre-defined areas.

This work can easily be extended to study the movement of scalars, such as water vapour. This is particularly important when considering the ventillation requirements in large chiller and cold rooms. The local vapour pressure turbulence levels, mean flow velocity and local temperature control the 'drying out' or dehydration rate of material.

Conclusions

This note gives some examples of what CFD can do for the food process industry. CDF is unlikely to replace experimental work, it is, however likely to reduce the amount of experimental work on fluid flow and heat and mass transfer. Further, CFD is likely to encourage better design of experimental equipment and better use of the hard data which is slowly becoming available in the food process area.

With the continuing improvements in the performance to cost ratio of the computer hardware combined with the versatile CFD software, it is likely that we will see a rapid adoption of the use of CFD by the food processing industry.

Acknowledgements

The author would like to acknowledge the work and contributions made by many CFDS members, including Dr B A Splawski, Dr N S Wilkes, Dr M J Tierney, and Mr R A Hieley. The examples given are the results of their labours. Thanks is also given to Dr D Oakley of SPS.

CONTINUITY, MOMENTUM and ENERGY EQUATIONS

Continuity

$$\frac{\partial \rho}{\partial t} + \frac{\partial \rho u_i}{\partial x_i} = 0$$

Momentum

$$\frac{\partial u_i}{\partial t} + \frac{\partial u_i u_j}{\partial x_i} = F_i - \frac{\partial p}{\partial x_i} + \frac{\partial}{\partial x_i}\{\mu_{eff}\partial \frac{u_i}{\partial x_i}\}$$

where

$$\mu_{eff} = \mu + \mu_t$$

and

$$\mu_t \frac{\partial u_i}{\partial x_i} = <u_i u_j>$$

Energy

$$\frac{\partial \phi}{\partial t} + \frac{\partial u_i \phi}{\partial x_i} = G_i + \frac{\partial}{\partial x_i}\{\kappa_{eff}\frac{\partial \phi}{\partial x_i}\}$$

where

$$\kappa_{eff} = \kappa + \kappa_t$$

and

$$\kappa_t \frac{\partial \phi}{\partial x_i} = <u_i \phi>$$

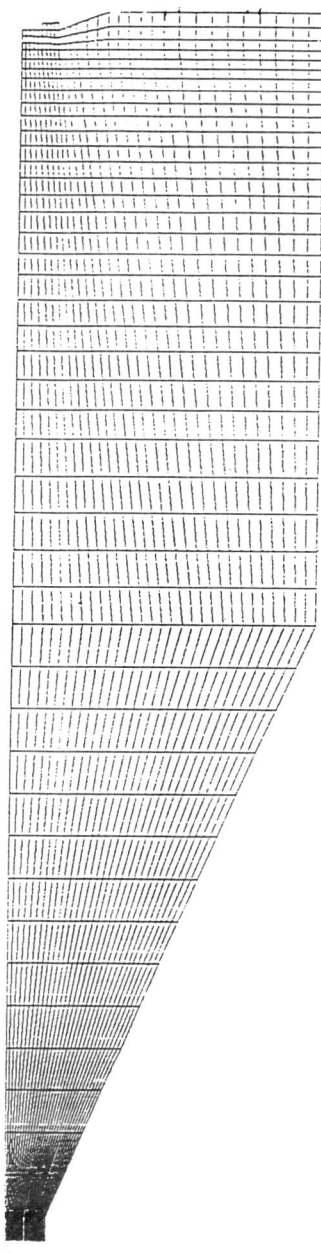

Figure 1 The FLOW3D grid used to model the spray dryer

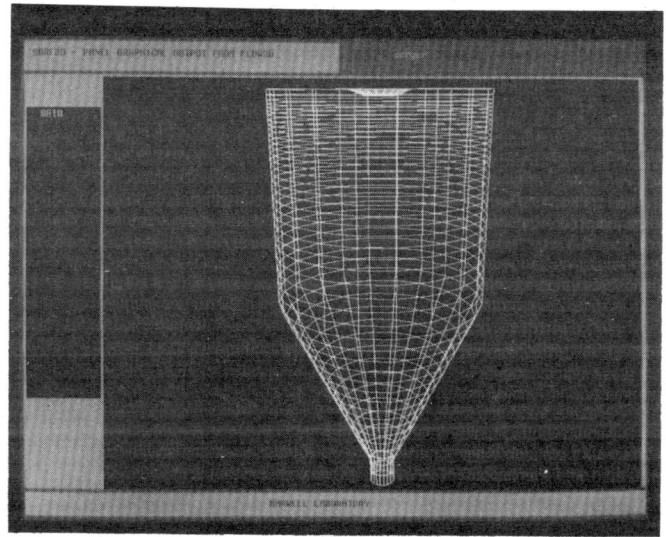

Figure 2   The spray dryer geometry (grid) in three dimensions

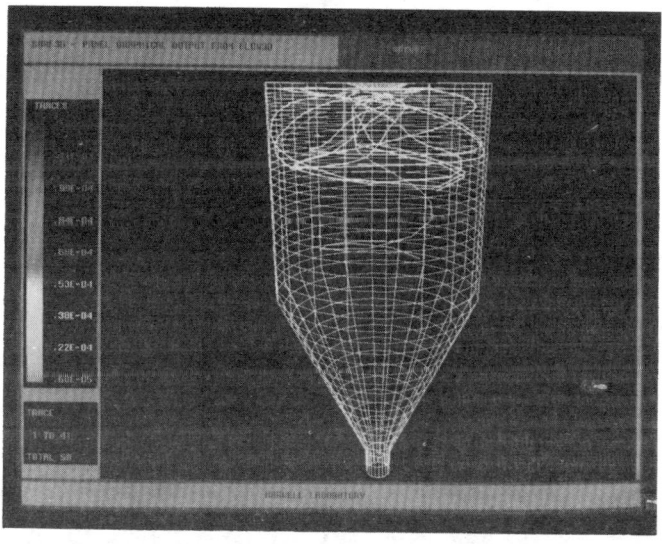

Figure 3   Some particle tracks of droplets within the spray dryer

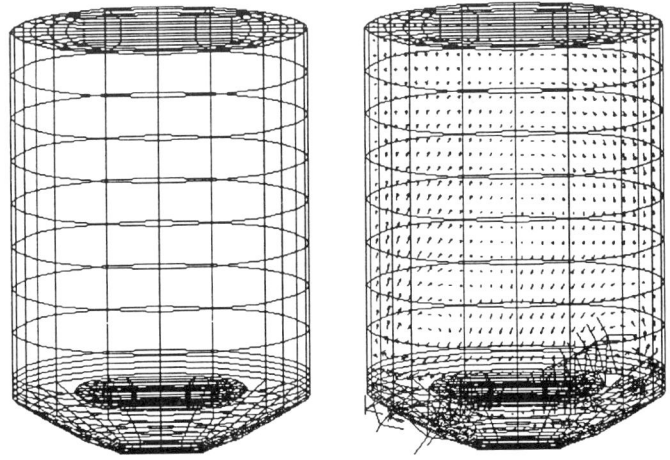

Figure 4   Velocity vectors and batch reactor identifying poor momentum transfer from the stirrer to the bulk fluid

Heating of solids containing water

When porous solids containing water are rapidly heated to high temperatures, the rate of heat penetration is governed both by the thermal properties of the solid, and by the phase change of the water content.

The prediction of heat transfer in this medium by analytical means is not easy, because of the moving interface between wet and dry regions, often with different thermal properties in each region. On the other hand it is possible to use conventional computer codes for heat transfer, if they can solve the heat conduction equation with temperature dependent properties. The heat absorbed by phase change can be simulated by using an enhanced heat capacity over an appropriate temperature range. The flexibility of a computational approach also allows further modelling, for example, to incorporate heat sources due to internal exothermic reactions, or boundary conditions to represent external heating conditions.

These techniques have been successfully used to develop models for heat penetration into cemented blocks during a fire, and also for the heat output from a large volume of setting cement due to its hydration exotherm.

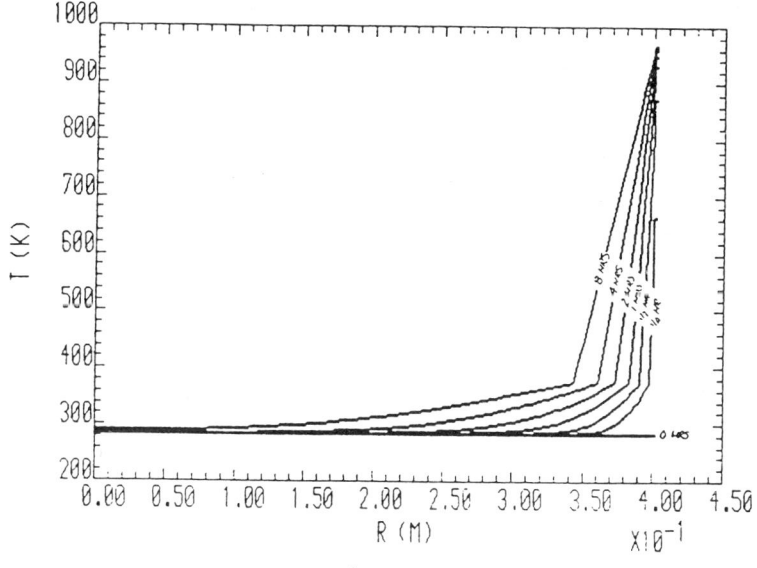

Figure 5

TYPICAL INSTANTANEOUS TEMPERATURE PROFILE FOR EXTERNALLY HEATED WET SOLID

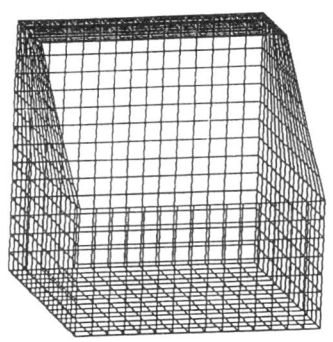

COMPUTATIONAL GRID

Figure 6

Example calculation of forced cooling in a chiller/display cabinet, using the CFDS code
FLOW3D

The unit size is 2m high x 2m wide x 2m deep. The computational grid is 15 x 14 x 15 grid cells. Two cells in the middle of the left panel are designated inlets with inflow at 1m/sec and 0°C. Two cells on the opposite panel are outlets. Side panels have a fixed temperature of 10°C, and the front window is represented by a fixed temperature boundary at 20°C. Computed flow and temperature patterns are shown at two heights. At mid-height the main flow feature is the current across the unit from the inlets to the outlets. Higher up there is weaker flow in the opposite direction.

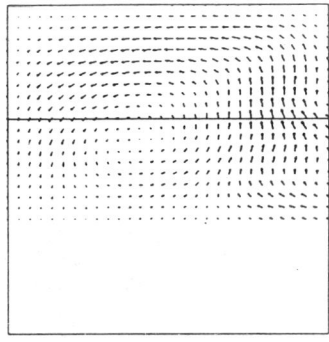

VELOCITY VECTORS AT HEIGHT 1.5 m

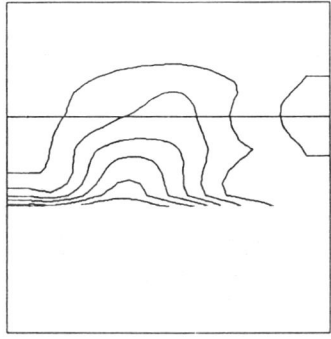

TEMPERATURE CONTOURS AT HEIGHT 1.5 m

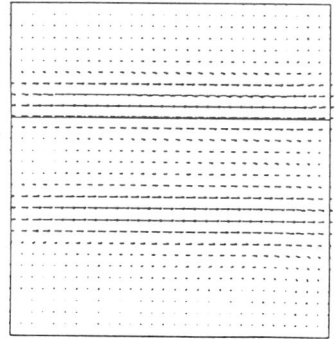

VELOCITY VECTORS AT HEIGHT 1 m

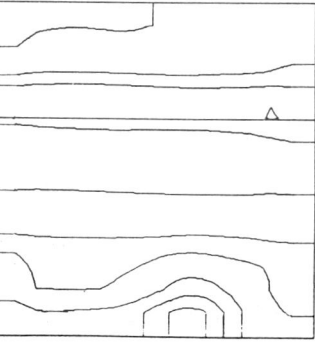

TEMPERATURE CONTOURS AT HEIGHT 1 m

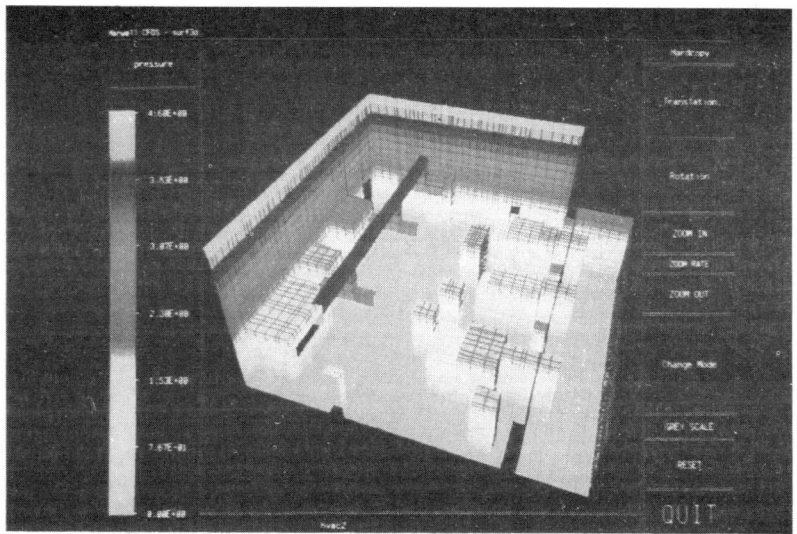

Figure 7   Geometry within a working environment in which food processing occurs

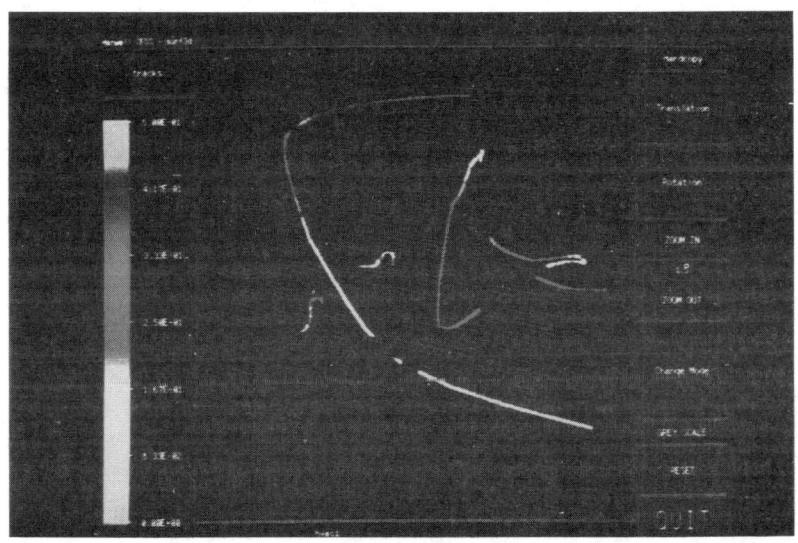

Figure 8   Particle tracks indicating ventilation flows within the working environment

A MONTE CARLO SIMULATION OF THE FLOW AND MIXING OF FOOD FLUIDS IN A CAVITY TRANSFER MIXER

JJ van der Meer[†] , PJ Fryer and CD Rielly

Abstract

The development of mixing under various design and operating conditions was studied experimentally in a cavity transfer mixer (CTM). Although the experiments provided some important results on macro-scale, distributive mixing in the CTM, the reduction in scale and intensity of segregation was so rapid that tracer concentration fluctuations fell below the resolution of the measurement equipment after only one or two cavity transfers. In order to gain further insight into the development of mixedness in the CTM, computer simulations, based on a simplified mathematical model of the flow, were performed. The model yielded realistic results for the increase in interfacial area between two miscible liquids, with increasing number of cavity transfers. Some rules for scale-up at (i) constant increase in the degree of mixedness, characterised by a mixing number, and, (ii) constant shear rate and constant shearing time, are also proposed.

The Cavity Transfer Mixer

The Cavity Transfer Mixer (CTM) is a continuous dynamic mixer, originally developed for plastics processing (Gale 1982) but which has now found some applications in the food industry. The geometry of the CTM shown in figure 1 consists of a rotating inner cylinder (rotor) which fits closely inside a stationary outer cylinder (stator). Both the outer surface of the rotor and the inner surface of the stator are covered with close-packed hemispherical cavities, off-set in the axial direction, such that a pressure gradient drives the fluid axially through the mixer from a cavity on the rotor to one on the stator, and so on until it leaves the mixer. Due to the rotor movement the angular position of the rotor cavities with respect to the stator cavities changes periodically, resulting in a helical flow direction from cavity to cavity. In the past CTMs have been developed for polymer processing with different shapes of cavities and different arrangements of the cavities on the surfaces of both the rotor and the stator.

For the mixer to be used effectively, its operation must be understood, however, only qualitative descriptions of mixing in the CTM have been presented so far (Gale 1990). The aim of this work is to develop a mathematical model which enables a calculation of the degree of mixedness in the CTM as a function of the number of rows of cavities. Such a model would be useful for optimizing the design and operating conditions, such as size, number of rows of cavities, throughput and rotational speed of the rotor, of the CTM. For this study a CTM with a perspex stator and a dural rotor was built; the perspex mixer was a 2 x scaled-up model of the pilot plant CTM shown in figure 1 (mixer dimensions are given in table 1). It consisted of hemispherical cavities in a hexagonal arrangement on the rotor and stator surfaces, with 6 cavities per circumferential row on both rotor and stator. As is usual for blending applications in the food industry, the CTM was independently motor driven and was fed by a pump.

Since the flow in the CTM is largely determined by relative tangential movement of the cavities, a Reynolds number was defined in terms of the rotational speed and the cavity dimensions. In this "cavity Reynolds number", Re_c, the diameter of the cavity, D_c, and the velocity of the rotor at the surface of the cavity are used as appropriate length and velocity scales

$$Re_c = \frac{\rho \cdot \pi D_r N \cdot D_c}{\mu} \tag{1}$$

where N is the rotational speed, D_r is the diameter of the rotor; μ is the viscosity and ρ is the density of the fluid. In industrial practice $Re_c \approx 10^2$, and so this work has concentrated on the mixing of Newtonian, miscible fluids with viscosities in the range of 0.01 - 1 Ns/m². Rotational speeds were chosen in the range of 4 - 60 rpm as to achieve these Reynolds numbers.

A qualitative description of the mixing mechanisms in the CTM

The perspex model was first used for flow visualisation studies of the flow pattern and cavity transfer mechanism. Dye was injected into one of the upstream cavities and the flow path through the mixer observed. Experiments showed that the annular gap between the rotor and the stator was wetted, but none of the dyed tracer entered this region. The flow in the CTM can thus be described as a repetitive combination of *cavity flow* in the cavities, followed by a *cross-cavity flow* in a predominantly radial direction across the annulus from one cavity into another in the next row up. For all of the operating conditions given in table 1 the dye streaks were smooth (no turbulent dispersion) and the flow pattern was observed to be laminar.

---

† Correspondence should be sent to J.J. van der Meer, Department of Chemical Engineering, University of Cambridge, Pembroke Street, CB2 3RA

Cavity flow. An axial pressure gradient drives fluid through the cavities; this axial flow is combined with a tangential movement due to momentum transfer at the 'open' surface of the cavity (contiguous with the annulus) because of the relative motion of the rotor and the stator. The combination of the axial pressure flow and tangential drag flow produces a helical flow within each cavity. The hemispherical shape of the cavities results in a small amount of extensional flow within the cavity. The extensional strain rates within the cavities are relatively low and the principle shear layer in the CTM is between the rotor and the stator. Moreover, analysis of the flow in a two dimensional model of a driven cavity shows that for large Reynolds numbers in laminar flow ($Re_c > 10^2$) the core of the fluid in the centre of the cavity rotates as a solid body (Van der Meer, 1990). In this inviscid core no mixing takes place since fluid particles are not displaced relatively to one another whilst rotating. The contribution of cavity flow to mixing in the CTM is therefore limited; its main effect is to reorientate fluid elements, prior to the cross-cavity flow.

Cross-cavity flow. In operation the rotor rotates at a constant speed giving a tangential shear field in the annular gap between rotor and stator, see figure 2. During transfer from a cavity into one opposite the fluid passes through this shear layer. Since the ratio of the rotor radius to the stator radius is near unity the shear rate in the annulus is approximately constant it is assumed that the cross-cavity flow passes through a region of simple shear.

Apart from this shear flow, cross-cavity flow is also extensional; the cross-sectional area available for flow within the cavities is not in general equal to the area for cross-cavity flow formed by the projection of the rotor cavities on the stator cavities (this area changes with time). The rotor and stator cavities are off-set asymmetrically, as can be seen from figure 3, so that the area ($A_1 + A_2$) for cross-cavity flow from rotor to stator is in general larger than A_3, the area for transfer from stator to rotor. This causes the flow from a rotor cavity to decelerate and the flow from a stator cavity to accelerate during cross-cavity flow. The exact rate of contraction and elongation depends on the angular position of the rotor, however, on average the cross-sectional area for a flow from a rotor cavity decreases by a factor of 0.4 and for flow from a stator cavity the area increases by a factor of 0.3. The elongation rates arising from this series of decelerations and accelerations are not very large and it is likely that their contribution to mixing is small, especially as part of the mixing effect achieved by accelerating extensional flow is lost by subsequent deceleration as the fluid enters the next cavity. In addition to the shear and extensional flow, distributive mixing is achieved by the redistribution of the fluid over the cavities in the next row up, see figure 3. This distributive mixing is further discussed in the experimental results section.

Theory of laminar mixing in shear flows

The concepts of the total interfacial surface between the fluid components and of the striation thickness of a segregated mixture are commonly used to assess the degree of mixedness of two miscible fluids in a laminar velocity field (Spencer and Wiley, 1951). The two quantities are related (if the mixture has a lamellar structure); one half of the interfacial area times the striation thickness is equal to the volume of the mixture. Theoretical work by Spencer and Wiley (1951) related the growth in interfacial area to the shear strain, γ, experienced in simple shear flow by

$$\frac{A_1}{A_o} = \sqrt{1 - \gamma \cos \alpha \cos \beta + \gamma^2 \cos^2 \alpha} \tag{2}$$

where A_o and A_1 are respectively the initial and final interfacial areas and α and β define the initial orientation of the fluid interface to the shear field. The ratio of interfacial area before and after shear is called the mixing number, M (Lewis and Mokhtarian, 1983). If the interface is orientated such that it is initially perpendicular to the shear field ($\alpha = 0$, $\beta = \pi/2$), giving the largest mixing effect, then eq. (2) becomes

$$M = \sqrt{1 + \gamma^2} \tag{3}$$

so that for large shear strains ($\gamma \gg 1$) $M \approx \gamma$. The validity of eq. (3) was demonstrated experimentally by Ng and Erwin (1979), who also showed that if fluid orientated perpendicular to a simple shear field was subjected to a large shear strain γ, then reorientated to its initial orientation and subjected again to a similar shear, the total increase in interfacial area was given by the product of the two individual mixing numbers: $M_1 = A_1 / A_0 = \gamma$, $M_2 = A_2 / A_1 = \gamma$, i.e.

$$M_t = M_1 \times M_2 = \gamma^2 \tag{4}$$

In general for a mixer, consisting of n identical shearing sections and with (n-1) reorientation sections in between, and whose mixing number per shearing section is some function of the shear strain, $f(\gamma)$, the total increase in interfacial area is given by

38

$$\frac{A_n}{A_0} = \prod_{i=1}^{n} M_i = M_1^n = (f(\gamma))^n \tag{5}$$

So the increase in interfacial area is an exponential function of the mixing number with the exponent equal to the total number of shearing sections the fluid passes through. This theory can be applied to the CTM. The shearing sections correspond to the shear flow in cross-cavity flow, whereas the reorientation sections correspond to helical flow within the cavities which reorientate the fluid approximately to its initial orientation to the shear field prior to the previous cross-cavity flow. This qualitative model for the development of mixing in the CTM has been described by Gale (1990), who also showed that the CTM obeys an exponential mixing relation when mixing PVC, as expressed by eq. (5). Quantitative data on the size of the total mixing number and its dependence on design and operation conditions of the CTM have not as yet been reported in the literature. This information would be useful for optimizing the design of the CTM; for example in specifying the minimum number of cavity rows required for a specified reduction in striation thickness. It is the aim of this work to produce this information using computational models of the flow and mixing in the CTM and validations with experiment.

Experiments on mixing

Experimental set up. The aim of experimental work in the perspex CTM was to measure the development of interfacial area along the mixer as a function of throughput and rotational speed. Full details are given by Van der Meer (1992). A continuous stream of an electrolyte tracer was introduced into the bulk flow through a needle in one of the cavities in the second cavity row on the stator. Conductivity measurements were made using micro probes at several cavities downstream of the injection cavity. The probes have a spatial resolution of approximately 1 mm, a frequency response (3 dB cut off) of 100 Hz and were sampled at a rate of 312.5 Hz. Dependent on the bulk flow rate (200-400 litre/h) measurements were taken under steady conditions for between 30 and 60 seconds. The conductivity data were stored and then converted into NaCl concentration profiles as a function of time, C(t).

To characterize quantitatively the structure of the mixture flowing past a conductivity probe, the concept of a 'scale of segregation' was used (Danckwerts, 1952; Nadav and Tadmor, 1973). The autocorrelation function, $R(\tau)$, can be calculated from C(t) as

$$R(\tau) = \frac{\overline{(C(t) - \overline{C}) \ (C(t + \tau) - \overline{C})}}{(C(t) - \overline{C})^2} \tag{6}$$

where $\overline{C}$ is the mean tracer concentration measured by the probe. High values of $R(\tau)$ indicate that any value of $(C(t) - \overline{C})$ at any time t is likely to be followed by an identical value of $(C(t) - \overline{C})$ at time $(t + \tau)$. Thus any regular fluctuation of period T in the signal, which would be expected for a lamellar structured mixture, would give $R(\tau)$ with alternating positive and negative values. High values of $R(\tau)$ would occur for τ = T, 2T,.. and low values for τ = T/2, 3T/2,..

The length scale of segregation, L_S, is the mean velocity, U, of the bulk fluid in the axial direction multiplied by the integral of $R(\tau)$, between pairs of concentrations a time τ apart, taken over values of t ranging from zero (where R(0) = 1) to a value of $\tau = \xi$ (where $R(\xi) = 0$)

$$L_s = U \int_0^\xi R(\tau) \, d\tau \tag{7}$$

Since we may treat the length scale of segregation as being equivalent to the striation thickness L_S is expected to decrease with distance down the mixer. Eq. (4) suggests that it should decrease in an exponential manner.

Experimental results. Conductivity measurements showed that in all rows on the stator downstream of the injection cavity the tracer was concentrated in only a limited number (about two out of six) of cavities per row. Figure 4 shows two typical correlograms for such cavities: one for a cavity in the third row and one for a cavity in the fifth row on the stator. For this experiment the bulk fluid used was 60 W% glycerol-water mixture with a viscosity of approximately 0.01 Ns/m^2. The tracer was a 100 g/l NaCl solution in the same glycerol-water mixture, i.e. with the same physical properties as the bulk flow. The rotational speed was 7.5 rpm which corresponded to Re_C = 300.

The regular pattern of positive and negative values in the correlogram shows that the fluid has a non-random structure. However the graph also shows the two correlograms having a similar periodicity of approximately 1.3 seconds. This was observed for all the correlograms calculated for stator cavities downstream of the injection cavity. This period of 1.3 seconds is equal to one sixth of the time required for a complete revolution of the rotor. Experiments at other operation conditions showed the correlograms to be dominated by the same period of

1/6N. Even though extra interfacial area must have been formed during cross-cavity flow no change in periodicity, and therefore length scale of segregation, was seen for signals from probes at different axial positions in the mixer. It appears that after two or three cross-cavity flows the striation thicknesses fell below the resolution of the conductivity probes.

The mechanism which causes a periodicity of 1/6N to appear in the downstream stator cavities is outlined in figure 5. The injection cavity is sampled by the cavities in the next row of the rotor at a frequency equal to six times the rotational speed of the rotor. It is assumed that the tracer moves in plug flow through the cavity, such that neighbouring cavities transfer the tracer at times 1/6N apart. Since the passing frequency of rotor cavities is 6N, then all of the tracer is deposited into one or two cavities in the next stator row, resulting in a striated system, and no further distribution takes place between stator cavities in the same row. Although this picture is somewhat idealised, experimentally the tracer is only detected in one or two cavities in the next stator row and the period of 1/6N in the correlogram would results from this lamellar structure. This mechanism repeats itself in subsequent rows, so that a characteristic frequency of N would be detected in all rotor cavities and 6N in all stator cavities. This is independent of the rotational speed and throughput, however, the position of the two cavities on stator row 3, relative to the injection position in row 1 would depend on the ratio NV/Q, where V is the cavity volume and Q is the volumetric flow rate.

These experiments demonstrated that a flow from a stator cavity is distributed between all the cavities in the next row on the rotor but subsequently recombined in one or two cavities on the next row of the stator. It can thus be concluded that distributive mixing in the CTM is very limited. For the complete CTM significant distributive mixing seems to be restricted to the first row of cavities on the rotor that slices the fluid as it flows into the mixer. Fluid flows along certain predetermined paths through the mixer and if large non-uniformities exist in the fluid entering the CTM it is unlikely that they would become mixed. This indicates that special attention must be taken for the design of the inlet system of the mixer. Therefore it may be concluded that there is little distributive mixing and that the shear flow in the cross-cavity flow is the main mixing mechanism.

Computer simulations of mixing in the CTM

Shear strain during cross-cavity flow. As described above, the total increase in interfacial area for fluid flowing through the mixer can be calculated from the product of the mixing numbers for each cross-cavity flow the fluid undergoes. To calculate the mixing numbers the following model was set up.

The velocity difference across the shear layer is approximately equal to the tangential velocity of the rotor at the annulus ($\pi D_r N$). The actual width, ΔR, of the shear layer may differ from the annular gap between the rotor and the stator and is unknown. Since $\Delta R \ll D_r / 2$, the shear rate $\dot{\gamma}$ is constant and can be expressed as

$$\dot{\gamma} \approx \frac{\pi D_r N}{\Delta R} \qquad (8)$$

The shear strain, γ, experienced during the cross-cavity flow can be found by multiplying the shear rate and the time, t, for the fluid to flow through the shear field

$$\gamma = \int_0^t \dot{\gamma}(t') \, dt' \approx \dot{\gamma} t \qquad (9)$$

The time t is equal to the width of the shear layer divided by the average velocity $<V>$ of the fluid during cross-cavity flow

$$t = \frac{\Delta R}{<V>} \qquad (10)$$

Whilst flowing through the CTM the fluid undergoes a number of cross-cavity flows (twelve for the perspex CTM). The shear strain, γ_i, experienced during the i-th cross-cavity flow follows from eqs. (8), (9) and (10)

$$\gamma_i = \frac{\pi D_i N}{<V_i>}, \quad i = 1,2,..12 \qquad (11)$$

Figure 3 shows that during a cross-cavity flow there are either one or two flow routes, depending on the relative cavity positions on the rotor and the stator. Moreover, the areas for cross-cavity flow also depend on relative cavity position so that there is a distribution of mean velocities for each cross-cavity flow and hence a distribution of shear strains (see eq. (11)). By summing up the shear strains for all the cross-cavity flows experienced by a fluid package, total strain histories of individual packages can be calculated at any axial position in the mixer. If this is repeated for a large number of fluid packages strain distribution functions (SDF) (Lidor and Tadmor, 1976) can be calculated as a function of axial position in the CTM. Similarly, from the product of the individual mixing numbers, the total mixing number can be calculated at any axial position in the CTM. Repeating this for a large number of fluid packages yields the distribution of these mixing numbers.

To calculate these distributions a computer program based on a Monte Carlo simulation technique was developed. The working of this program is outlined below, after the relations used to calculate the mean cross-cavity flow velocity and mixing numbers have been explained.

The mean velocity during cross-cavity flow. In cross-cavity flow, a fluid package can flow into either one or two cavities in the next row, depending on the angular position of the rotor. The mean velocity for flow into a single cavity follows from continuity. However, for flow into two cavities a relation is needed to describe the mean velocity in the two flow paths as a function of the bulk flow rate and the areas of overlap between rotor and stator cavity.

The axisymmetry of the cavity pattern makes it possible to model fluid flow from one cavity into either of two, distinct, opposite cavities, as a system in which fluid flows from one cavity into a single reservoir through two orifices of similar shapes and sizes as A_1 and A_2. A schematic drawing of this model is shown in figure 6. It is assumed that the pressure is equal in all cavities in a single row (i.e. there is no dependence of the pressure on tangential position, because the mixer is axisymmetric). Therefore the pressure drop, ΔP, over A_1 is equal to that over A_2. If $A_1 \neq A_2$ the difference in the area and circumference of the two regions results in a different fraction of fluid flowing through A_1 and A_2 and in two different mean velocities, $<V_1>$ and $<V_2>$. As there are six cavities per row the flow per cavity is one sixth of the total flow rate, Q. So continuity gives

$$\frac{Q}{6} = A_1 <V_1> + A_2 <V_2>$$
(12)

The cross-cavity flow is laminar and the flows through A_1 and A_2 are assumed similar to the flow through small straight channels of equal length, L. It is assumed that the Hagen-Poiseuille equation may be used to estimate the pressure drop for each flow

$$\frac{\Delta P}{L} = 2\mu <V_1> \left(\frac{S_1}{A_1}\right)^2 \qquad (13) \qquad\qquad \frac{\Delta P}{L} = 2\mu <V_2> \left(\frac{S_2}{A_2}\right)^2 \qquad (14)$$

where S_1 and S_2 are the circumferences of A_1 and A_2. Solving eqs. (12) - (14) for the velocity gives

$$<V_1> = \frac{\dfrac{Q}{6}}{A_2 \left(\dfrac{S_1}{A_1}\right)^2 \left(\dfrac{A_2}{S_2}\right)^2 + A_1}$$
(15)

An equivalent equation for $<V_2>$ follows by interchanging the indices 1 and 2. If the variation of A and S with time is known eq.(15) can be used to calculate velocities for fluid packages traced through the CTM.

Calculation of the mixing numbers. The effect of the strain during cross-cavity flow upon the increase in interfacial area is not the same for all cross-cavity flows, and so different mixing numbers for different cross-cavity flows must be defined. During the first cross-cavity flow the interfacial areas in the fluid packages have a more or less random orientation to the shear field in the annulus. The shearing of the fluid during this cross-cavity flow, however, partially aligns these interfaces (Erwin, 1978). In the following cavity flow the alignment achieved is expected to be more or less conserved so interfaces have an approximately perpendicular orientation to the shear field during the second cross-cavity flow. Alignment continues to improve for subsequent cross-cavity flows. For simplicity, it will be assumed that interfaces are randomly orientated in the first cross-cavity flow and all are perpendicular to the shear field in the following cross-cavity flows.

To calculate the mixing number for randomly orientated interfaces eq. (2) was rewritten in spherical coordinates and integrated numerically over all possible orientations of the interface for a number of shear strains. The result, averaged over all possible orientations, gives the first mixing number as a function of the shear strain and, it was found to be well described by the hyperbolic relation (Van der Meer, 1992)

$$M_1 = \sqrt{0.25 \left(\gamma^2 + 1.78\right)} + 0.33$$
(16)

The mixing numbers, M_2 to M_{12}, for the other cross-cavity flows are given by eq. (3). Thus for the increase in interfacial area of fluid package j through the complete CTM the total mixing number comes from the sum of eqs. (3) and (16)

$$\left(\frac{A_{12}}{A_0}\right)_j = \prod_{n=1}^{12} M_n = \left(\sqrt{0.25\left(\gamma_{1j}{}^2 + 1.78\right)} + 0.33\right) \times \prod_{i=2}^{12} \left(\sqrt{1 + \gamma_{ij}{}^2}\right)$$

(17)

where γ_{ij} is the shear strain of fluid package j during the i-th cross-cavity flow

$$\gamma_{ij} = \frac{\pi D_r N}{\langle V_{ij} \rangle}, \quad j = 1,2,..12$$

(18)

As can be seen from eqs. (15) - (18) in this model the shear strain, and therefore also the mixing numbers, are independent of the fluid viscosity and both M and γ increase with increasing rotational speed of the rotor and with decreasing throughput.

The simulation model. A Monte Carlo simulation of the CTM has been produced in which the mixer is modelled as two hexagonal arrays with the cavities at the node points, one array for the rotor and one for the stator. These arrays move relative to one another, corresponding to the angular movement of the rotor. The cylindrical shapes of the rotor and stator are simulated by introducing circular periodicity at the sides of the arrays. The computer program traces the path of fluid packages through the CTM, such that at any time their position in the arrays and the areas for cross-cavity flow are known.

During the residence time of a fluid package in a cavity the angular position of the rotor is changed according to the rotational speed of the rotor. After the fluid has spent one residence time in the cavity a cross-cavity flow occurs: the cross-sectional areas with the opposite cavity and the two mean cross-cavity velocities are calculated using eq. (15). The probability that a fluid package flows into either of the two opposite cavities is proportional to the fractional flow rate through the two cross-sectional areas. A uniformly distributed random generator is used for the decision making and residence times in the cavities are calculated assuming plug flow. All positions of the rotor cavities relative to the stator, when the fluid first enters, are equally likely and are also determined by the random number generator. For each fluid package a series of 12 cross-cavity velocities are calculated, which can then be used for the calculation of the strain and mixing number distribution as a function of the number of cross-cavity flows it experiences. It was found that in order to obtain smooth distributions approximately 10^5 flows of fluid packages through the mixer had to be simulated.

Simulation results. To illustrate the model, mixing in the perspex CTM, operating at a rotational speed of 30 rpm and at a throughput of 400 l/h was simulated. Figure 7 shows resulting SDF's, $g(\gamma)$, after 2, 4, 6, 8, 10 and 12 cross-cavity flows. These distributions have been normalised according to

$$\int_0^\infty g(\gamma)\, d\gamma = 1$$

(19)

The SDFs appear to be asymmetric and are characterised by a minimum shear strain (non-zero) and by infinitely high shear strains. These features arise from the existence of, respectively, a maximum mean cross-cavity velocity and infinitesimally small values of this velocity. From the SDF's an average shear strain per cross-cavity flow of 11.0 strain units is estimated.

Figure 8 shows the relative frequency distributions of the total mixing number. The distributions are placed on a logarithmic base and are approximately equally spaced from one another because of the exponential nature of the mixing process. The distributions are much broader than the corresponding SDF's because of the multiplication of the individual mixing numbers which are functions of γ. The distribution after n = 4 cross-cavity flows has a mixing number of approximately 7×10^3 at the peak and a minimum mixing number of 2×10^3.

Figure 9 shows the mixing numbers as a function of the number of cross-cavity flows. In the graph for any even number of cross-cavity flows, the lower symbol indicates the minimum mixing number and the upper symbol the mixing number at the peak of the distribution. The minimum mixing numbers are important to determine the minimum number of cross-cavity flows required for all the fluid to be mixed to a certain degree of homogeneity. If for example a reduction of length scale by a factor of 10^4 is required it can be seen from the graph that the lower line exceeds $M_n = 10^4$ from n > 5. At the operating conditions as specified for the simulation, the mixer should therefore at least have 5 cross-cavity flows: for the CTM of this study this implies 4 rotor and 3 stator rows of cavities.

Scale-up criteria for mixing in the CTM

The effect of scale-up on mixing can now be examined using this model as a basis. Two scale-up criteria are considered: (i) the same reduction in length scale, or a constant mixing number, at both scales of operation; and, (ii) the same total strain is experienced by the fluid at both scales, ie. both the strain rate and the time spent in

42

the shear layers are constant. In this discussion it is assumed that the mixers are geometrically similar, but that the number of rows (ie. the number of cross-cavity flows) may be changed to suit criteria (i) or (ii).

(i) Scaling-up with a constant mixing number. For large shear strains ($\gamma \gg 1$) eq. (17) shows that the total mixing number, M_t, is proportional to γ^n. The requirement to be met is therefore (see eq.(11))

$$\left(\pi D_r N \cdot \overline{\left(\frac{1}{\langle V \rangle}\right)}\right)^n = \text{constant} \tag{20}$$

The reciprocal mean cross-cavity velocity, averaged over the n cross-cavity flows and time, is assumed to be described by $1/\langle V \rangle_c$, where $\langle V \rangle_c$ is a 'characteristic' cross-cavity velocity. For geometrically scaled-up mixers $\langle V \rangle_c$ should be proportional to the flow rate Q divided by a length dimension squared, we can take for example

$$\langle V \rangle_c = \chi \frac{Q}{D_r^2} \tag{21}$$

where χ is a proportionality constant and is identical for both the model and the scaled-up version of the CTM. Its value can be estimated using the simulation results of the cross-cavity flow velocity distribution (not presented here) and for the mixer of this study $\chi = 2.8$. Substitution of eq. (21) into (20) gives the scale-up rule

$$\left(\frac{\pi D_{r,1}^3 N_1}{\chi Q_1}\right)^{n_1} = \left(\frac{\pi D_{r,2}^3 N_2}{\chi Q_2}\right)^{n_2} \tag{22}$$

where 1 and 2 refer to the two scales of the mixer. The special cases of equal numbers of rows, or equal CTM diameter may be easily derived from eq. (22).

Scaling-up with both constant shear rate and time spent in the shear layer. Constant scale-up of the shear rate (eq. (8)) requires

$$\frac{\pi D_r N}{\Delta R} = \text{constant} \tag{23}$$

The width of the shear layer, ΔR, is expected to change proportionally to the annular gap and thus scales-up proportionally to D_r. So the requirement becomes that

$$N_1 = N_2 \tag{24}$$

For the time spent in the shear layer to be constant, using the definition of the characteristic velocity, $\langle V \rangle_c$, (see eqs. (10)) follows

$$\frac{n \Delta R}{\langle V \rangle_c} = \text{constant} \tag{25}$$

which, after substitution of eq. (21), gives the scale-up rule

$$\frac{n_1 D_{r,1}^3}{Q_1} = \frac{n_2 D_{r,2}^3}{Q_2} \tag{26}$$

The shear strain remains constant if both eqs. (24) and (26) are met.

Conclusions

Theoretical and experimental results both show that elongational and distributive flow do not contribute significantly to mixing in the CTM. Therefore realistic calculations of the development of mixing in the CTM may be based on the mixing effect of shear flow in cross-cavity flow. The model set up to perform these calculations assumes that the degree of mixedness is an exponential function of the mixing number per cross-cavity flow with the exponent equal to the number of cross-cavity flows the fluid experiences. The mixing numbers are given as explicit functions of shear strain. The model therefore implies that the mixing achieved in the CTM is a function of rotational speed, throughput and number of cavity rows. It is also a function of the dimensions of the machine but only in so far as they concern the diameter of the rotor and the overlap between opposite cavities. The number of cavities per circumferential row is not important from the mixing point of view so long as they allow for the reorientation of the cavity flow prior to cross-cavity flow. The annular gap should be small enough to guide the fluid into the opposite cavities and to avoid leakage of fluid down the annulus.

An example computer simulation based on this model shows that the mixing is described by (broad) distributions of mixing numbers. To design CTMs it is important to know at least the minimum mixing number achieved so that the minimum number of cavity rows may be specified. The example simulation shows that application of the model yields realistic predictions of this minimum number of rows and the model may be used to define useful scale-up rules for mixing in the CTM.

Acknowledgements. J.J. van der Meer would like to acknowledge the financial support and encouragement of Unilever Research Laboratorium Vlaardingen (The Netherlands).

References
Danckwerts, P.V., 1951, Ind. Chem., **9**, 395.
Danckwerts, P.V., 1952, Appl. Sci. Res., **3**, 279.
Erwin, L., 1978, Pol. Eng. Sci, **18**, 572-576.
Erwin, L. and Mokhtarian, F., 1983, Pol. Eng. Sci, **18**, 572-576.
Gale, G.M., 1982, European patent application, 0048590.
Gale, G.M., 1990, Fluid Mixing IV, IChemE Symposium Series, **121**, 413-424.
Lidor, G. and Tadmor, Z., 1976, Pol. Eng. Sci., **16**, 450-462.
Nadav, N. and Tadmor, Z., 1973, Chem. Eng. Sci., **28**, 2115-2126.
Ng, K.Y. and Erwin, L., 1979, 37th ANTEC of the SPE, **25**, 214-244.
Spencer, R.S. and Wiley, R.M., 1951, J. Coll. Sci., **6**, 133-145.
Van der Meer, J.J., 1992, PhD. Thesis, Univ. of Cambridge, Dept. Chem. Eng, to be published.
Van der Meer, J.J., 1990, CPGS report, Univ. of Cambridge, Dept. Chem. Eng.

Latin symbols		Greek symbols	
A	Interfacial area, m^2	α, β	Angles defining orientation interfacial area, -
C	Concentration, kg/m^3	γ	Shear strain, -
D_c	Cavity diameter, m	$\dot{\gamma}$	Shear rate, s^{-1}
D_r	Rotor diameter, m	μ	Viscosity, Ns/m^2
L_s	Length scale of segregation, m	ρ	Density, kg/m^3
M	Mixing number, -	ξ	Correlation time at which $R(\xi) = 0$, s
n	Number of cross-cavity flows, -	χ	Proportionality constant for $<V>_c$, -
N	Rotational speed rotor, rev/s		
ΔP	Pressure drop, Pa	**Indices**	
Q	Volumetric flow rate, m^3/s	i	Identifies the cross-cavity flow, i = 1,2,..12
Re_c	Cavity Reynolds number	j	Identifies the fluid package
ΔR	Width of shear layer, m		
$R(\tau)$	Correlation function, -		
t	Time spent in shear layer, s		
U	Average flow velocity at probe tip, m/s		
$<V>,<V>_c$	Resp. mean and characteristic cross-cavity flow velocity, m/s		

Rotor diameter (mm)	130
Cavity diameter (mm)	60
Annular gap (mm)	0.15
No. cavities on the rotor	42
No. cavities on the stator	36
No. cavities per row	6
Rotational speed (rpm)	7.5 - 60
Throughput (l / h)	200 - 400
Viscosity (Ns / m^2)	0.01 - 1

Table 1. Characteristic dimensions and operation conditions of the perspex CTM.

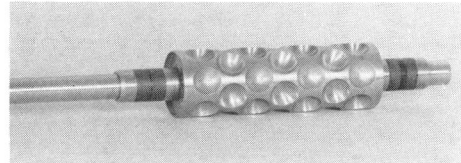

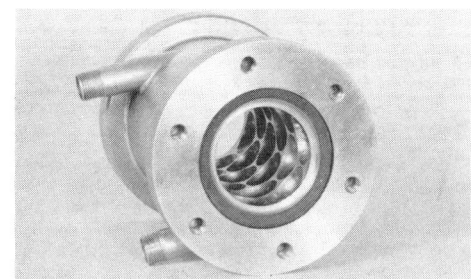

Fig.1 The rotor and stator of the pilot plant CTM.

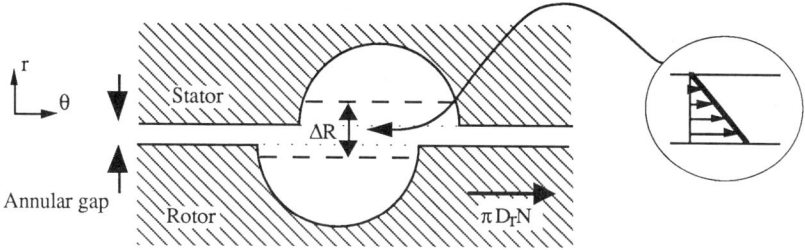

Fig.2 The shear layer in cross-cavity flow of width ΔR and constant shear rate $\dot{\gamma}$.

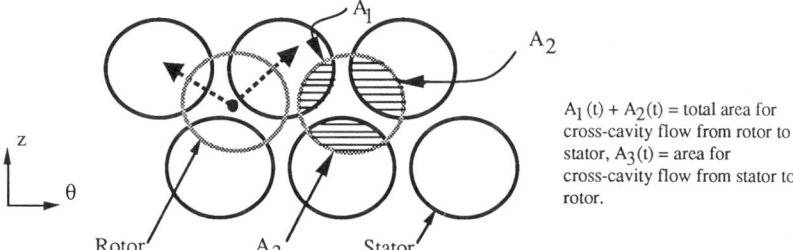

$A_1(t) + A_2(t)$ = total area for cross-cavity flow from rotor to stator, $A_3(t)$ = area for cross-cavity flow from stator to rotor.

Fig.3. Distributive and extensional flow in cross-cavity flow.

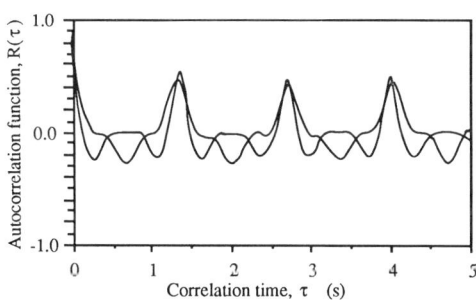

Fig. 4. Correlograms for a cavity in the third row and for a cavity in the fifth row on the stator.

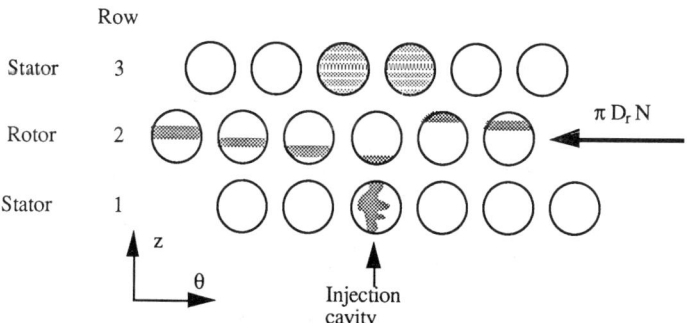

Fig.5. Distributive mixing in the CTM.

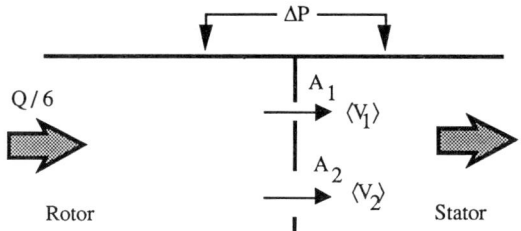

Fig. 6. Schematic drawing of the model used for the velocity calculations.

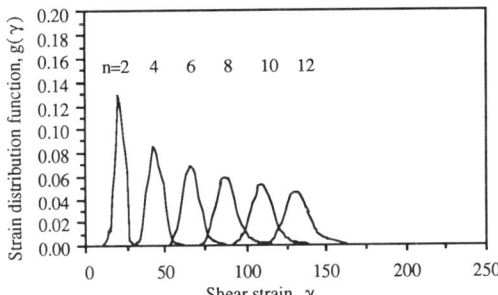

Fig. 7. Simulated strain distribution functions for even numbers of cross-cavity flows.

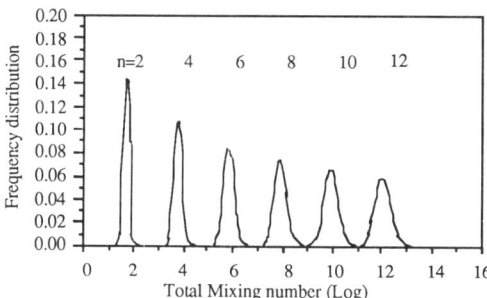

Fig. 8. Simulated distributions of the total mixing number for even numbers of cross-cavity flows.

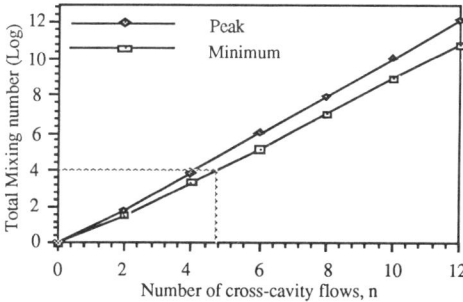

Fig. 9. The minimum and peak values of the total mixing number for even numbers of cross-cavity flows.

MODELLING THE EFFECT OF HEATED-AIR DRYING OF GRAINS ON THEIR QUALITY FOR BREAD BAKING AND FOR SEED

D M Bruce[*] and M E Nellist[*]

Models of drying of agricultural crops have been developed which enable moisture and temperature within the dryer to be calculated under steady and non-steady conditions. Sub-models of the loss of loaf volume and of seed viability, as a consequence of temperature and moisture experienced by the grains during drying, have been developed so that process simulation within quality constraints can be used to improve the design and control of grain dryers.

Keywords: dryer, wheat, mathematical model, simulation, viability, baking quality.

Introduction

The whole purpose of drying and cooling grain is to preserve its quality by reducing its equilibrium relative humidity and temperature to below the level at which micro-organisms and insects are active. Nevertheless, some deterioration may occur during, or be caused by, the drying. It is important, therefore, to understand and quantify the biological changes which occur under drying conditions.

In the UK, grain may be dried either in batch or continuous-flow dryers or in bulk-storage dryers of the in-bin or on-floor type. Typically batch and continuous dryers use air heated
to temperatures between 40 and 120°C to dry, and ambient air to cool the grain, within one half to 4 hours. Using as high an air temperature as possible has two advantages; the output rate of dried crop is maximised with the subsidiary benefits of less deterioration of crop waiting to be dried, less supervision time, etc., and the thermal efficiency of the dryer is increased. However, the quality of the grain will be damaged if its temperature becomes excessive, and this potential loss of quality, and therefore value, sets the upper bound to the drying air temperature. Drying times in heated-air dryers are too short for significant growth of mould or insects. However, in bulk-storage dryers which use drying air temperatures at or near ambient, drying times may be several weeks and care is needed to minimise growth of micro-organisms.

As grains have various end uses, there are many measures which are used in commerce to assess their quality, but only a few are relevant to detection of heat damage. Two of critical economic importance are bread baking quality, of which the primary determinant is the volume of the loaf per unit mass, and viability, i.e. the ability of the grains to germinate successfully. Viability, quantified by germination capacity, is the

[*]   **Silsoe Research Institute, Wrest Park, Silsoe, Bedford MK45 4HS**

appropriate measure for grain to be used as seed and similar to the test for grain to be malted for the food and drink industry, the first stage of malt production being steeping in water to start the germination process. Thus the quality parameters used in the research programme into quality loss on drying were loaf volume for wheat and germination capacity for wheat and barley.

Work at Silsoe Research Institute has concentrated on modelling the physics of the drying process in general, and simulating the process in specific designs of dryer so that the crop drying process could be improved. A significant contribution has been made to the design, operation and control of grain drying processes by combining basic work on material properties, modelling and simulation, and testing on small- and full-scale. Work is now focused on incorporating the biological constraints on the process of drying into the models, both of heated-air drying and also of near-ambient drying where mould growth rates are being studied.

This paper aims to present the approach taken to modelling of quality loss and to give examples of the use of models of baking quality and viability in dryer simulation.

Modelling the physical process of grain drying

Typically wheat and barley are harvested at a moisture content of around 18 - 22% wet basis, and rapeseed at 10 - 13%, at which the seeds are sufficiently hard and non-cohesive to be handled in bulk. Dryers use forced ventilation through packed beds of stationary or moving grains which have a porosity of some 40%. Drying of grains, which are hygroscopic, is diffusion-controlled and takes place in the falling rate period.

Modelling the process at steady state for the one-dimensional case involves deriving four ordinary differential equations from the heat and moisture balances between air and grain and the rates of exchange of heat and moisture. Such equations have been formulated, solved using finite difference method for one-dimensional flows of air and grain, and validated against experimental data for cross-flow (Nellist 1987) and mixed-flow (Bruce 1984) grain dryers. More comprehensive formulations have been derived but can be simplified under assumptions valid for grain drying conditions (Parry 1985). Further equations are needed if both the distribution of moisture and temperature within the particles are to be described or if an a non-steady state model is required.

Generally the air flow passing through the bed is not one-dimensional, but passes into and out of the bed via ducts. This two-dimensional flow of air has been modelled by equations based on Darcy's law and solved both by finite element (Cenkowski et al., 1990) and finite difference methods (Burfoot, D. Personal Communication). Because of its complex frictional flow behaviour the flow of grain around such ducts during drying has not been modelled, to the authors' knowledge.

In each case the essential point is that once the moisture and temperature of air and grain throughout the dryer have been calculated, the conditions which the grain experiences during drying can then be used to compute grain quality changes resulting from that moisture and temperature history. To compute the results sufficiently accurately, the temperature predictions must be accurate to within about 2°C because the reaction rate changes significantly within that span at the peak grain temperatures. Thus the heat transfer coefficient is crucial, particularly at the point of most intense heating which occurs when grain comes into close contact with the heated inlet air as it enters the grain bed. Mass transfer also contributes to temperature change because of evaporative cooling.

For most agricultural dryers a one-dimensional model of a single bed, or combination of beds, represents a dryer sufficiently well for performance calculations. A cross-flow dryer consists of one drying and one cooling bed unless the grain is inverted or mixed (Nellist, 1987). A dryer of the mixed-flow type (Fig.1) can be represented as a series of concurrent- and counter-flow beds (Bruce, 1984), for both the drying and cooling sections. However, this scheme omits a cross-flow element near the air inlet ducts which is important if, as here, grain temperature is of major concern. A new model representing the mixed-flow dryer by one dimensional blocks of all three types of flow is under development at Silsoe Research Institute.

In addition to the coefficients of heat and mass transfer, relationships are needed to represent the properties of the material, in particular the equilibrium between air and grain and, related to it, the latent heat of vaporisation of water from grain as a function of grain moisture content.

Modelling loss of grain viability

Because viability, as measured by the germination test (ISTA, 1985), is the primary measure of the quality of seed grain and is also closely correlated to baking quality (Bruce, 1992), it is the most important property reflecting thermal damage. Efforts to understand the mechanism of heat damage began when Groves (1917) carried out a series of treatments in which grain was heated but not dried. Later experiments, notably by Hutchinson (1944), Ptitsyn (1953), Lindberg and Sorensson (1959), Roberts (1960) and Roberts and Abdalla (1968), were also of this 'sealed' heating type. The virtue of such experiments is that because grain moisture content and temperature are held virtually constant, the only variable factor is exposure time. The results of 'sealed' heating tests are very repeatable and more easily interpreted than those from drying test, which where all three factors are varying together. It was found that grain temperature, moisture content and the exposure at which the viability was reduced below some threshold value could be related by either of Equations (1) and (2).

$$T_{cg} = a - b.\ln(t) - c.\ln(W) \qquad (1)$$

$$T_{cg} = a - b.\ln(t) - d.W \qquad (2)$$

The choice of threshold value varied. Hutchinson (1944) identified "the start of damage" and "complete kill", whilst Lindberg and Sorensson (1959) chose 90% viability.

For situations such as storage where grain temperature and moisture content remain more or less constant, this quantification of the critical temperature is extremely useful and capable of direct application. However it is not possible to apply this "threshold" approach to the dynamic conditions experienced by grain undergoing drying. An expression is needed for the rate of loss of quality as a function of the conditions and of the initial state of the grain, which can be integrated directly once the grain treatment history has been calculated.

For seed viability a successful approach has been made to determining the loss function. Studying the loss of viability with time in seed stored at constant conditions, Roberts (1960) realised that although the time scale varied with temperature and moisture, the pattern of seed deaths at the constant conditions was always the same. At first, the rate of death would be so low that changes in viability were difficult to detect. Gradually more seeds would begin to die and the death rate would accelerate to a maximum at which time half the seeds would have died. Thereafter it would necessarily decline. Thus seed deaths tend to be "normally distributed" in time, and graphs of the accumulated percentage of deaths (or more conveniently the percentage of seeds

49

remaining viable, i.e. the germination percentage) against time produce a sigmoid shaped curve typical of the normal probability integral (Fig.2a). Replacing probability, P, by the decimal value of the germination, G, we can write:

$$\frac{dG}{dX} = \frac{1}{\sqrt{2\pi}} \exp(-\tfrac{1}{2}X^2) \qquad (3)$$

which in integral form and inserting integration limits becomes

$$G = \frac{1}{\sqrt{2\pi}} \int_{-\infty}^{X} \exp(-\tfrac{1}{2}X^2)dX \qquad (4)$$

The quantity X, termed the standard normal deviate, is symmetrical about zero at the point $G = 0.5$ (i.e. $t = \bar{t}$). Also X has been found to vary linearly with t. Thus if we plot X against t (Fig.2b) the result is a straight line which can be described by Eqn. (5).

$$X = X_o - t/\sigma \qquad (5)$$

A branch of statistical analysis called 'probit' analysis (Finney 1971) is based upon Equations (4) and (5). Ellis and Roberts (1980) have coined the term 'probit viability' to describe values of X (X_o is treated as a constant). The standard deviation, σ, is a measure of the dispersion of the deaths about the mean drying time (or half life) and can be shown to be that time in which the germination would reduce from 84.1% to 50% under the prevailing, constant condition of moisture and temperature.

The first advantage of Eqn (5) is that it recognises that there may be a difference in initial viability, X_o, but that for a particular moisture content and temperature there will be a single death rate, $1/\sigma$, at any point on the transformed 'probit' curve. Grain with poor germination is more easily damaged than that of good quality and Table 1 shows how the probit behaviour explains this. For a germination of 99% one unit (or standard deviation) of 'probit' damage causes an 8.2% loss in germination; at 90% the same damage is equivalent to 28.9% loss. The second advantage is the finding by Ellis and Roberts (1981) that the value of σ was a function of seed moisture and temperature only and was not affected by the initial quality of the seed. In consequence it is possible to accumulate reductions in 'probit' from successive environments to estimate a total 'probit' loss. Therefore to use the 'probit' method, which is similar to using logarithms, the initial viability is first converted to its probit equivalent. Subtracting the accumulated loss from the initial 'probit' value gives the final 'probit' value; the final viability can then be found by converting 'probit' back again.

The computer simulations of batch and continuous-flow drying developed and used at Silsoe Research Institute all incorporate this procedure to calculate 'probit' loss. The routines work well but require better data defining σ and, particularly in the case of complex designs such as the mixed-flow, the improvement in grain temperature prediction in 2-D flow situations referred to previously. For cross-flow driers where final grain and air temperatures are virtually in equilibrium, predictions are more reliable. To avoid the need to assume an initial value of germination, the amount of damage caused by a grain dryer at given operating conditions can be characterised in terms of 'probit' loss rather than germination loss. For example, 65.5°C (150°F) is a safe drying air temperature for a well-designed cross-flow dryer drying from 20 - 15%. At these operating conditions in a simple cross-flow dryer with a drying to cooling ration of 3:1 the predicted probit loss is 0.028. To make this calculation the seed death rate, $1/\sigma$, was evaluated from Eqn.(6) derived from unpublished data from sealed heated tests on wheat at Silsoe Research Institute.

$$\sigma = \exp(40.2895 - 0.3178\ T - 5.896\ \ln(W)) \tag{6}$$

Table 1   Effect of initial viability on the loss of viability caused by the application of one standard deviation of 'probit' loss

Initial conditions		Final conditions		Loss of viability
G_o %	X_o	G_f %	X_f	$(G_o - G_f)$ %
99.990	3.72	99.67	2.72	0.317
99.90	3.09	98.17	2.09	1.73
99.0	2.33	90.8	1.33	8.23
97.0	1.88	81.1	0.88	15.9
90.0	1.28	61.1	0.28	28.9
80.0	0.84	43.7	-0.16	36.3

If we then determine other combinations of drying air temperature and initial and final moisture contents at which the probit loss is 0.028 we can draw the 'isoprobit' lines of Fig.3. These curves show that the safe drying temperature reduces with increasing initial moisture content and also with decreasing final moisture content. This is because of the increase in residence time necessary to remove additional water. Although not verified by physical experiment, circumstantial evidence suggests that this is a realistic envelope of safe temperatures for this type of dryer.

Modelling loss of bread baking quality of grains

Wheat protein when hydrolysed during the making of dough forms gluten, a visco-elastic substance capable of retaining fermentation gases. If sufficient protein is present the dough can rise to a commercially acceptable volume. If the protein has been heat damaged, the gluten formed is less elastic and can fracture, releasing gas and resulting in a loaf of lower volume and poor, crumbly texture. In a system used for evaluating loaves, loaf volume is a dominant element which can be accurately measured and so was used for study.

From previous work by Becker and Sallans (1956) it was known that the reduction in the volume, relative to control, of loaves baked from wheat subjected to sealed heating followed a logarithmic decay with time. Increasing the temperature or moisture content resulted in an increase in the rate of decay. The first stage of modelling was, then, to determine the form and coefficients of the loss function

$$-\frac{dQ}{dt} = f(T, M) \tag{7}$$

While this could in principle be done by sealed heating tests, the quantity of grain required for baking test loaves makes it impractical, and it is preferable to proceed directly to drying tests performed on thin layers of grain so each grain received the same treatment. By analysing a succession of samples taken during drying, or carrying out a series of progressively longer drying tests under identical conditions, loaf volumes can be determined at various treatment times. Sample conditions during drying must also be measured. From a number of such test series covering the moisture and temperature range of interest, the relationship between rate of loss of quality, wheat moisture and temperature can be determined.

Wassermann et al. (1981) and Bruce (1992) both performed such experiments, the results of which are in good agreement. Both experiments illustrate the rapid increase in damage rate with grain temperature between 70 and 80°C, and also the increase, less rapid, with grain initial moisture between 18 and 22% wet basis. Schreiber et al. (1981) fitted a model to Wassermann's data which predicted a constant rate of loss of specific loaf volume at given grain moisture and temperature.

$$- \frac{dQ}{dt} = k_o \exp (aT + bW) \tag{8}$$

Using a diffusion model (Bruce 1985) consisting of ten concentric, spherical shells to represent the drying behaviour of each grain, Bruce (1992) computed the rate of loss of relative loaf volume for each shell using a damage model with the decaying exponential form of Eqn (9). The mean relative loaf volume for t he whole 10 shell model was calculated at each point in time when the grain, dried in thin layers, had been sampled and a test loaf baked.

$$- \frac{dV_r}{dt} = V_r (41.4M_s + 140) \exp (-427000/(RT_s)) \tag{9}$$

The coefficients of the loss function for relative loaf volume, Eqn.9 were derived from 112 thin layer drying tests by non-linear optimisation, and validated by comparison with data of Wassermann et al. (1981). Fig.4 shows the agreement between relative loaf volume versus time predicted by Eqn (9) and the experimental data from 29 drying tests with wheat of initial m.c. $\approx$ 0.28 dry basis.

An advantage of representing the grain kernel as a series of shells is that intense drying, when gradients in temperature and moisture are present within the kernel, can be modelled. Designs of dryer such as the mixed-flow type subject grain to just such intense conditions at certain points so accurate prediction of damage rates in these conditions is an essential element of the next generation of dryer models.

Use of quality loss models

Work is in progress to validate both of these models of quality loss, incorporated in simulations of dryers which themselves have been thoroughly checked against test data from small- and full-scale machines. The limits to dryer performance imposed by the quality loss models can then be explored in a cost-effective way not possible by experiment alone. If a cost penalty can be placed on quality loss, the drying process can be optimised. The quality test used commercially for viability is a pass/fail test so the cost function is discontinuous, and the commercial limit must be incorporated in the optimisation scheme as a constraint.

If the interaction between grain, dryer design, dryer conditions and quality loss can be determined, this enables the critical design features to be determined and suitable operating conditions to be specified for any particular design. It also enables the dryer to be characterised in terms of the quality loss for comparison with other dryers, and independent of the initial quality of the grain. It is notable that, as the underlying loss functions are continuous, quality loss is occurring in all dryers so all dryers damage to some extent the crop passing through them. But, provided the loss is quantified, an economic optimum can be achieved between, on the one hand, lost quality and on the other, increased output and efficiency.

Dryers in practice do not operate at a single value of air temperature. Variations with time occur as a result of direct-firing burners switching in and out, and spatial variations occur across the plenum chamber as a result of imperfect air distribution. As the response to temperature of the grain quality loss is exponential (Eqns. 6 and 9) these fluctuations result in greater quality loss than a constant temperature equal to the mean. Therefore one use of the quality loss model is to define the limits within which these variations in temperature must be controlled.

Automatic control of moisture at discharge is normally achieved in grain dryers by altering the grain flow rate. This leads to increased exposure time for grain which is initially more moist and which is therefore more sensitive to heat as shown by Eqns. 3 and 9. Thus the action of reducing grain flow to achieve the target moisture would tend to reduce the quality of discharged grain unless the drying air temperature were also altered. This in turn changes the grain flow required to achieve a certain moisture reduction. Based on the physical models of dryers described earlier, Silsoe Research Institute has developed effective algorithms for moisture regulation to overcome the effect of moisture fluctuations, sometimes severe, in the input grain feedback-only (Whitfield 1988a and b) and feedback-plus-feedforward control algorithms (McFarlane and Bruce 1991, Bruce and McFarlane 1992) have been tested and taken up by industry. Incorporation of the quality loss calculations into the control algorithm would enable the controller to regulate the moisture, as now, but within acceptable quality loss bounds which would differ depending on the end use of the grain.

Conclusions

Because high grain quality is vital to economic cereal production, grain dryers must maintain the quality of the grain but, to operate with high throughput and high efficiency, they must use the highest possible safe temperature. The physics of drying has been modelled, and the performance of commercial designs of dryer has been computed successfully using beds of one-dimensional flow, but for dryers with complex air flow patterns, 2-D models will give more realistic predictions of grain temperature on which quality loss largely depends.

The rate of loss of seed viability and of the volume of bread loaves with time as a result of drying with heated air has been modelled as exponential functions of temperature and moisture content. Using the moisture and temperature throughout a dryer computed by the physical model, these quality loss functions can be integrated to yield the overall losses of quality caused by that drying process.

Whilst these models have been validated in small-scale tests, validation on commercial scale remains to be done. In addition to their use as aids to design and to specification of the most economic operating conditions, the models could be used to implement moisture regulation algorithms within bounds of acceptable quality loss.

Nomenclature

a	experimentally determined constant
b	" " " "
c	" " " "
d	" " " "
G	germination, decimal
k_o	experimentally determined constant
M	moisture content, dry basis
M_S	moisture content, dry basis, of a shell of the 10 shell grain model
Q	specific loaf volume, cm^3/g

R gas constant, $= 8.3143$ J/(Mol K)

t exposure time, s

$\bar{t}$ exposure time at which $G = 0.5$, i.e. half-life of the seed sample

T_{cg} critical temperature at which viability is reduced to the threshold value, °C

T grain temperature, °C

T_s temperature, K, of a shell of the 10 shell grain model

V loaf volume cm^3

V_{rs} contribution to relative loaf volume, V/V_c, of a shell of the 10 shell grain model

V_c loaf volume of control (unheated) sample, cm^3

W moisture content, % wet basis

X $(\bar{t} - t)/\sigma$

X_o value of X at $t = o$

σ standard deviation of distribution of seed death, s

References

Becker, H.A.; Sallans, H.R. (1956) Cereal Che., 33,254-265

Bruce,D.M. (1984) J. agric. Engng Res., 30(4),361-372

Bruce, D.M. (1985) J.agric. Engng Res., 32, 337-347

Bruce, D.M. (1992) (in press) J.agric. Engng Res.

Cenkowski, S.; Miketinac, M.J.; Kelm, A.W. 1990 Canadian Agric. Engng, 32, 85-90

Ellis,R.H.; Roberts,E.H. (1980) in Seed Production. pp 605-635. Ed. Hebblethwaite, P.D., Butterworths, London

Ellis,R.H.;Roberts,E.H. 1981 Seed Sci.& Technol, 9(2),373-409

Finney,D.J.(1971) Probit analysis. 3rd Edition. Cambridge University Press, Cambridge, UK

Groves,J.F. (1917) Botanical Gazette, 63 (3), 169-189.

Hutchinson,J.B. 1944 Journ. Soc. Chem. Industry, 63, 104-7.

International Seed Testing Association. (1985) Seed Science and Technology, 13(2), 307-355

Lindberg,J.E.;Sorensson,I. (1959) Journal of Royal Swedish Academy of Agriculture and Forestry, Supplement 1, Stockholm.

McFarlane, N.J.B.; Bruce, D.M. (1991) J.agric.Engng Res.,49,243-258

Nellist,M.E. (1987), J. agric. Engng Res., 37(1),43-57

Parry,J.L. (1985) J. agric. Engng Res., 32(1),1-29

Ptitsyn,S.D. (1953) Mekhan. I. Elektr. Sots sels.Khoz., No.3, 32-39. (NIAE Translation By E.Harris)

Roberts,E.H. (1960) Annals of Botany, 24(93), 12-31.

Roberts,E.H.;Abdalla,F.H. (1968) Ann. Bot. N.S., 32, 97-117.

Schreiber, H.; Muhlbauer, W.; Wassermann, L.; Kuppinger, H. (1981) Lebensm Unters. Forsch., 173,169-175

Wassermann.L.; Muhlbauer,W.; Schreiber,H. (1983) Getreide Mehl und Brot, 9, 268-274

Whitfield,R.D. (1988a) J.agric. Engng Res., 41, 275-287

Whitfield,R.D. (1988b) J.agric. Engng Res., 42, 289-299

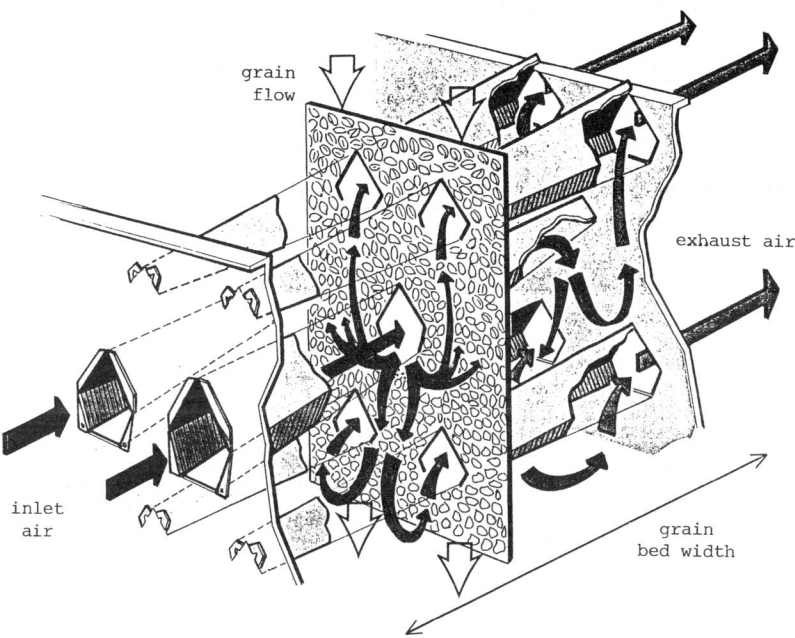

Fig.1. Schematic cut-away of part of a mixed-flow drying bed (by kind permission of Law Denis Engineering Ltd.) Solid arrows - air flow. Hollow arrows - grain flow.

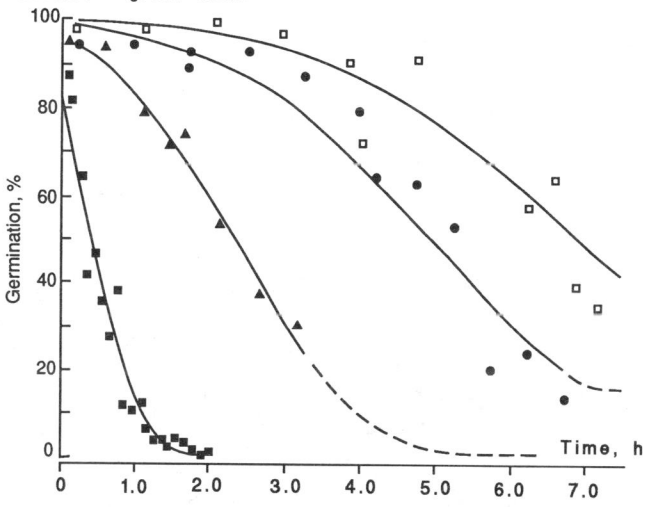

Fig.2a. Effect of exposure time on germination of wheat grains heated without evaporation at 60 C and at moisture contents of 22.1(■), 20.2(▲), 18.1(●) and 16.8(□) %w.b. Lines as fitted to linearised data in Fig.2b.

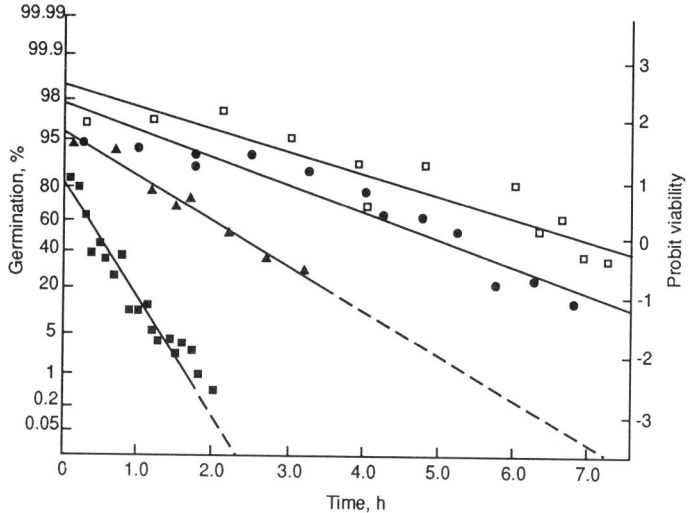

Fig.2b Data from Fig.2a plotted on a probability scale. Lines were fitted by the "probit" model. Key as Fig.2a.

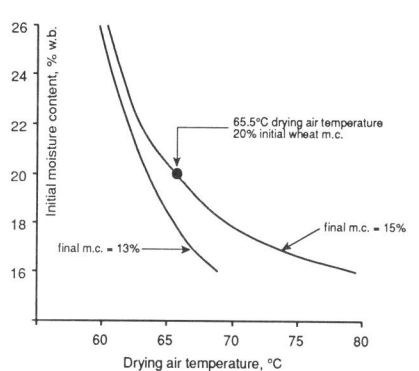

Fig.3. Computed safe drying air temperatures for an acceptable probit viability loss of 0.028, for milling wheat dried to final moisture contents of 15 and 13% in a simple cross-flow dryer.

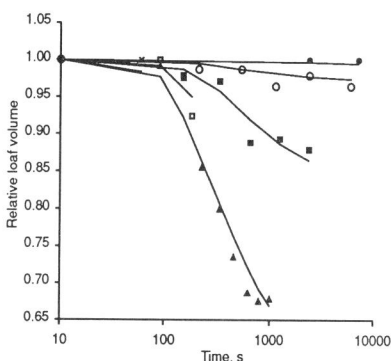

Fig.4. Experimental observations (symbols) and predictions (lines) of loaf relative volume for loaves baked from wheat samples dried in thin layers for various times. The predictions were made using Eqn.9. Wheat initial m.c. = 22% w.b. All samples were of variety Broom except (▲) which was variety Avalon. Key 65 C (●), 70 C (○), 75 C (■), 80 C (□), 80 C (▲), 85 C (×)

56

MODELLING AND SIMULATION OF A GLUCOSE-FRUCTOSE
SIMULATED MOVING-BED ADSORBER

M.L. Lameloise and V.Viard*

This work deals with the chromatographic separation of glucose and fructose by adsorption on gel type ion exchange resins, charged with Ca^{2+}. The modelling methodology and the experimental results are given for the fixed bed separation. On this basis, computer codes are developed to analyse the process of simulated moving bed adsorber. This analysis indicates interesting perspectives of applications for pilot plant control, to be studied in future work.

INTRODUCTION

The first part of this work reports the modelling of the chromatographic separation of glucose and fructose from invert sugar feedstock by adsorption on calcium gel type ion exchange resins. Experiments and fundamentals are discussed elsewhere (Viard and Lameloise, in press). The ability of the model to represent batch separation is demonstrated. We propose then to extend our knowledge to the industrial process of simulated moving bed adsorber. The economic advantage of a counter-current contact mode of liquid and solid is related for this separation to the small separation factor of the mixture. In order to keep it without the difficulties of solid motion and flow distribution, a semi-continuous process was first commercialized in the 1970's by the firm UOP, and is known as the SAREX process (Broughton and al., 1977). Models adopting either the continuous counter-current representation, or the semi-continuous sequential one, are developed for computer simulation of the process. This study highlights which investigations have still to be made with the aid of these models, as a tool for efficient development of a pilot plant.

I - MODELLING FIXED RESIN BED ADSORPTION OF GLUCOSE AND FRUCTOSE

Principle of adsorption

Orientation of hydroxyl groups in the sugar molecule is responsible for its ability to chelate with metallic cations, and for the stability of the resulting complex (Goulding, 1975 - Angyal and al., 1979). This is the basis of sugar separation techniques involving cationic ion exchange resins.

* Department Genie Industriel Alimentaire, E.N.S.I.A.,
1 av. des Olympiades, Massy F91305

In the case of glucose and fructose molecules, mutarotation leads to the composition at equilibrium and at 30°C (Shallenberger and Birch, 1975 - Hyvönen and al., 1977) :
- glucose : 36% α-glucopyranose and 64% β-glucopyranose,
- fructose : (traces) α-fructopyranose, 64% β-fructopyranose and
           36% β-fructofuranose.

For glucose, only the minor α-glucopyranose form is able to complex with calcium ions of the resin (one ax-eq pair), but may stay uncomplexed because of the law stability constant. The major fructose form β-fructopyranose can chelate with calcium. The two ax-eq pairs present in the molecule and the exocyclic hydroxyl group contribute to complex formation. These differences between glucose and fructose isomers lead fructose to be more retained than glucose by the resin column.

Measurement of parameters involved in the chromatographic separation

Modelling glucose-fructose separation on fixed-beds of ion-exchange resins of gel type was the first step of our study. This was accomplished by applying a classical chemical engineering methodology : realize independant experiments at the laboratory scale to obtain the physicochemical constants characteristic of the system (Costa and Rodrigues, 1985 - Rodrigues and Costa, 1986 - Rodrigues and al., 1989). These parameters are :
- capacity parameters : the equilibrium isotherms giving the equilibrium partition law between resin and liquid phases,
- dispersive parameters, ranging in two categories : kinetics (internal and external mass transfer rates) and hydrodynamics of liquid flow in the packed-bed.

The method employed here is not specific to linear systems unlike the moment analysis technique usually applied in the case of glucose and fructose (Ghim and Chang, 1982 - Sakiyama and al., 1985 - Ho and al., 1987) and enables the knowledge of the contribution of the involved phenomena to the chromatographic process. A similar study has been reported in the case of xylose and mannose (Carillon, 1987) but not yet for glucose and fructose.

The glucose and fructose equilibrium isotherms

They were measured by the frontal analysis technique, according to the principle described by Tondeur and al. (1989). Breakthrough curves were realized on a laboratory scale column (50 cm long and 5.3 cm^2 id). Mass balance on these curves in the case of monosolute solutions and for mixtures at various concentrations and compositions provided linear and independant isotherms over a large range of concentrations, including industrial concentrations of glucose and fructose in invert sugar. This result was obtained for the Duolite C204/2115 resin at 60°C and different resins and temperatures could then be rapidly characterized by applying the frontal analysis technique with successive steps of concentration of monosolute solutions. The isotherms are shown on figure 1. Comparison between partition coefficients for Duolite C204/2115 (471 μm) and C204/2078 (269 μm) at 60°C indicates no effect of resin size. Glucose partition coefficients have been shown not to be influenced by temperature whereas fructose equilibrium is markedly influenced by temperature. This leads fructose to be less retained in the chromatographic column at higher temperatures. This result is well supported by the studies of Hyvönen and al. (1977) concerning the influence of temperature on glucose and fructose tautomeric equilibria.

Hydrodynamics

Axial dispersion of solutes in the interstitial liquid phase is characterized by the axial Peclet number of the column :
$Pe = uL/D_L$, where D_L is the axial dispersion coefficient. The chromatographic column is modelled as a series of ideal mixing cells. For a great number of cells ($J>10$ in practice), this model is equivalent to the axially dispersed plug flow model with $Pe \cong 2J$ (Villermaux, 1981). The transfer function of the model is given by :

$$G(s) = (1+st_0/J)^{-J}, \quad \text{where } t_0 = \varepsilon V_b/F \text{ is the space time.}$$

In order to solve linear chromatographic models, we use the Fast Fourier Transform algorithm and the model parameters are obtained by fitting the experimental curve to the experimental one with Rosenbrock method.

The hydrodynamic study was realized with an interstitial tracer of the resin bed : Blue dextran, for which breakthrough curves were measured in the usual manner. A constant number of cells was obtained as a function of flowrate, in the case of the 50 cm long laboratory column. This is an experimental proof of the turbulent origin of the axial diffusivity, then proportional to the interstitial velocity of the liquid u. Studies on a one meter long column showed Peclet numbers proportional to column length. An example of experimental curve fitted with the mixing cells in series model is shown on figure 2. The results show that for sufficiently long columns the contribution of axial dispersion to band-broadening is small.

Kinetics

- Intraparticle resistance

The rate of diffusion of solutes in the resin beads was studied by contacting given volumes of resin and solution (in the ratio 1/10) in an agitated batch reactor. No effect of the agitation frequency on the first hand, and high values of calculated Biot numbers on the other hand, justified the hypothesis of negligible external resistance to mass transfer in the reactor. Kinetic curves are well represented by the homogeneous Fickian diffusion model (figure 3). Effective intraparticle diffusivities D_e were fitted on the experimental curves with the analytic solution of the model given by Crank (1967). We verified that the rate of diffusion of glucose and fructose in the resin phase is not a function of concentration. Influence of temperature is less marked for glucose, especially in the case of the Duolite C204/2115 resin. The other resins studied show diffusivities of both solutes higher at 60°C than at 30°C, leading to a ratio D_m/D_e of the order of 15. Glucose and fructose have very similar kinetic properties, with slightly higher glucose diffusivities.

- External resistance

Mass transfer rate in the laminar sublayer surrounding the particles can be approached by the way of semi-empirical correlations giving Sherwood number as a function of Schmidt and Reynolds numbers. Estimated values of Sherwood numbers indicate that the external resistance can be neglected. Biot numbers show that the overall transport of sugars is controlled by the intraparticle rate of diffusion. Comparison between chromatographic elution curves obtained with constant L/u ratio and for 25 and 50 cm high beds validate this hypothesis experimentally.

Fixed-bed separation

For each sugar, the last experiments give the parameters of the chromatographic column model : the capacity factor K', the hydrodynamic parameters t_0 and J and the internal transfer time constant t_d. The column

59

transfer function of the mixing cells in series with mass exchange model is given by (Villermaux, 1981) :

$$G(s) = \left(1 + \frac{st_0}{J} \left(\frac{K'}{1+t_d s} \right) \right)^{-J} \quad \text{with } K' = \frac{(1-\varepsilon)}{\varepsilon} K_d \quad \text{and } t_d = \frac{R_p^2}{15D_e}$$

On figures 4 and 5, the simulated curves are compared with the experimental ones, respectively in the case of pulse response experiments and in the case of an elution curve (square injection). They show satisfactory agreement and use can therefore be made of the measured parameters included in the model to study the industrial semi-continuous separation by simulated moving-bed process.

II - THE SIMULATED MOVING BED PROCESS : PRINCIPLE AND OPERATION

The semi-continuous adsorber

The simulated moving bed is a separation process involving a series of chromatographic columns (figure 6). A counter-current displacement of resin and liquid is not physically achieved, but simulated by a periodic rotation of input points (invert sugar feed point and water supply) and draw-off points (glucose and fructose enriched streams), from column to column co-currently to the liquid flow, at fixed time interval T. Examining the equivalent counter-current system shows that each of the four zones delimited by the input/output points fulfills a particular role (Broughton and al., 1977). Equilibrium data measured at the laboratory scale can be used to establish the operating counstraints of the system. These are obtained either by an analysis of solutes' flux in the equivalent counter-current system (Ching and al., 1985), or by an analysis of concentration fronts' velocities in the beds of the semi-continuous adsorber (Hashimoto and al., 1983) :

$$Q_4 < [\varepsilon + (1-\varepsilon)K_{dG}][V_b/T] < Q_2 < Q_3 < [\varepsilon + (1-\varepsilon)K_{dF}][V_b/T] < Q_1,$$

where T is the sequence time, Q_i the liquid flowrate in zone i, and V_b the volume of one column of the system.

Parts III and IV deal with computer simulation of the process, considering an eight columns system of 2.5 m each, packed with Dowex C326 resin. It is supposed, on the basis of the experimental hydrodynamic results obtained for a one meter long column, that Pe>>St. But in the case of a system for which this doesn't hold, similar work can be generalized. The independant behavior of glucose and fructose leads to duplicate calculations of the models for the two sugars. The system is supposed to be isothermal and operated at 60°C.

III - DESIGN APPROACH : THE COUNTER-CURRENT MODEL

In a given zone of the counter-current equivalent system (figure 6), with resin in plug-flow and liquid in axially dispersed plug-flow, the analytic solution of the linear model is known at steady state as a function of distance in the zone (Ruthven, 1984). In the case of Pe>>St, we obtain a linear relation between the input and output concentrations in resin and liquid phase in the zone :

$$c_s = A_n c_e + B_n q_e$$

$$\text{with } A_n = \frac{\gamma_n e^{St_n (1-\gamma_n)} - 1}{\gamma_n - 1} \quad \text{and } B_n = \frac{\gamma_n}{K_d(\gamma_n - 1)} (1 - e^{St_n (1-\gamma_n)})$$

Four equations of this type corresponding to the four sections are written. To calculate the concentrations in the glucose and fructose outputs for given operating conditions, additional equations are needed :
- a global mass balance per zone : $S (q_s - q_e) = L_n (c_s - c_e)$
- mass balance at the feed point : $Q_F c_F + L_2 c_2 = L_3 c_2'$
- and at the recirculation point : $L_4 c_4 = L_1 c_0$

A linear system of ten equations is thus obtained with ten unknowns : c_0, c_1, c_2, c_2', c_3, c_4, q_0, q_1, q_2 and q_3 and must be solved for each sugar. This simple model was programmed and solved with Lotus 1.2.3 software. Our aim was to develop a user's guide which could be used neither knowing the background of the calculations, nor the computer language. Helped and asked by a conversational menu, the user can modify some of the input variables to obtain a rough profile of the concentrations of glucose and fructose in the system, the output concentrations, purities and recoveries.

We used this guide for parametric studies of the counter-current system. The information provided by the model is restricted to the counter-current hypothetic process, which is strictly a stationary one, but gives a first investigation into the behavior of the characteristics of the products with the operating variables. It was verified by Ching and al. (1985) that the counter-current stationary profile is well correlated to the semi-continuous profile at the midpoint of the switch interval T. As the guide unables different configurations to be tested (repartition of the columns in the zones), it could be stated that it has little effect on the process performances. All other numerical simulations were concerned with two columns per zone. Figure 7 represents the effect of the recirculation flowrate on the performances for a set of sequence times T, all other flowrates being kept constant. T=24 min and Q_4=170 ml/min were conditions satisfying the operating counstraints. Such diagrams may be helful in choosing operating conditions but they also allow an interesting insight into the operating range in an operation and control procedure development goal. Ching and al. (1985) and Ho and al. (1987) defined a parameter α, the margin by which all the operating counstraints are satisfied. The influence of this parameter on the process performances enables a reduction in the input variables of the design problem. But, it fails in realizing an optimal design and in fact, reduces the degrees of liberty on the control point of view. Work has to be done in this area : define a commercial function to be studied under counstraints and as a function of the flowrates and sequence time. Optimum choice of the followed trajectory in the control strategy has although to be considered.

IV - TRANSIENT BEHAVIOR OF THE SMB PROCESS

The code
The real operating sequential mode of the process is numerically reproduced. Informations concerning the transient behavior (periodically stationary) can thus be obtained by the way of computer simulation. Between two permutations, the system consists of eight fixed-beds.
- each column is represented by the fixed-bed chromatographic model over the period [0,T] :
$$\frac{\partial c}{\partial \tau} = -\frac{T u}{L} \frac{\partial c}{\partial x} - \frac{K' T}{t_d} (c - c^*)$$
and
$$\frac{\partial c^*}{\partial \tau} = \frac{T}{t_d} (c - c^*)$$
where $\tau = t/T$ and $x = z/L$, and with given initial conditions (concentrations in each of the columns).

The first order partial derivatives in these equations are approximated using the finite difference technique, with a forward approximation for time derivatives and a backward one for spacial derivatives. Calculation of the concentrations in a column is thus realized at each node of a grid in space and time. The concentrations for column N are thus obtained by :

$$c_N(i,j+1) = \left(1 - \frac{K'T}{t_d}\,\Delta\tau - \frac{T\,\Delta\tau}{L\,\Delta x}\,u_N\right) c_N(i,j) + \left(\frac{T\,\Delta\tau}{L\,\Delta x}\,u_N\right) c_N(i-1,j)$$

$$+ \left(\frac{K'T}{t_d}\,\Delta\tau\right) c_N^*(i,j)$$

$$c_N^*(i,j+1) = \left(1 - \frac{T\,\Delta\tau}{t_d}\right) c_N^*(i,j) + \frac{T\,\Delta\tau}{t_d}\,c_N(i,j)$$

In these calculations, only time j must be memorized by the computer and can then be cancelled when j+1 has been calculated.

- One additional equation is needed for calculation of $c_N(i,j+1)$ and is obtained for columns 1, 3, 5 and 7 by mass-balance at the input and output points, and for columns 2, 4, 6 and 8 by continuity of concentrations with the end of the preceding column. At time t=0, the concentrations $c_N(i)$ and $c_N^*(i)$ are defined in the system and indicated in the computer program.

- At time T, the displacement of concentration matrix is done so that columns 1 to 8 are renumbered, the input and output points being considered fixed and the columns mobile in the calculations (contrary to the pilot case). The calculation is also initialized at time T. The number of sequences calculated by the computer is simply registered. After eight sequences, the procedure is repeated for a new cycle and so until the desired number of cycles has been operated.

Use of the code

The code allows the displacement of the concentration profile in the system during a sequence, as can be seen on figure 8. It shows the consequences of this displacement on the registered outputs : transient concentrations in the glucose and fructose enriched fractions.

It is also very interesting in studying the starting-up procedures of the process. The effect of preloading the system according to different schemes is represented on figure 9. We stress the fact that the recirculation flowrate is 5% greater than in figure 8, explaining the different stationary profile thus obtained. In figure 9a, the establishment of this profile from a system initially free of solute is shown, whereas figure 9b assumes that the two columns preceding the feed (3 and 4) are initially saturated with 40 g%ml glucose and fructose solution. In figure 9c, columns 3 and 4 contain fructose solution (40g%ml) and columns 5 and 6 glucose solution (40g%ml). Figure 9d sums up the advantage of the third procedure : concentration of glucose in the glucose-rich fraction is, from the start, closer to the steady state concentration, even if the number of cycles necessary to reach it is only slightly shorter.

Another interesting application is the study of the response of the system (for example, the glucose and fructose output concentrations) to a step change in one of the operating variable. For example, a rapid response (very sensible system) and a modest transient period are obtained consecutively to a 5% increase or decrease of the recirculation flowrate.

Our simulator appears as very useful for control perspectives and aid to an automatic monitoring of the process. In a control purpose, this code should be a powerful tool as an internal predictor code of the process. On the basis of this perspective, the rapid calculations possible with the code imply its ability to compensate for the lack of on-line sensors : to monitor the process with global on-line measurements (total concentrations) and punctual knowledge of detailed concentrations (HPLC off-line analysis).

CONCLUSION

The two approaches of computer simulation of the semi-continuous moving bed adsorber have proved to fulfill different functions : the first is essentially a design one, the other is an accurate simulator. Both are involved in an automation strategy. More work is needed in the optimal design of the operating variables. The semi-continuous model provides a detailed analysis of the transient behavior, and its coupling procedure with a pilot plant has to be investigated.

The general objective is the development of methodologies for modelling chromatographic processes in the food industry. The application objective is to make use of these tools for pilot plant control. These goals have to be reached in the case of glucose-fructose separation. This knowledge is essential for further generalization to more complicated systems.

NOMENCLATURE

A	column section	(m^2)
c	bulk liquid phase concentration	(g/l)
c^*	concentration at the surface of the particle, liquid side	(g/l)
D_e	intraparticle effective diffusivity	(m^2/s)
D_L	axial diffusivity	(m^2/s)
D_m	molecular liquid diffusivity	(m^2/s)
F	liquid flowrate	(m^3/s)
G	column transfer function	
i, j	space, time grid references	
J	number of mixing cells	
K_d	partition coefficient	
K'	capacity factor	
L	column length	(m)
	equivalent liquid flowrate in the counter-current model	(m^3/s)
Pe	Peclet number $(=uL/D_L)$	
q	solid phase concentrations in the counter-current system, see figure 6.	

Q	actual liquid flowrate in the SMB adsorber	(m^3/s)
R	particle radius	(m)
s^p	Laplace parameter	
S	solid flowrate	(m^3/s)
St	Stanton number $(=L/t_d u_s)$	
t	time	(s)
t_0	space time	(s)
t_d	intraparticle transfer time constant	(s)
T	sequence time	(s)
u	interstitial liquid velocity	(m/s)
u_s	hypothetical solid velocity $(=L/T)$	(m/s)
v	equivalent interstitial liquid velocity, counter current system	(m/s)
V_b	bed volume	(m^3)
x	normalized space abscissa $(=z/L)$	
z	space axial coordinate	(m)
γ	$= (1-\varepsilon) K_d u_s/\varepsilon v$	
τ	normalized time $(=t/T)$	
Δ	difference operator	

Subscripts :   G glucose, F fructose
              i or n =1,4 zone of the process (figure 6)

REFERENCES

Angyal, S.J., Bethell, G.S. and Beveridge, R.J., 1979, *Carbohyd Res*, 73: 9-18.

Broughton, D.B., Bieser, H.J., Berg, R.C. and Connel E.D., 1977, *La sucrerie belge*, 96: 155-162.

Carillon, T., 1987, Thèse de Docteur Ingénieur (INPT).

Ching, C.B., Ruthven, D.M. and Hidajat, K., 1985, *Chem Eng Sci*, 40: 1411-1417.

Costa, C. and Rodrigues, A., 1985, *AIChe J*, 31: 1645-1654.

Crank, J., 1967, *The Mathematics of diffusion*, pp 84-98 (Clarendon press, Oxford).

Ghim, Y.S. and Chang, H.N., 1982, *Ind Eng Chem Fund*, 21: 369-374.

Goulding, R.W., 1975, *J Chrom*, 103: 229-239.

Hashimoto, K., Adachi, S., Noujima, H. and Maruyama, H., *J Chem Eng Jap*, 16: 400-406.

Ho, C., Ching, C.B. and Ruthven D.M., 1987, *Ind Eng Chem Res*, 26: 1407-1412.

Hyvönen, L., Varo, P. and Koivistoinen, 1977, *J Food Sci*, 42: 652-659.

Rodrigues, A.E. and Costa, C., 1986, in *Ion exchange : Science and Technology*, ed Rodrigues A.E., pp 271-287 (Martinus Nijhoff Publishers, Dordrecht).

Rodrigues, A.E., Costa, C., Loureiro, J., Leitäo, A. and Ferreira R., 1989, in *Adsorption : Science and Technology*, eds Rodrigues A.E., LeVan M.D. and Tondeur D., pp 239-256 (Kluwer Academic Publishers, Dordrecht).

Ruthven, D.M., 1984, *Principles of adsorption and adsorption processes*, pp 380-386 (Wiley-interscience, New-York).

Sakiyama, T., Nakamura, K. and Yano, T., 1985, *Agric Biol Chem*, 49: 2619-2625.

Shallenberger, C.N. and Birch, K.M., 1975, in *Sugar Chemistry*, p 89 (Avi Publishing Company, Wesport).

Tondeur, D., Gorius, A. and Bailly, M., 1989, in *Adsorption : Science and Technology*, eds Rodrigues A.E., LeVan M.D. and Tondeur D., pp 115-148 (Kluwer Academic Publishers, Dordrecht).

Viard, V. and Lameloise, M.L., *J Food Eng*, in press.

Villermaux, J., 1981, in *Percolation Processes, Theory and Applications*, eds Rodrigues A. and Tondeur D., pp 83-140 (Sijthoff and Noordhoff Publishers, Alphen aan den Rijn).

ACKNOWLEDGEMENT

The authors are grateful to the French Ministry of Agriculture for its financial support.

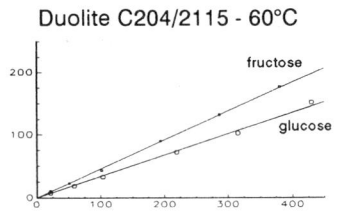

Duolite C204/2115 - 60°C

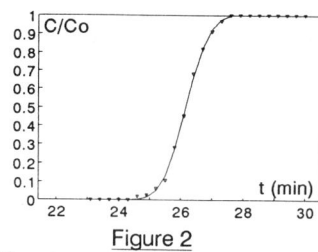

Figure 2
Blue dextran breakthrough curve.
Duolite C204/2078 resin,
▽ experimental points
— J=2010 cells, t =26 min.

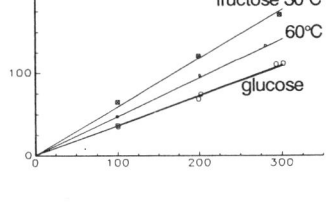

Duolite C204/2078 - 30 and 60°C

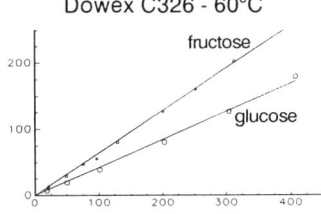

Dowex C326 - 60°C

Concentration in solution (g/l)
Figure 1
Equilibrium isotherms
glucose (o)
fructose (□)

Concentration in resin (g/l)

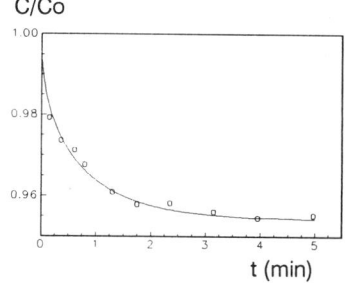

Figure 3
Batch kinetic adsorption curve.
Duolite C204/2115 resin,
fructose, 100 g/l, 30°C.
o experimental points
— De=0.45E-10 m²/s

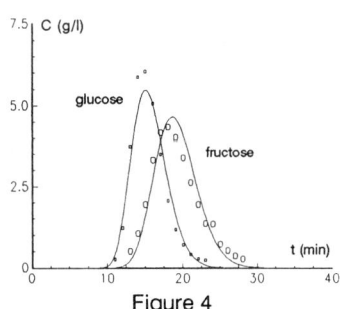

Figure 4
Pulse response : experience and
simulation.
injected volume = 1 ml, L=50 cm, 60°C,
F=10 ml/min, Co(G)=Co(F)=250 g/l.

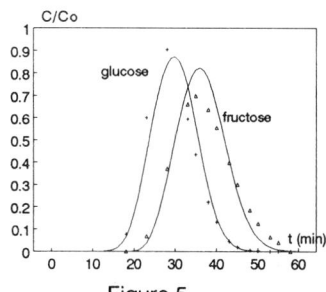

Figure 5
Glucose and fructose elution curve.
injected volume = 586.8 ml,
L=100 cm, 30°C, F=48.9 ml/min,
Co(G)=184.5 g/l, Co(F)=187.8 g/l.

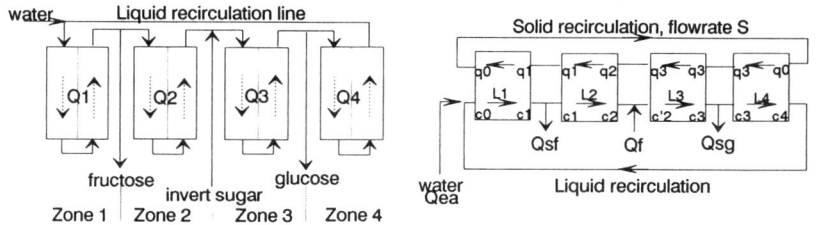

Figure 6
The simulated moving bed adsorber of eight columns,
and the equivalent counter-current representation (right).
Qi : actual flowrate in zone i, Li : equivalent flowrate
S : hypothetical liquid flowrate = $(1-\varepsilon)A(L/T)$

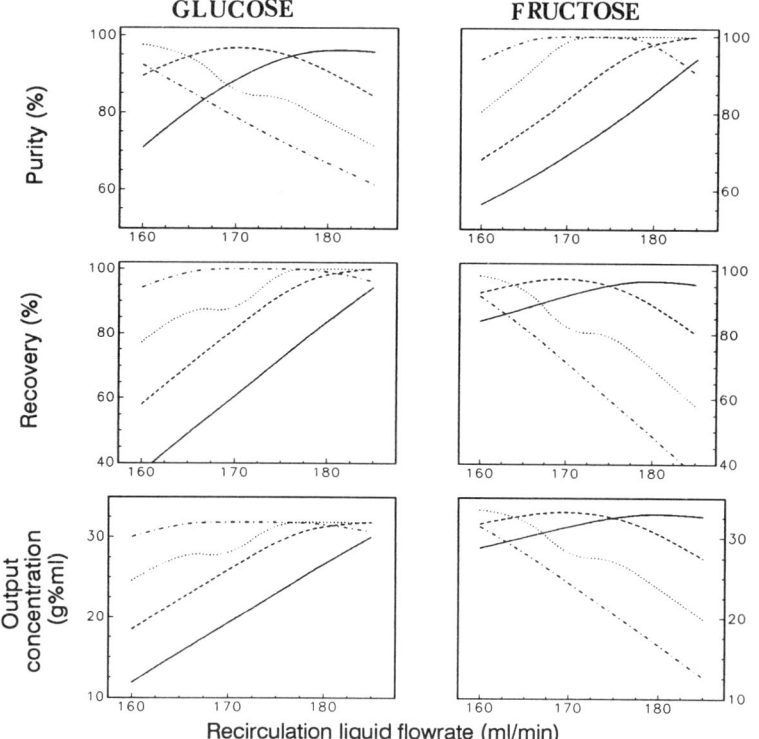

Figure 7
Influence of sequence time T and recirculation flowrate Q4
on the process performances.
T : 22 min (–), 23 min (- -), 24 min (····), 25 min (-·-).

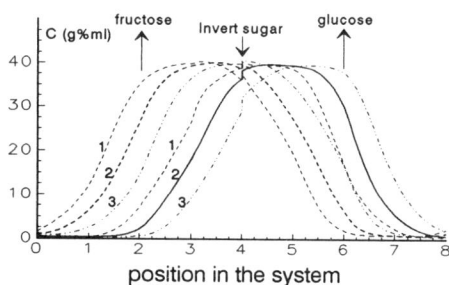

Figure 8
Steady state concentration profile
in the simulated moving bed.
1 start of a sequence
2 half of a sequence
3 end of a sequence

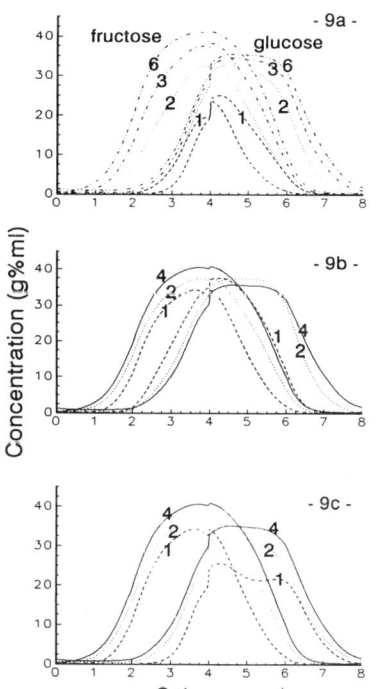

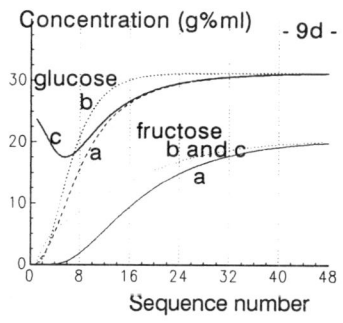

Figure 9
Influence of system preloading.
9a- empty adsorber
9b- two columns before feed-point
    saturated with invert sugar
9c- two columns before feed-point
    preloaded with fructose 40 g%ml
    and two after with glucose 40 g%ml
Numbers on curves denote cycle number,
for half of fifth sequence.
9d- evolution of glucose and fructose
    concentration in their respective
    draw-off lines.

AN AUTOMATED FERMENTATION SYSTEM FOR PECTINASE

PRODUCTION FROM WHEY PERMEATE

T.C. Arnot*, D.L. Pyle* and C.A. Zaror*

This paper outlines an automated pectinase production system suitable for integration into the dairy industry. A yeast fermentation with three commercial products is used as a model system at laboratory scale, with considerable potential for large-scale implementation. A two-tier hierarchical control system is used to maintain system stability with a feedback loop, and optimise productivity with a feedforward loop based on off-line measurements. This approach overcomes the very non-linear system dynamics and can accommodate probable variations in the feed stream.

Introduction

Pectinase enzymes are widely employed in the food industry for their ability to degrade pectin. They have a wide number of uses: removal of haze in wine must and cider, removal or stabilisation of cloud in fruit juices, preparation of vegetable hydrolysates and improvement of both extraction yield and efficiency in fruit juice preparation.

Pectinase is conventionally produced through fermentation of sugar beet residues or molasses by species of *Aspergillus*. This process has a number of problems related to the heterogeneous nature of the fermentation broth and the inherent difficulties of enzyme purification; possibilities for process automation, and therefore integration, are limited.

The yeast *Kluyveromyces marxianus* has been shown to actively secrete one of the four pectinase enzymes, an endo-polygalacturonase, to very high levels - up to 92% of the total broth protein (Phaff & Demain - 1951). The unicellular nature of yeast growth and the relatively pure enzyme product make this organism an ideal alternative to *Aspergillus*; both in terms of automation and process integration. Table 1 summarises the relative merits of the two systems.

Downstream processing has been shown to be extremely simple: centrifugation followed by adsorption chromatography gives over 95% yield and even greater retention of enzyme activity (Harsa - 1991). Both of the additional products, food grade biomass and ethanol, can be easily separated and are of commercial value.

* Biotechnology Group, Department of Food Science and Technology, University of Reading, Whiteknights, P.O. Box 226, Reading. RG6 2AP UK

Table 1: A comparison of the two pectinase production systems.

Aspergillus niger	*Kluyveromyces marxianus*
Solid or semi-submerged culture, predominantly batch but possibly fed-batch.	Continuous submerged culture therefore smaller volume and greater productivity.
Media include corn steep liquor, molasses and sugar beet residues. Pectin is required as an inducer.	Media include yeast extract and glucose, whey permeate, or plant mash juices. No inducer required.
Very mixed products - three pectinases as well as about sixty other hydrolytic enzymes. Therefore considerable problems with downstream processing and purification.	Single enzyme produced together with two other useful products: ethanol and biomass. Active secretion of the enzyme - 92% of broth protein - greatly reduces purification problems.
Pectinesterase activity results in the release of methanol, which must then be removed from food.	Pectinesterase is not produced so there are no problems with methanol production or removal.
Rather limited potential for future improvement or process development.	Many possibilities, notably as an expression system for foreign proteins.
Slow growth rate - 0.1 hr^{-1}	Fast growth rate - 0.43 hr^{-1}
Bad mixing characteristics lead to very difficult on-line monitoring of process conditions. Little hope for the application of control.	Good mixing characteristics allow on-line monitoring and considerable potential for the development of a number of control schemes.

This work presents the implementation of computer control to this fermentation process. A 386 desktop computer is interfaced to the fermenter via AD/DA converters and in-house software. This provides signal conditioning, data acquisition and process control during batch, fed-batch or continuous operation. A hierarchical feedback / feedforward control scheme allows manipulation of feed flow rate in response to fluctuations in on-line measurements of carbon dioxide in the fermenter exhaust gas; and manipulation of the feed concentration in response to off-line measurements and an optimisation model, based upon a validated kinetic model and mass balances. pH, temperature, agitation and gas flow rates are monitored by the computer but controlled by conventional fermenter hardware.

Experimental

Kluyveromyces marxianus (NCYC 587) was maintained on malt agar slope cultures at 4°C for up to 2 months. After this period fresh slope cultures were generated by inoculating a small loop-full of yeast into 100 mls of medium in a 250ml shake flask. The medium contained the following components made up in distilled water: anhydrous glucose - 50 g/l, yeast extract - 10 g/l, KH_2PO_4 - 1 g/l, $(NH_3)_2SO_4$ - 0.5 g/l and $MgSO_4.7H_2O$ - 1 g/l. The inoculum was grown at 30°C for 24 hours before inoculation of the fermenter, which contained the same medium. The fermenter was operated in continuous culture under anaerobic conditions at 30°C, pH 4.5 and 500 r.p.m.

The system was based around a Bioengineering KLF 2000 laboratory fermenter with a working volume of 1.25 litres, and a Victor V386A computer with an MSDOS 4.01a operating system and a 80387 maths co-processor. The RS232 serial port of the computer was modified to handle eight bi-directional channels, at a baud rate of 9600, using a 3D Digital Design and Development MITC9 multiplexer card in one of the expansion slots. Two of the serial channels were connected to Sartorius IB31D load cells to allow measurement of the weight change of the feed reservoirs with time, and therefore feedback control of the feed flow rate. A third serial channel was connected to a 3D "Thinklab" interface unit which featured eight 12 Bit analogue to digital input channels (0 - 5 volts), four 12 Bit digital to analogue output channels (4 - 20 mA), with a multiplexer and signal conditioning amplifiers. All connections were made with shielded cable to avoid interference from other electrical sources.

The input channels of the interface were connected to the fermenter control units to allow monitoring of pH, temperature and agitation. The gas flow rate was monitored and controlled by a Brooks Instruments 5850TR series mass flow controller which was also connected to the interface. Carbon dioxide concentration in the exhaust gas was measured on-line by an Analytical Development Company SB-200 infra-red analyser, 0-100 % CO_2 +/-2% of full scale. Oxygen-free nitrogen was passed through the fermenter head space as a carrier gas, having been filtered with 0.2 μm PTFE Gelman filters.

The output channels were connected to two Verder 326-S auto-control peristaltic pumps using neoprene tubing. Measurement of the feed reservoir weight changes with time allowed proportional feedback control of the feed flow rate. The feed flow rate and feed concentration could be independently manipulated by maintaining the feed reservoirs at different concentrations. The flow rates for the two pumps were calculated using a simple mass balance so that:

$$F_1 = F - F_2$$

$$F_2 = \frac{F(S_F - S_1)}{(S_2 - S_1)}$$

where S_1 and S_2 are the substrate concentrations in the two reservoirs (g/l), F_1 and F_2 are the flow rates for the two pumps (l/hr), and S_F and F are the required feed substrate concentrations and flow rates respectively. Figure 1 shows a simplified schematic of the fermenter system, with one of the load cells being omitted for clarity.

The system was monitored and controlled by in-house software written in Turbo Basic (version 1.1, Borland International Inc.) which allowed data collection and storage, real time graphical display and implementation of control actions. Process simulations were also written in Turbo Basic and the model was solved using the Runge-Kutta 4th order algorithm. Simulations were written for a Proportional Integral Derivative (PID) algorithm which was tested against simulated step changes in the process variables. The time constants for the PID algorithm were tuned using the well known ultimate sensitivity method (Ziegler & Nichols - 1942).

Mathematical Modelling

A particular feature of this fermentation is the inhibition of yeast growth by one of the products - ethanol. This interaction is of enormous complexity but has been successfully modelled using a simple un-structured extension to the Monod equation (Luong -1985) - equation 1 below. The dynamic behaviour of the continuous fermenter system can be modelled on the basis of mass balances:

$$\mu = \frac{\mu_{max} \, S}{(K_S + S)} (1 - (\frac{P}{P_{max}})^n)$$ (1)

$$\frac{dX}{dt} = X(\mu - D)$$ (2)

$$\frac{dS}{dt} = D(S_F - S) - \frac{\mu X}{Y_{(X/S)}}$$ (3)

$$\frac{dP}{dt} = \mu X Y_{(P/X)} - PD$$ (4)

$$\frac{dCO_2}{dt} = \mu X Y_{(C/X)} - \frac{G}{V} CO_2$$ (5)

$$\frac{dE}{dt} = \mu X Y_{(E/X)} - ED$$ (6)

An explanation of the symbols and the model parameters can be found in the Nomenclature section.
The model assumes that the reactor remains perfectly mixed and at constant volume. All of the CO_2 produced is carried out of the headspace by the inert nitrogen, and the level of dissolved CO_2 is assumed to be minimal and constant. Ethanol and water losses in the gas phase are neglected as it is assumed that they are stripped out in the exhaust condenser. The yield coefficients of all the variables, except the enzyme, were not found to vary with growth rate; the enzyme yield was found to have a logarithmic relationship with the growth rate of the form $Y_{(E/X)} = a * e^{(-b\mu)}$. Figure 2 shows the relationship between the model and experimental data for a set of steady state conditions.

The main feature of this graph is the rapid increase in substrate concentration, and the concomitant decrease in the concentrations of ethanol and biomass, above a dilution rate of about 0.175 hour^{-1}. This is a reflection of the non-competitive inhibition of growth by ethanol, as $\mu = D$, and has considerable implications for process productivity and control. Non-inhibited fermentations would typically show a much more linear relationship between the variables and dilution rate, almost until μ_{max} is reached.

Optimisation

The model was coupled with an objective cost function in order to predict the optimal operating conditions of the system (Arnot *et al* - 1991). The objective function was of the form:

$$Productivity = D(aX + bP + cE - dS) \qquad (7)$$

where a,b,c and d are the respective typical bulk costs (£/g) of the biomass, ethanol, enzyme and glucose. The function penalises residual glucose which would be one of the major expenses. Figure 3 shows the predicted productivity in (£/l/hour) against the values calculated from the experimental data in Figure 2, and highlights the dramatic reduction in productivity in the region where residual substrate becomes significant. Figure 4 shows a contour plot of productivity as a function of feed substrate concentration, S_F, and dilution rate, D. This graph clearly identifies the optimal operating conditions to be around 100-200 g/l feed concentration and a dilution rate of 0.075 to 0.1 hour^{-1}.

Process Control

The productivity graphs clearly identify the need to maintain the system at a steady state within quite tight limits. It can be seen that a relatively small increase in the amount of residual substrate causes a dramatic decrease in the process productivity. Such an increase is probable if the process were to be applied to an effluent stream such as whey permeate as fluctuations in the feed concentration are highly likely. The control objectives are therefore clearly defined:

    (i) to maintain steady state operation at the highest level of productivity;
    (ii) to combat probable fluctuations in the feed substrate concentration.

The rate of carbon dioxide production is dependent upon the growth rate of the yeast, which is in turn dependent upon the rate of substrate delivery. Steady state operation might therefore be achieved by relating feed flow rate to the measurements of carbon dioxide in the fermenter exhaust gas in a feedback control loop.

$$F_t = F_{t-1} + K_C \left[e_t - e_{t-1} + \frac{T_S}{\tau_I} e_t + \frac{\tau_D}{T_S}(e_t - 2e_{t-1} + e_{t-2}) \right] \qquad (8)$$

where:

$$e_t = (CO_2 \ setpoint - (CO_2)_t) \qquad (9)$$

The PID feedback algorithm was tuned by model simulations and found to be stable in operation up to the point where residual substrate became significant. At this point it can also be seen, from Figure 2, that the concentration of carbon dioxide in the exit gas begins to reduce. Below a dilution rate of about 0.18 hour^{-1}, increasing carbon dioxide levels will cause a decrease in the flow rate, but beyond this point the trend is reversed so that decreasing carbon dioxide levels will increase the flow rate, to the point where the biomass will be washed out and productivity reaches a minimum. The inevitable consequence of this behaviour is that if the process goes beyond this operating point the control action will become unstable unless the value of K_c, the controller gain, changes sign. This problem could be solved by simply placing an upper limit on the flow rate, or by using an adaptive gain scheme.

In addition to process stability, the productivity is very sensitive to the residual substrate concentration, as can be seen from Figure 4. It is therefore necessary to control this value within acceptable limits. At steady state it can be shown that:

$$S_F = S + \frac{G}{V \, Y_{(C/S)}} \, \frac{CO_2}{D} \tag{10}$$

If the values of S and CO_2 are used as set-points, chosen from the process model, S_F could be manipulated in response to fluctuations in D, which in turn would be mediated by the feedback loop. Since the time constant for hydraulic dynamics (ie. those determined by changes in the flow rate) is approximately 8 times smaller then those corresponding to a change in feed concentration, the feedforward loop was invoked at a lower frequency. It was also expanded to use off-line measurements of the process variables, viz biomass, glucose, ethanol and enzyme, and also the concentrations in the feed reservoirs. This hierarchical approach is shown in diagrammatical form in Figure 5. The lower level feedback loop is used to maintain stable operation by sampling at half-hourly intervals and controlling the flow rate in response to variations in on-line CO_2 measurements. The higher level feedforward loop would be implemented approximately four-hourly in response to off-line measurements and the optimisation model. In this way productivity can be adjusted to the highest level while also maintaining stable operation.

Conclusions

An alternative source of commercial food grade pectinase has been identified. The process kinetics have been successfully modelled, and a model-based optimisation protocol has been devised. The kinetic and optimisation models were combined with a conventional PID feedback loop to develop a novel control regime. This work has highlighted the problems of implementing conventional control schemes in product inhibited fermentations, and has shown the potential benefits of incorporating off-line information.

References

Arnot, T.C.; Zaror, C.A.; Pyle, D.L. (1991) Kinetic Modelling as a Tool for Fermentation Optimisation, presented at the International Symposium on Bioprocess Modelling and Control, University of Newcastle-upon-Tyne, UK.

Harsa, S. (1991) PhD Thesis - University of Reading.

Phaff, H.J.; Demain, A.L. (1956) Journal of Biological Chemistry 218, pp 875-884.

Ziegler, J.G; Nichols, N.B. (1942) Transactions of the American Society of Mechanical Engineers 64, pp 759-768.

Luong, J.H.T. (1985) Biotechnology and Bioengineering 27, pp 280-285.

Nomenclature

Process parameters:

a = bulk cost of biomass (£150/tonne -> £0.00015/g)
b = bulk cost of ethanol (£500/tonne -> £0.0005/g)
c = bulk cost of enzyme (£1300/10^6 Units -> £0.0013/Unit)
d = bulk cost of glucose (£1300/tonne -> £0.0013/g)
μ = specific growth rate (hour^{-1})
D = dilution rate (F/V - hour^{-1})
S = residual glucose concentration (g/l)
P = ethanol concentration (g/l)
X = biomass concentration (g/l)
E = enzyme activity (Units/l)
S_F = feed glucose concentration (initially 50 g/l)
F = feed flow rate (l/hour)
V = culture volume (1.25 l)
G = gas flow rate (22.5 l/hour)
K_C = controller gain (l/(%v/v h))
T_s = sampling interval, feedback loop (0.5 hours)
τ_I = reset time (hours)
τ_D = derivative time constant (hours)

Kinetic parameters:

μ_{max} = maximum specific growth rate (0.426 hour^{-1})
K_s = substrate utilisation constant (0.032 g/l)
P_{max} = maximum tolerable ethanol concentration (52.44 g/l)
n = inhibition constant (0.532)
$Y_{(X/S)}$ = biomass yield on substrate (0.04 g/g)
$Y_{(P/X)}$ = ethanol yield on biomass (9 g/g)
$Y_{(C/X)}$ = CO_2 yield on biomass (10.5 g/g)
$Y_{(E/X)}$ = enzyme yield on biomass (6039*e$^{(-11.18\,\mu)}$ Units/g)

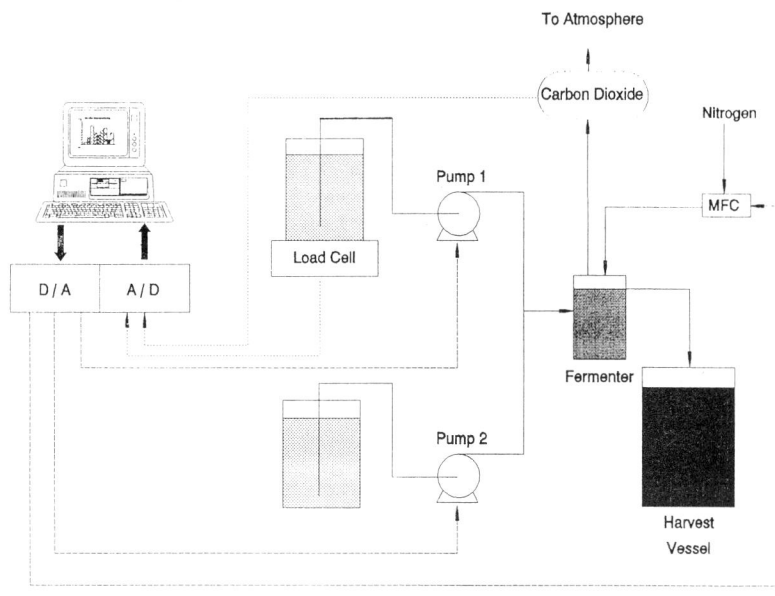

Figure 1:   Schematic diagram of the fermentation system showing lines of communication.

MFC = Mass Flow Controller

Figure 2:   Steady state variables against dilution rate in continuous culture of *Kluyveromyces marxianus*. Note that solid lines are from the model and the points are experimental data.

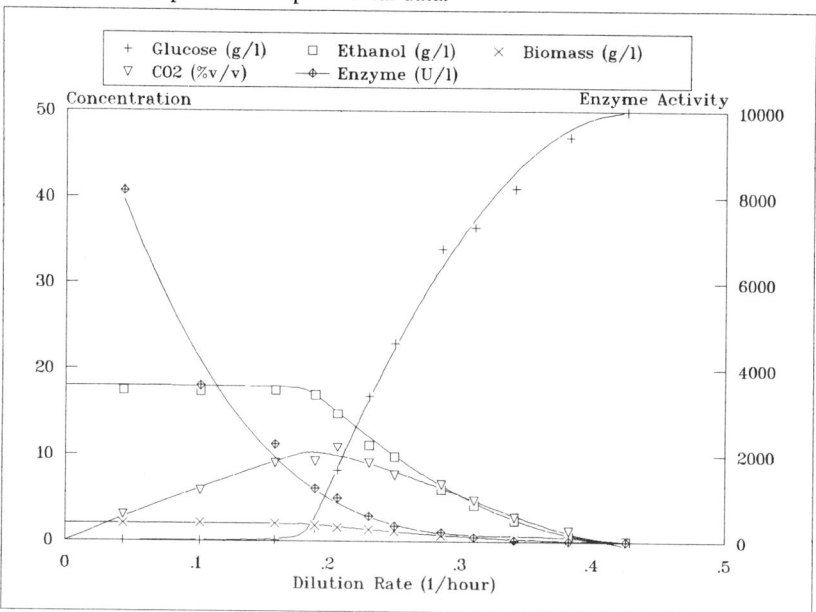

Figure 3:   Productivity against dilution rate for the same data as Figure 2. Note that the solid line is the model and the points are data.

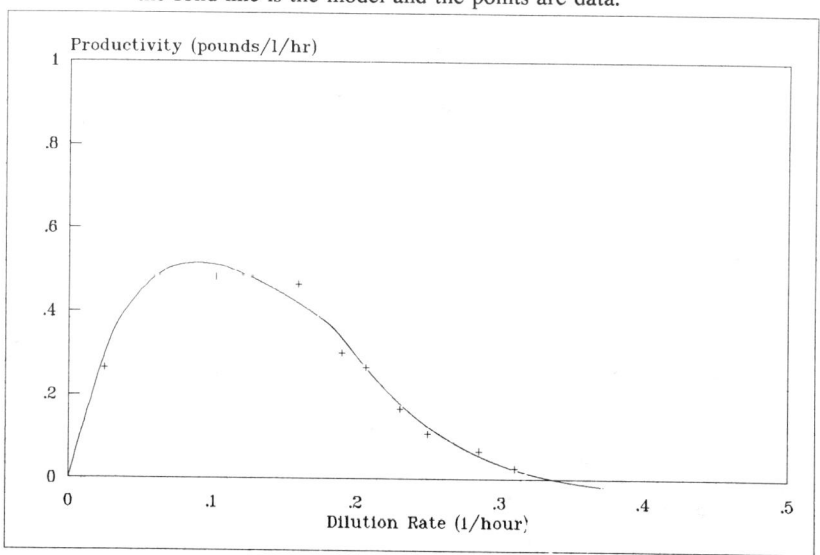

Figure 4: Contour plot of productivity (£/l/hr) as a function of feed concentration, S_F (g/l), and dilution rate, D (hour^{-1}). Data generated from the optimisation model.

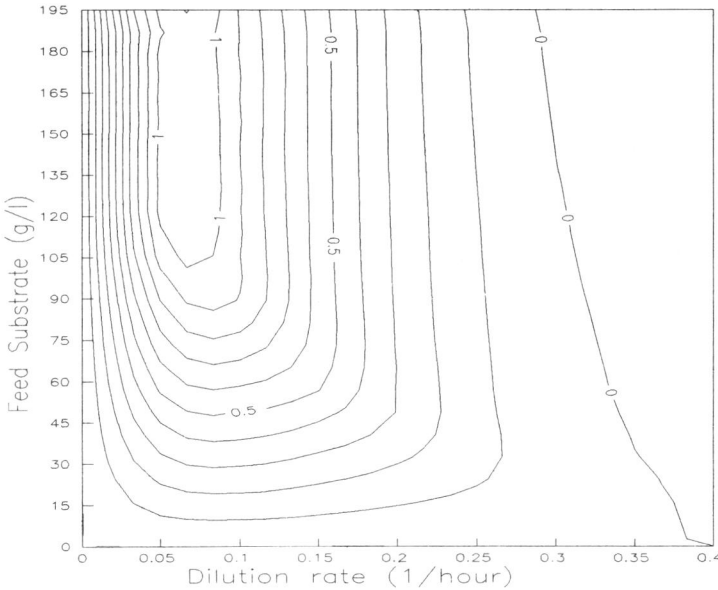

Figure 5: Schematic diagram of the hierarchical control scheme.

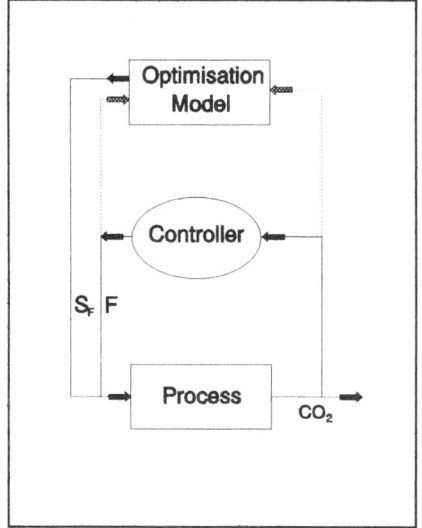

HEAT TRANSFER AND FLOW IN SOLID-LIQUID FOOD MIXTURES

L. ZHANG* , S. LIU*, J-P PAIN† and P J FRYER*

The application of High Temperature Short Time processes to solid-liquid mixtures requires an understanding of both the heating and cooling of the particles and the flow patterns of the two phases. Volumetric heating, by ohmic or microwave techniques is a more efficient way of sterilising particles than conventional heating. The ohmic heating of particle-liquid mixtures has been examined by assuming a homogeneous suspension of particles, and modelling a unit cell of the fluid. This approach cannot be used to model cooling, but an estimate of C-value accumulation can be made by assuming rapid liquid cooling. If the particle size is too large or the heat transfer coefficient between particle and fluid too low, product quality can be significantly impaired during cooling. The flow of food particles has been studied experimentally; turbulent flows can be correlated with the modified particle Froude number, but laminar flows are more complex.

INTRODUCTION

Amongst the reactions that take place in a food when it is heated are those which result in the death of microbes and microbial spores, giving sterility, and those which impair the quality of the final product. The activation energies of the two sets of reactions are such that, for a given level of product sterilisation, quality is maximised if the process is carried out at as high a temperature as possible (Hallstrom et al, 1988). High Temperature Short Time (HTST) (or Ultra-High Temperature (UHT)) processes, are thus favourable to food quality, and are now widespread. HTST processing requires rapid heat transfer.

Liquids can be continuously sterilised by passing the liquid through plate heat exchangers which provide high convective heat transfer coefficients (Lalande et al, 1991). Conventional techniques for particulate sterilisation attempt to have as high a heat transfer coefficient as possible between particle and fluid (Sastry, 1986). The application of HTST techniques to foods containing particles is more complex, since for all but very small particles, the process time to ensure sterility is the time required to conduct enough heat to the centre of the particle. Alternative techniques are thus necessary to enable rapid particle heating. Heating throughout the particle is possible using volumetric heating techniques such as microwave (Ayappa et al, 1991) or ohmic heating (de Alwis et al , 1989, de Alwis and Fryer, 1990), in which heat is generated within a food by the passage of electric field or current. In both cases, thermal conduction does not limit the heating process, so both particles and liquids can heat at similar rates, making the HTST processing of particle-liquid mixtures possible. Ohmic heating plants are now in commercial operation.

Commercial HTST plants consist of three sections, each of which contribute to the F and C values of the product. Food is first heated to the required temperature, is held at that temperature for long enough to ensure sterility, and is then rapidly cooled to room temperature. The role of the holding section is significantly different in conventional and volumetric heating plants. In conventional heating, the particle temperature lags behind the liquid, so the holding tube must be long enough to allow for thermal equilibration as well as the required hold time at the sterilisation temperature. However, in volumetric heating particle and liquid temperatures are similar, so there may be no need for thermal equilibration in the hold tube. Volumetric

*Department of Chemical Engineering, University of Cambridge.
†University of Compiegne, France.

heating methods transfer the heat transfer limitation from the heating to the cooling section.

Any continuous food process must be designed to sterilise the fastest moving part of the system whilst minimising the cooking of the slowest-moving part. De Alwis et al (1991) express this design problem in terms of two ratios, ϕ_F and ϕ_C;

$$\phi_F = \frac{F}{F_p} \quad \text{and} \quad \phi_C = \frac{C}{C_{max}}, \tag{1}$$

in which F_p is the minimum F value which must be achieved by the heating process and C_{max} is the C value beyond which the nutrition of the food will be damaged. ϕ_F and ϕ_C thus quantitatively reflect the sterility and the nutrition destruction level by cooking respectively. A satisfactory process can be described in terms of ϕ_F and ϕ_C : in each part of the system, if $\phi_F < 1$: the food is insufficiently sterile, whilst if $\phi_C > 1$, it is overcooked. The criteria for process acceptability are thus firstly that $\phi_F > 1$ throughout the product, and then that $\phi_C < 1$ throughout. Each point in the food must be processed for longer than t_{min}, the time at which $\phi_F = 1$, to give the required sterility, but for no longer than t_{max}, the time at which $\phi_C = 1$, to ensure the food is of satisfactory quality. Significantly higher quality is possible with volumetric heating.

Food mixtures undergoing HTST processing may contain >40% solids and particles up to 25 mm in diameter. The flow characteristics of viscous and particulate food products are complex, and little information is available. To ensure the microbiological safety of the process the speed of the fastest moving particle relative to the average particle velocity must be known. The fastest moving particle, with the shortest residence time, thus determines the process time, whilst the particle residence time distribution determines the quality of the final product. To ensure sterilisation in commercial practice, laminar flow is generally assumed; so the process is designed to sterilise material travelling at twice the mean flow velocity. This may well lead to significant overprocessing in practice.

To calculate ϕ_F and ϕ_C in conventional heating requires an understanding of the residence time distribution (RTD) of both phases, and of solid-liquid heat transfer. Neither of these problems is as well understood, although partial information is available both on particle RTD (Sastry and Zuritz, 1987, Dutta and Sastry, 1990, Liu et al, 1991) and on particle-liquid heat transfer coefficients (Chandarana et al, 1990, Merson et al, 1991). Additionally in volumetric heating it is necessary to predict the pattern of heat generation within the system. This paper describes work underway to study both heat transfer and flow in HTST processing, using both experiments and the ANSYS finite-element program. Research has concentrated on the ohmic heating process, but work on flow and cooling is of relevance to all continuous food processes.

HEAT GENERATION IN OHMIC PROCESSING

The equation which describes heat generation and transfer is

$$\nabla(\lambda\Delta T) + Q = \rho \, c_p \frac{dT}{dt} \tag{2}$$

where Q is the heat generation rate, zero for conventional heating. The factors which affect Q ($= \kappa |E_i|^2$) in ohmic heating are well understood (de Alwis et al, 1991); it is first necessary to know the distribution of electrical conductivity within the food, and then the field distribution can be found by solving Laplace's equation:

$$\nabla(\kappa \nabla V) = 0 \tag{3}$$

throughout the medium.

Analytical solutions to equation (2) are only available in very restricted cases. The worst temperature variation, and thus variation in F and C in the food, occurs in the case of no heat transfer. Under these conditions, equation (2) becomes

$$\frac{dT_i}{dt} = \frac{\kappa |E_i|^2}{\rho C_p} = G_i \qquad (4)$$

The factor G is generally useful, as it relates the heat generation within the food and its thermal capacity. If physical properties are assumed temperature independent, then equation (4) can be integrated to give T_i (t) = T_{i0} + G_i t , where T_{i0} is the initial temperature at point i and the variation of F and C found at point i as a function of time;

$$F_i (t) = \frac{\exp[\beta_F (T_{i0} - T_{ref} + G_i t)] - \exp[\beta_F (T_{i0} - T_{ref})]}{\beta_F G_i} \qquad (5)$$

$$C_i (t) = \frac{\exp[\beta_C (T_{i0} - T_{ref} + G_i t)] - \exp[\beta_C (T_{i0} - T_{ref})]}{\beta_C G_i} \qquad (6)$$

where $\beta_F = \ln(10)/Z_F$ and $\beta_C = \ln(10)/Z_C$.

The above equations can be used to put bounds on the variation in F and C within a given food product. The sterilisation time, at which $\phi_F >1$ throughout the material must be found. This is the time required to sterilise the slowest heating part of the food, i.e. where G = G_{min} ; G_{min} can be substituted into equation (5) to find t_{min} when F = F_p. The quality of the product can then be checked by finding the C at the fastest heating point, where G = G_{max} , and ensuring that $\phi_C <1$ using equation (6).

In reality, physical properties are functions of temperature, so the electric and thermal fields are coupled. Modelling of these coupled fields is possible but expensive in computer time (de Alwis and Fryer, 1990). Zhang and Fryer (1992) describe a simplification to improve the modelling of heat generation and find G for a solid-liquid mixture. If a homogeneous suspension of particles within the fluid is assumed, then the system can be modelled using ANSYS as in Figure 1, as a series of unit cells each containing particles. The cells are symmetrical, so that there is no current flow across the cell boundaries (A-A), and the voltage drop across each cell is the same. In consequence, each cell will heat identically, so that the simulation of one is representative of the whole.

The ratio

$$R_Q = \frac{\text{Heat generation rate; Q}}{\text{Heat generation in liquid were particle not present; } Q_u} \qquad (7)$$

can be used to display the variation in heat generation within the system. When $R_\kappa = \kappa_l/\kappa_s \neq 1$ heat generation will not be uniform. At the maximum and minimum heat generation points the heating rate can be very different from the rest of the phase; however, in practical situations about 80% of the material will heat at or near the average rate. As a demonstration of the use of the program, Figures (2) and (3) show plots of four parameters; $R_{Qmx} = Q_{mx}/Q_u$, $R_{Qmn} = Q_{mn}/Q_u$, $R_{Ql} = Q_l/Q_u$, $R_{Qs} = Q_s/Q_u$, plotted against solids fraction, where Q_{mx} and Q_{mn} are the maximum and minimum heat generation rate and Q_l and Q_s the volume average heat generation rates in the liquid and solid phase. Figure (4) shows a plot of R_Q for $R_\kappa = 0.75$ and a solids fraction of 6.5%, in which the heat generation within the particle is less than within the fluid, but regions of high heat generation form around the edges of the particle.

These values can be used in design together with estimates of the mixing within the liquid. The cell configuration shown gives maximum variation between liquid and solid (Zhang and Fryer, 1992). The average values Q_l and Q_s can be used to calculate the temperature change for infinitely large heat transfer within each phase, i.e. for a well mixed liquid phase. However, for a poorly mixed liquid phase or within the solid, Q_{mx} and Q_{mn} should be examined to determine the maximum possible under- and over-cooking in the two phases.

HEAT TRANSFER DURING COOLING

During heating and holding stages, the food will reach its required F-value. However, during cooling, both the F and C-values of the food material will continue to increase. C accumulated during cooling may damage overall product quality. This is especially important in volumetric heating techniques in which it is likely that particles will reach $\phi_F = 1$ before $\phi_C > 1$. In control of the ohmic heating process, it is useful if the electrical conductivity ratio is adjusted so that the particle temperature is equal to or exceeds that of the liquid. The liquid temperature can be readily measured in operation; if it is known that this is the lowest temperature in the material then it is simple to ensure that the process is sterile. However, excessive particle overheating will cause quality problems during cooling, as shown below.

Liquids can be quickly cooled by convective heat transfer; however, the solid particle cooling rate will be a function of the liquid-solid heat transfer coefficient, thermal diffusivity and the liquid temperature. The minimum C value accumulation during cooling can be estimated by assuming that at the start of cooling the surrounding liquid cools immediately to the final temperature T_c. To demonstrate possible C values which can result during cooling, a spherical particle surrounded by a coolant fluid has been modelled using ANSYS to solve the conduction equation

$$\alpha \left(\frac{\partial^2 T}{\partial r^2} + \frac{2}{r} \frac{\partial T}{\partial r} \right) = \frac{\partial T}{\partial t} \qquad (8)$$

where α is the thermal diffusivity, r is the radius variable , with the boundary condition:

$$h \left(T_s - T_b \right) = \lambda \frac{\partial T}{\partial r} \qquad (9)$$

where T_s and T_b are the solid/ liquid interface and liquid bulk temperatures and h is the convective heat transfer coefficient. Introducing nondimensional distance y = r/R, equation (8) becomes

$$\frac{\alpha}{R^2} \left(\frac{\partial^2 T}{\partial y^2} + \frac{2}{y} \frac{\partial T}{\partial y} \right) = \frac{\partial T}{\partial t} \qquad (10)$$

C value accumulation is a function of two system parameters: Biot number, Bi = hR/k and the time constant $\tau = R^2/\alpha$. Figures (5) and (6) show that the larger τ, and the smaller Bi, the greater the accumulation of C value during cooling. The C value at the centre of the particle is plotted against Bi and t for (i) a constant liquid coolant temperature 20°C and (ii) the initial particle temperature T_0 is assumed uniform and equal to 140 °C (iii) Z_c =33°C, T_{ref} = 100°C. C values increase with t and decrease with Bi, and several hundred minutes of C can be accumulated during cooling for even the best case. Ohmic heating involves the slow flow of solid-liquid mixtures; at low flow rates, the heat transfer coefficient will approach the limit of Nu = 2 (Chandarana et al, 1991) so that low Biot numbers are possible. Care must thus be taken to ensure that cooling rates are satisfactory and to model the whole process in quality calculations.

VELOCITY DISTRIBUTIONS OF FOOD PARTICLES

The models outlined above are designed to reflect good commercial practice in which the separation of liquid and solid phases must be avoided. It is not possible to predict the flow behaviour of foods theoretically. Analytical approaches are possible only for single particles in idealised circumstances (for example as discussed by Purdom and Richardson(1990)). Most work on hydraulic conveying has considered the flow of particles much denser than the liquid. Some information on the correlation of velocities in solid-liquid flows is available from Okuda (1981), who examined the flow patterns of coarse solid particles (plastic spheres 6-38mm diameter, specific gravity 1.050-1.440) in hydraulic transport in pipes of 50 and 100 mm pipe diameter, and fitted experimental velocity results to equations of the form:

$$v_r = \frac{v_p}{v_m} = 1 - \exp[- a \frac{d}{D} (Fr_p + b)] \tag{11}$$

where d and D are the particle and tube diameters, a and b are constants, v_r is the ratio of the particle and the mean fluid velocity, and Fr_p is the modified particle Froude number, defined in hydaulic conveying as:

$$Fr_p = \frac{v_m}{\sqrt{g\, d\, (s - 1)}} \tag{12}$$

where s is the ratio of the densities of the particles and the fluid, i.e. ρ_S/ρ_L. Several studies have been conducted on the residence time distribution of single phase fluids during continuous sterilization or pasteurization, such as Rao and Loncin (1974), Heppell (1985) and Rao (1987). Fewer studies on the flow of suspensions have been reported. Some particle residence times have been measured, for example by Richardson and Gaze (1986) and Alksgog (1991). Dutta and Sastry (1990) videotaped particles in systems of low solids fractions, about 0.8 %, in carboxy methylcellulose solutions during passage through a transparent holding tube similar to that of commercial processing systems. They considered that viscosity was the strongest factor affecting the velocity distribution.

Experiments have been conducted in a horizontal flow loop, with a test section consisting of a 5m length of 44mm i.d. perspex pipe, to study food flows in water and non-Newtonian fluids using various sizes, shapes and densities of particles (Liu et al, 1991). Particle velocities were detected by using metal detection coils. Particles of known size and density were wrapped with metal foil so their passage could be detected by coils mounted along the pipe, allowing particle velocities up to about 2 m/s to be measured in flows of any solids fraction with a relative error smaller than 3%. Experiments showed the sedimentation properties of the tracers to be indistinguishable from food particles of the same size and density. Two types of particle could be detected and distinguished in the same experiment. Food solids naturally contain a range of densities; in experiments with high solids fractions, the densities of the two tracers are chosen so that the density range of the food lies between them.

Observations of the flow behaviours of tracer particles and food flows show several types of flow patterns, similar to those of denser solids; as the liquid flow is increased from zero, a sedimented particle is first unaffected but then begins to slip along the pipe. The particle then begins to roll and bounce along the pipe (saltation) prior to full suspension.

The velocity ratio v_r does not correlate well with Reynolds number. For example, for the heaviest disc used, Re > 8000 was necessary to cause the particle to move, whilst for the majority of particles the velocity ratio was in the region of unity at this Reynolds number. Figure 7 shows results for the flow of a single particle in largely turbulent flows of water as the variation of v_r as a function of the particle Froude number. Several types of particle (cubes, spheres, cylinders and discs) of diameters between 5 and 13 mm and density between 1010 and 1400 kg/m³ were used. The data lies on a single curve. For $Fr_p > 5$ the particle velocity is comparable to that to the fluid, values of v_r between 0.9 and 1.2 being found; this corresponds to saltation and suspension of the particle. At the centreline of a turbulent fluid, the local velcoity is 20% greater than the mean velocity; it is thus possible for the particle to travel faster than the mean fluid velocity. For $Fr_p < 5$, however, the mean particle velocity decreases rapidly until for $Fr_p < 2$ the flow is insufficient to move the particle, leading to a velocity ratio of zero. The 503 data points were fitted with a correlation coefficient of 0.9 with the empirical equation:

$$v_r = \frac{Fr_p}{0.462\,Fr_p + 0.219} - 0.969 \tag{13}$$

More complex effects are seen in laminar flows. Experiments have been carried out in CMC for a wide range of tracers. Figure 8 shows typical results of v_r plotted against the modified Froude number for three cubic particles of densities 2%, 5% and 10% heavier than the liquid. The general shape of the curve is similar to Figure 7; however, higher v_r values of up to 1.6 are seen, and the data for the particles diverge for $Fr_p > 5$, with the lighter particle having the highest velocity. The velocity profile of a laminar flow is such that the centreline velocity is up to twice the mean velocity, so a suspended particle in a laminar flow will travel at higher v_r than in a turbulent flow. The velocity required to suspend the heaviest particle is such that the flow is turbulent, so the maximum v_r achieved is less. Particle flow is thus a function both of the Froude number and of the fluid flow pattern. As the particle fraction of solids increases, the velocity profile across the tube will become more uniform. Figure 9 shows a plot of the v_r for two particles of different density in a flow of 25% 10 mm diameter carrots in water suggesting that for $Fr_p > 10$ the flow is reasonably uniform. More work is needed to produce design correlations.

CONCLUSIONS

HTST processing of solid-liquid mixtures requires information on the heating, cooling and flow of food fluids. This paper has briefly described work in progress at Cambridge in all three areas. The successful design of a process requires that the flow be homogeneous throughout; it appears that particle sedimentation can be avoided if the system is chosen so that $Fr_p > 5$, and further work is under way to produce correlations for the behaviour of high solids fractions. Once the variation in particle flow, and thus residence time, is known, it is possible to predict the F and C value distribution within the product. Modelling heat generation is easier than modelling conventional heating if homogeneous flow is assumed, as the system is symmetrical. If the heating process is such that the solid temperature is comparable to that of the liquid, as in ohmic heating, then it is necessary to study cooling as well as heating processes to ensure maximum product quality.

ACKNOWLEGEMENTS
JPP wishes to that the EEC for the provision of a study grant during the duration of which this work was carried out. SL is supported by the British Council and by Sous-Chef Ltd. ZL is supported by AFRC. PJF is grateful for the provision of ANSYS at a University rate by Strucom Ltd., Croydon, UK.

REFERENCES
Alkskog, K.Technical developments in aseptic particle processing, presented at "Ambient Shelf Stable Products", Institute of Packaging, London. (1991)

Ayeppa, KG, Davis, HT, Crapiste, G, Davis, EA and Gordon, J. Microwave heating: an evaluation of power formulations, *Chem.Eng.Sci.*, **46**, 1005-1016, (1991).

Chandarana, DI, Gavin, A and Wheaton, FW. Particle/fluid interface heat transfer under UHT conditions at low particle/fluid relative velocities, *J. Food.Proc. Engng.*, **13**, 191 (1990).

de Alwis, AAP and Fryer, PJ. A finite element analysis of heat generation and transfer during ohmic heating of food,*Chem.Eng.Sci.*. **45**, 6, 1547-1560, (1990).

de Alwis, AAP, Halden, K and Fryer, PJ. Shape and conductivity effects in the ohmic heating of foods, *Chem.Eng.Res.Des.*, **67**, 159-168, (1989).

de Alwis, AAP, Zhang, L, and Fryer, PJ. Modelling sterilisation and quality in the ohmic heating process, to be published as Chapter 5 in*"Advances in Aseptic Processing Technologies"*, ed RK Singh and PE Nelson, Elsevier. (1991)

Dutta, B and Sastry, SK. Velocity distributions of food particle suspensions in holding tube flow: distribution characteristics and fastest-particle velocities, *J. Food Proc*, **55**, 1703-1710 (1990)

Hallstrom, B., Skjoldebrand, C. and Tragardh, C. *Heat Transfer & Food Products*. Elsevier, London (1988).

Heppel, NJ, Comparison of the residence time distributions of water and milk in an experimental UHT steriliser, *J.Food Eng.*, **4**, 71-84. (1985)

Liu, S, Pain, J-P, and Fryer, PJ. The flow and velocity distributions of single particles in liquids and their application in food processing, presented at Eurotherm #20, *Heat Transfer in Complex Fluids*, and submitted to*Entropie*.

Okuda, K.Trajectory and diffusion of particles in solid-liquid flow of slurry, *J. of Pipelines*, **3**, 211-233. (1981)

Purdom, GJ, and Richardson, SM. Lateral migration for the separation of dilute two-phase suspensions, *Fluid Mixing 4, IChemE Symp. Ser 121*, 297-308 (1990)

Rao, MA, and Loncin, M. Residence time distribution and its role in continuous pasteurisation, *Lebesnm. Wiss. u-Techn.*, **7**, 4-17. (1974)

Rao, MA. Predicting the flow properties of food suspensions of plant origin, *Food Technol.*, **41**, 85-87. (1987)

Rene, F, Leuliet, JC and Lalande, M. Heat transfer to Newtonian and non-Newtonian food fluids in plate heat exchangers: experimental and numerical approaches, *Trans. IChemE C*, **69**, 115-126.(1991)

Richardson, PS and Gaze, JE, Application of an alginate particle technique to the study of particle sterilisation under dynamic flow, Campden Tech. Memo. N° 429, (1986).

Sastry, SK, Mathematical evaluation of process schedules for aseptic processing of low-acid foods containing discrete particles, *J. Food Sci.*, **51**, 1323-1332,(1986).

Sastry, SK, and Zuritz, CA, A review of particle behaviour in tube flow; applications to aseptic processing, *J. Food Proc. Eng.*, **10**, 27-52, (1987).

Shah, SN and Lord, DL. Critical velocity correlations for slurry transport with non-Newtonian fluids, *AIChE. J.*, **37**, 863-870, (1991).

Stoforus, NG, and Merson, RL. Measurement of heat transfer coefficients in rotating liquid/particulate systems, *Biotechnol. Prog.*, **7**, 267-272 (1991)

Zhang, L and Fryer, PJ. Ohmic heating and cooling of two phase food materials, submitted to *Chem. Eng. Sci.* (1992)

NOMENCLATURE

a	constant	t_{max}	maximum process time (s)
b	constant	v	velocity (m/s)
Bi	particle Biot number	v_m	mean fluid velocity (m/s)
C	quality loss (min)	v_p	particle velocity (m/s)
C_{max}	maximum acceptable quality loss (min)	v_r	velocity ratio (v_p/v_m)
C_p	specific heat (kJ/kg K)	V	voltage (V)
d	particle diameter (m)	z	Temperature slope (K)
D	tube diameter (m)		
E	electric field (V/m)	ϕ_C	Quality ratio.
F	integrated lethality (min)	ϕ_F	Sterility ratio.
F_p	required lethality (min)	ρ	Density (kg/m^3)
Fr	modified Froude number	α	thermal diffusivity (m^2/s)
G	heating rate (°C/s)	β	factor in eqns (4) and (5) (K^{-1})
h	heat transfer coefficient (kW/m^{2}K)	κ	electrical conductivity (S/m)
Q	heat generation rate (W/m^3)	τ	time constant (s)
Q_l	mean heat generation in the liquid (W/m^3)	λ	thermal conductivity (W/mK)
Q_s	mean heat generation in the solid(W/m^3)		
Q_u	heat generation if no particles(W/m^3)		
r	radius (m)		
R_k	ratio of solid to liquid conductivity		
R	particle radius (m)	Subscript:	
R_Q	heat generation ratio		
t	time (s)	l	liquid
T	Temperature (K)	s	solid
T_b	Bulk temperature (K)	t	time (s)
T_c	Cooling temperature (K)	ref	reference
T_{ref}	Reference temperature (K)		
t_{min}	minimum process time (s)		

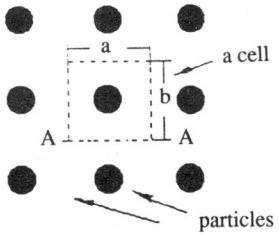

Figure 1:   A 2D sketch of the unit cell.

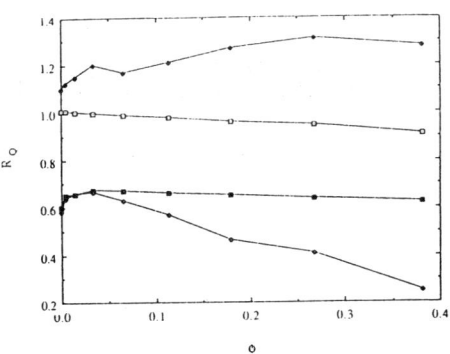

Figure 2: R_Q plotted against solid fraction ϕ for $R_\kappa = 0.5$.

        ● R_{Qmx} (in liquid)   ◇ R_{Qmn} (in particle)

        ◻ R_{Ql} (average in liquid)   ◼ R_{Qs} (average in particle)

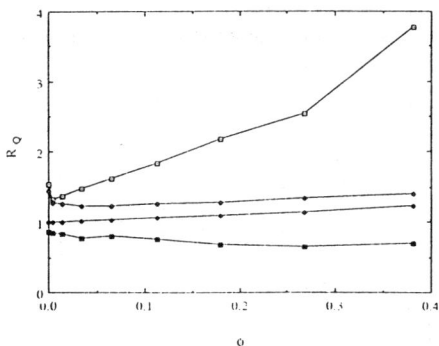

Figure 3: R_Q plotted against solid fraction ϕ for $R_\kappa = 2.0$.

        ◻ R_{Qmx} (in particle)   ◼ R_{Qmn} (in liquid)

        ● R_{Ql} (average in liquid)   ◇ R_{Qs} (average in particle)

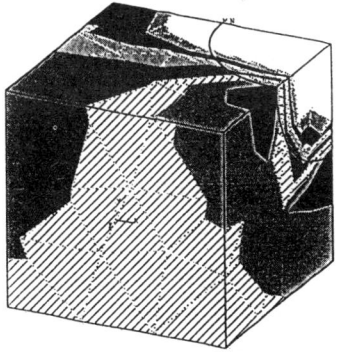

Figure 4:   Typical 3D ANSYS output: contours of R_Q for $R_\kappa = 0.75$ and solid fraction 6.5%. The darker the shading the higher the heat generation.

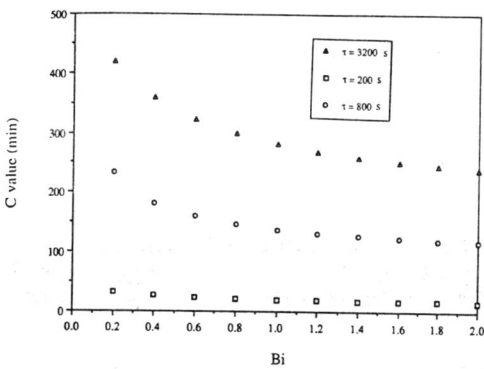

Figure 5:   C values plotted against Bi for three cooling time constants.

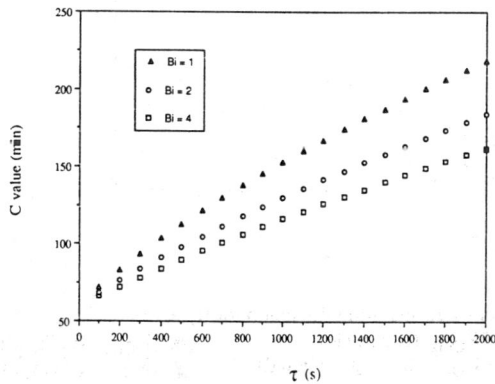

Figure 6:   C values plotted against cooling time for three Biot numbers.

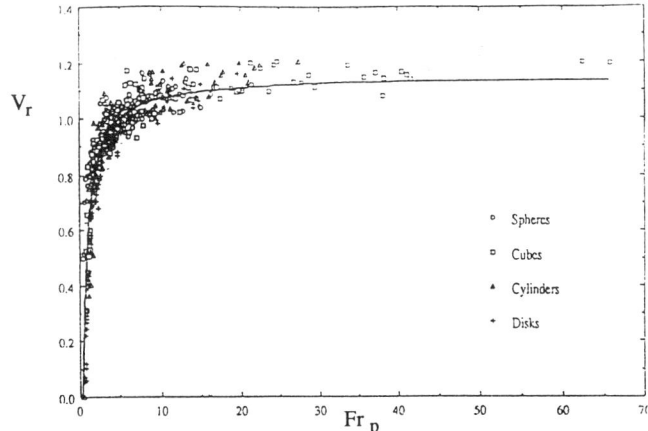

Figure 7: V_r for a single particle in water, showing equation (13).

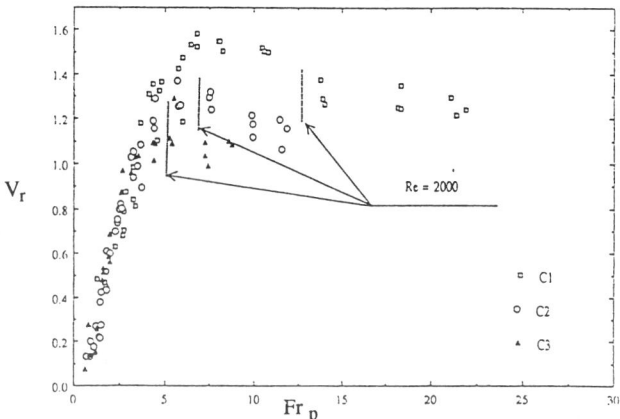

Figure 8: V_r for a single cubic particle in CMC. Specific gravity of particles: C1; 1.016. C2; 1.048. C3; 1.097.

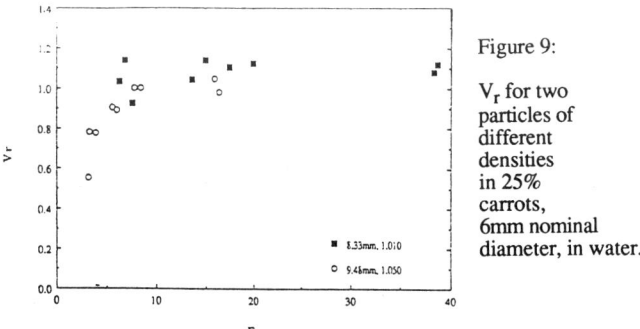

Figure 9:

V_r for two particles of different densities in 25% carrots, 6mm nominal diameter, in water.

HYGIENIC DESIGN - THE BASIS FOR COMPUTER CONTROLLED AUTOMATION

Albrecht Graßhoff
Institut für Verfahrenstechnik, Bundesanstalt für Milchforschung Kiel, Germany

Due to the fact, that economic and competitive food production requires modern processing equipment which, according to the state of engineering knowledge, applies all benefits of computerized automation, but excludes all risks of it. Thus, its uncontestable hygienic design is one of the presumptions to be met. The subject of this report is a review on the state of scientific work dealing with hygienic design questions. Furthermore, it has been investigated to which extent the scientific findings have made their way into industrial practice. On the basis of this review the requirements for further scientific activities are pointed out.

1.0 Introduction

>Hygienic Design< and >Product Hygiene< have become increasingly important terms in food processing. Food manufacturing and processing equipment has developed from small units, with predominantly manual work, up to industrial sized, entirely mechanically and automatically working plants. Therefore, now, hygienic design has a central role.

First guidelines for hygienic design of food processing equipment were given by legislation based on the ethical demand to minimize health risks in food consumption. Besides explicit formulations of this minimum demand, so called >exclusive rules< have been set up, by which the manufacturer of foods is prevented from neglecting the consumer's moral basic right. For example, in Germany it has been laid down in the "Lebensmittel- und Bedarfsgegenständegesetz (LMBG)" from 1974 which specifies in 5, paragraph 1, that

"Articles intended to be used in the production, treatment, in placing goods in the stream of commerce or in consumption of food or exert an influence on it ,,..., shall be used in such a manner that they do not transmit substances to food or its surface exept those that are harmless in terms of health, flavour and odour and are technically unavoidable" (31, paragraph 1).

Similar regulations are existing in the following European countries: Austria (1975), Belgium (1972), Bulgaria (1972), Denmark (1973 and 1978), Finland (1979), France (1973), Ireland (1936), Italia (1962 and 1973), The Netherlands (1935), Norway (1976), Spain (1967), Sweden (1967 and 1975), Switzerland (1979), United Kingdom (1955). (Source: World Health Organization Doc.No. 5 (Copenhagen)) /33, 55/.

Legal regulations for the consumer's protection date, with few exceptions, from the seventies. For the manufacturer of food, of course, such laws are of little help. They state what has to be avoided or omitted, but make no positive provisions to guarantee compliance with legal demands. Legislative orders can be creatively eluded. Another driving force is neededwhich induces the food manufacturer, as well as the food processing equipment industry, to deal seriously with terms like process hygiene or hygienic design. And of course, it is the interest to earn maximum profits. Good prices are achieved with high quality products. In food production, these distinguish themselves by a perfect hygienic quality, which can only be achieved with the aid of adequate food processing equipment.

To push through a good price for a high quality product on the market requires competitiveness, so production must be possible at minimum costs. Manpower, which is expensive and also a factor of insecurity, must be replaced by automatic machines with calculable characteristics. Nowadays, these are usually computer controlled.
Here it comes full circle. In the food area good products can only be produced economically, i.e. with automation, if the basic installation requirements have been met. Thus hygienic design becomes the basis for computer controlled automation.

The guiding principle underlying the basic idea of hygienic design is that contact surfaces of food processing equipment, tanks and pipes, valves, measurement and control device etc., will not cause microbial or chemical contamination. The term >contamination< is of latin origin (contaminare with the wider root >contangere = intensively contacting, soiling<) and is to be understood as unscheduled, or unintended soiling by material additives. Contaminants can be:

- impurities, which have deposited at the surfaces,
- chemical reaction products of the surfaces,
- abrasive particles of the product contacted surfaces,
- residues of cleaning, disinfecting or rinsing agents,
- chemical or microbiological altered residues of a preceding product batch.

The first activists were the manufacturers of equipment (e.g. in Germany, VDMA). They have, primarily for competitive reasons, elaborated standards to be considered in the making of food treatment and processing equipment. Observance of these standards should guarantee the plants' working in accordance with legal regulations. In Germany, recommendations of this kind are the DIN Standards (DIN = Deutsches Institut für Normung) and in France the AFNOR (Assosiation francaise de normalisation - French Association for Standardization). In the USA equipment and accessories for the food industry are made according to the "3-A-Standard" which is based on a concept developed in the twenties. Since then, particularly in the seventies, this has been continuously updated, according to the latest technical development. The 3-A-Standard is increasingly respected (for reasons of competitiveness?) by European manufacturers of equipment. However, there is no doubt the DIN-Norm is the more accurate standard at least in special cases.

The International Dairy Federation (IDF) has edited a users' guide for the industry, "Hygienic Design of Dairy Processing Equipment" (Bulletin No. 218/1987), in which constructive details, and also hints for food processing and the realization of monitoring procedures, are listed /31/. Similarly, partially detailed standards with emphasis laid on "cleaning and sanitizing" are existing in Australia for the meat, the poultry meat, the sea food and the egg handling and processing industry. These were edited by the Standards Association of Australia (SAA standards No. 2995 to 2998) in 1987. In order to promote the application of cleaning-in- place (CIP) in the food industry, and to reduce the environmental stress by lowering the quantities of cleaning chemicals, the technical report No. 18 (Dairy equipment - cleaning and disinfecting by CIP-processing) has been edited by the German Institut für Normung (DIN, 1988) /13/.

2.0 Factors influencing product adhesion and cleanability of solid surfaces

Product hygiene requires basic knowledge of the mechanisms of product or foreign material adhesion and detachment. Molecules and microbial cells adhere to chemically inert surfaces through *non-specific* physio-chemical adhesion mechanism (as opposed to the numerous *specific* intermolecular adhesion mechanisms of cell-cell adhesion) /38/. Two types of interactions are involved:

- electrostatic interactions, between net surface charges of double layers, can result in attraction (opposite signs) or repulsion (same signs). Estimation of surface charge and sign may be obtained by zeta-potential measurement. In case of high ionic strength, as in food products, surface charges are weak or even negligible.

- electrodynamic or Van-der-Waals interactions, between dipoles, induced dipoles, or dipoles and induced dipoles, result in attraction. Estimation of these interactions can be done by (i) thermodynamic measurements of surface free energies and (ii) a set of equations /41/.

According to the relative intensity of electrostatic and electrodynamic interactions, attraction or repulsion may occur, or both as a function of the distance between the surface and the molecule or the microorganism. Cells at about 10 nm distance may be in a situation of *reversible adhesion*, and can be removed by appropriate rinsing conditions. At <5nm, they are in a state of *irreversible adhesion*, there is no longer Brownian motion, and strong mechanical action is needed for removal. Modification of thermodynamic conditions enables irreversible adhesion to become reversible, and conversely.

2.1 Adhesion of molecules

Triggering of fouling of food plants surfaces is due to molecules which adhere irreversibly and form a so called *conditioning film*. The film hides the surface material more or less from other molecules of the food product, so that a new surface is "seen" from the bulk product. Cleaning aims at restoring the surface to initial "clean" condition, but fails sometimes. For example cleaning of stainless steel by chromsulfuric mixture (laboratory cleaning) gives rise to a *hydrophilic* surface (spontaneously wetted by water). Industrial cleaning by nitric acid, water and soda in succession, results in a *hydrophobic* one, partially wetted by water (but nevertheless clean in the sense of official regulation). Food product in the following run does no longer "see" naked stainless steel after industrial cleaning /17/.

Therefore, studies of fouling should take account of the presence of that first deposit layer, which in turn is fouled by deposition of other molecules. In addition, reactions take place inside the deposit: for example, protein denaturation and calcium phosphate precipitation on heating plates of pasteurizers and UHT sterilizers have been extensively studied in the past few years /37, 40, 43/. Owing to the wide variety of molecular species in food products, there will always be molecules capable of adhering to surface materials, whether in their initial state or not, whether hydrophobic (low surface free energy, like polymers or not perfectly cleaned stainless steel) or hydrophilic (high surface free energy, like glass or naked and clean metals). Nevertheless, energy needed for cleaning depends on the surface free energy of the material: each one of us can observe that saucepans coated with low free energy polymers are easily cleaned.

2.2 Adhesion of microorganisms

On surfaces covered by flowing liquid, reversible adhesion is more probable than irreversible /47/. Yet, an additional mechanism allows microorganisms to remain adhering: the production of a capsule of exocellular polymers (proteins, or, more frequently, polysaccharides forming the "glycocalyx"). Polymer threads come close to the surface, where they adhere irreversibly /44, 54/ (Fig. 1). Firmly attached microorganisms can then multiply and colonize the surface within a matrix of the polymer, thus forming a "slime layer" /29, 38/.

Concerning the primary step of adhesion, recent results with a variety of microorganisms confirm thermodynamic provisions: those with high free surface energy adhere more to hydrophilic materials, while those with low surface free energy adhere more to hydrophobic materials /41/. If macromolecules which modify the apparent surface energy of materials are excreted by microorganisms, thermodynamic models remain valid provided the new state of the surface is considered. Two such cases have been reported /2, 6, 7/:
(i) about the same adhesion extent, of the microorganism on various materials; and

(ii) no adhesion on any materials.

Microorganisms of food products have varied classes of surface free energies /19/. Bacteria have, in general, a high energy surface, whereas molds have a low one. However, it should be possible to reach a compromise for the material in order to limit microbial contamination.

3.0 Influencing the mechanisms of soil deposition

3.1 Surface tension

Adhesive forces are a function of surface energy properties. The lower these adhesive forces the easier it is to clean a solid surface, e.g. the surface is wettable by a liquid only if its surface energy exceeds that of the liquid. Clean mineral as well as metallic surfaces are generally wettable by water, many synthetic materials (plastics) are not, particularly polytetrafluoricethylene (PTFE). Its low surface energy (18 mN/m) means that PTFE is not wettable under practical conditions. Therefore PTFE offers the lowest soil adhesion property of all relevant materials /18/. (At a temperature of 20 °C water offers a surface energy value of about 72.8 mN/m, which can be reduced by addition of surface active agents to 40 to 50 mN/m).

3.2 Surface potential

NASSAUER /39/ has pointed out that surface potential has a considerable influence on adhesion of electrically charged product substances. Furthermore, he showed the surface energy value of some important materials, e.g. austenitic chrome nickel steel, to be variable within certain limits. He showed the fouling of an electro-polished chrome nickel steel surface by microorganisms was significantly higher if the surface was treated by strong oxidizing disinfectants after cleaning. I.e., its surface potential had been shifted into positive direction. This observation may be of some importance in connexion with surfaces, which at cleaning can be impacted with low flow stress only, e.g. the walls of large tanks or vessels.

3.3 Surface finish

Normally, for mechanical treatment, the smoother the surface, the easier the cleaning. Therefore, food processing equipment (in particular that used for liquid and/or perishable products), uses the smoothest possible surfaces, sometimes at considerable expense. Since objective criteria are lacking, the German Institute for Standardization (DIN) has, on the basis of practical experience, empirically laid down the minimum requirements for surface finish of stainless steel dairy plant components in contact with the product. This DIN Standard 11 480 from 1978 specifies different surface quality grades /9/. For grade 3 (obtained by precision grind, lapping, electropolishing or glass blasting) for requirements used in transportation, storage, production, processing and heat treatment of fluid milk, cheese milk, cheese curd, cream, fermented milk, mixed milk drinks and ice cream a mean roughness value between 0.1 and 0.4 μm is required. For aseptic methods and equipment for cultivating pure cultures the roughness mean shall be < 0.1 μm corresponding to grade 4 (polishing, lapping). For transportation and processing of raw milk, and milk driers, R_a values of 0.8 μm are considered sufficient. The R_a values are determined using electric brush analyzers in compliance with DIN 4768 /8/.

In USA, the 3-A-Sanitary Standard 01-06 from 1974 /52/, requirements for the finish of surfaces in contact with the product (e.g. for the storage tanks for milk and milk products), are less exactly defined. According to this standard the surfaces correspond to finish No.4 (precision grind using silicon carbide 150 grid (mesh/inch)). On the finish No.4 sample made available by Messrs. IRVING POLISHING, KENOSHA, Wisc., USA, the R_t values measured in parallel direction to the scratches were around 2 µm and the R_a values around 0.3 µm. In cross direction R_t = 6.0 µm and R_a = 0.5 µm were found. Experience has shown that objective characterization of surface finish, using prescribed grid numbers, is almost impossible. Great differences in polishing quality may result from inclusion of foreign substances on the surface of the grinding wheel, and from the individual working manner of the grinder and the grinding device. The indication of admissible limits complying with standard 11 480 are, however, clear and to be preferred to American practice.

TIMPERLEY /53/ has reported, without giving details of the method used, linear relationship between surface quality in pipelines (R_a = 0.5 to 2.5 µm), and the number of microorganisms present on the surface after standard cleaning. In 1983 HOFFMANN /26, 27/ has, for the first time, systematically investigated the functional relationships between surface quality and cleanability. Using branchless pipeleines with straight through flow (NW 50), and different surface roughness (R_a = 0.2 to 9.1 µm), he performed cleaning experiments with dried skim milk deposits. Parameters were the temperature, the cleaning solution, its velocity and the time to clean. Indicators were the spores of *Bacillus stearothermophilus* suspended in the skim milk and not eliminated during cleaning. They germinated and formed colonies after the cleaned pipe surface was covered with nutrient agar and incubated for 24 hours. Fig. 2 shows the influence of surface roughness on cleanability in pipes of different finish, reflected by the number of residual spores/cm after cleaning for 5 min. with 0.3 % NaOH of 70 °C and 0.2 m/s. The figure shows a correlation between surface roughness and cleanability. However, the influence of roughness especially in the low Ra range, should not be overestimated, the more so as in all experiments the residual bacterial numbers differed between roughest and smoothest surface only by 1 power of ten. In relation to the initial number of 50 000 bacteria/cm , the relative residual spore numbers ranged between 5×10^4 and 4.4×10^3. Hence, results of the experiments untertaken by HOFFMANN show, clearly, that requirements for surfaces as defined in compliance with DIN 11 480 (R_a below 0.4 or 0.8 µm) are absolutely sufficient and that there is no reason for additional requirements to be met in the sphere of food technology.

3.4 Flow conditions

Deposit formation and colonization of surfaces by microorganisms, and removal of contaminants, are, besides other criteria, dependent on *local flow conditions*. According to the KERN-SEATON-Model /35/ effective deposit formation is interpreted as being the difference between deposit formation and the removing mass flow. Cleaning has to be considered as a "deposit formation with negative sign". It is obvious that the removing mass flow is supported by introducing mechanical energy via the fluid flow /45, 46/. In a flow mechanical cleaning process the fluid flow serves mainly to

- supply and remove cleaning, disinfecting and rinsing solutions, both fresh and used,
- heat and impulse transport,
- remove chemically modified soil (swollen colloids, electrostatically charged soil particles, fat partially emulgified by surfactants, peptidized protein structures) from the solid surface to be cleaned,
- break down larger soil aggregates into smaller units,
- prevent sedimentation and redeposition of already removed soil particles.

The question relating to *minimal flow velocity* of the cleaning solution, which still ensures perfect cleaning, is not only a question of energy consumption. (It is known that energy consumption for pump circulation of the cleaning solution increases, approximately, with the square of flow velocity.) The designer of plant components (valves, manifolds etc.) needs relevant information about flow speeds to ensure optimal flow required.

BERTELSEN /3/, the IDF-Document 117 /30/ as well as the Intern. Ass. Milk Food /50/, concurrently indicate a value of 1.5 m/s or a minimal Reynolds number of 10.000, and relate this value to the pipe flow in a circuit. The DIN-Report 18 /13/ indicates a standard value of 1.5 - 2.0 m/s. If possible the flow velocity of the cleaning solutions should be higher than that of the product. /28/ and /21/ point out that objective characterization of the factor flow "mechanics" is not possible via flow velocity, but only by the wall shear stress which is not directly measurable.
Factor mechanics do not play an exclusive and dominant role in in-place cleaning processes. They are more important in purely mechanical processes (e.g. scrubbing, scraping, brushing, but also cleaning using water jets), demonstrated by the magnitude of the active shear forces. A comparative study /23/ established a friction shear stress of 1 250 N/m achieved by scrubbing with a cotton towel on a smooth PVC surface. In in-place-cleaning experiments in a flow channel, the values found were only between 1.0 and 12 N/m , with flow velocities ranging between 0.5 and 2.0 m/s. LADWIG /36/ has performed extensive measuremants of turbulence, and local wall shear stress, in the profile space of plate heat exchangers. In the central plate area values between 6 and 9 N/m were found in the luff side zone of a support point. In the turbulent region of the flow shadows in the lee side zone of a support, showing difficulties in obtaining satisfactory cleaning results in practice, the wall shear stress was between 0 and 4 N/m . Extremely high values exceeding 50 N/m were found in the distribution zone immediately at the slit entrance. The smooth straight through flow pipe (NW 50) /21/ indicates wall shear stresses between 0.19 and 7.5 N/m in the flow velocity range between 0.25 and 2.0 m/s, the flow being in all cases highly turbulent (Re 30.000 - 240.000). Cleaning experiments using a straight through pipe /28/ showed a wall shear stress of between 0.6 and 52 N/m (Re = 60.000 - 600.000) by considering surface roughness. This established a significant but not necessarily dominant influence of the factor mechanics on the whole soil removal process, for cleaning-in-place range of up to 10 N/m . This figure is possible in practice.

Of greater importance is, however, the fluid flow in connection with cleaning of *dead spaces*. Dead spaces are zones in branched pipeline systems connected to the main flow, which, however, does not circulate continously through them. Such stagnant zones are mainly located at complex valve assemblies and connecting mains to the storage tanks, if these are equipped with additional shut off devices. GRASSHOFF /20, 21/ has studied the flow behaviour of fluids in dead spaces and the influence of fluid movement on cleanability. He found that the *fluid exchange* (>rinsing behaviour) and the *local wall shear stress* (>cleaning behaviour) decreases very rapidly with increasing stagnant space depth. Here both processes correlate well with fluid movement in the main flow (Fig. 3). At a velocity of 1 m/s in the straight through flow pipe in a dead space of a relative depth $l/d = 1$ zones with wall shear forces of < 1/100 of the values in the main flow were found. At $l/d = 3$, the minimal values for the local shear stress were less the 1/500 of the values found for the straight through flow pipe at 1.0 m/s (Fig. 4).

Hence, the maximum permissible dead space depth is easily reached. Beyond these, the required rinsing times exceed the time needed for the individual steps in programme controlled CIP systems and are, therefore, not acceptable. The same is true for the local wall shear stress, which must be, throughout the stagnant space, high enough to prevent solid particles (also emulsified fat droplets) in the fluid flow to sediment on, or adhere to, the surfaces. If in a particular situation deeper stagnant spaces within cylindric pipeline systems cannot be avoided, e.g. if in-line measuring nozzles are installed, the problem associated with dead spaces can effectively be avoided by incorporating a flow divider /14/ according to Fig. 5.

Hence, calculating the required minimum velocity of the cleaning solution in CIP-circuits, for straight through flow pipes or geometrically simple surfaces, is insufficient. A numerical value for flow velocity in a more or less complex circuit can only be an *empirical value*, which allows the fluidic stagnant spaces still to be satisfactorily cleaned. Such an empirical value is 1,5 m/s, as mentioned before, where dead spaces are no deeper than $l/d = 1 + 2$.

4.0 Design of pipeline components

4.1 Connections

Critical points in cleanability of pipe lines, are the *joining elements* (pipe bends, T-pieces, diminishing pipes etc.). Here, welded connections have a clear advantage over the *rolled-in* type (e.g. DIN 11 851) /11/. Even most careful assembly cannot avoid slits at the joints of the rolled-in components, so that product residues or colonies of microorganisms can accumulate which survive the cleaning process and may be the cause of bacterial contamination /16/. HOFFMANN /27/, in his experiments, obtained distorted cleaning results caused by microorganisms accumulated in such rolled-in slits, and transmitted to the pipe surface by residual water during dismantling the test pipes. This distortion was independent of the surface roughness. After eliminating the slit by modifying the design, the amount of residual spores decreased each time by more than 1 power of ten after cleaning the test pipe. *Butt-welded* screw fittings with cylindrical guide, in connection with a suitable flushing gasket, allow interfacing without slit and misalignment at the screw fitting /56/. On the European market different types of pipe connections are offered. The main designs are presented in Fig. 6. They are standard screw fittings complying with

SMS (Sweden)'
DS (Denmark)
BS (Great Britain)
DIN (Germany)
ISO / IDF

and a clamped joint corresponding to ISO Standard designed by Alfa-Laval Flow Equipment. The pipe connections shown in the figure seal almost slitfree using the gaskets shown. The gaskets are deformed by pressing the two joining components together until tightness is achieved. Deformation is not limited by a metallic stop and is, therefore, only dependent on the starting torque of the screw fitting. A non-definable initial stress is produced, which becomes still greater by a possible thermal expansion stressing the pipe. This may lead to *permanent gasket deformation*, which may cause leakage if the thermal expansion stress is decreasing. Repeated tightening of the screw fittings can damage the gasket to an extent that crakcs form in which bacteria colonize, presenting risks for product quality /25/. New designs with metal stops and room for thermal expansion have been developed by several manufacturers /15/. The problem of mechanically damaged gaskets should, therefore, have been overcome.

4.2 Fittings, gaskets

The technological development of fittings which, besides straight-lined pipes, are needed for the assembly of complex pipeline systems (T- and cross-pieces, bends, reduction pieces, sight glasses etc.) can be considered finished. This applies, at least, to requirements of dimensions, quality and surface finish. The manufacturing dimensions are standardized according to DIN 11 852 /12/ (Germany, 1963) or to 3-A, Serial No. 08-09 (USA) /51/ and No. 08-17 (1983), respectively. By use of automated production to make the fittings, they are highly accurate and their design quality is excellent. Hence, they meet all requirements of food processing. Of course, fitting and coupling elements have to be welded as a unit with no use of rolled-in types.

Innovations may be done concerning the design of the sealings. On principle, the tightening of fitting/pipe is relatively uncomplicated, because it is a static problem. But mounting of the gasket must be free of spaces with undefinable dead zones which cannot be cleaned by CIP. The O-ring with a mounting slot according to DIN 3771 (American Standard AS 568 A), necessary in the total sphere of engineering and constructiion of chemical plants, is totally unsuitable for use in the product region of the food industry.

4.3 Valves

Evaluating the risks due to single components of CIP-cleaned food processing equipment the valves, of course, must be considered. The number of the valves on the market, intended for use in the food industry, is great and their design varies depending on their function. Therefore, it is not possible either to specify or to describe them. However, compared with smooth pipelines they represent a *markedly increased risk* as regards possible recontamination of the product passing through them. For valves intended to be used in the dairy industry guidelines have been elaborated by the department responsible for testing dairy equipment (Prüfstelle für milchwirtschaftliche Maschinen, Apparate, Geräte und Anlagen of the Federal Dairy Research Centre, Kiel) /42/ in collaboration with the manufacturers. If met, they will ensure hygienically perfect operation of the corresponding valves in brand new condition. However brand new valves do not absolutely exclude risk of recontamination. In studies on pneumatic double seat valves HAUSER and MICHEL /24/ found in all cases, including brand new valves, product *carry over phenomena* at the dynamic seal of the valve spindle in the shaft duct area. If the valves are not devised as aseptically operating bellow type valves, amounts of liquids or solids may pass through as adhesion film below the slit between gasket and valve stem with each lifting movement of the valve spindle. This is the so called *lift effect.* Since cleaning does not include the spindle regions outside the product zone nor the sealing space these represent with each to and fro movement, it is not possible to calculate the contamination risk. According to /22/, the quantitative extent of product carry-over, as a function of gasket type and spindle surface, ranges between 10^{-6} and 10^{-4} ml/lift. A dominant factor of influence is the *surface roughness of the spindle.* So, mechanical polishing (Ra = 0.04 μm, Rt = 0.2 μm) of a microfinished spindle (Ra = 0.15 μm, Rt = 1 μm) allowes the fluid carry-over rate to be reduced by the factor 20. A few years ago a survey of finishing of valve spindles (which had been carefully disassembled from brand new valves of several leading European manufacturers) showed that almost all of the subjects under control exhibited considerable faults, e.g. scratches, blowholes, grooves from machining. Even residues of broken lathe bent tools being thrashed at the spindle surface were found /22/. Since then, the valve makers have taken up the problem of product carry-over by moving valve stems. More attention has been paid to surface finish of the valve spindle. One maker has extended the final finishing steps, turning and fine polishing, to include a further finishing step in axial direction "honing". Other makers isolate the valve spindle from outside by means of a further case equipped with separate rinsing and steam connections, so that the product passing below the gasket into this zone is not contaminated by microorganisms from the ambient. During countermovement of the spindle into the product zone the extent of bacterial carryover is markedly lower, compared with valves without protective housing.

Spindle reversing valves designed for separating "incompatible" liquids must be devised as *double seat valves* equipped with leakage safety device. As the leakage zone might be a source of recontamination for the product zone, it must, therefore, be part of the CIP-program. The requirements to be met by seals and cleanability of the product zone do not allow the leakage between the valve disks to be devised in a manner particularly easy to clean. Studies performed by BUCHWALD /4/ have shown that it is not enough to briefly lift up the valve disks during cleaning of the product zone, allowing part of the cleaning solution to pass for aprox 1 - 2 sec. into the leakage zone. For this reason the valves made by a number of manufacturers are equipped with separate cleaning or rinsing connections, the cleaning fluid coming in via the valve spindle devised as a hollow body. The rinsing fluid drains from the spindle in the form of a tangential water jet. This ensures that stagnant or dammed zones are avoided within the leakage zone during circulation of cleaning and rinsing solutions and that this zone is perfectly cleaned.

Relatively new is the *shock-pressure protected valve* design and, depending on the system, the types offered by a number of manufacturers are very similar. The conventional types of spindle valves are devised so that the valve disk is unintentionally lifted, if a pressure impulse in the product pipeline system reaches a value exceeding the restoring force of the spring. Then amounts of the product pass into the leakage zone which is subsequently not rinsed any more. As a result uncontrolled accumulation may take place. Since the lower valve spindle is devised in the form of a piston with the diameter of the valve disk, the forces of a pressure shock after acting upon the upper and lower surfaces are compensated, and unintentional lifting of the valve disk does not take place. Due to the markedly larger surface of the pistonspindle compared with the conventional spindle, the new valves require the insulation against soiling from outside by means of the aforementioned protective housing.

The influence of the spindle gasket on product carry-over and recontamination was discussed at some length in the investigation of /22/. So the ideal gasket should meet the following criterions:

- completely accurate sealing in both directions,
- sealing zone without any dead spaces,
- slit-free fit in the housing,
- low internal pressure force,
- intensifying the pressure force by the system pressure,
- good stripping off at the gasket lip,
- high abrasion stability of the gliding area,
- low frictional index,
- chemical and thermal resistance.

Assessment of the gaskets used in practice, with reference to these criteria, show that the *ideal gasket* is *not yet on the market*. This fact may be demonstrated by the Fig. 7 and 8 showing the problem zones of the gaskets of two important German manufacturers. Both gaskets were dismounted from CIP-cleaned valves. Development of an improved spindle gasket is urgently required. Direction of this development (assembling the gasket as a "sandwich-compound" with a cylindrical PTFE sleeve and an elastomeric body) has been indicated at least in study /22/.

For aseptic operations, e.g. in UHT plants and sterile tanks, the measures described so far for eliminating product recontamination are not sufficient, because carry-over of contaminants to the spindle seal via the "lift-effect" cannot be excluded. This is only possible by *hermetic isolation* of the interior valve spaces against outer air *by a bellows.* The first aseptic valves were equipped with rubber-elastic membranes. At higher operation and sterilization temperatures, however, their shelf life was poor. Today the valves are equipped with PTFE or special steel (1.4571) bellows. The PTFE design has a guaranteed service life of at least 300 000 switching cycles and a temperature stability of up to 135 °C. With the special steel design equipped with a PTFE gasket, resistance to shock pressure of the bellows resulting from water and steam shocks at an operating temperature up to 160 °C, is ensured. Bellow-type valves are offered as two- and three-way stop valves as well as three-, four- and five-way reversing valves. Due to their construction, they are not suited for use in separation of incompatible fluids, because they are lacking the necessary leakage zones.

A valve type which is increasingly used in the food industry is the *butterfly or disk valve.* Because it is extremely short, for inspection and maintainance it can be removed from the fix-mounted pipeline without moving the latter. Due to its simple design it is relatively reliable and at least for simple circuit functions considerably cheaper compared with a spindle valve. For more complex circuit functions, several disk valves must be combined, which can, indeed, impair the price advantage. At first butterfly valves were designed as manual shut-off devices. Today they are normally motor-driven or equipped with a pneumatic master cylinder, and with a position reporting back device via microswitch or approximation sensors for both final positions. To meet the higher requirements for operating reliability in automated production plants of the food industry, the butterfly valves were also designed as leakage valves. Two systems are now on the market. Both systems allow cleaning and sterilization of the leakage zone when the disk is closed, so that contamination of the product is avoided when the disks are open. No study have been done on accumulation of soil residues with increasing operation time, or as a function of the number of valve operations in the sealing space of the disk spindle. These may be a source of possible product recontamination /34/.

Switching the product pipelines via *three-way cocks* with conegrinded stopcocks is rarely used today, because perfect cleaning is only possible when taken apart (COP = cleaning out of place). Frequent cleaning of such cocks is necessary because of the excessively high number of microscopic grooves on the cone-grinded surfaces of the stopcock and the housing, where microorganisms colonize together with lubrication grease. These are smeared again, with each switching operation, into contact with the medium. These surfaces are not included in the CIP process. The same is true for ball valves which have proven most suitable for use in chemical equipment. Because of hygiene problems they are not suited for use in food technology.

5.Conclusions

Efforts contributing to the hygienic design of food processing equipment are essentially airning at the increase of manufacturing economics, i.e.
- improvement of the hygiene quality of products
- elimination of incalculable risks,
- reduction of production costs.

These will be achieved only by considering both the processing equipment, and its operation, as an inseparable unit. Thus, a few words have to be dedicated to cleaning operations.

Cleaning in place (CIP) /10/ is the operation related to hygiene in the food industry where most of the progress has been made. The pioneer work has been done mainly in the dairy industry (inside of plants) and in the brewing industry (kegs and bottles). CIP has to be automatic to be efficient. Consequently, it is now controlled by microprocessors, extensively using on-line sensors for temperature, level, flow rate, pressure, position, etc. Sensors must be calibrated at fixed time intervals, and safety procedures must be implemented to avoid damage to the food product in case of failure. In addition, optimal cleaning can be done through specific on-line sensors measuring the concentration of cleaning or disinfection agents: pH-meter, redox potential-meter, chlorometers, etc. Also, one can measure the concentration of organic effluents in flowing fluids by optical density at the appropriate wavelength, and the degree of surface cleanliness can be deduced from the pressure drop measurement.

At the end of each CIP run, the efficiency of cleaning and disinfection must be estimated. Here in contrast, there has been no recent progress. Old, classical, and poorly effective techniques are usually used: visual inspection of cleaned surfaces, contact agar plates or smears for monitoring residual microorganisms /1/. Research work must be done on developing efficient methods for assessment of both equipment cleanability and cleaning process efficiency. These procedures are the last to be monitored manually. May be application of progressive knowledge of surface physics and surface chemistry, combined with advanced technologies of semiconductors and microelectronics, will lead to a CIP-controller chip, enabling automated cleaning efficiency monitoring.

References:

1. BELLON-FONTAINE, M.-N.; CERF, O.: Nettoyage et désinfection dans les industries alimentaires, APRIA, Paris (1988)

2. BELONN-FONTAINE, M.-N.; MOZES, N.; VAN DER MEI, H. C.; SJOLLEMA, H. J.; CERF, O.; ROUXHET, P. G.; BUSSCHER, H. J.: Cell Biophysics 17 (1) 93-106 (1990)

3. BERTELSEN, E.: Milchwissenschaft 29 (5) 111 (1974)

4. BUCHWALD, B.: Brauwelt 122 (12) 526-528 (1982)

5. BUSAK+LUYKEN: Handbuch "Dichtungen, Führungen", Stuttgart (1985)

6. BUSSCHER, H. J.; BELLON-FONTAINE, M.-N.; MOZES, N.; VAN DER MEI, H. C.; SJOLLEMA, H. J.; CERF, O.; ROUXHET, P. G.: Biofouling 2 (1) 55-63 (1990)

7. BUSSCHER, H. J.; BELLON-FONTAINE, M. N.; MOZES, N.; VAN DER MEI, H. C.; SJOLLEMA, H. J.; ROUXHET, P. G.; CERF, O.: Journal of Microbiological Methods 12 (2) 101-115 (1990)

8. Deutsches Institut für Normung (DIN) e. V.: DIN 4768, Erfassung der Rauheiten von Oberflächen mit elektrischen Tastschnittgeräten (1968).

9. Deutsches Institut für Normung (DIN) e. V.: DIN 11 480, Milchwirtschaftliche Maschinen in Molkereibetrieben - Oberflächen (1978)

10. Deutsches Institut für Normung (DIN) e. V.: DIN 11 483, Milchwirtschaftliche Anlagen - Reinigung und Desinfektion (1986)

11. Deutsches Institut für Normung (DIN) e. V.: DIN 11 851, Getränke und Milchwirtschaftsarmaturen - Rohrverschraubungen aus nichtrostendem Stahl (1964)

12. Deutsches Institut für Normung (DIN) e. V.: DIN 11 852, Getränke- und Milchwirtschaftsarmaturen - Formstücke aus nichtrostendem Stahl (1963)

13. Deutsches Institut für Normung (DIN) e. V.: DIN-Fachbericht 18, Milchwirtschaftliche Anlagen, Reinigung und Desinfektion nach dem CIP-Verfahren. Beuth Verlag GmbH, Berlin - Köln (1988)

14. Deutsches Patent 3207 239 C2 v. 18.09.1986

15. Deutsches Patent 2910 684 C2 v. 1.10.1981

16. DREWS, M.; GRASSHOFF, A.; HAGEMEISTER, H.; PFEUFFER, M.; REUTER, H.; SUHREN, G.; THOMASOW, J.; TOLLE, A.; WIETBRAUK, H.: Kieler Milchwirtschaftliche Forschungsberichte 35 (2) 107-236 (1983)

17. DUPEYRAT, M.; LABBÉ, J. P.; MICHEL, F.; BILLOUDET, F.; DAUFIN, G.: Le Lait 67 465-486 (1987)

18. FRANCK, R.; WIECZOREK, H.: Kunststoffe im Lebensmittelverkehr - Empfehlungen des Bundesgesundheitsamtes - Textausgabe, Carl Heymanns Verlag KG, Köln-Berlin-Bonn-München (1987)

19. GERSON, D. F. and ZAJIC, J. E.: The biophysics of cellular adhesion. In: Immobilized Microbial Cells, ed. K. Venkatsubramanian, Ann. Chem. Soc. Symp. Series, 106 pp. 29-57 (1979)

20. GRASSHOFF, A.: Kieler Milchwirtschaftliche Forschungsberichte 32 (4) 273-298 (1980)

21. GRASSHOFF, A.: Kieler Milchwirtschaftliche Forschungsberichte 35 (4) 471-492 (1983)

22. GRASSHOFF, A.: Kieler Milchwirtschaftliche Forschungsberichte 38 (1) 3-38 (1986)

23. GRASSHOFF, A.: Kieler Milchwirtschaftliche Forschungsberichte 40 (3) 139-177 (1988)

24. HAUSER, G.; MICHEL, R.: Zeitschr.f.Lebensmitteltechnol. u. -verfahrenstechnik (ZFL) 35 (1) 40-45 (1984)

25. HAUSER, G.; MICHEL, R.; SOMMER, K.: Deutsche Milchwirtschaft 36 (51/52) 1733-1738 (1985)

26. HOFFMANN, W.: Kieler Milchwirtschaftliche Forschungsberichte 34 (4) 363-379 (1982)

27. HOFFMANN, W.: "Zirkulationsreinigen (CIP) von geraden Rohren in Abhängigkeit von Oberflächenrauheit und anderen Einflußfaktoren." Dissertation Universität Kiel (1983)

28. HOFFMANN, W.: Milchwissenschaft 39 (11) 645-647 (1984)

29. HUGO, W.B.; PALLENT, L. J.; GRANT, D. J. W.; DENYER, S. P.; DAVIES, A.: Letters Appl. Microbiol. 2 37-42 (1986)

30. INTERNATIONAL DAIRY FEDERATION: Bulletin "Automated cleaning and disinfection of milk storage and processing plants", Doc. 117 (1979)

31. INTERNATIONAL DAIRY FEDERATION: Bulletin "Hygienic design of dairy processing equipment", Doc. 218 (1987)

32. ISOARD, P.: Guide de la biocontamination, APRIA, Paris (1988)

33. JOHNSON, R. (Edit.): World Health Organization: "Public Health in Europe - 14 - Food Safety Services". Copenhagen 1981

34. KARPINSKI, J. L.; BRADLEY, R. L.: J. Food Protect. **51** (5) 364-368 (1988)

35. KERN, D. O.; SEATON, R. E.: Chem. Eng. **4** (May) 258 (1959)

36. LADWIG, H.-P.: "Strömung und örtlicher Wärmeübergang in Plattenwärmeaustauschern". Dissertation Universität Kiel (1981)

37. LECLERCQ-PERLAT, M.-N.: "Etude du nettoyage des echangeurs a plaques destines a la pasteurisation et a la sterilisation a ultra-haute-temperature du lait." Thesis, University of Lille I (1986)

38. MARSHALL, K.C.: In: Bacterial Adhesion, ed. D.C. Savage and M. Fletcher, Plenum Press, London, 133-162 (1985)

39. NASSAUER, J.: "Adsorption und Haftung an Oberflächen und Membranen". Habilitationsschrift Technische Universität München - Weihenstephan (1985)

40. PERLAT, M. N.; LALANDE, M.; CORRIEU, G.: Le Lait **66** 31-64 (1986)

41. PRATT-TERPSTRA, I.H.; WEERKAMP, A. H.; BUSSCHER, H. J.:J. Gen. Microbiol. **133** 3199-3206 (1987)

42. Prüfstelle für Milchwirtschaftliche Maschinen, Apparate und Anlagen der Bundesanstalt für Milchforschung, Kiel: Kieler Milchwirtschaftliche Forschungsberichte **26** 175-178 (1974)

43. RENÉ, F.; LEULIET, J. C.; GOLDBERG, M.; LALANDE, M.: Le Lait **68** 85-102 (1988)

44. RÖNNER, U.; HUSMARK, U.; HENRIKSSON, A.: J. Appl. Bact. **69** 550-556 (1990)

45. SANDU, C.;PLETT, E. A.; LUND, D.: ZFL **36** (3) 180-189 (1985)

46. SANDU, C; LUND, D.: Am. Inst. Chem. Eng. **78** (218) 12-30 (1982)

47. SJOLLEMA, J.; BUSSCHER, H. J.; WEERKAMP, A. H.: J. Microbiol. Methods **9** 79-90 (1989)

48. The International Commission on Microbiological Specifications for Foods, Micro-organisms in Foods, 4. Application of the hazard analysis critical control point (HACCP) system to ensure microbiological safety and quality, Blackwell Scientific Publications, Oxford (1988)

49. 3-A Sanitary Standards for multiple-use rubber and rubber-like materials used as product contact surfaces in dairy equipment. Serial #18-00. J. Milk Food Technol **26** (1) 5-6 (1963)

50. 3-A accepted practices for permanently installed productpipelines and cleaning systems. J. Milk Food Technol. **29** 95 (1966)

51. 3-A Sanitary Standards for fittings used on milk and milk products equipment and used on sanitary lines conducting milk and milk products. Serial #08-09. J. Milk Food Technol. **33** (4) 137-160 (1970)

52. 3-A Sanitary Standards for Storage Tanks for Milk and Milk Products. Serial #01-06. J. Milk Food Technol. **37** (1) 56-61 (1974)

53. TIMPERLEY, D.A.: J. Soc. Dairy Technol. **34** (1) 6-14 (1981)

54. VAN LOOSDRECHT, M. C. M.; LYKLEMA, J.; NORDE, W. and ZEHNDER, A. J. B.: Microb. Ecol. **17** (1) 1-16 (1989)

55. WORLD HEALTH ORGANIZATION: European Cooperation of Environmental Health Aspects of the Control of Chemicals. Copenhagen 1982

56. ZAHRER, S.: Pharm. Ind. **44** 1093-1096 (1982)

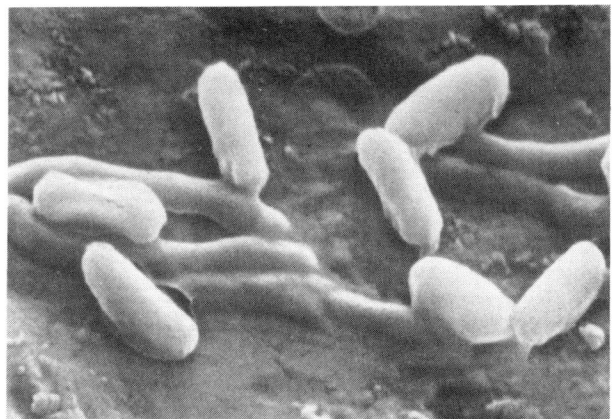

Fig. 1: Spores of *Bac. stearothermophilus* adhering to a stainless steel surface

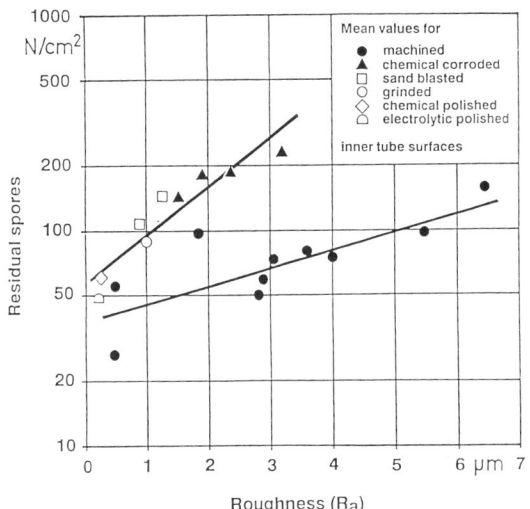

Fig. 2: Influence of the surface roughness on the cleanability of a stainless steel surface /27/.

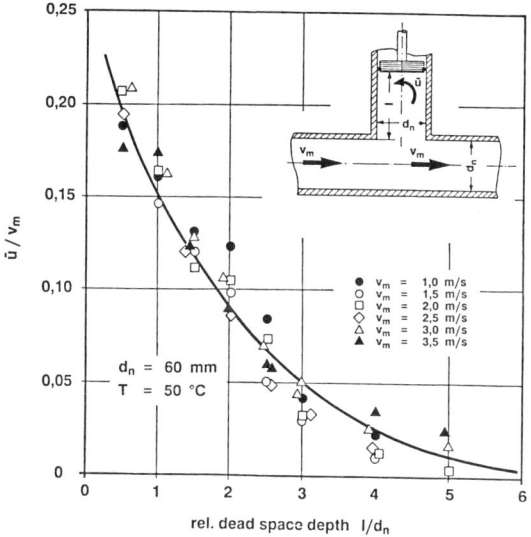

Fig. 3: Fluid motion in a dead space /20/.

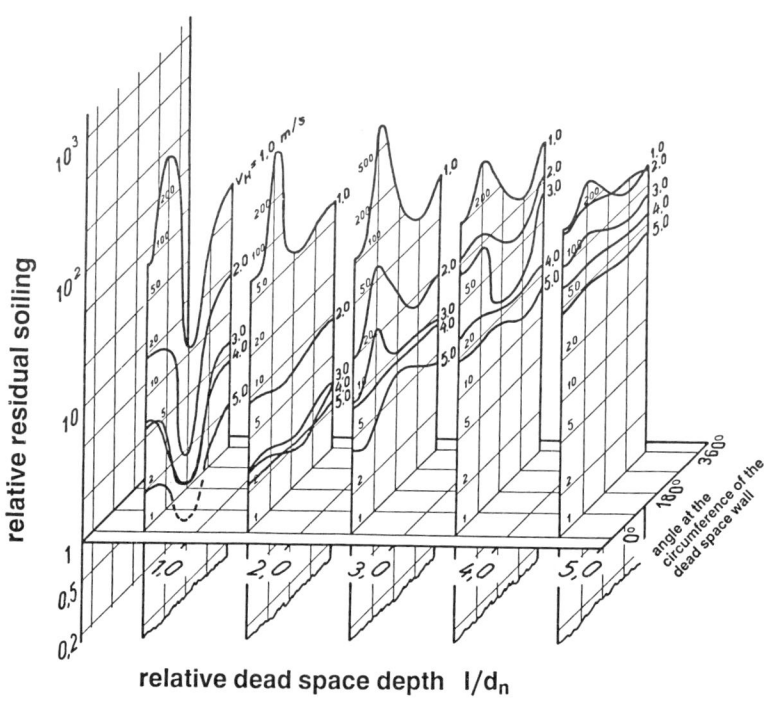

Fig. 4: Local cleaning behaviour of a dead space /21/.

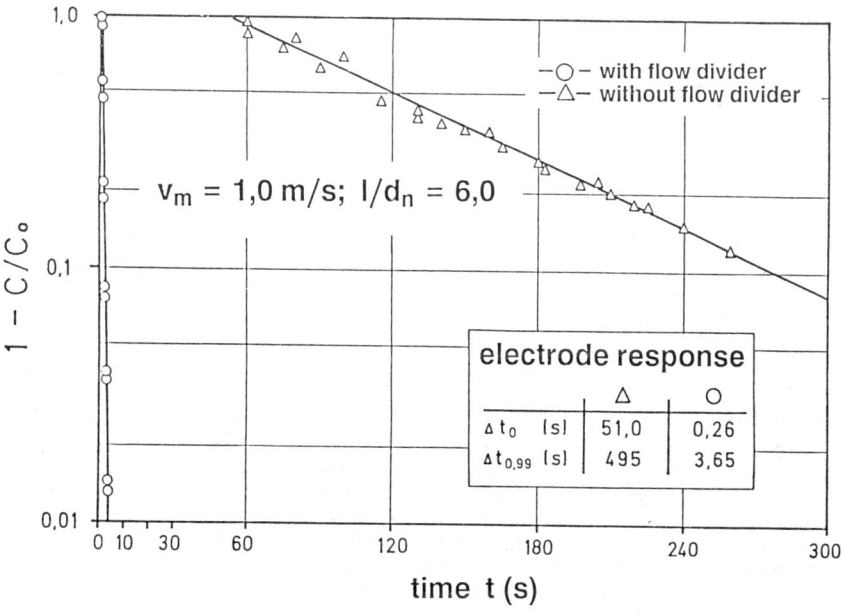

$v_m = 1,0$ m/s; $l/d_n = 6,0$

- —O— with flow divider
- —△— without flow divider

electrode response

	△	O
Δt_0 (s)	51,0	0,26
$\Delta t_{0,99}$ (s)	495	3,65

y-axis: $1 - C/C_o$

x-axis: time t (s)

in-line measuring nozzle

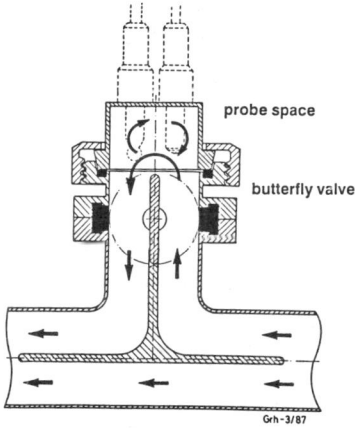

probe space

butterfly valve

Grh-3/87

Fig. 5: Solving the dead space problem by a flow divider /14/.

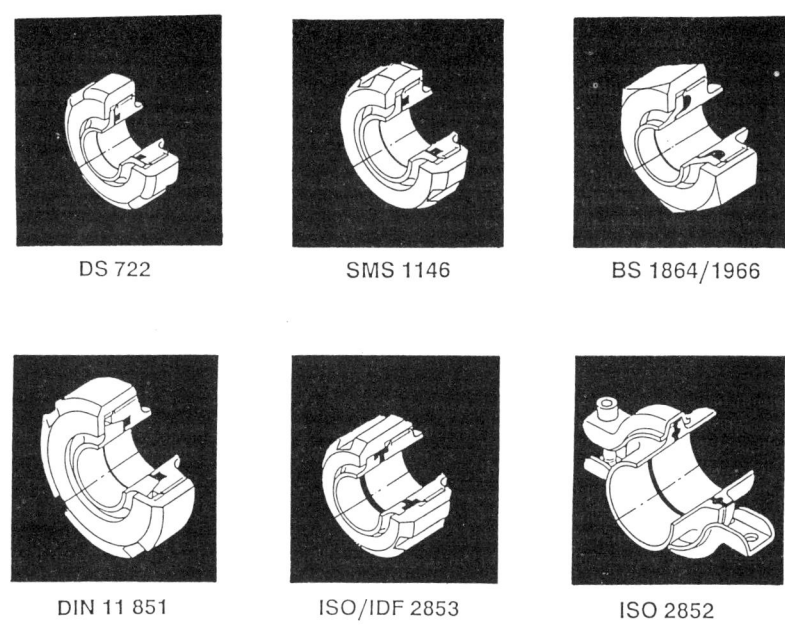

DS 722   SMS 1146   BS 1864/1966

DIN 11 851   ISO/IDF 2853   ISO 2852

Fig. 6: Examples of slit free milking pipe couplings

Fig. 7: Abrasives of a double seat valve spindle gasket /22/.

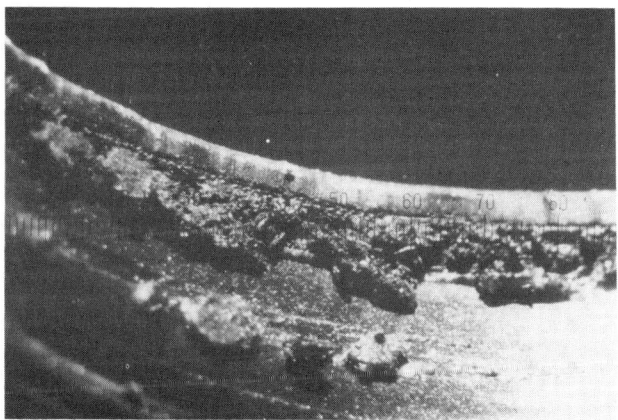

Fig. 8: Accumulation of abrasives and grease in a
dead space of a double seat valve spindle gasket /22/.

The monitoring and control of disinfection processes.

A.P.M.Hasting[*], I.W.Burns[*], G de Goederen[**], P.Luijendijk[**]

Peracetic acid (PAA) is becoming increasingly widely
used in disinfection processes due to its particularly
favourable combination of microbial activity and
environmental safety. Quality assurance of the disinfection
process requires that the concentration of PAA be
monitored and a novel sensor has been developed, based
on manufacturing techniques used in the electronics
industry. Practical experience with the system has
confirmed the accuracy and reliability of the sensor
and shown that it can be used to control a disinfection
recovery system and improve quality assurance.

Introduction

The food industry is facing ever increasing legislative and commercial pressures for the hygiene standards within the industry to be improved as consumers demand minimally processed, preservative free products with an extended shelf life. Manufacturers continue to look for more cost effective processes by minimising downtime and thus increasing plant operation cycles whilst retaining a high degree of quality assurance. These trends place an increasing emphasis on hygienic design and operation and the need for an improved understanding and awareness of all aspects related to hygienic operation. Cleaning and disinfection play a key role in the total hygienic operation of a process but are not always given the attention they merit.

The disinfection process

Disinfection is a process which reduces the number of microorganisms within a system to a level which is not harmful to health or the quality of the food. The process does not destroy all microorganisms in the same way as a process such as sterilisation; for example bacterial spores may not necessarily be destroyed. However, after disinfection, the system should not result in recontamination of the product coming into contact with it. Disinfection is generally carried out after cleaning by thermal or chemical means. For thermal disinfection steam or hot water is used depending on the plant being treated, with temperatures of up to 100°C for disinfection and 120°C - 140°C for sterilisation.

[*]   Unilever Research, Sharnbrook, Bedford, UK

[**]   Lever Industrial, Development and Application Centre, Maarssen, Holland

There are a wide range of chemicals available for disinfection some of which are described in Table 1.

Table 1. Chemical disinfection products.

Chemical group	Examples	Actual products
Halogens	Iodine Chlorine	Iodophors - iodine reacted with suitable carrier 1. Inorganic containing hypochlorites eg NaOCl 2. Organic chlorine release agents eg Trichloroisocyanurate
Cationics	Quaternary ammonium compounds Biguanides Amphoterics	Didecyl dimethyl ammonium chloride Polyhexamethylene biguanide n alkyl betane
Acid Anionics	Anionic surfactant	Sodium lauryl sulphate/ Phosphoric acid
Peroxygen compounds	Peroxide Peroxyacids	Hydrogen peroxide 1. Peracetic acid 2. Performic acid
Alkalis		Sodium hydroxide

With such a variety of chemicals available, it is not suprising that there are several mechanisms associated with the disinfection process. These range from oxidation of the microbial proteins in the case of chlorine compounds, to disruption of the cell membrane by quaternary ammonium compounds. Probably the most widely used disinfectant in the food industry at present is sodium hypochlorite, which is cheap, readily available and effective. However it is potentially corrosive and its use is being increasingly questioned on environmental grounds. There is therefore an increasing demand for chemicals that are both effective disinfectants as well as environmentally safe and of the disinfectants available, peracetic acid is being increasingly widely used in industrial applications (1-2) due to its particularly favourable combination of properties.

- broad spectrum of microbial activity at low concentrations (3-5)
- effective at low temperatures (6)
- environmentally safe, degrades to oxygen, carbon dioxide and water
- good chemical and physical stability (-10°C - 40°C)
- non foaming
- good rinsability
- some tolerance of organic soil

It is also necessary to appreciate that a suitable chemical alone is insufficient and that a total systems approach is essential, so that the chemical can be effectively delivered to the plant being disinfected, monitored, controlled and recorded to provide a high level of quality assurance and hygiene security. The ability to be able to measure the concentration of peracetic acid is therefore an integral step in its application.

Measurement approaches

Peracetic acid(PAA) is formed by the reaction of acetic acid and hydrogen peroxide of a mineral

$$CH_3COOH + H_2O_2 \rightleftharpoons CH_3CO_3H + H_2O \qquad (1)$$

Peracetic acid disinfectants are therefore an equilibrium mixture of acetic acid, peroxide and peracetic acid and the concentration cannot be determined by a single titration due to the presence of the peroxide. It is therefore necessary to remove the peroxide by means of potassium permanganate followed by titration of peracetic acid with potassium iodide and sodium thiosulphate. Whilst an automatic titrator may therefore be technically feasible for control of the disinfection process, the costs are likely to be prohibitive. Another potential approach would be to use conductivity, although the low conductivity of the disinfectant solution would require addition of a tracer to enable this method to be considered. Such an approach could give an indirect measurement of peracetic acid but any differences in relative concentration of PAA to the tracer due to for example breakdown of the PAA would result in a false and potentially overoptimistic reading. This could then pose the serious risk of an inadequate disinfection process being delivered to the plant. It was therefore decided that a direct measurement technique would be preferred and such a technique has been developed, utilising an electrochemical (amperometric) measurement, figure 1. The concentration in the reaction mixture can be monitored by measuring the current at a working electrode subject to a fixed potential. Since the disinfectant contains acetic acid and hydrogen peroxide, it was also necessary to ensure that such a measurement could adequately differentiate between the components of the solution. Figure 2 shows that there is a good differentiation between the measured current for PAA and acetic acid/hydrogen peroxide mixtures indicating that the measurement principle is valid.

The complete sensor system incorporates working, counter and reference electrodes as well as pH, redox and temperature. Standard industrial instruments are used where possible but a novel sensor was developed for the working and counter electrodes based on manufacturing techniques developed for the electronics industry. The components were then incorporated into a sensor assembly through which disinfection solution could be passed, care being taken to ensure the design of the assembly itself was hygienic. The complete sensor system is shown in figure 3 with the signals from the sensors being fed to a head amplifier which is connected in turn to a control unit via a multicore screened cable. The actual concentration of PAA is calculated and the data can be downloaded to a PC or printer if so desired. In addition the calculated concentration can be used to activate an appropriate control function such as operation of a dosing pump if outside the set point, as well as appropriate alarms and management information on disinfectant usage.

Practical application

Laboratory trials indicated that the system functioned reliably and the measured concentrations from the sensor correlated satisfactorily with the values obtained by titration. It was therefore decided to install a prototype in a factory and a system was therefore installed in a continental cheese factory. Disinfectants can either be used on a single use or recovery basis in the same way as CIP detergents. Recovery systems are commonly used in Europe and concentration monitoring is particularly important in such installations, where the concentration can fall significantly over a period of time due to dilution and loss of disinfectant from the circuit. The factory used a recovery system and the sensor system was installed in a recirculation loop around the batch tank as shown in figure 4. Prior to installation of the sensor, operation of the recovery system was as follows:

1. At start of week, fill recovery tank with water and add PAA disinfectant to give a nominal concentration of 600 ppm.
2. At end of each days production, refill tank to replenish liquid lost during the day and add PAA to bring overall tank concentration to nominally 300 ppm.
3. At end of week, completely drain recovery tank.

PAA concentrations were determined by titration.

The sensor was initially used to monitor rather than control conditions in the batch tank in order to build confidence in the total system. PAA concentrations determined by the sensor closely matched the concentrations of batch tank samples analysed by titration, Table 2.

Table 2.   Comparison of PAA concentrations in recovery tank measured using sensor and conventional titration.

Sample	PAA concentration determined by sensor ppm	PAA concentration determined by titration ppm
1	220	250
2	255	250
3	260	260
4	255	270
5	220	235
6	300	300
7	375	400
8	310	310
9	350	350

Typical data obtained when using the PAA sensor to monitor the batch tank is shown in figure 5. This indicated that during the course of even one day the PAA concentration fell rapidly and for a large part of the time, the concentration delivered to the plant was wholly inadequate to assure the quality of the disinfection process. This posed a potentially serious risk to the microbiological quality of the products processed within the factory and the customer considered that automatic control of the system was essential.

When operating in control mode, a level of PAA below the set point activated the dosing pump feeding disinfectant into the recovery tank. Since there was a significant time lag between dosing in PAA and the concentration in the recovery tank reaching equilibrium, the dosing pump was activated for a fixed period after which a built in time delay allowed equilibration of the tank concentration. Since the relative quantities of PAA dosed in at any time were small compared to the size of the recovery vessel, it was also necessary to ensure that there was a adequate flow through the recirculation line to assist in mixing PAA into the bulk solution. The time lags incorporated into such a control system inevitably slowed the response of the system to changes in concentration and hence affected the quality of the control. Although, the very presence of a substantial recovery tank volume means that changes in PAA concentration are relatively slow, figure 6 indicates that the control system is capable of maintaining the concentration at a level which provided assurance of the disinfection process. It was also possible to operate the total system at a lower concentration set point (240 ppm), when under controlled conditions, due to the greater confidence the system provided. It is not automatically the case that the PAA usage will be less, since in the uncontrolled case there is less than 100 ppm PAA for the majority of the time. However, in the controlled situation it is feasible to further reduce the concentration set point, whilst maintaining assured disinfection and under these conditions it may be possible to reduce the level of PAA usage, Table 3.

Table 3. Comparative usage of PAA in manual and controlled applications.

	Manual operation PAA levels (ppm) Start day 1 600 Start days 2-5 300	Automatic control PAA set point 240 ppm
Predicted PAA utilisation per week for a prototype system (litres of 6% solution)	120	84
% of time recovery tank concentration is less than 100ppm PAA	46	0

The true capabilities of the system have by no means yet been fully explored. Improved control may well be achievable by the use of feed forward techniques for example. In addition, one of the most potentially powerful features of such a system is in conjunction with appropriate process models and diagnostic facilities, to monitor and interpret the operation of the disinfection and cleaning in place process.

Conclusions.

1.   An electrochemical technique has been developed to monitor concentrations of peracetic acid in a disinfection process.

2.   Satisfactory agreement has been obtained between the concentrations measured by the sensor and those measured by conventional titration.

3.   Practical experience with the system indicates that peracetic acid concentrations can be used to control a disinfection recovery system leading to improved assurance that adequate disinfection processes have been achieved.

References

1.   Baldry MJC and Dickinson K (1983) Speciality Chemicals 3, 30, 17-19

2.   Fraser JAL (1986) Chemspec Bacs Symp 65-69

3.   Ito KA, Seeger ML and Lee WH (1972) J Appl Bact 35, 479-483

4.   Merka V and Dvorak J (1968) J Hyg Epid Micro Immuno 12, 115-121

5.   Han BH, Schornick G and Loncin M (1980) JFood Proc Pres 4, 95-110

6.   Jones LA, Hoffman RK and Phillips CR (1967) Appl Micro 15(2), 357-362

Figure 1. Electrochemical Measurement Principle

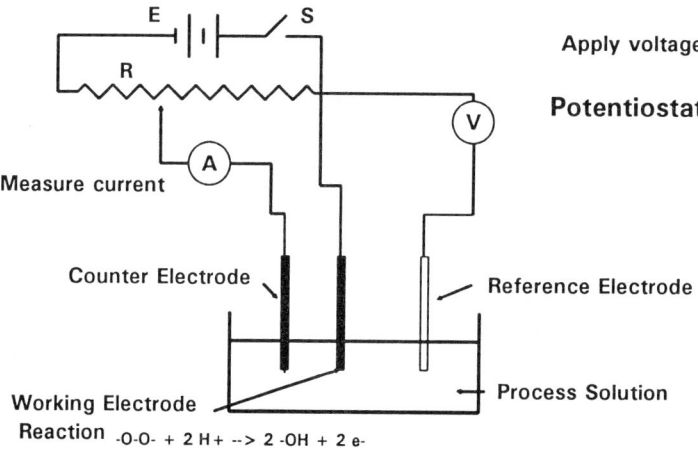

Reaction $-O-O- + 2H+ \rightarrow 2 -OH + 2 e-$

Figure 2. Comparative values of Currents

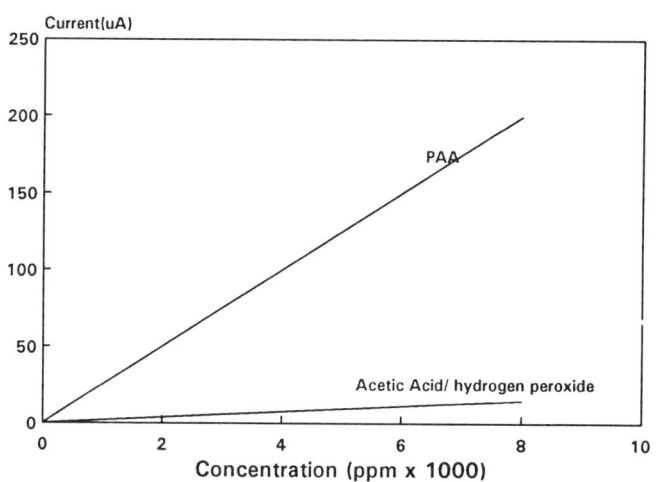

Figure 3. Basic Components of PAA Sensor System

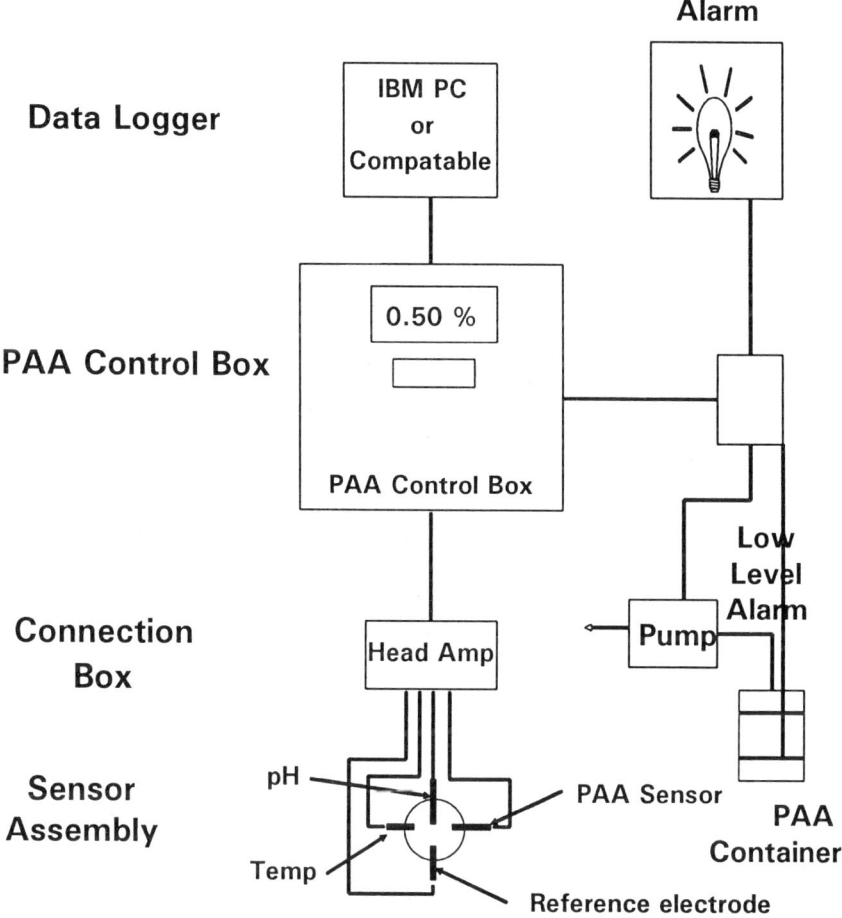

FIGURE 4. SENSOR ARRANGEMENT IN FACTORY

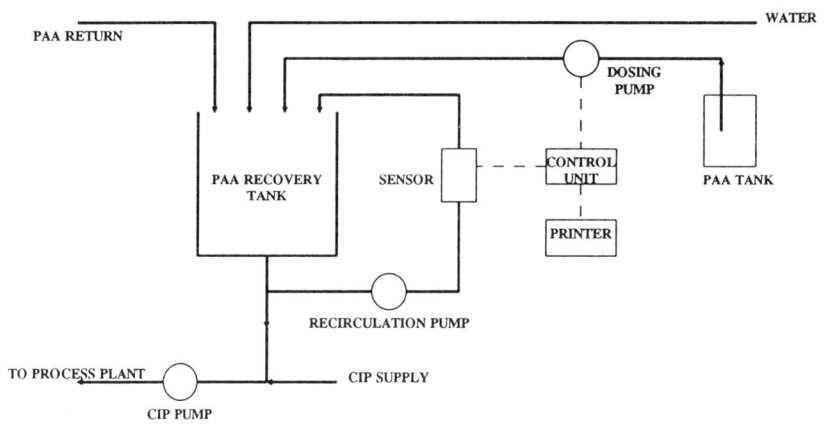

Figure 5. Manual Addition of PAA

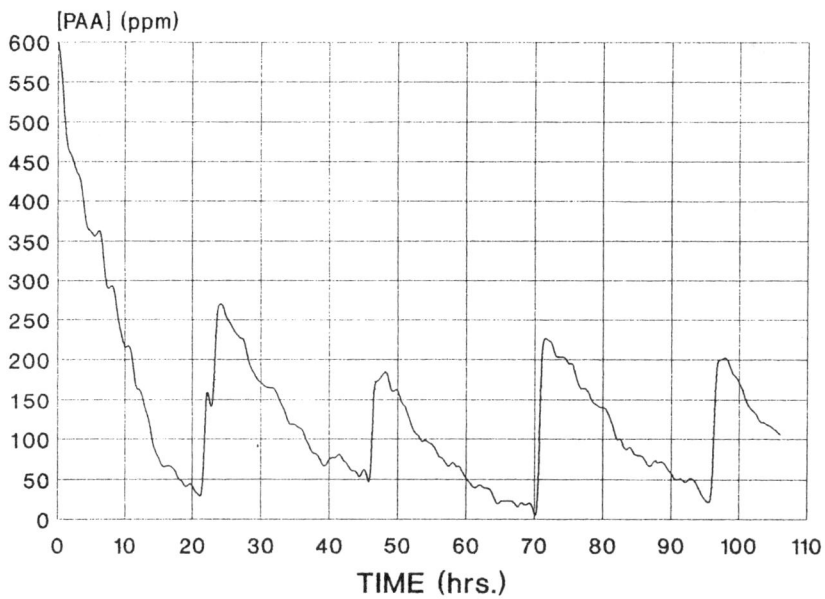

Figure 6. Automatic Control of PAA Concentration

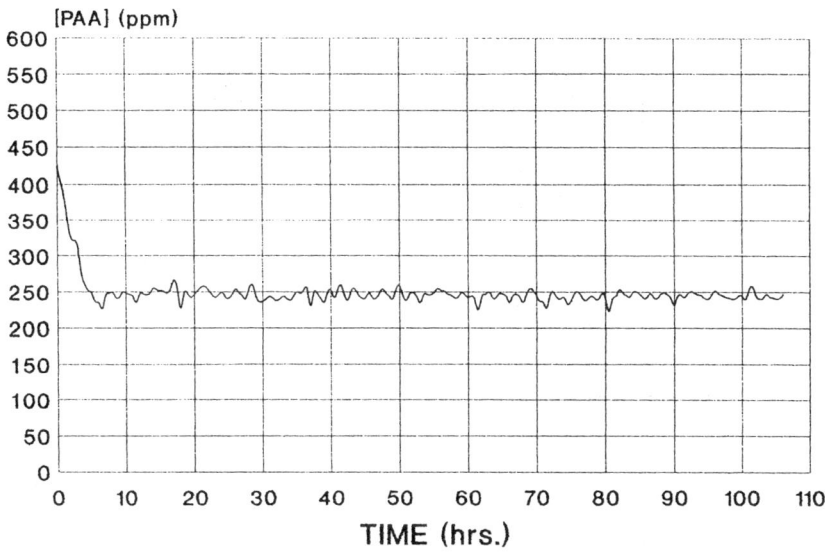

"HEATPROC" - AN EXPERT SYSTEM FOR THE ASSESSMENT

OF PASTEURIZATION PLANTS FOR MILK.

W. RIEDER, Dipl.-Ing, MSc, MIFST *)

An algorithm has been developed for the assessment of milk pasteurization plants with regard to (i) product safety, (ii) product quality, and (iii) energy economy. The most outstanding scientific principle involved is the P*-concept characterizing processes differing in terms of time and temperature as to microorganism death rate. The practicability of the system devised could be demonstrated using process data obtained from three different types of plants including HTST and flash processing.

Introduction

An expert system is said to represent a group of computer programs, along with knowledge, information and databases, which act together to address problems that might otherwise be solved by human consultants (Alberico & Micco 1990). Some applications developed for the food industries have been reviewed recently (Whitney 1990).

Pasteurization is a process applied to raw milk in order to (i) destroy pathogenic microorganisms and (ii) extend shelf-life whilst minimizing changes in the natural state of the product. A generally agreed definition has been provided by IDF as used in the UK (Staal 1986).

Considering a given process it is necessary to check regularly whether the goal of the procedure has been matched. In case of continuous plate-heat-exchange-pasteurization of milk this is commonly performed by measuring the product's temperature at the end of the holding section and automatic recording of the results. Supposing the legal requirements in the UK (71.7° C for at least 15 s) have not been matched the under heat-treated and thus unsafe product will be diverted back to the balance tank for reprocessing. A negative score in the phosphatase test confirms the reliability of the process on the finished product (Tolle 1983). Hygienic plant management downstream the actual holding equipment and bacteriological examinations (low total plate count/TPC and

*) Grand Metropolitan Foods Europe (GMFE), South Ruislip (UK)
   At present: Nestle-Austria, A-1051 Vienna

coliforms not detectable) eventually ensure that customers will get their product free of post processing contaminations.

While this may do fairly well in most practical situations we have chosen a more basic approach including various mathematical calculations in order to balance product safety, product quality, and energy economy in an optimal manner. Moreover such a program might serve as a model tool for future work on expert systems dealing with thermal processing of foods.

Materials and Methods

Hardware

IBM-compatible microcomputer with Intel 80386SX processor, 16 mHz frequency, 2 MB RAM, 40 mB hard disc, two floppy disc drives (5.25 inches 1.2 mB or 3.5 inches 1.44 mB alternatively, VGA card 512 kB 16 bit, 1024/768 high resolution colour screen, IBM graphics printer 5152.

System-Software

MS-DOS 4.0 as operating system and Crystal 3.5 as an expert-system-shell. The latter represents a fourth-generation language written in "C". It is supplied by Intelligent Environment Ltd, Richmond (UK).

Knowledge Engineering

Knowledge acquisition was accomplished by interviewing GMFE's Corporate Technical Centre expert on thermal processing of dairy products, Mr. D. Hancock, supported by consultation of various textbooks and papers (references given in the text), data provided by Alfa Laval Ltd. (Anonymous 1987) and, additionally, personal communication with the APV Company (Berry 1990) and Leatherhead Food RA's Information Technology Group (Robinson 1990).

Application software development was carried out using the tree structure model and the top-down method, starting with the conclusion working down to the various sub-modules ("backward-chaining"). Subprograms themselves have been written according to the suggestions provided by Nassi & Shneiderman in a widely agreed way of "structured programming" (Schneider 1985).

Results

The program created reveals main features commonly included in an expert system, such as rules, facts, database handling, inference chaining for reaching a conclusion, and clear design of the user interface (Daly 1988), although still embracing a pure scientific (i.e. algorithmic) rather than a heuristic (i.e. processing of "rules of thumb") approach. In this context facts are process data taken from a pasteurization plant entered by the user into Heatproc which may change with each consultation of the system. Rules represent names calling certain subprograms depending upon input data and resulting figures of calculations achieved automatically. Conclusions are drawn within the output section in a way sketched in Table 2 and 3. Heatproc occupies 52.36 kB in the RAM (random access memory) or on the magnetic disc. The data stored volatilely in the input variables and arrays may be saved permanently in a dBASE file and consequently the system is able to communicate with dBASE via an interface. The actual program starts with a main menu, offering input, calculation, and output section.

All input parameters employed are readily available, i.e. the time–temperature profile of the process (s,°C), the mass flow rate of the product (kg/h or kg/s), and the diameter of the holding tube (m or mm). Residence times may be measured by the injection method (Lewis 1986) or, more easily, taken from the supplier's manual. Alternatively the average residence time (tav, s) might be calculated by dividing the volume of the section under concern (m3) by the volumetric flow rate (m3/s). Times in context of Heatproc mean minimal residence times (tmin, s). Under circular pipe flow there is an empirical relationship between these parameters, i.e. tmin = 0.83 tav (assuming turbulent flow conditions, Lewis 1986).

Temperatures may be taken from thermocouple readings. In order to get the mass flow rate (m') the amount of milk streaming through the plant within a certain time can be collected in a bucket, weighed and m' is calculated by dividing mass by time. Alternatively m' may be taken from readings of calibrated flow meters. The inner diameter of the holding tube may be measured by means of sliding callipers.

Certain physical parameters which will be needed for some calculations carried out have already been written into the program including dynamic viscosity (0.0006 Pa.s for milk of 0.5% fat and 0.00075 Pa.s in case of full cream milk of 3.6% fat), density (1013 kg/m3 and 1008 kg/m3 in respect), both adapted from Kessler 1988 and Lewis 1986 & 1987, and decimal reduction time of Listeria monocytogenes (0.9 s) which had been derived by experiment by Bradshaw et al. 1985 (all data taken at 72°C). The calculation section comprises 4 distinct modules employing the equations arranged in Table 1.

The P*-concept enables the comparison of any given time–temperature profile including heating, holding, and cooling with that stipulated as reference parameters by IDF 1986 (72°C, 15 s) similarly to the well established Fo-concept employed when dealing with UHT (ultra high temperature) or sterilization tasks. Thus P* is a dimensionless number characterizing the pasteurization effect of milk. When applying the reference conditions to raw milk it is generally agreed that this will ensure a product free of Mycobacterium tuberculosis and other pathogenic organisms whilst losses in nutritional and sensorial quality will be minimal (inactivation of vitamins less then 3%, denaturation

Equation Number	Scientific Principle	Symbol	Calculation	Dimension
(1)	Comparison of time-temp. conditions with a reference process (P-Star)	P*	$= \int_{0}^{t} \dfrac{1}{tp^*(1)} \, dt$	-
(1a)	P*-fraction exerted in a particular second		$\log tp^*(1) =$ $14885/(273+T)-41.97$	-
(2)	Number of decimal reduction cycles for a particular organism (D(t) = decimal reduction time in s for this org. at 72°C)	NDR	$= \dfrac{15}{D(t)} \, p^*$	-
(3)	Reynold's number (n = dyn. viscosity in Pa.s)	Re	$= \dfrac{vav \; S \; D}{n}$	-
(3a)	Average velocity of any particle streaming through the holding tube	vav	$= \dfrac{Q'}{A}$	m/s
(3b)	Volumetric flow rate (m' = mass flow rate in kg/s and S is density at 72° C in kg/m3)	Q'	$= \dfrac{m'}{S}$	m3/s
(3c)	Cross section area (circle formula)	A	$= \dfrac{D^2 \, \pi}{4}$	m2
(4)	Regeneration efficiency (Temperatures taken from time-temp. profile, Fig.1, explanation inside the text)	RE%	$= \dfrac{T(2)-T(1)}{T(3)-T(1)} \; 100$	%

Table 1: Arrangement of concepts and formulas applied in the evaluation of pasteurization plants. Equations adapted from Kessler 1988 and Lewis 1986 & 1987.

of β-lactoglobulin less than 5%). To check this for any pasteurization treatment on hand of the time–temperature parameters used means the computation of the definite integral given in equation (1) and comparison of the result with that obtained under reference conditions which is said to be one by definition. P* may be described as the integrated heat impact over the whole process starting at time nought continuing up to time character t. Since a common HTST (high temperature short time) plate–heat–exchanger is built up of several sections and the thermal and flow conditions may change completely when any particle is moving from one section to another, the integral is a non–continuous

one. Wilbey 1990 determines P* by graphical estimation of
each P*-fraction exerted in one particular second and
summarizing this over the whole process assuming linear time-
temperature conditions in each section including a linear
temperature drop in the holding tube. We, more accurately,
use equation (1a), valid within a temperature range of at
maximum 90°C. Equation (1) has been derived by transformation
of the common Arrhenius-law describing temperature dependency
of reaction velocity by Nassauer & Kessler 1986 assuming an
activation energy of 285 kJ/mol for microorganism death rate.

Hence the algorithm able to calculate all this automatically
starts with the conversion of the input temperature from
Celsius into Kelvin ("conversion loop"). In loop-one the
heater-section dealt with is fixed (heating, holding,
cooling) and the section-time is calculated. In loop two the
P*-number of any particular section is calculated by means of
equation (1a) and summarized for each section. Finally the
P*-values of each section are added ending up with the total
P* over the whole process. Now the surrounding-loop is
completed by skipping back to the calculation-menu, so that
we end up with four loops framed into each other in the
described manner.

The number of decimal reduction cycles for a particular
organism is calculated according to equation (2) employing
the P* number computed. This equation has been derived by
reformulating the law for microorganism death rate in
thermal processing of biological materials (Rieder 1990).

Reynold's number which describes the flow characteristics of
the fluid is computed automatically by option (3) of the
calculation section. Equation (3) applies to circular pipe
flow, therefore - and since residence time distribution in
slits is more complex than in pipes - Heatproc must not be
used for plants equipped with plate-type holding sections.
However, the latter ones are obsolete and rarely used in
modern process lines.

Regeneration efficiency has been defined as the amount of
heat supplied by regeneration divided by the total heat
requirement assuming no regeneration (Lewis 1986 & 1987). The
calculation of regeneration efficiency (equation 4) employs
$T(1)$ (temp. after storage in °C), $T(2)$ (temp. after
regeneration warming), and $T(3)$ (temp. after heating by means
of hot water, that is equivalent to begin of holding).

The inference engine which forms the essential part of an
expert system is included into the output section of the
program. Since the P*-concept is only applicable when really
good turbulent streaming conditions are achieved (referring
to Re > 12 000) (Nassauer & Kessler 1986) this is checked
first of all. Supposing that prerequisite is not fulfilled, a
construction failure has taken place when designing the
holding tube. In this case the pipe has to be replaced by
another one with adjusted dimensions or, provided Re lies
just below the limit, the throughput might be increased.

In any case it is assumed that the raw milk processed by the plant is heat stable and of at least moderate bacteriological quality (i.e. TPC of < 300 000 cfu (colony forming units)/ml, pH > 6.6). Cleaning and dismantling of the plant for visual inspection of the plates must be carried out regularly in order to make sure that there is no leakage or fouling regardless of the outcome of the Heatproc calculations.

An assessment of the plant with regard to product safety and product quality will be provided depending upon the calculated effective value of P* in a way given in Table 2. The number of decimal reduction cycles of Listeria monocytogenes is estimated in order to supply an idea, of how much this pathogenic organism is reduced by the conditions applied. The conclusion drawing in the energy economy section is performed in a straightforward way employing simply the regeneration efficiency of the plant (Table 3). Finally the user gets the results of all calculations computed and a certificate assessing the process is provided exhibited on either the screen or on a printout, alternatively.

The usefulness of the concept devised has been demonstrated by employing data taken from an APV–Junior pilot scale HTST–plant installed at Reading University's food processing area (process 1), data from a typical commercial scale HTST–pasteurization apparatus (process 2), and assumed data for a flash pasteurization process (process 3). The mass flow rates entered into Heatproc are 480 kg/h for process 1, 12 000 kg/h for process 2, and 10 000 kg/h for process 3. The diameters for the holding tubes are 0.023 m, 0.066 m, and 0.050 m in respect. The time–temperature conditions are given graphically (Figure 1). The figures calculated by Heatproc will be shown in Table 4. The substrate processed by these plants is skimmed milk.

Range of P*	Comment
P* < 1.00	underprocessed and thus unsafe product: increase t - T conditions
P* = 1.00-1.30	good quality, but not really safe, since there is not much margin: increase t - T conditions slightly
P* = 1.31-2.00	optimum range: high product safety and good quality
P* = 2.01-10.00	overprocessed: safe product, but perhaps mild cooked flavour: relax t - T conditions
P* > 10	severely overprocessed: safe product, but probably cooked flavour, losses of vitamins, waste of energy: relax t - T conditions

Table 2: Display of chosen comments serving as conclusions with regard to product safety and quality aspects depending upon certain P*-values calculated by the system.

Range of REX	C o m m e n t
<75	poor energy economy, improve regeneration conditions
75-90	moderate energy economy, check regeneration conditions
>90	good energy economy

Table 3: Arrangement of chosen comments for energy economy representing the conclusion drawing depending upon the figures for regeneration efficiency calculated by Heatproc.

Principle	APV-Junior (1)	Commercial HTST (2)	Flash-Past. (3)
Re	12 302	107 178	117 896
P*-total	1.46	4.23	14.06
P*(1)-heating	0.14	0.21	0.96
P*(2)-holding	1.23	3.79	12.28
P*(3)-cooling	0.09	0.23	0.82
NOR	24.8	72.1	263.5
REX	78.5	94.2	62.5

Table 4: Depiction of some characteristic process parameters calculated automatically for skimmed milk streaming through three different types of pasteurization plants.

Discussion

In 1976 the working group on artificial intelligence of Stanford University, California, succeeded in introducing Mycin as the first appropriate knowledge-base dealing with diagnosis and treatment of infectious blood diseases (Buchanan & Shortliffe 1984). This system has served as a model for many successors. Formulated in the if-clause form the matter of how Heatproc comes to its conclusion with regard to product safety and quality aspects will be compared with an example taken from the Mycin experiments of the early 1970ies (Table 5).

From Table 4 it is to be seen that P* for the pilot plant is situated between 1.3 and 2.0, thus a safe product of excellent quality is produced. The commercial scale plant provides a safe but overprocessed product (P* between 2.0 and 10.0). Flash processing ends up with a severely overprocessed product (P* above 10.0) which may probably have a certain undesireable cooked flavour. These findings are in good accordance with Kessler 1987 who has recognised a certain

---

MYCIN (Stanford Univ. 1976)	HEATPROC (GMFE/Reading Univ. 1990)

IF strain is gram positive	IF Re is greater then 12 000
AND morphology is coccus	AND P* is greater then 1.3
AND growth is chains	AND P* is smaller then 2.0
THEN suggestive evidence that	THEN process is well controlled
organism is streptococcus	and a safe and good quality
	product is manufactured.

Table 5: Comparision of two significant rules of the Mycin experiments 1976 (Buchanan & Shortliffe 1984) and the Heatproc creation 1990 (Rieder 1990).

tendency to end up with overprocessed products under practice circumstances. According to that author overprocessing does not increase keeping quality! However, none of the plants yields an underprocessed product (i.e. all P* values above 1.0 and 1.3 in respect).

Due to the logarithmic nature of equation (1a) the enhancement of temperature causes an exponential increase of P* whilst changes in holding time end up with a simple proportional alteration of P* merely. This may clearly be demonstrated on hand of the profiles: process 2 (holding of tmin = 32 s at 74 °C) has twice the holding time and 1.02 times temperature impact of process 1 (holding of tmin = 16 s at 72.5 °C). However, P*-holding increases from 1.23 (process 1) to 3.79 (process 2) which is 3.1 times. This behaviour is of course even much more pronounced in case of process 3 (holding tmin = 5.0 s at 85 °C) where 0.31 times holding time of process 1 and 1.17 times temperature impact of process 1 exhibit an P*-holding of 12.28 which is in fact 10 times higher than that of process 1. Consequently contribution of P* for heating and cooling to the total one is low for process 1 and 2 (0.23 and 0.44 in respect) but more distinct in case of process 3 (1.78) although the latter one has the flashing connexion with short residence times in these sections. Figure 2 depicts the P*-values discussed in a bloc diagram.

Listeria monocytogenes has been chosen as an example for a pathogenic bacteria due to recent publicity mainly. This, of course, is just an example and you may calculate such figures similarly for any organism for which the decimal reduction time at the given temperature and the substratum under concern (i.e. milk in our case) has been estimated correctly by experiment. When comparing our findings (NDR of 24.8 − 263.5 for processes 1 − 3) with the common 12−D concept of UHT or sterilization processing (i.e. 12 decimal reduction cycles for Clostridium botulinum spores referring to Fo of 2.4 in low acid foods, Lewis 1987) we are by far on the safe side in any case. These findings again reveal a tendency to overprocessing. Accordingly detections of L. monocytogenes in pasteurized milk or dairy products manufactured from pasteurized milk as a raw matter indicate post pasteurization contaminations.

Turbulence is good in any case due to Reynold's numbers above 12 000 for processes 1 − 3 (Re = 12 302 − 117 896). However, for process 2 and 3 Re lies between 100 000 and 150 000 which has been reported to be the optimal region (Stadler 1985) whereas process one is just above the minimal requirements.

Regeneration efficiency is highly depending upon connexion of the plates and the way how the product streams through the plant: Excellent for the commercial scale (94%) due to a long regeneration section, moderate for the junior type (79%), where energy economy aspects are less important because of the relatively low total energy consumption due to the small scale of the plant, and poor looking at flashing (63%) because of short regeneration and long heating sections, which lies in the nature of this process. Further aspects of regeneration efficiency have already been discussed elsewhere (Wilbey 1990).

The expert system installed at present provides a useful guide to the expected outcome of practical applications of the data provided. Further development work might probably deal with aspects not yet covered by Heatproc at this stage such as technological purposes of pasteurized milk serving as a raw matter for further processing (eg. different desired degree of whey protein denaturation in cheesemaking and in yoghurt production) or unit operations commonly combined with pasteurization purposes like separation and homogenization. In future power and steam requirement for the heating section, the overall heat transfer coefficient in the distinct sections, or electrical energy needed for pumping purposes, and energy needed for providing the cooling water should be included into the energy consumption section. Reaction kinetical aspects of changes of technological, sensorial or nutritional importance could be taken into account employing equations given by Kessler 1988. Further prospects might be updating the system for cream processing which needs dealing with non Newtonian behaviour of viscosity and being aware that too high turbulence should be avoided because of possible damage of fat droplets. Finally the development of a similar program dealing with UHT and sterilization tasks would require slight adaptions only.

Acknowledgments

I wish to acknowledge GMFE's Dr. Phil Perkins for initiating this project and providing the necessary facilities. Thanks to Dr.-Ing. W. Walenta of Univ. of Science, Dept. of Food Engineering and Dairy Technology, Munich−Weihenstephan, Germany, for revising the manuscript.

Figures

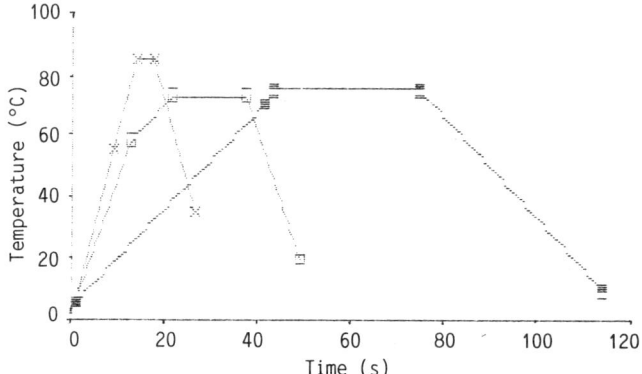

Figure 1: Time-temperature profiles of different pasteurization processes. (□) means APV-Junior (process 1), (■) means commercial HTST (process 2), (x) means flash procedure (process 3).

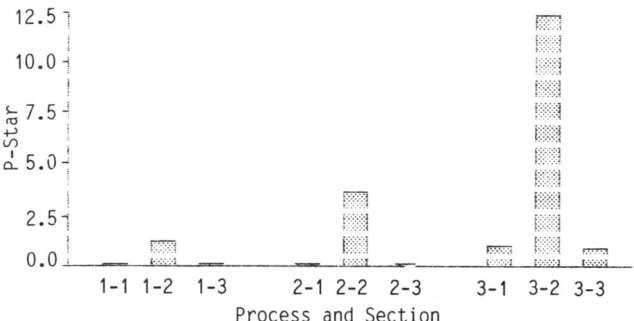

Figure 2: Arrangement of P*-fractions exerted in different sections of plate-heat-exchanger-plants with regard to various types of pasteurization processes. 1-1 means process 1, section 1 (heating), 1-2 means process 1, section 2 (holding), 1-3 means process 1, section 3 (cooling) etc. Regeneration warming has no significant influence and is neglected therefore.

References

Alberico, R. & Micco, M. (1990). Expert systems,IX, Meckler, London.
Anonymous (1989). The off-shelf-plate-heat-exchangers, pamphlet by Alfa Laval & Co Ltd., Brentford (UK).
Berry, N. (1990). Pers. comm. with APV Baker Ltd., Crawley (UK).
Bradshaw, J.G., Peeler, J.T. & Corwin, J.J. (1985). J. Food Prot. 48/9, 743-745.
Buchanan, B. & Shortliffe, E. (1984). Rule-based expert systems, Addison Wesley Publ., Reading (Mass).
Cerf, O. (1986). In Internat. Dairy Fed. (IDF): Monogr. on past. milk, 2-4, Bull. 200, Brussel.
Daly, D. (1988). Expert systems introduced, 6-30, Chartwell Bratt, Lund.
Kessler, H.G. (1987). Deutsche Molkereizeitung 6/87, 146-153.
Kessler, H.G. (1988). Lebensmittel- und Bioverfahrenstechnik, Molkereitechnologie, 31-41 and 132-191, Univ. of Sc. and Technol. Publ., Munich.
Lewis, M.J. (1986). In Robinson, R.K. (Ed.): Mod. dairy technol. Vol. 1., 1-51, Elsevier, London.
Lewis, M.J. (1987). Phys. prop. of foods and food proc. syst., 17-136 and 200-323, Ellis Horwood, Chichester.
Nassauer, J. & Kessler, H.G. (1986). In Internat. Dairy Fed. (IDF): Monogr. on past. milk, 84-86, Bull. 200, Brussel.
Rieder, W. (1990). Knowledge-based computer systems and some possible applications in the food and dairy industries, Master's Thesis, Reading Univ. (UK).
Robinson, A. (1990). Pers. comm. with Leatherhead Food Res. Ass., Inform. Technol. Group, Leatherhead (UK).
Schneider, W. (1985). Strukturiertes Programmieren in BASIC, 27-46, Vieweg, Braunschweig.
Staal, P. (1986). In Internat. Dairy Fed. (IDF): Monogr. on past. milk, 71-80, Bull. 200, Brussel.
Stadler, J.J. (1985). Nestec Techn. Inf. Bull. 1/85, 67-74, Vevey (Switzerland).
Tolle, A. (1983). In Gravert, H.O.: Die Milch, 211-306, Ulmer, Stuttgart.
Whitney, C.F. (1990). In Spiess, W.E. & Schubert, H. (Eds.): Engineering and food, Vol. 1, 900-908, Elsevier, London.
Wilbey, R.A. (1990). Food Technol. Internat. Europe 1990, 49-52, Inst. of Food Sc. & Technol. (IFST), London.

Nomenclature

Symbols and dimensions have already been given in the text. All calculations carried out employ SI-units.

USE OF IN-LINE SENSORS AND CLOSED-LOOP CONTROL FOR FOOD MANUFACTURING PROCESSES

IAN McFARLANE*

Advances in sensor technology have led to the development of new in-line sensors and analysers, and to improvements in reliability. Together these extend the feasibility of automatic control and reduce the cost of upkeep. The paper reviews the implications for different sectors of food manufacture, with examples of recent investment in control and automation.

INTRODUCTION

Advances in micro-electronics and computing in the last decade have strengthened the incentives for automation of food manufacturing processes. This paper gives examples of innovations which have been reported since an earlier review (McFarlane, 1983).

Investment in automation offers several forms of payback:

1 Yield. Process variability, caused for example by seasonal variation in ingredient properties, leads to fluctuations in the final moisture content, pack weight, or other measures of product quality. Automatic control will approximately halve the standard deviation of a controlled variable.

2 Waste. Compared with conventional mechanisation, an automatic control system can reduce the quantity of out-of-spec product at a grade change.

3 Operator productivity. Automation systems offer a net saving of 10 to 20% of direct labour. Operators who are retrained to work with automation equipment find high levels of job satisfaction, and any displaced labour can usually be absorbed within the organisation.

4 Fuel efficiency. Automation of start up sequences and optimisation of thermal efficiencies may save about 10% of fuel costs.

*Beaconsfield Instrument Company Limited

5 Product quality. During the 1980s there has been much interest in the application of computer-based data recording as a means to ensure product quality. Terms such as SPC (statistical process control) and SQC (statistical quality control) are used to identify systematic methods for quality assurance. The value of such innovations can be estimated by assuming a marginally higher sales value for a quality assured product. In any sector where quality can command a premium for a given grade of product, this corresponds to a significant improvement in profitability.

6 Hygiene. Automatic cleaning and sterilisation of equipment offer hygiene assurance, and modern control equipment is itself more compact, and consequently more convenient to clean. For example, Wander Ltd have automated the dispensing of ingredients for their 'Ovaltine' product using GE Fanuc equipment with pneumatic and electrical lines carried in one sheath.

7 Environment. 'Green' concern has been another trend of the 1980s, with attention to the environment extending beyond the workplace. There are a few examples of plants being constructed on green field sites partly to satisfy environmental requirements. A plant to process 10 000 hams/h has been built by Campofrio near Burgos in Spain (opened in 1990), where elimination of harmful effluent has been guaranteed by process automation designed by the French supplier Tecnal, with support to the value of FF45 million under a European community 'Eureka' scheme.

8 Throughput. The uprating of plant throughput is a further possible source of benefit related to the introduction of automation. It is often possible to run a plant above its original production rate by using automatic control to bring the plant slightly closer to the upper limits of speed and capacity. It may also be possible to run the plant for a greater proportion of 'unsocial' hours if the manning levels are reduced by use of automation. Both these possibilities only apply if there is a market for the additional production, in which case the increased capacity may allow the building of additional plant to be postponed. Golden Vale Food Products, Co Cork, re-instrumented the control room of its butter factory with Honeywell LeaderLine electronic controllers, releasing the space formerly occupied by the 6m long control desk installed 15 years previously.

In estimating the value of benefits such as increased yield and throughput, high added value provides the strongest incentive for scientific process control.

ADVANCES IN SENSORS
There are applications in the food industry for almost all the standard techniques for measuring physical quantities in-line. The most common requirements are for measuring temperature, flow and level (or contents), and compact hygienic versions of standard transducers are continually being introduced.

Thermocouples are particularly suitable for in-line temperature measurement, being inherently small, accurate and reliable. VanDeVoort et al (1987) describe a means for using a thermocouple shielded with conducting braid inside a microwave oven. Other means for measuring inside microwave chambers include observing the temperature sensitive fluorescence of phosphors by fibre optic probes.

Techniques for measurement of flow are much more diverse than those for temperature. A wide variety of requirements for flow measurement are encountered in food processing operations. The choice of measuring device depends on the flowrate, viscosity, temperature, conductivity and corrosiveness of the fluid to be measured, and also on the accuracy needed, taking account of the possible presence of entrained air and other factors. Compensation calculations are carried out with dedicated microsystems incorporated by the instrument supplier. Flowmetering using Coriolis force on a vibrating curved pipe is particularly suitable for food industry applications; chocolate manufacturers have been able to use it to make direct measurement of flow rates for the first time.

Level, or contents gauging, is the third of the common measuring requirements in the food industry. Among other methods, ultrasonic depth gauges offer a convenient method for surface position sensing for liquids, particularly in stirred tanks where the surface is disturbed intermittently. The strain gauge pressure transducers used to measure hydrostatic head are available in hygienic mounting suitable for general purpose pressure measurement, for example, in retorts.

Measurements of variables such as viscosity, pH, conductivity, humidity, density and colour are more specialised, and have required the development of transducers specially for food applications. A Schlumberger liquid density transducer, for example, has been fitted with an entrained gas circuit to measure the density of aerated marshmallow at 75 C; it operates at pressures from 1 to 5 bar, and is used to control air injection.

Moisture measurement is one of the main applications for near-infrared (NIR) inspection devices. Infrared instruments, adapted and simplified to measure moisture only, are available from several manufacturers. Scott and Pickles (1991) report the use of on-line NIR reflectance at the new Weetabix Corby no 2 plant to improve product quality and operational efficiency, by applying statistical process control to the sensor data.

A disadvantage of IR moisture measurement is that the radiation only penetrates about 1mm into the material being inspected. For many purposes, and particularly where steep moisture gradients are present immediately after a heat process, it is preferable to select a method which measures total moisture, or at least one which penetrates below the exposed surface. Change of dielectric constant with moisture content provides the principle of most electrical moisture meters. For radio frequency measurements, electrodes may be flat or cylindrical, and fringe-field patterns are used for one-sided access. Microwave moisture meters operate in the frequency range 1-30 GHz. They differ from radio frequency meters chiefly in that the radiation needs a waveguide, strip-line guide, or horn antenna.

Progress with the many potential applications of chemical sensors, in food processing and elsewhere, has been stimulated recent government backed joint ventures. Various field trials have been conducted with immobilised enzyme sensors, and applications are certain to become established with the next few years. Hulley (1988) reviews progress in this field.

Legislation in the USA concerning sulfites in food has created a demand for rapid analysis. Kim et al (1987) describe a technique for combining rapid extraction with ion exclusion chromatography, which was applied successfully to coconut, potato, dried fruit and wine vinegar products. Automatic sampling may soon enable elaborate technology of this type to be incorporated in-line.

BULK PROCESSING
Processing of starch, raw sugar, and oils and fats include methods which have much in common with industrial production of bulk chemicals, and producers have the advantage of large investments made by the chemical industry in process control.

The French government and industry reacted swiftly to the embargo placed on soybean exports by the US authorities at the time of the petroleum crisis in the 1970s. Uzzan (1989) reports that, in a co-ordinated program covering many aspects of edible oil production, the research centre CETIOM created a two stage process for rapeseed dehulling, and the French Petroleum Institute with the research centre ITERG devised a method for lowering the linoleic acid content of rape oil from 10% to a level below the limit of 2% allowed for frying oils in France.

Moran (1991) describes the manufacture of reduced and low fat spreads. If the aqueous phase has sufficient viscosity then water-in-oil emulsions are crystallised in scraped surface heat exchangers as in margarine production. Low viscosity products start as oil-in-water emulsion, part crystallised in a scraped wall exchanger, and then become water-in-oil in stirred jacketed units with high speed rotors. Important parameters include initial oil droplet size, solids level in the fat, and concentration of oil in the emulsion. NIR reflectance spectroscopy is well established for in-line control of oil, protein and moisture in rape oil products (Campbell, 1984). VanDenBergh Foods have commissioned a new computer controlled solvent fractionation plant at Joliet, Illinois. Refrigeration, fractionation, evaporation and tank

farms are all controlled from a single control desk. Solid
fat content is monitored automatically by NMR with robotic
sampling; the instrument measures the liquid phase, and then
the sample is solidified at 0 C for one hour, remeasured, and
then measured again at 30 minute intervals at 10, 20, 25, 30
and 35 C. The new plant incorporates Unilever's worldwide
experience with edible oil processing (Pszczola, 1991).

The scraped surface heat exchanger is one of several types of
equipment for high temperature short time (HTST)
sterilisation. The lethal effect of heat on bacteria is a
logarithmic function of temperature. It has been known since
the 1950s that nutrient degradation is less strongly
temperature dependent than lethality. In a famous study,
Feliciotti and Esselen (1957) published data which is
summarised in figure 1. The figure shows that bacteria may
survive treatment for several minutes at 120 C which would
destroy a proportion of the nutrient, but by contrast a few
seconds at 140 C will destroy the bacteria while leaving the
nutrient almost unaffected. Similar patterns apply for other
quality/lethality situations - a short exposure at high
temperature is generally better than longer times at lower
temperatures for preserving quality during sterilisation.
Equipment suppliers have developed several methods for HTST
treatment. Heppell (1990) compares scraped-surface with
plate and tubular heat exchangers and steam injection, and
with another method, APV ohmic heating, which is outlined in
the next section.

Each dairy that has been built or re-equipped in the 1980s
has been able to take advantage of central computer control
of the various temperature critical operations such as cream
separation, milk standardisation, butter manufacture and
spray drying. All these are carried out, under computer
control, at the Whitland creamery in South Wales, opened by
the Milk Marketing Board in 1986.

New beverage products have stimulated the introduction of
control technology. Brent Walker Breweries worked with
Alfa-Laval to produce low alcohol 'Stud Lite', in which a
strong flavour is preserved by evaporating at low
temperature. Alfa-Laval have also applied advances in
evaporator design to fruit juice concentration; a three
stage, five pass design with thermocompression over the first
two stages, and with second stage condensate taken directly
to a distillation column for aroma preservation, offers both
thermal efficiency and flavour retention. Units are capable
of concentrating cloudy apple juice to 55 Brix operating at
below 50 C.

Enzyme technology has evolved to become an integral part of the food industry. The 1970s brought major breakthroughs in the sweetener and dairy industries due to the design of immobilised enzyme reactors. Wassermann (1990) notes that in high fructose corn syrup (HFCS) and other processes there is a great potential for further improvements which may be enabled by instrumentation and control, for example by 'programming' two or more catalytically distinct enzymes to function simultaneously. IN HFCS manufacture, a streamlined process might entail combining starch saccharification and isomeration so that glucose amylase and glucose isomerase may function simultaneously.

A malting process operated by Munton and Fison for production of 38 different kinds of malt has kilns which have been fitted with automatic control for temperature, flow and proportion of recirculation of air. Additionally, hot water pressure at the inlet to each heat exchanger is controlled to maximise the heat available to the kiln where demand is greatest. The control scheme has improved production efficiency, energy usage and product quality.

Continuous production of beer has been the subject of research for many years. Lommi et al (1990) describe the development at the VTT laboratory, Finland, of a brewing process using an immobilised yeast reactor system (fig 2). A critical stage of the process is the conversion by heat treatment of the diacetyl precursor alpha-acetolactate to diacetyl. The controlled time-temperature conditions for this also serve to pasteurise the feed to the maturation vessels.

There are various processes which benefit from the installation of on-line analysers with automatic sampling lines. Nishinari et al (1989) describe a method for glucose determination during enzymatic hydrolysis of starch in real time by NIR spectroscopy. Absorbance at 2008nm decreases with increasing reaction time, corresponding to the shortening of starch molecular chains by the breaking of alpha-1,4 glucosidic links in dextrins. Comparison with HPLC analysis gave correlation with glucose concentration in the range 1.5 to 5.2% to within 0.1%.

An example of on-line sampling for NIR analysis during flour milling is the NIROS system (Maris, 1990) developed at the Flour Milling and Baking Research Association (FMBRA). The addition of gluten, together with lecithin and soya, has enabled UK millers to increase the proportion of home grown wheat by 40% to about 87% since the mid 1970s. The FMBRA on-line system is used to control the gluten addition at a number of larger mills.

UNIFORM PRODUCTS
There are several classes of foods processed in large
quantity which are not homogeneous, and are consequently not
capable of being blended and standardised in tanks or silos;
for example meat and fish products, bread biscuits and cakes,
and many snack foods. The restriction of not being able to
blend these after processing imposes the need to attempt to
control the process so that each item or particle of product
is always maintained within specification.

One outstanding development of the 1980s has been the
commercialisation of electrical resistance heating (as
applied to metal billets, for example) for heating fluid
foodstuffs. Although the idea was patented in the USA in
1897, and used during the 1930s in the USA for pasteurising
milk, it was the Electricity Council, in work at the
Capenhurst research centre, who demonstrated the possibility
of use for other food applications. APV were licensed in
1984 to use the Electricity Council work, and APV sponsored
work at Cambridge on a static heating cell and a new food
conductivity meter working at 50Hz (Fryer and de Alwis,
1989). The electrode assembly for continuous processing is
shown in figure 3. Food enters the column at 70 C, is raised
to 140 C in about 70 seconds, and cooled to 25 C in 15
minutes in a tube-in-tube water jacketed cooler. The first
commercial installation is at Sous Chef, Deeside, where it is
used for manufacturing the 'Quality Cuisine' range of ready
meals for restaurants.

Extrusion is one of the most versatile operations in food
processing and there are many reported studies of models of
particular applications of the process. Design of controls
for extruders includes the difficulty of making measurements
within the barrel. A strip-line sensor for measuring
moisture by microwave attenuation has been fitted to a pilot
extruder at the Institute of Food Research, Norwich (Chouiki
et al, 1987). Good correlation between attenuation and
moisture content was found for maize grits, but not for maize
flour. The problem in the case of flour appears to be the
distortion of the fringe field by uneven moisture
distribution, which is known to affect various moisture
sensors based on microwave techniques. Moisture control by
feedback control using dead-time compensation is described by
Levine et al (1986), and provides a good illustration of the
stability of this type of feedback control in the presence of
modelling errors. Dead-time compensation has also been
demonstrated in the control of baking ovens, with similar
encouraging conclusions, described in an earlier paper
(McFarlane, 1984). Some of the recent proprietary control
packages now include dead-time compensation as a standard
facility; it is easily within the capacity of any real time
computer to provide such an algorithm.

Several studies of control of mixing and oven control systems for bakeries have been published in the 1980s. Roller and Tscheuschener (1990) review optimisation of dough mixing, and Malkki et al (1984) have summarised the conclusions of four coordinated research projects on the optimisation of the baking process. A consensus is now emerging that energy input is as important a parameter as temperature during mixing, dough piece forming and in continuous ovens. If the oven is modelled as a unit operation, there is a close correspondence between the moisture balance and the heat balance. The main consideration in dynamic control of ovens is adjustment for the change in load during gaps in production.

PORTIONED PRODUCTS
For whole meat and fish products, fruits, vegetables and nuts, and for some prepared meals, the main requirements for sensing and control are to keep the structure and flavour of the items as nearly as possible in 'fresh' condition. Coupled with this is the requirement for conformance with weights and measures and with health and safety regulations, mainly met by use of checkweighers and metal detectors. Technical progress has been made during the 1980s in all these areas.

Modified atmosphere packaging is now in widespread use for meat, fish, fresh pasta and some cheese and bakery goods. St Ivel cheeses, for example, are packed at Westbury, Wiltshire, using Rose Forgrove flowpack machines designed to cope with the irregular wedge shaped pieces. Each pack is flushed with inert gas, giving residual oxygen content of less than 1% and this approximately doubles the shelf life. Gas consumption is continuously monitored. Inert gas packaging requires a relatively impermeable pack. In contrast, the living tissue of respiring fresh fruits and vegetables consumes oxygen and produces carbon dioxide and water vapour. Optimum storage depends on use of a suitably permeable film with appropriate ratio of product weight to film area. A joint program of work by the Institute of Food Research, Norwich and the Institute of Horticultural Research, East Malling, has resulted in recommendations for apple packaging which enables packs to stabilise at 5 to 6% carbon dioxide and 5 to 10% oxygen, at which apples remain firm and crisp and retain flavour.

There is very widespread current interest in Hazard Analysis and Critical Control Point (HACCP) systems, particularly in relation to meat and poultry inspection. This form of control calls for more rapid analytical and microbiological tests, which at present are laboratory based. The progress referred to above in robotic sampling for automatic analysis of bulk fluids is likely to lead to the development of automation of analytical tests on meat and poultry.

The introduction in the UK of EC 'average weight' regulations for food packaging stimulated the introduction of a range of microprocessor-equipped in-line checkweighers. Most suppliers now provide printed and/or transmitted statistical summaries of pack weights in addition to the basic function of rejecting underweight items. Checkweigher technology has also incorporated sensitive low-drift weigh cells; it is this technical feature which has enabled the introduction of the elegant Ishida equipment for combining loads held momentarily in intermediate weigh pans, to dispense optimum pack contents in high speed bag or box filling operations.

Metal detectors are comparable in design and complexity to checkweighers, and it is often convenient to install metal detectors close to checkweighers, as a position in the production process where it is possible to pass all product through a small aperture. Manufacturers would welcome the availability of X-ray or other means for non-metallic foreign body detectors in similar physical format to checkweighers and metal detectors, but the means to achieve such detection remains elusive.

INTEGRATED CONTROL

Equipment suppliers provide built-in sensors and controls with most individual units of food processing equipment. The facilities frequently include options for data communication with the users' own information systems. This still leaves food manufacturers with the difficult task of making their own arrangements to combine production information from numerous different sources, to present it to process operators and to use it in production reports. In many food factories data collection and recording is done by manual form-filling, while others have invested in management information systems only to find that when new equipment is installed the associated on-line data cannot easily be incorporated.

One way to avoid this unsatisfactory situation is to insist that all new equipment be interfaced to a proprietary electrical system, such as that offered by Allen-Bradley, Gould-Modicon or Texas Instruments. As well as being costly, this policy has the disadvantage of weakening the reliability of the data paths which pass through a series of interfaces. Equipment suppliers recognise that rapid technological change is taking place and most now offer embedded intelligence in new subsystems to permit re-configuration. Another development which will be of great benefit to users is the imminent adoption of a 'fieldbus' standard for inter-communication between sensors and process control equipment. Standards already exist for computer networks, but the 'fieldbus' will have specific features to ensure reliability, integrity and fail-safe modes for equipment being used to control automatic plant.

CONCLUSION

Automation is well established in dairies, wet corn milling and processing of edible oils and fats. Investment in automation of other forms of food manufacture is gradually increasing, assisted by improvements in the availability and reliability of suitable in-line sensors. The rate at which processes can be automated is limited by the applications work necessary to introduce control schemes for all the great diversity of food processing operations.

ILLUSTRATIONS
fig 1 - lethality diagram
fig 2 - continuous brewing diagram
fig 3 - APV ohmic heater

REFERENCES
Campbell SJ (1984) 'Quality control in a Canola crushing plant' JAOCS 61(6)1097-1101

Chouiki S Ferdinand JM Smith AC Kent M (1987) 'Microwave sensor for moisture measurement in an extruder' J Fd Eng 6, 113-121

Fearn T, P Maris P (1991) 'An application of Box-Jenkins methodology in control of gluten addition in flour mills' J App Stats 40(3), 477-484

Fryer P deAlwis A (1989) 'APV ohmic heating process' Chem & Ind (19)630-34

Heppell N (1990) 'Comparison of different UHT processing equipment' Euro Fd & Drk Rev (1)12-14

Hulley B (1988) 'Chemical sensors - an overview' Meas & Control 21, 44-47

Kim H-J Park G Y Kim Y-K (1987) 'Analysis of sulfites by ion exclusion chromatography' Fd Tech 41(1)85-91

Levine L Symes S Weimer J (1986) 'Automatic control of moisture in food extruders' J Fd Eng 8, 97-115

Lommi H Gronqvist A Pajunen E (1990) 'Immobilised yeast beer reactor' Fd Tech 44(7)128-33

McFarlane I (1983) 'Automatic control of food manufacturing processes' Elsevier Applied Science

McFarlane I (1984) 'Dead-time controller applied to interacting feedback loops on a baking oven' Trans Inst Meas & Control 6(1)46-52

Malkki Y Seibel W Skjoldebrand C Rask O (1984) 'Optimisation of the baking process' in 'Thermal processing and quality of foods' Elsevier, London

Maris P (1990) 'On-line control of flour protein content' Proc ACoFoP II, paper 1.7

Moran (1991) 'Developments in yellow fat spreads' Chem & Ind (11)379-83

Nishinari K Cho RK Iwamoto M (1989) 'NIR monitoring of starch hydrolysis' Starke 41(3)110-112

Pszczola DE (1991) 'New plant for vegetable oil based ingredients' Fd Tech 45(1)136-8

Roller T Tscheuschner H-D (1990) 'Control and optimisation of dough mixing process' Proc ACoFoP II, paper 2.8

Scott M Pickles J (1991) 'Continuous measurement of moisture' Fd Mfr 66(2) 45-6

Uzzan A (1989) 'French oils and fats industry' Chem & Ind (19)623-29

Van de Voort FR Laureano M Smith JP (1987) 'Temperature measurement in microwave ovens' J Can IFST 4, 279-84

Wasserman BP (1990) 'Enzyme technology progress and prospects' Fd Tech 44(4)118-22

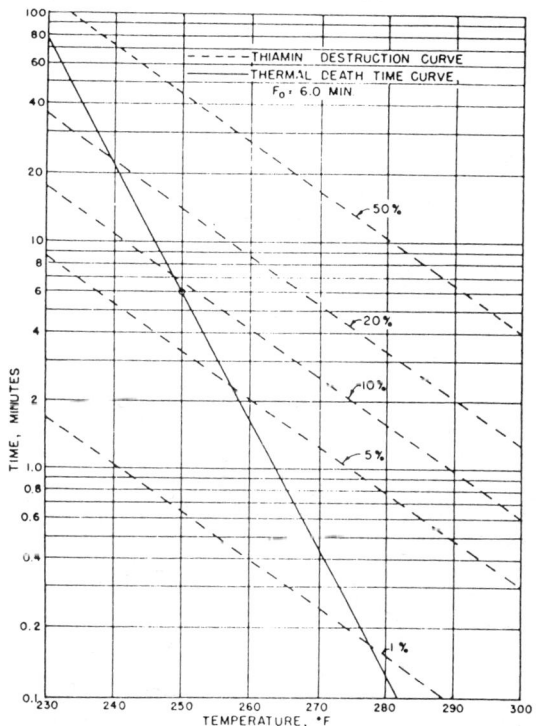

Fig 1 - THERMAL DESTRUCTION OF NUTRIENT AND BACTERIA
(after Feliciotti and Esselen, 1957)

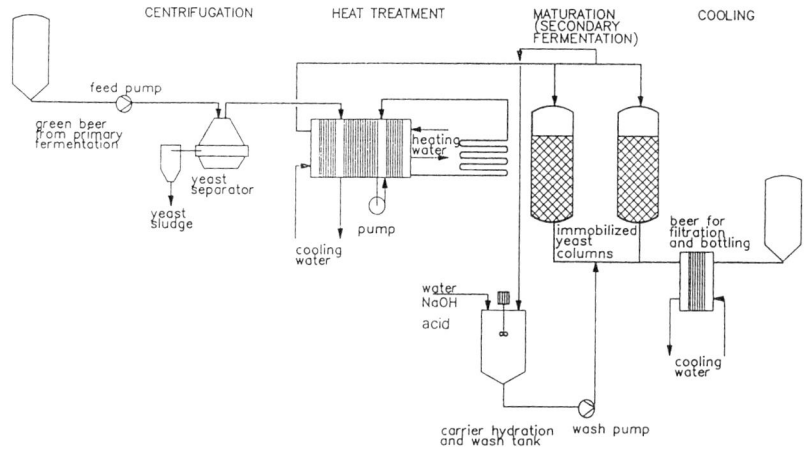

Fig 2 - CONTINUOUS BREWING (from Lommi et al, 1990)

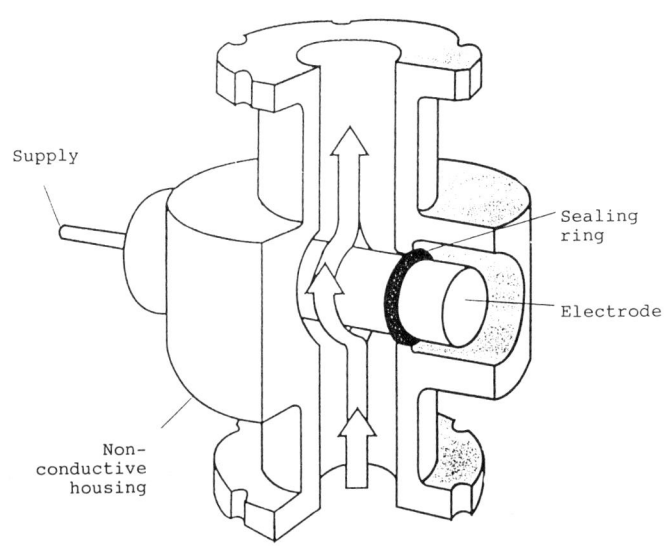

Fig 3 - OHMIC HEATER

DEVELOPING AN ON-LINE, COMPUTERISED SPC SYSTEM TO CONTROL PRODUCT QUALITY IN

A BREAKFAST CEREAL PROCESS.

J. Pickles *

Three on-line moisture analysers and an automatic bulk
density sampler were integrated with a personal computer
to monitor product quality in a flaked cereal process.
A SCADA package was configured to display the information,
plot control charts and alarm when the process runs out of
control. The benefits and difficulties incurred in
developing the system are reviewed.

Keywords: SPC, SQC, Moisture Analysers, SCADA,
On-line Samplers, Calibration.

Introduction

A new semi-continuous breakfast cereal process was installed and
commissioned to produce three different varieties of flaked products. The
major unit operations are shown in the simplified process flowsheet of
figure 1. The sequencing of the batch unit operations are controlled
automatically by local PLC's and many of the continuous process conditions
(eg. drying and toasting temperatures) are automatically controlled to predetermined set points by local closed loop (PID) controllers. However, akin
to many other food processes (1), it was not possible to install an overall
system to automatically control product quality.

Long and variable process residence times (8 - 21 hours) made it essential
to establish an effective, early warning product quality control system.
To this end, samples of product were routinely collected as frequently as
was practical and from every convenient sampling point throughout the
process. The quality of each sample was tested off-line for up to five
quantifiable characteristics. This data, gathered over several months of
production, was used to characterise the performance of the process.
Furthermore, from a statistical analysis of the data, five characteristics
were identified as being key to controlling finished product quality and
therefore warranted routine measurement (identified in figure 1).

Preliminary statistical process control (SPC) limits were calculated for
two of the key quality characteristics (granule weight and bulk density).
The process operators were trained to plot their measurements on ready
printed Individuals and Moving Range charts and they were instructed to take
control action only if points fell outside the control limits or if there
was a run of seven points all above/below target.

* Weetabix Ltd., Burton Latimer, Northants.

This limited use of SPC charts proved to be effective and well within the operators capability. The quantity of product scrapped because the bulk density fell out of specification was virtually eliminated and the regularly recalculated control limits narrowed to the point at which they appeared to reflect only inherent noise. However, the move to adopt control charts for the other three key quality characteristics was hindered by the intensive, manual effort required. Indeed, this has been seen as one of the major obstacles to the progress of SPC company wide. To mitigate this deterrent, significant progress has been made to date in automating and extending this SPC system. This paper reviews these latter developments.

System Hardware

An overview of the hardware configuration is given in figure 1. The first item to be installed was a robot which automatically samples and weighs a fixed volume of flake at regular intervals. A small PLC controls the measuring cycle and a micro processor calculates the bulk density of the flake. Several mechanical modifications to the unit were required after installation to improve its robustness and to contain the overflow and spillage of product generated during operation. This unit is expected to replace the off-line, manual bulk density measurements.

An on-line moisture monitoring system (System 55*) was installed to replace off-line moisture measurements. The system consists of three near infrared reflectance sensing heads that are wired to a dust tight, central display cabinet which houses the electronic control units for the moisture gauges, a 286PC with a 40MB hard disk and a VDU. The cabinet was sited local to the finished flake inspection belt where production staff regularly assess the sensory quality characteristics of the product (i.e. appearance and taste).

User access to the system is through a standard QUERTY keyboard which is attached to the display cabinet and covered with a flexible membrane to prevent the ingress of dust. Off-line bulk density measurements were manually keyed into the system before the on-line sampler was integrated. Although off-line granule weight measurements are currently keyed into the system, there is a plan to integrate an electronic weighing balance in the near future to assist with this.

It was found that the 640KB RAM capacity of the 286 PC was not sufficient to accommodate the full software configuration requirements. Consequently, the PC was upgraded to a 386 processor with 2 MB of extended RAM.

Sensor Calibration

A constant off-set was programmed into the automatic sampler's calculation of bulk density to bring the displayed value into line with off-line measurements. This discrepancy was attributed to the differences between the sampling techniques and sample container geometries. Correcting the sampler's display was favoured because all product bulk density measurements and specification limits company wide are based on the off-line technique and this remains the back-up method in the event of sampler and/or system failure.

* From Infrared Engineering Ltd., Maldon, Essex.

The finished flake infrared moisture gauge was calibrated on-line by varying the toaster temperature set points to induce changes in flake moisture content. Samples of flake were collected after each set point change, analysed off-line using the standard laboratory oven drying method, and the results compared with the recorded gauge display readings to calculate the required calibration settings. The results indicate an accuracy of ± 0.16% (absolute moisture content on a wet basis) with respect to the lab. reference test.

To date, the calibration of the other two upstream moisture gauges is still in progress. When completed, these gauges are expected to replace off-line measurements which use infrared drying balances.

<u>System Software</u>

The System 55 was supplied with a configurable SCADA package (Paragon 500*) which has an optional SPC module. The system supplier had utilised Paragon's driver development kit to construct an RS485 driver to communicate with their infrared moisture meters.

The automatic bulk density sampler was initially supplied with a serial communications protocol that was not compatible with any of the drivers supported by Paragon. It was considered more cost effective to contract the supplier to modify the sampler's software to adopt one of the more common protocols supported by Paragon.

<u>Graphical Display Configuration</u>

With very little training (1 day) it was possible to use Paragon's mouse driven, icon based display builder to construct demonstration display page formats. These were approved by the Plant Shift Superintendent before the System 55 was fully configured and commissioned. Further configuration modifications have been made to improve the display formats but these could not be done in runtime mode.

For easy overview, a "main display page" was configured containing real time bar graphs and digital displays of the present values of all five monitored parameters. Data entry boxes were also configured on this display page to facilitate keyboard entry of off-line bulk density and granule weight measurements. Separate minute counters are also displayed for each off-line measurement to indicate the time elapsed since the last entry. These counters automatically reset to zero when new results are entered and change colour when they exceed a preset time to indicate that a measurement is overdue. Digital switching facilities were also configured on the main page to allow the user to activate/inactivate the monitoring of data from any of the on-line moisture analysers. This feature is used during start-up/shut-down when material may not be present at these locations in the process.

Access to historical data through the standard Paragon SPC charts in runtime was found to be too slow. Paragon treats these charts as historical files and stores the information on the hard disk in batches of about four data values at a time. Only information written to disk may be viewed. There can be a significant delay therefore before the most recent batch of four data values can be viewed. To resolve this problem, a trend graph display page was configured for each parameter. Using standard function keys the

* From Intec Controls Ltd., Chichester.

user can scroll between three preset time periods for the trend (i.e. last 30 mins., 4 or 8 hours). The SPC charts are accessed to view older data. Pick fields were configured on each display page to allow the user to rapidly switch to different pages.

An alarm page was also configured to clearly identify all pending alarms. This page is automatically triggered if any new alarm occurs.

SPC Configuration

Paragon's standard SPC module supports the classical $\overline{X}$ and R charts. However, Individuals and Moving Range charts are considered more appropriate for the Process Industry (2) and the paper versions of these charts were successfully established before the System 55 was installed. For continuity, it was considered important to retain these types of charts. To resolve this problem, a Paragon data manipulation strategy was developed and configured to plot Individuals and Moving Range points on the standard $\overline{X}$ and R charts. The mathematical basis for this transformation and a brief description of the differences between $\overline{X}$ and R charts and Individuals and Moving Range charts are given in the appendix.

Paragon offers a control limit recalculation facility which is based on the following standard formulae:

$$\text{Control Limits for } \overline{X} = \overline{\overline{X}} \pm A.\overline{R} \qquad (1)$$

$$\text{Upper Control Limit for } R = D.\overline{R} \qquad (2) \; (LCL = 0 \text{ for } n \leqslant 6).$$

It has been calculated that if the above equations are applied, as they stand, to the transformation given in the appendix, then they substantially under-estimate the span between the control limits by 62% and 21% for the Individuals and Moving Range control charts respectively. This presents the serious problem of unjustified control action being taken. To resolve this the historical SPC files are copied onto floppy disk and transferred to an office PC for analysis. A standard Paragon programme file allows the data to be converted into spreadsheet format. In this way, the control limits are regularly reassessed. The new control limits are then programmed as fixed values into the Paragon SPC modules such that the correct limits are displayed on the Individuals control chart.

Data Entry Validation

For the off-line bulk density measurements each point on the Individuals control chart is in fact an average of four replicated measurements. Replication was necessary to reduce the variation attributed to the test method and therefore make the chart more sensitive to underlying process changes. From past data an acceptable threshold value was calculated for the range between a set of four replicates (effectively an upper control limit using equation 2). Ranges greater than this threshold are attributed to human or test equipment error (eg. keyboard entry mistake or the balance not correctly tared etc.) effecting at least one of the four replicated measurements. In these cases, the operators are instructed to reject the results and repeat the measurements.

To configure Paragon to automate this data entry validation procedure required a fairly complex control strategy. Colour changes are automatically triggered on the main display as each new replicate result is entered. An alarm message is automatically displayed if the range between

148

the four replicates exceeds the preset threshold. Otherwise, the average is automatically calculated and used to update the various bulk density displays and control charts.

SPC Alarm Configuration

Paragon recognises 10 different "out of control" conditions. These trigger a pooled digital alarm. The user must be familiar with these conditions and must interrogate the control chart to determine which condition(s) triggered the alarm. However, when the paper control charts were first established, it was found that adopting only a few standard conditions was sufficient to maintain adequate control, namely points outside control limits and, for the Individuals chart only, a run of seven consecutive points falling either all above or all below the target line. The operators were familiar and understood the significance of these rules and, for continuity, it was considered important to automate only these rules.

To resolve this problem, separate alarm strategies were configured for each individual "out of control" condition and these were replicated for each key product quality parameter. In addition, automatic "out of specification" alarm strategies were also configured for the two finished flake quality parameters (bulk density and moisture content). These alarm features added significantly to the complexity of the overall control strategy and necessitated upgrading the memory capacity of the PC.

User Reaction

The familiarity of the process operators with off-line measurements and paper control charts greatly facilitated the introduction of this automation. Retraining requirements were minimal (a few hours for each shift) and there appeared to be a positive attitude towards the reduction in manual effort required to sample, test and chart off-line measurements.

Conclusion

This project has demonstrated that it is feasible to automate an SPC/SQC system through the use of on-line sensing and computer technology for a relatively modest capital outlay. This has benefited Weetabix by considerably reducing the manual effort involved in SPC and facilitated the extension of SPC to control additional product quality characteristics.

While it is encouraging to find SCADA packages supporting SPC, the software writers are urged to recognise that the classical $\bar{X}$ and R charts are less appropriate for food processes than other types of charts (eg moving averages/ranges and CUSUM etc). Also SPC should be treated as a real-time control tool and not just for historical data analysis.

In-house familiarity and experience in configuring the SCADA package has also been beneficial. It has improved awareness of the package's capability, facilitated trouble shooting, enabled rapid improvements to be made to the system and provided a benchmark with which to compare other SCADA packages.

The memory limitation of PC's should not be underestimated.

Acknowledgements

1. L. Hindle of Infrared Engeering Ltd. for configuring a large part of
   the System 55's control strategy and display formats and for providing
   valuable commissioning assistance.

2. P. Gomes of Intec Controls Corporation for devising and configuring the
   Paragon control strategy to plot Individual and Moving Range points on
   the standard $\bar{X}$ and R charts.

3. M. Groves of Intec Controls Ltd. for configuring the Paragon alarm
   strategy for the run of seven above/below target alarm.

4. T. Leschallas of Eltek Systems Ltd. for co-ordinating the upgrading of
   the PC and integrating it with the automatic bulk density sampler.

5. Silsoe Research Institute of the Agriculture and Food Research
   Council for designing and modifying the automatic bulk density sampler
   and assisting in integrating it with the System 55.

References

1. Flintham, T, 1989, Technical Audits and Data Analysis Training Course
   T076, Leatherhead Food Research Association.

2. Caulcutt, R, 1990, I. Chem. E. Symposium Papers No. 6, Use of SPC in
   the Process Industries.

Nomenclature

A,D	= constants from statistical tables which depend only on sample size.
ECU	= Electronic Control Unit.
KB	= Kilo-Byte.
LCL	= Lower Control Limit.
MB	= Mega-Byte.
PC	= Personal Computer.
PID	= Proportional, Integral and Derivative.
PLC	= Programmable Logic Controller.
RAM	= Random Access Memory.
R	= Range.
$\bar{R}$	= Mean range.
SCADA	= Supervisory Control and Data Acquisition.
SPC/SQC	= Statistical Process/Quality Control.
UCL	= Upper Control Limit.
VDU	= Visual Display Unit.
$\bar{X}$	= Mean Value
$\bar{\bar{X}}$	= Overall Mean Value.

FIGURE 1

PROCESS FLOWSHEET

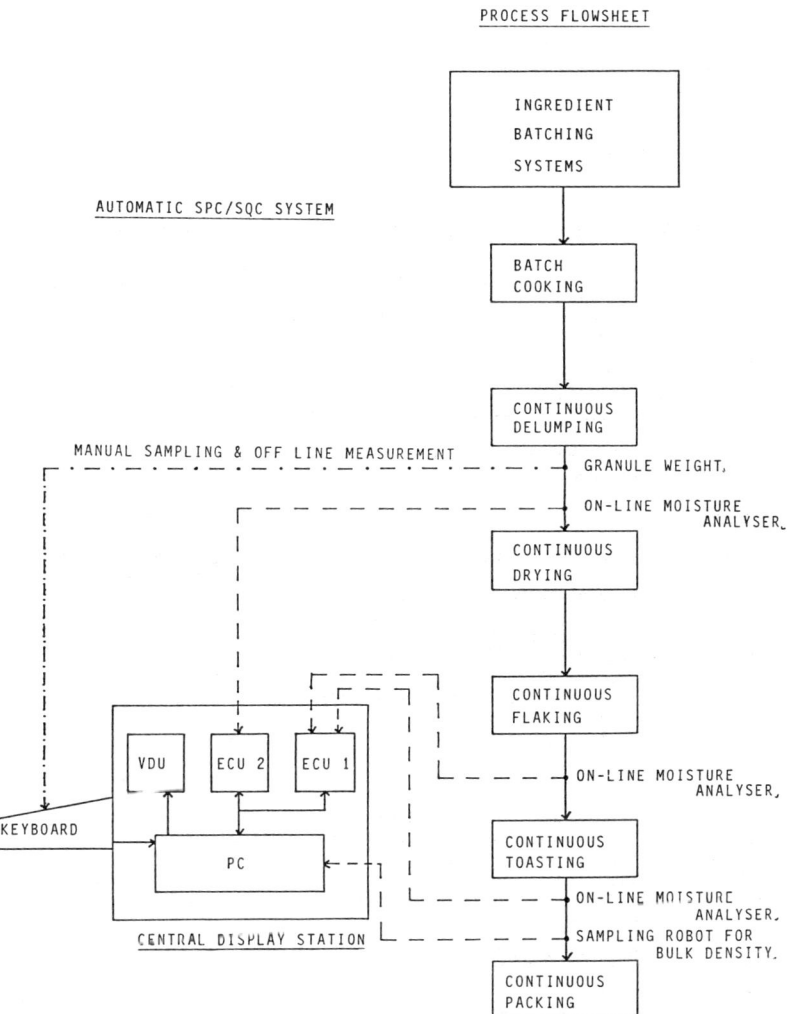

Appendix

Control Chart Description and Conversion

Classical $\overline{X}$ and R Charts

These charts are useful for monitoring the quality of discrete objects. A group (size n) of these objects is sampled and the quality of each object is measured. By denoting the value of the i'th measurement as X_i then the sample produces a set of n measurements: X_1, X_2,.......X_i...X_n. The group average ($\overline{X}$) and range (R) are then calculated as follows:

$$\overline{X} = \frac{1}{n} \sum_{i=1}^{n} X_i$$

R = Largest X_i - Smallest X_i for all i.

After a suitable time interval (say t minutes) another group of objects is sampled and measured and the new group average ($\overline{X}$) and range (R) is calculated. Traditionally the $\overline{X}$'s and R's are plotted chronologically on separate graphs that are drawn on the same page, one above the other.

Individuals and Moving Range Charts

By contrast, these charts are useful in monitoring quality if only one measurement can be made at each time interval. The individual measurement is plotted on one graph (i.e. instead of $\overline{X}$) and the moving range is plotted on the other graph (i.e. instead of R). The moving range is defined as the positive difference between consecutive individual measurements.

If the measurements are made at regular time intervals (t minutes apart) then these measurements can be denoted as : X_o, X_t, X_{2t}, X_{3t}, etc. The first moving range is calculated after the first time interval as follows:

$$\text{Moving Range} = \begin{cases} 0 & \text{if } X_t = X_o \\ X_t - X_o & \text{if } X_t > X_o \\ X_o - X_t & \text{if } X_t < X_o \end{cases}$$

Conversion

In this paper individuals and moving range charts are required but the standard SPC module used by the selected SCADA package only calculates and plots classical $\overline{X}$ and R charts. A mathematical transformation scheme was therefore developed such that the standard SPC module could be used to plot individual and moving ranges on the $\overline{X}$ and R charts.

Individual measurements are made at regular time intervals (t minutes apart). The values of the measurements are denoted as : X_o, X_t, X_{2t} ... etc. After the first time interval a group of three values are calculated as follows:

$$X_A = X_t + \tfrac{1}{2}(X_t - X_o)$$
$$X_B = X_t - \tfrac{1}{2}(X_t - X_o)$$
$$X_C = X_t$$

These three values are then used to represent a group of measurements that are fed into the SPC module which calculates the group average ($\overline{X}$) and range (R). The transformation formulae defined above is such that the group average equals the individual measurement (X_t) because the terms involving X_0 cancel :

viz. $\overline{X} = \dfrac{X_A + X_B + X_C}{3} = \dfrac{[X_t + \frac{1}{2}(X_t - X_0)] + [X_t - \frac{1}{2}(X_t - X_0)] + X_t}{3} = X_t$

Similarly the transformations also mean that the group range equals the moving range of the individual measurements. This can be demonstrated by considering the three possibilities:

1. $X_t = X_0$ i.e. moving range = 0

In this case, the three transformations become :

$X_A = X_t$
$X_B = X_t$
$X_C = X_t$

The range (R) of this group therefore equals zero which is the same as the moving range.

2. $X_t > X_0$ i.e. moving range = $X_t - X_0$

In this case, by inspecting the transformation formulae, the following condition must hold : $X_A > X_C > X_B$. The group range is then calculated as follows:

   R = Largest (X_A) - Smallest (X_B)

i.e. $R = [X_t + \frac{1}{2}(X_t - X_0)] - [X_t - \frac{1}{2}(X_t - X_0)] = X_t - X_0$

which is the same as the moving range.

3. $X_t < X_0$ i.e. moving range = $X_0 - X_t$

Considering the transformation then, by inspection, the following condition must hold: $X_B > X_C > X_A$

then : $R = X_B - X_A = X_0 - X_t$ which is the same as the moving range.

Thus, by making a similar transformation after each new individual measurement, the SPC module plots the individuals and moving ranges on the $\overline{X}$ and R charts.

IMAGE CAPTURE AND ANALYSIS TECHNIQUES
FOR ON-LINE QUALITY MONITORING

J.V. Stafford and B. Ambler*

Automatic visual inspection of dry particulate food materials may be carried out on-line using CCD video cameras for image capture and suitable image analysis software algorithms to provide statistical information or 100% inspection of the product. This paper describes some of the problems and possible solutions in capturing images and developing suitable algorithms for analysis so that characteristics such as object size and shape may be determined and defects detected.

1.   Introduction

Optical inspection in the visible spectrum of dry particulate materials on food processing lines is desirable or essential for quality control, foreign body detection and to monitor process performance. Manual inspection has the shortcomings of subjectivity, variable performance and high labour cost. 100% inspection is not possible for high throughput, low value materials. Computer vision techniques are increasingly being used in the process industries to automate inspection at all stages along the process line. Computer vision involves the capturing of images of the material by suitable sensors such as CCD video cameras and the analysis of images by software algorithms. The technique is more easily applied to the well specified and repeatable shapes on mass production lines in the engineering industry and to larger well-defined objects in the food industry, such as cakes, packets or bottles. However, the technique is being increasingly developed to characterise and identify biological objects and is finding application in areas such as fruit and vegetable grading lines (Marchant et al, 1989), animal identification (Schofield 1990) and soil structure (Stafford and Ambler, 1990). Like biological objects, dry particulate materials in the food industry are not clearly defined in terms of shape, size or surface topography but fall into more general classes which may be identified by the human eye but which are much more difficult to interpret by computer vision.

Although image analysis systems are available for use under quality control laboratory conditions on material samples, there are a number of problems in applying image

---

* Sensor Systems Group, Silsoe Research Institute, Wrest Park, Silsoe, Beds, MK45 4HS

capture and analysis as an on-line technique. This paper describes some of the problems in capturing images from a moving stream of material and developments of software algorithms to analyse dry particulates for size, shape and the presence of defects.

2. The image capture problem

In order to analyse an image to identify required characteristics of the particulate material, it is necessary to capture the image. This may readily be done by using a CCD (charge coupled device) video camera optimized in the visible spectrum as an imaging sensor. In order to ease the task of analysing images by software algorithms, it is desirable to enhance the image viewed by the camera. For imaging on-line, account must be taken of illumination conditions, the background to the particulate material and the fact that the material is moving at speeds of up to several metres per second. The motion of the material means that images must be "frozen" for successful analysis. We have successfully achieved this by employing what may be described as an "electronic shutter". Essentially the image is gated out of the CCD array over a set time period equivalent to a 'shutter speed' of typically $1/1000$ s.

To obtain a useful image, the material must contrast with its background. With material conveyed on a belt this can be achieved by a suitable choice of belt colour, although in a processing plant, we have observed that discoloration of the belt can give rise to problems in analysing the image. Where particulate material is conveyed by gravity or pneumatically, we have obtained sufficient contrast by front illumination of the particulates. In both types of systems, material is frequently conveyed at a high mass flow rate so that the camera views the top layer only of a multi-layer stream. The image analysis task is considerably reduced if the camera views a mono-layer only. Speeding up of the conveyor belt in the imaging area and other techniques may be used to achieve this state. Alternatively, for statistical analysis, a sub-sample of the main stream may be channelled through the imaging area in such a way that a mono-layer only is presented to the camera. The analysis task is then reduced to discriminating between touching and overlapping objects.

3. The development of image analysis algorithms

3.1 Analysis equipment

One set of equipment was based on an MC 68000 VME development system and an Imaging Technology framestore and colour monitor. Software for this system was programmed in Forth. The second system was based on a 386 PC with co-processor and a Data Translation framestore. This system was programmed in C. The video signal from the CCD camera was digitized into 512 x 512 pixel images with a pixel grey level resolution of 8 bits.

3.2 Thresholding and contrast enhancement

The image data was binarised into two grey levels to separate objects (the particulate material) from background according to a manually or automatically selected threshold. This was achieved by feeding the image data through an input look-up table (LUT) that converted the data to background or object according to the threshold level programmed into the LUT. To compensate for changes in ambient light that affect the choice of threshold level, the contrast of the stored image data was enhanced so that the image contrast was spread over the full 8 bit resolution (256 grey levels) available prior to binarisation. Contrast enhancement was achieved automatically by using the lowest (I_l) and highest (I_h) grey level intensities in the image to modify each pixel intensity (P_m) according to

$$P_m = 256 \frac{(P_0 - I_l)}{(I_h - I_l)}$$

where P_0 is the original pixel intensity.

3.3   Discrimination and edge detection

In order to extract object size and shape information from an image, the object has to be identified. An object in a binary image can be completely described by its boundary. Identification of objects in an image captured from a process line is confounded by the fact that adjacent objects touch and/or overlap. Thus, the discrimination of individual objects was undertaken in two stages. Firstly, all boundaries ("internal" and "external") of each object cluster in the image were defined. Criteria were then applied to each cluster of objects to discriminate single objects within each cluster.

An object boundary may be described by a series of vectors; a technique that is known as chain coding. The technique has been described by Freeman (1974). From a given starting point on the object boundary, the direction to the next boundary pixel is represented as a vector code which may, for instance, be an 8-way code (analogous to an 8-point compass). The chain code is progressed around the boundary of the object until it returns to the start coordinate, storing direction vectors as it moves from boundary pixel to boundary pixel. The Freeman chain code was implemented for the images captured on the process line by scanning the binarised image data from left to right starting at the bottom line until a background-to-object transition was detected. Clusters of objects were thus progressively identified and defined by a chain code.

A modified chain coding technique was devised to improve the accuracy for calculation of object area. The chain code as described above assumes that the edge of the object is at the centre of the boundary pixels. More accurately, the edge of the object is the mid-point between adjacent boundary and background pixels. The modified technique used a 2x2 pixel mask to produce a chain code to define the outer edge of the object. As before, the lowest pixel of an object was found by scanning from left to right starting at the bottom line. The pixel to the left of the start pixel, together with the two immediately below, formed the mask that was progressively moved round the outer edge of the object. The direction that the mask was moved and the vector code recorded depended on which of the pixels in the mask were at object level and which at background level.

Chain coding identified and defined separated object clusters. Within each cluster, the individual particulates are touching and overlapping one another. A procedure was devised to identify individual objects. The objects were generally of circular form and so the criterion used for separating objects was the "gradient" of the edge code. The gradient was determined by differencing adjacent code vectors. The resulting series of codes were called the curvature code. The curvature code for approximately circular objects is either positive or zero. Where, however, two objects are touching (Fig. 1a), the curvature code is negative. Thus, the sign of the code was used to identify where two particulates touched or overlapped. Because minor distortions around the edge of an approximately circular object may result in a negative curvature code, the code was compared at each point with the average of the previous six codes and had to be more negative than a set value to be indicative of an intersect point (indicated in Fig. 1b by dots). In the simple case of two touching particles, a line can be drawn through the two detected intersect points to separate the particles. However, for the more general case, constraints had to be imposed to ensure that cuts were made between "opposing" intersect points. The two constraints applied were (1) the cutting line must not be longer than a given fraction of the diameter of an average sized object, and (2) the curvature codes at the intersect points must be approximately opposing. The resulting 'separated' objects are shown in Figs. 1c and 1d.

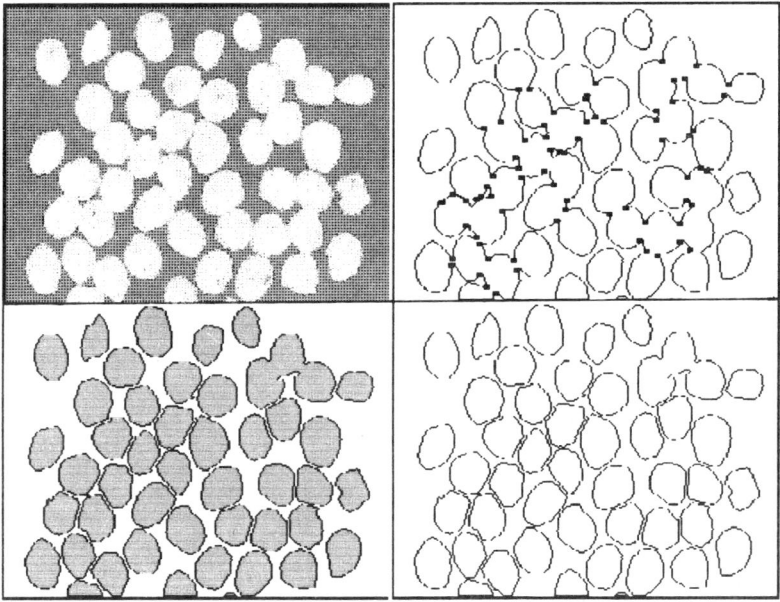

Figure 1. Stages in discriminating touching and overlapping objects
a. original image, b. object intersect points,
c. separated objects, d. outlines of separated objects

With a cluster of touching particulates, there are often background pixels inside the cluster. To identify matching intersect points, it was necessary to know whether the point lay on an outer or an inner boundary of the cluster. This was easily determined when establishing the chain code as the pixel below the start pixel was "background" when the boundary was an outer one and "object" if it was an inner one.

For complex clusters, a single pass of the image data through the algorithms was insufficient to separate all touching and overlapping particulates. In practice, it was found that three passes through the algorithms were necessary with the constraints being made tighter at the second and third pass. The constraints that had to be used are described in Section 4.2.

3.4 Characteristics in 3 dimensions

For some applications, such as the extruded material shown in Fig. 2a, it is necessary not only to have information on the "top" surface area and shape but also on the thickness of the particulate. Methods were devised to extract this 3-D information from 2-D images. The procedure used was to enhance the contrast difference between the edges and the top surface of the particulates and then use a double thresholding technique in the image analysis procedure to discriminate thickness from top surface characteristics.

Images were captured by angling the video camera to the perpendicular to the scene with the objects on a black non-reflecting surface illuminated from directly overhead. As shown in Fig. 2a, this resulted in contrasting the edges from the tops of the objects, although the difference was more subtle than that between object and background.

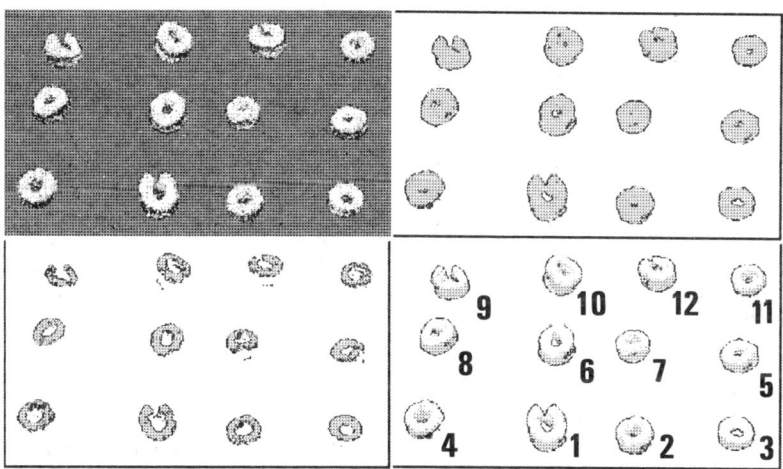

Figure 2.   Stages in analysis of 3D objects
a. original image, b. whole objects extracted,
c. top surfaces extracted, d. reconstituted objects

Contrast enhancement of the image allowed two fixed threshold levels to be determined to produce two binary images, the whole of the object (Fig. 2b) and the top surface (Fig. 2c). Subtracting the top surface from the object image resulted in a thickness image (Fig. 2d). Analysis of shape, area and thickness could then be applied to individual objects.

Object thickness could only be determined on the imaged side of the objects. However, an indication of uniformity of thickness could be determined by capturing and analysing a series of images with the camera at different orientations to the scene perpendicular.

3.5 Surface topography

The surface topography of larger objects such as cakes or biscuits (or smaller particulates using microscope objectives on the video camera) can be characterised using image analysis.

Although it may not be possible to define the required surface topography, such a characterisation may be useful as a "black box sensor" in relating, for example, sensory perception to process variables. A method of characterising surface topography by image analysis has been described by Stafford and Ambler (1990) in relation to the surface condition of agricultural seedbeds. Their analysis could equally be applied to some materials in the food processing industry.

The essence of the analysis was to use a line scanning technique to obtain transects of grey level variation at equally spaced intervals across the surface. These transects were then analysed to dimension surface features and output size distribution and statistics. In the case of the seedbeds, the surface features were aggregates in the surface. Full details of the analysis procedure are given in the paper.

4. Applications and results

4.1 Flake thickness

The first application was the requirement to control the thickness of flaked corn on-line. The flakes are produced by a flaking roller where the pressure and roller gap could be varied to affect flake thickness. Thickness can be determined off-line in a quality control lab but image analysis held the promise of monitoring thickness on-line. It was believed that thickness was related to flake surface area as the corn nibs or extruded corn pellets used as input to the flaking roll were of reasonably consistent volume.

Flakes were sampled under varying flaking roll conditions and each sample was then subjected to both image capture (static) analysis and to conventional thickness measurement in the quality control lab. The modified chain coding algorithms described in Section 3.3 were applied to the images. Flake areas were determined and an equivalent mean diameter calculated. Mean diameter is plotted against flake thickness in Fig. 3 which shows a reasonable correlation between the two parameters and hence supports the potential of image analysis for on-line monitoring of thickness.

4.2   Touching and overlapping objects

In order to illustrate the separation algorithms described in Section 3.3, extruded sliced rice material of generally circular form was used.   Before analysis, the system was calibrated using a 50 x 50 mm white card and a typical sample was selected and processed to give a sample diameter for the separation algorithm.   The image was first binarised and then objects were chain coded and the intersect points were identified. The constraints referred to in Section 3.3 were applied to determine valid cut points from spurious ones.   The image data was subjected to three passes through the separation algorithms with the constraints being increased at each pass as shown in Table 1.

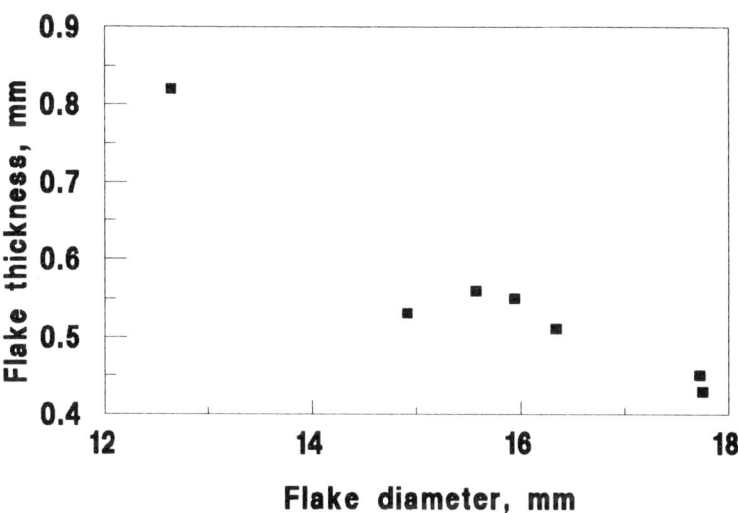

Figure 3. Relationship between flake diameter and thickness

Pass	Maximum cutting distance as proportion of sample diameter	Negative acceptance level of curvature code
1	0.4	-1.5
2	0.7	-1.5
3	0.7	-1.3

Table 1. Separation algorithm constraints

To test the separation algorithms, static tests were undertaken with 20 particulates placed in the image viewing area.   They were placed sequentially in 5 different arrangements varying from no objects touching to 20 touching. The results of the test are shown in Table 2.

Number of touching objects	Estimated number detected	Average object area (mm^2)
0	20	48.8
5	20	48.8
10	20	48.6
15	20	47.9
20	20	46.9

Table 2. Analysis of touching objects

The potential of the separation algorithms for separating particulates within an image was thus demonstrated.

Object	Top area	Top perimeter	hole area	hole perimeter	thickness	Circularity function
1	1523	237	21	14	17	0.58
2	1443	135	238	74	14	1.00
3	1301	136	163	44	6	0.94
4	1507	154	315	67	12	0.89
5	1103	124	99	37	17	0.95
6	1456	129	183	53	15	1.05
7	999	105	141	49	16	1.07
8	1140	115	168	49	19	1.04
9	469	149	24	19	23	0.52
10	1232	120	263	70	21	1.04
11	1108	117	277	64	11	1.01
12	856	158	0	0	23	0.66

Table 3. Characteristics of extruded particulates (dimensions in pixels)

4.3   Characteristics in 3 dimensions

Extruded hoop shaped particulates similar to those shown in Fig. 2a were used to illustrate the image capture and analysis techniques described in Section 3.4 for 3-D characteristics. The information required was thickness, top surface area, hole size and presence of defects such as the cracks evident in 3 of the particulates in Fig. 2a. The double thresholding technique described in Section 3.4 was applied to the image data to extract first the top surface of the particulates and then the complete (angled) view of the particulates. In each case, the outlines were chain coded and the two images were then subtracted, as shown in Fig. 2d. The top surface area and hole area could then be calculated and the thickness determined. Defects were detected by assuming that "perfect" particulates had a circular top surface. The circumference of a circle of equivalent area to the top surface area was calculated and the peripheral length of the top surface was determined. A circularity function was then calculated as the ratio of circumference to the peripheral length. The results of the analysis on the 12 particulates in Fig. 2d are shown in Table 3. The presence of defects was indicated by a circularity factor < <1 (objects 1, 9 and 12).

4.4 Surface topography

The potential of image analysis to determine size distribution of surface features was demonstrated by Stafford and Ambler (1990) for agricultural seedbeds. Typical seedbeds are shown in Fig. 4 and a comparison of mean weight diameter of surface aggregates determined by image analysis and mechanical sieve analyses is shown in Fig. 5. The regression line through the points indicates that the image analysis was biased towards larger particles. This was because of particle sorting resulting in larger particles being in the surface layer - the layer viewed by the imaging camera. In contrast, sieving was carried out over the top 100mm depth of particles.

Figure 4. Seedbed surface topography

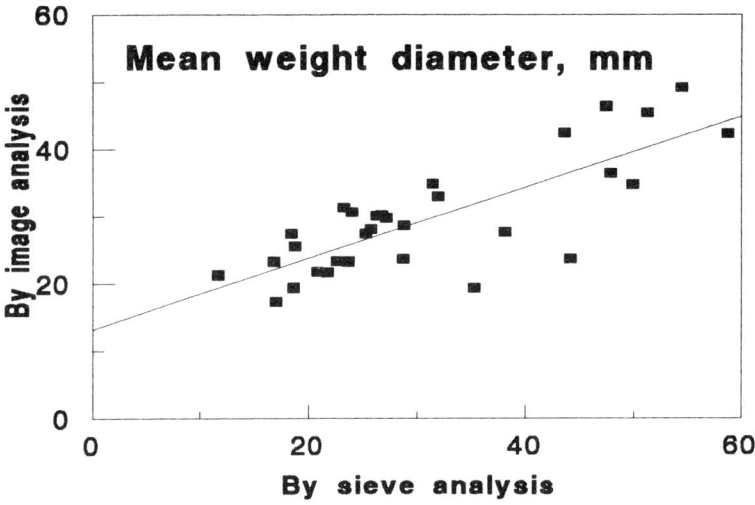

Figure 5. Sizes of surface topography features

5. Conclusions

The work reported in this paper has demonstrated the potential of image capture and analysis techniques to determine characteristics of dry particulate food materials, such as area, perimeter, thickness and defect detection. Example applications of the techniques have been carried out on static samples. However, it has been shown that problems in capturing images of sufficient quality on-line such as freezing images, image illumination and discrimination of touching and overlapping objects can be solved. Thus, image capture and analysis has been shown to be a potential tool for on-line statistical analysis of processed materials allowing the monitoring of quality and the effect of upstream process variables. With improvement in processing speeds, such as by the use of parallel processing, 100% quality inspection of dry particulate process materials should be possible.

6. References

Freeman, H. 1974. Computing Surveys 6 (1)

Marchant, J.A., Onyango, C.M. and Elipe, E. 1989. Proceedings of the 2nd international conference 'Agrotique 89', Bordeaux, 26-28 September 1989 (Editors: Sagasne J.P. and Villeger, A.) Teknea, Marseilles, France, 41-52

Schofield, C.P. 1990. Journal of Agricultural Engineering Research 47 (4) 287-296

Stafford, J.V. and Ambler, B. 1990. Proc. I. Mech. E. C419 123-129

INTEGRATED CONTROL DEVELOPMENT
FOR FOOD INDUSTRY

G. REYMAN*

An approach towards integrated control development to design a new process or improve the existing one is described. The importance of this methodological approach and especially proper choice of a process model is shown on an example of modelling and control of a fed-batch yeast fermentation. A new modelling and control strategy is described based on analysis and determination of metabolic switches of the yeast culture.

Introduction

This paper is motivated by a growing gap between academic research and industrial practice on the field of food process control. A vast amount of reported new and improved control algorithms is not reflected in number of successful and working implementations in Food Industry. Moreover, there is still an existing gap between control engineers and chemical engineers way of thinking. Most control engineers textbooks (and as a result their attitude towards a process) start from a given linear model and little attention is given to various types of modelling and other process control aspects. Based on a given linear model all identification and control principles are presented. The same applies to new techniques developed in the control community. On the other hand most of chemical engineers think in a steady state framework, neglecting disturbances and their influence on plant behaviour. This leads often to design of processes which operate in ill-conditioned operating points. This leads to a conclusion that process control improvement cannot be considered only in terms of applying a given control technique. The current acceptance of control techniques in Japan is limited to two techniques: various modifications of PID (also self-tuning PID) and Model Predictive Controllers (Morari (1991)). In European food companies the practical use is mostly restricted to the former technique. What are the reasons of this situation ? In contrary to the Chemical Industry, the Food Industry is characterized by use of large number of various production processes of various nature and complexity, where controlled process parameters depend on changing raw materials quality and end product specifications. Typically availability of on-line process/product quality sensors and the knowledge of underlying process dynamics and raw material-product relations are limited. These are the main reasons why there have been relatively few attempts to develop a generic control strategy to cope with the required process performance, which would be suitable for a broad range of Food Industry processes. In fact, in the opinion of the author, control strategy development for a specific food production process should be oriented towards this specific process. This means that an integrated control development approach should be followed in place of picking and implementing a particular control technique.

Such integrated control development should consist of the following main steps: determination of control performance requirements, collecting process data, analysis of process instrumentation, analysis of process input/output responses, improvement of the primary control strategy, dynamic modelling of the process, development of supervisory control strategy specific for a given process, testing and tuning of the developed control strategy/controller by simulation, implementation of the pre-tuned controller.

The above specified steps should be obviously implemented on a different way for new processes under design and in another for existing processes where control improvements are essential.

* Unilever Research, Vlaardingen, The Netherlands

This integrated approach is presented on an example of control development for an existing fed-batch yeast fermentation process. A fed-batch fermentation of yeast was chosen as an illustrative example because it has a lot of features common for various other difficult to control Food Industry processes. Some of these features are: a complex nonlinear dynamics, measurement problems (lack of reliable sensors, long time responses, etc), dependence on raw material quality, whole range of products, process irreversibility in terms of obtaining a given product quality, primary (environmental) as well as quality parameters to be controlled, process disturbances (e.g.: antifoam and base addition). Special attention is paid on various possible models based on different degree of process knowledge and use of these models for determining of the controller structure.

Integrated control development

Let us concentrate on main steps of control development. Each step will be illustrated on a fed-batch fermentation of bakers' yeast.

1. Control performance requirements

This step is critical for a success in a control improvement. Basically several aspects should be taken into account: process objectives in terms of productivity and product quality, existing processing and instrumentation limitations, economical factors and safety issues. Analysis of the above aspects with obvious weighing of their importance should result in a final control performance index expressed in terms of end product and operating conditions specification. For most food processes end product quality is measured infrequently off-line and these measurements are rarely incorporated in control schemes. However, quality parameters specification should be used when determining operating conditions. This may lead to infrequent adjustment of process setpoins (manually by operators - common practice) or using inferential control schemes.

For fed-batch yeast fermentation following control requirements have been determined:

- the batch phase should be performed as quick as possible using minimum of energy yielding a standard amount of yeast
- the transition to a fed-batch phase should be smooth and non delayed
- the fed-batch phase should assure optimal growth until nitrogen limitation occurs
- during this phase nutrient and energy should be optimized

These requirements has been translated to specific setpoints for environmental parameters: pH, temperature and foam level. Instrumentation limitations have led to choice of RQ and DOT as controlled parameters for the switch between batch and fed-batch phases and during the fed-batch phase.

2. Collecting process data

Proper process data collection is a necessary and mostly overlooked step in a process analysis and controller design procedure. Inventorization of sensors and actuators used in a plant or laboratory leads usually to better choice of instrumentation to be used or their replacement on the early stage of process control improvement. The most important instrumentation features to be looked at are: range and linearity, hysteresis, accuracy, time delays (some are large because of used bypassing), proper placement etc. To obtain the determined control performance it is important to assure proper measured/controlled signals analogue prefiltering, scaling and sampling (frequency and equidistant samples). This will avoid problems of proper process analysis and model identification.

3. Analysis of process instrumentation

Process instrumentation finally chosen and implemented to measure/control the process should be analyzed prior to development of the controller. It is important to determine all essential characteristics: as static as dynamic because this data can be then used for adequate prefiltering or precompensating of signals. In this way the designed controller will be instrumentation independent and thus transferable for other plants.

For control of fed-batch fermentation the off-gas analysis instrumentation and substrate pumps are usually the crucial elements of the plant which may cause a lot of trouble during implementation stage if not taking their characteristics into account. See for example problems caused by non zero flow rate by minimal signal to the pump in Wang et al. (1979) and by drift in CO_2 measurement in Dekkers and Voetter (1985).

4. Analysis of input/output responses

The aim of analysis of input/output process responses is twofold. Firstly, to properly design experiments for process identification and secondly, to obtain information for tuning of primary process controllers. Based on step and staircase signal responses it is possible to determine process gains, largest process time, time delays, and process bandwidth. This information should be used for proper pseudo-random-binary-noise-signal (PRBNS) experiment design in terms of this signal amplitude, basic frequency and duration (Backx and Damen (1989)).

5. Primary control improvement

The usual laboratory and industrial practice are process control systems with factory PID settings. Usually during the commissioning proper control of primary process parameters as temperature and pH is seen as not relevant and other issues prevail. Afterwards there is either no time to tune PID settings or there is nobody around with control expertise required. The primary parameters are therefore often poorly controlled. Based on input/output response data it is mostly easy to improve primary control applying one of standard tuning methods.

6. Dynamic process modelling

Basically a model can be used for process analysis, process optimization, process simulation in open loop, controller design and process simulation in closed loop. Dependent on a model aim appropriate model class should be chosen. From the point of control design it is important to obtain reliable model for simulation and appropriate control reference model.

A key issue in any kind of process modelling to be further used for process control should be incorporating of the a priori knowledge of the process.

Depending on the level of complexity, structured and unstructured systems of fermentation models care usually distinguished. Unstructured models describe the overall observed microbial response. Typically this kind of models are reduced to linear class of models giving the advantage of straightforward use of classical control synthesis techniques: Dekkers and Voetter (1985), Williams et al. (1986) and Wu et al. (1987). No provision is made for changes in the internal composition of the cells when the metabolism is shifted. The structured models take into account the various cellular processes i.e activities of specific enzymes, which are important in the process. An advantage of structured models is their potential for predicting the relationship between the different metabolic processes and the effects of disturbances on the overall microbial process. A disadvantage of structured models is that they require thorough investigation of the internal cell metabolism which often leads to very complex and highly nonlinear models (Steinmeyer and Shuler (1989), Dellgardt et al. (1991). Simpler structured models are mostly satisfactory for fermentation analysis, simulation and control design purposes: Sonnleitner and Käppeli (1986), Sweere (1988), Enfors et al. (1990), Bastin and Dochain (1990).

Recently encouraging results have been reported on application of expert system techniques to fed-batch fermentation modelling: Konstantinov and Yoshida (1990) and Halme and Visala (1991). Very promising modelling technique applying artificial neural networks (ANN) was applied to fed-batch fermentation by e.g. Thibault and van Breusegem (1991). Morris et al. (1991) compared ANN and model based estimation techniques. ANN approach showed to be very attractive because of capability of capturing process nonlinearities and generic structure. However, several questions remain to be answered before their general use. On the other hand, linear model based estimator study showed that this approach should adopt nonlinear model based technique.

For this study a structured model based on hypothesis of Sonnleitner and Käppeli (1986) and extended by Sweere (1988), and proved by Enfors et al. (1990) was chosen. This model proved to be excellent means for extensive analysis based on open loop as well as closed loop simulations: Reyman (1991). Three various control reference models will be handled in more detail: structured model, linear model, and model based on metabolic considerations leading to determination of three basic fed-batch fermentation states.

When a given model structure is determined it is essential to prove validity of the model in terms of matching the process data. Data obtained from e.g. PRBNS experiments should be first pre-processed independent of model structure (it is also essential when using ANN model structure). Primary signal processing involves peak shaving, trend determination and correction, scaling and offset correction, filtering, time delay correction and sample rate reduction (Backx and Damen (1989)). Various identification techniques could be used to estimate unknown model parameters. For identification and validation of identified models tolls available in Matlab, and Signal Processing and Identification Toolboxes has been used (The Mathworks (1989)).

7. Development of supervisory control strategy

Based on the process reference model optimal trajectories for process inputs, outputs and states can be determined to minimize a given product quality and process performance index. Determination of optimal trajectories is not handled here. Interested reader is referred to e.g. Dekkers (1982), Johnson (1987), Chen and Chwang (1990), and Bellgardt (1991). To ensure desired tracking of the designed trajectory an appropriate controller should de developed. Various types of controllers have been implemented for fed-batch fermentation. Most of them base on a linear model, e.g.: Dekkers and Voetter (1985), Williams et al. (1986), Wu et al. (1987), Keulers and Reyman (1991). Nonlinear model reference control strategy based on a structured model was discussed in Montague et al. (1986), Bastin and Dochain (1990), Bastin (1991), and Reyman (1991). Controllers, based on other types of unstructured models, incorporating essential a priori process knowledge are presented in Wang et al. (1979) and O'Connor et al. (1991). A priori process knowledge is extensively used in knowledge based systems approaches which can be eventually used for real time control: Konstantinov and Yoshida (1990), and Halme and Visala (1991). The ANN based control concept which is becoming very popular has until now one major disadvantage of neglecting most of all a priori process knowledge and treating the fed-batch fermentation as a black-box system. A priori knowledge might be used for choice of an appropriate ANN structure and for ANN pruning.

In this paper three various control concepts will be discussed in greater detail:

    i.   - Model Reference Adaptive Control (MRAC) based on reduced structured model
    ii. - Generalized Predictive Control (GPC) based on a linear model
    iii. - Adaptive Discrete Stochastic Control (ADSC) based on a metabolic state transition model

8. Controller testing and implementation

Choice and synthesis of a particular controller should be followed by extensive simulation study and pretuning. This holds especially for food industry while in most processes where modern control techniques would be implemented the process quality of a whole batch can be affected by even short transition to undesired process conditions. This is so because these processes are irreversible in terms of obtainable end product quality. For continuous processes excessive disturbances would usually lead to loss of the product and very often to shutdown and subsequent startup of the process. Well identified and validated dynamic model of the process used for controller testing and tuning will save usually a lot of waste material, and time.

On the other hand the hardware/software implementation should be considered very carefully as well. It will be advisable to consult one of specialized system houses at least at this stage. Otherwise, there are some possibilities for smaller applications, e.g. downloading the developed controller to a PLC. Unilever Research, Vlaardingen developed an interface PC/AT with Matlab and fermenter system.

The need of signal galvanic separation caused choice of Opto22 for interfacing all necessary fermentation manipulated inputs and measured outputs. This solution has obviously one great advantage: once developed and tested controller in the Matlab analysis/simulation environment might be readily used for real-time control, thus saving rewriting of the software in a format/language specific for used control system.

Fed-batch fermentation modelling

In this paper three types of possible fed-batch models are presented to illustrate various possible control design approaches. The key issue is choice of the a priori process knowledge. MRAC based on a structured model was supposed to work very well and was a preferred sound technique for biotechnologists. Much simpler linear model, where the process information was used only for determination of polynomial orders and time delays lead to development of GPC. This controller was supposed to give less accurate trajectory tracking, but on other hand should be more robust (unmodelled dynamics and disturbances) than MRAC and of more generic use for other similar processes. The ADSC was developed in Unilever Research, Vlaardingen to demonstrate an alternative approach based on relevant process knowledge: metabolic conditions and transitions from one to other metabolic state.

i. Structured model

The model is derived from the recently published hypothesis of Sonnleitner and Käppeli (1986) and incorporates recent results of Sweere (1988). Enfors et al. (1990) proved this theory. This simple structured model is based on the response of yeast to a glucose pulse during the fermentation assuming limited respiratory capacity. Stoichiometric equations of the growth of bakers' yeast on glucose and/or ethanol are given below for oxidative - {1} and {3} - and reductive {2} metabolic pathways:

{1} $C_6H_{12}O_6 + aO_2 + b \bullet nx[NH_3] \rightarrow bC_1H_{hx}O_{ox}N_{nx} + cCO_2 + dH_2O$

{2} $C_6H_{12}O_6 + g \bullet nx[NH_3] \rightarrow gC_1H_{hx}O_{ox}N_{nx} + hCO_2 + iH_2O + jC_2H_6O$

{3} $C_2H_6O + kO_2 + p \bullet nx[NH_3] \rightarrow pC_1H_{hx}O_{ox}N_{nx} + mCO_2 + nH_2O$

The composition of biomass grown on glucose does not change significantly if ethanol is either co-consumed or produced. The above equation set has three degrees of freedom and requires an empirical or mathematical estimation of three stoichiometric parameters: b,g and p.

The limited respiration capacity of the yeast cells depends on the availability of dissolved oxygen in the broth and can be represented as a bottleneck (see Sonleitner and Käppeli (1986)). Let us consider three different situations (cases) with respect to filling the above bottleneck with two possible substrates: glucose and ethanol.

CASE 1. If there is a mixture of glucose and ethanol in the medium and the glucose flux does not require maximal respiration (subcritical glucose flux) the specific rate of the oxidative pathway {1} will be determined by the glucose consumption rate. The glucose consumption rate follows Monod kinetics. In this case no ethanol is produced, so the rate of pathway {2} will be zero. The residual respiration capacity can be utilized for ethanol growth. If there is no oxygen limitation then the ethanol consumption follows Monod kinetics. The priority of glucose consumption over ethanol consumption can be formulated as inhibition by freely available glucose.

CASE 2. Same as CASE 1 but the ethanol uptake is limited by the residual respiration capacity.

CASE 3. When the glucose flux is sufficiently high to exceed the respiration capacity (supracritical glucose flux) the respiration capacity of the yeast cells limits the specific rate of pathway {1} and all the oxygen will be used via this pathway. No oxygen is left for pathway {3} so this pathway rate is zero. The remainder of the glucose flux which could not be metabolized via pathway {1} will be utilized according to the reductive pathway {2}. In order to obtain high biomass productivity and quality this case is the desired one and should be maintained during fermentation by the particular control strategy employed, assuming the remainder of the glucose flux is minimal.

For all the above cases, it can be stated - referring to the Monod kinetics - that the maximum specific consumption rates are not constant but are functions of the culturing conditions. To describe the gradual changes in maximum consumption rates of glucose, oxygen and ethanol approach of Sweere (1988) is adopted. In this approach induction or repression of the enzyme synthesis for a certain group of reactions was modelled. If oxygen is present the synthesis of oxidation capacity is induced by an increase in the substrate concentration.

The synthesis of enzymes responsible for the growth on glucose was modelled as well. The formation of enzymes inducing the growth on ethanol is suppressed by glucose and induced by ethanol. Because no ethanol is consumed under anaerobic conditions, enzyme synthesis will also occur in the presence of oxygen.

Solving the balance equations for the chemical states and of total mass (see Roels (1983)) results in a set of first order, nonlinear, differential equations describing the growth process of bakers' yeast. The set of differential equations of the chemical states can be reduced because the pH in the culture is kept constant. This operating condition allows the carbon dioxide balance to be ignored, because the dissociation of carbon dioxide into bicarbonate is negligible at a Ph 5 or lower. Therefore the carbon dioxide production rate (CPR) may be considered to equal the carbon dioxide transfer rate (CTR). The nitrogen and water balances are not included in the model, as they do not affect the other balances. The above reasoning leads to a set of balance equations for glucose (G), biomass (X), ethanol (E) and dissolved oxygen (DOT), and volume (V). This model was validated on a glucose pulse. After reduction to the CASE 3 it was used as a reference for development of the MRAC (Reyman (1991)).

ii. Linear model

The GPC controller is based on a Controlled Auto-Regressive with Integrated Moving Average (CARIMA) model (for theory see Clarke (1987))

$$z_{n+1} = a_0 z_n + a_1 z_{n-1} + \ldots + a_k z_{n-k} + b_0 u_n + b_1 u_{n-1} + \ldots + b_m u_{n-m} + (c_0 \epsilon_n + c_2 \epsilon_{n-1} + \ldots + c_l \epsilon_{n-1})/p$$

where

k, m and l - polynomial orders,
z_n - the current estimate of DOT or RQ respectively,
u_n - the currently applied input, stirrer speed rate or glucose flow rate respectively,
ϵ_i, i = n-m,...,n - Gaussian noise terms
p - the operator $1\text{-}q^{-1}$

iii. Model based on metabolic states transition

On the basis of the analysis of processes taking place during the fed-batch fermentation it can be concluded that the fermentation physiological conditions on the macro scale can be represented by a state given by one of the three above defined cases. Knowing the current state, it is then easy to determine a control strategy for a next fixed time horizon. Motivated by the structured model analysis let us define three fermentation states:

state one - ethanol production in the presence of excess glucose with respect to the limiting oxygen bottleneck,
state two - optimal growth on glucose, i.e., optimal fitting of the glucose flux into the oxygen bottleneck,
state three - consumption of ethanol by insufficient glucose flux to fill the whole oxygen bottleneck.

For the states transitions a Markov chain description is proposed and for description of measurement mechanism probability density function set is appropriate.

Let $n = 0,1,\ldots$ denote a current time moment of the controlled Markov chain. At each time n characteristic features of the current state are measured. On the basis of the current measurement x_n an action should be chosen and executed. Let us use the following denotations :

$S = \{ 1,2,\ldots,M \}$ - the finite state space ,

$K = \{ 1,2,...,r \}$ - the finite set of actions ,

$x_n \in X$, X is a closed bounded set in the Euclidean space R^r.

All random variables are denoted in bold type contrary to their realizations. Let also denote

$$\bar{b}_n \equiv (b_0,...,b_n) \ , \qquad \bar{b}_n \in \bar{B}_{n+1} = \prod_{n+1} B \qquad (1)$$

The behaviour of the system is governed by the set of transition probabilities

$$P(j_{n+1}=j|j_n=i,k_n=k) \equiv p_{ij}^k(\phi) \quad , \quad P(j_0=0) \equiv p_j \qquad (2)$$

where j_n is the state of the system and k_n is the action executed, $\phi \in \Phi$ is the unknown true parameter, and Φ is a closed bounded set in the Euclidean space, R^t , $t <= M(M-1)r$. The measurement x_n of the state j_n is given by the conditional probability densities vector

$$\bar{f}(x_n=x|j_n=j,j_{n-1},...j_0) = f(x|j,\alpha) \quad , \qquad j=1,...,M \qquad (3)$$

where $\bar{f}$ is a probability density of x_n , $(j_n, j_{n-1} ,...,j_0)$ is given, $\alpha \in A$ is the unknown true parameter, where A is a closed bounded set in the Euclidean space R^M .

Model based controllers

Based on the above described fed-batch fermentation models three controllers has been developed and tested in the Matlab package. Here only a short outline of MRAC and GPC will be given. Interested reader can refer to Reyman (1991) for all details and results. Here only the novel ADSC approach will be described in more detail.

i. Model Reference Adaptive Controller

Once the structured dynamic process model is known, it is possible to develop MRAC which uses the process dynamics information. In the case of the fermentation process two main problems have been encountered during evaluation of the MRAC. First of all the above presented structured model is highly nonlinear. The type of nonlinearity caused by metabolic shifts affecting specific growth limits, cannot be easily incorporated into the structure of the MRAC. As stated earlier maintaining the conditions of CASE 3, with possibly minimal glucose flow outside the oxygen bottleneck will lead to the desired growth. Therefore the reference model,used to construct the MRAC, was simplified to CASE 3. Four state variables are to be controlled by MRAC: DOT, and biomass, ethanol and glucose concentrations in the broth. A difficulty of the model reference approach lies in the need for on-line estimation of various unknown parameters. In our case, two of them are constant stoichiometric parameters b and g and the other two are time varying maximum specific growth rates. Because of this use of the MRAC technique is based on the best estimation approach combining the extended Kalman filtering (EKF) and recursive least squares (RLS) algorithms.

Several of such bootstrap structures have been constructed and tested by simulation. The technique finally selected combines EKF for fermentation state estimates (biomass, glucose, and ethanol concentrations, DOT and volume) and for the constant parameters. The DOT sampling rate has been used as an update rate and therefore for all states but DOT a prediction between measurements scheme of Bellgardt et al.(1986) has been used. A multivariable RLS has been applied for estimation of two time varying parameters - maximum specific growth and consumption rates on oxygen and glucose. Ethanol concentration was well filtered and there was only a negligible constant offset between the simulated biomass concentration and its EKF estimate. However, the offset for both maximum specific growth rates increased with time because there were not enough measured variables available. If the total fermentation state was known at a given moment, the reference model with estimated parameters allowed the use of a simple One-Step-Ahead Predictive Controller (OSAPC). This controller has been extended with integral action to assure reduction of an offset from desired trajectory.

The estimation of states was very good while unknown parameter estimates gradually diverge. This divergence is critical for the controller in the case of wrong initial estimates or strong process disturbances. Extensive simulation studies shown very good results (see Figure 1), but because of the sensitivity to process disturbances this controller has not been tested experimentally at this stage. The above mentioned problems can be solved by incorporating on-line measurements of biomass and glucose to decrease the number of unknown states to be estimated. This, however, is dependent on the availability of accurate and reliable sensors.

ii. Generalized Predictive Control

The Generalized Predictive Control (GPC) principle of Clarke et al. (1987) is based on the prediction of the future behaviour of the process using the linear model for the system under control. This means that the entire knowledge of the model is merely used to establish degrees of linear models. The GPC controls two measurable process variables, DOT and RQ, on predetermined trajectories. To achieve the required growth rate RQ is controlled at a given value by manipulating the glucose feed rate. To maintain proper respiratory conditions the DOT is controlled at a given level by manipulating the stirrer speed and air flow rates. This multiloop structure was chosen based on the assumption that there hardly exists significant dependence between DOT and RQ if the value of DOT stays between 10% and 20% of saturation and RQ is maintained between 0.9 and 1.2. The other reason of the multiloop structure is different sampling frequency for DOT and RQ implying difficulties in realization of a multi-input multi-output structure.

Simulation results were very promising. The DOT was maintained at the required level until the stirrer speed rate reached its maximum allowable value. The RQ level was controlled well until stirrer speed saturation but then its maintenance was quite troublesome. After about three hours the required level was reached again but at the end of the simulation period this could not be maintained due to the lack of oxygen. The biomass concentration increased exponentially (as required) until the oxygen level decreased due to stirrer speed saturation which caused the further linear biomass concentration increase.

The strength of the GPC technique lies in adapting an assumed simple linear model to the process conditions and the possibility of applying GPC for single loops. The latter is very important when the DOT was sampled by a factor 20 times faster than the RQ.

Successful simulations of the GPC controller have lead to implementation of this technique in a stand alone controller and experimental tests in the fermentation laboratory of Unilever Research, Vlaardingen. The simulation experience and first experiments with the GPC show that this technique is highly advantageous compared to traditional open loop control. Tuning, however is quite time consuming and complex. Also shorter learning period is required which will lead to better setpoint tracking. It was shown experimentally that the applied GPC has good disturbance rejection properties (see Figure 2).

iii. Adaptive Discrete Stochastic Controller

In a case of known process transition probabilities and probability density functions (modelling measurements) the control strategy can be decomposed into two steps. First, the current state is recognized and then, assuming the recognized state to be the true one, a receding horizon dynamic programming controller is applied to minimize the following finite horizon performance index

$$Q_N = E \sum_{n=0}^{N-1} c_n(j_n, k_n) \tag{4}$$

where $c_n(j,k)$ is the local cost incurred by execution of the action k when the current state at the time n is j.

To use all the past information about the process for proper state recognition the contextual recognition algorithm is used to minimize the risk:

$$R_N = E\sum_{n=0}^{N} L(i_n, j_n) \ , \tag{5}$$

$$L(i,j) = \begin{cases} 0 & if \quad i=j \\ 1 & if \quad i \neq j \end{cases} \tag{6}$$

$$i_n = arg \ \{ \ \max_{\lambda}[d_n(\lambda, \bar{x}_n, \bar{k}_{n-1})] \ \}$$

$$i_0 = arg \ \{ \ \max_{\lambda}[d_0(\lambda, x_0)] \ \} \tag{7}$$

where i_n is the recognized state. The following recursive contextual recognition algorithm was obtained where

$$d_n(\lambda, \bar{x}_n, \bar{k}_{n-1}) = \frac{f(x_n|\lambda, \alpha)\sum_{j=1}^{M} p_{j\lambda}^{k_{n-1}}(\phi)d_{n-1}(j, \bar{x}_{n-1}, \bar{k}_{n-2})}{\sum_{\lambda=1}^{M} f(x_n|\lambda, \alpha)\sum_{j=1}^{M} p_{j\lambda}^{k_{n-1}}(\phi)d_{n-1}(j, \bar{x}_{n-1}, \bar{k}_{n-2})} \tag{8}$$

with

$$d_0(\lambda, x_0) \equiv f(x_0|\lambda, \alpha)p_\lambda \tag{9}$$

Assuming that the recognized state is a true one the following simple control algorithm minimizing (4), given a new estimate ϕ_n at the time n determines the optimal action to be realized

$$H_n : S \rightarrow K \quad , \quad k_n = H_n(i_n). \tag{10}$$

The decision table H_n may be easily obtained by solving the following dynamic programming problem

$$V_1(i) = \min_{k\in K}[c_{N-1}(i,k)] \tag{11}$$

$$V_{N-\lambda}(i) = \min_{k\in K}[c_\lambda(i,k) + \sum_{j=1}^{M} V_{N-\lambda-1}(j)p_{ij}^k(\phi)] \ , \quad \lambda=N-2,\ldots,n. \tag{12}$$

After the decision table H_n is calculated the first action of this table according to the currently recognized state i: $k_1 = H_1(i)$ is realized and the procedure (15-16) repeated (receding horizon control).

In reality probabilities of transitions and density functions distributions are unknown. Some of the unknown parameters can be left as tuning parameters to achieve required controller performance.

Two fermentation parameters which give some information about yeast growth conditions and about the current fermentation state has been chosen: dissolved oxygen tension (DOT) and respiratory quotient (RQ). The same multi-rate, multi-loop controller structure as for GPC was applied. Above reasoning leads to separate definitions of state for DOT and RQ loop. For DOT loop $j=1$ denotes state one, $j=2$ state two and $j=3$ state three. However for RQ, $j=1$ denotes state three, $j=2$ state two and $j=3$ state one. This definition leads to uniform definition of control actions for both loops: $k=1$ denotes incremental flow increase, $k=2$ exponential incremental ('normal') increase and $k=3$ flow decrease. A rough target trajectory should be defined (e.g. a trajectory which would be followed in an open loop fermentation with no disturbances).

Form this target trajectory and required initial conditions 'normal' exponentially growing increments for stirrer and glucose flow can be easily calculated. These increments are then implemented if the fermentation state is two (optimal growth). For the definition of the performance index (4) costs c_n should be given. For a desired time horizon of about ten scanning cycli, ten values should be defined. The most practical approach is to weight stronger undesired transitions, and assign weight equal to zero to transitions which are desired. This results in

$$c_n(j_n,k_n) = \alpha^{N-i}c(j,k) \quad , \quad i = n,...,N \tag{13}$$

where n denotes a current time and $0 < \underline{\alpha} < 1$. For e.g. state $j=1$

$$c(1,k) = \begin{cases} 0 & \text{if } k=1 \\ \gamma & \text{if } k=2 \\ 1 & \text{if } k=3 \end{cases} \quad , \quad 0 < \gamma < 1 \tag{14}$$

where for the state $j=1$, $k=1$ denotes required action, $k=2$ 'normal growth' action and $k=3$ undesired action. For other states the c values are defined in the same way.

Initial values of transition probabilities were obtained from discussions with process operators. To relate measurements with three defined states, probability density functions were used. It seemed logical to represent the measurement of a state two by a normal distribution with the mean equal to the required current setpoint and deviation set equal to allowable deviation from this setpoint. Both parameters are however free with respect to further tuning if required. Measurement of state one and state three are given by lognormal distributions. For the state one the density function is modified - given for our purposes by a symmetric function equal to zero for negative arguments. Mean values are set to zero and initial deviation equal to one (other tuning parameters). These deviation values are estimated on-line during run of the controller.

Using the above values in the ADSC controller during several simulation trials led to very good results. Results of control of RQ and DOT where RQ was measured every 5 minutes with 1% noise, and DOT was measured every 20 seconds with 1% noise are given in Figure 3. The batch phase took about 22 hours. An intelligent switch based on analysis of DOT and RQ trends was implemented and started ADSC at that time. From that moment on DOT was maintained on 20% of saturation. RQ was controlled on 1.07 until 40 hours and then the RQ setpoint was changed to 1.05 to assure no ethanol formation at the last fermentation phase. The controller showed to be noise insensitive and to be able to smoothly track RQ setpoint changes. The latter is essential from the point of view of optimal RQ trajectories (see Dekkers and Voetter (1985)).

On the basis of these very promising results it has been decided to implement ADSC in the real-time fermentation control. To use fully the already developed Matlab and C software, an interface was built between the Matlab program and fermentation process. DOT and RQ as well as control parameters: stirrer speed rate, air flow rate and glucose flow rate are read/written by an Opto22 interface. To facilitate monitoring and tuning a graphical interface and real-time editor was developed in Matlab environment using C modules.

It is already obvious that ADSC can cope with complex quality and economic performance indices and not only minimize the output error as PID controllers. Recognition and informing about the current fermentation state is possible which may give better insight into the fermentation course. This feature is certainly not supported by other control techniques. The noise filtering is an intrinsic feature of DSC because of its specific modelling approach. Process noises are modelled and adapted to by the Markov chain transition probabilities and measurement noises by normal and lognormal density functions characterizing the measurement mechanism. Simulation proves very good tracking behaviour and disturbance rejection capability and stability of the closed loop superior to these of MRAC, GPC and PID. ADSC in the present form cannot optimally deal with constraints on input variables or states. ADSC can cope with varying process dynamics using the built-in learning mechanism whereas GPC must be extended by implementing e.g. RLS filter which decreases the stability of the system.

Conclusions

A integrated control improvement strategy has been outlined. Assuming that there are no major process design errors, this methodology might help in achieving the processing objectives. Attention should be paid to modelling of the process dynamics. Various modelling techniques are available. One should always remember what is the ultimate goal of process modelling and therefore incorporate a priori knowledge at this stage if available. A novel modelling and control technique has been proposed which has proved to be applicable for processes where characteristic process conditions (states) can be distinguished and during the process transitions might take place between these states.

The essential step in the process control improvement is proper understanding of process objectives and translating them into control requirements. Less important is a specific control technique used, assuming the design steps are carefully executed and given controller properly implemented. However, even if the particular controller fulfils the determined requirements the final test is the acceptance by be process engineers and operators. Therefore these people should be engaged from the very beginning and in as many development steps as possible.

References

Agrawal, P., Koshy, G., Ramseier, M. (1989), An algorithm for operating a fed-batch fermenter at optimum specific-growth rate, Biotechnology and Bioengineering, 33, 115-125.

Backx, T., Damen, A. (1989), Identification of industrial MIMO processes for fixed controllers, Journal A, 30, 3-11.

Bastin, G. (1991), Nonlinear and adaptive control in biotechnology: a tutorial, ECC 91 European Control Conference, Grenoble.

Bastin, G., Dochain, D. (1990), On-line estimation and adaptive control of bioreactors, Elsevier.

Bellgardt, K.-H., Kuhlmann, W., Meyer, H.-D., Schügerl, K., Thoma, M. (1986), Application of an extended Kalman filter for state estimation of a yeast fermentation, IEE Proc., 133/Pt.D., 226-234.

Bellgardt, K.-H., Yuan, J.-Q., Jiang, W.-S., Deckwer, W.-D (1991), Optimum quality control of a baker's yeast production process, ECC 91 European Control Conference, Grenoble.

Dekkers R.M., Voetter, M. (1985), Adaptive control of a fed-batch baker's yeast fermentation, Proc. 1st IFAC Symp. on Modelling and Control of Biotechnological Processes, Noordwijkerhout, Pergamon Press, pp. 103-110.

Chen, C.-T., Hwang, C. (1990), Optimal on-off control for fed-batch fermentation processes, Industrial and Engineering Chemistry Research, 29, 1869-1875.

Clarke, D.W., Mohtadi, C., Tuffs, P.S. (1987), Generalized predictive control - Part 1 and Part 2., Automatica, 23, 137-160.

Enfors, S.-O., Hedenberg, J., Olsson, K. (1990), Simulation of the dynamics in the baker's yeast process, Bioprocess Engineering, 5, 191-198.

Halme, A., Visala, A. (1991), Combining symbolic and numerical information in modelling the state of biotechnological processes, European Control Conference ECC '91, Grenoble.

Johnson, A. (1987), The control of fed-batch fermentation processes - A survey, Automatica, 23, 691-705.

Keulers, M., Reyman, G. (1991), The application of the GPC algorithm to a fed-batch fermentation process.- A simulation study, Proc. European Simulation Multiconference, Copenhegen, pp. 879-884.

Konstantinov, K.B., Yoshida, T., (1990), An expert system for control of fermentation processes as variable structure plants, J. of Fermentation and Bioengineering, 70, 48-57.

Montague, G.A., Morris, A.J., Wright, A.R., Aynsley, M., Ward, A.C. (1986), Online estimation and adaptive control of penicillin fermentation, Proc. IEE, 133/Pt.D., 240-246.

Morari, M. (1991), The role of theory in control practice, American Control Conference ACC '91, Boston.

Morris, A.J., Montague, G.A., Tham, M.T., Aynsley, M., Di Massimo, C., Lant, P. (1991), Towards improved process supervision - algorithms and knowledge based systems, Proc. 4th Int. Conf. on Chemical Process Control, Texas.

O'Connor, G.M., Sanchez-Riera, F., Cooney, C.L. (1991) Design and evaluation of control strategies for high cell density, Biotechnology and Bioengineering, to appear.

Reyman, G. (1991), Modelling and Control of fed-batch bakers' yeast fermentation, Food Control, to appear.

Roels, J.A. (1983), Energetics and Kinetics in Biotechnology, Elsevier Biomedical Press, Amsterdam.

Sonnleitner, B., Käppeli, O. (1986), Growth of Saccharomyces Cerevisiae is controlled by its limited respiration capacity: formulation and verification of a hypothesis, Biotechnology and Bioengineering, 28, 927-937.

Steinmeyer, D.E., Shuler, M.L. (1989), Structured model for Saccharomyces Cerevisiae, Chemical Engineering Science, 44, 2017-2030.

Sweere, A.P.J. (1988), Response of bakers' yeast to transient environmental conditions relevant to large-scale fermentation processes, Ph.D. Thesis, Drukkerij Elinkwijk, Utrecht.

The Mathworks Inc. (1989), Pro-Matlab for VAX/VMS Computers, User's Guide.

Thibault, J., van Breusegem, V. (1991), Modelling, prediction and control of fermentation processes via neural networks, ECC 91 European Control Conference, Grenoble.

Wang, H.Y., Cooney, C.L., Wang, D.I.C. (1979), Computer control of bakers' yeast production, Biotechnology and Bioengineering, 21, 975-995.

Williams, D., Yousepfour, Wellington, P. (1986), On-line adaptive control of a fermentation of Saccharomyces cerevisiae, Biotechnology and Bioprocessing, 28, 631-645.

Wu, W.-T., Jang, W.-D., Wu, S.-C. (1987), On-line control for cultivation of Saccharomyces cerevisiae via weighted moving identification, The Chemical Engineering Journal, 36, B1-B6.

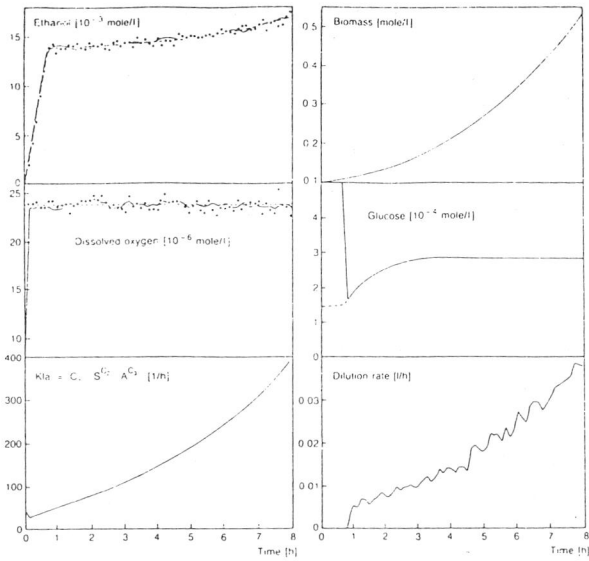

Figure 1. MRAC — simulation results.

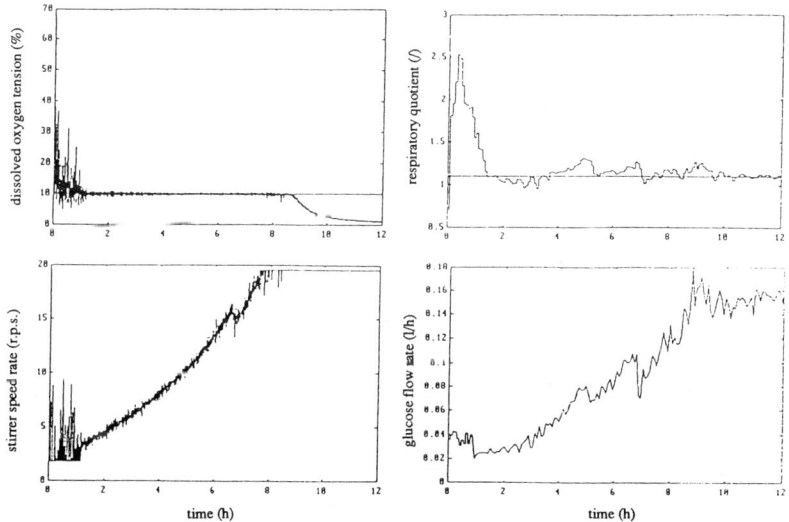

Figure 2. GPC — experimental results (10 1 fermenter).

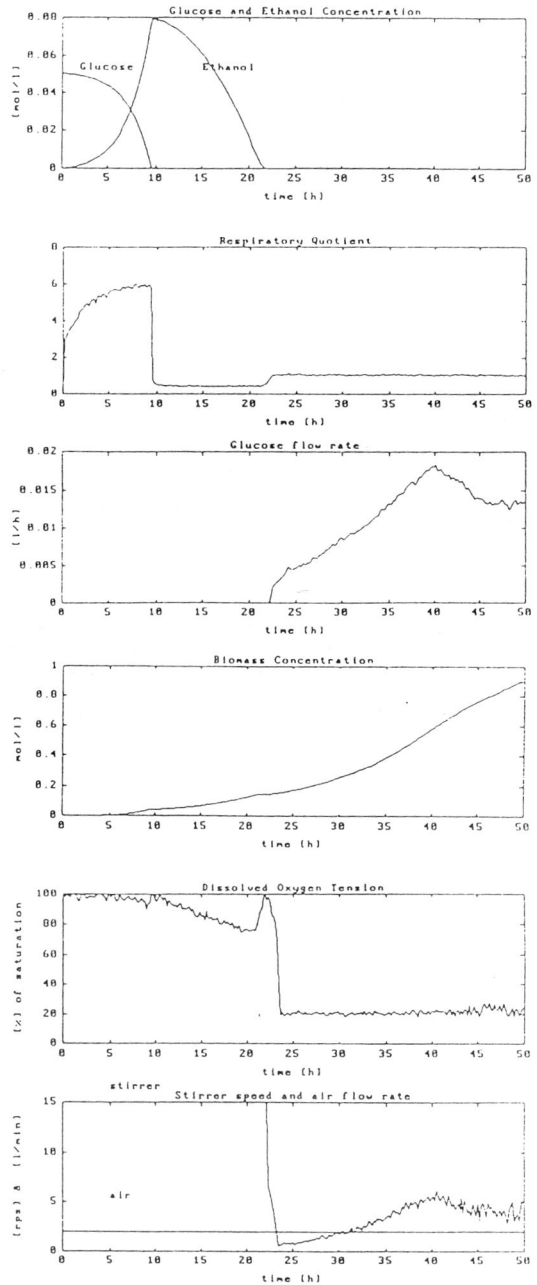

Figure 3. ADSC — simulation results. At about 22 h switch from batch to fed-batch phase took place

AUTOMATION RESEARCH ON A FOOD PROCESSING PILOT PLANT

S. Macchietto *

A computer controlled, multipurpose batch pilot plant is described for research on control, automation, and flexible production techniques in the food industry.
Current research activities are presented, with particular reference to: off-line production scheduling techniques; the automated execution and supervisory control of production schedules; Computer Aided Synthesis and validation of operating procedures.

Keywords: automation, flexible production, batch processing, scheduling, CIM

Introduction

In the process industries at large there are significant trends towards greater integration of many traditionally independent functions. At the operations end, this involves closer interaction between sales, marketing and administrative functions (order forecasting and acceptance, supplies procurement, product distribution, etc.), plantwide operations management functions (allocation of production facilities to products and production scheduling, maintenance planning, etc.) and process control functions (achieving and maintaining optimal process conditions under normal and emergency situations, etc.). The driving forces are the competitive advantages deriving from shorter "order-to-supply" times, more efficient utilisation of existing plant resources and raw materials, and the ability to achieve more consistent, higher quality products through better control.
At the engineering end, a similar integration trend, generically labelled as "concurrent engineering", addresses the need to shorten the "design-to-build" cycle. The functions involved are process and product design and development, plant design and construction, development and implementation of control and automation systems, etc. Here contracting rather than operating companies are typically concerned, but the driving forces still stem ultimately from the need to respond to or anticipate changes in product demands, prices, legislative constraints and production technologies in advance of the competition.
The current buzzword for all these trends is the much abused, ill-defined and all-encompassing CIM (Computer Integrated Manufacturing), borrowed from the discrete parts manufacturing industries. Problems, however, have been reported in the straight application of discrete manufacturing techniques such as MRP II and Just-In-Time in the process industry, due to the presence and/or different importance of resource constraints, continuous flows, continuous changes in materials upon processing, recycle flows, etc. It thus appears that a fair amount of adaptation and outright new developments are required (no doubt leading to the introduction of a big P, for process, somewhere in the acronym).

---

* Centre for Process Systems Engineering, Imperial College, London SW7 2BY - UK

The food industry is in many respects particularly affected by these trends. It is typically closer to the end user markets than, say, most chemical producers. The number of end products for a food company is often very large and changing frequently. Product demands and raw material supplies are subject to the vagaries of consumer fads, weather conditions, and salmonella scares, which can cause very large perturbations very quickly. Margins are often tightly squeezed between the prices paid by powerful buyers, such as the large supermarket chains and highly regulated raw material costs (e.g. milk, fixed by the Milk Marketing Board, or other agricoltural products). It is now common for supermarkets to have highly sophisticated stock control systems, enabling them to accurately target orders for next day delivery at specified times, thus shifting the costs of inventories to their suppliers.

In the food industry many processes are conducted in a batch mode. This is specially suited for small productions, seasonal products, processes involving many steps and/or solids handling, frequent changes in formulation, and production to demand. Products may require common equipment, ingredients, personnel and utilities, with more than one product being produced in the same plant at different times (multiproduct plants) or concurrently (multipurpose plants). Batch processes are not unique to the food industry, (they are also common in the fine chemicals and pharmaceutical industries), but some special challenges are due, for example, to the presence of cleaning-in-place (CIP) circuits, limited storage life of intermediates, etc. The design and operation of such plants is particularly complex and difficult, since the design, operation and control aspects all interact quite strongly.

All these aspects reinforce the need for very tight integration, at the plant operations level, between production management and process control systems, and for flexible plants, highly responsive to external demands and constraints. At the engineering level, the onus is on contractors/suppliers to build plants which offer the required level of flexibility, incorporating control and decision support systems suited to such environment. To ensure rapid, reliable and cost effective implementation, the solutions provided must be as generic and "portable" as possible, with only a minimum of configuration effort required, and this only where specific process knowledge is involved. This calls for powerful general purpose techniques rather than ad-hoc development.

Of course, the food industry is responding to these challenges, with a number of interesting full scale applications reported and others, no doubt, kept well in the closet for proprietary reasons. However, there are still significant problems to be solved and corresponding opportunities to be gained, enabled by the rapid advances in the last few years of supporting technologies such as data aquisition, data bases, computers and communication networks, graphical interfaces, etc. and by the fast evolution in computer aided techniques for optimisation, scheduling, optimal control, etc.

Within the Centre for Process Systems Engineering, several fundamental research projects address many of the problems discussed above. To support this research and to provide an experimental test bed for flexible manufacturing methods a small pilot plant facility suitable for food processing has been built in the Centre. This facility is described in Section 2.
The research projects underway include the development of techniques for optimal planning and scheduling of multipurpose production facilities, for supervisory management and control of such plants, and for linking the two in a generic way to provide integrated off-line and on-line (re)scheduling functions. Projects are also dealing with the design and development aspects of flexible, multipurpose plant and associated control systems. These activities are discussed briefly, and current results presented, in section 3, with more details on the individual projects available elsewhere (1).

Pilot plant description

a) Equipment

The pilot plant was designed to hygienic standards as required for food production, is entirely constructed in stainless steel and operates in batch mode. It is computer controlled and its operation is highly automated, although some operations still require manual intervention. This is not untypical of most food plants. A schematic diagram of the plant is given in figure 1. The design is centered around a main reactor vessel operating up to moderate pressure (4 bar), with two feed and two product tanks; all vessels have 100 l capacity. The product vessels in particular can also be utilized to carry out certain processing tasks (e.g. decanting, cooling and heating). Additional liquid feed systems permit the controlled dosing of additives into the reactor for process and pH control purposes. Solids and premixed slurries can be fed in two different ways. The reactor is built on load cells which can be used to weigh the amounts charged or discharged from it and a sampling port permits the withdrawal of small amounts of material for analysis. A torque measurement on the agitator provides an indirect way of monitoring the viscosity of the contents. The reactor can be heated/cooled in several ways: by direct steam sparging; by passing steam through the reactor jacket; by circulating water through the jacket (cooling water or water heated by recirculation through a plate heat exchanger); finally, by external recirculation of the reactor contents through a second plate heat exchanger with primary heating or cooling.

The contents of each vessel can be transferred to any other vessel. The two feed tanks have discharge flow control using variable speed positive displacement pumps and batch totalising facilities whereas the other transfer pumps have variable speed only. Transfers may be carried out simultaneously, except where they share common pipework. Flow paths are set up by means of Flow Separate Plates (FSP), where a movable U shaped pipe section is manually positioned to join two fixed ports. This is a common way, in the food industry, to make sure that various portions of a plant are physically segregated and undesired contamination is prevented without using valve manifolds. FSPs are often used, for example, in distribution systems where several upstream vessels feed several downstream ones.

In addition to the main process circuits, a 'cleaning in place' (CIP) system enables sections of the plant to be individually cleaned. Each cleaning operation typically consists of a pre-rinse of cold water, followed by recirculation of a hot caustic solution, and a final water rinse. The cleaning system has its own equipment and associated controls for keeping the cleaning solution at the required level, strength and temperature.

For obvious practical (and budgetary) reasons the plant has only a limited number of vessels. Several processes and process variations, however, can be devised to run on the available equipment. Each process typically involves many steps, some of which share the same equipment items, pipework and utilities. Several batches of some products can be produced before cleaning is due, while with other products a cleaning must be performed after each batch. Changeover between products will usually require intermediate cleaning, with its own demands on available plant resources. Although there is only a single reactor, concurrent operation of two batches of the same product, or even of distinct products can be performed, provided the equipment is allocated wisely and the various steps are carefully scheduled. However, on at least one occasion, during the initial simulation testing of the control system according to a manually generated production script, a gridlock situation was (quite involuntarily) reached where transfers could not be done because a cleaning was required, and this could not be performed because some vessels were occupied! This highlights the general need for scheduling techniques which can not only take into account detailed operational models and constraints (and this already excludes most existing methods), but can do so on-line when the control system detects changes due to delays, equipment failures, new requirements, etc.

The plant was designed by APV using a 3D CAD system (PROVUE 3D), resulting in a comprehensive mechanical model of individual plant items, subsystems and full plant assembly stored in a relational database. The plant was delivered to us fully assembled on a skid, and was simply put in place and connected to prepositioned utility terminals, ready for commissioning (after some minor realignments).

b) Control system
The plant is controlled by an industrial distributed control system (ACCOS, supplied by APV Automation). The system configuration is schematically illustrated in figure 2. At the lowest level a small ACCOS 30 computer carries out and monitors several control sequences, interacting with the plant through a number of interface cards running individual control loops and handling digital and analogue I/O. The ACCOS 30 computer communicates via a proprietary network link with an ACCOS 300 computer, which hosts most of the supervisory monitoring and management functions. This Unix based computer can be further linked to other systems and peripheral devices through several supported communication protocols. Our present configuration includes a main graphics terminal for regular process monitoring, with a logging printer, a plotter and two 386 PCs running a number of application programs (more on this later). An Ethernet connection to the general College computing network will be implemented as soon as the wiring to the pilot plant area is completed. This will provide access in particular to the Centre's own network of workstations and servers for more computer intensive calculations.

Control sequences are implemented in the proprietary PARACODE language. An interesting feature is that the code itself can be inspected and edited on-line, if necessary, from a remote station. This permits maintainance of existing sequences without interrupting normal plant operation.
All control sequences were designed jointly with APV in such a way as to provide the maximum flexibility for supervisory control and future modification. In practice, this involved a careful structuring of the sequences into small independent primitive units with well defined parameters, building more complex sequences from these primitives, and so on, according to the current standards for batch control. At the top level, 38 sequences permit the execution of all our current processes. Sequences are normally initiated by an operator entry from the main control screen, although this can also be done from other programs.

A second feature is the presence of a simulation card. This diverts control signal communication from the final control elements and measuring devices in the actual plant, to some other destination through a serial communication link. In particular we plan to run, at the other end of this link, a detailed real-time dynamic model of the plant, resident in one of the local PCs or in a remote workstation, and developed in a suitable general purpose simulation language such as SPEEDUP (2). When operating in simulation mode the simulation will provide (to the accuracy of the model used) all the responses normally obtained from the plant. The simulation mode will be particularly useful for the assessment and validation of new control sequences and plant modifications at the development stage, to assist in the evaluation of new operating procedures, for operator training and to provide an on-line decision support tool for plant operators, as detailed in (3) for an earlier implementation of this concept. Work on the development of a detailed plant model for a starch conversion process has just started.
In order to test the ability to interface the control system with external application programs, we have developed our own graphical operator interface

(as a WINDOWS application) running in one of the local PCs. Here, the operator manipulates the plant exclusively through graphical diagrams (figure 3a). By clicking on a plant item (say, the reactor vessel) all possible sequences that can be run involving that item are displayed, again in a graphical form. For example, figure 3b shows the available reactor heating sequences, displayed when the "reactor" and "heat" icons are selected from the main plant display. For a particular sequence, default parameters are automatically shown, and it is possible to easily include help displays with related information, etc. Information returned from the plant is also easily included in plant status and dialog windows, to show, for example, active sequences, the latest alarms, etc.

The speed of communications across the interface is excellent, giving essentially the same response times as the dedicated screens of the control system itself. The new interface has very rapidly become the primary way of running the plant and will certainly be used whenever students are involved.

The ACCOS 300 provides, in addition to the usual control functions such as graphic displays, trending, etc., an interesting maintenance database package where a maintenance history record is maintained for each plant item. We have now defined maintenance policies for all mechanical items in the plant. For example, the manufacturers of some valves recommend that certain parts be serviced or replaced after so many operations. These are automatically monitored when the plant is running and a maintenance report is issued periodically or on request with the forthcoming maintenance requirements, supplier contacts, etc. In addition, the ACCOS30 control computer stores the initial response or grace time of each automatic valve and pump when first operated. Their response is then monitored in subsequent operations, and relevant sequences are alarmed when the respose of any item degrades beyond a defined threshold.

One of the applications running on the ACCOS300 computer, but accessed from the PC terminals is Batch Manager, an APV program for batch planning and scheduling. It allows the definition of plant configuration and production models for one or more plants, receives and processes orders for various products and customers, breaks the orders down into batches, sequences the batches and produces a detailed production schedule using a finite capacity scheduler which takes into account the current and predicted availability of all resources (equipment, utilities, storage levels, personnel, etc.). The intermediate and final schedules are presented as Gantt charts (figure 4 gives an example for a small yoghurt plant), with other reports available. Information are held on a relational database and all interactions with the planner/scheduler are through highly interactive graphic displays.

We are currently building a Batch Manager model of our pilot plant to support the pilot plant planner/scheduler/operator in off-line mode. The provision of on-line scheduling support is discussed in the next section.

c) Processes

The plant can be used to run several food processes, of which the enzymatic conversion of starch to sugars is the main one. This is a two-step process, involving first the gelatinization of starch in a water solution at a temperature of about 80C, followed by starch degradation upon addition of an active enzyme. Initial runs have been conducted with a well known commercial enzyme (alpha-amylase). Several variations of this basic process are easily generated depending on the choice of enzymes and operating procedures used, leading to a variety of products (e.g. dextrines, cyclodextrines) and processing times. For the purposes of studying the flexible operation of a multipurpose plant, we will adopt several of these variations in our slate of processes. A separate project, aimed at studying the effect of enzymes and process conditions on product distributions and yields is also under way, jointly with reserchers in the Department of Chemical and Biochemical Engineering at University College, London, but it is outside the scope of this paper and will not be further discussed here.

A second very different process is the production of an emulsion of oil and water, followed by separation of the two phases and subsequent recovery, as far as is possible, of the initial ingredients.

In addition, we can generate an endless variety of processes involving heating, cooling, dosing, pH adjustment, mixing and splitting of inexpensive ingredients (water?) with process variability generated artificially by introducing known disturbances. For example, a variety of exothermic reactions may be mimicked by using water and a programmed profile of steam injection from the sparger, while temperature control is performed using the reactor jacket (this can also be used to test advanced control methods). Of course, we can introduce changes in formulations, and require production to a variety of self imposed demand patterns and operating constraints.

In summary, the plant has sufficient built-in flexibility and complexity to pose realistic operational problems at the production planning, detailed production scheduling, operations management and control levels. It will enable to reproduce qualitatively, if not in shere size, the problems of operating multiproduct and, in more restricted way, multipurpose plants and it will provide a good test environment for the automation and flexible production techniques currently under development within the Centre.

Current research activities

Three specific problems and solution approaches of relevance to the food industry are discussed here:

a. Detailed operations scheduling in response to changing demand of products, changes in formulations, utility and equipment availability, cleaning requirements, etc.
b. The automated execution and supervisory control of the production schedules with on line rescheduling of all batches in light of actual plant events.
c. The Computer Aided Synthesis of operating procedures and sequences to be implemented on the control system.

a) Detailed Operation Scheduling
Mathematical production scheduling methods offer the promise of rigorous, optimal solutions. However, methods with a discrete parts manufacturing origin usually fail to model very essential aspects present in process and food plants, in particular the presence of constraints on capacity of vessels, utilities and personnel, and continuous flows. Knowledge based scheduling systems typically incorporate rules to enable the scheduling system to mimic the choices made by an expert (human) scheduler. These can be effective in the consistent application of the current policies, but provide no guarantee they are the best possible ones (keeping in mind the very low plant utilisation levels often achieved in practice). In particular, there may be difficulties in handling unusual situations, for which effective rules are lacking.
Research on scheduling in the Centre is in two complementary directions. The first addresses the optimal operations scheduling using a rigorous mathematical formulation and Mixed Integer Linear Programming solution approach, typically with an economic objective function and a variety of constraints. Unlike other methods, it relies on a much more realistic operations model which includes most of the complexity of chemical and food plants. The resulting mathematical problems are formidable in size but current work has shown that with careful attention to the solution techniques (and ever more powerful number crunchers) optimal solutions can be achieved for problems with several thousand variables in reasonable times (of the order of a few minutes to half hour, on a SUN Sparc2

workstation). To contain problem size, however, the algorithms rely on a discretisation of time to a resolution of, say, half an hour for a daily production schedule (4, 5). The mathematical formulation lends itself to extensions towards batch plant design (where having or not having a specific vessel is an additional choice) and longer term planning.

Developments along the second direction (6) consider a continuous time representation, and leave some decisions (such as the order of batches) to the operator (or scheduler program), but will then produce a schedule wich satisfies operational feasibility constraints in detail, including complex simultaneous transfers, continuous operations, tasks involving several processing vessels and utilities, etc. This is done from a general problem definition in a high level language, which includes the separate definition of plant resources (vessels and connections), operating procedures (in terms of primitive "phases"), production requirements, and operating constraints (such as resource availability). Each of the definitions may be changed independently to study, for example, the effect of a different plant configuration on the detailed schedule. The algorithm used does not guarantee optimality, but is fast and can be used interactively by a planner/operator (or scheduler program) taking the top level decisions. A supervisory batch management system (SUPERBATCH) was developed to incorporate these ideas and a number of industrial case studies have been successfully carried out, including a study of the daily production scheduling in one of the largest dairy plants in the UK. Figure 5 shows the output, in the form of a Gantt chart, of a (very) detailed scheduling exercise for producing a single batch of emulsion in our pilot plant. Without going into the details, this is a difficult problem to solve since it involves scheduling both the main process and the cleaning through some common pipework, with simultaneous selection of flowpaths though the Flow Separate Plates (shown in Figure 5 in terms of the utilisation profile of individual ports). This example shows that resource contention is managed well within SUPERBATCH. This technology has been incorporated by APV in their Batch Manager program described above.

We are obviously interested in the integration of mathematical methods for off line design, long range planning and coarse scheduling based on economic optimisation with the detailed off-line and on line scheduling methods to ensure and maintain operational feasibility. Major challenges arise from the need to ensure consistency between the various problem representations and levels of aggregation in the models used in the various planning, scheduling and control functions. Some preliminary work (8) has shown that an effective integration can indeed be achieved.

b) On line supervisory batch management
A particular feature of the SUPERBATCH system described above is that once a detailed operations schedule has been produced (off line) for the current problem, this schedule can be automatically executed on a target control system, with SUPERBATCH initiating the sequences to be carried out by the control system, monitoring the progress of the schedule, as reported by sequence status and other signals from the control system and rescheduling on-line all batches in light of actual plant events. In order for SUPERBATCH to talk to the control system, the correspondence must be established between its own model "phases" and associated parameters, and the control sequences and associated tags. Suitable sections in the SUPERBATCH definition language allow the easy configuration of this interface. A prototype system demonstrating this approach has been in operation now for almost three years, interfaced with IBM's RTPMS as the control system controlling three other pilot plants in the Department of Chemical Engineering laboratory. None of these plants however, is of a batch nature, and the new pilot plant now provides the opportunity to implement and verify these ideas on an actual multipurpose plant. As already noted, the control sequences in

the new plant have been designed with this in mind and some required software development is being carried out at present.

c) Synthesis of operating procedures and sequences

The development of control software for a batch plant (from broad functional specifications and descriptions of the intended operating procedures to detailed sequence control code) is a very engineering intensive and error prone activity, involving both process and control engineering knowledge. There is considerable interest in any method that will improve productivity and reduce errors. Our objective here is to develop both specifications (if not actual code) for the individual sequences required to run a plant, and operating procedures (in terms of those sequences) required to achieve a more complex goal. The operating procedures should be defined in such a way that they could be automatically carried out by a supervisory management system. We have posed the problem as follows: given a process description (in terms of *tasks* to be performed to reach various *states*), a plant description (vessels and their type, their connections, and their suitability to perform the various tasks), and operating constraints, develop the control sequences necessary to achieve specified goals.

This is clearly a big problem, nonetheless we are working on a prototype system (CAPS, for Computer Aided Procedure Synthesis) which does just that. CAPS first breaks down the overall problem into a series of smaller goals (using, incidentally, the same mathematical optimisation programs mentioned earlier) and identifies the required master procedures and sequences. Then for each unknown sequence it produces a set of specifications. The last function is performed by a rule based system and requires flowsheet information (such as is usually available from a P&I diagram), plus preferred control strategies, additional constraints, etc. Figure 6 gives an example of the type of specification for a sequence that CAPS can produce (this particular sequence refers to the dairy plant mentioned previously). In fact, the phases required to run the emulsion process and the entire SUPERBATCH input which produced figure 5 were automatically generated by CAPS. Further details are given in References (7, 8).

Conclusions

The overall goal of the research described is to develop and test techniques supporting the entire range of activites, from preliminary plant and control system design, to the development of control system software and finally to planning and scheduling techniques which can assist production decisions both off line and on line, for flexible, multipurpose production plants. We are not only concerned with individual tools, but also, and increasingly with their integration. The new pilot plant described in this paper will be an excellent test bed and demonstration facility for flexible production techniques. It is expected these will be particularly relevant to the food industry. It is envisaged that the plant will be used also for teaching.

Acknowledgements

This work was partially funded by SERC/AFRC. Contributions to the pilot plant project by APV Baker are gratefully acknowledged. Particular thanks to B. Westwood, L. Zhenhai, C. Crooks and A. Barnes

References

1) Centre for Process Systems Engineering, Imperial College (Sept. 1991) *Second Annual Report*.
2) Pantelides, C C, (1988) *Comput. Chem. Engng.*, **12**, 745-755.
3) Macchietto S., Matzopoulos M. and Stuart G. (1987) pp. 669-677 in *Computer Aided Process Operations*', G. V. Reklaitis and H. D. Spriggs Eds., Elsevier, Amsterdam.

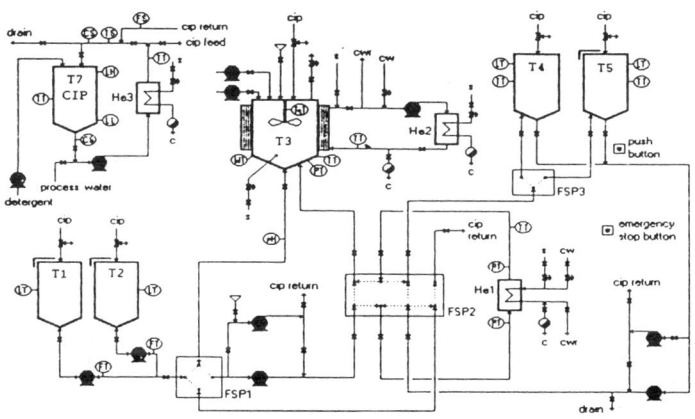

Figure 1. Schematic diagram of the pilot plant

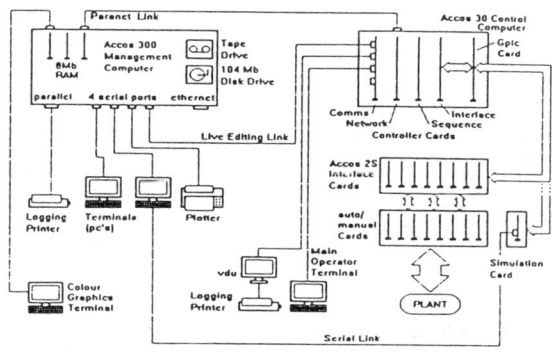

Figure 2. Schematic diagram of the control system

a)

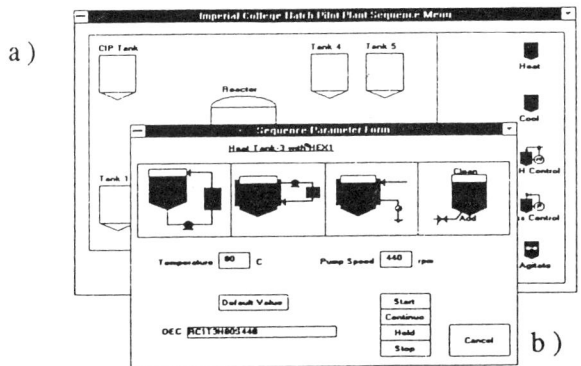

b)

Figure 3. Graphical interface to the plant a) main plant vessels diagram
b) selecting and initiating a reactor heating sequence

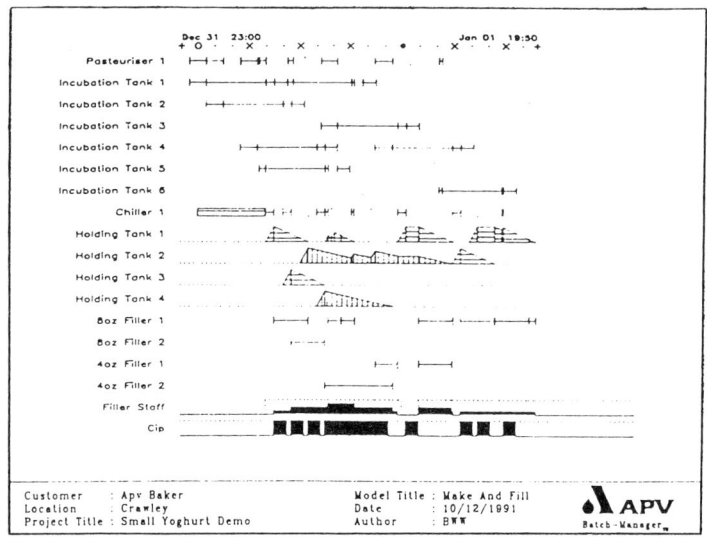

Figure 4. Batch Manager schedule for a day's operation in a small yoghurt plant

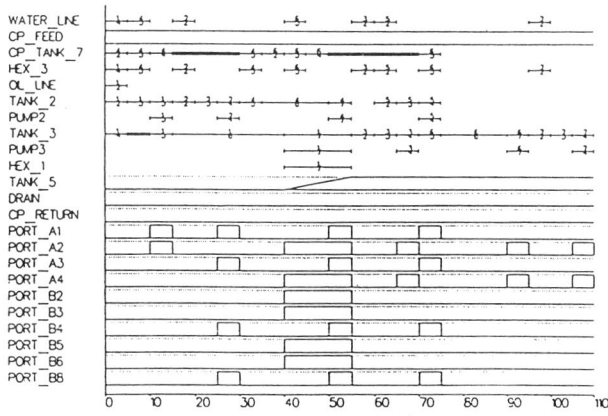

Figure 5. Gantt chart of a detailed operations schedule for the pilot plant

Phase Past_Skim is of type TRANSFER with heat exchange.
    Its action is to transfer 4549.4 units of material of composition
        [skim,100] from skim_silo to vat1
        by the path: [skim_silo, v01, p01, v05, past1, v06, v09, v10, v11, vat1]
        with heating to 80 degrees.
The corresponding control instructions for this phase are:
Interlock to "Closed" items: [v07, v08, v13, v16, v19, v12, v28]
Interlock items: [skim_silo, v01, p01, v05, past1, v06, v09, v10, v11, vat1]
Sequence Instructions:

1. open_valve(v01)	2. open_valve(v05)
3. open_valve(v06)	4. open_valve(v09)
5. open_valve(v10)	6. open_valve(v11)
7. turn_on_pump(p01)	8. start_hx(past1, 80)

Termination Condition: Wait_for_transfer_time(90)
Termination Instructions:

1. turn_off_hx(past1)	2. turn_off_pump(p01)
3. close_valve(v01)	4. close_valve(v05)
5. close_valve(v06)	6. close_valve(v09)
7. close_valve(v10)	8. close_valve(v11)

Uninterlock items: [skim_silo, v01, p01, v05, past1, v06, v09, v10, v11, vat1,
                       v07, v08, v13, v16, v19, v12, v28]

Figure 6. Example of a Phase Control Sequence Generated by CAPS

MEASUREMENT OF CAN ROTATION DURING CONTINUOUS ROTARY

PROCESSES AND ITS INFLUENCE ON PROCESS VALUES

P.M. Withers and P.S. Richardson*

An electronic device was designed and constructed to accurately measure the rotation of cans during continuous rotary processes.

The device was used to investigate the parameters that could affect can rotation and the effect of rotation on the lethality of the process. During the course of the work, a number of factors were identified which directly affected the rotation of the can. It was found, for example, that the presence of water in the steriliser could reduce the number of rotations by up to 50%. It was also ascertained that a reduction in the number of rotations during the process reduced the effectiveness of the heat process.

Introduction

Certain types of rotary steriliser allow cans of product to rotate freely for at least part of the time during processing. If the product exhibits some degree of convection heating, then this rotation will cause agitation of the product, which will increase the rate of heat transfer into the product and thus increase the sterilisation effect, or lethality, of the process. Therefore, any factors which affect the rotation of the can of product will also have some effect on the lethality.

The objective of this work was to develop an electronic device capable of recording the total number of rotations experienced by a can of product during a continuous rotary sterilisation process. The device was then used to investigate and quantify the effects of factors likely to influence can rotation during processing, such as the presence of water in the bottom of the steriliser vessel.

The prototype device was able to record accurately the number of can rotations during a process at a rate of up to three can rotations per second at temperatures up to 125°C. The device was fitted inside a can. The can was then ballasted with water or product to allow accurate simulation of the physical behaviour of a normal can of product.

Rotation Counter

The construction of the counter is discussed in three parts: the rotation sensor, the electronic counter, and the battery.

*   Campden Food and Drink Research Association, Chipping Campden, Glos, GL55 6LD, UK

The rotation sensor was designed to monitor can rotation in either direction at the required temperature and likely rotation rate. The sensing element chosen was a miniature mercury tilt switch. The sensor system consisted of two switches arranged 180° apart and perpendicular to the longitudinal axis of the can. This arrangement meant that both switches operated once per can revolution. The output from each switch was passed through a low pass filter, the time constant of which was selected to give a response rate of 3 revs/sec, while providing a high degree of noise immunity. The outputs from both filters were used to operate the SET and RESET inputs of a switching circuit. The output from this circuit cycled once per revolution of the rotation counter.

The counter itself had to have sufficient capacity to record the number of revolutions experienced in any rotary process. A 16-bit binary counter was chosen, giving a possible total count of 65,535 revolutions. The counter was formed from four 4-bit binary counters connected in cascade and driven by the rotation sensor such that the value stored in the counter was incremented once per revolution. The data was output from the counter as a 16-bit binary word.

The battery was required to operate at temperatures up to 125°C, while supplying power to operate the counter for sufficient time plus an additional safety margin, approximately 5 hours in total. The battery used in the prototype was a lithium manganese dioxide primary cell. This had a nominal terminal voltage of 3.0 V at a rate of 160 mAh.

The components used in the construction of the rotating counter were either rated at or had been tested at 125°C. This meant that there was no need to provide any form of thermal insulation for the electronics. The layout of the counter is shown in Diagram 1.

Housing

The housing was required to protect the electronics from moisture and to allow mounting of the unit inside the can. The housing consisted of a stainless steel tubular body with aluminium end caps. The electronic circuit board was located inside the housing via plastic guides. The housing was subsequently located inside the can by a threaded gland assembly fitted through a hole in the can end. The opposite end of the housing was located by three stainless steel wire fingers. This ensured that the unit was securely located, preventing false counts being recorded due to the counter moving within the can, and that the housing was not mounted eccentrically in the can which could cause atypical rotation patterns. The layout of the housing in the can is shown in Diagram 2.

Read-out Unit

The read-out unit was used to read the binary data from the counter at the end of a process and convert it into a decimal value which could be displayed, giving a reading of the total number of rotations that the counter had experienced during the thermal process.

Experiments and Results

In order to test and evaluate the counter, a range of trials was conducted using both full size sterilisers and pilot scale simulators. For all trials the counters were installed in cans in the fashion detailed in the description of the housing above.

Simulator trials: a series of trials was carried out using the counter in a pilot scale rotary steriliser simulator in order to assess the counter's ability to function as intended under normal processing conditions, as experienced in a full size steriliser.

The counters were secured within three-piece A2 cans and processed in the simulator using a variety of times and temperatures. The range of experiments and results are shown in Table 1.

Buoyancy trials: trials were conducted using the simulator mentioned above, the objective being to ascertain whether the counter was able to indicate the presence of water within the steriliser vessels. In order to do this, the can containing the counter was made buoyant, such that it would float when submerged rather than roll as it would normally do in the absence of water. In this way the presence of water should be indicated by a reduced count. Different levels of water were used and a trial with the simulator empty of water provided a reference count. The results are shown in Table 2.

Trials in full size reel and spiral sterilisers: a series of trials were conducted in a full size reel and spiral steriliser which consisted of preheat, processing and cooling vessels. The first and last of these are normally half filled with water. The reel speed was nominally 3 revs/min and two-piece ET cans were used throughout. The work was conducted in two parts: calibration trials at ambient temperature and trials under normal processing conditions.

Calibration trials: four cans containing counters were used for each trial. These were ballasted with water to a realistic fill weight. The first run was carried out with the entire steriliser empty, the second with the cooling vessel half full of water, and the third with both the preheat and cooling vessels half full of water. All runs were at ambient temperature. The results are summarised in Table 3.

Trials under normal process conditions: these trials were carried out in the same way as the calibration trials, but the steriliser was used under normal processing conditions, e.g. a temperature in the processing vessel of approximately 120°C. The results are shown in Table 4. Note that the third run was carried out in a different but apparently identical steriliser using the same processing conditions.

Discussion

From observations made during the trials carried out in the simulator, otherwise identical cans demonstrated different rates of rotation, and it was concluded that this could be due to the effect of different can pockets within the simulator reel. This variation resulted in the calculated range of values shown in the expected count column of Table 1. Since the results obtained fell into the expected ranges, it was felt that the counters accurately recorded the number of revolutions that those cans had experienced.

The results of the buoyancy trials showed that a counter in a buoyant can was capable of indicating the presence of water inside a steriliser shell provided that the water was of sufficient depth to allow the can to float rather than roll on the can guide rails. It was essential, however, to know the likely number of revolutions that the can would undergo in the absence of water in order to make an assessment of the amount of water present.

The trials carried out in the full size simulator showed that the presence of water in a shell approximately halved the number of revolutions that the can experienced in that shell when compared to an empty shell. A prediction was made for the results of the third trial, with preheat and cooling shells half filled with water, based on the results obtained in the second trial. The close agreement between the predicted and actual values would tend to confirm the effect that the presence of water had on the rotation of the cans in this instance.

Trials carried out under normal processing conditions showed that the counters were immune to the effects of temperature. The third trial was carried out in a different but apparently identical steriliser using the same processing conditions. The difference in counts between this and the other steriliser indicated some difference between them that was influencing can rotation. This may have been caused by differences in wear or corrosion.

The factors that may influence can rotation are not limited to those mentioned above. Also to be considered are the effects of different sizes and types of can, types of product (e.g. solid, liquid, or particulate), type of process, and the design of the steriliser itself. Connected with the last of these is the question of wear or corrosion in the steriliser. Another area of uncertainty arose when comparing simulators to full size sterilisers, and the effect of such things as thermocouple probes in cans used in experimental work.

A more fundamental question was that of the effect of can rotation on the lethality of the process received by a can of product in a rotary process. For convection or part convection heating packs, the effectiveness of heat transfer into the product depends partly upon its agitation, caused in this case by the rotation of the can. Therefore, any reduction in the number of rotations will affect directly the lethality of the process recovered by the affected cans. Reductions in rotation could be caused by any of the factors discussed above.

The device discussed in this document has been shown in the course of the work to be a suitable means of investigating the above factors. To this end it has a number of applications. It may be used for QA/QC purposes, to provide a daily or weekly record of steriliser performance in terms of can rotation. Longer term testing would enable monitoring of the steriliser in terms of wear or corrosion. The device could also be used in research work using simulators and full size sterilisers. However, the counter described can only give a total count of the number of revolutions that it has undergone. While this is useful in itself, and quite useable as discussed, it does mean that the examination of can rotation in small sections of the steriliser is very difficult if not impossible. To enable a more detailed analysis to be made, the development of a logging version of the counter would be desirable. This device would sense the rotations in the same way as the existing counter but would store the total count in a memory at predetermined intervals. The data could then be retrieved at the end of a process via a simple computer interface and presented as required, e.g. as a time/rotation history.

Conclusion

The device produced as a result of this work was successful in fulfilling the original objective. It became apparent during the course of the evaluation of the counter that a number of factors, some not previously considered, affected the rotation of cans in rotary sterilisers.

Table 1: Simulator Trials

Unit No.	Temp (°C)	Reel Speed (rpm)	Process Duration (minutes)	Estimated[1] Count	Actual[2] Count
1	124	3	32	260-390	359
4	124	3	32	260-390	350
1	123	3	34	300-500	321
2	123	3	34	300-500	314
4	122	3	15	135-225	170
6	122	3	15	135-225	131
1	122	3	15	135-225	176
4	122	3	15	135-225	187
5	122	3	15	135-225	185
6	122	3	15	135-225	179
4	122	3	15	135-225	193
5	122	3	15	135-225	198
6	122	3	15	135-225	195
4	122	3	30	270-450	342
5	122	3	30	270-450	361
4	122	4	15	240-270	255
5	122	4	15	240-270	248

1   Calculated from the reel diameter and pitch, and the can size
2   As recorded by the counter

Table 2: Buoyancy Trials

Unit No.	No. of Rotations After 30 Minutes		
	Simulator Half Full	Simulator One Third Full	Simulator Empty
1	63	64	224
2	63		
4	68	64	187
5	65		
6	67		

Table 3: Full Size Steriliser
Calibration Trial

Trial No.	Unit No.	Counter Reading at End of Process	Process Conditions[1]
1	5	1279	Empty
	6	1290	Process time: 69 mins
			Predicted count 1200-1600
2	1	1130	Cooler half full
	2	1143	Process time: 69 mins
	5	1150	
	6	1102	
3	1	854	Preheat and cooler half full
	2	904	Process time: 69 mins
	5	921	Predicted count 900
	6	863	

[1] All processes carried out with steriliser at ambient temperature (approximately 20°C)

Table 4: Full Size Steriliser
Process Trial

Trial No.	Unit No.	Counter Reading at End of Process	Process Conditions
1	1	932	Cooker "C"
	2	921	Process time: 69 mins
	5	882	Process temp: 119°C
2	1	981	Cooker "C"
	2	923	Process time: 69 mins
	5	918	Process temp: 119°C
3	1	826	Cooker "A"
	2	877	Process time: 69 mins
	6	873	Process temp: 119°C

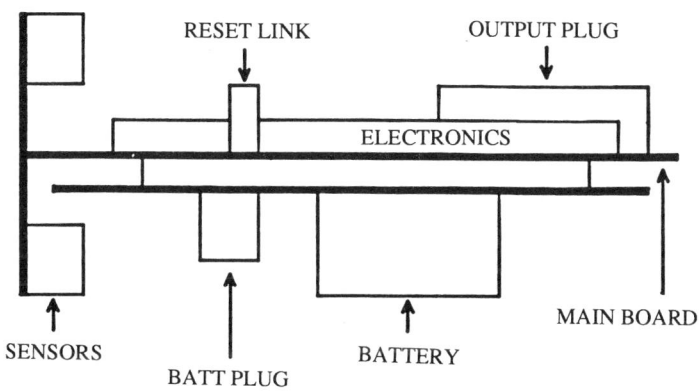

Diagram 1: Layout of can Rotation Counter

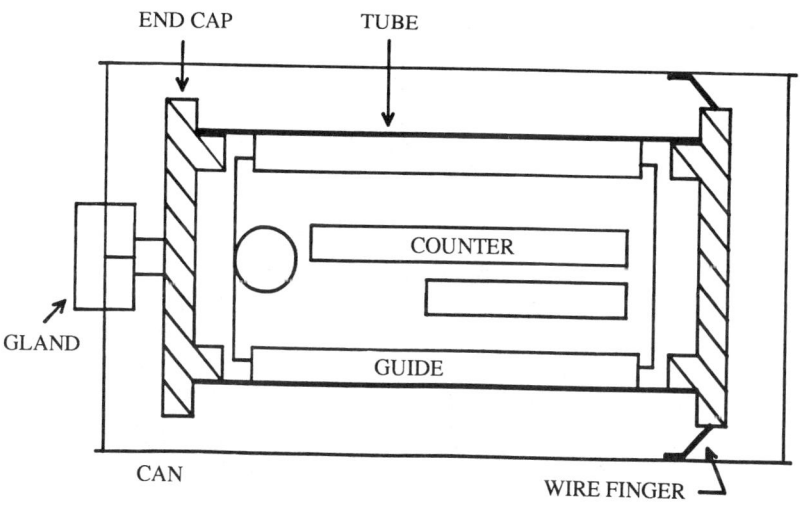

Diagram 2: Layout of Housing in Can

THE USE OF THE TUBE VISCOMETER TO PROVIDE ACCURATE RHEOLOGY DATA FOR THE MODELLING OF HEAT TRANSFER INTO FOOD PARTICULATES DURING UHT PROCESSING

G.S. Tucker*

During UHT processing of foods containing discrete particles (> 3 mm), it is imperative to understand the behaviour of the materials in terms of flow and heat transfer, in order that the commercial sterility of the product is ensured. This paper describes one approach which used a finite difference model to predict heat transfer rates into the particulate matter, and a tube viscometer to measure apparent viscosity of the food. By accurately measuring viscosity under continuous flow conditions, it will be possible to predict with more confidence the fluid/ particulate heat transfer coefficient. This variable is critical in controlling heat transfer rates into the food particulates, and as such a more accurate model will result.

Introduction

Aseptic processing is being extended to a greater range of foodstuffs as processing and packaging innovations continue to be developed. The processing of particulates under dynamic flow conditions has gained rapid prominence with these developments. A major concern with the development of these thermal processes is to ensure that an adequate sterilisation value is achieved at the centre of the particulates, while at the same time maintaining the sensory and nutritional qualities of the product. Presently there is no experimental technique available to verify the commercial sterility of heterogeneous products processed in continuous flow other than by microbiological means (Dallyn *et al*, 1977; Gaze *et al*, 1988; Gaze *et al*, 1989) in which a known number of spores are encapsulated in an alginate bead and the bead exposed to the thermal process. This is because of the difficulty in measuring the temperature at the centre of a particulate as it travels through a continuous process. Predictive models are, therefore, very important in estimating the particulate centre temperature during heating, holding and cooling when designing a process.

The objectives of this work were twofold. Firstly, a finite difference model was written for predictions of lethality achieved at the centre of rectangular, cylindrical and spherical particulates as they travel through a continuous process. Having validated the model, a tube viscometer was constructed to provide accurate experimental data for the model. Viscosity data under continuous flow conditions has not been extensively researched; therefore, the needs of the particulate model provided an excellent opportunity to perform this research. The results from the tube viscometer were used to provide a better estimate of the fluid/particulate heat transfer coefficient, which is a variable that has been proved critical, but difficult to calculate accurately.

*   Campden Food and Drink Research Association, Chipping Campden, Glos, GL55 6LD, UK

Heat Transfer Considerations

When heterogeneous foods are heated using a scraped-surface heat exchanger, the particulates exhibit a thermal lag compared to the fluid. Unlike the heating of canned foods in condensing steam, whereby heat transfer from the steam to the can is extremely good, particulates in a liquid do not experience such ideal heating conditions. There is no latent heat of condensation in a hot liquid, as is present using condensing steam, and generally the liquid portion must be highly viscous to create the buoyancy necessary to prevent settling. Under these conditions, the surface heat transfer coefficient for the fluid/particulate interface is greatly reduced from the canning situation, and therefore becomes vital in quantifying heat penetration from the fluid to the particulate. At present there is no way of accurately measuring the temperature of a continuously moving particulate, and therefore models with a term for the convective boundary condition (which includes the fluid/particulate surface heat transfer coefficient) must be used in the estimation of the centre temperature.

The finite difference model (McKenna and Tucker, 1990) allowed for the use of a convective fluid/particulate heat transfer coefficient derived from the Ranz-Marshall (1952) relationship equation.

$$Nu = 2 + 0.6 \, Re_s^{0.5} \, Pr^{0.33} \qquad \qquad \text{..... (1)}$$

This equation (1) is valid for Newtonian flow past a single sphere. For non-Newtonian flow the Reynolds and Prandtl numbers are replaced by their generalised equivalents (Skelland, 1967), which contain the rheology parameters. Thus, for power fluids the consistency coefficient for pipe flow, K, and the flow behaviour index, n, are introduced into the calculation of surface heat transfer coefficient.

If the relative velocity between the fluid and particulate is zero, the equation (1) simplifies to $Nu = 2.0$. It is difficult to measure the actual fluid to particulate relative velocity but, in most cases, this would be greater than zero. When calculating the heat transfer coefficient, the thermophysical properties of the fluid in the equation should be calculated at the specific temperature used in the process. For this reason, the tube viscometer was constructed (McKenna, 1990) and is shown in Figure 1.

A number of authors have developed a finite difference method to determine the rate of heat transfer into the centre of a particulate (Sawada and Merson, 1986; Aström et al, 1988; Chandarana et al, 1989; Chandarana and Gavin, 1989; Chang and Toledo, 1989; and Lee et al, 1990a). Previous work carried out at Campden Food and Drink Research Association (Tucker and Clark, 1989) documents the use of the finite difference method for conduction heating of cylindrical and rectangular shaped cans in static retorts. This finite difference technique was used as the basis of the predictive model which has been developed (McKenna and Tucker, 1990) for this work. Results for the model are presented in McKenna and Tucker (1991), for a range of particle Biot numbers from 5 to 51 obtained using Sylgard 184 (Dow Corning Ltd) particulates. The experimental work used single particulates suspended in a flowing medium (water). Future work will involve a range of food carrier fluids for the particulates and develop heat transfer equations for non-Newtonian flow conditions. Investigations will also be carried out as to whether the single-particulate model for heat transfer is suitable for high solids concentration mixtures. and how the heat transfer coefficient changes during the heating and cooling cycles.

Flow Considerations

The first published work on fluid flow patterns in pipes was done by Reynolds (1883), who injected streams of dye into the moving fluid. Reynolds correlated his data using a dimensionless group universally known as the Reynolds number. The Reynolds number has been widely used in the study of fluid mechanics in order to characterise the flow nature of a fluid as that fluid travels through a pipe. When considering the food industry, and more specifically the area of continuous thermal processing with particulate matter, the majority of fluids tend to display laminar flow characteristics. This is primarily because of the need to create buoyancy forces sufficient to keep the particulate matter in suspension.

The design of a continuous flow plant to produce such products, and its effectiveness in producing a high quality sterile product, are greatly influenced by the flow properties of the product. Reliable rheological data is required for the design of continuous processes in terms of being able to predict flow rates and pressure drops in pipes and to correctly size pumps. There is considerable data for the rheological properties of liquid foods without particulate matter using rotational viscometers (Harper and Lebermann, 1962; Holdsworth, 1971; Rao, 1977; Rao et al, 1981; Crandall et al, 1982). However, when the range of products is extended to include particulate matter in a carrier fluid, the use of conventional viscometers is not possible and in-line techniques are required. A tube viscometer similar to the one used in this study was used by Self et al (1990) and also by Dail and Steffe (1990a and b) to measure rheological properties using such an in-line technique. Both groups used starch solutions of varying concentrations as their liquid product. To date only one study has been reported that concerns particulate matter within a liquid carrier fluid. This was done by Bhamidipati and Singh (1990), who used peas in tomato sauce to represent a model system for their work, and compared their results to those both with and without peas.

Most liquid foods exhibit non-Newtonian flow behaviour, with the greater proportion of these showing pseudoplastic or shear thinning properties. For pseudoplastic foods the relationship between shear stress and shear rate can be defined using the power law:

$$\tau = k.D^n \qquad \qquad \dots \dots \quad (2)$$

For Newtonian fluids the flow behaviour index, n, is always 1.0, and the consistency coefficient, k, becomes the dynamic viscosity. For pseudoplastic foods the value of n will be below 1.0, and for other fluids n generally lies between 0 and 2.

With reference to equation (2) for power law fluids, it is possible to relate the wall shear stress to the wall shear rate using variables which can be measured, such as pressure drop and flow rate (Holland, 1973):

$$\frac{d.\Delta P}{4L} = k.\left(\frac{32Q}{\pi d^3}\right)^n \left(\frac{3n+1}{4n}\right)^n \qquad \dots \dots \quad (3)$$

It is common practice to correlate non-Newtonian flow data for pipes of circular cross-section by taking logarithms in order to remove the power index in equation (3) and thus allow the equation to be represented by a straight line graph. Each of the variables in equation (3) can be measured over a length of pipe, and from the gradient and intercept of the straight line graph, the constants k and n determined.

A plot of $\ln(d.\Delta P/4L)$ on the ordinate axis against $\ln(8Q/\pi d^3)$ on the abscissa will give a straight line for power law fluids, and from this the constants n and k determined:

1. Gradient = n

2. Intercept, $K = k\left(\dfrac{3n+1}{n}\right)^n$

To establish the flow regime of the fluid through the tube viscometer, Metzner and Reed (1955) established a generalised Reynolds number which incorporated the power law constants:

$$Re_{gen} = \frac{D^n.u^{2-n}.\rho}{K.8^{n-1}}$$

A value of $Re_{gen} < 2,100$ represents flow within the laminar regime (Skelland, 1967) and therefore the generalised Reynolds number was calculated for each trial. For those fluids exhibiting laminar flow, the apparent viscosity, μ_a, can be obtained from the following equation:

$$\mu_a = K.\left(\frac{32Q}{\pi d^3}\right)^{n-1}$$

This value for apparent viscosity will have been determined at process conditions, therefore providing the finite difference model with the accurate data required.

Results and Discussions

Figure 2 shows an example of the results from the tube viscometer taken at 50°C for 10% w/w peas in a 5% Colflo 67 starch solution as the carrier fluid. The mixture shows good modelling agreement using the power law, with an $R^2 = 0.987$, giving $n = 0.51$ and $k = 2.31$ kg m^{-1} s^{n-2}. Table 1 presents this data and also highlights the relationship between shear stress, shear rate and apparent viscosity.

At the time of writing, the tube viscometer has been extensively used for homogeneous foods such as starch solutions, gravies, tomato soup, bechamel sauce and lobster bisque. Some of the results for these products at temperatures up to 60°C are given in Figures 3 and 4 in terms of the relationship between shear rate and apparent viscosity. The initial work using peas as an example of particulate matter (in a 5% Colflo 67 carrier fluid) appears very promising. To date, pea concentrations up to 15% have been successfully pumped around the tube viscometer and the power law used to model the results. As the pea concentration was increased from 5% to 15%, the consistency coefficient, k, was found to increase, and the flow behaviour index, n, decreased. For data at 50°C the flow behaviour was found to get less Newtonian as the pea concentration increased from 5 to 15%. These results are shown in Table 2. At fixed pea concentrations, both k and n were found to decrease with increasing temperature in the range 35°C to 50°C. Much work is needed in this area to investigate different particulate materials and fluids. The rheology work presented here used the power law to successfully model peas in starch, but it is likely that other models will need to be used for different foods or even new models developed. This research, however, has provided a proven method which may allow some of these questions to be answered.

Conclusions

The use of mathematical models to predict heat transfer rates into food particulates will provide the thermal processor with an invaluable tool to ensure adequate product safety. However, a model is only as good as the data inputted to that model. Therefore, techniques such as the tube viscometer enable more accurate data to be collected, which will subsequently improve the model results. Also, gaining a better idea of the magnitude of the fluid/particulate heat transfer coefficient will assist in determining the critical control points for a continuous process. These are essential for process engineers to develop computer control systems that can only operate if the experimental data provided is reliable and the models employed suitably validated.

References

Aström, A., Ohlsson, T., Skjöldebrand, C. and Falk, C. (1988). In Proceedings of the International Symposium on "Progress in Food Preservation Processes," Vol. 2, Centre for Education and Research of Food and Chemical Industries, Brussels, Belgium, p29.

Bhamidipati, S. and Singh, R.K. (1990). Journal of Food Process Engineering 12, 275.

Chandarana, D.I. and Gavin III, A. (1989). Journal of Food Science 54 (1), 198.

Chandarana, D.I., Gavin III, A. and Wheaton, F.W. (1989). Food Technology 43 (3), 137.

Chang, S.Y. and Toledo, R.T. (1989). Journal of Food Science 54 (4), 1017.

Crandall, P.G., Chen, C.S. and Carter, R.D. (1982). Food Technology 36 (5), 245.

Dail, R.V. and Steffe, J.F. (1990a). Journal of Food Science 55 (6), 1660.

Dail, R.V. and Steffe, J.F. (1990b). Journal of Food Science 55 (6), 1764.

Dallyn, H., Falloon, W.C. and Bean, P.G. (1977). Laboratory Practice 26 (10), 773.

Gaze, J.E., Carter, J., Brown, G.D. and Thomas, J.D. (1988) Technical Memorandum No. 508, Campden Food and Drink Research Association, Chipping Campden, Glos, UK.

Gaze, J.E., Spence, L. and Brown, G.D. (1989). Technical Memorandum No. 547, Campden Food and Drink Research Association, Chipping Campden, Glos, UK.

Harper, J.C. and Lebermann, K.W. (1962). Proceedings of the 1st International Conference on Food Science and Technology 1, 719.

Holdsworth, S.D. (1971). Journal of Texture Studies 2, 393.

Holland, F.A. (1973). Fluid Flow for Chemical Engineers, Edward Arnold Publishers Ltd, London, UK.

Lee, J.H., Singh, R.K. and Larkin, J.W. (1990). Journal of Food Engineering 11, 67-92.

McKenna, A.B. (1990). Technical Memorandum No. 605, Campden Food and Drink Research Association, Chipping Campden, Glos, UK.

McKenna, A.B. and Tucker, G.S. (1990). Technical Memorandum No. 587, Campden Food and Drink Research Association, Chipping Campden, Glos, UK.

McKenna, A.B. and Tucker, G.S. (1991). Food Control $\underline{2}$, 224.

Metzner, A.B. and Reed, J.C. (1955). American Chemical Engineering Journal $\underline{1}$, 434.

Ranz, W.E. and Marshall, W.K. Jr (1952). Chemical Engineering Progress $\underline{48}$ (4), 173.

Rao, M.A. (1977). Journal of Texture Studies $\underline{8}$, 257.

Rao, M.A., Bourne, M.C. and Cooley, H.J. (1981). Journal of Texture Studies $\underline{12}$, 521.

Reynolds, O. (1883). Proceedings Royal Society (London), A, $\underline{174}$, 935.

Sawada, H. and Merson, R.L. (1986). 4th International Congress - "Food Engineering and Process Applications", Vol. 1, Eds. le Maguer, M. and Jelen, P., Applied Science Publishers, New York, USA, p569.

Self, K.P., Wilkins, T.J., Morley, M.J. and Bailey, C. (1990). Journal of Food Engineering $\underline{11}$, 291.

Skelland, A.H.P. (1967). Non-Newtonian Flow and Heat Transfer, John Wiley, New York, USA.

Tucker, G.S. and Clark, P. (1989). Technical Memorandum No. 529, Campden Food and Drink Research Association, Chipping Campden, Glos, UK.

Nomenclature

d	Internal pipe diameter, m
D	Shear rate, s^{-1}
k	General consistency coefficient, $kg\ m^{-1}\ s^{n-2}$
K	Consistency coefficient for pipe flow, $kg\ m^{-1}\ s^{n-2}$
L	Pipe length, m
n	Flow behaviour index
Nu	Nusselt number
ΔP	Pressure drop, $N\ m^{-2}$
Pr	Prandtl number
Q	Flow rate, $m^3\ s^{-1}$
Re_s	Reynolds number for the sphere
Re_{gen}	Generalised Reynolds number
τ	Shear stress, $N\ m^{-2}$
μ_a	Apparent viscosity, $N\ s\ m^{-2}$

Table 1: Rheological Properties of
Liquid/Solid Foods using a Tube Viscometer

Product: 5% Starch (Colflo 67)
with 10% Fresh Peas at 50.0°C

K	=	2.86	k	=	2.31
n	=	0.51	n	=	0.51

Volumetric Flow Rate (l/min)	Pressure Drop (mbar)	Shear Stress (N/m^2)	Shear Rate (s^{-1})	Apparent Viscosity $(N\ s/m^2)$
16.0	41.0	15.2	31.7	0.596
16.4	41.0	15.2	32.5	0.589
20.0	44.0	16.4	39.7	0.532
23.1	48.0	17.8	45.8	0.494
26.1	50.0	18.6	51.8	0.464
30.0	54.0	20.1	59.5	0.432
30.8	55.0	20.5	61.1	0.426
33.3	58.0	21.6	66.1	0.410
35.3	61.0	22.7	70.0	0.398
37.5	63.0	23.4	74.4	0.385
42.1	67.0	24.9	83.5	0.363

Table 2: Rheological Properties of Peas
in Starch for Changing Solids Concentration

Pea Concentration (%)	Consistency Coefficient, K $(kg^{m-1}\ s^{n-2})$	Flow Behaviour Index, n
5	2.14	0.54
10	2.85	0.51
15	4.15	0.44

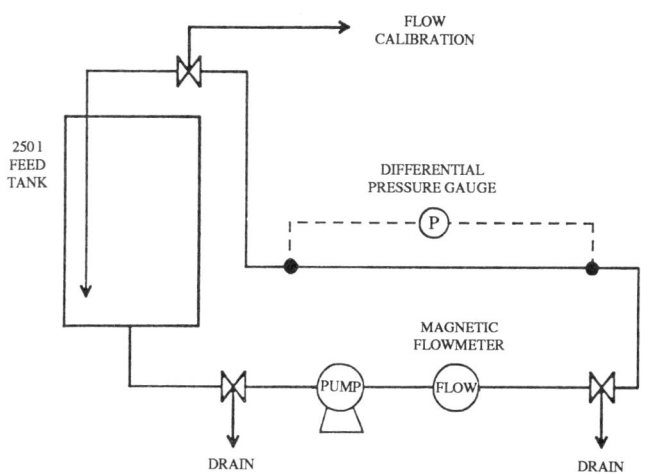

FIGURE 1

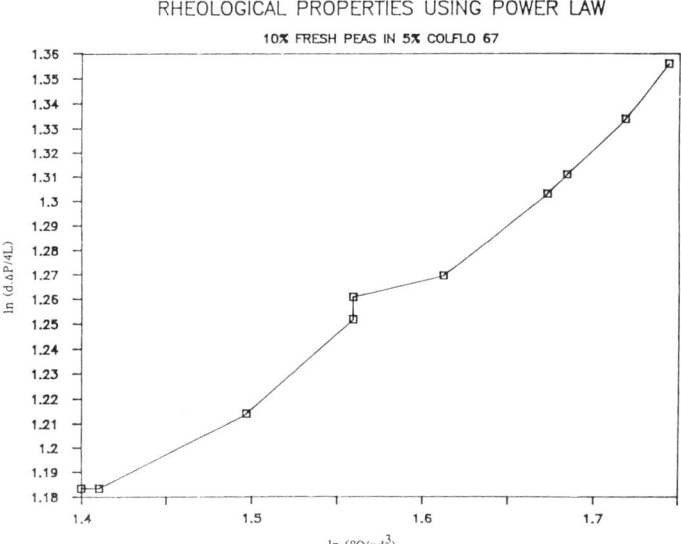

FIGURE 2

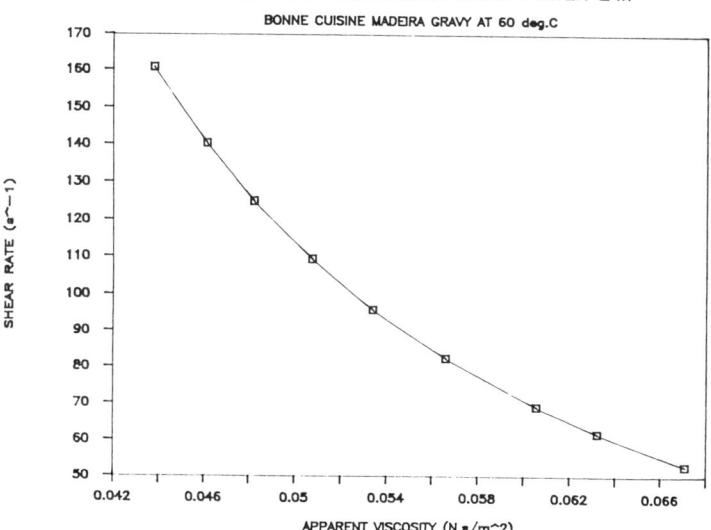

FIGURE 3

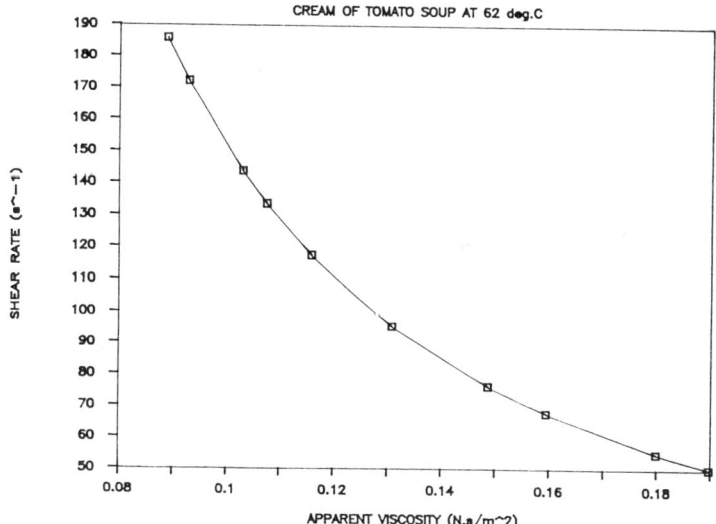

FIGURE 4

SIMULATION AND MODELLING OF CONTAINER STERILISATION PROCESSES AND THE APPLICATION OF DERIVED VALUE CONTROL TECHNIQUE

G.M. Scott*

This paper outlines some of the recent developments in the computer simulation of container sterilisation processes and how these simulation techniques can be applied in a real time process control environment to carry out derived value control.

Introduction

Simulation is the imitation of real life processes. In order to successfully simulate a process, knowledge concerning the underlying physical operations has to be known. When the mode of simulation is mathematical modelling, the knowledge required to model the process is the mathematical representation of that process, e.g. for the case of container sterilisation, the sterilisation process is achieved by the conduction of heat from an ambient source into the container. The mechanism of this heat conduction is described by Fourier's partial differential equations.

Derived value control is the control of a process plant based on parameters that are not directly measurable but are calculated from variables that can be measured. For the sterilisation of containers it is not practical or desirable to measure the temperature at the centre of the container. This temperature can be calculated using a heat penetration model which predicts container centre temperature based on the ambient temperature of the process. From this knowledge, the process can be controlled accordingly.

This paper outlines the application of a finite difference approximation for heat transfer by conduction into a container of cylindrical geometry to the dynamic computer simulation of a hydrostatic cooker and discusses how computer simulation can be included in the control loop to effect derived value control.

* Campden Food and Drink Research Association, Chipping Campden, Glos, GL55 6LD, UK

Heat Penetration Models

Various heat penetration models have been developed for the prediction of temperature within food containers of various geometries during thermal processing. A comprehensive review of such models is given in Tucker (1991). One of the most widely used methods of modelling the heat penetration is by using a finite difference method. This method is a mathematical solution of the Fourier equation describing the heat penetration into the container. It is this method of solution that has been chosen for this paper.

Process Modelling in a Computer Environment

To effectively simulate container sterilisation processes using a finite difference method, a computer is required to carry out the numerous time consuming calculations required at each time step of the modelling procedure. In the early days of process modelling, these finite difference procedures took many hours on a main-frame computer to complete, but with the advances in computer technology in recent years, the run time of these programs has been reduced to minutes even on a PC. Recent advances in the fields of multi-tasking software, transputer technology and parallel processing has reduced the run time even further to the point where the models will run in real time, i.e. the output from the model is calculated virtually instantaneously after the input has been read in.

Modelling of Batch and Continuous Processes

Up until recently, most of the applications of process modelling have been applied to batch processes such as batch retorting. In these examples, it is assumed that all containers within the batch receive the same thermal process and any process deviations affect all the containers in the same way. It is therefore necessary only to model one container per batch and take this to be representative of the whole batch. The next progressive step is to extend this modelling technique to continuous cookers such as hydrostatic cookers. In the modelling of such processes, it is no longer possible to model just one container. Within a continuous cooker there will be, at any one point in time, containers in different processing environments depending on their position within the cooker. Also, process deviations will affect containers differently depending on their position and time inside the cooker. To simulate such a process it is necessary to model the heat penetration into a number of containers to ensure a fair representation of the whole process.

As an example of a computer simulation using finite difference approximation for a continuous cooker, a model to predict the effects of heat penetration into containers process in a hydrostatic cooker was developed (Scott, 1992).

Hydrostatic Cooker Model

A hydrostatic cooker is a continuous cooker (see Figure 1) comprising of four sections: the pre-heat leg; the steam chamber; the pre-cool leg and the cooling section. Passing through the cooker there is a carrier belt which transports the containers through the cooker system. A more detailed description of a hydrostatic cooker is given in Atherton *et al* (1981).

As mentioned previously, in order to successfully model the hydrostatic cooker the effects of heat penetration into more than one container have to be considered. The problem is amplified by considering the fact that containers are continuously entering the cooker prior to processing, and also continuously leaving the cooker after processing. The first problem was solved by considering the hardware set-up of the cooker and then deciding the minimum number of containers required to be representative of all the containers in the process at any point in time of interest. The simplest way of ensuring that this is achieved is to view the cooker in terms of the belt length in each section of the cooker. These belt lengths can be assumed to be constant, so are not affected by deviations in process conditions. Therefore the minimum number of containers, at any point in time, required to model the cooker must be calculated to ensure that there is always at least one can in each section of the cooker being modelled. This can be calculated using equation 1:

$$Nc = INTEGER \left(\frac{TLb}{Lbmin} + 0.5 \right) + 1 \qquad \dots \dots \quad (1)$$

where   Nc   = Minimum number of cans
        TLb   = Total belt length in hydrostat (m)
        LBmin = Shortest sectional belt length in hydrostat (m)

The second problem was a logistical problem of solving the heat penetration via a finite difference approximation for a number of containers at the same time, and was solved in the structuring and development of the hydrostatic cooker computer simulation program. The hydrostatic cooker computer simulation program was written such that it offered a dynamic simulation of the process, i.e. the process variables (namely the speed of the carrier belt and the process temperatures) were supplied on a real-time basis. This method of simulation was chosen as it lends itself to derived value control applications.

The model was compared against experimental results from a heat penetration study on a can of baked beans in tomato sauce. Figure 2 shows a comparison of the time-temperature profiles for the experimental and model results. For the early stages of heating, the model predicts experimental accurately, though there is a slight under-prediction during the latter stages of heating. The maximum difference between experimental and model temperatures was 3°C, with an average difference of approximately 1°C. These discrepancies can be accounted for by the mode of heating for baked beans in tomato sauce being partially convective as well as conductive, whilst the model assumes pure conduction.

Requirements for Derived Value Control

When considering the use of derived value control, two questions must be answered. Firstly, can the process variable of interest be measured directly? If the answer is no, then derived value control is a possible means of process control. Secondly, is there a process model available that will derive the process variable of interest based on measurable process parameters? If the answer is yes, then derived value control is a definite means for process control.

Since, by definition, derived value control requires a process model to calculate the immeasurable process parameters, it is a basic requirement that this predictive model be included in the control loop. Figure 3 shows a basic control diagram for a derived value control loop.

Sterilisation Processes: An Example of a Derived Value Control Application

To illustrate the underlying principles of derived value control, two examples of in-container sterilisation will be used as a process suited to such a control technique. The examples chosen are cans processed in a batch retort and cans processed in a hydrostatic cooker. In both cases the processes are to be controlled using container centre temperature (and by inference, F, the in-container sterility) as the control variable. Since it is impractical to measure the container centre temperature directly, it is calculated or "derived" by measuring the processing environment temperature. The can centre temperature is calculated based on this value using a dynamic, real time heat penetration model.

Derived Value Control of a Batch Retort

In the processing of cans in a batch retort, the main control decision suited to derived value control is when to stop the heating stage and commence with cooling. The criterion for this decision is whether a certain value of F, the in-container sterility, has been reached during the heating stage. If this F value has been achieved, then cooling can commence. The normal way of establishing when to start the cooling stage is by heat penetration studies. From these heat penetration studies, a processing schedule is devised, i.e. the operator knows how long to heat the containers for before starting cooling to ensure the desired F is achieved at the end of heating. Unfortunately, this heating time does not take into account deviations in environment heating temperature. An increase in environment temperature can lead to overprocessing, resulting in the deterioration of product organoleptic quality. A decrease in this temperature could result in the product not reaching commercial sterility, hence being unfit for consumption. Including a heat penetration model to calculate centre temperature (and F) based on environment temperature into the control loop, it is possible to ensure that, even in the event of environment temperature deviation, the onset of cooling will only occur when the desired F has been reached.

This application of derived value control was demonstrated by Bown (1985) within a multi-tasking computer system, whereby the heat penetration model was one task amongst a series of tasks dedicated to control action. Scott (1991) discussed the application of such control within a distributed control system where all control actions were supervised by a supervisory process control package and the heat penetration model was resident on a separate computer interfaced to the supervisory system.

Derived Value Control of a Hydrostatic Cooker

The application of derived value control to a hydrostatic cooker is more complex as there are various process variables to base the control on and various different control strategies available. But, in this example, derived value control will be applied to the control of the carrier belt based on in-container sterility. The main process variable that affects in-container sterility is deviations in steam temperature within the steam chamber. The normal practice in the event of a drop in steam temperature is to stop the carrier belt until the processing temperature is re-established. When this temperature is re-established, the belt is either held for an extra length of time or restarted straight away, depending on the length of belt stoppage. The action the operator takes, i.e. when to restart the belt, is based on extensive heat penetration studies. These studies establish the appropriate action to be taken in the event of a process deviation to ensure commercial sterility is achieved. The drawback with this method is that there is a possibility that some containers may be overprocessed and some may be underprocessed. The containers will therefore have to be disposed of. The only method of establishing which containers are unfit for consumption is by a microbiological/quality analysis. What is required is a method of monitoring the in-container sterility value at various points throughout the cooker. Then, in the event of a process deviation, predicting forward in time the final F value when cans at these points are fully processed.

This is possible by using a computer to dynamically model the heat penetration into a number of containers throughout the hydrostat based on the temperatures within each of the processing sections. When a drop in steam pressure occurs, the carrier belt is stopped. The time the carrier belt is restarted is based on the computer model, which predicts the final F value of all the containers it is modelling based on the operating conditions of the cooker at that point in time. If the model is supplied with maximum and minimum acceptable final F values, then via optimization the model can "decide" when the carrier belt should be started, and restopped if necessary, to minimise the number of containers that are under- and overprocessed. This starting and restopping of the belt may occur before the steam temperature is re-established, resulting in an increased can throughput.

This example is purely illustrative and, if applied practically to a hydrostat, will require further additions to the process model, such as a model of bacteria growth/ death kinetics. But it does highlight one application of derived value control as a method of minimizing product spoilage due to process deviations.

Conclusion

It is evident that derived value control offers the food industry a powerful tool for controlling sterilisation processes. There is now, readily available, low cost and powerful computing hardware on which process heat penetration models can be run in real time. These calculated temperatures can then be fed into a control strategy and the corresponding control action taken.

References

Atherton, D. and Austin, G. (1981). Technical Manual No. 5, Part 1, Campden Food and Drink Research Association, Chipping Campden, Glos, UK.

Bown, G. (1985). Technical Memorandum No. 391, Campden Food and Drink Research Association, Chipping Campden, Glos, UK.

Scott, G.M. (1991). Technical Memorandum No. 623, Campden Food and Drink Research Association, Chipping Campden, Glos, UK.

Scott, G.M. (1992). Technical Memorandum (to be published), Campden Food and Drink Research Association, Chipping Campden, Glos, UK.

Tucker, G.S. (1991). Technical Bulletin No. 79, Campden Food and Drink Research Association, Chipping Campden, Glos, UK.

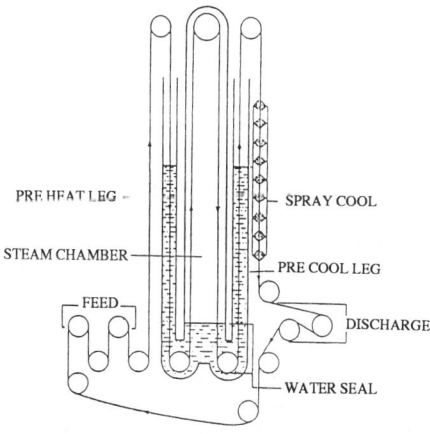

FIGURE 1: HYDROSTATIC COOKER

213

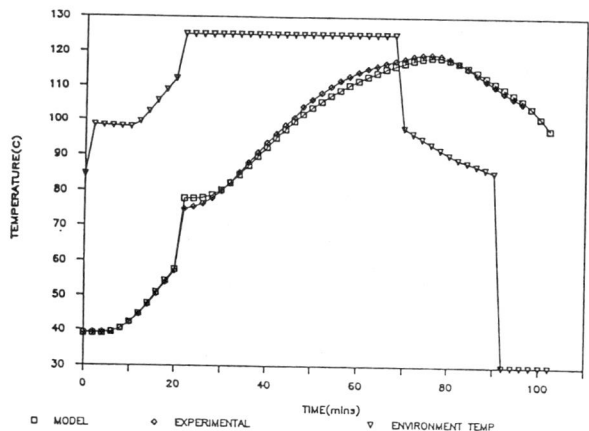

FIGURE 2: TIME/TEMPERATURE
PROFILE IN HYDROSTAT

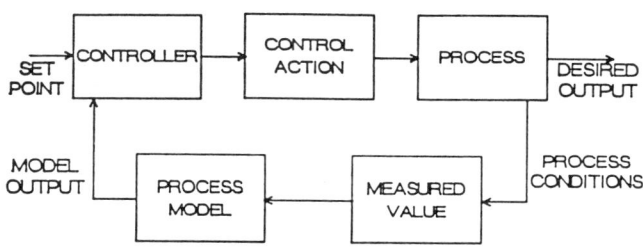

FIGURE 3: CONTROL LOOP FOR
DERIVED VALUE CONTROL

THE MODELLING OF FOOD SHELF LIFE AND PACKAGE
PERFORMANCE, USING COMPUTER SPREADSHEETS

G D HAYES

Recent research studies have demonstrated that
long-term moisture-gain experiments are no longer
required to predict food shelf life and package
performance. In fact the only data required is
(1) the moisture-sorption isotherm data, (2) the
package properties and (3) the external
conditions. A simple technique is outlined
whereby the food stability and shelf life may be
modelled using readily available computer
spreadsheet software.

Introduction

Although the modern food package is designed to serve many
functions including marketing, labelling and consumer
information delivery, the primary function of the package
remains to preserve the product quality and extend the shelf
life. In particular the protection of the food from moisture
exchange has developed from ancient times and become the basis
for a number of food preservation techniques.

Thus water is of great importance in food preservation,
particularly free or unbound water such that the single most
important physical/chemical property of any food material with
respect to shelf life, is the water activity. At a constant
temperature a unique relationship exists between moisture
content and water activity of a specific food, depending upon
its method of preparation. This "food fingerprint profile" is
depicted by the moisture sorption isotherm of the food.

The protection of foods from moisture exchange is an ancient
practice in food preservation, but only since the introduction
of polymeric based package materials in the 1940s have
numerous studies been published about the influence of the
water vapour transmission rate (WVTR) on the shelf life of
foods (ref 1).

Dept.of Food & Consumer Technology,Manchester Polytechnic.

Water in food exerts a vapour pressure. The size of the vapour depends on

(1) the amount of water present
(2) the temperature
(3) the concentration of dissolved solutes (particularly salts and sugars) in the water

Water activity is defined as the ratio of the vapour pressure of water in a food to the saturated vapour pressure of water at the same temperature:

$$a_W = \frac{P}{P_o} \tag{1}$$

where P(Pa) is vapour pressure of the food and P_o(Pa) the vapour pressure of pure water at the same temperature. Pa represents the SI unit of pressure (Pascals)

and

$$a_W = \%ERH \qquad \text{Where ERH Denotes} \qquad (2)$$
$$\text{the equilibrium}$$
$$\text{relative humidity}$$

The movement of water vapour from a food to the surrounding air depends upon both the moisture content and composition of the food, and the temperature and humidity of the air. At a constant temperature the moisture content of food changes until it comes into equilibrium with water vapour in the surrounding air. The food then neither gains nor loses weight on storage under those conditions. This is called the *equilibrium moisture content* of the food and the relative

humidity of the storage atmosphere is known as the *equilibrium relative humidity*. When different values of relative humidity versus equilibrium moisture content are plotted, a curve known as a *water sorption isotherm* is obtained (Fig.1.).

a_W is related to the moisture content by the Brunauer-Emmett-Teller(BET) equation

$$\frac{a_W}{M(1 - a_W)} = \frac{1}{M_1 C} + \frac{C - 1}{M_1 C} a_W \tag{3}$$

where a_W is the water activity, M the moisture as percentage dry weight, M_1 the moisture (dry-weight basis) of a monomolecular layer and C a constant.

All foods follow a specific moisture versus a_W curve. The moisture sorption isotherm is an extremely useful tool for the food scientist/engineer since it can be used to predict and model the food shelf life and package properties. For instance the studies of the rates of chemical reactions in foods have shown that there is a moisture content below which the rates of quality loss are negligible. This moisture content m_o corresponds to the monolayer value, as determined from the BET equation, and is generally around an a_W of 0.2 - 0.4. Similarly the crispness or hardness of dry foods, the caking properties and the microbiological resistance may be predicted.

The basic principle governing the transmission of water vapour through a flexible film is given by Fick's first law of diffusion, combined with Henry's law for gas solution at low concentration. Under steady-state conditions for water vapour, the rate of transport across a membrane becomes:

$$\frac{dw}{d\theta} = \left[\frac{k}{x}\right] A \left[P_1 - P_2\right] \qquad (4)$$

where

$\dfrac{dw}{d\theta}$ = amount of moisture passing through per unit time

k = film permeability grammes-mm/m² day mmHg

x = film thickness. mm

A = package area m²

p_1-p_2 = vapour pressure driving force

The standard method used to determine $k/_\lambda$ is to monitor the driving force for a given area and measure the weight change or moisture change as a function of time. A plot of the amount transported versus time results in a straight line, the slope of which is:

$$slope = \left[\frac{k}{x}\right] A \left[p_1 - p_2\right] \qquad (5)$$

Many packaging specialists use WVTR in preference to a_W, the difference being that in using WVTR one needs to divide by the driving force Δp. However, since for the purpose of shelf-life predictions the vapour pressure driving force can rarely be constant, WVTR will not be used in our spreadsheet model.

$$WVTR = \frac{slope}{area} = \frac{gH_2O}{day\ m^2} \qquad (6)$$

Based upon the above theory, simple equations have been derived to estimate the gain or loss of moisture for a food held in a semi-permeable package. In particular, Karel (ref 2) simplified the problem by suggesting that the isotherm can be treated as a linear function in the range between the initial moisture content m_i and the critical moisture content m_c.

Using this linear isotherm, the solution to the integral of equation 4 is exact and becomes:

$$\theta_{gain} = \frac{\ln\left[\dfrac{m_c - m_i}{m_c - m}\right]}{\left(\dfrac{k}{x}\right)\left(\dfrac{A}{W_s}\right)\left(\dfrac{p_o}{b}\right)} \qquad (7)$$

or

$$\theta_{loss} = \frac{\ln\left[\dfrac{m_i - m_c}{m - m_c}\right]}{\left(\dfrac{k}{x}\right)\left(\dfrac{A}{W_s}\right)\left(\dfrac{p_o}{b}\right)} \qquad (8)$$

Where m_i = initial moisture content in dry basis (g water/g solids).

m_c = equilibrium moisture from the linear isotherm (the moisture level the product would reach with no package)

m = moisture at any time θ

W_s = grammes of dry solids in the package

p_o = vapour pressure of pure water at storage temperature

A = package area m^2

b = slope of the water sorption isotherm (g water/g solids).

Experimental Details

From the foregoing discussion it can be appreciated that in order to predict the shelf-life of a range of packaged foods, under specified storage conditions, only the two points m_i and m_c on the water sorption isotherm are required. Although the purpose of this report is primarily to demonstrate the ease at which food shelf-life and stability can be modelled using a computer spreadsheet, research work is being carried out at Manchester Polytechnic in an attempt to predict the shelf-life of a commercial cornflakes product. Indeed, the design of a computer-linked continuous-food shelf-life monitoring system has been proposed (ref 3).

The Crispness of dry, cereal-based foods (e.g. crisps, cornflakes, crackers) is a strong function of water activity, and in fact for most cereal-based products significant loss of crispness occurs between the a_w range 0.4 - 0.45. For practical water sorption measurements the reader is invited to read the book entitled "Moisture Sorption. Practical Aspects of Isotherm Measurement and Use". (ref 4), in which the preparation of recommended saturated salt solutions is described, covering the relative humidity range from 11.15% - 90.26%.

The initial moisture content of the cornflakes have been determined by conventional loss-in-weight (Carter-Simon Oven) techniques. Similarly, the critical moisture level may be determined. The initial crispness\texture and the critical crispness\texture can be determined using organoleptic tests supported by computerized shear\texture tests (Analisa. Stable MicroSystems). The water activity determinations will be carried out using a laboratory hygrometer (Rotronic Hygroskop DT). In Table 1 the critical maximum water activity values for some dry foods are listed (ref 5).

Table 1

Critical Maximum Water Activity (a_w) Values for Some Dry Foods

Food		Reason
Baking soda	0.65	Caking loss of leavening
Crackers	80.4	Crispness to soggy
Dry eggs	0.30	Quality?
Gelatin	0.45	Quality?
Hard candy	0.30	Stickiness
Chocolate	0.70	Microbial growth
Dry potato	0.11	Rancidity?
Flour	0.65	Mould
Oatmeal	0.25	Quality?
Nonfat dry milk	0.30	Caking
Dry soup mix	0.60	Microbial growth
Soluble coffee	0.45	Caking
Pasta	0.60	Microbial growth
Dried beef	0.72	Microbial growth
Dry vegetables	0.25-0.4	Quality?
Dry fruits	0.60-0.65	Microbial growth

Adapted from Heiss (4)

Spreadsheet Details

In order to achieve an efficient spreadsheet design it is
advisable to plan the structure of the spreadsheet beforehand,
on paper. Assuming that we have completed our laboratory
water-sorption tests, we could:

1. Enter the water sorption isotherm data and calculate the
    slope between the initial moisture level (m_i) and the
    critical moisture level (m_c).

2. Calculate the slope of the unaccomplished moisture gain
    lines using the packaging type data, the area to solids
    ratio and the environmental conditions.

3. Calculate the time to reach the critical moisture using
    the formula:

$$\Theta_g = \frac{\ln\left[\dfrac{m_c - m_i}{m_c - m}\right]}{\left(\dfrac{k}{x}\right)\left(\dfrac{A}{W_s}\right)\left(\dfrac{P_o}{b}\right)} \qquad (9)$$

For example, using the water sorption data relating to potato chips cited in the literature (ref 4).

1. Calculation of the slope of the water sorption isotherm, using commercially available software (e.g. SuperCalc5, Computer Associates).

	A	B	C	D	E	F	G	H	I	J
1	WATER SORPTION DATA.				POTATO CHIPS					
2										
3	WATER CONTENT				a_W	REGRESSION OUTPUT				
4	gH$_2$O/g solids									
5	0.01				0.06					
6	0.018				0.1					
7	0.024				0.2					
8	0.032				0.3					
9	0.042				0.4					
10	0.046				0.45					
11										
12										

After input of the data (X and Y values), on the //Data, Analysis, Regression, command will output the regression calculation as shown above.

2. The calculation of the slope of the unaccomplished moisture gain line, using the packaging data and the environment conditons can be accomplished easily within the spreadsheet, perhaps by expanding the cell width using the format opotion.

   Thus, after entering all the data (m$_e$, m$_i$, m, A, W$_s$, P$_o$ and b) into the appropriate columns of the spreadsheet, the computer could be asked to perform the major calculations:

   (i)   ln(Me-Mi)/(Me-M)

   (ii)   (k/x)(A/Ws)(Po/b)

   (iii) Θg = $^{(i)}/_{(ii)}$

The spreadsheet data and calculations are given in Table II, in which the first five models use data and examples from the cited literature.

Example 1. Prediction of the shelf life of potato chips in a polythene package at 50%RH and 73°F.

Example 2. Similar calculation of the shelf life of potato chips at 90%RH and 100°F.

Example 3. Determination of the optimum k/x value for a shelf life of 90 days (potato chips).

Example 4. Potato chips in a polyethylene A package - low W$_s$ value.

Example 5.   Potato chips in a mylar A package - low W_s
                   value.

Examples 6 - 11.
                   Shelf life predictions over a range of $k/_x$
                   values and 50%RH.

Examples 11 - 17.

                   Shelf life predictions over a range of $k/_x$
                   values and 90%RH.

Conclusions

Although the experimental procedure outlined was very simple
the implications of such a technique may be profound since, by
using similarly designed spreadsheets the QA or product
development scientist can rapidly anticipate or predict the
food stability during storage.

Using the spreadsheet application of the linear isotherm, the
quality assurance scientist/engineer could carry out the
following tasks:

1.   Evaluate the effects of pinholes on film permeability:
2.   Conduct accelerated shelf life tests:
3.   Fix the initial moisture content of the food in line with
      product costs:
4.   Evaluate the effect of package size and V/A ratio on
      shelf life:
5.   Determine the optimum air velocity during storage:
6.   Evaluate the shelf life of frozen foods.

The product development engineer could use a similar technique
to fix the optimum water content and package properties for
any particular market and distribution link, for their newly
developed products. The monitoring of product stability
throughout the extended distribution links could become
increasingly important, post 1992.

List of References

1.   Labuza. T.P. 1981. Cereal Foods World. P335-343.

2.   Karel. M. Cereal Foods World. P341.

3.   Hayes. G. 1991. Continuous measurement of food quality.
          Longman Cartermill.

4.   Labuza. T.P. 1984. American Association of Cereal
      Chemists.

5.   Heiss. R. Shelf life determination. Mod.Packag.
      31(8): 119, 1958.

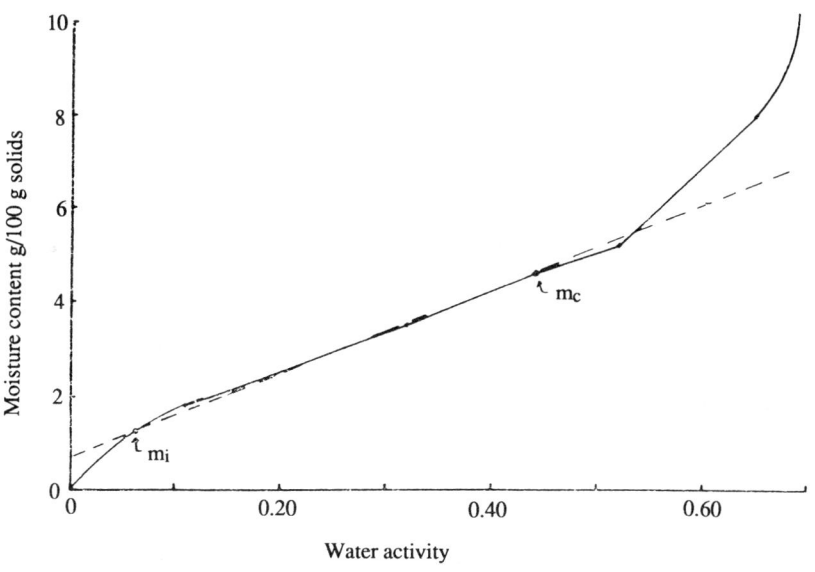

Figure 1. Moisture sorption isotherm for potato chips at 22°C

TABLE II SPREADSHEET RESULTS

	Me	Ni	M	k/x	A	Ws	Po	b	ln(Me-Mi)/(Me-M)	(k/x)(A/Ws)(Po/b)	Θg
1	0.06	0.01	0.05	0.01	0.1	100	22.2	0.1	1.6094	0.00222	725
2	0.11	0.01	0.05	0.01	0.1	100	49.2	0.1	0.5108	0.00492	103.8
3	0.0505	0.01	0.046	0.3	0.1	84.37	20.82	0.087	2.197	7.323	90
4	0.095	0.01	0.046	0.073	0.0290	8.53	42.2	0.088	0.55	0.119	4.6
5	0.095	0.01	0.046	0.1185	0.0290	8.99	42.2	0.088	0.55	0.1903	2.9
6	0.06	0.01	0.05	0.01	0.1	100	22.2	0.1	1.6094	0.00222	724.97
7	0.06	0.01	0.05	0.02	0.1	100	22.2	0.1	1.6094	0.00444	362.48
8	0.06	0.01	0.05	0.04	0.1	100	22.2	0.1	1.6094	0.00888	181.24
9	0.06	0.01	0.05	0.06	0.1	100	22.2	0.1	1.6094	0.01332	120.82
10	0.06	0.01	0.05	0.08	0.1	100	22.2	0.1	1.6094	0.01776	90.62
11	0.06	0.01	0.05	0.1	0.1	100	22.2	0.1	1.6094	0.0222	72.49
12	0.06	0.01	0.05	0.01	0.1	100	44.4	0.1	1.6094	0.00444	362.48
13	0.06	0.01	0.05	0.02	0.1	100	44.4	0.1	1.6094	0.00888	181.24
14	0.06	0.01	0.05	0.04	0.1	100	44.4	0.1	1.6094	0.01776	90.62
15	0.06	0.01	0.05	0.06	0.1	100	44.4	0.1	1.6094	0.02664	60.41
16	0.06	0.01	0.05	0.08	0.1	100	44.4	0.1	1.6094	0.03552	45.31
17	0.06	0.01	0.05	0.1	0.1	100	44.4	0.1	1.6094	0.0444	36.25

A SIMULATION MODEL FOR CALCULATING OF NUTRIENT LOSSES DURING BLANCHING

A. Andersson* and R. Öste*

A well-defined artificial food with a known diffusion
coefficient and specific heat and thermal conductivities
is required for testing new mathematical models and
methods of solution. This paper presents physical data of
such an artificial food. A simulation model that links
heat transfer with diffusion is also proposed.

Introduction

Fruits and vegetables are sometimes blanched in hot water or steam
partly for the purpose of inactivating enzymes, which otherwise might
cause a quality deterioration during handling and storage. Blanching also
has other advantages for example, the blanching of potatoes prior to
frying gives improved texture of the final product, reduction of fat
absorption, and better colour of fried products by decreasing the reducing
sugar content on the surface of the potato. From the nutritive point of
view, the blanching may cause a reduced quality. It is well known that
during blanching there is a considerable loss of soluble components, such
as, water-soluble vitamins and minerals, into the blanching water.
Nutritive substances sensitive to heat, like thiamine and vitamin C, can
also be chemically degraded. These chemical reactions are often cut of
apparent first or second order.

A simulation model for calculating the loss of nutritive substances
upon blanching needs to link heat transfer, diffusion, and chemical
reactions of the first and second order. Mathematical modelling of
blanching has to take into account that the diffusion coefficient and the
reaction coefficient are temperature-dependent. Simpler models disregard
temperature and concentration gradients within the foodstuff, particulary
if the foodstuff is very small (Ryley et al., 1990). Other workers have
calculated with a constant diffusion coefficient (Garrote et al., 1986).
Alzamora et al. (1985) and Califano & Calvelo (1983) have incorporated
temperature and concentration gradients in the model for a one-dimensional
spherical food shape. All of these models assume that there are constant
thermal properties throughout the process. The present paper presents a
simulation model that links heat transfer, diffusion, and chemical
reactions of the first and the second order for some geometries. The model

* Department of Food Chemistry, Chemical Center, Lund, Sweden.

can process temperature and concentration gradients and temperature dependent thermal conductivity, specific heat, diffusion coefficient, and reaction coefficient. This paper mainly deals with the linkage of heat transfer to diffusion in a finite cylinder.

All of these mathematical models require information about the diffusion coefficient for each solute and the effect of the temperature on these coefficients. Unfortunately, most of the published data on vitamin retention are endpoint data - information collected at the beginning and at the end of a process. Very little has been published on the temperature dependence of the apparent diffusion coefficient. However, the temperature dependence of the diffusion coefficients of certain nutrient solutes in potato (Garrote et al., 1986), carrot (Selman et al., 1983), and peas (Alzamora et al., 1985) has been published. Unfortunately, these values cannot be used to test a new mathematical model because the value of the diffusion coefficient varies with the time of harvest, with the part of the vegetable being used, and with the length of storage before the experiment. There is also a need to improve the method of solving of the different existing mathematical models that calculate nutrient losses during blanching. To be able to test these new mathematical models and solution methods, a well-defined artificial food with a known diffusion coefficient and specific heat and thermal conductivities was needed. This paper presents physical data of such an artificial food. A 5% agarose gel was chosen because of the stability and the capacity of enduring high blanching temperatures without shrinking or swelling of the gel. Such a gel can be moulded to any desired geometry.

Theory

To study the linkage of heat transfer to diffusion of the simulation model, experiments were carried out with cylindrical agarose gels.

Equations of the finite cylinder:

A nonstationary heat transfer in a finite cylinder that is symmetrical around its own axis can be described by the following differential equation (Smith, 1985):

$$\rho * c_p * \frac{dT}{dt} = \frac{1}{r} * \frac{d}{dr}(r * k * \frac{dT}{dr}) + \frac{d}{dz}(k * \frac{dT}{dz}) \qquad (1)$$

if the heat of reaction is negligible. The corresponding initial and boundary conditions are as follows:

$$t = 0 ; \quad \text{In the entire cylinder ;} \quad T = T_o \qquad (2)$$

$$t > 0 ; \quad r = R \text{ or } z = Z ; \quad h * (T_f - T) = k * dT/dr \qquad (3)$$

$$t > 0 ; \quad r = 0 ; \quad dT/dr = 0 \qquad (4)$$

Fick's second law of diffusion under unsteady-state conditions can be written as follows for a finite cylinder if no chemical reactions occur (Crank, 1975):

$$\frac{dC}{dt} = \frac{1}{r} * \frac{d}{dr}(r * D * \frac{dC}{dr}) + \frac{d}{dz}(D * \frac{dC}{dz}) \qquad (5)$$

where D is the apparent diffusion coefficient of thiamine in an 5% agarose gel. The following initial and boundary conditions were presumed:

$$t = 0 ; \quad \text{In the entire cylinder ;} \quad C = C_o \quad (6)$$

$$t > 0 ; \quad r = R \text{ or } z = Z ; \quad C_B = C_f \text{ or}$$

$$k_c*(C_f-C) = D*dC/dr \quad (7)$$

$$t > 0 ; \quad r = 0 ; \quad dC/dr = 0 \quad (8)$$

where C_B is the thiamine concentrations in the outer layer and C_f the thiamine concentration in the blanching water.

Solution method:

The partial differential equations were transfered to discretization equations with the control volume method (Patankar, 1980), which is a type of finite difference method. The calculation domain (the food geometry) was divided into a number of nonoverlapping control volumes, so that there was one control volume surrounding each grid point. The differential equations were then integrated over each control volume. Piecewise profiles expressed the variation of the temperature, and the concentration between the grid points were used to evaluate the required integrals. This resulted in the discretization equations containing the values of the temperature and the concentration for a group of grid points. Those discretization equations were then solved implicitly for the sphere and other one-dimensional problems and solved explicitly for the finite cylinder and other multi-dimensional problems. The reason for the using an implicit method for the one-dimensional problem was the possibility of forming a tridiagonal matrix at every time-step, which could be solved handily with Thomas Tri Diagonal Algorithm (von Rosenberg, 1971).

The heat transfer equation affects the mass transfer equation through the diffusions coefficient, which is temperature-dependent; therefore, the heat transfer equation was solved first in each time-step. Then, the arithmetic mean temperature profile for the time-step was calculated from the previous and the new temperature profiles. The arithmetic mean temperatures were used to calculate the diffusion coefficients in various parts of the agarose gel, and then the diffusion equations were solved.

The simulation model:

A program was written in Turbo Pascal that linked heat transfer, diffusion, and chemical reactions of the first and the second order. The model could execute calculations for infinite slabs, infinite and finite cylinders, spheres, infinite rods and blocks, and five different types of boundary conditions. The program could also process temperature-dependent thermal conductivity, specific heat, diffusion coefficient, and reaction coefficient.

Results and Discussion

Information about the methods and the analyses that were used is available from the authors.

Physical data of the agarose gel:

Apparent diffusion coefficient: The results of the measurement of the apparent diffusion coefficient are presented in Figure 1. Mathematically, the temperature dependence of the apparent diffusion coefficient can be excellently described by the Stoke-Einstein equation (Skelland, 1974):

$$D_T = K*T/\mu_w \quad (9)$$

In this equation μ_w is the water viscosity at temperature T and K is a constant that depends on the system. For this system, K was $1.72*10^{-15}$

kgm/s^2K. Stoke-Einstein's equation actually applies to large molecules in diluted solutions. It usually does not apply to solid foodstuffs due to their heterogeneous structure (presence of membranes, skins, envelopes, layers, networks, pores, etc.), but it seems to apply to thiamine diffusion in a 5% agarose gel, as can be seen in Figure 1.

Thermal properties: The specific heat of the agarose gel can be determined by using of an approximation formula invented by Choi and Ohos (1983):

$$c_p = 4.180*x_w + 1.711*x_p + 1.928*x_f + 1.547*x_c + 0.908*x_a \qquad (10)$$

There is plenty of other approximation formulas that can be used. In general, they give the same value for the specific heat of the agarose gel. There are also approximation formulas for the thermal conductivity of the agarose gel, but these gave different values (0.22 to 0.75 W/m°C). Bowman's (1970) estimation formula gave the best agreement between the experimental and the simulated temperature:

$$k = 0.081 + 0.568*x_w \qquad (11)$$

Object of blanching:

The purpose of the blanching experiments performed in the present study was to evaluate the integration of heat transfer with diffusion in the simulation model. To reduce sources of error not directly linked to the simulation model, an artificial food in the form of a moulded agarose gel was employed. This allowed the use of well-defined geometrical shapes. Further, a known and uniform initial thiamine concentration in the blanching experiments was easy to establish. Another advantage was that agarose gels do not shrink or swell at temperatures below 85°C (Fennema, 1985).

Blanching of cylinders:

The blanching experiments were carried out with two different types of cylinders: a small cylinder with a length of 50mm and a diameter of 15mm, and a large disc with a length of 15mm and a diameter of 38mm. The leaching losses through the top and bottom surfaces for the small cylinder were negligible compared with the losses through the mantle surface. In the large disc the area of the top and bottom exceeded the area of the mantle surface. This resulted in considerable losses through the terminal ends of the disc.

Figure 2 shows the measured and simulated time-retention curves for blanching of the small cylinder at 80°C. The figure shows a good correspondence between the experimental values and the values of the simulation with the boundary condition $C_B = C_f = 0$. The mass transfer coefficient needed to be $40.0*10^{-6}$ m/s to give an acceptable result. The large surface/volume ratio for the cylinder caused considerable thiamine losses. Blanching for 20 minutes gave a thiamine retention of 56.4% according to the simulation ($C_B = C_f = 0$), whereas the experimental blanching gave a thiamine retention of 55.9%. The standard deviations between the measured values and the simulation curves were 1.0% ($C_B = 0$) and 1.7% for $k_c = 40.0*10^{-6}$ m/s.

In Figure 3 the results of the blanching of a disc at 80°C are shown. The final thiamine retention was about 65% both for the simulation ($C_B = C_f = 0$) and for the experimental blanching. The standard deviations between the measured values and the simulation curves were 1.0% ($C_B = 0$) and 0.9% for $k_c = 40.0*10^{-6}$ m/s. In the time interval 0-200 seconds, the simulations gave a lower thiamine retention than the measured values. Figure 4 shows that the measured values for blanching of the cylinder and the disc were scattered around the optimal line. This indicated that the linking of heat transfer to solute mass transfer for two-dimensional symmetrical cylinders was satisfactory.

As previuosly stated, the mass transfer coefficient had to be $40*10^{-6}$ m/s to give a good correspondence with the experimentally measured values. This corresponds to a heat transfer coefficient of 2900W/m^2°C.

Conclusions

This study has shown the possibility of integrating heat transfer with mass transfer in an agarose gel given the apparent diffusion coefficient by Stoke-Einstein's equation. However, in most foodstuffs the temperature dependence of the diffusion coefficient is more complex than in the agarose gel due to denaturation of the materials. Still, many research works have shown that the temperature dependence of the diffusion coefficient can be approximatively described by Stoke-Einstein's equation or an Arrhenius type of equation. Thus, the present model may potentially be applied on foodstuffs.

In ongoing research of the simulation model, the integration of chemical reactions to heat transfer and diffusion is being studied. The results of this research will be presented later.

Nomenclature

C	= thiamine concentration in the agarose sphere (g/dm^3 gel)	
C_B	= thiamine concentration at the surface of the agarose gel (g/dm^3)	
C_f	= thiamine concentration in the blanching water (g/dm^3)	
c_p	= specific heat (J/kg°C)	
D_T	= apparent diffusion coefficient of thiamine in the agarose gel (m^2/s)	
h	= heat transfer coefficient (W/m^2°C)	
k	= thermal conductivity (W/m°C)	
k_c	= mass transfer coefficient (m/s)	
K	= constant	
r	= radius (m)	
t	= time (s)	
T	= temperature (°C)	
T_o	= initial temperature (°C)	
T_f	= fluid temperature (°C)	
$x_{w,p,f,c,a}$	= weight fraction of water, protein, fat, carbohydrates, ash	
μ_w	= water viscosity	

References

Alzamora, S.M., Hough, G. and Chirife, J. 1985. J. Food Technol. 20:251

Bowman, R.C. 1970. M.Sc. thesis. Leeds University, Leeds, UK.

Califano, A.N. and Calvelo, A. 1983. J. Food Sci. 48:220.

Choi, Y. and Okos, M.R. 1983. Trans. ASAE 26(1):305-311.

Crank, J. 1975. "The Mathematics of Diffusion.", Oxford University Press.

Fennema, O.R. 1985. "Food Chemistry.", 2nd ed. Dekker, New York, NY.

Garrote, R.L., Silva, E.R. and Bertone, R.A. 1986. Lebenm.-Wiss.u.Technol. 19: 263.

Patankar, S.V. 1980. "Numerical Heat Transfer and Fluid Flow." McGraw-Hill Book Company, Washington.

Ryley, J., Abdel-Kader, Z. and Lamb, J. 1990. Trends in Nutrition and Food Policy, 96. Proceedings of the 7th IUFOST, Singapore.

Selman, J.D., Rice, R. and Abdul-Rezzak, R.K. 1983. J. Food Sci. 18:427.

Skelland, A.H.P. 1974. "Diffusional Mass Transfer." J.Wiley & Sons. NY.

Smith, G.D. 1985. "Numerical Solution of Partial Differential Equations: Finite Difference Methods.", 3rd ed. Oxford University Press.

Von Rosenberg, D.U. 1971. "Methods for the Numerical Solution of Partial Differential Equations." Elsevier, New York, NY.

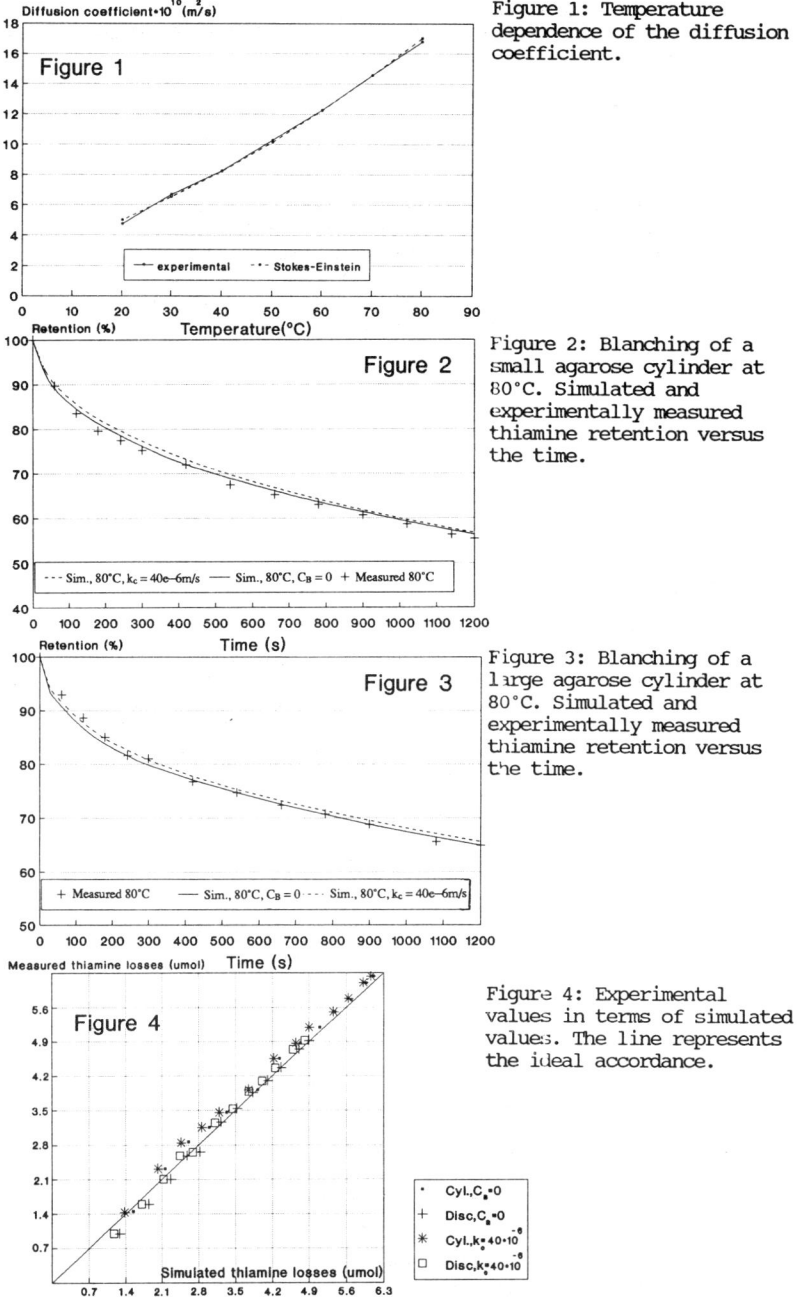

Figure 1: Temperature dependence of the diffusion coefficient.

Figure 2: Blanching of a small agarose cylinder at 80°C. Simulated and experimentally measured thiamine retention versus the time.

Figure 3: Blanching of a large agarose cylinder at 80°C. Simulated and experimentally measured thiamine retention versus the time.

Figure 4: Experimental values in terms of simulated values. The line represents the ideal accordance.

MODELLING THE EFFECTS OF WATER CONTENT ON THE EXTRUSION-COOKING OF CEREAL
FLOURS.

D.A. Janes[*]

With consideration of the results from recent pilot
plant studies, a simple phenomenological model is
derived, which simulates the kinky relationship
between the feed moisture content of cereal-based
formulations and the texture characteristics of the
resulting extrusion-cooked products.

INTRODUCTION

Previous studies on the extrusion cooking of cereals under moderate conditions
have shown, that of all the determining process parameters, the feed moisture
content is the most influential on the size of directly expanded
extrudates[1,2], and that the mouth-feel characteristics of extrusion-cooked
grain-based foods are related to both the foam structure and the
physicochemical form of the biopolymers in the foam wall fragments[3]. General
food process simulator computer programs exist[4], which aim to predict product
composition and texture, but mathematical models are needed for the simulation
of the individual unit operations.

Cooking rate is very dependent on the reaction rate between water and the
starch components, amylose and amylopectin, but is also influenced by the rate
of water diffusion in the cooked layer. There is a fairly extensive body of
literature[5,6] on the mathematical modelling of thermo-mechanical extruders,
and attempts have been made to model the diffusion and reactions between
starch and water in counter-rotating twin screw extruders[7]. However, the
complexity of the transport processes in the screw channels means either the
models are to simple to have any theoretically-based predictive capacity on
product characteristics; or the applicability of more sophisticated models,
which have generally evolved from research in plastic processing, to extrusion
cooking, is limited by the lack of physicochemical models of the food
materials and the relevant property data, particularly over a range of
realistic conditions. Therefore to elucidate the cooking behaviour over a
wider range, a short-cut description of the key processes occurring in the
amylaceous mix, has been adopted here, in an effort to reproduce the variation
of extrudate texture, cooked from aqueous and farinaceous mixes.

[*] FAST Team, School of Chemical Engineering, University of Birmingham, P.O.
Box 363, Edgbaston, Birmingham B15 2TT.

THE MODEL

Work with a range of cereals has shown that many shape and texture characteristics per unit mass of cooked extrudates show a twin-peaked non-linear relationship with initial water content (*e.g.* Figure 1). Although the turning values for say gas cell number and the length-to-width ratio may not coincide, they do lie within the so called intermediate moisture content range - 21% to 28% moisture content (wet basis). The 'cooking' in thermo-mechanical extruders of farinaceous mixes, is mostly determined by the changes to the starch fraction[2,3]. The plasticating process is initiated by the rupture of hydrogen bonds between poly-(1,4)-alpha-glucan chains, followed by the reformation of junction zones between starch molecules. The diffusion of water through the outer gelled layers retards the cooking rate within granules. Because the moisture steps between bonding sites through the oxygenated biopolymer, the diffusion process is likely to exhibit an Arrhenius characteristics. Subsequently the polymers are dispersed and finally they begin to degrade. All this makes for a complex chain of events, but assuming for a pure starch and water mix, that the rate of 'cooking' depends on the initial concentration of starch and the availability of water, which is assumed to be proportional to the moisture content, the kinetics can be expressed by:

$$r_C = \frac{-dC_S}{dt} = k \cdot C_S^a \cdot C_W^b \tag{1}.$$

If over limited extents 'cooking' can be described by pseudo-first order kinetics with respect to each component, as with the gelatinization of starch in excess water[8], then:

$$r_C = k \cdot C_W \cdot C_W^2 \tag{2}.$$

Observation of the extrusion-cooking kinetics is complicated because of the considerable quantities of autogenous heat dissipated from the mechanical mechanisms within a cooker-extruder. Work on the rheology of the starch-based melts has shown that the consistency of melts and, thus the viscous heating, declines with increasing moisture content[9,10]. Flour particles consist of agglomerates of starch granules embedded within a protein matrix and the size of the starch granule appears to influence the rate at which flour-based throughputs plasticate (another important determinant is the endosperm 'hardness' of wheat flours) and thus critical to the behaviour of an extrusion cooking system. The importance of the powder's frictional coefficient has been demonstrated in simulation studies[6]. With wetter mixes, the influence of capillary action between the granules is likely to increase cohesive and adhesive forces, which may counter autogenous heating advantage of drier mixes, but not negate it. All else being equal, the temperature in starch melts will be a function of the starch concentration, as a result of internal heating; thus,

$$T = f(1 - C_W) \tag{3}.$$

Putting this into an Arrhenius type relationship,

$$k \propto e^{\frac{\lambda}{C_W - 1}} \tag{4}.$$

Combining (2) and (4) and introducing a proportionality constant gives an expression for an extrudate characteristic, that is a function of the rate of cooking, $f(r_C)$,

$$f(r_C) = B \cdot e^{\frac{\lambda}{C_W - 1}} \cdot (C_W - C_W^2) \tag{5}.$$

Parameters A and B will vary for different extrudate characteristic. Taking values of 0.165 and 21 for A and B in the model, Figure 2 depicts a simulation of the relationship between the extruder feed composition and the degree of cook of the extrudate. The model indicates a phenomenological explanation for the serpentine trend in directly expanded extrudate specific volume, with a local minimum between the 20% and 25% moisture contents (wet basis).

CONCLUSIONS

The extrusion cooking process has been broken down into three regimes: low, intermediate, and high, according to the moisture content of the feed. This model implies that the morphology of the regimes exists, because the water has two main functions: to react with the starch; and to lubricate the passage of the throughput and thus control the quantity of autogenous heat input. Because the expansion of extrudates depends on the mobility of exuded starch biopolymer chains, product characteristics, such as size and crumb texture, hinge on the hydrogen-bonding reactions and thus are non-linear, bi-maxima functions of the starch/water ratio in the feed.

REFERENCES

1) Seiler, K., Weipert, & Seibel, W., (1980) In: Linko, P., (ed.) "*Food Process Engineering*" $\underline{1}$:808-820, Applied Science, London.

2) Guy, R.C.E., Janes, D.A., & Nkwanyuo, W.E., (1989) *C.O.S.T. 91 (Subgroup 1) Workshop "Progress in Extrusion Cooking"*, (Montpellier, France, May).

3) Guy, R.C.E. & Horne, A.W., (1988) In: Blanshard, J.M.V. & Mitchell, J.R., (eds) "*Food structure: its creation and evaluation*", :331-349, Butterworths, London.

4) Kozempel M., Craig, J.C., Sullivan, J.F., Damert, W., (1988) *Biotechnol. Prog.* $\underline{4}$:63-67.

5) Roberts, S.A. & Guy, R.C.E., (1986) *J. Food Eng.* $\underline{5}$, :7-30.

6) Tayeb J., Vergnes, B., & Della Valle, G., (1989) *J. Food Sci.* $\underline{54}$, :1047-1056.

7) Pieters, C.E., (1989) *Engineering Foundation Conference "Mixing 12"*, (Missouri, August).

8) Lund, D.B. & Wirakartakusumah, M., (1984) In: McKenna, B.M., (ed.) "*Engineering and Food*" $\underline{1}$:425-432, Elsevier Applied Science, London.

9) Castle, J., Guy, R.C.E., Hastilow, P.A.P., & Janes, D.A., (1990) In: Oliver D.R. (ed.). *3rd European Rheology Conference*, :85-87, Elsevier Applied Science, London.

10) Wang, S.M., Bouvier, J.M. & Gelus, M., (1990) *Int. J. Food Sci. Technol.* $\underline{25}$:129-139.

NOMENCLATURE

A,B	constants
a,b	stoichiometric constants
C_S	concentration of starch
C_W	concentration of water
k	rate constant (s^{-1})
r_C	rate of cooking (s^{-1})
T	melt temperature $(°K)$

FIGURES

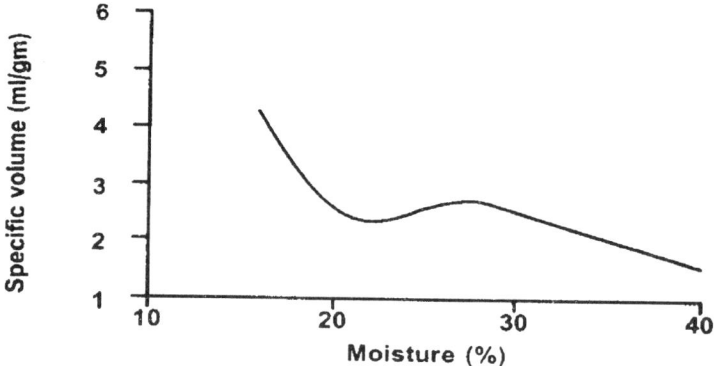

Figure 1 Specific volume of wheat flour extrudate at screw speed 300 r.p.m.,
feed rate 800g/min (Fig. 3^2).

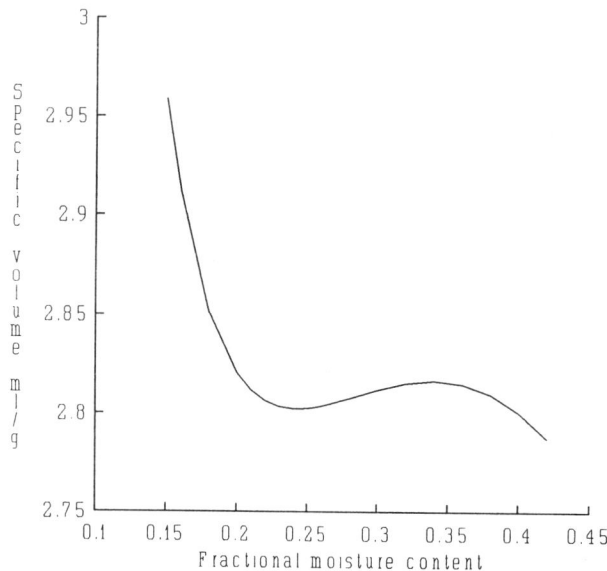

Figure 2 Simulation of variation in extrudate size with moisture content with
parameters: A = 0.165; B = 21.

COST BENEFITS THROUGH SUGAR REFINERY SIMULATION

P C Mitchell*

Computer simulations of sugar refinery plant are being developed to facilitate the making of quicker and more accurate daily operating decisions based on reliable processing cost predictions.

Not all stages in the sugar refining process can be modelled using a theoretical approach. The modelling objectives for the affination processing stage were achieved using an empirical approach. A user friendly interface for the affination simulation was provided through the Ten-Core Software package.

INTRODUCTION

Raw cane sugar is processed to remove undesirable impurities such as ash and colour leaving a refined white sugar with a sucrose content in excess of 99.95% by weight. Typically 75 to 90% of the raw sugar impurities are contained in a viscous solution which coats the crystal. The first processing stage, known as affination, aims to remove this sticky coat without dissolving any of the crystal. The affination product known as washed sugar undergoes processing to remove impurities contained within the crystal. The by-product known as affination syrup undergoes processing to recover dissolved sucrose.

The affination process requires the raw cane sugar to be continuously mixed with a warm syrup. The resulting crystal and syrup mixture undergoes further mixing to ensure adequate softening of the crystal coat before it is fed to one of a bank of batch centrifugals which carry out the combined deliquoring and washing operations. The latter involves spraying process water for a fixed period of time onto the wall of sugar while the centrifugal basket is rotating at or near its top speed. Typically 95% of the syrup removed during centrifugal filtration is recycled for mixing with further raw cane sugar. Typically forty minutes is the combined residence time from raw cane sugar intake to washed sugar discharge. Efficient operation of the affination process is facilitated by sophisticated sequential control, on line computer data logging and raw cane sugar quality analysis on a once every four hours basis.

* The University of Ulster,
  Department of Mechanical & Industrial Engineering

THE NEED TO MODEL AFFINATION

The economics of raw cane sugar refining depends largely on the efficiency of Affination Station operation. If the raw cane sugar is over-washed, partial crystal dissolution will result thereby sending excess sucrose to the Recovery Station. The consequences are an increased steam use and the inability to recover some of this excess sucrose as the high value white sugar product. On the other hand, if the raw cane sugar is under-washed, the excess impurity loading will adversely affect the performance of downstream Refining Stations. The impurity loading on the final white sugar boiling is particularly critical. The consequences of under-washing could be that the final boiling product does not meet the specification thereby requiring product reprocessing. Of the two, it is under-washing which results not only in the greater cost penalty but also greater production difficulties.

There is an economic balance between under-washing and over-washing in Affination Station operation which is specifiable by a target washed sugar impurity level. This target must be adjusted in response to variations in raw cane sugar quality and the level of impurity loading on downstream refining operations. Although the effect of most process changes on washed sugar quality are known within minutes, it is three to four hours before the effect on syrup purity and two days before the overall impact on recovery and refining operations are known. Such is the process complexity in terms of recycle streams and unit operation residence times that there is a tendency for those directing Affination Station operations to minimise condition changes and to favour over-washing. Steady state simulation has the potential not only to give an immediate picture of affination performance but also overall refinery performance.

Donovan (1986) indicated that for a major sugar refinery, with a 600,000 tonne per annum capacity, the ability to select affination conditions for varying raw cane sugar qualities which consistently met impurity removal targets, offered savings of £192,000 per annum through reduced steam use and reduced sugar loss. A significant proportion of these savings could be obtained by developing an Affination Station simulation and linking it with appropriate cost functions for other stations in the refinery. The full potential savings, plus others attributable to each individual station, could be obtained by developing an overall refinery simulation.

COMPUTER MODEL

Selection of Method

Perry (1973) cites that theoretical predictions of the behaviour of solid-liquid mixtures in a centrifugal filter have met with limited success. The theory is well developed for incompressible cake, bulk filtration rates but not for residual moisture predictions. The extent of crystal sucrose dissolution and washed sugar air drying during centrifugal filtration and washing add to the difficulties in developing a theoretical model for the affination process.

The approach adopted was to develop a global affination model using empirical equations in conjunction with stream material and enthalpy balances. Correlations for the required physical and enthalpy property data were expressed as a function of temperature and sucrose concentration. No theoretical equations were used to model the complex equilibrium, mass and heat transfer processes. Instead empirical equations for the following three performance indicators were derived from plant data -

.   Liquor coat impurity removal efficiency based on ash (%)
.   Affination syrup purity (% by weight sucrose on soluble solids)
.   Affination syrup brix (% by weight soluble solids)

The independent variables in these multiple regression equations were significant process conditions and raw material characteristics at the 95% confidence level. The form of the regression equations for all three performance indicators which involve no interaction terms is given in equation 1.

$$y = a + b_1x_1 + b_2x_2 + b_3x_3 + \quad \ldots\ldots\ldots\ldots \quad (1)$$

The affination model was structured so as to permit the simultaneous solution of all equations.

Outline of Programme

The affination model calculates the stream compositions, steam requirements, performance indicators and processing costs associated with a specific set of process conditions and raw sugar characteristics. Process and cost assumptions have been made for refining operations outside the affination process. Stream mass balances cover the five components of water, sucrose, ash, invert and organics.

There is an extensive Affination Station performance data base for raw sugars from nineteen countries of origin. The model user can look at this historic data and run the model on one of three input date types.

.   Historic data for an individual raw sugar cargo
.   Historic data for a specific country of origin
.   The latest or user specified raw sugar cargo

The user is prompted for the data required to run the model and is always given the acceptable range of the input value. The user can select from a number of output reports.

The commercial package Ten-Core was selected to provide the necessary user-interface. This allowed an interactive approach to data input, calculations and the output of results. Graphics, plant mimic diagrams and colour were used in the presentation of results.

RESULTS AND DISCUSSIONS

The Affination Station project took six man months of development work to satisfy the following objective -

Develop a computer simulation of the Affination Station to be used by factory management for the selection of economical operation conditions

Detailed discussions with factory managers, production supervisors and process operators were required to gain the necessary process and production expertise to plan the project. Preliminary data collection and multiple regression analysis on historic production records did not result in significant correlations at the 95% confidence level for the three performance indicators.

This was attributed to two factors -

. The records did not contain all the identified influence variables
. There was uncertainty concerning the match between process conditions and raw material characteristics

Planned primary data collection on the affination process followed after obtaining expert advice on orthogonal experimental design to minimise the interactions between independent variables.

It was essential to get the most information from the minimal amount of work and with minimal disruption to production. On-line instrumentation, with computer data capture capability, was essential to enable the matching of process stream samples with process conditions. The production trails covered four raw sugar cargoes under different levels of -

. Affination Syrup Temperature
. Total Soluble Solids Concentration of the Crystal and Syrup Mixture
. Centrifugal Basket Load
. Centrifugal Wash Time

Regression analysis yielded correlations, significant at the 95% confidence level and with a regression coefficient greater than 0.9, for all three performance predictors. The observed versus predicted plot for the ash removal efficiency correlation is shown in Figure 1. Further testing of these correlations was carried out using historic data. The predictive capability proved to be good except for low purity raw cane sugar cargoes whose countries of origin were not covered in the data collection.

CONCLUSIONS AND RECOMMENDATIONS

The property database and library of unit operations incorporated within many commercial "Steady State" simulation packages do not meet the modelling needs for the sugar affination process. Planned data collection on the affination process provided the basis for a functional "empirical" model.

Functionality is only one essential aspect of simulation. The user-interface is equally important. Ten-Core, an interactive package, has good user-friendly features and is capable of supporting an empirical model for a process section. The user demands of the affination simulation required that processing costs be linked to operating conditions and that the model be able to run on historic as well as actual data.

The affination simulation was installed and commissioned in the factory for management use. It was recommended that production personnel collect operational data on a select few country of origin raw sugar cargoes whose performance was not precisely predicted by the model. Once sufficient data had been collected it would be analysed by development personnel. A second version of the simulation software would be produced taking into account additional performance prediction empirical equations and recommendations for change made by factory management users. It was also recommended that the simulation be adapted for future use at plant level, accepting on-line process data input, and at management level as part of the overall refinery simulation.

ACKNOWLEDGEMENTS

The author would like to thank Dr Mike Donovan, Dr Gordon Walker, Mr Bill Raiola and Mr Alan Parry for their guidance and support during the Affination Station simulation project

REFERENCES

1   Lyle, O. (1957). Technology for Sugar Refinery Workers,
    3rd Edition, 346-351, Chapman & Hall, London

2   Donovan, M. (1986), Tate & Lyle Group R & D Memorandum
    hjc/0659K/22.05.86

3   Perry, R.H. and Chilton, C.H. (1973), Chemical Engineers'
    Handbook, 5th edition, 19-98, McGraw-Hill Kogakusha Ltd, Tokyo

NOMENCLATURE

a	Model fitting coefficient for the regression constant
b_1	Model fitting coefficient for the i th independent variable
x_i	The i th independent variable
y	Dependent variable

Figure 1 : Results for the affination efficiency correlation

MODEL FITTING RESULTS

VARIABLE	COEFFICIENT	STND. ERROR	T-VALUE	PROB(>"T")
CONSTANT	-1436.336348	93.457535	-15.3689	.0000
POLARISATION	15.171579	0.945866	16.0399	.0000
MOISTURE	48.323459	5.154564	9.3749	.0000
WASH TIME	2.705621	0.172976	15.6414	.0000
SEQUENCE TIME	-0.799937	0.122648	-6.5222	.0000
BASKET LOAD	-0.170023	0.040611	-4.1867	.0002

ANALYSIS OF VARIANCE FOR THE FULL REGRESSION

SOURCE	SUM OF SQUARES	DF	MEAN SQUARE	F-RATIO	PROB(>F)
MODEL	1921.0686	5	384.2137	111.3555	.0000
ERROR	103.51003	30	3.45033		
TOTAL (CORR.)	2024.5787	35			

R-SQUARED = 0.948873
R-SQUARED (ADJ. FOR D.F.) = 0.940352
STND. ERROR OF EST. = 1.85751

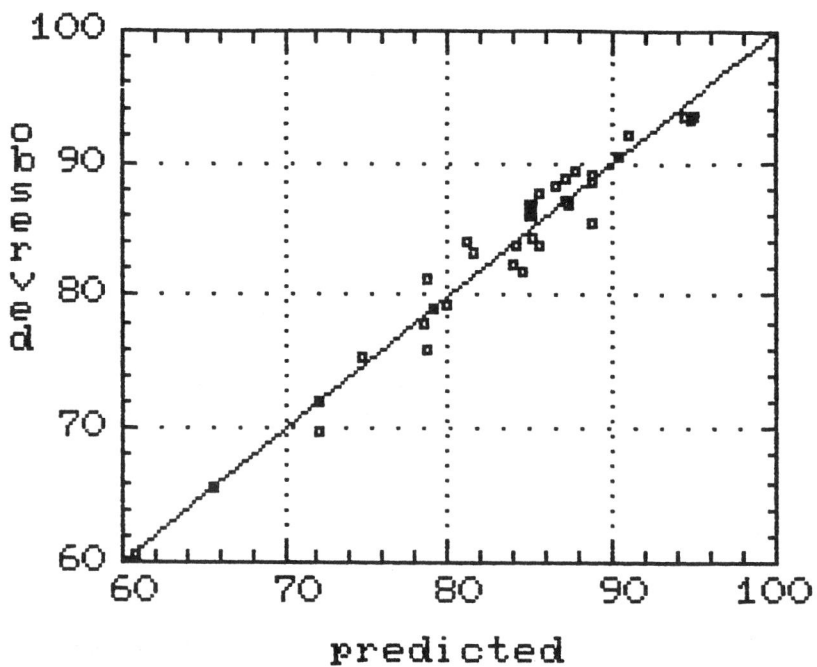

COMPUTER CONTROLLED OPERATION OF A TWIN SCREW FOOD EXTRUDER

M.K. Kulshreshtha, D.J. Jukes and C.A. Zaror *

This paper reports on the computer controlled operation of an extruder featuring automatic data acquisition, start-up and shut down. The details of instrumentation, calibration and control software are presented. The practical aspects of signal noise and digital filtering are discussed. The extruder operation was satisfactory under computer control.

INTRODUCTION

The use of computers to control the operation of industrial units has enabled increased product quality and process flexibility. In the case of extrusion cooking, maintaining stable operation is an essential requirement for consistent product quality. Unfortunately, key quality control variables cannot be measured on-line due to the lack of appropriate sensors, and industrial systems rely mostly on the operator knowledge of the process. Moreover, the process involves complex interactions between energy, mass and momentum transfer and physico-chemical transformations, which are poorly understood (Kulshreshtha et al, 1991). The introduction of computer controlled operation should provide a better monitoring and regulation of the process.

However, more often than not, practitioners have found that implementing computerised production systems may lead to serious drawbacks. For example, the process hardware, including sensors and actuators, may be inadequate for direct interfacing and require expensive upgrading; also, apropriate software for data communication between the extruder and the computer has to be developed. This paper addresses these questions and reports on a successful implementation of computer control operation of a Baker-Perkins twin screw extruder. The main components of the hardware and software are presented followed by a discussion on the uses of mathematical models as a tool for computer control.

HARDWARE

A Baker-Perkins twin screw extruder, Model MPF 50, was interfaced to an 8086-based computer, as shown in Figure 1 (Kulshreshtha, 1991). The die pressure and temperature, temperature profile along the barrel, and the torque can be recorded

* Department of Food Science and Technology, University of Reading, Reading (UK)

continuously, whereas the screw speed, the feed rate, and the water addition rate can be set by computer.

The data acquisition and control interface consists of an 8-channel A/D converter for +10V dc differential input, 4-channel D/A converter for 0-10V dc output, 8-channel digital input and 4 relay outputs. The interface unit communicates with the computer through a RS232C serial link. A 16-channel multiplexer amplifier, with cold junction compensation, is used for the temperature measurements. The melt-temperature profile, including the die temperature, is recorded using seven K-type thermocouples connected to the A/D converter through the multiplexer amplifier. The feed rate is controlled by changing the rotational speed of the feeder motor. The speed of feeder and the twin screws are controlled by a 0-10V dc outputs from D/A converter. The moisture content is controlled by varying the water addition rate using a water pump, controllable by a 0-3V dc signal from the D/A converter. Appropriate signal conditioning is provided for all signals.

SIGNAL NOISE AND FILTERING

The data obtained from the data acquisition system was very noisy, showing random spikes and high frequency noise. The spikes were generally attributed to high amplification, surrounding machinery and/or mains-borne electrical interference. The spikes were eliminated by putting a limit on the permissible magnitude of change from one sampling instant to another. The limit was decided on the basis of process knowledge. An exponential filter (Seborg et al, 1989) successfully minimised the random noise.

SOFTWARE

A computer program, written in turbo-BASIC, for operating the extruder was developed and successfully implemented. The program enables automatic start-up and shut-down of the extruder, data acquisition, opening and closing of data files, and the change of the extruder operating conditions from a menu driven environment. It also incorporates the control laws for feedback control of selected output variables. The software employs a modular design. The function of the main modules is described below.

Data Acquisition: The function of this module is to input process data, filter out the noise component, display it on the screen, and, optionally, store the data in the appropriate data files for further data processing eg. off-line modelling and optimization (Kulshreshtha et al, 1992).

Data File Management: These are routines for data file management which open and close the data files.

Changing the Operating Conditions: This module allows the operator to change the current operating conditions i.e. the screw speed, the mass flow rate and the moisture content of the feed.

Automatic Start-up of Extruder: A smooth and successful start-up of an extruder requires considerable practice. A hasty start-up leads to a sudden buildup of excessive torque resulting in stoppage of extruder. A cautious approach requires a long start-up and process stabilization period. The automatic start-up procedure is based on the controlled adjustment of the extruder start-up variables, under computer monitoring of torque and die pressure. The logic of the start-up routine is similar to one used by Ferdinand et al (1987) and is represented in Figure 2.

Automatic Shut-down of Extruder: Normally, the shut-down of extruders does not pose as much difficulty as the start-up. However, a too quick cutting down of dry feed may result in die blockage. Similarly, experiments show that a sudden increase of moisture content may also lead to die blockage. The logic flow diagram of the automatic shut-down is represented in Figure 3.

Process Control: It contains the control law to be used in a feedback control loop; in this study, the die pressure is controlled manipulating the feed flow rate, using a PID algorithm. More sophisticated model-based algorithms can be easily incorporated.

MODEL-BASED SET-POINT ADJUSTMENT

One of the main advantages of using a computer-based system to control extrusion cooking is that it enables the use of mathematical models to regulate unmeasured product quality to a desired value (Kulshreshtha *et al*, 1991). Indeed, if the quantitative relationship between measurable inputs and outputs and product quality is known, then the set point of the controlled output can be continuously adjusted to maintain production within an acceptable range of consistent quality. Preliminary simulation studies, using a dynamic model based on first principles, showed a considerable improvement in performance when model-based set point adjusment was used (Kulshreshtha, 1991). Implementation of such a scheme is only feasible if all relevant measurable variables can be logged into the computer and used in the on-line calculation of the required output set-point.

CONCLUSIONS

This study illustrates the use of computers to upgrade the operational features of extruders. It provides enhanced monitoring facilities which facilitates off-line data processing and, at the same time, allows the use of mathematical models to assist in the implementation of more efficient control schemes.

The automatic control system proved to be robust under a wide range of experimental conditions and, in all cases, start up and shut down were trouble free.

Finally, this study has also highlighted the need to use well designed and structured software, which maximises flexibility and efficiency. Clearly documented modular software allows expandability and further refinements can be implemented with minimum modifications. This work forms the basis of a continuing programme on computer control of extruder.

REFERENCES

Ferdinand J.M., Holley M.L., Prescott E.H.A., Richmond P., Smith A.C. (1988), In "Automatic control and Optimization of Food Processes, pp. 519-531, Elsevier Applied Science Publ., London.

Kulshreshtha M.K., Zaror C.A., Jukes D.J. (1991), J. of Food Control 2, 2, pp. 80-86.

Kulshreshtha M.K., Zaror C.A.Jukes D.J., Pyle D.L. (1992), "A Generalized Steady State Model for Twin Screw Extruders", J. Inst. Chem. Engrs. (Part C), in press.

Kulshreshtha, M.K. (1991), "Modelling and Control of a Twin Screw Food Extruder", PhD Thesis, University of Reading, Reading, UK

Seborg D.E., Edgar T.F., Mellichamp D.A. (1989), "Process Dynamics and Control", John Wiley & Sons, NY

NOMENCLATURE

FR : Feed Flow Rate (kg/h)   SS : Screw Speed (rpm)
MC : Moisture Content (% w.b.) TRQ : Torque (%)   WR : Water Feed Rate (kg/h)

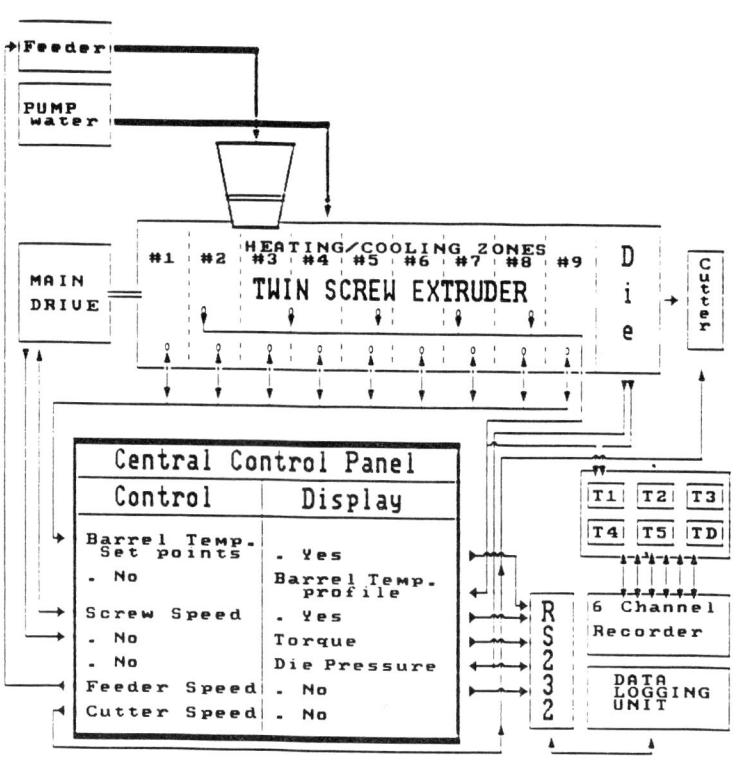

FIGURE 1
COMPUTER CONTROLLED BAKER-PERKINS
TWIN SCREW EXTRUDER

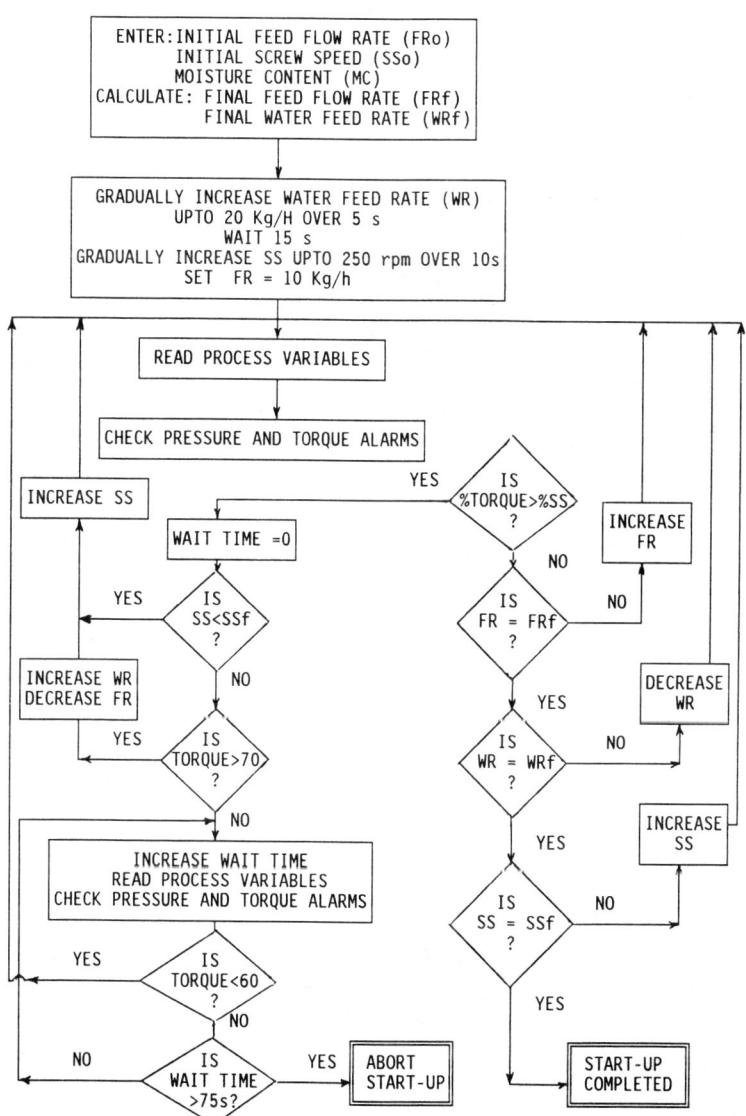

FIGURE 2: FLOW DIAGRAM OF AUTOMATIC START-UP

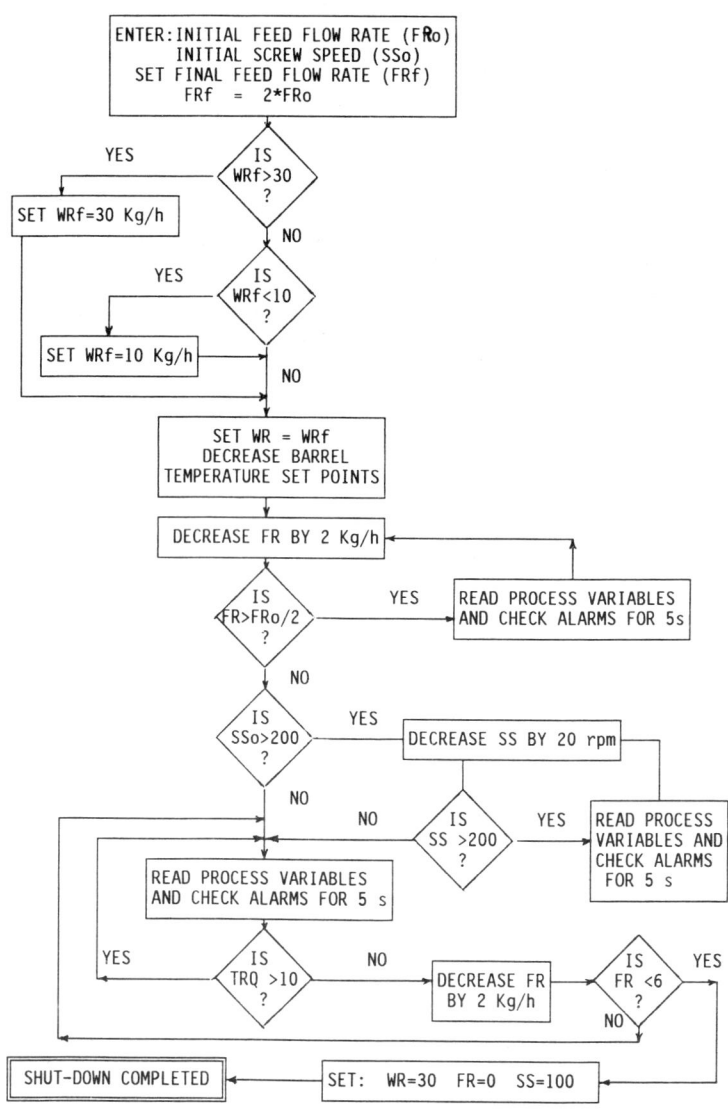

FIGURE 3: FLOW DIAGRAM OF AUTOMATIC SHUT-DOWN

SIMULATION OF HEAT TRANSFER IN FOODS WITH STOCHASTIC INITIAL AND BOUNDARY CONDITIONS

Bart M. Nicolaï and Josse De Baerdemaeker [1]

A numerical method for the computation of mean values and variances of the transient temperature field in heated foods with stochastic process parameters (initial temperature, surface heat transfer coefficient, ambient temperature) is proposed. This method is based on the finite element formulation of the heat conduction equation and is computationally less demanding than the Monte Carlo method. Simulations indicate that the stochastic fluctuations of the process parameters may cause a considerable level of uncertainty in the predicted temperatures and consequently also in the effect of the heat treatment.

INTRODUCTION

For the optimization of the thermal processing of foods the temperature evolution within the food during heating or cooling has to be known. During the last decades the emphasis has gone to the simulation of conduction heat transfer as an alternative to the time consuming and expensive experimental measurements. For conduction-type foods the mathematical model for heat transfer, the Fourier equation with appropriate initial and boundary conditions, has to be solved numerically which is accomplished using a finite difference [1] or finite element technique [2],[3].

Recently some methods have been proposed for the computation of the propagation of *random variable* fluctuations on the thermophysical properties (thermal conductivity and heat capacity) and the process conditions (surface heat transfer coeffient, initial and ambient temperature) through the heat transfer process [6,7,8]. For this purpose it was assumed that these parameters may vary when comparing different heated objects [4],[5], but are deterministic within a given object in a specific process environment. For example, the initial temperature of the raw materials may vary quite a lot between different batches, depending on the transport conditions where the temperature within the refrigerated vehicle may be higher in summer than in winter.

The process conditions may also change in time in a more or less noisy and unpredictable way. For example, when new products are brought into a chilling cabinet or an oven at unpredictable moments of time, the ambient temperature may rise temporarily. The pattern of air circulation may also alter resulting in changes of the surface heat transfer coefficient. Together with other unpredictable disturbances this results in time fluctuations of the process variables around their mean values. In this case they can be considered as *stochastic processes*. Two methods for the computation of heat transfer with random variable initial temperature and stochastic ambient temperature and surface heat transfer coefficient are discussed here.

FINITE ELEMENT FORMULATION OF THE HEAT CONDUCTION EQUATION

Transient linear heat conduction in isotropic media in the absence of heat generation is governed by the Fourier equation which is given in the cartesian coordinate system by

$$\mathcal{L}(T) = k\nabla^2 T - \rho c \frac{\partial T}{\partial t} = 0 \qquad (1)$$

where $\mathcal{L}$ a parabolic partial differential operator, T is the temperature [K], k the thermal conductivity [W/m.K] and ρc the volumetric heat capacity [J/m^{3}K]. The initial condition is defined as

$$T(x,y,z,t) = T_0(x,y,z) \qquad \text{at} \quad t = t_0 \qquad (2)$$

[1] Agricultural Engineering Department, K.U.Leuven, Kardinaal Mercierlaan 92, B-3001 Heverlee, Belgium

On the boundary surface Γ of the heated object specified temperature and convection boundary conditions may occur.

$$T(x,y,z,t) = T_\infty(x,y,z,t) \qquad \text{on } \Gamma_D \qquad (3)$$

$$k\frac{\partial}{\partial n}T(x,y,z,t) = h\left(T_\infty\ (x,y,z,t) - T(x,y,z,t)\right) \qquad \text{on } \Gamma_C \qquad (4)$$

with n the outward normal to the surface, h the convection coefficient [W/m^{2}K], T_∞ the (known) ambient temperature and $\Gamma = \Gamma_D \cup \Gamma_C$. For $h \to \infty$ the convection boundary condition tends to a specified temperature boundary condition and hence only convection boundary conditions will be dealt with. Nonlinear boundary conditions such as radiation are not considered here. In the finite element method [9] the continuum is subdivided in (finite) elements of variable size and shape which are interconnected in a finite number m of nodal points. In every element the unknown temperature can be approximated by a low order interpolating polynomial in such a way that the temperature is uniquely defined in terms of the (approximate) temperatures $u_i(t)$ at the nodes. It is possible to show [9] that the unknown nodal temperature vector $\mathbf{u} = [u_1, \ldots, u_m]^T$ is the solution of the following linear differential system:

$$\mathbf{C\dot{u}} + \mathbf{Ku} = \mathbf{f} \qquad (5)$$

with $\mathbf{C}$ the capacity matrix and $\mathbf{K}$ the conductivity matrix, both $m \times m$ - matrices and $\mathbf{f}$ a $m \times 1$ vector. $\mathbf{C}$ involves ρc, $\mathbf{K}$ involves k and h, $\mathbf{f}$ involves T_∞ and h. In the DOT finite element code [10] equation 5 is solved using an implicit Euler finite difference method.

STOCHASTIC ANALYSIS

A common formalism for describing time dependent random phenomena such as T_∞ and h is that of a stochastic process [11]. To avoid the difficulties of the Itô calculus inherent in *white* noise processes only colored Gaussian stochastic processes are dealt with here. It is further assumed, without loss of generality, that the stochastic processes $x(t)$ are stationary first order Markov processes with autocorrelation function

$$P(\tau) \stackrel{\Delta}{=} \mathcal{E}\left(x(t)x(t+\tau)\right) = \sigma^2 \exp(-|\tau|/\alpha) \qquad (6)$$

where $\mathcal{E}$ is the mean value operator, σ^2 the variance and α the correlation time which is a measure of the time interval in which two samples of the process are more or less correlated. For $\alpha \to 0$ the process approaches white noise; for $\alpha \to \infty$ the stochastic process reduces to an ordinary random variable. A first order Markov process is the most simple correlated stochastic process. It may be used when the variable varies unpredictably but more or less smoothly during time. The degree of smoothness can be adjusted by the parameter α.

A conceptually simple method for the simulation of heat transfer with stochastic boundary and initial conditions is the Monte Carlo approach in which a set of stochastic process conditions is generated. For each element of the set the heat transfer process is solved and in the end the mean values and variances of the temperature for a given place and time are estimated by classical statistical means. A major drawback of the Monte Carlo method is the large amount of CPU time which is required when the number of Monte Carlo steps is increased to decrease the variance of the estimates. An alternative method is based on stochastic systems theory.

Stochastic ambient temperature In case of a stochastic ambient temperature equation 5 can be considered as a linear system with a stochastic input T_∞ and random initial condition because the right hand side of equation 5 is a linear function of the ambient temperature. Applying the mean value operator to this system with initial condition 2 and interchanging order of the differential and mean value operator yields

$$\dot{\bar{\mathbf{u}}} = -\mathbf{C}^{-1}\mathbf{K}\bar{\mathbf{u}} + \mathbf{C}^{-1}\bar{\mathbf{f}} \qquad (7)$$

with initial condition

$$\bar{\mathbf{u}}_t = \mathcal{E}(\mathbf{u}_0) \qquad \text{for} \quad t = 0 \qquad (8)$$

in which the bar on top of $\bar{\mathbf{f}}$ denotes that it is constructed with the mean value $\overline{T}_\infty$ of T_∞. This means that the the mean value of the temperatures at the nodal points can be found by solving the original heat transfer process with mean values for the ambient temperature and mean initial temperature. A Taylor expansion of $\mathbf{f}$ around $\bar{\mathbf{f}}$ yields

$$\mathbf{f} - \bar{\mathbf{f}} = \frac{\partial \bar{\mathbf{f}}}{\partial T_\infty}\Delta T_\infty \stackrel{\Delta}{=} \left.\frac{\partial \mathbf{f}}{\partial T_\infty}\right|_{\overline{T}_\infty} \Delta T_\infty \qquad (9)$$

because higher derivatives vanish as a consequence of the construction of $\mathbf{f}$. From equation 5, 7 and 9 it follows that

$$\Delta\dot{\mathbf{u}} = -\mathbf{C}^{-1}\mathbf{K}\Delta\mathbf{u} + \mathbf{C}^{-1}\frac{\partial \bar{\mathbf{f}}}{\partial T_\infty}\Delta T_\infty \qquad (10)$$

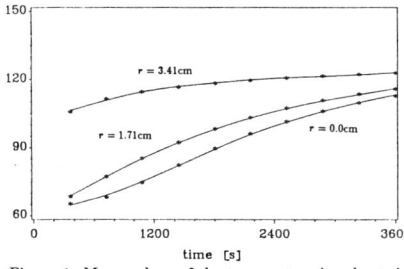

Figure 1. Mean values of the temperature in a heated Al-can with random variable initial temperature at three different locations. ——— : Variance propagation algorithm; $\star$: Monte Carlo solution

Figure 2. Variances of the temperature in a heated Al-can with random variable initial temperature at three different locations. Same legend as Figure 1.

in which Δ denotes the deviation with respect to the corresponding mean. ΔT_∞ is assumed to be a first order stationary Gaussian Markov process with mean equal to zero, variance $\sigma^2_{T_\infty} = \sigma^2_{\Delta T_\infty}$ and correlation time α_{T_∞}. ΔT_∞ can be described by the following differential equation [11]:

$$\Delta \dot{T}_\infty(t) = -\Delta T_\infty(t)/\alpha_{T_\infty} + \sigma_{T_\infty}\sqrt{2/\alpha_{T_\infty}}\ w(t) \tag{11}$$

where the mean and the variance of ΔT_∞ are initially respectively equal to 0 and $\sigma^2_{T_\infty}$ and $w(t)$ is a zero mean Gaussian white noise process with standard variance σ^2_w equal to unity. Equation 10 and 11 can be combined to the following system:

$$\dot{x}(t) = \mathbf{F}\mathbf{x}(t) + \mathbf{G}w(t) \tag{12}$$

with

$$\mathbf{x} = [\ \Delta\mathbf{u}^T\ \Delta T_\infty\ ]^T \tag{13}$$

$$\mathbf{F} = \begin{bmatrix} -\mathbf{C}^{-1}\mathbf{K} & \mathbf{C}^{-1}\partial\mathbf{f}/\partial T_\infty \\ \mathbf{0}_{1\times m} & -1/\alpha_{T_\infty} \end{bmatrix} \quad (14) \qquad \mathbf{G} = \begin{bmatrix} \mathbf{0}_{1\times m} & \sigma_{T_\infty}\sqrt{2/\alpha_{T_\infty}} \end{bmatrix}^T \tag{15}$$

and $\mathbf{0}_{1\times m}$ a $1\times m$ zero vector. The transpose of a vector or a matrix is denoted by the superscript ^{T}. It is known from stochastic systems theory that the variance matrix $\mathbf{V_x}$ of the solution of 12 obeys the following *Lyapunov* matrix differential equation

$$\dot{\mathbf{V}}_\mathbf{x}(t) = \mathbf{F}\mathbf{V}_\mathbf{x}(t) + \mathbf{V}_\mathbf{x}(t)\mathbf{F}^T + \mathbf{G}\sigma^2_w\mathbf{G}^T \tag{16}$$

with

$$\mathbf{V_x} \triangleq \mathcal{E}\left(\begin{bmatrix}\Delta\mathbf{u}\\\Delta T_\infty\end{bmatrix}[\Delta\mathbf{u}^T\ \Delta T_\infty]^T\right) = \begin{bmatrix}\mathbf{V}_{\Delta\mathbf{u}} & \mathbf{V}_{\Delta\mathbf{u},\Delta T_\infty}\\\mathbf{V}^T_{\Delta\mathbf{u},\Delta T_\infty} & \sigma^2_{T_\infty}\end{bmatrix} \tag{17}$$

in which $\mathbf{V}_{\Delta\mathbf{u}}$ is the variance matrix of $\Delta\mathbf{u}$ and $\mathbf{V}_{\Delta\mathbf{u},\Delta T_\infty}$ the covariance matrix of $\Delta\mathbf{u}$ and ΔT_∞ . The diagonal elements of $\mathbf{V}_{\Delta\mathbf{u}}$ are the variances of the nodal temperatures u_i. After some manipulations the following *variance propagation algorithm* for $\mathbf{V}_{\Delta\mathbf{u}}$ and $\mathbf{V}_{\Delta\mathbf{u},\Delta T_\infty}$ is obtained

$$\dot{\mathbf{V}}_{\Delta\mathbf{u},\Delta T_\infty} = -\mathbf{C}^{-1}\mathbf{K}\mathbf{V}_{\Delta\mathbf{u},\Delta T_\infty} + \mathbf{C}^{-1}\frac{\partial\overline{\mathbf{f}}}{\partial T_\infty}\sigma^2_{T_\infty} - \frac{\mathbf{V}_{\Delta\mathbf{u},\Delta T_\infty}}{\alpha_{T_\infty}} \tag{18}$$

$$\dot{\mathbf{V}}_{\Delta\mathbf{u}} = -\mathbf{C}^{-1}\mathbf{K}\mathbf{V}_{\Delta\mathbf{u}} - \mathbf{V}_{\Delta\mathbf{u}}\mathbf{K}^T\mathbf{C}^{-T} + \mathbf{C}^{-1}\frac{\partial\overline{\mathbf{f}}}{\partial T_\infty}\mathbf{V}^T_{\Delta\mathbf{u},\Delta T_\infty} + \mathbf{V}_{\Delta\mathbf{u},\Delta T_\infty}\frac{\partial\overline{\mathbf{f}}}{\partial T_\infty}^T\mathbf{C}^{-T} \tag{19}$$

The initial $\mathbf{V}_{\Delta\mathbf{u}}$ is equal to the variance matrix of the random initial temperature, the initial $\mathbf{V}_{\Delta\mathbf{u},\Delta T_\infty}$ is equal to a $1\times m$ zero vector because it is assumed that the initial temperature is not correlated with the ambient temperature. Lyapunov equation 19 is discretized with an explicit Euler finite difference scheme and equation 18 with an implicit scheme. The *explicit* discretization of 19 reduces the computational effort considerably but may lead to numerical instabilities if the time step is to large.

Stochastic surface heat transfer coefficient In the case of a stochastic surface heat transfer coefficient h with mean $\overline{h}$, variance σ^2_h and correlation time α_h a complication arises because both $\mathbf{K}$ and $\mathbf{f}$ are functions of h. Equation 5 can now be interpreted as a system which is nonlinear in the control variable h. Linearizing 5 around the mean control variable $\overline{h}$ and the corresponding solution denoted by

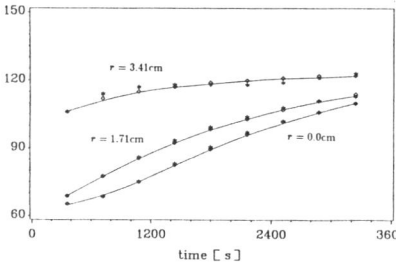

Figure 3. Mean values of the temperature in a heated Al-can with stochastic ambient temperature at three different locations. ▬▬ : Variance propagation algorithm; ⋆ : Monte Carlo with 100 runs; ⋄ : Monte Carlo with 1000 runs

Figure 4. Variances of the temperature in a heated Al-can with stochastic ambient temperature at three different locations. Same legend as Figure 3.

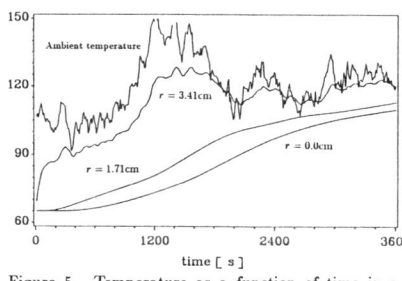

Figure 5. Temperature as a function of time in a heated Al-can with stochastic ambient temperature at three different locations

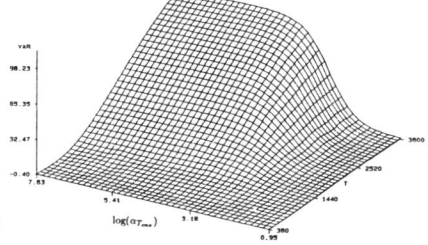

Figure 6. Variance of the temperature in the center of a heated Al-can with stochastic ambient temperature as a function of time and correlation time

$\overline{\mathbf{u}}$ yields

$$\Delta\dot{\mathbf{u}} \approx -\mathbf{C}^{-1}\mathbf{K}\Delta\mathbf{u} + \left(-\mathbf{C}^{-1}\frac{\partial\overline{\mathbf{K}}}{\partial h}\overline{\mathbf{u}} + \mathbf{C}^{-1}\frac{\partial\overline{\mathbf{f}}}{\partial h}\right)\Delta h \qquad (20)$$

After applying the mean value operator on 20 it becomes clear that $\overline{\mathbf{u}}$ is indeed the first order approximation of the mean value of $\mathbf{u}$. Comparing equation 20 with equation 10, it is seen that a derivation can be made that is similar to the case of a stochastic ambient temperature. In equations 19 and 18 $\mathbf{V}_{\Delta\mathbf{u},\Delta T_\infty}$, α_{T_∞} and $\sigma_{T_\infty}^2$ should be replaced by respectively $\mathbf{V}_{\Delta\mathbf{u},\Delta h}$, α_h and σ_h^2. Also, $\partial\overline{\mathbf{f}}/\partial T_\infty$ should be replaced by the expression $\partial\overline{\mathbf{f}}/\partial h - (\partial\overline{\mathbf{K}}/\partial h)\,\overline{\mathbf{u}}$. Note that in case h is completely white the stochastic Itô calculus must be used.

NUMERICAL RESULTS AND DISCUSSION

Simulations have been carried out in order to compare the results for the mean values and variances obtained by the numerical scheme which was presented above with those obtained by the Monte Carlo method.

The testproblem consisted of a Al-can (radius $r_0 = 3.41$ cm, height $L = 10.2$ cm) filled with a 30 % solids content tomato concentrate with k=0.542 W/m.K and ρc=3.89 10^6 J/m^3.K. The following process conditions were applied: $\overline{T}_0 = 65$ °C, $\overline{T}_\infty = 125$°C, $\overline{h} = 100$ W/m^{2}K.

All programs have been coded in FORTRAN. The random sequences for the Monte Carlo simulations were generated using NAG routines G05EAF and G05EZF.

In Figure 1 and 2 the mean temperatures and variances in three locations, computed with both the variance propagation algorithm and the Monte Carlo method, are shown for the testproblem with a homogeneous random initial temperature ($\sigma_{T_0}/\overline{T}_0 = 0.1$) and deterministic ambient temperature and surface heat transfer coefficient. It is clear that the results of both methods agree well. Not unexpectedly, the large initial variance eventually fades out but may still be significant for intermediate process times.

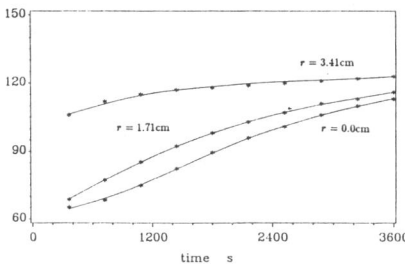

Figure 7. Mean values of the temperature in a heated Al-can with stochastic surface heat transfer coefficient at three different locations. Same legend as Figure 1. solution

Figure 8. Variances of the temperature in a heated Al-can with stochastic surface heat transfer coefficient at three different locations. Same legend as Figure 1.

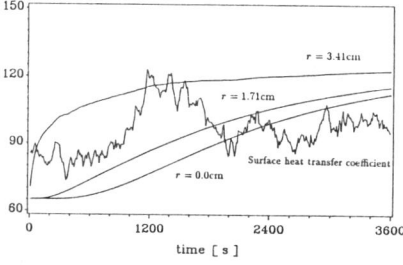

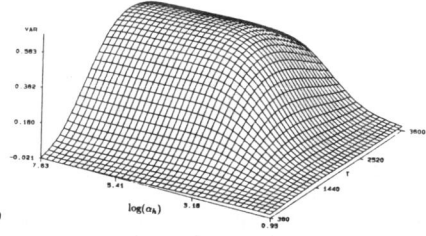

Figure 9. Temperature as a function of time in a heated Al-can with a stochastic surface heat transfer coefficient at three different locations

Figure 10. Variance of the temperature in the center of a heated Al-can with stochastic stochastic surface heat transfer coefficient as a function of time and correlation time

In Figure 3 and 4 the mean temperatures and variances are shown for the testproblem with stochastic ambient temperature ($\sigma_{T_\infty}/\overline{T}_\infty = 0.1$, $\alpha_{T_\infty} = 360$s) and deterministic initial temperature and surface heat transfer coefficient. In a first Monte Carlo experiment 100 runs were carried out, in a second experiment 1000 runs. It is clear that variances of the second Monte Carlo experiment agree very well with these computed with the variance propagation algorithm. However, the variances computed with the first Monte Carlo experiment are much more scattered indicating that the number of runs was not sufficient.

In Figure 5 a particular solution is shown for the above heat transfer problem in different locations. It is clear that the surface temperature course is very rugged. The food acts as a filter so that the temperature course in the more interior points is rather smooth.

The variances are also a function of the correlation length which is obvious from Figure 6. For correlation times smaller than 100 s the variances remain very small but increase rapidly with increasing correlation times For correlation times comparable to the duration of the process the variances in this example become very large. In Figure 7 and 8 the mean temperatures and variances are shown for the testproblem with stochastic surface heat transfer coefficient ($\sigma_h/\overline{h} = 0.1$, $\alpha_h = 360$s) and deterministic initial and ambient temperature. Because of the huge amount of CPU time which was needed with only 100 runs no larger Monte Carlo experiment has been carried out. The variances computed with the Monte Carlo method are again not very accurate for this small number of runs. It can be seen that, compared to the stochastic ambient temperature case, the variances are two orders of magnitude smaller.

In Figure 9 a particular solution is shown for the above heat transfer problem in different locations. Even at the surface the temperature course is very smooth. In Figure 10 the variance in the center of the can is shown as a function of the heating time and the correlation time. The same conclusions can be drawn as in the case of a stochastic ambient temperature.

CONCLUSION

A variance propagation algorithm for the computation of conduction heat transfer with stochastic initial and ambient temperature and surface heat transfer coefficient has been derived. It is based on the space discretisation of the heat conduction equation by a finite element method. The stochastic systems theory is applied to the resulting linear or linearized system. For this purpose the process parameters mentioned above were considered as stochastic inputs to this system. The stochastic processes were assumed to be stationary, Gaussian and first order Markov.

The mean values and variances of the temperature within the container computed by this algorithm agreed well with those computed with the Monte Carlo method. A relatively large number of Monte Carlo runs (1000) was required in order to achieve a reasonable accuracy.

The simulations showed that uncertainties on the initial temperature eventually fade out during the heat transfer process but may be still significant for intermediate process times. The variances of the temperature within the food heated with a stochastic ambient temperature increase during the process and may become as large as the variance of the ambient temperature, depending on the correlation length. A stochastic surface heat transfer coefficient causes only small temperature variances within the heated food. The temperature variances show then a maximum for intermediate process times.

It is clear that the uncertainty on the process temperatures inside the food results in an uncertainty on the net effect of the thermal treatment. For example, the thermal inactivation of micro–organisms is highly dependent on the temperature. It may be expected therefore that the uncertainty on the inner food temperatures will be amplified resulting in a very large uncertainty on the ultimate F–value. This topic is currently investigated further by the authors.

The incorporation of uncertainty propagation methods in heat transfer simulations of foods is a new approach which may be considered as a first step in the development of stochastic reliability methods in food process engineering.

ACKNOWLEDGEMENTS

This study has been performed as a part of FLAIR (Food Linked Agro-Industrial Research) project AGRF-CT91-0047 (DTEE). The authors wish to thank the European Communities for the financial support.

REFERENCES

1 Teixeira, A.A., J.R. Dixon, J.W. Zahradnik, and G.E. Zinsmeister. *Food Technology* **25**: 137-142, 1969.

2 De Baerdemaeker, J., R.P. Singh and L.J. Segerlind. *Food Process Engineering* **1**: 37-50, 1977.

3 Naveh, D., I.J. Kopelman and I.I. Pflug. *Journal of Food Science* **48**: 1086-1093, 1983.

4 Meffert, H.F. In G. Vos (ed) *Physical Properties of Foods*, Applied Science Publishers, London-New York, 229-267, 1983.

5 James, S. and J. Evans. In P. Zeuthen, J.C. Cheftel, C. Eriksson, T.R. Gormley, P. Linko and K. Paulus (eds) *Processing and Quality of Foods*, Elsevier Applied Science Vol. 3, 273–278, 1990.

6 De Baerdemaeker, J. and B.M. Nicolaï. In Singh R. and A. Medina (eds) *Food Properties and Computer-Aided Engineering of Food Processing Systems*. Kluwer Academic Publishers, Dordrecht-Boston-London, 557-563, 1988.

7 Nicolaï B. M. and J. De Baerdemaeker. In Mosekilde (ed) *Modelling and Simulation* 1991, 887-892.

8 Nicolaï B. M. and J. De Baerdemaeker. *Proceedings of the International Workshop on the Role of Food Engineering Research in the Development of Indonesian Food Industry*, Jakarta, 2–9 september 1991.

9 Segerlind, L.J.: *Applied Finite Element Analysis*. J.Wiley and Sons, Inc., 1976.

10 Polivka R.M. and E.L. Wilson. Report no. UC SESM 76-2, 1976. Dept. of Civil Engineering, University of California, Berkeley, California.

11 Melsa J.L. and A.P. Sage. *An Introduction to Probability and Stochastic Processes*. Prentice-Hall, Englewood Cliffs, New Jersey, 1973.

NOMENCLATURE

α	: correlation length		L	: height of can [m]
$\mathbf{C}$	: capacity matrix		$\mathcal{L}$	: parabolic partial differential operator
$\mathbf{V}$	: variance matrix		m	: number of nodes
Δt	: time step [s]		n	: outward normal
$\mathcal{E}$	: mean value operator		r	: distance to the centre of the can [m]
ϵ	: residu		r_0	: radius of can [m]
$\mathbf{f}$	: thermal load vector		ρc	: volumetric heat capacity [J/m³.K]
Γ_C	: convection boundary condition surface		σ	: standard deviation
Γ_D	: fixed temperature boundary condition surface		t	: time [s]
Γ	: boundary surface		T	: temperature [K]
h	: surface heat transfer coefficient [W/m².K]		T_∞	: environmental temperature [K]
k	: thermal conductivity [W/m.K]		T_0	: initial temperature function
$\mathbf{K}$	: conductivity matrix		$\mathbf{u}$	: nodal temperature vector

Simulation of Thermal Food Processing Operations

de Alwis A A P, Varley J and Niranjan K

Abstract

Thermal processing is a major preservation technique employed by the food processing industry. The need for computer simulation of such processes hardly needs to be emphasised in the present climate. An important feature of food processing operations is the existence of *quality* and *sterility* constraints. It is essential that they are incorporated into relevant mathematical models which describe heat, mass and momentum transfer.

Simulation of two thermal processing operations is considered here using SPEEDUP™ as the process simulator. Models for blanching and in-container sterilisation are developed on the basis of mass and energy balances. Important stages in the development of models for SPEEDUP are also considered in this paper.

Introduction

Simulation of two thermal processing techniques (i)canning and (ii)blanching commonly used in food processing industry is considered in this paper. Biological changes are continuously taking place in foods and these may have adverse effects on both quality and safety. If process models developed for food processing are to have any practical value, they must be able to handle the inherent dynamic nature of food operations. Food processing is a low profit, high volume industry and improved methods of operation are continually being sought. Computer aided techniques such as computer intergrated manufacturing (CIM) have been used for line management and material handling schemes in the food industry but as yet, they have had little impact on the engineering aspects of the processes themselves: theoretical models could be used to improve process efficiency and for process optimisation. In systems such as CIM, the emphasis is on improving the usage of an existing system, rather than developing a fundamental understanding of the process itself. The successful implementation of existing models, rather than the building of entirely new models, is reported. The integration of such models into SPEEDUP™, an equation based simulator, being the primary objective of the work described here.

SPEEDUP™ system

The main software tool used in this study is SPEEDUP™, an equation-based process simulator. The SPEEDUP (Simulating Program for Evaluating and Evolutionary Design of Unsteady state Processes) system (Sargent *et al*, 1982) is the product of work at Imperial College, London. SPEEDUP is a multi-function simulator which is designed to model systems which can be represented by a set of equations. As a simulator having an equation-oriented approach, it is based on representing process units as sets of equations. SPEEDUP has been designed to solve a variety of problems including steady-state, optimisation, parameter estimation and dynamic operation within an interactive environment. The structure of the SPEEDUP system is given in Figure 1

Department of Food Science and Technology, University of Reading, Whiteknights, PO Box 226, Reading, RG6 2AP.

Mathematical modelling of any process requires quantitative mathematical expressions for the behaviour of physical, biological and other complex chemical phenomena. Such equations must also be easily solvable. SPEEDUP provides an efficient robust system which allows the user to obtain solutions to a set of derived equations. A selection of numerical methods for solution phase is available in the "Maths routines" of the simulator.

At present, the SPEEDUP 'library' contains only a few models of use to the food processing industry, further models must therefore be developed. In this study, SPEEDUP is used as the tool in model building and testing for thermal processes found in the food industry. These developed models will be incorporated into the SPEEDUP library.

Figure 1 SPEEDUP™ : *Structure of the simulator*

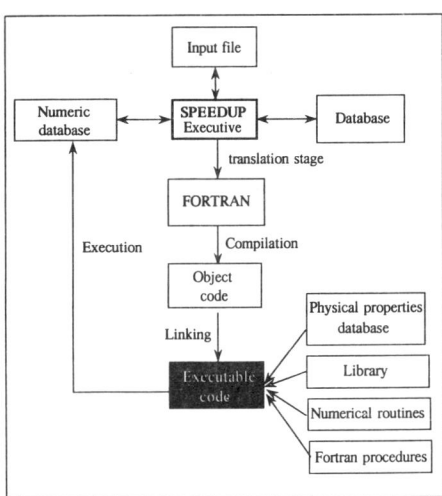

In-container sterilisation (Canning)

Introduction

Canning is one of the most widely used thermal operations in the food industry and is still a major thermal preservation process. Development of operational methods for in-container sterilisation which improve the safety and the quality of its products is an area of major research interest.

Initial developments in predictive modelling of canning have included the use of semi-analytical approaches which use 'f' and 'j' values (Ball and Olson, 1957). Such approaches can be applied to conduction and convection heating in systems with regular geometries. These techniques have served the industry well. As the use of analytical or semi-analytical techniques is fairly limited, numerical methods which are more flexible and robust are required in general for solving realistic problems (Tucker and Holdsworth, 1991).

The first numerical model to simulate thermal processing of conduction-heated canned foods was developed by Teixeira *et al* (1969) for cylindrical containers (solids). The model was based on the mathematical coupling of (i) first-order reaction kinetics, describing the thermal inactivation of microorganisms, with (ii) a numerical solution of the two dimensional heat conduction equation for a finite cylinder. Later modifications to this model are reported by Manson, Zahradnik and Stumbo (1970) and Manson, Stumbo and Zahradnik (1974): these modifications allow for rectangular and pear-shaped container geometries. Manson and Cullen (1974) have further developed this model to include liquid foods containing suspended particles. However, computer hardware costs and capabilities available at that time prevented these models being used within an industrial environment; a factor of less importance today.

Heat transfer model for in-container sterilisation

A major objective of any canning process is to achieve a pre-set level of bacterial sterility. The process lethality, measured in terms of an F_0 value, is given by;

$$F_0 = \int_0^t 10^{\frac{(T-T_{ref})}{z}} dt \tag{1}$$

where F_0 is the integrated lethality (min); t is the time of processing; T is the temperature at the measurement point (usually selected is the slowest heating point); T_{ref} is the reference temperature (121.1 °C) and z is the inverse gradient determined from a graph of the logarithm of the decimal reduction time plotted against temperature. This formula continues to be used even though there are certain limitations when using a single value for z.

The changes in quality attributes of products can be expressed by a 'C_0', which is defined as;

$$C_0 = \int_0^t 10^{\frac{(T-T_{ref})}{z_c}} dt \tag{2}$$

Mansfield(1962) first used this concept for degradation of quality attributes. The formulation is basically similar to the F_0 value with the reference temperature (T_{ref}) being 100°C. z_c indicates the temperature sensitivity of the attribute in question. z_c values are not as easily determined as the corresponding z values for F_0 calculations, as the quality attributes of a food are subjective. Some examples of z_c are given in Holdsworth (1985).

The objective function, which expresses the end point for a sterilisation process having three stages (heating, holding and cooling) is given by the minimisation of;

$$F_0(t) = \int_{t=0}^{t=HT} 10^{[(T-121.1)/z]} dt + \int_{t=HT}^{t=EHT} 10^{[(T-121.1)/z]} dt + \int_{t=EHT}^{t=CT} 10^{[(T-121.1)/z]} dt \tag{3}$$

The above equation expresses the contribution to lethality from possible three phases of a thermal preservation operation. For a canning operation, the second integral is not relevant. The constraints to this objective function are;

Safety constraints: $F_0(t) \geq (F_0)_{min}$ (4)

Quality constraints: $C_0(t) \leq (C_0)_{max}$ (5)

$F_0(t)$ and $C_0(t)$ give the sterility and level of quality at any time t. $(F_0)_{min}$ is the minimum sterility required at the slowest heating point of the system and $(C_0)_{max}$ is the maximum loss in quality that can be tolerated.

The transient temperature T is a function of the transient retort temperature T_R, the dimensions of the container and the thermal diffusivity of the can contents. Thermal diffusivity varies with temperature making the problem non-linear. For conduction heating in a cylindrical container, assuming constant thermal diffusivity, the governing heat conduction equation in cylindrical coordinates is (Teixeira, 1989);

$$\frac{1}{\alpha} \frac{\partial T}{\partial t} = \frac{\partial^2 T}{\partial h^2} + \frac{1}{r} \frac{\partial T}{\partial r} + \frac{\partial^2 T}{\partial r^2} \tag{6}$$

where α is the thermal diffusivity and h and r are the vertical and radial coordinates respectively.

This equation is subject to the following initial and boundary conditions;

$$T = T_i \ (t = 0); \tag{7}$$

$$T_{boundary} = T_R(t) \ (t > 0); \tag{8}$$

where T_i the initial temperature and $T_{boundary}$ is the temperature at the boundary condition which is determined by the retort temperature profile.

No external heat transfer resistances are considered as very high heat transfer coefficients are associated with condensing steam, which is the usual heating medium, and internal heat transfer resistances will therefore be limiting.

The explicit finite difference form of the partial derivatives expressed in Equation (6) yields (Teixeira, 1989);

$$T_{ij}^{t+\Delta t} = T_{ij}^t + \frac{\alpha \Delta t}{\Delta r^2} \left[T_{i-1,j} - 2T_{ij} + T_{i+1,j} \right]^t$$
$$+ \frac{\alpha \Delta t}{2r\Delta r} \left[T_{i-1,j} - T_{i+1,j} \right]^t$$
$$+ \frac{\alpha \Delta t}{\Delta h^2} \left[T_{i,j-1} - 2T_{ij} + T_{i,j+1} \right]^t \tag{9}$$

where i and j denote the sequence of radial and vertical increments away from the can wall and mid-plane. The above equation expresses the temperature at a point inside the cylinder at time ($t+\Delta t$), in terms of the temperature of the immediately surrounding points at time t. The expression uses characteristic dimensions of the can, a selected number of radial and vertical increments and the thermal diffusivity of its contents. Variations in thermal diffusivity with temperature have been incorporated. The number and relative sizes of space and time intervals chosen to obtain the finite difference grid for a cylinder governs the mathematical stability of computed values for temperature. For stability it is necessary to observe conditions expressed in Eqs. (10) and (11) (Croft and Lilley, 1977).

(radial Fourier number) $\dfrac{\alpha \Delta t}{\Delta r^2} \leq \dfrac{1}{4}$ \hfill (10)

(vertical Fourier number) $\dfrac{\alpha \Delta t}{\Delta h^2} \leq \dfrac{1}{4}$ \hfill (11)

Integration of the heat transfer model into SPEEDUP

Within SPEEDUP the finite difference scheme is handled in a procedure which communicates with the main executable code. The stability constraints given above (Equations (10) and (11)) are evaluated within the executable code of SPEEDUP from updated diffusivity values (α) and are then passed to the procedure. Once the temperature distribution has been determined from Equation (9) F_o and C_o values can be evaluated.

The availability of a numerical model similar to that outlined above, allows determination of F_o in a real time situation: T(t) is calculated from the finite difference approximation to Equation (9) from on-line measurements of the retort temperature and known values for the required physical properties. On-line model based control thus becomes a feasible option.

Results

Figures 2 and 3 show a typical temperature plot and corresponding F_o and C_o values obtained from transient heating of a can containing a meat sample with an initial thermal diffusivity of 1.2×10^{-8} m^2/s. The variation in C_o indicates a low quality for the canned food material, when the required F_o is achieved: longer processing times lead to significant reductions in product quality. This knowledge has prompted the food industry's current move towards the use of high temperature short time (HTST) processes, wherever possible.

Future Work

The above discussion gives an indication of the initial work in developing the SPEEDUP model library to handle a thermal processing operation. The model discussed above is very simple and must be extended to cope with the wide range of problems arising in in-container sterilisation. Models which can handle processes with a range of retort temperature functions, a variety of geometrical configurations (*eg* retort pouches), a range of solid/liquid ratios, complete heating and cooling cycles and which take into account lag times during processing, effects of can wall material and thickness, finite heat transfer coefficients at sides of the container, effect of head space, convection effects are needed.

Any process models generated will be verified by using static and rotary retorts which are available in the department.

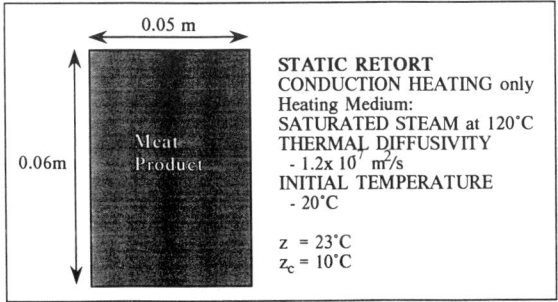

Figure 2(a) Simulation input data

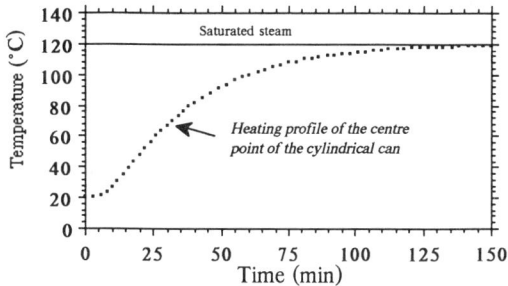

Figure 2(b) Transient temperature profile at the geometric centre

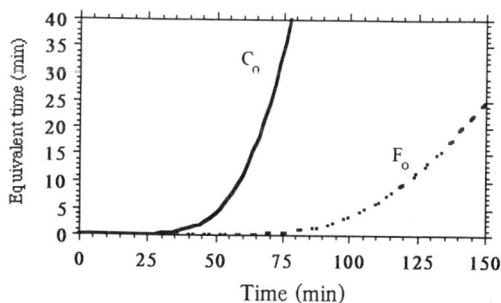

Figure 3 F_o and C_o variation with processing time at the geometric centre

BLANCHING

Introduction

In the blanching process, a food material is rapidly heated to a predetermined temperature and then held at this temperature for a specific time before being, either cooled rapidly, or passed immediately to the next processing stage. Blanching is an important operation in vegetable processing. The aim of the process is to prevent the deterioration of vegetables which usually starts at the time of harvest. Enzymatic activity, which continues after harvesting, breaks down the plant tissue, and it is therefore important to inactivate any enzymes present. The time between harvesting and enzyme inactivation is critical to the quality of the final product.

Desired effects of blanching include enzyme inactivation *via* temperature inhibition and food sterilisation, whilst adverse effects include leaching of soluble solids, loss of nutrients such as ascorbic acid, loss of intercellular gases and changes in the sensory properties and microscopic structure of, for example vegetables. The extent to which any of these changes occur is influenced by the combined heat and mass transfer processes, which take place during the process. From the point of view of product quality, any adverse effects of blanching should be minimised.

Potato blanching is widely used in the food sector and has therefore been a subject of interest for a considerable time. Important objectives of an industrial potato-blanching process include deactivation of enzymes and reduction of the glucose/fructose content. Reduction in sugar helps in product colour control during subsequent frying. For products such as crisps or chips, the process has further functions; starch in the surface layer gelatinizes and reduces fat absorption, reducing the fat content of the final product. Also, because the potato is partly cooked by blanching, subsequent frying times are reduced. The blanching operation for potatoes consists of submerging raw potatoes in hot water; this hot water is recirculated through a heat exchanger to provide the energy to heat the raw potatoes to the required blanch temperature. The potatoes may not initially be at ambient temperature due to pre-treatment operations, *eg* lye peeling. Water is added to the blancher and overflows, thus controlling the sugar content in the blanch water.

Predictive models for potato blanching have been proposed by Calfano and Calvelo, (1983) and Kozempel *et al* (1981ab). The mass transfer model developed by Kozempel *et al* (1981ab) is implemented below to calculate leaching of components from blanched food material. Though the model has been developed for potato blanching it is equally applicable to other foods.

Mass transfer model for blanching

In the development of their model Kozempel *et al* (1981a) assumed that the blanching unit is completely stirred. This assumption is valid if the ratio of water circulation rate to overall throughput for the system is high. During blanching leaching of solutes takes place. Leaching is usually controlled by internal diffusion. This process is adequately described by Fick's second law: the rate controlling step for leaching of sugar from potatoes is diffusion within the solid. Using Fick's second law of diffusion it is possible to obtain the solute concentration for a slab geometry.

The solute concentration within the solid due to diffusion for a slab of finite thickness L is given by (Yang and Brier, 1958);

$$C = C_e + (C_1 - C_e) \frac{8}{\pi^2} \sum_{m=0}^{\infty} \frac{1}{(2m+1)^2} \exp\left[-D(2m+1)^2 \pi^2 \tau / L^2\right] \qquad (12)$$

where C is exit average solute concentration in the juice within the potato, C_e is equilibrium solute concentration in the juice within the potato, C_1 is the initial solute concentration in the potato juice, D is the diffusion constant, L is a characteristic dimension of the solid (thickness), m is a positive integer and τ is the extraction residence time.

For $(D\tau/L^2)$ larger than 0.1, all terms of the series solution, except the first, can usually be neglected with little error (Schwartzberg, 1975). The maximum concentration that the solute can reach is the solute concentration in the juice of the feed potatoes (C_1). At equilibrium the solute concentration in the blanch water is equal to the equilibrium solute concentration in the juice which then helps to relate the blanch solute concentration to that of it within the solid.

The mathematical model describing the loss of solute from potatoes during hot water blanching is obtained from a component material balance over the blancher unit (see Figure 4);

$$\frac{dS}{dt} = \left[\frac{Fa(C_1-S)\psi + W(S_1-S)}{V\rho + (Fa\tau/2)\psi} \right] \qquad (13)$$

where dS/dt is the rate of change of concentration of solute in blanch water, W is mass flow rate of solids, a is the moisture content, F is liquid mass flow rate, S_1 is the solute concentration in the inlet water, ρ is the density of the blanch water, V is the volume of the blancher.

$$\psi = 1 - \frac{8}{\pi^2} \exp(-\pi^2 D\tau / L^2) \qquad (14)$$

For steady state conditions, a solution of Equation (13) can be obtained by setting $dS/dt = 0$.

The following assumptions are inherent in the derivation of the above equations: slab geometry, instantaneous solubilization of the solute in the reject solution, complete absence of external mass transfer resistances, no chemical reactions are involved, the process is isothermal, no shrinkage of the food material, there are no interactions between the solute and the solution, the solid structure or other solute material and the equilibrium concentration can be adequately described. Also the accumulation of solute in the juice within the solid is the arithmetic average $(C_1+C)/2$.

The ERRC Food Process Simulator (Kozempel et al 1991), a process simulator available for studying the Potato Flake Process, has implemented the steady state blanching model. The detailed steps in derivation of the model are given by Yang and Brier (1958) and Kozempel et al (1981ab).

For non-ideal flow patterns the exit concentration can be modified to;
$$S = \alpha_f S_B + (1-\alpha_f)S_P \qquad (15)$$

where α_f is the fraction of flow which is back mixed. S_B and S_P are the solute concentrations for complete back mixing and plug flow respectively.

Integration of mass transfer model into SPEEDUP

All parameters in the model except C_1 and D are process parameters. C_1 is the effective solute concentration in the juice within the solid and has to be experimentally determined. This actually will be a quality or compositional parameter associated with the raw material. To use the model it is first necessary to know the solute concentrations within the food solids and the appropriate diffusion constants. Usually the latter has to be determined from experimental data and subsequent parameter estimation in SPEEDUP parameter estimation mode.

Mass transfer within the blancher unit is represented by the set of derived equations (13-14) given above.

Results

Simulation results from a dynamic run are given in Figure 5 with initial input data in Table 1, which shows the variation of soluble solids and sugar concentrations in the blanch water. Though some leaching effects are desirable (eg glucose leaching in potato blanching), some are not (eg leaching of soluble solids). Introduction of recycling could be used to reduce the leaching losses by reducing the concentration driving force present when new solid feed is introduced to the system.

Table 1: INPUT DATA

Solid feed rate	- 5.442 kg/hr
Liquid feed rate	- 42.3 kg/hr
Moisture content	- 0.45
Extraction time	- 5 hr
Inlet water temperature	- 93°C
Blancher fill volume	- 0.75 m^3
Inlet feed soluble solids	- 0.012 kg/kg
Inlet glucose concentration	- 0.03 kg/kg
Diffusivity	- 4.057 (glucose) cm^2/hr
	- 0.274 (soluble solids) cm^2/hr
Sample thickness	- 0.95 cm

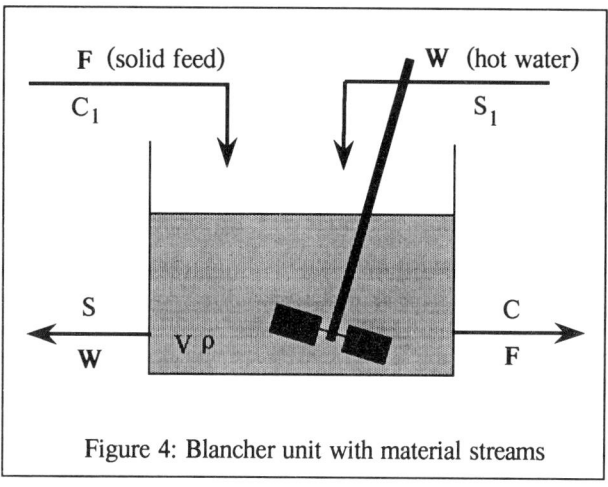

Figure 4: Blancher unit with material streams

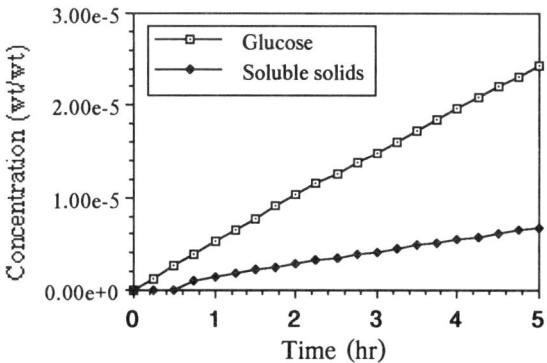

Figure 5 Variation of soluble solids and sugar concentration in blanch water with extraction residence time

Future Work

The blanching model discussed above will be developed further to take into consideration variations in geometry and non-isothermal effects (transient temperature distributions and enzyme kinetics). Optimisation studies will also be undertaken.

Nomenclature

$(C_o)_{max}$	minimum acceptable process quality
$(F_o)_{min}$	minimum sterility required at the slowest heating point
a	moisture content
C	exit solute concentration in the juice within the potato
C_1	initial solute concentration in the potato juice
C_e	equilibrium solute concentration in the juice within the potato
C_o	process quality
CT	end of cooling period
D	diffusivity
EHT	end of holding period
f	absolute value of inverse slope of u vs t line
F_o	process lethality
h	vertical coordinate
HT	end of heating period
j	intercept of u vs t line
L	characteristic dimension of the solids
M	moisture content
m	positive integer
P	solid feed rate
r	radial coordinate
S	solute concentration in the exit water and within the blancher
S_1	solute concentration in the inlet water
S_B	solute concentration for complete back mixing
S_P	solute concentration for non-ideal or plug flow
T	temperature
t	time
$T_{boundary}$	temperature at the boundary condition
T_i	initial temperature
T_{ij}	temperature at position i,j
T_R	retort temperature
T_{ref}	reference temperature
u	transformed temperature = $(T_\infty - T)/(T_0 - T)$
V	volume of blanch water
W	volume of the blancher (fill volume)
z	inverse gradient of log decimal reduction time vs temperature
z_c	inverse gradient of log change in quality parameter vs temperature

Greek symbols

α	thermal diffusivity
α_f	fraction of flow which is back mixed
ρ	density of blanch water
τ	extraction residence time

References

Ball, CO and Olson, FCW (1957), *Sterilisation in Food Technology*, McGraw Hill, NY.

Califano, AN and Calvelo, A (1983), Heat and mass transfer during warm water blanching of potatoes, *J Food Science*, **48**, 220-225.

Croft, DR and Lilley, DG (1977), *Heat transfer calculations using finite difference equations*, Applied Science Publications, London.

Holdsworth, SD (1985), Optimisation of Thermal processing - A review, *J Food Engineering*, 4, 89.

Kozempel, MF; Sullivan, JF and Craig, JC Jr (1981a), Model for Blanching Potatoes and other Vegetables, *Lebensm-Wiss U-Technol*, **14**, 6, 331-335.

Kozempel, MF; Sullivan, JF and Craig, JC Jr (1981b), Effect of temperature on the model for blanching potatoes and other vegetables, *Lebensm-Wiss U-Technol,* 16, 6, 338-342.

Lamberg, I and Olsson, (1989), Starch gelatinization temperatures within potato during blanching, *Int J of Food Science and Technology,* 24, 487-494.

Mansfield, T (1962), High Temperature Short Time sterilisation, *Procs 1st Int Congress on Food Science and Technology,* Gordon and Breach, 311.

Manson, JE and Cullen JF (1974), Thermal process simulation for aseptic processing of foods containing discrete particulate matter, *J Food Science,* 39, 1084-1089.

Manson, JE; Stumbo, CR and Zahradnik, JW (1974), Evaluation of thermal processes for conduction-heating foods in pear shaped containers, *J Food Science,* 39, 276.

Manson, JE; Zahradnik, JW and Stumbo, CR (1970), Evaluation of lethality and nutrient retention of conduction-heating food in rectangular containers, *Food Technology,* 24, 11, 109-113.

Schwartzberg, HG (1975), Mathematical analysis of solubilization kinetics and diffusion in foods, *J Food Science,* 40, 211-213.

Teixeira, AA (1989), Computer simulation of thermal processing for canned food sterilisation, in *Food properties and computer-aided engineering of food processing systems,* Singh RP and Medina AG (Eds), 543-552.

Teixeira, AA; Dixon, JR; Zahradnik, JW and Zinsmeister, GE (1969), Computer optimization of nutrient retention in the thermal processing of conduction-heated foods, *Food Technology,* 23, 6, 137.

Tucker, GS and Holdsworth, SD (1991), Mathematical modelling of sterilisation and cooking processes for heat preserved foods, *Food and Bioproducts processing, Trans Inst Chem Engrs,* 69, Part C, 5-12.

Yang, HH and Brier, J (1958), Extraction of sugar from beets, *AIChE Journal,* 4, 453.

Sargent, RWH; Perkins, JD and Thomas, S (1982), SPEEDUP: Simulation program for the economic evaluation and design of unified processes, in *Computer-aided Process Plant Design,* Leesley, ME (ed), Gulph, Houston, 1982.

MODELLING SPRAY EVAPORATION
USING EQUATION ORIENTED PROCESS SIMULATORS

AAP de Alwis and CA Zaror

ABSTRACT

The food industry is under increasing pressure to implement advanced computer-based tools for design and optimisation. Equation oriented simulation packages, such as SPEEDUP™, have been successfully used in conventional chemical processes. However, their application for the description of food manufacturing processes has been hindered by the lack of appropriate models and the limited data on physical and chemical properties and rate parameters. This paper illustrates the use of such a model based simulator to predict the steady state and dynamic operation of spray dryers. Droplet evaporation is characterised by a combination of mass and energy transfer. The extent of moisture removal is determined by a range of transport parameters and flow patterns within the dryer. A simplified model is presented here which features mass and energy balances and variable physical properties. Also introduced is the modelling approach adopted in trying to reduce the complex nature of spray drying when building models into SPEEDUP.

INTRODUCTION

Dehydration of foods by spray drying is becoming increasingly popular in large scale drying operations where short residence times (3 to 30 seconds) and low product temperatures are advantageous, as in the case of thermally labile liquid food products. It is used in the production of several food products, notably powdered milk and instant coffee preparations. It features rapid evaporation rates due to very large heat/mass transfer area and most of the water evaporates at the adiabatic saturation temperature.

Spray drying is quite a complex process to be simulated, due to the various phenomena involving transfer processes (Figs. 1 and 2). The complex nature of heat, mass and momentum transfer requires quite sophisticated mathematical descriptions. For spray drying of foods the main points of interest are knowing the (Kerkhof, 1977);

       1) The drying history of single particles
       2) The movement of particles in the dryer
       3) The effects of particle size distribution
       4) The loss of volatile flavour compounds
       5) Thermal degradation of heat labile compounds.

From a process control point of view, the control of the solid product moisture content is key to the success of the process. However, on-line measurement of solid powder moisture content is difficult due to the lack of robust sensors appropriate for automatic process control. Alternatively, most control schemes use the outlet air temperature as a direct on-line measure of the product quality, since it is a direct function of the water evaporation rate. The outlet air and the dried solid product are not in equilibrium and as such the air humidity cannot be directly related to that of the product.

This paper focuses on the control of product moisture, using a model based scheme which accounts for changes in the relationship between product moisture content and air outlet temperature. The model has been incorporated into SPEEDUP™, an equation oriented process simulator. The paper describes the dynamic model for spray drying which has been incorporated into SPEEDUP and looks at the future developments.

Department of Food Science and Technology, University of Reading
PO Box 226, Reading, BERKS, RG6 2AP

SPEEDUP™

The SPEEDUP (Simulating Program for Evaluating and Evolutionary Design of Unsteady state Processes) system (Perkins and Sargent, 1981; Sargent et al, 1982) is the product of work at Imperial College, London. SPEEDUP is a multi-function simulator. That it can perform comfortably in many operational roles is shown in Fig 3. SPEEDUP is designed to model systems which can be represented by a set of equations. To calculate a flowsheet, the equations describing individual process units are assembled, and iteratively solved using standard numerical techniques.

Mathematical modelling of processes involve expressing the behaviour of physical, biological and other complex phenomena quantitatively in mathematical terms. It is not always easy however, to solve these when expressed as a set of equations. SPEEDUP provides and efficient robust system whereby solutions could be obtained without the need to be concerned about the method of solving. This makes it a very suitable modelling tool.

Most of the early work was conducted on steady state process simulators. However, the dynamic behaviour is also more important, especially to study the process stability and dynamics in the face of changes in the operating point, start-up and shut-down (Zaror and Perez-Correa, 1991). Moreover, the synthesis of process control schemes is based on a knowledge of the process dynamics.

In this paper, the spray drying process is analysed from two ways i) Macroscopic modelling and (ii) Microscopic modelling. Preliminary results are presented here. This two way approach makes it possible to reduce the complexity to a minimum. Quite detailed aspects of the drying process will be analysed by the microscopic approach whereas the overall effects are considered in the macroscopic approach (Fig. 4). Once both types of modelling has been brought into a successful completion, it is intended to have a complete integrated model finally by unifying the two results.

The developed models have been tested using a pilot scale Kestner Spray Dryer (evaporative capacity 35 kg water/h), featuring a centrifugal atomiser (12000 rpm), using skimmed milk as a raw material.

DYNAMIC MODELLING OF SPRAY DRYING - *Macroscopic Approach*

Mathematical modelling of spray dryers has been the subject of research for many decades. Typically, spray drying models have been formulated to predict the effect of atomisation conditions on spray size distribution and to describe droplet trajectories to infer the extent of drying for a given dryer geometry or residence time (Dlouhy and Gauvin, 1960; Gluckert, 1962; Goffredl and Crosby, 1983; Katta and Gauvin, 1975 and Zbicinski, Grabowski, Strumillo, Kiraly and Krzanowski, 1988). It has long been recognised that a complete description of the process is too involved given the complexity of flow patterns and interactions between the spray and the drying medium, coupling between mass and energy transfer and nonuniform (and time varying) particle shape and size distribution (Masters, 1985). Therefore, many simplifying assumptions may be required to obtain models which are mathematically tractable, and some (or all) of the following assumptions are often made:

a) the relative velocity of particles with respect to the air is neglected;

b) in the case of cocurrent dryers equipped with centrifugal atomisers, recirculation is so great that idealised mixed-flow can be assumed; on the other hand, tower cocurrent dryers with nozzle atomisers may be approximated by plug flow;

c) particles are assumed to be spherical, monosized, and with constant diameter;

d) the particle temperature (in the dryer and outlet) is assumed to be uniform and equal to the adiabatic saturation (wet bulb) temperature, and vapour pressure lowering effects are neglected; the particle physical properties are assumed constant;

e) heat losses to the surroundings are neglected.

Dynamic model.

The spray dryer studied here is a cocurrent centrifugal atomiser spray dryer. Preliminary residence time and temperature distribution measurements showed that recirculation currents in the dryer are very large which justifies the assumption of a perfectly mixed system. Experiments conducted also show that the dried product temperature is very near the wet bulb temperature of the outlet air. Therefore, as a first approximation, the model developed below is based on the assumptions listed above, though some of these may be relaxed at a later stage of model development. The governing equations are based on overall unsteady mass and energy balances for the gas phase. The extent of moisture removal from the spray particles depends on the mechanisms governing the rate of evaporation and the residence time during which evaporation takes place. This is discussed in the section of microscopic modelling. Setting the datum temperature equal to the adiabatic saturation (wet bulb) temperature (T_{sat}), the following energy and mass balances are obtained.

$$\frac{d[M_A c_{AO}(T_o - T_{sat})]}{dt} = G[c_{Ai}(T_i - T_{sat}) - c_{AO}(T_o - T_{sat})$$

$$+ \lambda_{sat}(H_i - H_o)] + F_s c_{si}(T_F - T_{sat}) \tag{1}$$

$$\frac{d[M_A H_o]}{dt} = G(H_i - H_o) + F_s(X_i - X_o) \tag{2}$$

These equations are complemented by the equilibrium conditions:
A linear water sorption isotherm is used here.

$$X_E = m H_{OS} \tag{3}$$

The particle size is mainly a function of atomiser design, speed of rotation, and feed flowrate. The Volume-surface (Sauter) mean diameter of a spray droplet in centrifugal atomizers is often expressed as (Masters, 1985)

$$d = b(F_F)^{0.24} / (N)^{0.83}$$

$$\text{with } F_F = (1 + X_i) F_s \tag{4}$$

where d is the droplet diameter (m), N is the atomizer rotation speed (rev/min) and b is a constant particular to the atomizer design. The flow rates are expressed in kg s^{-1}. This is one of the most commonly used mean diameters in spray drying operations. The calculation assumes that spray droplets or particles to be spherical.

Finally, the adiabatic saturation equilibrium between the air temperature and absolute humidity is given by :
Adiabatic saturation equilibrium

$$H_o = H_{sat} - (T_o - T_{sat}) C_{Asat} / \lambda_{sat} \tag{5}$$

This dynamic model can be easily extended to steady state conditions by setting the accumulation terms of equations (1) and (2) equal to zero.

The experimental and simulated dynamic response to a 25% step increase in the feed flowrate is shown in Fig 5. It can be seen that there is a good agreement between the experiments and predictions.

Integration of the dynamic model in SPEEDUP

The dynamic model described in equations 1-5 constitute the basic model in SPEEDUP. The solution of this mixed ordinary differential-algebraic equation (DAE) system is handled by its solution scheme. A typical REPORT presentation from a dynamic run is given in Fig. 6. For dynamic runs, times or time slices may be specified.

Dynamic modelling of Spray drying: *Microscopic Modelling*

Modelling evaporation:

Microscopic modelling looks into the details of the process. However, the more information you need, the deeper that you have to look into the problem and also the more complex the process of analysis.

The evaporative process during spray drying can be explained as follows. As soon as the spray comes into contact with the hot medium, heat is transferred by convection from the hotter environment to the particle's surface producing evaporation; the vapourised water is transported into the air by convection through the boundary layer that surrounds each particle. Initially, the boundary film is saturated with vapour and the rate of evaporation will be limited by external heat transfer and will be proportional to the temperature difference between the surrounding air and the film's temperature. This is the so called constant rate stage, and will continue as long as there is sufficient water in the particle to quickly replenish that lost by evaporation. During this stage, the particle is at the adiabatic saturation temperature. Once the moisture content attains a characteristic critical value, the water content is too low to maintain the particle's surface saturated, and a dry shell forms at the surface. The evaporation rate is now limited by the diffusion of moisture through this shell, whose thickness increases with time, causing a decrease in the evaporation rate. It is called, the falling rate period, and will continue until moisture reaches a final equilibrium value. These evaporation mechanisms have been thoroughly studied and there are well established models to describe both stages (Dlouhy and Gauvin, 1960; Masters, 1985; Ranz and Marshall, 1952; Perry and Green, 1984, Clement et al, 1991).

The two drying stages of a particle can be calculated from particle size distributions and combined with flow trajectories, it is possible to determine the residence time distribution patterns. The type of spray dryer and the type of atomiser are influential in setting up the particle size distributions and flow patterns. From the point of view of quality, to prevent aroma loses and other volatiles. These areas of looking closely at what is going on during spray drying constitute microscopic modelling of the process. This work is also being undertaken with the intention of later integration to a fully developed model with flexibility to add different sets of conditions.

Spray evaporation

For spherical particles, the following relationships have been commonly applied:

Constant rate stage: $X > X_c$

$$\frac{dX}{dt} = \left(\frac{-12k_A}{d^2\rho_s\lambda_{sat}}\right)(T_o - T_{sat}) \tag{6}$$

Falling rate stage: $X \leq X_c$

$$\frac{dX}{dt} = \left(\frac{-4\pi^2}{d^2}\right)D_e(X - X_E) \tag{7}$$

The diffusion coefficient has to be determined empirically. The effective diffusivity depends on the physical structure of the solid, atomisation conditions and drying rate, and may vary during drying. For this study diffusion coefficient data was taken from the literature. The D_e was expressed as (from Perry and Green, 1984):

$$D_e = 1.38 \times 10^{-11} T(K) - 1.55 \times 10^{-9} \ (m^2 s^{-1}) \tag{8}$$

These two equations can be solved for various diameter spherical particles for drying time calculations. The characteristics of particle size distributions possible can be obtained by solving equations similar to 4. A typical drying curve given by a SPEEDUP simulation for a sprayed particle experiencing both drying stages is given in Fig 7. The implicit discontinuity that is present during solving these two equations will be handled by SPEEDUP internally.

Conclusions

SPEEDUP can be used to model the dynamics of spray driers, using lumped parameter models. The equation-based simulator can easily handle a set of ordinary differential algebraic system. This model can be used as part of an advanced control scheme to maintain operational stability in the face of changing process parameters. This forms part of a future publication by the authors.

NOMENCLATURE

b	atomiser parameter	G	mass flow rate of bone dry air
c_{Ao}	humid heat of outlet air	H	air absolute humidity
c_{Asat}	humid heat of air at saturation conditions	k	thermal conductivity
c_{So}	composite specific heat of product	m	solid moisture equilibrium constant
c_A	specific heat capacity of dry air	M	hold-up in the dryer chamber
c_s	specific heat capacity of bone dry solid	N	atomiser rotation speed
c_v	specific heat capacity of water vapour	P_w	vapour pressure
c_w	specific heat capacity of liquid water	t	time
d	particle diameter	T	temperature
D_e	effective diffusivity	X	moisture content (kg water/kg solids)
F_s	solids flowrate (d.b.)	λ_{sat}	latent heat of vaporisation
F_F	liquid flowrate (d.b.)	ρ_s	density

Subscripts

A	air	C	critical
E	equilibrium	F	liquid feed
i	inlet	O	outlet
sat	saturation	S	solid

REFERENCES

Clement, KH; Hallstrom, A; Dich, HC; Le, CM; Mortensen, J. and Thomsen, HA (1991), On the dynamic behaviour of spray dryers, *Trans. IChemE*, **69**, Part A, 245-252.

Dlouhy J. and Gauvin W.H.(1960), Heat and Mass Transfer in Spray Drying, *AIChE Journal*, , 29-34.

Gluckert F.A.(1962), A Theoretical Correlation of Spray Dryer Performance, *AIChE Journal*, , 460-466.

Goffredl R.A. and Crosby E.J.(1983), Limiting Analytical Relationships for Prediction of Spray Dryer Performance, *Ind. Engn. Chem. Process Des. Dev.*, **22**, 665-672.

Katta S. and Gauvin W.H.(1975), Some Fundamental Aspects of Spray Drying, *AIChE Journal*, **21**, 1, 143-152

Kerkhof, JAM (1977), Simplified methods for the description of the spray drying of liquid foods, Procs of the EFChE mini symposium on *Mathematical Modelling in Food Processing*, Sweden, 377.

Marshall W.R.(1955), *Trans. Amer. Soc. Mech. Eng.*,77, 11, 1377.

Masters K. (1985), *Spray Drying Handbook*, 4th Ed., G. Godwin Ltd., London

Perkins, JD and Sargent RWH (1982), SPEEDUP: A computer program for steady-state and dynamic simulation of chemical processes, in *Selected Topics in Computer-Aided Process Design and Analysis*, Mah, RSH and Reklaitis, GV (eds), AIChE Symp. Ser., 78, 1.

Perry R H. and Green D.(1984), *Perry's Chemical Engineers Handbook*, 6th Ed., McGraw Hill International .

Ranz W.E. and Marshall W.R.(1952), *Chem. Eng. Prog.*, **48**, 3, 141-146.

Sargent, RWH; Perkins, JD and Thomas, S (1982), SPEEDUP: Simulation program for the economic evaluation and design of unified processes, in *Computer-aided Process Plant Design*, Leesley, ME (ed), Gulph, Houston, 1982.

Zbicinski I., Grabowski S., Strumillo C., Kiraly L., Krzanowski W.(1988), Mathematical Modelling of Spray Drying, *Comput. Chem. Engng*, **12**, 2/3, 209-214

Zaror, CA and Perez-Correa, JR (1991), Model based control of centrifugal atomizer spray drying, *Food Control*, **2**, 3, 170-175.

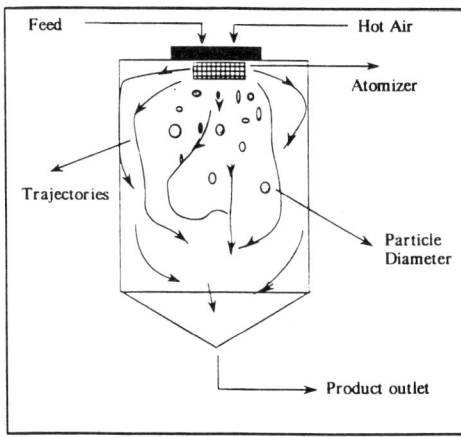

Figure 1: Spray Drying
- *Complex interactions*

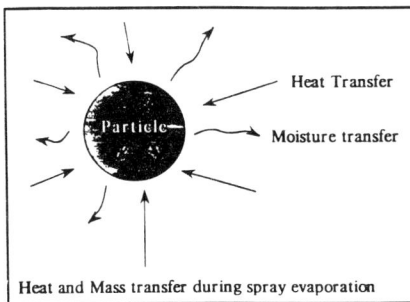

Figure 2: Drying of a droplet
Simultaneous heat and mass transfer

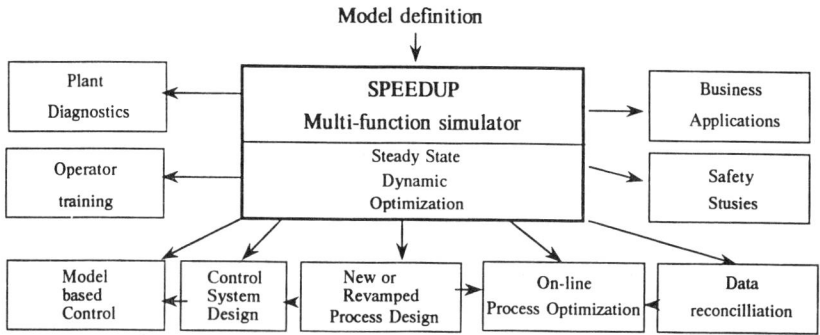

Figure 3: SPEEDUP capabilities

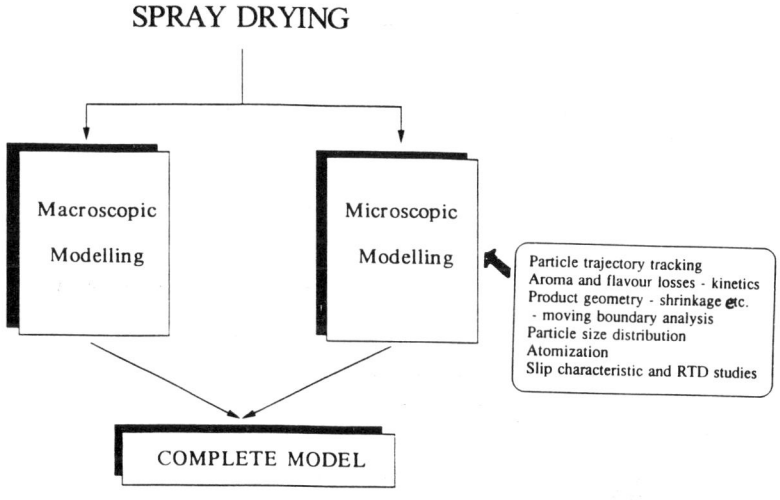

Figure 4: Modelling strategy of Spray Drying

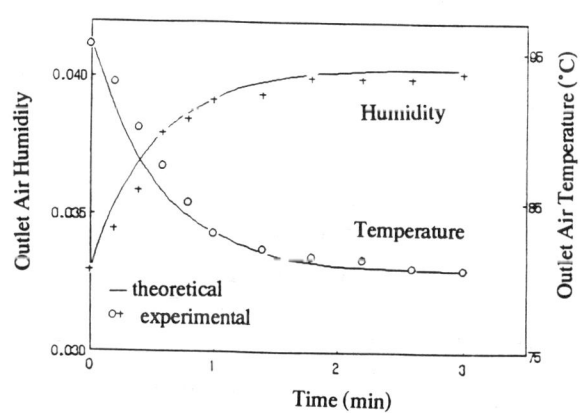

Figure 5: Response to step change of 25% in feed flow-rate

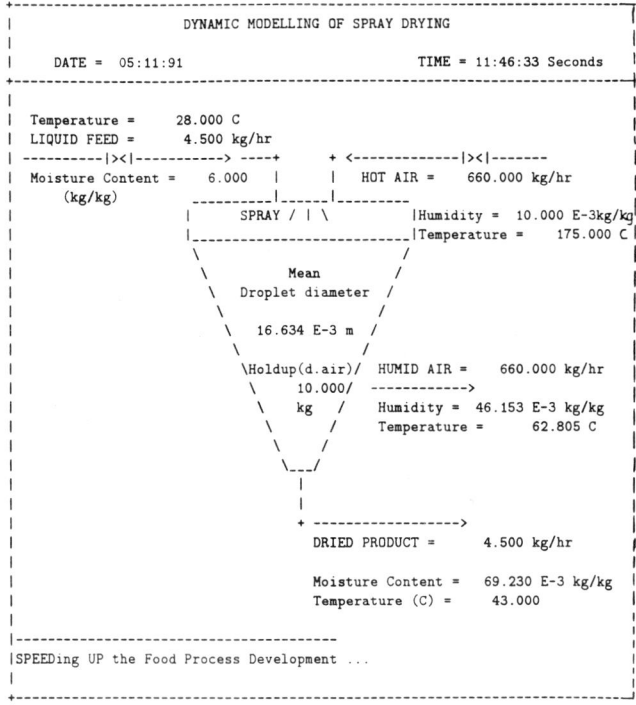

Figure 6: SPEEDUP REPORT from a dynamic simulation run

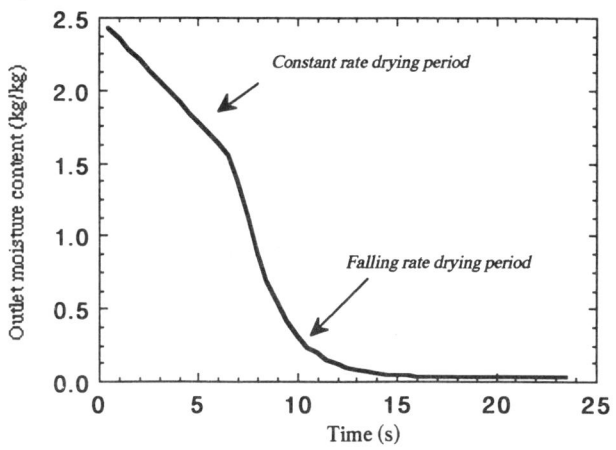

Figure 7: Simulated drying curve of a droplet

OPTIMIZING THERMAL PROCESSES OF CONDUCTION HEATED FOODS : GENERALIZED EQUATIONS FOR OPTIMAL PROCESSING TEMPERATURES

HENDRICKX, M. [*], SILVA, C. [+], OLIVEIRA, F. [+] AND TOBBACK, P. [*]

Optimal sterilization temperatures, for maximum surface quality retention, were calculated as a function of : (i) product properties (thermal diffusivity and z-value) (ii) processing conditions (geometry and dimensions of the food, surface heat transfer coefficient, initial product temperature and retort come up time) and (iii) processing criteria (target-F_0-value). From this theoretical study generalized empirical relations relating optimal temperatures and all relevant variables were formulated and presented. Applications in classical canning are illustrated in detail.

INTRODUCTION

Numerical modelling of heat transfer and thermal inactivation kinetics was first used, as a tool to optimize overall quality and nutrient retention of conduction heated foods, by Teixeira et. al.[1]. Temperature is the lethal agent and its rate of change can be controlled through the design variables : heating medium time-temperature profile, material properties, food geometry and dimensions [2]. When an objective function is specified it is possible to obtain a unique optimal time-temperature profile. The objective function can be based on economical aspects (e.g. energy requirements [3], processing time [4]), or on quality and nutrient retention.

Most of the research work in this area is devoted to processing conditions minimizing the thermal degradation of nutrients or other quality attributes. The optimization of quality becomes possible because microorganisms are less heat resistant than quality factors [6]. Aseptic packaging plants and rotary sterilization use the principle of high-temperature / short-time processing (HTST). However, slow heat transfer in conduction heated foods as well as the thermal resistance of some enzymes limit the applicability of this principle [7].

Optimal processing temperatures have been calculated to maximize surface [4,8,9,10,11,12,13] or volume average quality retention [1,2,4,8,9,10,14,15,16,17,18, 19,20]. Surface quality is of interest when appearance and odour are to be considered, while volume average quality is of interest for taste, consistency or nutrient retention [8]. Most of these studies consider an infinite surface heat transfer coefficient. Although variable sterilization temperatures as compared to optimal constant retort temperature profiles do not

* Katholieke Universiteit Leuven, Laboratory of Food Technology, Kardinaal Mercierlaan 92, 3001 Heverlee, Belgium.
+ Escolo Superior de Biotecnologia, Rua Dr. Antonio Bernardino de Almeida, 4200 Porto, Portugal.
Author M. Hendrickx is Senior Research Assistant with the Belgian 'National Fund for Scientific Research', NFSR.

improve significantly optimum volume average quality, [2,4,15,17,18] surface quality factor retention can be substantially increased [4].

MATERIALS AND METHODS

Kinetics and heat transfer model

First order inactivation kinetics (both for microorganisms and quality attributes) was assumed, expressed as a decimal reduction time D_{ref} and a z-value.

The time-temperature distribution within a three-dimensional food product was described by the 2nd law of Fourier. The model assumptions were (i) heat transfer into the food was by pure conduction, (ii) the food product was homogeneous, and isotropic (iii) initial temperature of the food (T_o) was uniform. (iv) the heating medium time-temperature profile was a step function, with zero come-up-time and the cooling temperature was set equal to 20°C, (v) a constant and uniform surface overall heat transfer coefficient. This overall coefficient accounted for the packaging material (e.g. plastic) and heating medium thermal resistance.

The ANSYS finite element package (revision 4.4 on PC) [21] was used. Two-dimensional axisymmetric elements (2-D isoparametric thermal solid element STIF55) were used. The procedure for calculating the centre sterilization value and surface cook-value followed the standard steps of preprocessing, solution and postprocessing. In the postprocessing step the centre F_o-value and the surface C-value were calculated. A macro file was written to calculate the heating rate factor f_h.

Optimization approach

Sterilization temperature during the holding period was the design variable, surface cook-value (C_s) was the objective function.

$$C_s = \int_0^{t'} 10^{(Ts-100)/zq} \, dt$$

A specified target sterilizing value (F_t) in the coldest spot was the constraint.

RESULTS AND DISCUSSION

Based on calculations for one-dimensional geometries, generalized (semi)-empirical formulas relating optimal sterilization temperature with all relevant processing variables were developed. Both cases with and without surface resistance were considered. The resulting regression equations are illustrated in Table 1 and more details are given in [12,13]. In a next step, the equations were tested for three-dimensional shapes. In these simulations a CUT=0, and T_o = 10 °C were used, because these variable had a small influence on the optimum [12,13]. Typical results for cylindrical containers were presented in Table 2, 3 and 4. Different food properties, processing conditions and processing criteria were included.

Infinite surface heat transfer coefficient

24 case studies, finite cylinders with different sizes, F_t and z_q-values were executed (Table 2). The range of input-values are representative for practical situations. A mean food thermal diffusivity, of 1.6×10^{-7} m²/s, was used. The Biot number was set equal to infinite. Calculated optimal processing temperatures were compared with values predicted by the generalized (semi)-empirical formulas (Table 3). The generalized equation (Eq. 1 in Table 1) predicted optimal sterilization temperatures with an error smaller than ±0.7°C. Predicted values are correct within the accuracy of simulation results.

TABLE 1 : GENERALIZED (SEMI)-EMPIRICAL FORMULAS TO CALCULATE OPTIMAL STERILIZATION TEMPERATURES AS A FUNCTION OF RELEVANT VARIABLES [12,13].

Infinite surface heat transfer coefficient

$$T_{op} = 86.68 + 9.73*\log(F_t/f_h) + 10.46*\ln(z_q) + 0.025*T_o \qquad 1$$

Finite heat transfer coefficient

$$T_{op} = a + b*\log(F_t/f_h) + c*\ln(z_q) + d/Bi + e*z_q/Bi$$

Geometry	a	b	c	d	e	Equation No.
Inf. slab	91.37	9.71	9.32	-6.58	1.15	2
Inf. cyl	90.96	9.83	9.34	-4.73	1.20	3
Sphere	90.79	9.72	9.30	-3.72	1.24	4

All geometries, finite surface heat transfer coefficient

$$T_{op} = 124.18 + 9.70*\log(F_t*RF) + 9.57*\ln(z_q) - 9.22/Bi$$
$$+ 1.15*z_q/Bi - 8.61*2^{(\bar{V}/(A.L))} \qquad 5$$

TABLE 2 : OPTIMAL PROCESSING TEMPERATURES (°C) FOR CASES STUDIES WITH *NO SURFACE RESISTANCE TO HEAT TRANSFER.*

Case No.	r ($m*10^3$)	H ($m*10^3$)	z_q (°C)	F_t (min)	f_h (min)	T_{op}^{Eq1} (°C)	T_{op} (°C)
1	36.5	15.5	25	3	16.40	113.4	113.5
2	36.5	15.5	25	9	16.40	118.0	118.0
3	36.5	15.5	25	15	16.40	120.2	120.0
4	36.5	15.5	33	3	16.40	116.3	115.5
5	36.5	15.5	33	9	16.40	120.9	120.5
6	36.5	15.5	33	15	16.40	123.1	123.0
7	36.5	29.0	25	3	32.95	110.5	110.5
8	36.5	29.0	25	9	32.95	115.1	115.0
9	36.5	29.0	25	15	32.95	117.3	117.0
10	36.5	29.0	33	3	32.95	113.4	113.0
11	36.5	29.0	33	9	32.95	118.0	118.0
12	36.5	29.0	33	15	32.95	120.2	120.0
13	36.5	54.0	25	3	46.22	109.0	108.5
14	36.5	54.0	25	9	46.22	113.7	113.5
15	36.5	54.0	25	15	46.22	115.8	116.0
16	36.5	54.0	33	3	46.22	111.9	111.5
17	36.5	54.0	33	9	46.22	116.6	116.0
18	36.5	54.0	33	15	46.22	118.7	118.5
19	49.5	59.5	25	3	78.41	106.8	106.5
20	49.5	59.5	25	9	78.41	111.4	111.5
21	49.5	59.5	25	15	78.41	113.6	113.5
22	49.5	59.5	33	3	78.41	109.7	109.0
23	49.5	59.5	33	9	78.41	114.3	114.0
24	49.5	59.5	33	15	78.41	116.5	116.0
25	36.5	27.5	25	6	31.33	113.6	113.5

Finite surface heat transfer coefficient

9 cases with a finite surface heat transfer coefficient as described in Table 3 were studied. Processing temperatures optimizing surface C-values were calculated at two positions B (top of cylinder along the axial symmetry axis) and D (side wall). Optimal temperatures are dependent on surface position. Case No.1 size showed differences of more than 10°C for positions B and D while for Case No.5 both optima are equal. Also Case No.9 has optimal temperatures identical in the two locations. Comparing the half-height to radius ratio for the three sizes, it could be concluded that cylinders for which this ratio approaches one have more uniform optimum surface quality distribution.

Calculation results were compared to the values predicted by the generalized (semi)-empirical formulas (Table 5). The formulas in terms f_h estimated optimum temperatures in positions B and D with an error smaller than ± 0.5°C. This error is within the accuracy of calculations. Although a generalized formula (in terms of the parameter f_h) independent of geometry is not available, the equations for one-dimensional shapes proved to estimate reasonably well the optimal temperatures for finite cylinders. The generalized formula, in terms of RF estimated the optimum with absolute errors between 0.1 to 3°C. Although this equation does not predict accurately the optimum, it can be a useful tool (when f_h is unknown) to estimate the first guess in an optimization study.

CONCLUSIONS

Optimal processing temperatures, for conduction heated foods packaged in cylindrical containers with and without surface resistance to heat transfer, were calculated using the software package ANSYS. Optimal temperatures, maximizing surface quality, were compared with values predicted by generalized (semi)-empirical formulas. The generalized formulas can be successfully used to predict optimal processing conditions. For cases with finite surface heat transfer coefficient, the optimum depends on the position at the surface.

TABLE 3 : SIMULATIONS INPUT DATA FOR CASE STUDIES WITH *FINITE SURFACE RESISTANCE TO HEAT TRANSFER*

Case No.	r $(m*10^3)$	H (m^2/s)	α (m^2/s)	z_q (°C)	F_t (min)	h (W/m2/K)	f_h (min)	H/r
1	36.5	15.5	1.65×10^{-7}	30	3	100	27.55	0.43
2	36.5	15.5	1.65×10^{-7}	30	9	100	27.55	0.43
3	36.5	15.5	1.65×10^{-7}	30	15	100	27.55	0.43
4	36.5	54.0	1.70×10^{-7}	45	3	200	53.42	1.48
5	36.5	54.0	1.70×10^{-7}	45	9	200	53.42	1.48
6	36.5	54.0	1.70×10^{-7}	45	15	200	53.42	1.48
7	49.5	59.5	0.98×10^{-7}	20	3	500	127.2	1.20
8	49.5	59.5	0.98×10^{-7}	20	9	500	127.2	1.20
9	49.5	59.5	0.98×10^{-7}	20	15	500	127.2	1.20

ACKNOWLEDGMENTS

Authors C. Silva and F. Oliveira acknowledge JNICT - Junta Nacional de Investigação Científica e Tecnológica.

TABLE 4 : OPTIMAL PROCESSING TEMPERATURES (°C) FOR CASE STUDIES WITH FINITE SURFACE RESISTANCE TO HEAT TRANSFER.

Position B

Case	V/(A.r)	Bi^1	$T_{op}Eq2$	$T_{op}Eq3$	$T_{op}Eq5$	T_{op}
1	0.23	5.70	118.6	118.7	117.8	119.0
2	0.23	5.70	123.2	123.4	122.5	123.0
3	0.23	5.70	125.3	125.5	124.6	125.5
4	0.37	9.53	119.5	119.4	120.8	119.0
5	0.37	9.53	124.1	124.0	125.4	124.0
6	0.37	9.53	126.3	126.3	127.6	125.5
7	0.35	62.25	103.7	103.2	104.1	103.0
8	0.35	62.25	108.3	107.9	108.7	108.0
9	0.35	62.25	110.5	110.0	110.8	110.0

Position D

Case	V/(A.H)	Bi^2	$T_{op}Eq2$	$T_{op}Eq3$	$T_{op}Eq5$	T_{op}
1	0.54	2.42	125.2	126.2	128.6	125.5
2	0.54	2.42	129.8	130.8	133.3	130.0
3	0.54	2.42	131.9	132.9	135.4	132.5
4	0.25	14.09	117.9	117.7	116.9	119.0
5	0.25	14.09	122.5	122.4	121.6	124.0
6	0.25	14.09	124.7	124.6	123.7	125.5
7	0.29	74.82	103.7	103.2	102.9	103.0
8	0.29	74.82	108.3	107.8	107.5	108.0
9	0.29	74.82	110.4	110.0	109.7	110.0

[1] characteristic dimension = radius
[2] characteristic dimension = half-height

REFERENCES

1   Teixeira, A.A., Dixon, J.R., Zahradnik, J.W. and Zinsmeister, G.E. 1969, Food Technology, 23(6):137-142
2   Teixeira, A.A., Zinsmeister, G.E. and Zahradnik, J.W. 1975, Journal of Food Science, 40:656-659
3   Barreiro, J.A., Perez, C.R. and Guariguata, C. 1984, Journal of Food Engineering, 3:27-37
4   Banga, J.R., Perez-Martin, R.I., Gallardo, J.M. and Casares, J.J. 1991, Journal of Food Engineering, 14:25-51
5   Lund, D.B. 1982, Food Technology, 7:97-100
6   Lund, D.B. 1977, Food Technology, 2:71-78
7   Saguy, I. 1988, Journal of Food Science, 53:306-310
8   Ohlsson, T. 1980a, Journal of Food Science, 45:848-852
9   Ohlsson, T. 1980b, Journal of Food Science, 45:1517-1521
10   Ohlsson, T. 1980c, In : *Food Process Engineering*, Applied Science Publishers, U.K., 137-145

11   Hendrickx, M., Van Genechten, K. and Tobback, P. 1989, Optimizing quality attributes of conduction heated foods, a simulation approach. Presented in : ICEF 5, Cologne, Germany, May 25 - June 3.

12   Hendrickx, M., Silva, C., Oliveira, F. and Tobback, P. 1991, Submitted for publication in Journal of Food Engineering.

13   Silva, C., Hendrickx, M., Oliveira, F. and Tobback, P. 1991, Journal of Food Science, in press.

14   Thijssen, H.A.C., Kerkhof, P.J.A.M. and Liefkens, A.A.A. 1978, Journal of Food Science, 43:1096-1101

15   Saguy, I. and Karel, M. 1979, Journal of Food Science, 44:1485-1490

16   Thijssen, H.A.C. and Kochen, L.H.P. 1980, Journal of Food Science, 45:1267-1272.

17   Martens, T. 1980, Mathematical model of heat processing in flat containers. Ph.D. thesis, Katholieke Universiteit Leuven, Belgium.

18   Nadkarni, M.M. and Hatton, T.A. 1985, Journal of Food Science, 50:1312-1321

19   Tucker, G.S. and Holdsworth, S.D. 1990, IChemE conference paper, Bath, Elsevier Applied Science, London, 59-74

20   Tucker, G.S. and Holdsworth, S.D. 1991, Trans IChemE, 69(3):5-12

21   DeSalvo, G.J. and Gorman, R.W. 1989, ANSYS - Engineering Analysis System - User's manual, Swanson Analysis Systems, Inc., Houston, Pennsylvania.

NOMENCLATURE

Bi Biot number (= $h * L / \lambda$) (dimensionless)

c_s cook-value at the surface (min)

D_{ref} decimal reduction time at the reference temperature, T_{ref} (min)

f_h slope factor of a heating curve (min)

F_0 sterilizing value at reference temperature 121.15°C and zm=10°C (min)

F_t target sterilizing value at reference temperature 121.15°C and Zm=10°C (min)

h heat transfer coefficient ($W/m^2/K$)

H cylinder half-height (m)

L characteristic length (m) (radius of an infinite cylinder or sphere and half-thickness of an infinite slab)

r cylinder radius (m)

RF Reduced Fourier number (= α / L^2) (s^{-1})

t' total processing time (min)

T temperature (°C)

T_0 initial temperature of the product (°C)

T_{op} optimal processing temperature (°C)

T_{ref} reference temperature (°C)

T_s temperature at the surface (°C)

z_m z-value for the microorganism (°C)

z_q z-value for the quality factor (°C)

α thermal diffusivity (m^2/s)

BRIDGING THE GAP - PROCESS PLANT SCHEDULING FOR BOTH DESIGN AND OPERATION.

C.M.Jakeman*

Many food processing plants are difficult to schedule as the scheduled tasks compete for resources, such as empty tanks or cleaning systems. A scheduling tool designed specifically for operating these plants has proved its value in another role as a fundamental part of the design and implementation of complex plant. In this way, the needs of production are built-in to the design process bridging the communication gap between design and production.

Introduction

Process plants have special operating constraints which are not present in parts manufacturing, such as the filling and draining of tanks and the use of automatic clean-in-place (CIP) equipment. Many plants have several stages of processing, producing a number of intermediate materials and a much larger number (eg>100) of final products. This is a common situation in the dairy and beverage industries.

These production requirements lead to a flexible arrangement of intermediate storage tanks, fillers and CIP systems (see Figure 1). Because little of the equipment is dedicated, the product batches will be competing for equipment and other limited resources such as staff or chilled water.

The planner's task is to schedule the production to minimise the delays due to this competition, whilst meeting delivery deadlines and avoiding waste due to over-long storage etc.. The quantity of data and the need for 'what if?' operation means that the planner must rely on a computer-based scheduling tool to carry out his work effectively.

Integrating Design and Production

The computer-based scheduling tool used to manage the production of process plants must contain detailed information about all the practical constraints of operating the plant as well as procedures for making products and lists of products to be made. This information is, of course, also needed by the process plant supplier in order to specify, design and automate a new plant.

*APV Baker Ltd., Peterborough and Crawley

Until now, this information has only been available as written notes. But once the information is held in the computer-based form as needed by a computer-based scheduler (ref 1), it can be used as the basis for much of the design work. This is the principle of the five advanced engineering techniques described below.

The immediate benefit is that these stages of design are all using the same information, which minimises mistakes and makes changes easier. Customer and supplier both benefit from the higher quality and quicker time to delivery that these techniques can provide.

1. Proposal Design

At the proposal stage, the supplier must devise an arrangement of equipment which will meet the customer's expectations for capital cost, running costs, etc.. There are other expectations which are less easy to quantify, such as flexibility and resilience. Does the supplier propose 2 large tanks or 4 smaller ones? The computer-based scheduler can be used to quantify the flexibility of the plant by calculating the output achieved using different arrangements of equipment (see figure 2). Other difficult questions which can be answered in this way include the sizing of services such as steam or chilled water. For example, is it worth increasing the size of the boiler to avoid delays when processors compete for steam?

2. CAD and Automation

Once the specification has been accepted then the plant must be designed. This will specify all the vessels, pipes, valves, pumps, instruments and their connections (see Figure 3) and ultimately lay them out in 3 dimensions. The quantity of data and the need for 'what if?' operation means that the designer must rely on a computer-based design tool (CAD) to carry out his work effectively.

This connectivity information is vital to the next stage. When combined with the scheduling database on how to operate the plant, we now have all the information (once again in computer form) which the automation engineer needs to write the control programs which will automate the process plant.

In fact, research work has shown that it will be possible to generate control programs by computer using this data. See the paper Applications of Operating Procedure Synthesis in The Food Industry, C.A. Crooks and S. Macchietto (also published at this seminar) and also Ref. 2 for details of this research.

3. Testing

Control systems for automated process plant are always specific to a customer's requirements. They may be highly complex, supporting perhaps 2,000 - 4,000 input and output devices, and therefore require thorough testing.

Control software needs to be tested both for normal and abnormal operation. For example, the control system must take the correct action when a valve fails to operate. Testing is done by operating switches and knobs (or entering equivalent instructions into a computer) to simulate the response of the plant to the control operations. For each check, the simulated plant must be driven to the right situation before the failure mode can be tested. Furthermore, whenever the control software is changed, the tests must be repeated exactly to confirm that the change is satisfactory.

In the absence of support tools, testing is therefore repetitive, expensive and prone to error. Fortunately it is now possible to develop these tools. The scheduler can be used to drive the plant through every possible operation and this sequence can be repeated whenever re-testing is needed. The procedure synthesis technique above is also able to carry out all the functional checks needed, ensuring that all the valves have been driven to the right state before processing starts. The final element is a simple control system which will simulate the feedback from valves, level switches and other instruments.

4. Training

A food processing company will use training for several purposes; for new operating staff or to prepare for new processes, procedures or equipment. Exactly the same arrangement of equipment which was used to test the automation of the plant can now be used to provide training. In fact, if a supplier cannot provide this style of training, his test procedures may be lacking also!

5. Documentation

The equipment supplied by the main contractor must include specification documents setting out how the plant works. As with testing, this is a lengthy procedure and again prone to error. However, with our new techniques, we now have all the information on the operation of the plant in a computer database. Reports can be generated from the database listing all the conditions for normal and exceptional operations much more quickly than by hand.

Areas for Research

Our scheduling products, based on algorithms licensed from Imperial College, have been successfully proven in daily scheduling and also in proposal design. Research into generating control software has produced promising results. The areas of testing and documentation are ready to be researched.

Conclusion

We have shown how the operating information necessary to schedule a process plant has value for the supplier of process plants. Not only does it provide quantitative answers to difficult questions at the tendering stage, but the information can be extended during the design cycle to drive the later stages of automation design, documentation and testing. The benefits are fewer errors and quicker time to delivery.

References

1. COTT B.J. 1989   An integrated Computer-Aided Production
                     Management System for Batch Chemical
                     Processes. Imperial College of Science,
                     Technology and Medicine.

2. CROOKS A.C, SHAH N., PANTELIDES C.C., MACCHIETTO S.
                     A combined MILP and Logic-based Approach
                     To The Synthesis of Operating Procedures
                     for Batch Plants. Imperial College of
                     Science.

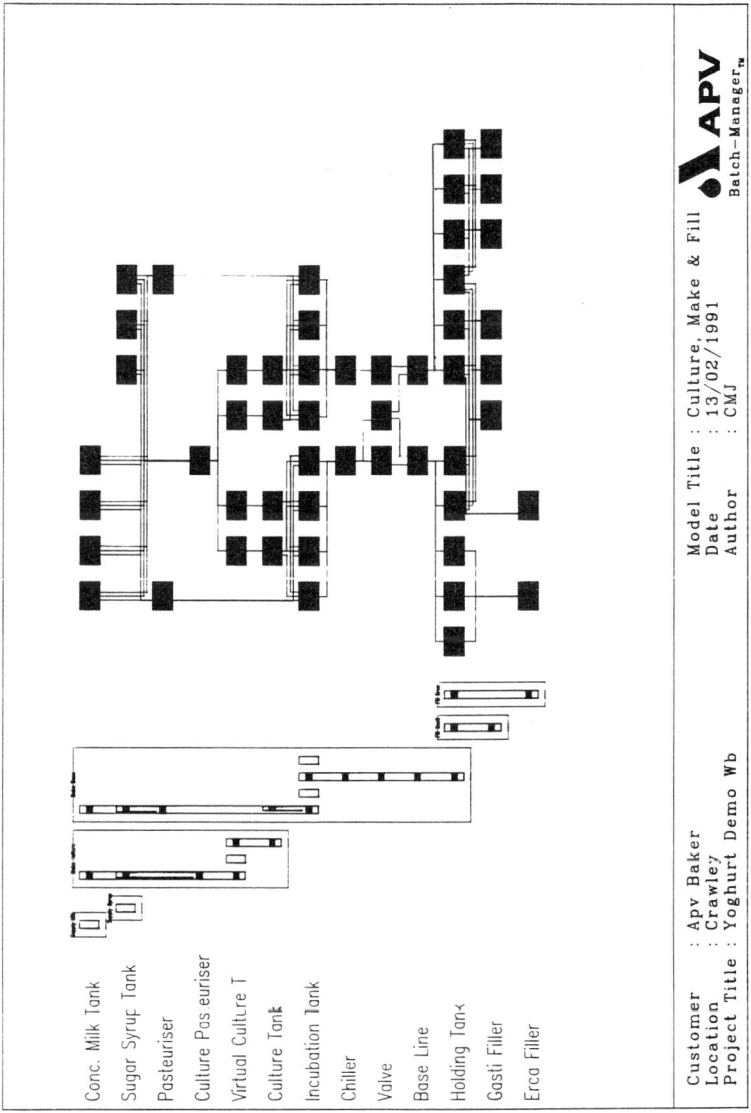

Conc. Milk Tank
Sugar Syrup Tank
Pasteuriser
Culture Pas euriser
Virtual Culture T
Culture Tank
Incubation Tank
Chiller
Valve
Base Line
Holding Tank
Gasti Filler
Erca Filler

Model Title : Culture, Make & Fill
Date   : 13/02/1991
Author   : CMJ

Customer   : Apv Baker
Location   : Crawley
Project Title : Yoghurt Demo Wb

APV
Batch-Manager™

Figure 1 – Procedures and Equipment for a Yogurt Plant

The right side of the diagram shows the major plant items. Note that some connections between items are missing; a scheduler must respect this constraint.

The left side shows procedures for filling silos, making culture and yogurt base and for filling both types of filler.

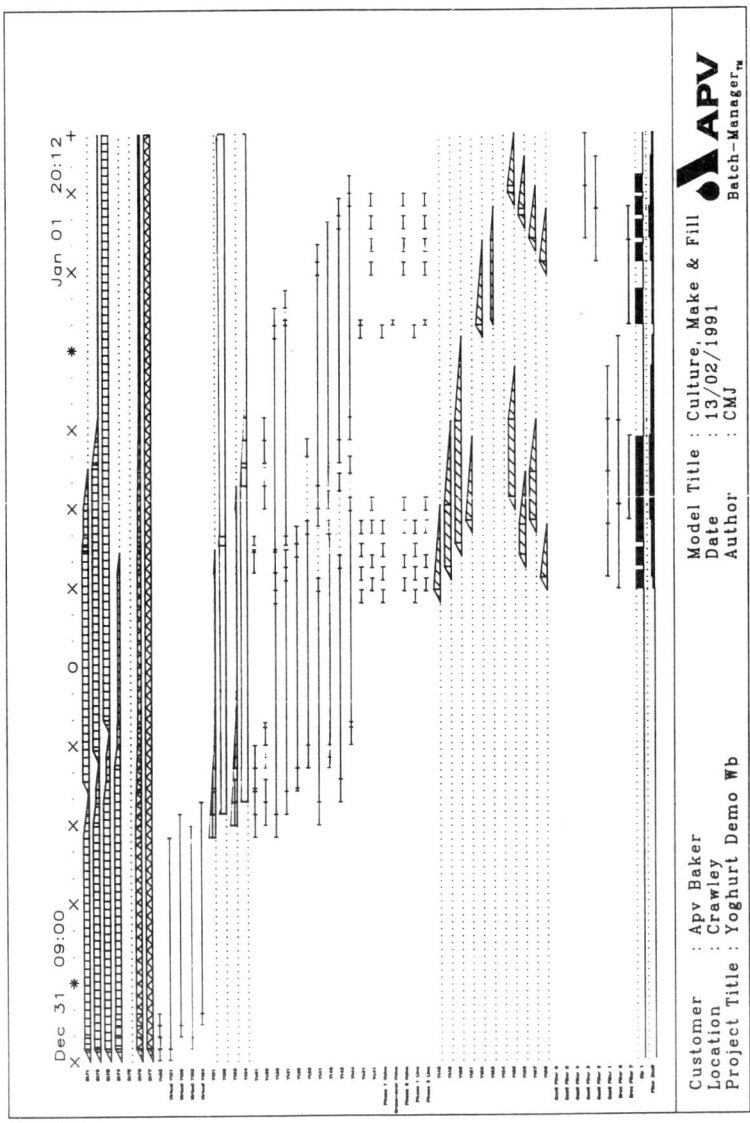

Figure 2 — A schedule for the plant in Figure 1

This schedule shows the levels in tanks, the operation of processing equipment and, at the bottom, the use of labour. In this example, the incubation of the yogurt base dominates the schedule.

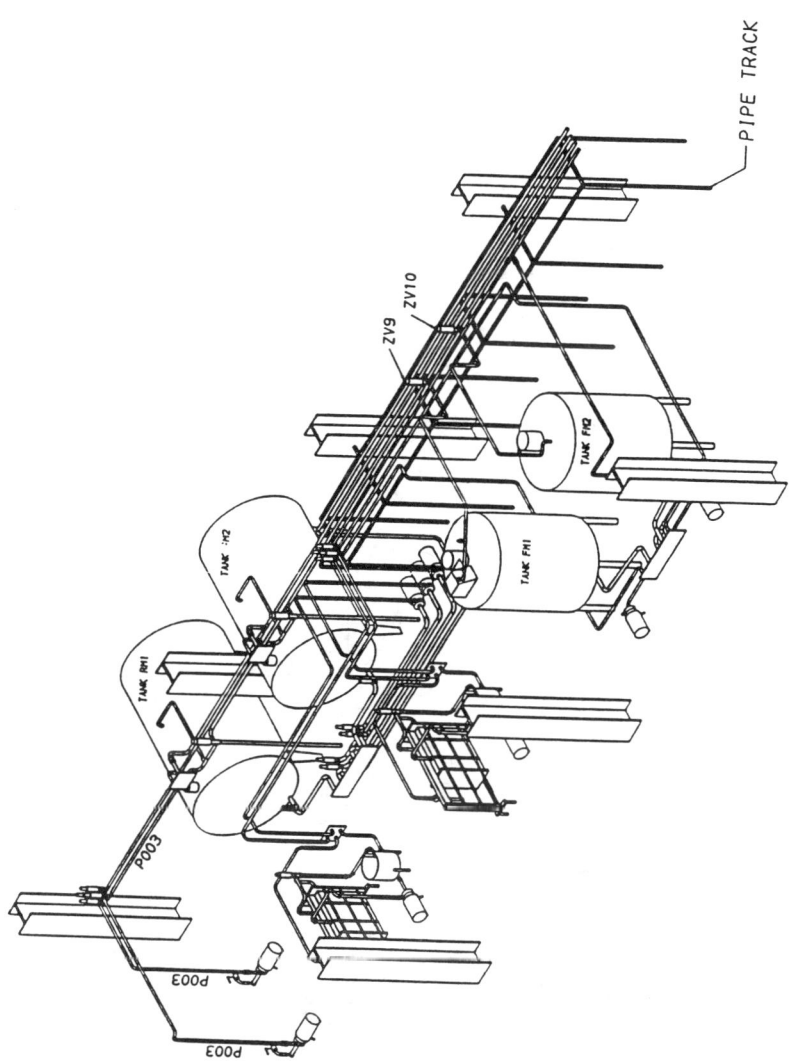

Figure 3 - Computer-Aided Design

Sample output from a computer-aided design system. A full-size plant will contain many thousands of components whose connections, part nos. etc. will be stored in the CAD database.

PIG CARCASE WEIGHING AND CLASSIFICATION -
PRACTICAL EXPERIENCES AND VISIONS FOR THE FUTURE

T.J.R. COOPER*

The Northern Ireland pigmeat processing industry was in
the forefront in 1970 when automatic weighing and data
recording equipment was installed at the classification
carcase stations of all ten plants. The equipment has
since been expanded and updated. For the future,
instrumentation for measuring and recording fat
thickness, muscle depth and meat quality, together with
the associated computer power is seen as having a
dominant role. The extension of automatic weighing and
classification on the killing line to an integrated
system of data capture throughout each plant is an
elusive but vital goal.

Introduction

Small changes in yield i.e. the percentage final product in relation
to raw material, due to processing, evaporation, drip or quality
rejects significantly influence overall profitability.[1] The
monitoring and control of product yield and quality are dependent on
responsive and accurate measurement of mass, volumetric flow and
temperature as well as chemical and physical parameters relevant to
the particular product. Not only is the recorded data an essential
part of an efficient production process, it is a means of
establishing confidence between the processor and producer, customer
and legislative bodies.

In pigmeat processing, as for other species there are many
additional demands. The ability to keep track of livestock from
birth to slaughter is a key factor in quality control. This
requires failsafe identification of animals to assess breeding
improvements, disease control programmes and drug residue monitoring
and traceability. Visual schemes for carcase classification i.e.
fat thickness and conformation, have been replaced in the pigmeat
sector, by instrumentation and computers.

*The Queen's University of Belfast

Early Experiences with Automatic Weighing and Data Capture Equipment

The author has, since 1968, been involved in specifying, developing and maintaining automatic weighing and data capture systems for the Northern Ireland pigmeat industry. This work has been carried out in conjunction with the Pigs Marketing Board, the Department of Agriculture for Northern Ireland and Ulster Curers' Association.

The three parties (PMB, DANI and UCA), having seen automatic weighing and data capture in operation in the "SCAN" group of meat plants in Sweden, proceeded to investigate and to purchase similar equipment for the N.I. pig slaughterlines. The Swedish "TELEMATIC" equipment was installed and commissioned by the manufacturers, Stathmos Lindell in the ten N.I. plants over twelve weeks in 1970. After a decade of satisfactory service the systems were overtaken by technology and so a second generation was introduced.

Second Generation of Equipment

The existing data capture equipment includes, one, two (Fig.1) or three terminals (depending on factory), printer, disc drive and overhead display printer.[2] The Danish "Scanvaegt" terminals have performed well in the N.I. factories. Not so, the double disc drives which had to convert data from the ASC II format to IBM in order to suit the computer used by the Pigs Marketing Board for producer payments. Weaknesses in the electronic equipment were overcome by designing the systems to meet all contingencies.

Measurement of Fat Thickness, Muscle Depth and Meat Quality

In 1990 each system was modified to predict and record the percentage lean meat in each carcase at the point of classification. This was to meet an EC Commission Regulation whereby carcases were to have percentage lean meat recorded and stamped with a letter E, U, R, O or P depending on the percentage.[3] Various nationalities had different formulae approved. In Ulster, this was based on carcase weight and the fat thickness taken 6.5 cm horizontally from the line at which the carcase was split and vertically at the last rib. The "Ulster" Fat probe had been used in all the N.I. pig slaughterlines on a production basis since 1973. A Mark II version had gone into operation with the second generation of equipment in 1981. (Fig.2)

Electronic probes for the measurement of fat thickness and muscle depth have been developed in Denmark, Canada and New Zealand.[4-7] In Europe though, they must conform to an authorised standard, i.e. "...... on a representative sample of the national or regional pigmeat production concerned ...... consisting of at least 120 carcases of which the lean meat has been ascertained .... if the coefficient of determination is greater than 0.64 .... subject to the residual standard error of estimate being less than 2.5 ..."

A further parameter to include at the classification station is that of predicting ultimate pH. While measurements of muscle colour or

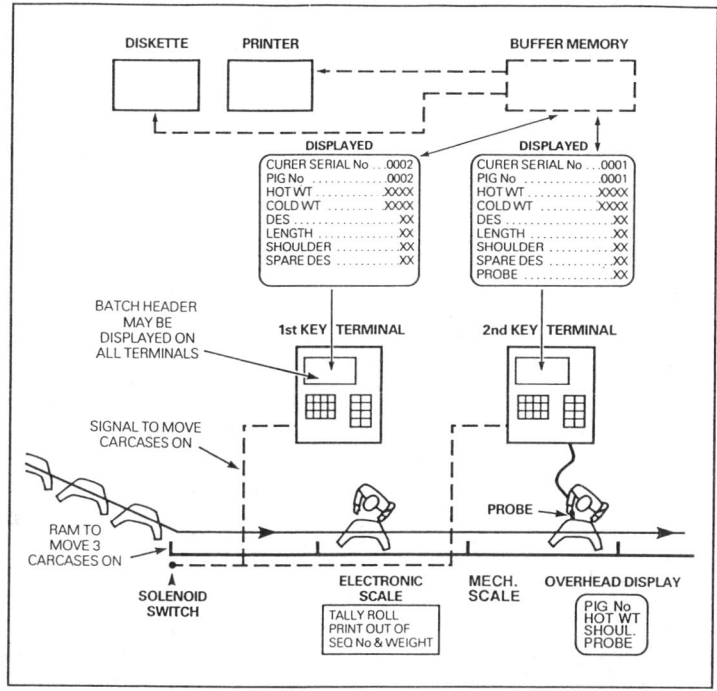

Fig. 1. Automatic Weighing and Recording on the Killing Line

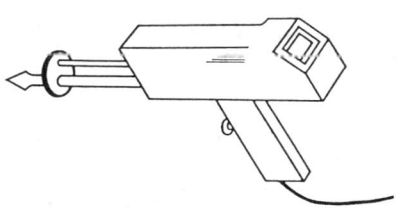

Fig. 2. Electronic Probe

reflectance may highlight extreme cases such values recorded 45 minutes post mortem are not a reliable indication of ultimate quality. High or low pH producing dark firm dry (DFD) or pale soft exudative (PSE) pork respectively are major quality problems which need to be identified as early as possible in the process.[8,9]

Future Developments

Automatic weighing, percentage lean meat prediction and recording of general classification data have reached an advanced stage of development. In the past, such systems have tended to centre around the weighing equipment. For the future though, instrumentation for measuring and recording fat thickness, muscle depth, lean meat content and muscle quality is seen as having the dominant role. The computer power to analyse these parameters has the potential for recording other classification data with the flexibility of reprogramming "in house" when required.

In Denmark, objective and operator independent lean/fat classification of the complete carcase and of the major cuts has been installed, using lean and fat measurements in eighteen positions per carcase - hind leg, middle and fore-end.[10] However, the capital cost of such a system is prohibitive to all but the largest plants. In the longer term, carcase scanning, e.g. using ultrasound for objective assessment of conformation, fat thickness and lean meat content is a possible alternative for further development.[11,12]

The extrapolation of ultimate pH post rigor only 45 minutes post mortem presents difficulties. There is much work to be done in this area to use data on colour, reflectance, pH and temperature at this early stage of the process.[13] The ability to keep track of the live animal from birth to slaughter, assess breeding improvements, control disease, police drug residues and monitor ante-mortem handling are crucial aspects and is within the scope of present technology.

The industry cannot afford not to continuously monitor such additional parameters as:-

(a) weight loss during carcase and offal chilling
(b) butchery yield
(c) brine uptake
(d) curing loss
(e) cooking loss
(f) weight loss during conditioning for slicing
(g) slicing yield

related to applied and product temperatures.[14]

Conclusions

1. The continuous monitoring of product yield and quality are crucial to the profitability of the food processing industry, and in establishing confidence between producers, processors and legislative bodies.
2. Although automatic weighing and data capture systems were successfully introduced into the meat processing industry in Sweden twenty five years ago, integrated systems have still not been universally adopted.
3. Whereas classification systems have tended in the past to centre around the weighing equipment, instrumentation for measuring and recording lean meat percentage and quality, together with the associated computer power is seen as having a dominant role in the future.
4. The main reason for delayed progress is attributed to a lack of confidence within the processing sector in specifying and sourcing reliable data capture and associated product conveying equipment to meet the rigorous and changing needs of the industry.

Acknowledgements

The author is indebted to Mr D Wright, until recently, Chief Livestock Officer, Department of Agriculture for Northern Ireland and Mr J.A. Gilliland, Computer Manager, Pigs Marketing Board (Northern Ireland) with whom the writer has worked closely on the first, then the second and so far, the proposed third generation of automatic weighing and classification data capture equipment for the Ulster Curer's Association.

References

1. ANON (1983). Meat Industry (3) 34

2. WRIGHT D, (1984). Proc. Meat and Livestock Commission Seminar, York 51-54

3. ANON (1985). Draft E.C. Regulation VI/4142/83-EN Rev 5. 3.

4. KEMPSTER A.J., CHADWICK J.P. & JONES D.W. (1985). British Society of Animal Production, 323-329

5. FORTIN A, JONES S.D.M. & HAWORTH C.R. (1984). Meat Science (10), 131-144

6. MATZKE P, PESCHKE W, AVERDUNK, G, BLENDL H, SAVERER G, GUNTER I, HUBER I (1986). Die Fleischwirtschaft 66 (3), 391-397

7. ALLEN P, (1985). Meat Research Department Report Dublin 30-32

8. BORSBOOM P.C.F., BOSCH J.J., KOEMAN R.P.T. (1988). Process Optical Measurements (1012) 206-211

9. ANDERSON J.R., BORGGAARD C & BARTON-GADE P, (1989). Proc. 35 Int. Congress 20-25 Aug. 208-219

10. DURINCK A (1990). Pigs-Misset, May/June 12-13

11. WOODS, J (1991). Meat Industry (5) 19

12. NEWMAN P.B. (1983). Food (12) 45-49

13. CHADWICK J (1990). Meat Industry (6) 33

14. CLAUSEN V (1984). Proc. Meat and Livestock Commission Seminar, York 35-50

CONTROLLED RIPENING AND DRYING CONCEPT FOR DRY SAUSAGE MANUFACTURING

A. LANDVOGT *

The influence of internal and external parameters on ripening and drying of dry sausage is discussed. Developing new, improved approaches in ripening and drying control requires detailed knowledge of the still unknown dynamic behaviour of the process. The new concept is based on data acquisition of the selected ripening parameters by on-line sensor detection in the dry sausage (in-situ). These data allow continuous recalculation of the ideal external ripening and drying climate.

Introduction

The technology of dry sausage manufacturing is mainly based on empirical principles, formed by trial and error through the centuries. The history can be traced back to the ancient Romans.

Salt, potassium nitrate and spices were mixed with comminuted meat and fat and stuffed into natural casings. The manufacturing took place only in the wintertime, because cold weather and dry climate conditions supported the following ripening and drying stage for weeks or months. The growth of moulds was suppressed by smoking. Therefore the dry sausage (salami) was seen as a wintersausage which could not be stored over the warm summer months.

A lot of craftsmanship and experience was necessary to select the best raw materials and to choose the right climate conditions at the right time to produce a stable product. The possibilities to adjust the climate were very limited. They could only choose between cold cellars or warm attics. The temperature and air change was adjusted by opening or closing windows and doors. Relative humidity was either not controlled at all or influenced by sprinkling some water in the drying room.

The four season manufacturing was first realized with the invention of cooling systems in combination with heating and humidification systems. The result was a ripening and drying chamber. Here a constant climate could be set, independent from the local weather conditions.

With the introduction of process control equipment, the user could preset his desired process parameters (temperature and humidity), which were adjusted within more or less

---

* VEMAG Anlagenbau GmbH, Weserstraße 32, W-2810 Verden/ Aller, Germany

narrow limits. If the finished product was of an acceptable quality, the empirical settings were recorded and automatically adjusted in further processes as time and product based plans.

At present dry sausage ripening is still controlled in this way. This control system is better than manual control, because continuous supervision could be eliminated. But it still lacks the possibility to include the ripening and drying sausage to complete the control cycle (WEISENFELS, 1990).

Meanwhile the needs of the industry have changed, but all the above mentioned problems of selecting the right climate are even more important than before. Large scale batch processes with ripening and drying chambers of several tons capacity are required. Here an incomplete process control system can lead to an unstable product with real hygienic problems, which, for these large batch sizes, bear a high financial risk for the producer. Although the present way of control is well established, its limitations are clearly seen.

Biotechnological point of view

In a more sophisticated way, dry sausage ripening can be seen as a complex long-term solid-state-fermentation. This sensitive biotechnological system is influenced by a lot of internal (ingredients, recipe) and external (climate) parameters. In terms of food process engineering the fermentation can be devided into a ripening stage and a drying stage, but the transitions are not distinct.

Meat and fat are comminuted, carrying a variety of unwanted microorganisms. To lower water activity and to inhibit the spontaneous microflora nitrite curing salt is added. Some starter cultures together with some sugars initiate and accelerate the ripening stage by establishing a well adapted, fast growing, competitive microflora. The *Lactobacillaceae* convert the sugar into latic acid, resulting in a pH drop. The acidification activity mainly depends on the strain, the amount and kind of sugar, the temperature and the water activity of the sausage, which has previously been discussed in detail (LANDVOGT and FISCHER, 1990; 1991) (Figure 1).
In the drying stage the temperature, relative humidity and air velocity play a determining part (MONAGLE et al,. 1974; PALUMBO et al., 1977; STIEBING and RÖDEL, 1987) (Figure 3).

It is obvious that fermentation and drying set different goals. The optimum balance of both is difficult to maintain. High relative humidities or low air velocities can result in mould growth at the surface. Strict drying conditions (low relative humidity or high air velocity) may cause case hardening due to denatured meat proteins.

Further imponderabilities arise from the lack of standardization. Inevitable changes in raw materials and naturally variable ingredients as well as the sometimes varying activity of starters can influence the whole process in an unpredictable way. A successfully established ripening pattern can not be simply transferred to another casing diameter. The settings in one plant would lead to different results in another plant on other equipment. All this goes to show that the interaction of internal and external parameters is to complex to be expressed as a general model. The change of one parameter effects many of the remaining ones.

New approach in control

Because of the previous discussion it is clearly seen that the scope for influencing the *internal* parameters is strictly limited (Figure 1). It ends with the stuffing of the casings and is therefore not available to continuous control strategies (except water, fat and protein standardization by NIR). It seems more promising to focus on the understanding of the dynamic changes of the product itself, while changing the *external* parameters (Figure 3), instead of sticking to the rigid course of the event and time based ripening plan.

According to the principles of GMP (Good Manufacturing Practice), ISO 9000 and HACCP (Hazard Analysis and Critical Control Point) it is necessary to control upstream from the beginning of ripening to get a complete documentation at every stage of the process. This is also in line with the requirements of product liability. The measurements need to be made at a stage where control action is possible to correct, rather than reject out of specification product. It is important for the success of introducing new control equipment in the industry that the control action is of commercial significance for the customer.

Most of all the applicable sensors deserve special consideration. Inexpert handling of sensors in the harsh reality of daily industry use often prevent the correct implementation of measurements. Therefore they should be shelf equipment, lightly modified for the special needs of the meat industry. The system must be robustly engineered and capable of absolute calibration (PEARSON, 1991).

The aim is to control the process by continuous acquisition of selected fundamental fermentation parameters, resulting in a feedback to the product by optimizing the ripening climate (Figure 2). Thereby the acidification, measured as pH in situ at the sausage, is controlled by the temperature, while the relative humidity and air velocity are used to control the course of drying, expressed as weight-loss and superficial water activity of the sausage.

Although much is known about single details influencing the process, there is a great lack of knowledge about the dynamic behaviour of the process. A physical properties library simply does not exist. Therefore extensive trials had to be conducted to clarify the influence of changing external parameters on the course of drying. Depending on these results, control principles were developed, calculating time and energy saving process parameters. These control strategies must be well suited to the biological kinetics of starter cultures and to the physical influence of climate.

First results

In order to get a first basic experience with the handling of the sensors, the new control system was implemented in a plant of a dry sausage manufacturer. Here it was used first of all only as a continuous data acquisition unit, but with off-line evaluation of the process.

Already this procedure (without controlling) gave a deep insight into the performance of the process, resulting in some instant proposals for process improvement; i. e. valuable informations could be given to optimize the heating of different casing sizes.

The system was also capable of detecting areas of low air circulation, which lead to delayed drying in some parts of the batch. Furthermore the influence of variable air velocities on the superficial water activity could be identified (Figure 4).

Conclusions

The developed control strategy will lead to a general optimization of ripening and drying and has the following benefits:
- Increase of microbiological safety (prevents mould growth)
- Minimization of energy costs
- Increase of yield by closer control of the limits
- Easier start up of new equipment by pure physical parameters
- Application of control strategies for industry as well as for butchers workshops.
- Optimization, analysis, comparison, transfer and scale-up of established ripening patterns is possible
- Application of control strategy can be transferred to other manufacturing processes (Cheese ripening, fish and meat drying, wood drying)
- Simulation of drying and ripening courses
- The principles can be used for the design of new equipment

References

LANDVOGT, A. and A. FISCHER (1990) Fleischwirtschaft 70 (10), 1134-1140

LANDVOGT, A. and A. FISCHER (1991) Fleischwirtschaft 71 (1), 32-35

MONAGLE, C. W., TOLEDO, R. T. and R. L. SAFFLE (1974) Journal of Food Science 39, 602-604

PALUMBO, S. A., KOMANOWSKY, M., METZGER, V. and J. L. SMITH (1977) Journal of Food Science 42, 1029-1033

PEARSON, C. A. (1991) Prozessmeßtechnik in der Lebensmittelindustrie, GMA-Bericht 19, VDI/VDE-Gesellschaft Meß- und Automatisierungstechnik (GMA), Düsseldorf

WEISENFELS, M. (1990) Fleischwirtschaft 70 (11), 1250-1265

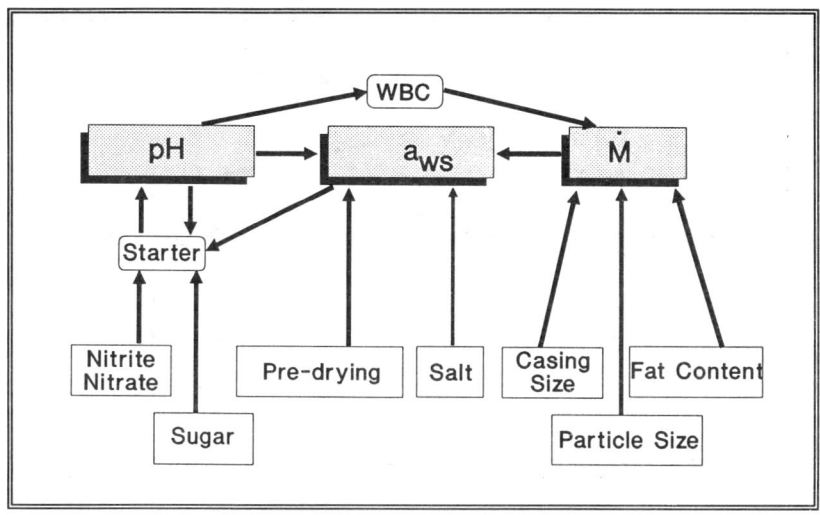

Figure 1: Influence of internal ripening parameters (recipe) on the controlled fermentation parameters pH, superficial water activity (a_{ws}) and mass flux (M). WBC (Water Binding Capacity).

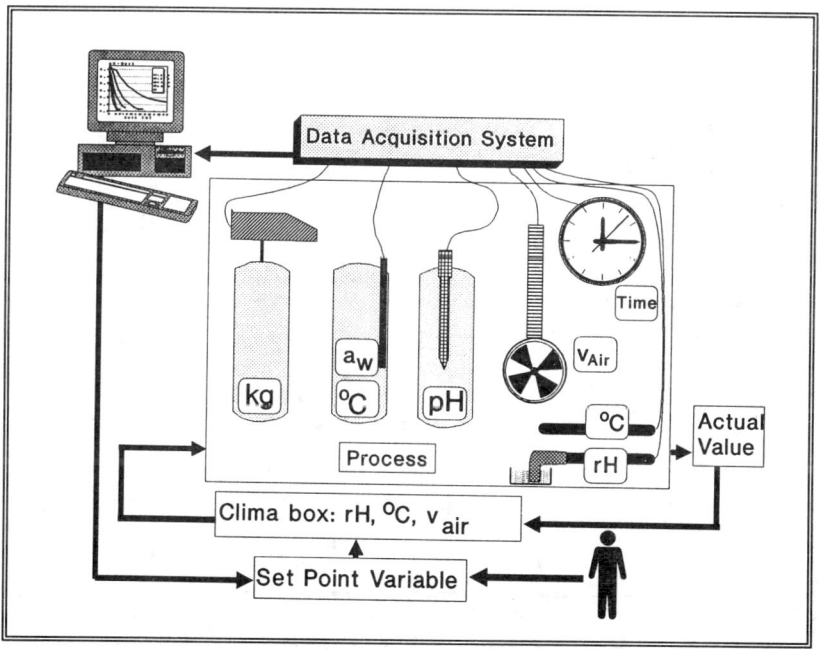

Figure 2: Control system dry sausage ripening

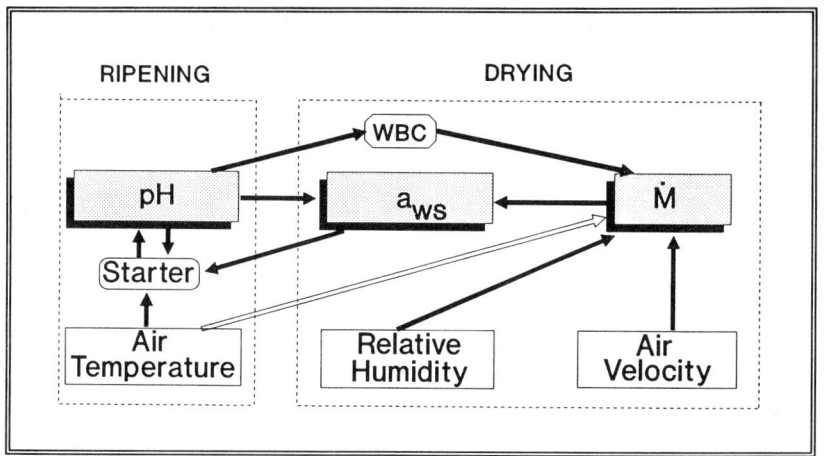

Figure 3: Influence of external ripening parameters on the controlled fermentation parameters pH, superficial water activity (a_{ws}) and mass flux ($\dot{M}$). WBC (Water Binding Capacity).

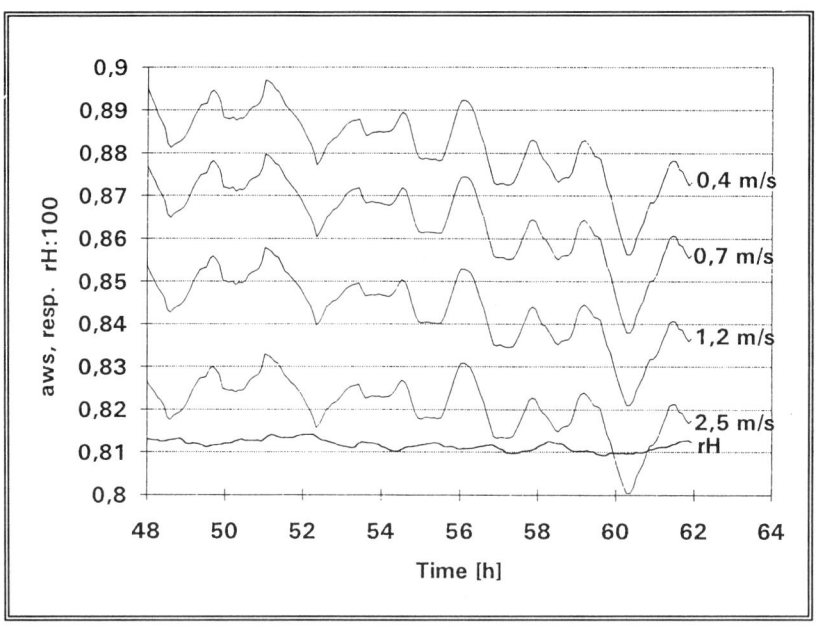

Figure 4: Influence of different air velocities on the superficial water activity (a_{ws}) of sausage at 20 °C and constant relative humidity (rH).

THE IMPORTANCE OF RHEOLOGY FOR HEAT TRANSFER AND MEMBRANE FILTRATION

R W FIELD*, P AIMAR** and M PRITCHARD***

Some results of research on transport phenomena are described. Although fundamental in nature, they are relevant to design. The first concerns the effect of boundary layer viscosity upon heat transfer, wherein it is important to distinguish between heating and cooling duties. The second demonstrates that a large membrane surface viscosity, due to concentration polarisation can, through its influence on mass transfer, lead to a limiting flux independent of other effects. However, increases in bulk viscosity can be beneficial.

Introduction

Hydrodynamic theory is presented to describe the phenomenon of limiting flux in heat exchangers and membrane processes. An analysis based upon a development of film theory shows that the variation of viscosity with concentration will lead to a limiting flux of either heat or mass. Typical relationships between viscosity and concentration are then used to develop practical versions of the limiting condition.

In heat transfer, following Seider and Tate (1936), it is well recognised that the film heat transfer coefficient is influenced by boundary layer viscosity. On empirical grounds they correlated their data on the basis that:

$$Nu/Nu_0 = (\mu_b/\mu_w)^z \tag{1}$$

where $z = 0.14$. Subsequently others have made a distinction between heating and cooling duties. A critical reading of the heat transfer literature suggests that there is no reason to alter the conclusions of Petukhov (1970) that $z = 0.11$ for heating duties ($\mu_w/\mu_b < 1$) and $z = 0.25$ for cooling duties ($\mu_w/\mu_b > 1$). Furthermore recent work by Field (1990) has provided a theoretical basis for a correction factor that is applicable for $\mu_w > \mu_b$. The approximate form is:

$$Nu/Nu_0 = F = (\mu_b/\mu_w)^{0.27} \tag{2}$$

and with regard to heat transfer, it is in good agreement with previous experimental work (Fig 1). The predicted exponent depends slightly on the viscosity ratio, and for $\mu_w >> \mu_b$ the following more complex expression of the correction factor is applicable:

*   School of Chemical Engineering, University of Bath, UK
**   LGC, URA–CNRS, Université Paul Sabatier, Toulouse, France
***   presently New Zealand Dairy Research Institute, NZ

$$F = \{\frac{\mu_b}{\mu_w} \frac{4(6e^\alpha - \alpha^3 - 3\alpha^2 - 6\alpha - 6)}{\alpha^4}\}^{\frac{1}{3}} \tag{3}$$

In the present paper this work will be extended to show that theoretically there is a limiting heat flux. The design implications are briefly discussed.

Related equations are relevant for mass transfer, and have, together with one particular form of a viscosity–concentration relationship, been used by Aimar and Field (1991) to develop a relationship in excellent agreement with some classical literature. An alternative expression and some new data are presented at the end of the next section.

Lastly, some recent work at Bath by Pritchard (1990) has shown that an increase in the viscosity of the bulk fluid can counteract the detrimental effect of a high viscosity boundary layer by transferring more shear stress to the boundary layer. The behaviour has been successfully modelled using an expression for the laminar mass transfer coefficient that incorporates concentration dependent, pseudoplastic flow properties. As shown later, the flux can actually increase at high concentrations.

Recent developments

(a) Heat transfer

Consider a cooling duty. Now the transport of heat from the process side to the coolant consists of three steps:

(1) transport through the process side boundary layer:

$$q = h_p (T_b - T_{w1}) \tag{4}$$

(2) conduction across the fouling layers and through the heat transfer surface:

$$q = (T_{w1} - T_{w2}) / R \tag{5}$$

(3) transport through the coolant–side boundary layer:

$$q = h_c (T_{w2} - T_c) \tag{6}$$

Under normal conditions, the various resistances and the overall temperature driving force determine the heat flux, q. Generally it is reasonable to assume that q is unbounded. However, if h_p is a decreasing function of temperature, the heat flux can reach a maximum value.

Writing $(T_b - T_{w1})$ as ΔT:

$$dq/d(\Delta T) = (d[h_p]/d[\Delta T]) \Delta T + h_p \tag{7}$$

The theoretical condition for a limiting flux is given by $dq/d(\Delta T) = 0$. Now if, following equation (2),

$$h_p = h_{po} (\mu_b/\mu_w)^{0.27} \tag{8}$$

a practical version of the limiting condition is:

$$- \frac{dh_p}{d\mu_w} \frac{d\mu_w}{d(\Delta T)} = h_p/\Delta T \tag{9}$$

ie

$$0.27 \, d\mu_w/d(\Delta T) = \mu_w/\Delta T \tag{10}$$

Following others (eg Bird, Stewart and Lightfoot, 1960), and assuming that for a liquid:

$$\mu = \mu_0 \exp(-\alpha [T-T_0]) \tag{11}$$

one can write:

$$\mu_w = \mu_b \exp(-\alpha [T_{w1}-T_b])$$
$$= \mu_b \exp(\alpha \Delta T) \tag{12}$$

Therefore $\quad d\mu_w/d(\Delta T) = \alpha \mu_w \tag{13}$

Combining equations (10) and (13) gives a particular version of the limiting condition:

$$0.27 \, \alpha \, \Delta T = 1 \tag{14}$$

An expression for h_p at the limiting flux can be determined by combining equations (8), (12) and (14). It then follows that the theoretical maximum heat flux is:

$$q_{max} = \frac{h_{po}}{\exp(1)} \frac{1}{0.27\alpha} = 1.36 \, h_{po}/\alpha \tag{15}$$

(b) Mass transfer in membrane systems

Aimar and Sanchez (1986) have been shown that some functions give a relationship between viscosity and concentration, from which an analytical solution can be obtained, even though the viscosity–concentration relationships themselves do not have any theoretical meaning. For example, an assumption relating viscosity to concentration is that considered by Clifton et al (1984), namely:

$$\mu = \mu_0 \exp(\gamma C) \tag{16}$$

Three typical values of γ are as follows:

whey proteins:	$\gamma = 14.3 \times 10^{-3}$ if C is in g/kg	(after Jonsson, 1984)
albumin:	$\gamma = 7 \times 10^{-3}$	(Aimar et al, 1989)
gelatin (60°C):	$\gamma = 24 \times 10^{-3}$	(Schüler, 1989)

Using the relationship in equation (16) and an analysis similar to that in section (a), Aimar and Field (1991) showed that the value of the mass transfer coefficient under limiting conditions would lie between 40% and 80% of the standard coefficient, k_0. They also obtained the following expression for the limiting flux:

$$J_{lim} = k_0 \left[\exp(\gamma z C_b)(1-\frac{C_w}{C_b}) \right] \frac{1}{\gamma z C_{w,lim}} \tag{17}$$

The limiting flux predicted by this model has been plotted versus the reduced concentration in Figure 2. The typical decrease in flux with bulk concentration and viscosity is predicted. More surprising is the apparent linear behaviour in semi-logarithmic co-ordinates over a wide range of reduced concentrations. Therefore this part of the curve does not disagree with the gel theory, and the numerous experimental observations which accord with it. However in addition, the present model predicts an upward curvature of the curve, and non–zero fluxes at large bulk concentrations. This accords with some work of Porter (1988).

According to the assumptions, the curve in Figure 2 should work for any solution whose viscosity fits an expression of the form given by equation (16). It is also of interest to consider alternative expressions. (Aimar, 1987) included:

$$\mu = \mu_s + \mu_0 C^V \tag{18}$$

The corresponding limiting flux, given that μ_s can be neglected, is

$$J_{lim} = k_0/[vz \exp(1)] \tag{19}$$

Table 1 shows the values of J_{lim}/k_0 for various values of v and z. One can see that, for systems where equation (18) is applicable, there is a theoretical limit for J_{lim} which is of the same order of magnitude as k_0. It is also predicted that the limiting flux is independent of bulk concentration. Although the values in the table vary over a moderate range, depending on the system, z, and on the rheological properties, v, z will probably be about 0.27 for the reasons given earlier. Thus the limiting flux at the midpoint of the range of greatest interest is about 0.5 k_0.

		values of v:	
	2	3	4
values of z:			
0.14	1.314	0.876	0.657
0.25	0.735	0.490	0.368
0.27	0.681	0.454	0.341

Table 1   Values of J_{lim}/k_0 for various values of v and z

The absence of a bulk concentration effect upon J_{lim} is rare. However, Breslau and Kilcullen (1977) reported that they were able to confirm repeatedly an ultrafiltration flux that was independent of the concentration factor up to concentration factors of 24x. This trend can be attributed to the combined effects of the rheology at high shear ($>24,000$ s^{-1}) and pH 3.0, and the low transmembrane pressure (1.2 bar). These data and those for other conditions is reproduced in Figure 3.

Discussion

Regarding heat transfer, the change in the value of z, depending upon whether the duty is one of heating or cooling, is of significance; the predicted value of the process heat transfer coefficient is easily altered by 20%. Although in practice the temperature driving force for q_{max} is unlikely to be reached (eg a viscous fluid with $\alpha = 0.05$ gives a value of 74 ˚C), a 10 ˚C increase in the temperature driving force brings significantly decreasing returns beyond a value of 20 ˚C. This is quantified in Table 2.

$\Delta T(1)$, K	10	20	30	40	50	60
$q/h_{po}(2)$, K	8.7	15.3	20.0	23.3	25.5	26.7

(1) This is not the overall temperature driving force; it is the temperature difference between wall and bulk process fluid
(2) q/h_{po} equates to the effective temperature difference on the process side

Table 2   Effect of viscosity variation upon heat transfer
($\alpha = 0.05$;   z = 0.27)

Regarding mass transfer in membrane systems, equation (19) can be dangerously misleading when used to predict limiting fluxes. Aimar (1987) has shown that equation (18) is a valid expression for the viscosity of dextran T70 solutions; over the range of 0–300 g/kg, the value of v is 2.76. The above analysis would then suggest that the limiting fluxes are independent of dextran concentration. This is not so. Thus the choice of viscosity–concentration relationships, which do not have theoretical meaning, must be made with great care.

The data of Breslau and Kilcullen (1977) and the work of Pritchard (1990) suggests that beneficial improvements in flux may be obtained at high shear stresses. Limitations on space preclude a discussion of this work. Those interested should consult Pritchard *et al* (1992).

Conclusions

1   A large temperature driving force is not beneficial for cooling duties.

2   The Seider–Tate correction factor $z = 0.14$ is inaccurate for cooling duties; a better value is $z = 0.25$–0.27.

3   In membrane systems the rheology can lead to a limiting flux. Quantitative expressions depend upon the viscosity–concentration relationship. It must be selected with care.

4   At high concentrations the use of high shear rates may give significant increases in flux.

Nomenclature

C	concentration of solute	**Greek**
F	viscosity correction factor	α constant in viscosity–distance relationship
h	film heat transfer coefficient	
J	flux through membrane	γ constant in viscosity–conc^n relationship (as eqn 16)
k	mass transfer coefficient	
k_0	mass transfer coefficient at bulk conditions	δ_c thickness of conc^n boundary layer
Nu	Nusselt number	μ viscosity
Pr	Prandtl number	
q	heat flux	**Subscripts**
R	heat transfer resistance	b bulk
T	temperature	c coolant side
v	constant in viscosity–conc^n relationship (as eqn 18)	lim limiting
		p process side
y	distance from membrane	w wall/membrane–fluid interface
z	index reflecting effect of viscosity changes	w_1 process side of wall
		w_2 coolant side of wall

References

Aimar, P (1987), Thesis, Université Paul Sabatier, Toulouse, France

Aimar, P and Field, R W (1991), *Chem Eng Sci*, 47

Aimar, P and Sanchez, V (1986), *Ind Eng Chem Fundam*, 25, 789

Aimar, P, Turner, N M and Howell, J A (1989), *Chem Eng Res Des*, 67, 255

Bird, R B, Stewart, W E and Lightfoot, E N (1960), Transport Phenomena, John Wiley & Sons, New York

Breslau, B R and Kilcullen, B M (1977), *J Dairy Sci*, 60, 1379–1386

Clifton, M J, Abidine, N, Aptel, P and Sanchez, V (1984), *J Memb Sci*, 21, 233

Field, R W (1990), *Chem Eng Sci*, 45, 1343

Jonsson, G (1984), *Desalination*, 51, 61

Petukhov, B S (1970), Heat transfer and friction in turbulent pipe flow, in Advances in Heat Transfer, 6 (edited by J P Hartnett and T F Irvine, Jr), pp503–564

Porter, M C (1988), Membrane filtration in Handbook of Separation Techniques for Chemical Engineers, (edited by P A Schweitzer), McGraw–Hill, New York

Pritchard, M (1990), PhD Thesis, University of Bath, UK

Pritchard, M, Howell, J A and Field, R W (1992), Paper accepted for oral presentation to 'Engineering of Membrane Processes' in Garmisch–Partenkirchen, Germany

Seider, E N and Tate G E (1936), *Ind. Engng Chem*, 25, 1429–1435

Schüler, T (1989), *Diplomarbeit*, Aachen, FRG

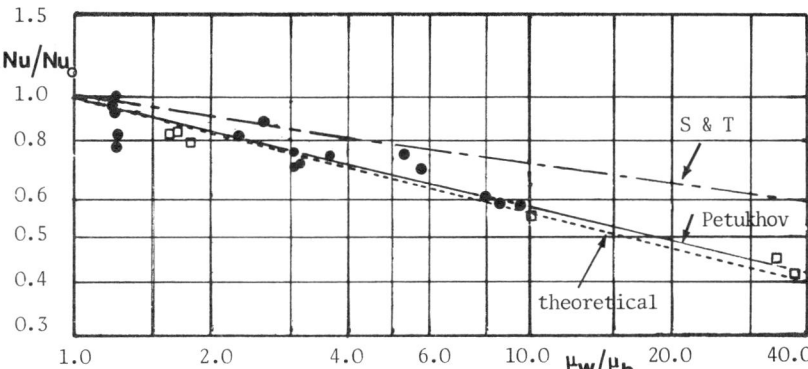

Figure 1   Comparison of two empirical viscosity factors (Seider and Tate z = 0.14; Petukhov z = 0.25) with theoretical curve. Data from Petukhov (1970)

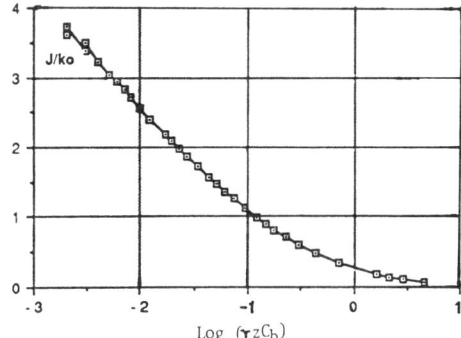

Figure 2

Predicted variation of limiting value of J/k_o with reduced concentration $\gamma z C_b$

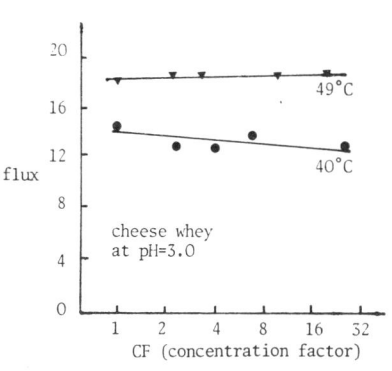

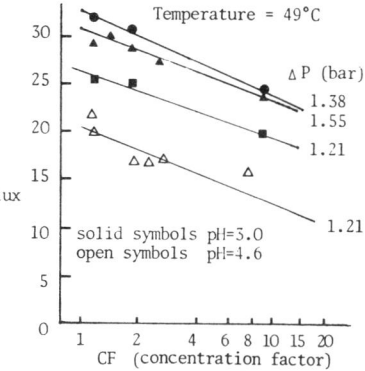

Figure 3(a) Ultrafiltration flux (GSFD) as a function of concentration factor CF at shear rates ≈ 24,000 s⁻¹. Note that flux approximately independent of CF

Figure 3(b) Ultrafiltration flux (GSFD) as a function of concentration factor and transmembrane pressure. Shear rate ≈ 9,000s⁻¹. Note expected dependence of flux on CF

COOKING TIMES AND WEIGHT LOSSES IN MEAT COOKING

M J Swain and S J James*

The results of three separate investigations are presented, the cooking of small meat joints, the cooking of whole poultry and the cooking and cooling of large meat joints to illustrate the effects of factors that influence cooking time and weight loss. In commercial cooking operations the safety need to achieve a minimum final temperature often conflicts with the economic requirements of low weight loss. The experiments show that there is no single process that will meet both aims. The results indicate that very small changes in operating conditions can considerably influence the weight loss and hence the economics of the operation.

Introduction

The main objectives of caterers and manufacturers of cooked meat are to produce economically products that are microbiologically safe and of high organoleptic quality. For safety, a minimum temperature-time treatment should be achieved during cooking followed by sufficiently rapid cooling to minimize growth of surviving organisms. These processes should incorporate good handling procedures designed to eliminate bacterial contamination. For a cooking operation to be economic it should achieve high throughputs (ie. short cooking and cooling processes), incur low weight losses, use the lowest cost raw materials and require both minimal capital investment and kitchen/factory floor space.

In practice these requirements are often in conflict because weight loss tends to increase with meat temperature and heating time. Furthermore the relationship between cooking temperature, time and tenderness is complex and it is generally accepted that poor quality meats, rich in collagen, should be cooked at low temperatures for long times. Few design data are available to cooked meat producers, especially those processing large joints (up to 8kg), which would enable them to specify an optimum cooking and cooling treatment.

Most studies of cooking methods and conditions have generally been carried out with small joints and high operating temperatures typical of those used in domestic situations. Few studies have compared the heating times and weight losses of large joints processed by different commercial systems. Currently there is no UK legislation that specifies a minimum temperature that has to be achieved during a cooking process. The Food Hygiene (Amendment) Regulations 1990 specify a minimum temperature of 63°C for certain foods if they are to be sold hot. The Chilled Food Association Chilled Food Guidelines and the DHSS Cook-Chill and Cook-Freeze Guidelines recommend a minimum temperature of 70°C for at least 2 minutes during cooking.

* Food Refrigeration and Process Engineering Research Centre, University of Bristol, Churchill Building, Langford, BS18 7DY

Data from three investigations are presented to illustrate some of the relationships that have been revealed. The investigations cover weight loss from small meat joints during forced convection air cooking, cooking of whole poultry and a comparison of different cooking and cooling systems for a range of larger joints.

Cooking of Small Meat Joints

M. semitendinosus muscles were removed from beef carcasses that had been chilled and held in air at -1°C for 3 days. The muscles were trimmed of visible fat and wrapped in acrylic sheet to form cylinders approximately 85mm in diameter. They were then frozen in air at -20°C and stored for at least 20 days until required. Muscles were then tempered for 3 days at -4°C before 80mm cylinders 160mm long were removed using a large cork borer. After thawing to 5°C a multi-point thermocouple probe was inserted through the geometric centre of the cylinder through the longitudinal axis. The probe was then attached to a metal support so that the cylinder was positioned at the centre of a forced convection cooking tunnel. The other end of the support was attached to a balance. Meat and air temperature were then recorded at 5 or 15 minute intervals to ±0.25°C and the weight to 0.1g at 30 minute intervals. Replicated trials were carried out at cooking temperatures of 65.5, 117.5 and 175°C and air velocities of 0.15, 0.3, 0.45 and 0.6m/s.

The relationship between time and minimum temperature and percentage weight loss are shown in Figures 1 and 2 respectively. As expected minimum temperature increases with increase in time, air temperature and air velocity. Weight loss increases with time and the rate of weight loss increases both with increased air temperature and in general with increased air velocity. In commercial practice it is quite possible for air velocities in different parts of a large oven to span the range used in these investigations. The results show that differences in air velocity can have a substantial effect on the final temperature of the meat and the percentage weight loss. For example after heating for 100 minutes in air at 175°C, the minimum meat temperature is 67°C in air at 0.15m/s and 75°C at 0.6m/s. Corresponding weight losses are 18 and 30%. Variations in weight loss of this magnitude would lead to substantial differences in the quality of the meat cooked in an oven with this degree of variation in air velocity. To the process operator relying solely on air temperature control, all the meat joints would appear to have received the same cooking treatment.

Although meat is often cooked for a set time the time has usually been chosen so that a known minimum internal temperature has been exceeded. When these results were analysed in terms of weight loss to a minimum internal temperature no relationship between weight loss and air velocity was revealed. However, air temperature did have a significant effect on weight loss (Figure 3). Cooking to a lowest internal temperature of 75°C the lowest weight loss (mean 28%) achieved in air at 175°C was approximately 7% less than in air at 117.5°C.

Cooking of Whole Poultry

Whole chicken carcasses (dressed weight approximately 1kg) were cooked to a minimum internal temperature of 80°C in forced convection wet (dew point 75°C) and dry air at air temperatures of 120, 150, 180 and 210°C and air velocities of 0.5, 1.0 and 2.0m/s. Multi-point temperature probes were used to measure temperature profiles during cooking.

The influence of oven temperature on cooking time is clearly demonstrated in Figure 4. Raising the oven temperature from 120 to 210°C reduces the cooking time by a factor of approximately two under all conditions. At least 70% of this reduction is achieved during a 30°C increase in oven temperature from 120 to 150°C. At a set oven temperature the use of wet air produces a substantial reduction in cooking time over that produced using dry air. The reduction is between 15 and 25 minutes at 120°C and approximately 10 minutes at 210°C. Increasing the air velocity by a factor of four, from 0.5 to 2m/s, produces a maximum reduction of 30 minutes in the cooking time at 120°C. At 210°C the maximum reduction is less than 10 minutes.

Weight loss increases with increase in temperature (Figure 5), with a minimum of approximately 15% in wet and 20% in dry air at 120°C to a maximum of 24 and 34% respectively at 210°C. In most conditions weight loss increased with increase in air velocity. The effect of was most pronounced at low temperatures and in wet air. The use of wet rather than dry air substantially reduced weight loss.

Cooking and Cooling of Large Meat Joints

Three types of beef joint (slabs from M. semitendinosus, silversides and forequarters), boned-out ham and boned-out turkey joints were used in this study. Silverside (mean 2.7kg) and forequarter joints (mean 2.7kg) were prepared to produce rolled joints approximately 110mm in diameter and M. semitendinosus to produce slabs (50x90x210mm, 0.94kg). Boned-out ham (mean 7.1kg) and turkey (mean 6.4kg) joints were obtained from a local producer. All the joints were frozen and thawed before cooking.

Three cooking and cooling methods (convective air cooking and cooling, water immersion cooking and cooling, and pressure cooking and vacuum cooling) were compared. In the convection method, each joint was cooked in air at 120°C, 0.5m/s and 75°C dew point followed by cooling in air at 0°C and 1.2m/s. Before immersion processing joints were vacuum packed and then heated in agitated water at 95°C then cooled in water at 0°C. Pressure cooking was carried out in a vessel operating at 1.03 bar followed by vacuum cooling. All the joints were cooked from 5°C to an internal temperature of 75°C for beef, 80°C for ham and 85°C for turkey then cooled to a maximum internal temperature of 10°C.

Temperatures were measured throughout cooking and cooling using multi-point sensors and the joints weighed before and after cooking for convection and pressure treatments, and after cooling.

The results (Table 2) show that pressure cooking is always substantially faster than either of the other two cooking methods and was always twice as fast as the slowest cooking method. With the small M. semitendinosus joints immersion cooking was faster than convection cooking but there was no significant difference between immersion and convection cooking times for the larger silverside and forequarter joints. With the large turkey and ham joints convection cooking was significantly faster than immersion.

Weight losses after convection cooking were always lower than after pressure cooking with a mean difference of 8.5%. Overall weight losses after convection or immersion cooking and cooling were not significantly different when processing any of the beef joints. The pressure/vacuum technique produced significantly greater overall weight losses than either convection or immersion processing. Mean weight losses for all treatments for convection, immersion and pressure/vacuum were 31.3, 27.5 and 45.8% respectively.

Table 2. Processing times and weight losses from meat under cooking and cooling regimes

Type of joint	Cooking		Cooling		Overall	
Processing conditions	Time (mins)	Weight loss (%)	Time (mins)	Weight loss (%)	Time (mins)	Weight loss (%)
Beef M.Semi.						
Convection	120	26.6	150	2.7	270	29.3
Immersion	71	-	100	-	171	32.7
Pressure/vacuum	50	32.4	52	9.5	102	41.8
Beef forequarter						
Convection	225	26.7	390	2.3	615	28.9
Immersion	208	-	282	-	489	25.5
Pressure/vacuum	110	38.0	43	7.9	153	45.9
Beef silverside						
Convection	219	28.4	338	3.3	557	31.8
Immersion	227	-	240	-	467	30.0
Pressure/vacuum	104	39.2	61	7.4	165	46.6
Boneless turkey						
Convection	360	32.7	526	1.8	886	34.5
Immersion	457	-	411	-	867	25.9
Pressure/vacuum	207	37.8	36	7.8	243	46.7
Boneless ham						
Convection	389	29.9	761	2.2	1150	32.1
Immersion	429	-	456	-	885	23.6
Pressure/vacuum	203	39.6	57	8.6	260	48.2

Although higher throughputs can be achieved using the pressure/vacuum process the high weight losses may be prohibitive for commercial use with thick joints. Increased losses during pressure cooking are probably due to the high surface temperatures achieved during the process and evaporative loss during vacuum cooling is an inherent part of the process. However, it would be interesting to see if the addition of intermittent water sprays could reduce weight loss. It is possible that a hybrid system, possibly using convection cooking in bags followed by immersion cooling, could optimise yields with large joints.

Conclusions

The results demonstrate the importance of good cooking practice and oven design. Very small changes in process control variables can make significant differences to the yield and hence profitability of the cooking operation and can also result in large variations in the quality of the final product. It is clear that the designer and manufacturer of commercial cooking equipment should pay particular attention to the variation in air velocity within the working section of cookers and the instructions for their use to minimise these differences.

The experiments have shown that there is no single process that will meet both aims of the commercial cooked meat producer, ie. to achieve a minimum final temperature needed for microbiological safety and low weight loss for economic reasons. The importance of considering the effect of the combined process of cooking and subsequent cooling on overall weight loss has also been demonstrated. There is no advantage in optimising the cooking process if any gains made are subsequently lost in the cooling phase.

There appears to be tremendous opportunity and scope for industry to improve the efficiency and quality of meat cooking through better monitoring and control of the process. Without close monitoring of weight loss after cooking there can be no measure of what effect changes in control settings are having and how economic the operation is. This may seem a fairly obvious statement but few producers of cooked meat routinely measure anything other than a few temperatures. The cooking of meat is considered by some to be an art and consequently in practice operations tend to be evolved rather than designed. However, due to the pressure of meeting production targets and high labour costs it is unlikely that a company has the luxury of time available to systematically modify their cooking process to find the optimum running conditions. This is where in the short term research establishments with suitable equipment (such as computer controlled data logging and industrial scale pilot plant) can provide assistance in monitoring current practice and supply empirical process design data and in the longer term improve the computer modelling and prediction techniques to a level that they are of more immediate use to the industry as they have proved to be in the area of meat refrigeration.

Figure 1. Minimum temperature in an 80mm diameter by 160mm long meat cylinder cooked in air at 65.5, 117.5 and 175°C and air velocities of 0.15, 0.3, 0.45 and 0.6m/s.

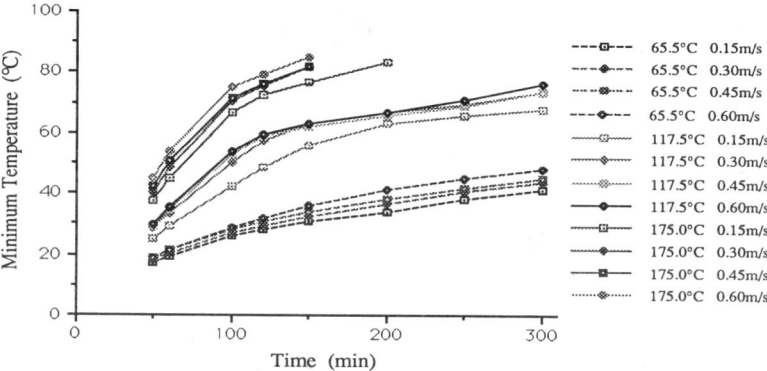

Figure 2. Percentage weight loss from an 80mm diameter by 160mm long meat cylinder cooked in air at 65.5, 117.5 and 175°

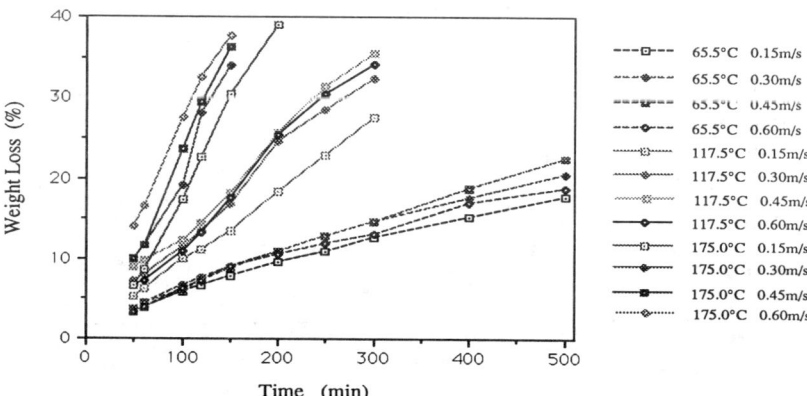

Figure 3. Percentage weight loss from 80mm diameter by 160mm long meat cylinder cooked in air at 65.5,117.5 and 175°to a lowest internal temperature.

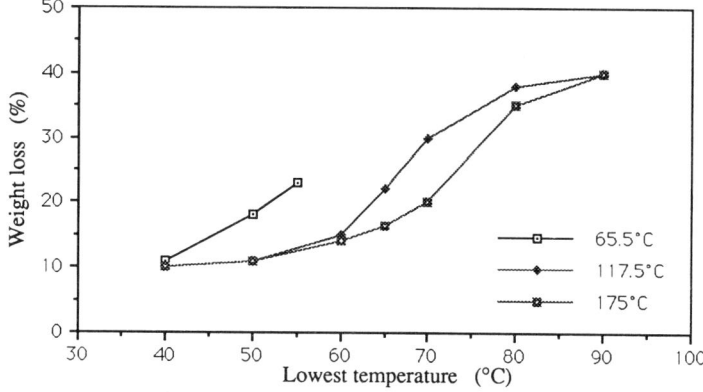

Figure 4. Cooking time of poultry to a minimum internal temperature of 80°C

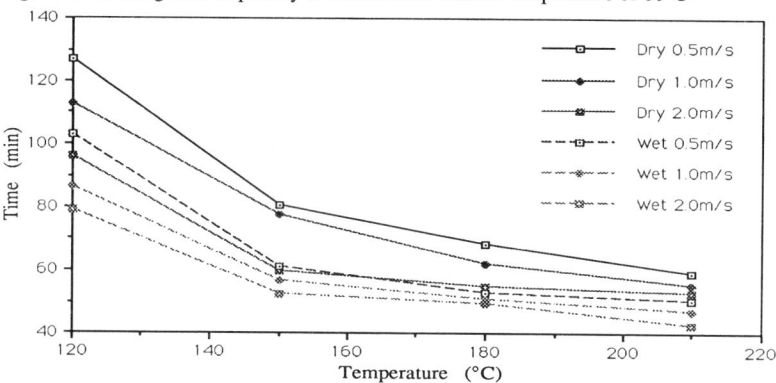

Figure 5. Percentage weight loss during cooking of poultry

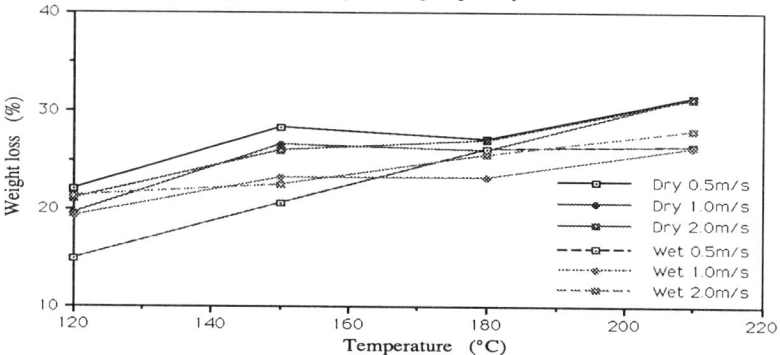

THE ENERGY CONSUMPTION IN MEAT PLANTS WITH SLAUGHTERHOUSES.

D. M. Holder and A.J. Gigiel*

A procedure for surveying the energy consumption of meat plants is evaluated with the results from twenty sites presented. Energy consumption per Tonne of production differs markedly between plants producing similar products. The range for electricity was 0.28 to 1.25 GJ/Tonne and for oil and/ or gas consumption 0.34 to 1.76 GJ/Tonne due to differences in processing operations. Targets for reducing sites specific consumption are suggested and the impact of energy savings on profits are discussed. If site mean specific consumptions were reduced to the targets, the total annual savings would be 0.14 million GJ, costing £1.3 million. Extending the surveys findings to the UK industry the estimated consumption is 3.4 million GJ/year, costing £21 million. The potential for UK energy savings based on the surveys findings is 1.6 million GJ, costing £10 million per year.

Introduction

The UK meat industry slaughters cows, sheep and pigs and processes the carcass meat for the production of fresh beef, veal, lamb, mutton, pork, ham, bacon, and offal. It produces 2.47 million tonnes of fresh meat with a total retail value of £5,311 million (MLC, 1990).

An economic survey of British plants concluded that there was low added value in slaughtering and producing meat products resulting in reduced profits. The scope for profit improvement could be achieved from increased operating efficiency (MLC, 1989c). The same survey found, as a percentage of income, that sites energy costs were of the same magnitude as profits, indicating the potential increase in profits from reduced energy consumption.

Many meat plants have little information on their energy usage due to poor accounting procedures and no submetering of process consumption. This masks the importance of using energy efficiently and hinder designers, engineers and suppliers trying to quantify the savings from implementing energy efficient measures.

An energy consumption survey of twenty meat plants with slaughterhouses was undertaken. The aims of the survey were to;
1. determine the amount of energy used.
2. determine the variation in energy consumption for a range of meat processors.
3. provide a reference for assessing the effects of changes on energy consumption.
4. enable targets for energy reduction to be set.

Energy data was collected by questionnaire and site visits, noting the range of operations, and analysing the data. This method was chosen because a range of consumptions from a variety of sites would be found.

A schematic diagram for a meat processing plant, is shown in Figure 1. Plants which only cut and package the meat are not considered. Their are few published sources on the energy consumption by process for the British industry, and the diagram is based on plants in the US (Brown et al, 1985) and New Zealand (Edwards et al, 1977) which are similar to British plants.

* Food Refrigeration and Process Engineering Research Centre. University of Bristol, Churchill Building, Langford.

The principal operations are mechanical processing and handling in a batch process, slaughtering and dressing animals with cutters, blowers, hoists and conveyors powered by compressed air and electrical motors.

This is then followed by carcass cooling. The refrigeration plant is the major electrical consumer (typically 65 to 90% of site electricity consumption). For each refrigerated room a self contained direct expansion packaged unit comprising compressor, evaporator, and condenser is installed, but some sites had a centralised compressor and condenser plant.

The carcasses are held and stored between 24 and 48h at 0 to 4°C in refrigerated rooms to reduce their temperature. Depending on the product range of the site the carcasses may then be sold for wholesale or further cut for packing in boxes or shrink film. The cutting room contains electric motored conveyors and cutters, although the majority of cutting is done manually and packaged by compressed air powered equipment. This is a continuous operation in air conditioned halls at 10°C minimising products temperature rise.

The meat products are then returned in batches to chilled stores set at 0 to 4°C for chilled dispatch or sent into freezers or blast freezers set at below -18°C for between 24 and 48h. Once frozen the meat products are held in a cold store at -18°C awaiting dispatch. The loading and dispatch areas are air conditioned to 10°C to minimise product temperature rise. Sites will also consume electricity for pumps and agitators in by-product plants, lights and auxiliary equipment.

Oil and/or gas is used in water heating for, "sterilising" (80°C), washdown (65°C), carcass washing (45°C) and office space heating. Sites with pig slaughtering lines also have a scalding tank of hot water for dehairing, and the remaining hair is singed off the carcass using a flame burning a fuel gas. Sites with by-products plants will have an additional heat load to evaporate water from the by-products.

Methodology
The survey design was limited to collecting available data common to each plant from site energy bills showing consumption and costs, and production records. Twenty meat plants were surveyed in 1988, and a minimum of twelve continuous months data was sought.

The production data available for all sites was the monthly number of animals slaughtered, enabling the average total weight of carcass meat (the common product before meat cutting operations) to be calculated. The Production Level (PL) was defined as the total weight of carcass meat imported to each site per month:

$$PL = (W_c.N_c + W_p.N_p + W_s.N_s) + W_c$$

where; subscripts c, p, and s = cattle, pigs, and sheep.
W = average dressed carcass weight of each species, (Table 1).
N = number of head of each species.
W_c = total weight of carcass meat (non-specific) bought into the cutting plant .

Table 1
British national average dressed carcass weights (MLC. 1988, 1989a and b).

Species	Average dressed carcass weight (kg)
Cattle, (inc Cows,Heifers, Steers)	270
Heifers / Steers only	247 / 297
Pigs, (inc Sows / Boars)	63
Sows / Boars only	145 / 136
Sheep, (inc Lambs, Ewes, Rams)	18

To relate invoiced energy consumption to measured production a common time interval of a calender month was chosen as this was the minimum period for the electricity meter readings.

To convert the energy consumption, and production figures to calender monthly data, each were cumulatively plotted against time elapsed from the beginning of the survey period (Figure 2). A Cubic Spline function was constrained to pass through each data point so that the increment was 'smoothed' without masking monthly fluctuations.

The monthly cumulative figures were then obtained by interpolating for the beginning and end of each month from the curve and the monthly consumption and production from the difference in the cumulative totals. Energy consumption was then converted from their metered units to the equivalent energy content (GJ). The Specific Electricity and Oil and/or Gas Consumption (SEC and SOGC) were then calculated by dividing the monthly energy consumption by the monthly Production Level.

Results

The greatest mean SEC was for site 20 (1.248 GJ/Tonne) and was over 4 times that for the smallest at site 7, (0.284 GJ/Tonne), (Figure 3). The mean specific costs ranged from 0.307 to 1.156 p/kg, (1988 prices, p/kg * 10 = £/Tonne). Within each site, monthly specific consumptions vary considerably. For site 1 it varies from 0.438 to 1.871 GJ per Tonne of production, (Figure 4).

Analysis of the sites monthly electricity consumptions (not SECs) revealed two different ($p < 0.05$) classes of operators. Primary types (P) which only slaughter and chill carcasses with small amounts of manual cutting operations. Secondary (S) which had additional facilities for large scale meat cutting and packaging lines (S1) and sometimes by-product processing (S2). The mean monthly specific electricity consumption for Primary and Secondary Operators respectively was 0.436 and 0.774 GJ/Tonne respectively.

The greatest mean specific oil and/or gas consumption was for site 11 (1.760 GJ/Tonne) and was over 5 times the consumption for the smallest at site 16 (0.338 GJ/Tonne). The SOGC consumptions range from 0.216 to 2.064 GJ/Tonne and costs from 0.098 to 0.390 p/kg (1988 prices, p/kg * 10 = £/Tonne), (Figure 5). For each site, monthly SOGCs vary considerably, for site 1, from 0.216 to 1.489 GJ per Tonne of production, (Figure 6).

Monthly oil and/or gas consumption (not SOGC) increased ($p < 0.05$) with production level, but did not differ ($p < 0.05$) between Operations groups. The grand mean SOGC was 0.819 GJ/Tonne and did not differ ($p < 0.05$) due to Production Level or Operations.

Electricity was 41% of the total consumption but 73% of total energy costs. The ratio of costs to profit was calculated using survey results of 12 sites in 1987 (MLC, 1988c). This found that the mean profit was £2.20 /Tonne (range £10.3 /Tonne loss to £42 /Tonne profit). The electricity costs are 2.5 and 3.5 times the mean profit, (Figure 7).

SECs varied considerably between sites. The mean SEC for site 1 is over 2.5 times that for site 5, and its consumption compares unfavourably with the Grand Mean for Primary Operators. Its high energy costs cannot be considered as minor production overheads.

Because processing operations affect electricity consumption this must be taken into account when setting targets for consumption. These are found from the minimum mean SECs and SOGCs, (Table 2). If the mean specific energy consumption at sites were reduced to the targets, (Table 2) then the mean total annual savings for the twenty sites would be 0.14 million GJ costing £1.3 million.

Assuming the sample of sites is representative of the whole UK industry, it is estimated that a total of 3.4 million GJ of energy per year are consumed, costing £21 million per year. If all UK sites achieved the lowest 'similar' site mean specific consumption, the estimated UK mean total annual energy savings would be 1.6 million GJ, with cost savings of £10 million.

Table 2.

Specific energy consumption targets for meat plants

	SEC Target (GJ/Tonne)	SOGC Target (GJ/Tonne)
Primary Operators	0.284	0.338
Secondary, S1 Operators	0.617	0.338
Secondary, S2 Operators	(0.724)[a]	_b

Subscripts a; minimum monthly consumption for site 20.

b; no target because of by-product plant in operation at site 20.

Conclusions
The survey has shown that the method was effective in finding the energy consumption for a range of meat plants using their site records. It also found differences between sites that cannot be accounted for by variability in the dataset or with processing operations and production level, but was due to excess energy consumption. The information presented should prompt the industry to assess sites performance in comparison to others and encourage further investigations into reducing energy consumption by using the energy targets suggested.

References
Brown H. Hammel B. and Hedman B. (1985). Energy Analysis of 108 Industrial Processes. *US Dept of Energy*, Contract Nos E(11-1) 2862.

Edwards B. Fleming A. Oliver D. Muir B. and Dunn S. (1977). Survey of energy use at Hellaby Northland Works. *MIRINZ*, Report 653.

MLC. (1988). Beef Yearbook (1987). *Meat and Livestock Commission Economics Information Service*. (UK).

MLC. (1989)a. Sheep Yearbook (1988). *Meat and Livestock Commission Economics Information Service*. (UK).

MLC. (1989)b. Pig Yearbook (1988). *Meat and Livestock Commission Economics Information Service*. (UK).

MLC. (1989)c. The slaughtering industry in Great Britain (1988). *Meat and Livestock Commission Economics Information Service*. (UK).

MLC. (1991). The slaughtering industry in Great Britain (1990). *Meat and Livestock Commission Economics Information Service*. (UK).

Figures
Fig. 1. Schematic diagram of meat processing plant. (Showing typical energy consumptions of the processing operations and production flow from left to right).

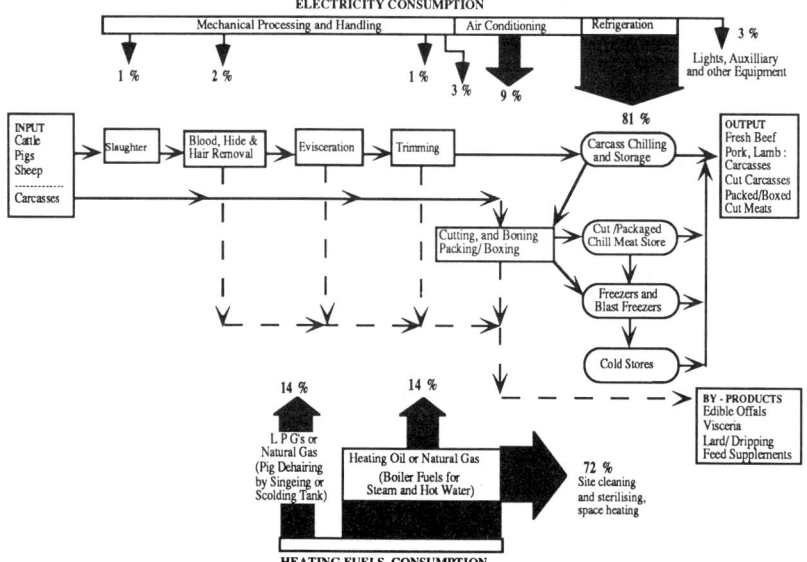

Fig. 2. An illustration of the cubic spline polynomial used for curve fitting.

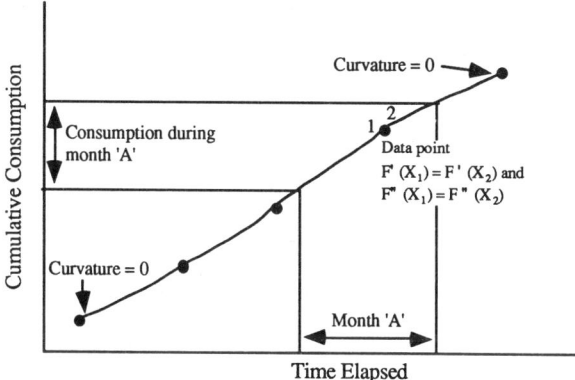

Fig. 3. Mean SEC and specific costs against site.

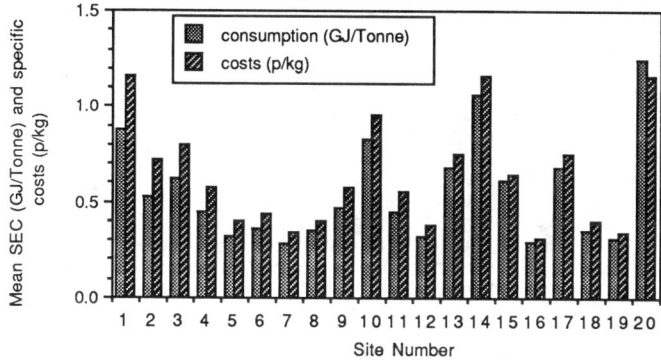

Fig. 4. Maximum and minimum SEC against site.

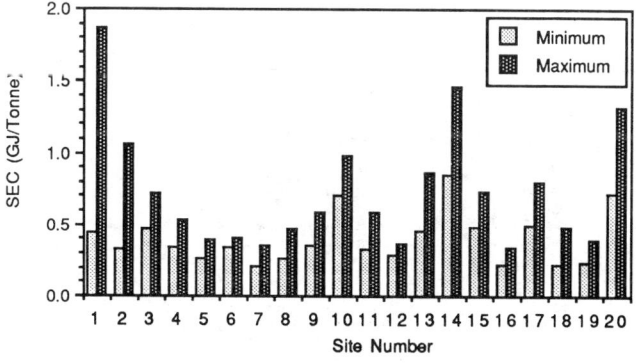

Fig. 5. Mean SOGC and specific costs against site. (N.A. denotes data unavailable)

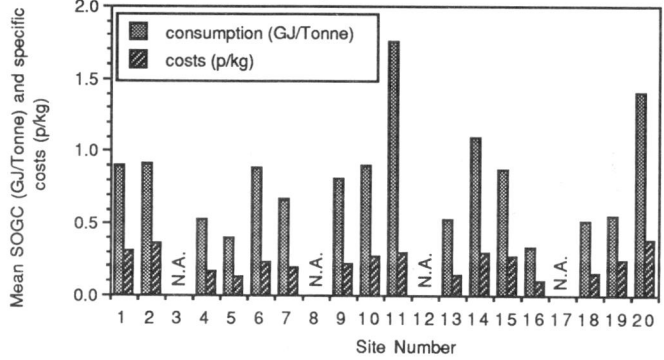

Fig. 6. Maximum and minimum SOGC against site.

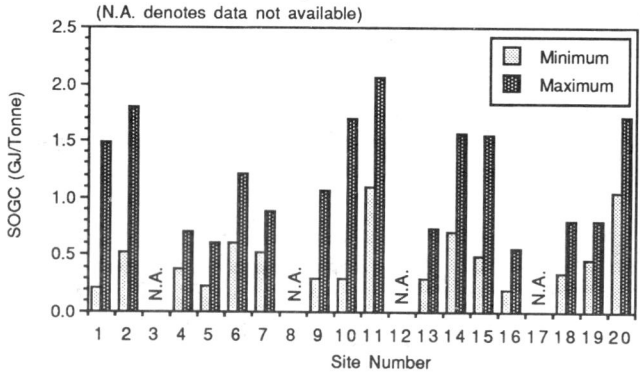

Fig. 7. The ratio of specific energy costs to profits.

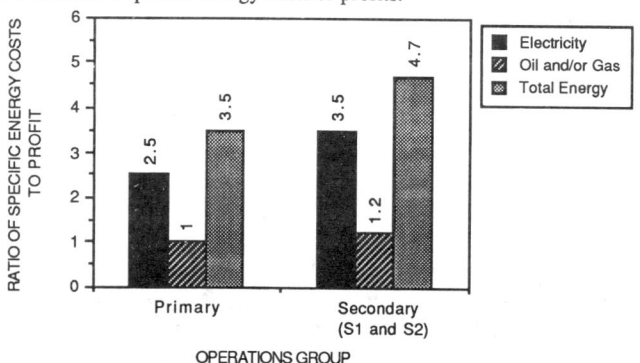

A MODEL FOR SOLID-LIQUID DISCHARGE

B O Mills Lamptey*

A mechanistic model has been developed to describe the flow of solid-liquid mixtures from a conical hopper. The model was developed from theories (Davidson and Nedderman [1983] and Thorpe [1984]) originally proposed for the discharge of dry powders from hoppers which have been pressurised by a gas.

The model predicts both the solid and liquid discharge rates and the discharge fractions for given operating conditions, such as driving force, fluid viscosity, orifice to particle diameter ratio, density ratio of the solid-liquid mixture and hopper half-angle. Simulations, which have been performed to investigate the relative effects of the input variables, indicate that the discharge rates and discharge fractions are particularly sensitive to the density ratio, orifice to particle diameter ratio and liquid viscosity. However, for values of orifice to particle diameter ratios greater than 40, no significant influence was observed on the discharge fraction.

Physical explanations are given for the above results which have been confirmed experimentally by Mills Lamptey [1991]. It is concluded that the model may be employed in process design and control of solid-liquid discharge, and also serve as the basis for modelling flow through other geometries such as dished-bottomed tanks with standpipes.

Introduction

Prior to the 1980's the food industry had been a low technology industry, and to some extent it still is. With the number of professional engineers in the food industry on the increase, utilization of computers in processing, design and simulation are transforming the the industry. Proven techniques and well established methods which have been employed in the oil, gas, and chemical industries, are now being applied in the food industry with much success. Current computer applications are in computer aided design (Havlik et al. [1989]), mathematical modelling and quality control. This paper addresses the modelling of the flow of solid-liquid mixtures out of storage vessels, namely conical hoppers. One potential application of this work is in aseptic processing of wet particulate foods (Mills Lamptey [1991]).

In designing aseptic processing systems it is important to understand which process parameters control discharge rates (which must be set at a value appropriate to the filler), the discharge solids fraction (which needs to be consistent and high for a considerable number of potential products which are presently tinned, such as peas in brine, carrot and potato curry, fruit cocktail, pineapple chunks in syrup etc.), and the residence time distribution (which will affect the product quality, and possibly safety). Thus it is essential that the flow behaviour of these foods is properly understood to fully exploit aseptic technology. The model presented describes the discharge process and as such enables the limitations of the system to be defined. It is a mechanistic model and is based on theories originally proposed for dry granular materials. It can be classified as being a continuum model as opposed to one which models individual particle movements.

* Silsoe Research Institute, Process Engineering Division, Wrest Park, Silsoe, Bedford MK45 4HS

Mathematical modelling

A detailed mathematical model of the flow of solid-liquid mixtures is given by Mills Lamptey [1991] and Mills Lamptey and Thorpe [1991a]. This mechanistic model includes phenomena which are peculiar to the flow of solid-liquid mixtures through constrictions. Percolation of the liquid through the moving solid particles is accounted for, and the energy loss associated with this is estimated from a slightly modified version of the Ergun equation. The reduction in the effective orifice size for solid flow but not for liquids, (the effect of the empty annulus, Beverloo et al [1961]) has been taken into account.

Also as a result of the drag force on the solid particles due to percolation of the liquid, and the accelerating effects of the liquid on the solid particles, an additional body force (identical to that used by Crewdson et al. [1977]) was added to the weight of the material in a force-momentum balance. The model generally solves two equations in order to predict the solid and liquid discharge rates; one (Equation 1) describes the pressure profile of the interstitial liquid and the other (Equation 2) is the force-momentum balance for an element of mixture within the hopper.

$$\frac{dP}{dr} = \frac{2\rho_L z^{*2}}{e^2 r^5} + \frac{s_1}{r^2}\left(\frac{z*}{e} - \frac{a*}{1-e}\right)\left(\frac{1-e}{e}\right)^2 + \frac{s_2\rho_L}{r^4}\left(\frac{z*}{e} - \frac{a^*}{1-e}\right)^2\left(\frac{1-e}{e}\right) \quad (1)$$

$$\frac{d\sigma}{dr} + \frac{2(1-K)\sigma}{r} = \frac{2\rho_s a^{*2}}{(1-e)r^5} - \rho_s(1-e)g + \rho_L(1-e)g$$

$$- \frac{s_1}{r^2}\left(\frac{z*}{e} - \frac{a*}{1-e}\right)\left(\frac{1-e}{e}\right)^2 - \frac{s_2\rho_L}{r^4}\left(\frac{z*}{e} - \frac{a^*}{1-e}\right)^2\left(\frac{1-e}{e}\right) \quad (2)$$

$$- \frac{2\rho_L(1-e)z^{*2}}{e^2 r^5}$$

On the right hand side of equation (1), the first term is due to acceleration of the liquid, and the last two terms are due to percolation. The terms on the right hand side of equation (2) represent the following: the first term is related to the stress component on the element, the second term is related to the acceleration of the solid particles, and the third term represents the weight of the material. The last four terms are associated with the additional body force which is said to result from the drag force and acceleration of the liquid.

To obtain values for the discharge rates, simultaneous solution for z^* and a (i.e. parameters related to the liquid and solid discharge rates respectively) in equations (1) and (2) was procured. This could be achieved by employing the Nag library routine DO2SAF. The following boundary conditions were used.

At $r = \infty$ (i.e. well away from the orifice plane)
     $P = \Delta P$ and $\sigma = 0$

and $r = r_o$ (i.e. at the orifice)
     $p = 0$ and $\sigma = 0$

Note that the displacement thickness effect is incorporated in the following manner:

$$r_{ok} = \frac{D_o - kdp}{2 \, Sin \, \theta_w} \text{ is used to replace}$$

$r_o = \dfrac{D_o}{2 \, Sin \, \theta_w}$ in the resulting algebraic equation from equation (2) only. The discharge rates (L and W) are then calculated using the values of z^* and a^* (see nomenclature).

It should be noted that the model is applicable only to solid-liquid mixtures with a low viscosity liquid, $\mu < 0.05$ N s m^{-2}, i.e. up to 50 times the viscosity of water) (Mills Lamptey [1991]).

Simulations

A number of simulations have been performed to consider different operating conditions. The effect on the discharge fraction and flow rates of changes in the pressure or driving force, the fluid viscosity, and the ratio of orifice to particle diameter and the ratio of solid to liquid density were investigated.

The conditions used in the simulations are given in Table 1.

Changes in dimensionless pressure increase

The effect of changes in the driving force (the dimensionless pressure increase) on the liquid discharge fraction (d) is shown in Fig 1. together with the effect of including the displacement thickness/empty annulus. The simulations reveal a significant difference in the discharge fraction at low values of the driving pressure, whilst at higher values the discharge fraction is constant. These simulated results compare well with the experimental results of Mills Lamptey [1991]. The considerable rise in the liquid fraction at low pressures for both curves is because, for mixtures with a high density ratio, the gravitational force is dominant in this region and causes the solid particles to fall through the liquid, decreasing the liquid fraction.

Taking account of the displacement thickness reduces the effective area available for solids flow but not for liquid flow, thus giving rise to a bigger increase in the liquid fraction in the upper curve. In the lower curve, the variation in the discharge fraction is purely due to percolation of the interstitial fluid.

Changes in density ratio, ρ^*

To demonstrate the effect of the relative density on the discharge fraction, two density ratios were used in the simulation (Fig.2). A value of 2.95 is typical of a glass ballatoni and water mixture and 1.2 is for a model food such as peas in brine. Although the values of discharge fractions are different at high pressure, at low pressure there is a noticeably larger rise in the discharge fraction for the high density ratio curve compared to the lower density ratio curve. The explanation for these effects are at low pressures the gravitational force is dominant and is larger for the solid particles with the high density ratio. Hence the particles tend to fall through the liquid which leads to a lower liquid discharge fraction, but at high pressures the liquid rather tends to percolate through the particles which then result in a high liquid discharge fraction. In the case of the lower density ratio, the effect of the gravitational force is not that great, and as such, the change in the discharge fraction is minimal.

The pressure profile of the liquid within the hopper ()

The dimensionless pressure (Π) is plotted as functions of the dimensionless inverse radial distance (R) in Fig.3. This profile is typical for these examples of solid-liquid mixtures. The simulation shows that most of the pressure drop occurs in the vicinity of the orifice, as found in experiments, Mills Lamptey and Thorpe [1991b].

Changes in the orifice to particle diameter ratio, D'

The effect of changes in the ratio of orifice to particle diameter, Do/dp denoted as D', on the discharge fraction (a). In order to simplify the explanation given below the term solid discharge fraction β will be introduced. β is simply defined as follows: $\beta = 1 - a$. From Fig.4a, it can be seen that an increase in D' results in an increase in solid discharge fraction, β. This is due to the existence of the empty annulus which decreases the effective area A' available for solids flow but not that for liquid flow. The increase in D' leads to an increase in A* {the ratio of the area available to solids (A') flow to the total orifice (A)}, which results in more solids flow (Fig. 4(b)).

$$\frac{A'}{A} = A^* = \left(\frac{D_o - kd_p}{D_o}\right)^2 = \left(1 - \frac{kd_p}{D_o}\right)^2 = \left(1 - \frac{k}{D'}\right)^2 \qquad (4)$$

In these simulations the particle size was held constant and the orifice diameter altered. This simulation scheme was preferred to avoid the complicating effect of different degrees of percolation as a result of changes in particle size. The three curves shown in Fig.4(a) represent different particle sizes (0.5, 1 and 4 mm diameter). The slight differences in the curves reflects the changes in the displacement thickness. The larger the particle size, the larger the empty annulus thickness, and hence a smaller effective area for the flow of larger particles. For values of D' greater than 40, the discharge fraction is found to be almost constant: this is the region in which A* is virtually independent of D' (Fig. 4(b)).

Changes in liquid viscosity, μ

An increase in the liquid viscosity results in a decrease in the liquid fraction. The simple explanation is that, the more viscous liquid percolates more slowly through the solid particles. This simulation is shown in Fig.5.

Future work

Further work is required in the modelling of high viscous mixtures as the current model is inadequate in describing the flow characteristics (Mills Lamptey [1991]). Work is already under way at Silsoe Research Institute to incorporate the effects of particle shape and size distribution. These two parameters are likely to affect the relationship between the discharge rates and the pressure gradient which is employed in the model.

Conclusions

1. The simulations from the model are in agreement with experiments carried out by Mills Lamptey [1991].

D' _____ ratio of orifice to particle diameter $D' = \dfrac{D_o}{d_p}$

d_p _____ particle diameter (m)

e _____ voidage fraction

g _____ the acceleration due to gravity (ms^{-2})

K _____ interparticle frictional constant often known as Rankine's coefficient of earth pressure

$$K = \frac{1 + \sin \phi}{1 - \sin \phi}$$

k _____ the empty annulus constant

L _____ liquid flowrate (kg s^{-1})

P _____ interstitial fluid pressure (N m^{-2})

R _____ dimensionless inverse radial distance $R = \dfrac{r_o}{r}$

r _____ radial co-ordinate (m)

s_1 _____ constant in the Ergun equation (kgm^{-3} s^{-1}) $s_1 = \dfrac{150\mu}{d_p^2}$

s_2 _____ constant in the Ergun equation (m^{-1}) $s_2 = \dfrac{1.75}{d_p}$

W _____ solids flowrate (kg s^{-1})

z^* _____ alternative liquid flowrate parameter (m^3 s^{-1})

$$z^* = \frac{L}{\rho_L 2\pi(1 - \cos \theta_w)}$$

Greek

α _____ volumetric liquid discharge fraction

β _____ volumetric solid discharge fractions

ϕ _____ internal angle of friction

Π _____ dimensionless interstitial liquid pressure $\Pi = \dfrac{P}{\rho_L g r_o}$

π _____ 3.1416

θ_w _____ hopper half-angle

ρ _____ density (kg m^{-3})

ρ^* _____ ratio of solid to liquid density

Σ _____ dimensionless normal stress $\Sigma = \dfrac{\sigma}{\rho_L g r_o}$

σ _____ normal stress (N m^{-2})

μ _____ liquid viscosity (Ns m^{-2})

Δ _____ a difference

Subscripts

o _____ orifice

ok _____ effective orifice

L _____ liquid

s _____ solid

2. The simulations, which have been performed to investigate the relative effects of the input variables, indicate that the discharge rates and discharge fractions are particularly sensitive to the density ratio, orifice to particle diameter ratio D' and liquid viscosity. However, for values of D' greater than 40, no significant influence was observed on the discharge fractions.

3. The model may be employed in process design and control of solid-liquid discharge, and also serve as the basis for modelling flow through other geometries such as dished-bottomed tanks with standpipes.

REFERENCES

Beverloo, W. A.; Leniger, H.A.; Van de Velde, J. 1961, The flow of granular solids through orifices. Chemical Engineering Science, **15**, 260.

Crewdson, B.J.; Ormond, A.L; Nedderman, R.M. 1977, Air-impeded discharge of fine particles from a hopper. Powder Technology, **16**, 179.

Davidson, J.F.; Nedderman, R.M., 1973, The hour glass theory of hopper flow. Transactions of the Institution of Chemical Engineers **51**, 29.

Ergun, S., 1952, Fluid flow through packed columns. Chemical Engineering Progress **48**, 89.

Havlik, S.; Deer, L; Okos, M.R., 1969, Computer-aided engineering in the food industry. Food properties and Computer-Aided Engineering of Food Processing Systems, (Eds Singh, R P and Medina, A G) 507-533. Kluwer Academic Publishers.

Mills Lamptey, B.O.; Thorpe, R.B. 1991a, The discharge of solid-liquid mixtures from hoppers. Chemical Engineering Science **46** (9) 2197-2212.

Mills Lamptey, B.O.; Thorpe, R.B., 1991b, The application of dimensionless analysis to the scale-up of discharging solid-liquid mixtures from hoppers and storage vessels. Submitted to Food & Bioproducts Processing.

Mills Lamptey, B.O., 1991, The discharge of solid-liquid mixtures from storage vessels. Chemical Engineering PhD Thesis, University of Cambridge.

Thorpe, R.B., 1984, Air-augmented flow of granular materials through orifices. Chemical Engineering PhD Thesis, University of Cambridge.

NOMENCLATURE

A	_____	total orifice area
A'	_____	effective orifice area
A*	_____	ratio of effective orifice area to total orifice area
a*	_____	alternative solids flow rate parameters (m^{3}s^{-1})

$$a^* = \frac{W}{\rho_s \, 2\pi(1 - \cos\theta_w)}$$

D	_____	a diameter (m)
d	_____	differential

Table 1

Table of conditions used in simulations

Figure Number	1	2	3	4a	4b	5
e	0.430	0.430	0.430	0.430	0.430	0.430
D_o(m) x 10^3	5.0	5.0	10.0	5.0	5.0	10.0
d_p(m) x 10^3	1.0	1.0	1.0	0.5,1.0,4.0	1.0	1.0
ρ_s(kg/m³)	2950	2950,1200	1100	2950	2950	2950
ρ_L(kg/m³)	1000	1000	1000	1000	1000	1000
ΔP (Nm^{-2})	-	-	1000	-	-	-
k	1.5,0.0	1.5	1.5	1.5	1.5	1.5,0.0
μ (Ns m^{-2})	0.001	0.001	0.001	0.001	0.001	0.001
K	7.0	7.0	7.0	7.0	7.0	7.0

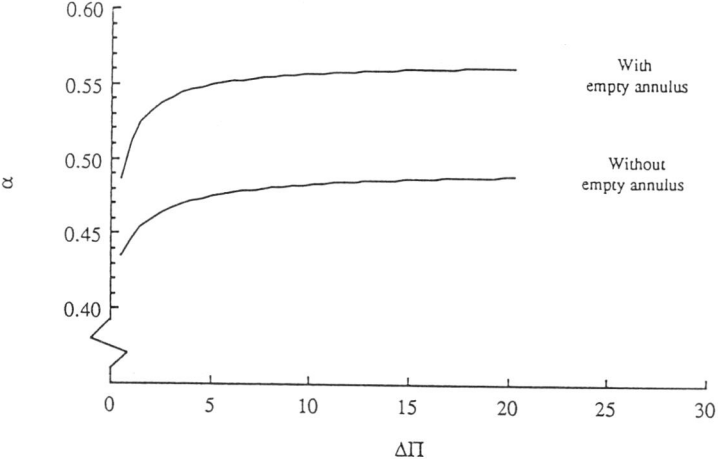

Figure 1. Simulation* of changes in the dimensionless driving pressure on the liquid discharge fraction for glass ballotini in water (with/without empty annulus).

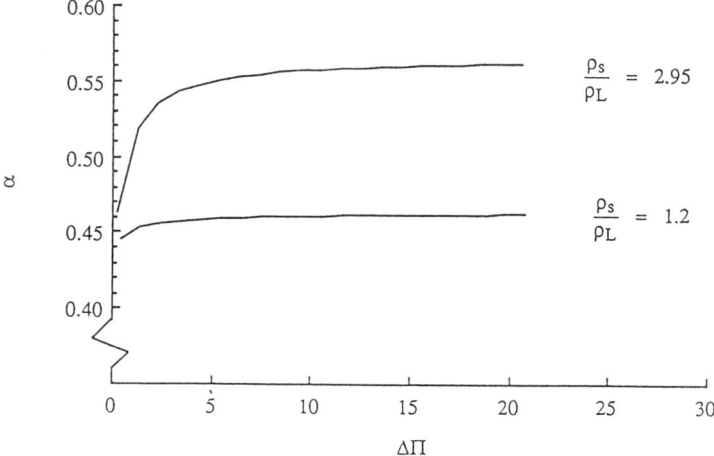

Figure 2. Simulation* of changes in the dimensionless driving pressure increase on the liquid discharge fraction illustrating the contrasting profiles of mixtures with a high and low density ratio.

*See Table 1 for conditions used in simulation.

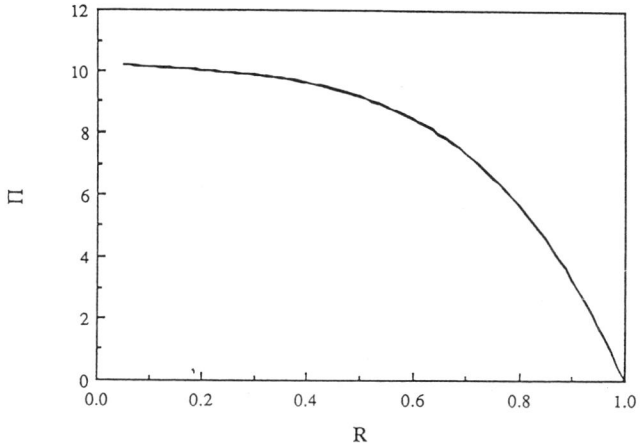

Figure 3. A simulation* of the stress and pressure profiles.

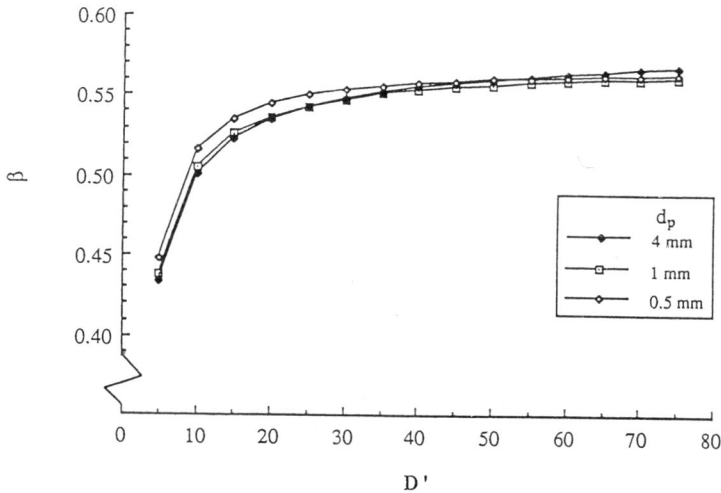

Figure 4a. Simulations of changes in the orifice to particle diameter ratio on the solid discharge fraction.

*See Table 1 for conditions used in simulation.

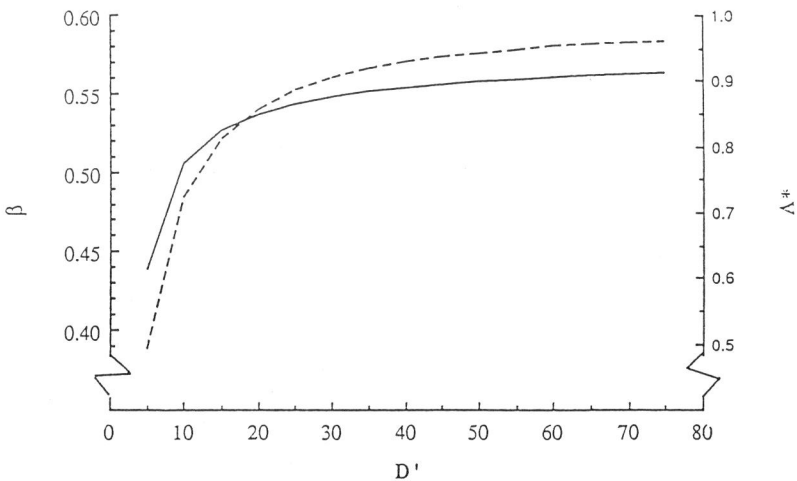

Figure 4b. Plot illustating the empty annulus effect with changes in D' for simulation shown in Figure 4a. {(----)A area available to solids flow/total area; (_____)β}

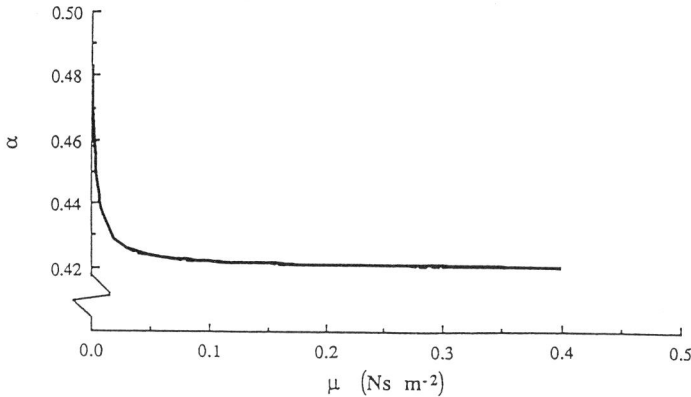

Figure 5. Simulation* of the effect on the liquid discharge fraction with changes in liquid viscosity.

*See Table 1 for conditions used in simulation.

AN ANALYTICAL MODEL FOR THE
CLEANING OF FOOD PROCESS PLANT

M R BIRD[†] and P J FRYER[††]

The ubiquitous and tenacious nature of fouling deposit in the food industry necessitates frequent cleaning. Any increase in understanding cleaning mechanisms will improve the hygienic operation of process plant, and a reduction in cleaning solution consumption has the benefit of a reduced environmental impact, and a consequent reduction in effluent treatment costs. Experiments have been carried out to study the removal of whey and whole milk protein deposits from stainless steel surfaces by chemical cleaning agents. Results are presented which show the favourable effect of temperature and flow rate, and the existence of an optimum cleaning solution concentration. Deposit removal occurs by the swelling and subsequent breakup of material into aggregates. The process has been modelled using a simple analytical approach.

THE CLEANING OF PROCESS PLANT

Food plant must be kept as clean as is practically possible. During processing plant can become contaminated both microbiologically and by fouling deposit caused by thermal degradation of the food stream. Cleaning is needed both for microbiological reasons and to restore the pressure drop and heat transfer characteristics of process plant. Complex cleaning-in-place (CIP) techniques have been developed empirically; although cleaning is common in the food industry, the kinetics and processes involved are poorly understood. Two types of treatment are used (Timperley and Smeulders, 1987):

- *two stage* cleaning using both acid and alkali, commonly sodium hydroxide, followed, after rinsing, with nitric or phosphoric acid.
- *single stage* cleaning with formulated detergents, which contain compounds to enhance cleaning, such as surface active and chelating agents.

These cleaning chemicals are expensive and in some cases environmentally damaging (Graßhoff, 1988). In addition, the time spent cleaning can be substantial. An increased understanding of the kinetics of cleaning which lead to a reduction in chemical usage or plant down time would be industrially useful. The mechanisms of fouling from milk fluids at pasteurisation temperatures is reasonably well understood (Belmar-Beiny et al, 1991). Both proteins (mainly ß-lactoglobulin) and minerals (mainly calcium phosphate) are deposited. The final deposit, seen in Figure 1, consists of protein aggregates c.a. 1 - 5µm in diameter. Lalande et al (1985) used ß-lactoglobulin denaturation kinetics to model fouling, but the controlling step appears to be protein aggregation, either in the bulk or on the wall (Gotham et al, 1989, Lalande and René, 1988). The rate of fouling is a function of bulk and heating surface temperatures, fluid flow rate and system chemistry. Cleaning is also a multistage process (Sandu et al, 1985). A fouled system consists of three phases, the fouled surface, the deposit and the cleaning solution, and cleaning involves steps which may be controlled by mass transfer, diffusion and reaction. Cleaning agent moves to the solid-liquid interface, and contacts the deposit. The solution then wets and reacts with the deposit, which is then removed. Any of these steps can control the overall process. This paper outlines experimental work to study cleaning and describes a simple model which can be used to analyse the cleaning process. Full details

[†]School of Chemical Engineering, University of Bath,.
[††]Department of Chemical Engineering, University of Cambridge.

are given in Bird (1992); the aim of the work is the development of models which can be used in the hygienic design of process plant.

EXPERIMENTAL

The cleaning process is difficult to study. Bird and Fryer (1991) report an experimental study in which the cleaning of a reproducible and uniform deposit was studied as function of temperature, Reynolds number and cleaning agent (sodium hydroxide) concentration. Two sets of apparatus were used; the first was a fouling rig in which a 2m length of stainless steel tube could be uniformly fouled by whey proteins, and the second was a cleaning rig in which sections of the fouled tube were cleaned under known conditions. The rate of removal of protein was measured by assaying the liquid leaving the stainless steel test section. The cleaning of a fouled stainless steel plate was also studied visually in a glass apparatus.

Cleaning experiments were conducted on both whey and whole milk soils over a wide range of thermo-hydraulic conditions. Figure 2 shows a typical cleaning curve; the rate of removal of deposit is first low and then builds up to a maximum before falling back to zero. The figure also shows the parameters used to characterise the process; the peak cleaning rate, the time to the peak rate, and the overall cleaning time, defined as the time for removal to fall to 2% of the maximum value. It was found that:

(i)   the removal of deposit was non-uniform; on contact with sodium hydroxide, a swollen translucent layer developed on the surface of the deposit which became thicker until all the deposit had swelled. Cleaning occurred by the removal of aggregates from this layer rather than uniformly,

(ii)   the temperature dependence of the cleaning process was considerable. The time to clean decreased dramatically on increasing the temperature, being typically three times shorter at 70°C than at 50°C.

(iii) the cleaning rate increased as a smooth function of increasing liquid velocity,

(iv)   cleaning showed a complex concentration dependence. There is an optimal concentration of sodium hydroxide of 0.5wt%, which results in the shortest cleaning time. The time to clean a surface using 2wt% sodium hydroxide was over three times as long as when 0.5% caustic was used.

Figure 3 shows the cleaning time of a whey protein soil as a function of sodium hydroxide concentration, at 50°C and a velocity of 0.174m/s, Re = 1730. The presence of a concentration optimum can be clearly seen. Too high a sodium hydroxide concentration gives a swelled deposit which is difficult to remove. Figures 4-6 show SEMs of the surface of the deposit contacted with concentrations of 0.1, 0.5 and 2wt% sodium hydroxide at 50°C for 2 minutes. Figure 4 shows that at a low concentration, sodium hydroxide reacts with the deposit to create a smooth surface, which may well be difficult to remove. In the region of the optimum, at 0.5wt%, Figure 5 shows that the deposit has been transformed into a more open, cellular structure of a high voidage. The use of 2wt% sodium hydroxide, which is sometimes recommended for industrial practice, produces a matrix where the cellular structure is still present, but the voidage is significantly reduced in comparison to Figure 5. Visually, the use of 2wt% sodium hydroxide turns the deposit from a creamy white to a burnt brown colour. The rate of removal of this brown layer is very low.

MODELLING

Experiments have demonstrated that the cleaning process takes place in two stages (i) the transformation of deposit by sodium hydroxide into a form which can be removed, and (ii) the removal of that deposit in aggregates by fluid shear. The process can be modelled using Monte Carlo techniques (Bird et al, 1992), but its essential features can be studied using a model kept deliberately simple but which reflects the events seen during visualisation. The aim of the model is to determine temperature and velocity effects on cleaning, rather than analyse the complex chemistry of cleaning illustrated above. Perlat (1986) describes a complex set of four differential equations to model diffusion and reaction in a two-layered deposit. Here we choose a simpler set of two equations. The deposit, of initial thickness δ, is considered as two layers: an upper layer of swelled deposit which can be removed, of thickness $x\delta$, and a lower layer of thickness $y\delta$ of deposit which is not yet removable. The equations governing the rate of change of thickness of the two layers are simply expressed as:

$$\frac{dy\delta}{dt} = -k_y \tag{1}$$

$$\frac{dx\delta}{dt} = k_y - k_x\, x\delta \tag{2}$$

i.e. that the rate of change of non-removable deposit y to removable deposit x is constant, and the rate of loss of removable deposit is proportional to the thickness of that deposit. Equation (2) can be integrated to give:

$$x = \frac{k_y}{\delta k_x}(1 - \exp(-k_x t)) \tag{3}$$

and the rate of removal can then be written as:-

$$\text{Rate of removal} = R = k_x\ \delta x = k_y(1 - \exp(-k_x t)) \qquad 0 < t < t^* \tag{4}$$

Equation (4) will apply until all the deposit has changed into a removable form at $t^* = \delta/k_y$. The maximum rate of removal occurs at $t = t^*$:-

$$R_{max} = k_x\ \delta x_{max} = k_y\left(1 - \exp\left[-\frac{\delta k_x}{k_y}\right]\right) \tag{5}$$

For $t > t^*$ the rate of removal falls with x:

$$x = x_{max} \exp(-k_x(t - t^*)); \quad R = R_{max} \exp(-k_x(t - t^*)) \quad t > t^* \tag{6}$$

The combination of equations (4) and (6) gives the cleaning curve , as shown in Figure 7. The model gives a similar shape to that found experimentally. Although it must represent a considerable simplification of the actual processes which are occuring, it has the advantage of simplicity. Some parts of the curve are functions of only one kinetic process:

(i)   the time to reach the maximum cleaning rate is dependent on the time required to convert all the deposit to a removable form, i.e. on k_y rather than both processes,

(ii) the drop from the peak removal rate depends only on the removal process, i.e. on k_x; for example, the time for the removal rate to drop to half that of the peak rate is $t_{1/2}$ so that:-

$$k_x = \frac{\ln 2}{t_{1/2}} \tag{7}$$

In contrast, both the initial rate of increase of the cleaning rate and the overall cleaning time are functions of both kinetic processes. This suggests that it might be better to analyse and model sections of cleaning curve rather than whole curves.

Experimental data can be simply analysed using this model to examine the variation of k_x and k_y. Figures 8 and 9 show these parameters plotted as Arrhenius functions of temperature, for a whey protein deposit cleaned with a 1 wt% sodium hydroxide solution at a velocity of 0.174 m/s. A reasonable straight line fit is produced in both cases; activation energies of 46 and 59 kJ/mole are found for the swelling and removal processes respectively.

These activation energies are lower than would be expected for reaction processes. It might be expected that the removal rate is mass transfer controlled; the low activation energy for the transformation of bound to removable deposit suggests that this may also be diffusion controlled.

CONCLUSIONS

Experiments have been conducted to investigate the variation of cleaning rate with process variables. The time to clean a surface appears to be a very stong function of the concentration of sodium hydroxide; considerable differences can be seen in the morphology of deposits treated with different concentrations. The process has been modelled using a higly simplistic approach which suggests that the rate-controlling processes are diffusion rather than reaction based. More sophisticated models are under development.

ACKNOWLEDGEMENTS

The authors wish to acknowledge the financial support of Lever Industrial and the SERC, together with the assistance of Dr APM Hasting of URL Colworth.

REFERENCES

Belmar-Beiny, MT, Gotham, SM, Fryer, PJ and Pritchard, AM, 1991, 'The effect of Reynolds number and fluid inlet temperature in whey protein fouling', presented at AIChemE Food Engineering Conf., Chicago, IL, March 1991, and submitted to *J.Fd.Eng.* (1991).

Bird, MR, 1992, PhD dissertation to be submitted, University of Cambridge.

Bird, MR and Fryer, PJ,1991, 'An experimental study of the cleaning of surfaces fouled by whey proteins,*Trans. IChemE C*, **69**, 13-21.

Bird, MR, Gladden, LF and Fryer, PJ, 1992, *Chem. Eng. Sci.* in preparation.

Grashoff, A, 1988, 'Zum Einflug der chemischen Komponenten alkalischer Reiniger auf die Kinetik der Ablosung festverkrusteter Belage aus Milchbestandteilen von Erhitzerplatten' *Kieler Milchwirtschaftliche Forschungberichte*, **40**, 3, 139.

Gotham, SM, Fryer, PJ and Pritchard, AM, 1989, 'Model studies of food fouling' in HG Kessler and DB Lund (eds.)*Fouling and Cleaning in Food Processing,* pp 1-13 (Munich Univ., FRG)

Lalande, M and Rene, F, 1988, 'Fouling by milk and dairy products and cleaning of heat exchange surfaces' in L Melo, TR Bott, and CA Bernardo (eds) *Fouling Science and Technology,* NATO ASI E 145, 557, (Kluwer, Amsterdam).

Lalande, M, Tissier, JP and Corrieu,G, 1985, 'Fouling of heat transfer related to b-lactoglobulin denaturation during heat processing of milk' *Biotech.Prog.*, 1,131.

Perlat, MN,1986, 'Etude du nettoyage des exchangeurs a plaques destines a la pasteurisation et a la sterilisation a ultra-haute-temperature du lait' Ph.D thesis UST 1 Lille, France.

Sandu, S, Lund, D, and Plett, EA, 1985, 'Fouling and cleaning of heat exchangers- a definition of terms' in DB Lund, C Sandu, and EA Plett (eds)*Fouling and Cleaning in Food Processing,* pp 3-21 (University of Wisconsin, USA).

Timperley, DA, and Smeulders, CNM, Cleaning of dairy HTST plate heat exchangers: comparison of single and two stage procedures *J.Soc. Dairy Tech.*, **40**,1, 4, (1987).

NOMENCLATURE

k_x	first order rate constant	s^{-1}
k_y	zero order rate constant	$m\ s^{-1}$
R	rate of removal	$m\ s^{-1}$
R_{max}	maximum removal rate	$m\ s^{-1}$
t	time	s
t^*	time to reach maximum removal rate	s
$t_{1/2}$	time for the removal rate to drop to half of the maximum	s
x	fraction of initial deposit thickness which has swollen	-
x_{max}	maximum thickness fraction of swollen deposit	-
y	fraction of initial deposit thickness which is unswollen	-
δ	initial deposit thickness	m

Figure 1. SEM of deposit formed from a 3.5wt% whey protein solution under pasteurisation conditions.

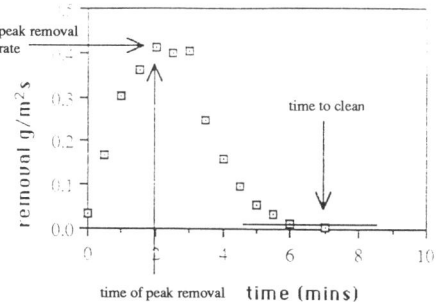

Figure 2. Typical cleaning curve showing whey protein soil cleaned with 1wt% NaOH at 70°C and 0.175m/s.

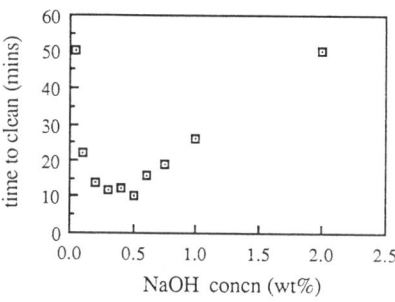

Figure 3. Time to clean as a function of NaOH concentration, showing the existence of an optimum. For whey protein deposit cleaned at 50°C and 0.174 m/s.

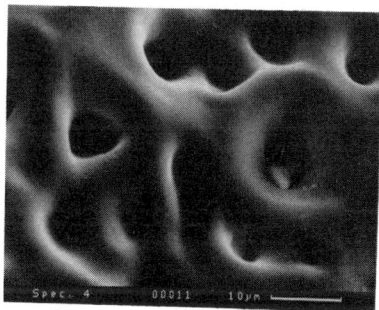

Figure 4. SEM of whey protein deposit surface contacted with 0.1wt% NaOH at 50°C for 2 minutes.

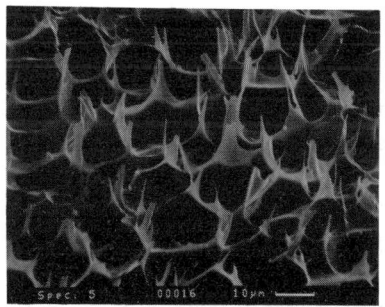

Figure 5. Deposit contacted with 0.5wt% NaOH at 50°C for 2 minutes.

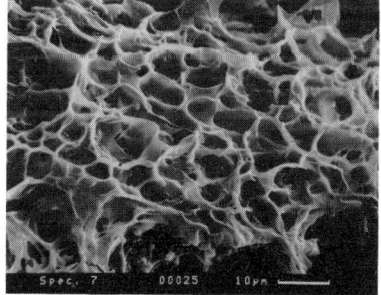

Figure 6. Deposit contacted with 2.0wt% NaOH at 50°C for 2 minutes.

329

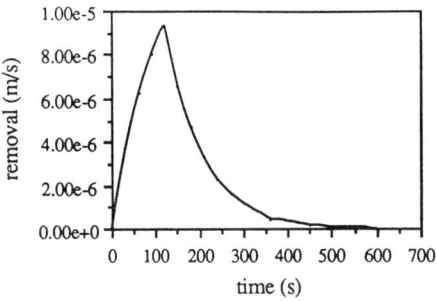

Figure 7. Cleaning curve predicted by analytical
model for conditions shown experimentally in figure 2.

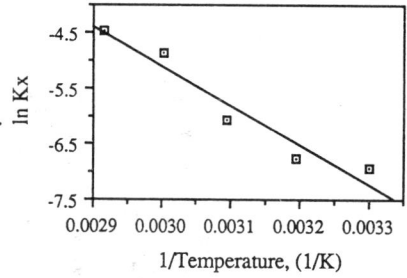

Figure 8. k_y plotted as an Arrhenius function
of temperature for whey protein deposit cleaned with
1wt% NaOH at 0.174m/s.

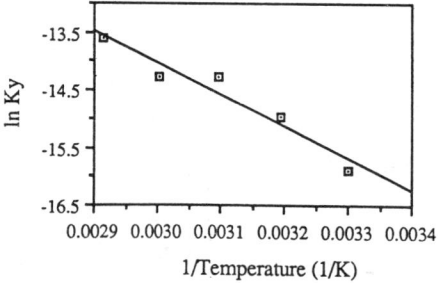

Figure 9. k_x plotted as an Arrhenius function of
temperature for whey deposit cleaned with
1wt% NaOH at 0.174m/s.

ULTRASONICS - THE APPLICATION TO

TEMPERATURE MEASUREMENT IN THE FOOD INDUSTRY

P.S. Richardson*

Ultrasonic technology offers the potential for many measurements, in particular non-invasive measurements based on measurement of sound velocity or alternative. The measurement of temperature is centred around the dependence of the velocity of ultrasound in a material in the temperature of that material. Two systems are described, the first being an invasive probe with demonstrated accuracy of better than ±0.5°C, and the second a non-invasive system with demonstrated accuracy of ±1°C for a range of flow velocities.

1. Introduction

Temperature measurement is central to many food processing operations in order to ensure the microbiological and organoleptic quality of food products. Traditionally, electrical methods have been used to measure temperatures, including thermocouples, thermistors and platinum resistance thermometers. These devices are not always the most suitable for a given application; for example, in microwave ovens the electrical field will interact with the sensor, so causing erroneous readings. Hygienic design of the sensor systems is often required, for example in the case of aseptic processing. An ultrasonic sensor offers potential solutions to both these problems in that it can be installed so that the sensing is achieved non-invasively and non-intrusively, and also for microwave environments when the electrical components would be physically separated from the electrical fields. In concept, ultrasonic temperature measurement is possible because the variation of the velocity of ultrasound in a body is dependent on the temperature of the body, and so measurements of time of flight by transmission or reflection can be used to infer the temperature of the medium under test. In our invasive sensor the temperature coefficient of expansion also contributed to the change in time of flight with temperature.

Previous work has illustrated the application of ultrasonic techniques to temperature measurement (Richardson, 1989), although at higher temperatures and at lower levels of resolution than would be required for the food industry.

*   Campden Food and Drink Research Association, Chipping Campden, Glos, GL55 6LD, UK

2. Experimental Programme and Equipment

The signal generator used was a Hewlett Packard 8116A, which allowed the generation of both continuous and burst signals in a variety of waveforms at frequencies up to 50 MHz. In order to perform the analysis of the waveform, it was necessary to have a high frequency oscilloscope which had sufficient resolution to capture the signal. A LeCroy 9400 oscilloscope was chosen because of its capabilities in this area and its potential for general purpose interface bus (GPIB) control, allowing remote operation and further data capture and analysis. A pre-amplifier was used to enhance the reflected signals entering the LeCroy 9400. The equipment layout is shown in Figure 1. Both the signal generator and the oscilloscope were controllable on the GPIB interface, allowing data handling within software, together with further data analysis. Commercially available double ultrasonic transducers were used for all experiments (Sonatest TMP3 transducers). One useful feature within the LeCroy 9400 oscilloscope was its ability to trigger off the desired part of the echo train. This permitted measurements of the time of flight in the sensing tip of the temperature to be made independently from the time of flight in the transmission rod. This facility was not required for the measurement technique used for the non-invasive sensor.

The principle of operation of the invasive sensor is illustrated in Figure 1. The probe consists of a rod of two different metals, brass and magnesium, chosen for their low attenuation of ultrasound. The magnesium tip was chosen for its high coefficient of linear expansion with temperature. It was decided to use a 5 MHz burst of ultrasound for this work because of the narrow pulse width that could be achieved. The materials chosen for the sensor designs exhibited a degree of acoustic mi· atch in order that some of the sound would be reflected from the transmission rod/sensing tip boundary. If the mismatch had been too great, no sound would enter the sensing tip. However, it if was too small, none would be reflected at the joint between rod and tip. In selecting materials for the sensing tip, it was necessary to consider the interaction of the temperature coefficient of thermal expansion and velocity.

It was found that the effect of the coefficients of expansion and velocity operate in opposite ways to provide the characteristic response of the velocity of ultrasound in the given material to changes in temperature.

Various shapes of rod were investigated (Figure 2), i.e. parallel and tapered, to determine the optimum shape for the transmission rod, so minimising side wall reflections. Rod 4 was selected for further trials and calibration for temperature measurement.

2.1 Invasive Sensor Development

For both invasive and non-invasive systems, it is possible to calculate the position of the echo train as a function of temperature based on physical data about the transmission of ultrasound in the medium concerned.

Consider rod 4 illustrated in Figure 2.

By triggering off the first echo, it is possible to evaluate the change in the tip echo positions as a function of temperature, i.e. the change in time of flight per degree Kelvin:

1st echo	6.79E-10 seconds
2nd echo	1.36E-09 seconds
3rd echo	2.04E-09 seconds

4th echo	2.72E-09 seconds
5th echo	3.39E-09 seconds

For maximum sensitivity in terms of timer resolution on the oscilloscope (0.01 nS), the highest order detectable echo should be used for the temperature measurement, because of the increased path length and hence greater change in time of flight for a given change in temperature because of the greater number of passes that the sound will have made in the tip.

To test the invasive sensor, the equipment described in section 2 was set to produce a 16 V burst of ultrasound of frequency 5.86 MHz and width 9 pulses. The oscilloscope was set to trigger off the first echo returning to it, so negating any temperature effects in the transmission rod.

The sensing tip was immersed in a temperature controlled water bath along with calibrated platinum resistance thermometers. A position in the fifth echo was nominated and tracked as the temperature was changed in the water bath. Sufficient time was allowed between each change for the bath to equilibrate.

2.2   Non-invasive Sensor Development

Similarly, ultrasonics offers a technique of non-invasive temperature measurement which may be interpreted in terms of bulk product temperature. The principle of the sensor is the same as for the invasive probe, but here there is no transmission rod or tip. The measurement is made directly by recording the change in the velocity of ultrasound in the product itself as a function of temperature.

Consider the flow rig illustrated in Figure 3.

Assuming a linear characteristic of the change in velocity of ultrasound in water with temperature in this temperature range, the change in time of flight per degree centigrade is 0.03 μs per pass, so, as before, there is an advantage in using a higher order echo to gain a greater sensitivity to velocity changes due to temperature.

The tests for the non-invasive sensor are illustrated in Figure 3. The 5 MHz dual probe was attached to the outside of a 2" pipe (vertical) in which water was flowing. The temperature of the water was controlled and monitored conventionally with a calibrated type-T thermocouple close to the point where the ultrasonic temperature measurement was taking place. The experimental rig is illustrated in Figure 3. The temperature of the water in the rig was varied between 285 K and 333 K, and also the flow of water varied between 15 l min^{-1} and 60 l min^{-1}. Four of the echo positions were recorded together, with a strong peak in the third echo. The effect of flowrate on the time of flight measured was found to be very small over this range of flowrate. In the case of the third echo, it was found to change the echo position by 0.02 μs between 15 l min^{-1} and 60 l min^{-1} for a given temperature. This is equivalent to a plant throughput of between 900 l hr^{-1} and 3600 l hr^{-1}. This could be a potential source of error if very high levels of accuracy, e.g. better than $\pm$ 0.1 K were being required. If this was the case, a correlation of time of flight with temperature and flowrate would be required. Consideration of the curvature in the velocity versus temperature graph for water would play an important part in calibrating the sensor over a wide range of temperature and would improve the accuracy of the system.

3.   Results, Discussion and Conclusion

Invasive sensor: the results for the measurement of variation of time of flight with temperature are plotted in Figure 4. The value of change in time per degree Kelvin was found to be 0.038 μs/K.

Considering first the invasive probe, the potential application cited was to the temperature measurement in microwave ovens. A possible installation technique may involve the ultrasonic transducer being attached to the outside of the oven cavity, with a liquid filled transmission rod attached to the inside surface and the sensing tip embedded in the food product that is to be tested. Such an installation has the advantage of having the electronics outside the microwave field, physically separated from the electric field environment. One reason for some of the errors in the experimental work to date are the difficulties in creating an optically parallel joint between the tip and the transmission rod. The use of epoxy resins is quite good from the ultrasonic viewpoint. However, their use at elevated temperatures may be limited because of bond structure causes, which may be the reason for the deviation from the straight line above 340 K.

Non-invasive sensor: a frequency of 5.14 MHz was used with a sound burst of width 14 cycles. Figure 5 represents the time change of a point within the second echo within the echo train (i.e. in the product). The observed value, based on the regressed results, is 0.060 μS/K. Statistical analysis of the results shows an R^2 value of 0.9898. If a wider temperature range had been investigated, it is likely that a polynomial fit would be more appropriate, as the velocity of sound as a function of temperature in water is not linear.

The non-invasive probe will have many applications in the food industry, providing the propagation of the ultrasound is not adversely affected by some of the food components. Likely applications would be to milk and fruit juice processing lines or to beer lines, providing that gas breakout could be prevented as this would make the technique impossible to use. It must be stressed that the application of an ultrasonic thermometer, although non-invasive in its operation, is unlikely to be a strap-on device because of the need for careful engineering of the cell in which the temperature measurement will be made. The non-invasive measuring technique has appeal in that it is totally hygienic and currently has no competitor. One difficulty is the need to calibrate the probe for each and every product, as the temperature sensing is achieved by looking at changes in the propagation of sound in the product. Other considerations must include the robustness of the ultrasonic transducer in terms of likely factory wash-down regimes and also the mechanism for attaching the transducer to the surface of the measurement cell in order to ensure a good and reliable bond for the transmission and receipt of ultrasound. It may be that seasonal variations in products is another consideration if they would affect the propagation of ultrasound. Tests are currently under way to evaluate the technique at higher temperatures for application to aseptic processing lines.

Acknowledgement

The contribution of the Department of Trade and Industry in partly funding this project is gratefully acknowledged.

References

Gopalsami, N. and Raptis, A.C. (1983). Proceedings of Ultrasonic Symposium, Atlanta, Georgia, USA, pp856-859.

Kay, G.W.C. and Labye, T.H. (1986). Tables of physical and chemical constants, 15th edition, Bath Avon Press, UK.

Landolt, H. and Bornstein, R. (1966). New Series 1966.

Lynnworth, L.C. and Papadakis, E.P. (1970). Proceedings of the 1970 Ultrasonics Symposium, San Francisco, California, USA, pp83-93.

Mayer, A.M. (1873). Phil. Mag. 45, 18.

Richardson, P.S. (1989). Food Manufacture, June, 43-46.

Richardson, P.S. (1989). Technical Memorandum No. 542, Campden Food and Drink Research Association, Chipping Campden, Glos, UK.

Satyabala, S.P., Madhusudan Rao, J., Sampath Kumar, J. and Mallikarjun Rao, S.P. (1980). Acoustic Letters 3 (1), 182.

Tasman, H.A. and Schmidt, H.E. (1972). High Temperatures - High Pressures 4 (4), 477-481.

Wilson, W.D. (1959). Journal of Acoustic Society of America 31 (8), 1067-1072.

Wiskersheim, K.A. (1988). Proceedings of Microwave Pack '88, London, UK.

Experimental Equipment

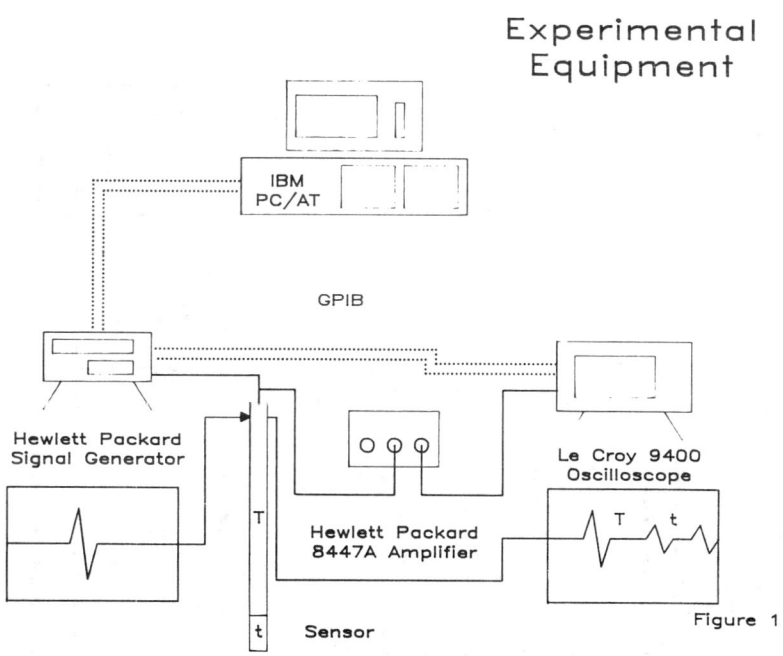

Figure 1

Design of Invasive Sensor

Examples Used for Sensor Development

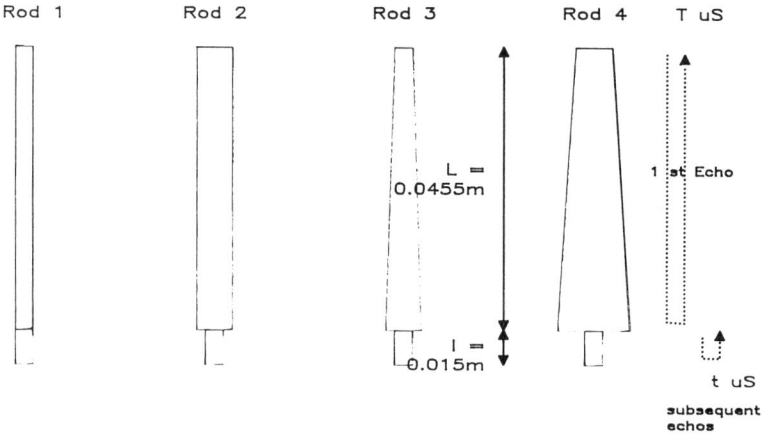

Figure 2

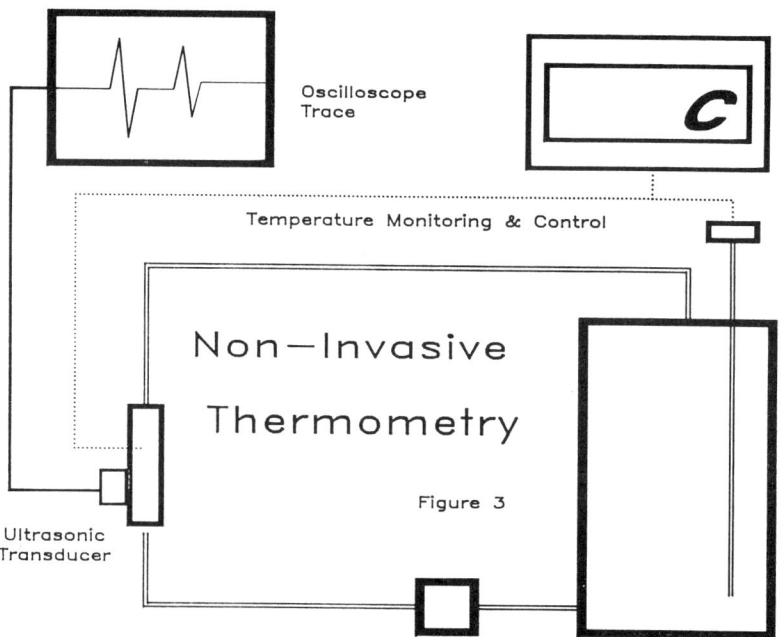

Figure 3

Ultrasonic Thermometer

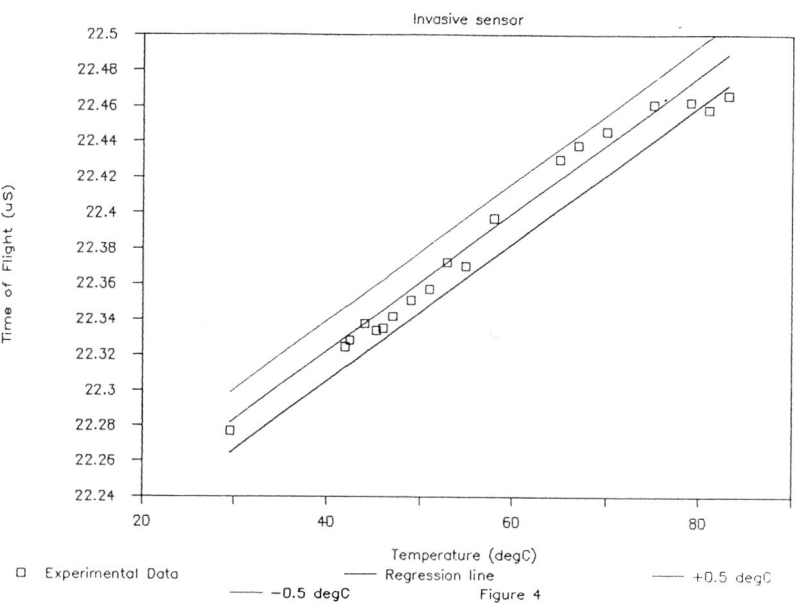

Figure 4

Ultrasonic Thermometer

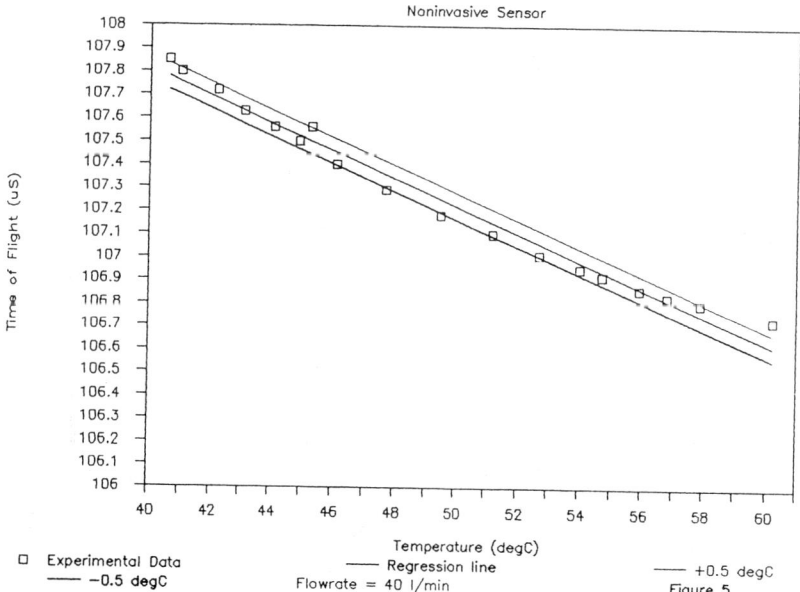

Figure 5

QUALITY ASSURANCE AND ENGINEERING TROUBLE SHOOTING USING
DATA LOGGERS IN THE BAKED FOODS INDUSTRIES.

M.E.WILLIAMSON *

Techniques are described for monitoring
process temperature profiles in baking
equipment using multichannel data loggers.
Particular reference is made to comparison
of profiles with standards and analysis of
hot and cold spots.

Introduction

Many commercial bakery production facilities use partially
automated processing equipment. After the ingredients have
been mixed to form the dough, individual dough pieces are
created for further processing to produce the final
product. Examples are biscuits, cakes, pies and bread. (1)

Two common processes are baking and cooling. Here the dough
pieces are transported on conveyors through tunnels which
are typically 800-3000 mm wide and up to 130 metres long.
Temperatures in these tunnels are controlled in zones,
often with separate set points above and below the
conveyor.

Two types of variability in finished product
characteristics (eg: weight, colour, moisture content,
shape, texture) are common problems for bakers (2):

1. Variability over time. Temperature setpoints are kept at
or close to some pre-determined profile which may be
trimmed as a result of direct observations of the product.
There are often conflicting opinions regarding which
temperature setpoints should be adjusted to correct
specific problems. Time dependant variability can be
gradual or occur as step changes.
For the operators, who see only the temperature values
displayed on their zonal temperature controllers, true
assessment of real time processing conditions is not
reliable using these instruments. Table 1 identifies some

* Fylde Thermal Engineering Limited

common causes of error between displayed temperatures and actual process temperatures.

2. Variability across the width of the conveyor. The severity of these variations may fluctuate, but if present they can not usually be eliminated using the controls available to the operator. Engineering modifications are often required to even out the heat and mass transfer occurring across the width of the tunnel.

For the maintenance engineers this presents a real problem in identifying where to start to look for the fault. On a 100 metre long oven, for example, much of the insulation may have to be removed, as well as hundreds of burners and possibly the conveyor.

A device that can ride the conveyor with the dough pieces and measure temperatures as it passes through a tunnel provides invaluable information for analysing both these problems. Using thermocouple technology, it's calibration can be easily checked against a known millivolt reference source at regular intervals without interfering with production. Such a device could be passed through the oven regularly on a shift by shift basis for quality assurance purposes, and used to compare conditions with established standard conditions. It could also be used by Maintenance Engineers to pin point problems, and by Design Engineers to test and optimise new tunnel designs.

FTE *Scorpion* Data Logging System

Extensive tests have been carried out over the last five years, using full scale tunnels, to develop a suitable device for use in the bakery environment.

The *Scorpion* data logger is a well insulated miniature circuit board that can communicate via an RS232 serial link to any IBM compatible personal computer. It has twenty type T thermocouples connected to it, which are arranged to measure ten conveyor temperatures and ten air temperatures above the conveyor. The sensors are mounted on a bar that spans the width of the conveyor so that readings can be taken across the width of the tunnel. The device is initialised by temporarily connecting it to the PC, and is then placed on the conveyor during a momentary gap in production. Once recovered at the out feed of the tunnel, the data logger is reconnected to the PC and the temperature data is automatically extracted. Graphical representation of the data is also generated at this time, and the data is saved to disk.

Results obtained so far have been encouraging. Figure 1 shows profiles from an exercise carried out on a ribbon burner natural convection/radiation biscuit oven in Toronto, Canada which revealed an unusual dip in the temperature profile. The associated thermal shock to the product was considered to be undesirable, and so a team of Maintenance Engineers stripped off the thermal insulation and outer cladding in the area of the oven corresponding to the dip. It was found that, during a recent modification to the oven, the inner bake chamber had not been rewelded. Cold air from the bakery was being sucked into the bake chamber at this point due to the negative pressure inside the chamber. The chamber was rewelded and the dip in the profile was eliminated, all within 24 hours.

Figure 2 shows the profiles obtained from a forced convection oven producing the same product on two different days, six months apart. It can be seen that there are significant differences, which may be attributable to a combination of factors (see table 1). This information enabled the bakery to re-establish their baking profile. An analysis of the spread of temperatures at any particular point compared to those in figure 1 reveals one of the major benefits of using forced convection systems. In a well designed forced convection system, heat transfer can be very even across the width of the conveyor.

Figure 3 shows a typical output from the quality assurance software package. It analyses the process temperatures both above and below the dough pieces and also analyses hot and cold spots within the oven, again for both top and bottom temperatures. The operator has a data base of standard profiles built into the software (these have been previously measured using the data logger and confirmed as standards so that they are saved for future reference).

Conclusions

A combination of electronic circuitry, suitable sensors and software data analysis packages have been developed for use in bakery heat transfer tunnels.

The information generated by the system has proved to correlate well with tunnel conditions and configurations and is therefore proven as a trouble shooting tool.

The use of the system as a quality assurance tool is currently being evaluated by several major biscuit manufacturers in the UK and in North America. Preliminary results are indicating acceptance by plant operators that the system enhances their understanding and control of processing equipment.

Acknowledgements

Burtons Gold Medal Biscuits have been actively involved in the development of the *Scorpion* system in the United Kingdom. Particular thanks are due to Mr Tom Docherty who had the foresight to see the value of the system.
Nabisco Biscuit Company in the United States of America have been willing partners in the testing of the quality assurance software.

References

(1)   Hallstrom B., Skjoldebrand C., Tragardu C. 1991
      Heat Transfer and Food Products
      Elsevier Applied Science London & New York

(2)   Wade P. 1988
      Biscuits, Cookies and Cracker Vol 1
      Elsevier Applied Science London & New York

TABLE 1

COMMON   CAUSES   OF   INCONSISTENCIES   BETWEEN   DISPLAYED
TEMPERATURES   AND   ACTUAL   PROCESSING   TEMPERATURES   FOR
CONTROLLERS USED ON ZONED BAKERY HEAT TRANSFER TUNNELS.

The sensors connected to the temperature controllers are
typically measuring at one point within a long section of
tunnel. This represents some arbitrary temperature between
the burner flames (>1000 C) and the centre of the dough
pieces (<=100 C)

Step Changes

-    Sudden movement of the temperature controller sensor
     in relation to the position of heat sources and heat
     sinks in the oven. Repositioning of the sensor after
     maintenance or physical impact during an oven jam-up
     are common causes.
-    Switching on or off of individual burners located
     close to the temperature controller sensor.
-    Opening or closing of inspection doors close to the
     temperature controller sensor.
-    Adjustments to the extraction or turbulence systems
     (if fitted).
-    Recalibration or replacement of any part of the
     temperature control instrumentation.
-    Engineering modifications to any part of the oven or
     its control systems.

Gradual Changes

-    Deterioration of the surface characteristics of the
     temperature controller sensor causing changes in the
     response to radiated energy.
-    Calibration drift in any part of the temperature
     control instrumentation.
-    Seasonal variations in the bakery ambient conditions
     affecting heat loss from the oven outer surfaces.
-    Deterioration of oven insulation due to age or
     accidental water spillage affecting heat loss from
     the outer surfaces of the oven.
-    Variable deterioration of thermal output for
     individual burners within a zone.

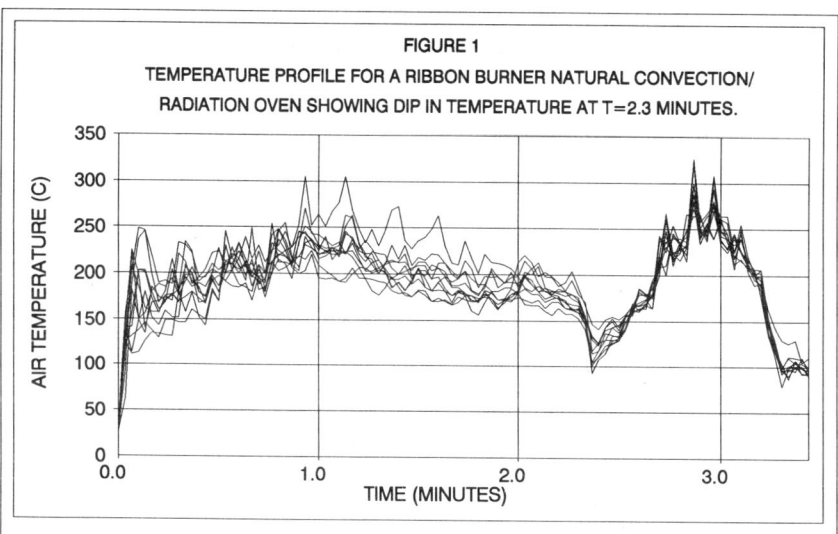

FIGURE 1

TEMPERATURE PROFILE FOR A RIBBON BURNER NATURAL CONVECTION/
RADIATION OVEN SHOWING DIP IN TEMPERATURE AT T=2.3 MINUTES.

FIGURE 2

TEMPERATURE PROFILE ON TWO DIFFERENT DAYS FOR THE SAME
PRODUCT BEING BAKED ON THE SAME FORCED CONVECTION OVEN.

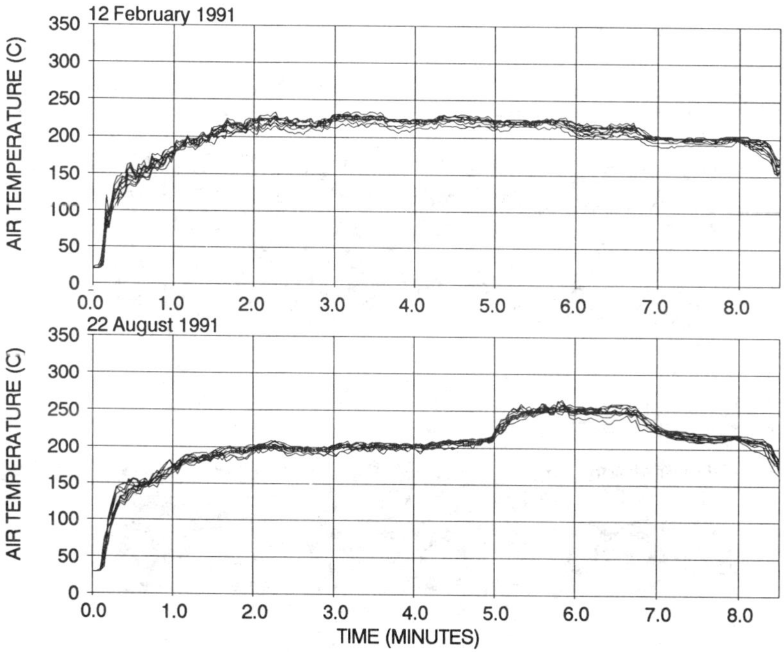

12 February 1991

22 August 1991

FIGURE 3

SCORPION QUALITY ASSURANCE SOFTWARE SCREEN DISPLAYS

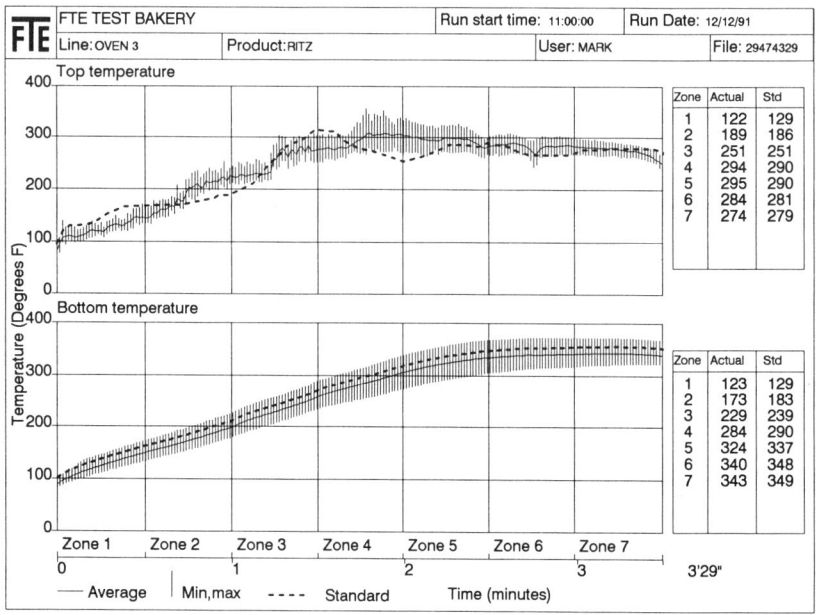

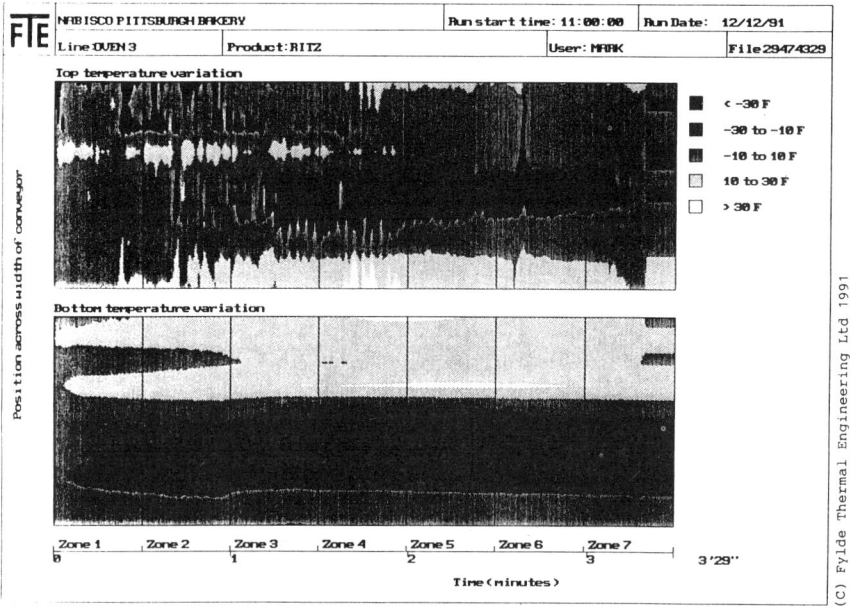

(C) Fylde Thermal Engineering Ltd 1991

THERMAL DATA STORAGE SYSTEM FOR FOOD FREEZING TUNNELS

W B BALD, Wolfson Unit for Applied Cryobiology, Dept of Biology &
P G LONG , York Electronics Centre, Dept of Electronics, University of York

Summary
The design and development of a prototype device for sampling the thermal characteristics of different food freezing tunnels is described. Initial tests show the variations in temperature and the heat transfer coefficient which have been measured in a liquid nitrogen tunnel and a static cold store. Further development of the software is proceeding to enable the device to be used for estimating freezing times of different products in varying food freezing environments.

Introduction
In order to improve the efficiency of both air blast and cryogenic food freezing tunnels and to predict the frozen state of products during their passage through the tunnel, the thermal characteristics of the tunnel must be known. This involves not only measuring the variation in temperature throughout the tunnel length but also determining variations in the heat transfer coefficient at different locations.

In addition to the size of the product and its thermal properties, the rate at which any particular product freezes is also dependent on the heat transfer coefficient multiplied by the instantaneous temperature difference between product and coolant.

This paper describes the development of a prototype thermal data storage system which is being used to monitor the thermal characteristics of different food freezing tunnels. The data stored in the device can be transferred on to a suitable PC (personal computer) where the temperature and heat transfer coefficients can be displayed as functions of time or location within the tunnel. The software is currently being extended to enable product freezing times to be estimated for different products which should improve the economic use of freezing tunnels.

Thermal Design

The basic principle underlying the design of the device is the application of the so called "lumped theory" of transient heat conduction to determine the heat transfer coefficient ($\bar{h}$) within any cooling medium. This theory shows that for any high thermal conductivity material the thermal gradients within the material are negligible provided the Biot modulus $B_i<<1$.

If, therefore, a probe of high conductivity material such as copper or aluminium is cooled during transport through a freezing tunnel, the relationship between the heat transfer coefficient and the cooling rate at any instant is given by

$$\bar{h} = \rho c \left(\frac{V}{A}\right) \frac{dT/dt}{(T-T_\infty)} \qquad (1)$$

where the various symbols are defined in the nomenclature

For a spherical copper probe equ (1) reduces to

$$\bar{h} = 0.51D \frac{dT/dt}{(T - T_\infty)} \qquad (2)$$

where D is measured in cms.

The device shown in figure 1 measures the temperature inside the probe T and the coolant temperature adjacent to the probe T_∞ during its passage through the tunnel. From these values the probe cooling rate dT/dt can be calculated at any instant and the corresponding heat transfer coefficient determined using equ (2).

Different probe diameters can be used for different tunnel designs depending on the tunnel's nominal operating temperature and the product passage time.

Electronic Design

The electronic unit stores the temperatures from the centre of the copper probe and the coolant temperature adjacent to the probe. It is also capable of storing the temperatures from up to four other thermocouple probes which may be inserted, by the user, into food products. The sampling interval is 0.25 seconds, allowing a total of 3600 consecutive points to be stored for each probe. The maximum time corresponding to this value is 15 minutes.

The unit contains a small microprocessor which samples the outputs from each probe, converts the values into temperatures and stores the results. Subsequently it also controls the unloading process when connected to the master computer. A calibration routine is also included to cater for physical variations from one probe to another.

The unit is powered from rechargeable batteries which are recharged when the unit is connected to the computer via the power supply.

The special low-profile insulated housing is capable of protecting the electronic circuits for up to 15 minutes at -200°C, still maintaining the full data recording facility and resolution of 0.1°C necessary for accurate heat transfer coefficient determination.

Results
Figure 2 shows the output from the device after its passage through a straight-belt, liquid nitrogen freezing tunnel. The lower curves are the recorded temperatures in the tunnel stream (T_∞) and in the probe as functions of passage time in the tunnel. The upper curve shows the variations in heat transfer coefficient at different locations within the tunnel.

Figure 3 shows the corresponding results obtained by placing the device in a static cold freezing chamber maintained at - 50°C. Again the upper curve illustrates the variations in heat transfer coefficient which occur in the chamber at the chosen locations.

Conclusions
1.   Initial tests on the prototype thermal data storage system show that the "lumped theory" approach is satisfactory for measuring transient heat transfer coefficients in food freezing tunnels. Figures 2 and 3 illustrate the typical variations which occur in different freezing environments.

2.   Further development of the software is currently being carried out to use the data of figures 2 and 3 to determine freezing times in real food products.

3.   The derived results obtained from this device can be used to ascertain surface boundary conditions which are necessary to predict cooling rates within products and to ascertain basic tunnel design parameters.

Acknowledgement
The authors wish to acknowledge the financial assistance provided by Air Products PLC in the part funding of this project and also design contributions from G. Cole, M. Chaplin and N. Bowyer.

Nomenclature

A	surface area of probe	(m^2)
c	specific heat of probe material	(KJ/KgC)
D	probe diameter	(m)
$\overline{h}$	heat transfer coefficient	(KW/m^2C)
T	instantaneous probe temperature	(C)
T_∞	bulk coolant temperature	(C)
dT/dt probe cooling rate		(C/s)
V	probe volume	(m^3)
ρ	density of probe material	(Kg/m^3)

Figure 1a External view of monitoring unit

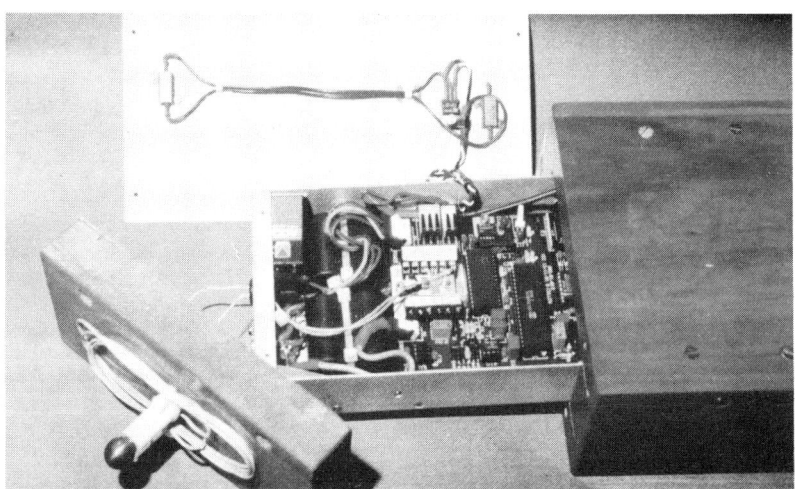

Figure 1b Exploded view of monitoring unit

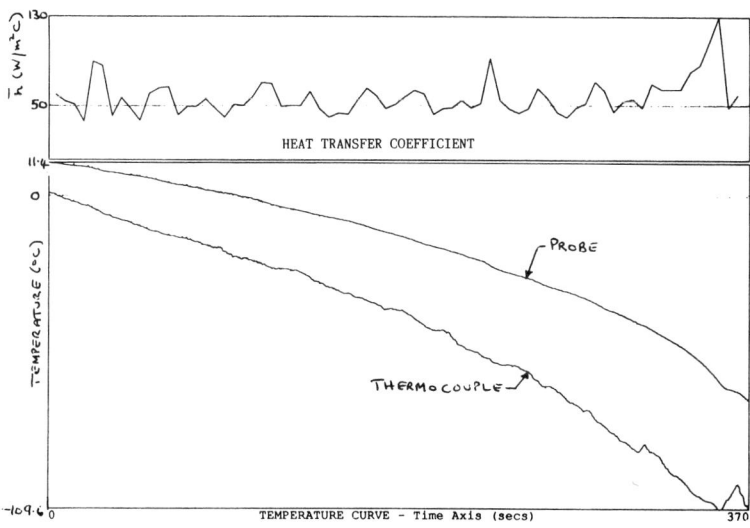

FIGURE 2

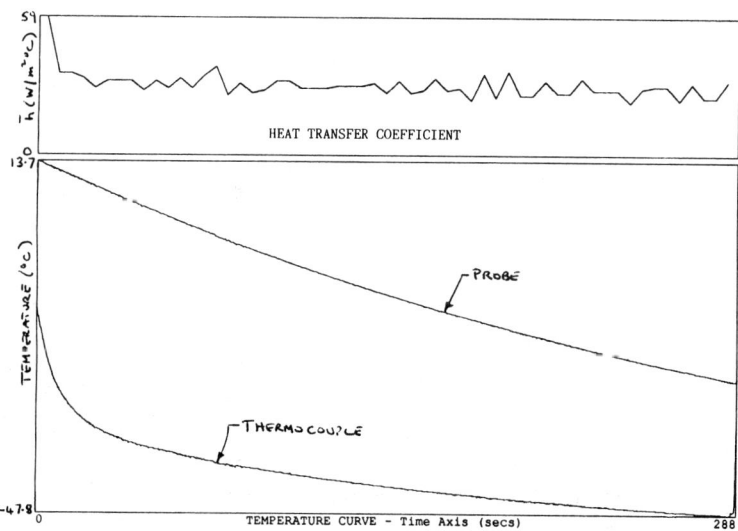

FIGURE 3

TRAVELLING HEAT FLUX SENSOR

IAN McFARLANE *

The paper describes the development of a
portable travelling heat flux sensor for
measuring the rate of heat transfer at the
baking surface in ovens used for bread, biscuits
and cakes. The work follows earlier work by the
Flour Milling and Baking Research Association on
heat flux measurement. The paper includes
results of tests in electric and gas fired pilot
scale ovens.

INTRODUCTION

In baking ovens, the time required for baking is well-known to
correlate with the rate of heat transfer into the product.
Sato et al (1987) measured the heat transfer into an aluminium
cylinder and reported correlation with baking of sponge cakes
in a laboratory oven, and Shibukawa et al (1989) reported
correlation of heat transfer measured by a similar method with
browning of cookies.

Christensen et al (1984) measured the energy absorbed in bread
baking and reported correlation with crust colour and
evaporation of moisture. Unklesbay and Unklesbay (1985)
studied the rapid baking of pizza bases in an infra-red tunnel
oven, Wade (1987) reported the accelerated baking of a wide
range of biscuit products using infra-red radiation with a
peak wavelength of 1200nm, and Skoldebrand and Andersson
(1989) demonstrated reduced baking times for bread using a
two-stage infra-red baking process. These studies show that
the baking process can be optimised for a very wide range of
products by consideration of factors affecting the rate of
heat transfer to the bulk of the product. In the present work,
conducted in collaboration with the Flour Milling and Baking
Research Association (FMBRA), Chorleywood, and with support
from the Energy Efficiency Office, Energy Technical Support
Unit (ETSU), Harwell Laboratory, a portable sensor has been
developed for direct measurement of heat transfer in any form
of baking process, enabling for example comparison to be made
between the efficiency of different forms of heat transfer at
different stages of baking.

*Beaconsfield Instrument Company Limited

The development of a travelling sensor follows work
extending over several years by Lawson and others at FMBRA,
which led to a fixed-point heat flux sensor. This fixed
point device has been fitted to a number of electric and
gas fired biscuit and bread ovens, and has demonstrated
further correlations between heat flux and product quality
(McFarlane 1989).

EQUIPMENT
The fixed point sensors have a surface with emissivity
similar to that of a flour-based product during baking
exposed in the baking chamber. The surface temperature is
maintained at a temperature similar to the temperature
reached within the bulk of the product during baking
(typically in the range 95 to 98 deg C). Thus the surface
experiences the same combination of convection and
radiation heat input as does the surface of the baked
product at an equivalent stage during baking.

Heat flux at the surface is proportional to the temperature
difference between two sensors mounted at each end of a
short calibrated heat path joining the exposed surface to a
heat sink whose temperature is controlled so as to maintain
the exposed surface at 95 to 98 deg C.

Fixed point probes constructed to date have a response time
of the order of one minute. This is fast enough to respond
to the slowly changing conditions at a particular position
within an oven, but not fast enough for a travelling probe.

The Beaconsfield Instrument fixed point Q-dot probe uses a
solid cylindrical sensor with an exposed surface area of
10 sq cm and the heat collected (up to 40 watts) is removed
from the baking chamber using a heat pipe. The travelling
probe developed for the present work has a flat square
sensor with an exposed upper surface area of 1.5 sq cm
(fig 1). The response time is correspondingly reduced.
The portable sensor is part of an assembly with overall
dimensions 640 x 200 x 50 mm which also includes an
insulated battery powered proprietary data logger. Data is
recorded during use at programmable intervals of 2 to 20
seconds, and subsequently transmitted to a desk-top or
portable computer for analysis.

There is limited electrical power available in such a
battery powered system, and the portable sensor is
consequently not equipped with temperature control for the
exposed surface. Instead the data is subsequently corrected
for the difference between the actual temperature TS at the
surface and the nominal temperature of 95C. For most ovens
or processes, a linear correction is sufficient. In
exceptional sets of conditions within the baking chamber,
it is possible to make successive passes with the sensor to
collect data with TS < 95C and then with TS > 95C, and
calculate the heat flux at TS = 95C by interpolation.

CALIBRATION
There are two methods for calibration. One method
uses a transfer standard, and is applicable for the
fixed point as well as for the portable style of
sensor.

The secondary method, for the portable sensor only, is
based on integrating the heat collected by measuring
the temperature rise in the associated heat sink of
which the heat capacity has previously been measured.

A flat cylindrical chamber has been built for primary
calibration, 800 mm diameter and 120 mm in height,
controllable in temperature between 90 and 250C and
with controllable circumferential air velocity from
0.5 to 5m/sec. A 20g copper test slab with an
embedded Pt resistance thermometer, with exposed
surface of 10.5 sq cm and heat capacity (found by
calorimetry) of 2.05 cal/deg, is lowered into the
circumferential air stream at preselected air
velocities and air temperatures. The rate of increase
of slab temperature in deg/sec as the slab reaches 95C
is noted. By this means a set of chamber conditions
was established giving known rates of heat transfer as
follows:

Air temp	Air velocity	Rate of change of slab temp	Heat flux
deg C	m/sec	deg/sec	watts/sq/cm
120	0.5	.17	.15
	3.0	.25	.22
150	0.5	.52	.45
	3.0	.69	.60
180	0.5	1.05	.91
	3.0	1.22	1.06

The fixed and portable sensors are initially calibrated by
exposing the sensor surfaces in the circumferential air
stream of the test chamber at each of these known sets of
conditions.

The calibration of the portable sensor can be verified when
in use by noting that the 1500g mild steel heat sink has a
heat capacity (also found by calorimetry) of 190 cal/deg.
Thus, when the 1.5 sq cm exposed surface is collecting
1 watt/sq cm, the heat sink will absorb 1.5 joules/sec, and
warm up at the rate of (1.5 x 60)/(4.18 x 190) or
0.113 deg/min.

RESULTS
The portable sensor has been used in two ovens
equipped with impingement nozzles, one electric and
one gas-fired. In both cases comparison was made
between conditions of maximum and minimum pressure in
the plenum chambers upstream from the nozzles.

Oven A is a two zone electric oven in the biscuit
bakery at FMBRA. Fig 2a shows the heat flux and
chamber temperature data for 6 minutes bake time, with
oven settings:

	Zone 1	2	
Zone temperature	184	176	C
Plenum damper setting	1/2	1/2	

Fig 2b shows data for the same oven, about 45 minutes
later, with the circulation reduced in zone 1 and
increased in zone 2.

Zone temperature	186	196	C
Plenum damper setting	closed	open	

Oven B is a three zone gas fired pilot oven at Spooner
Vicars, Ilkley. Fig 3a shows the heat flux and
chamber temperature data for 6 minutes bake time, with
oven settings:

	Zone 1	2	3	
Plenum temperature	205	205	205	C
Plenum pressure	.22	.24	.29	in wg

Fig 3b shows data for the same oven, about 30 minutes
later, with the plenum pressures increased in all 3 zones.

Plenum temperature	205	205	205	C
Plenum pressure	.66	.93	.87	in wg

DISCUSSION
Both the test ovens have means to alter the height of the
nozzles above the baking surface. During the tests with
oven A, the nozzles were set at a low height, about 100mm
above the baking surface. At half or full circulation
settings, the effect of individual nozzles can be seen in
the heat flux data. It can be seen from fig 2 that closing
dampers in the first half of the oven and opening them in
the second half approximately doubles the rate of heat
transfer in the second half relative to the first, while
the temperatures remain within +/- 15 deg of each other.

The results to date cover only a small part of the range of conditions encountered in baking ovens, but they strongly support the conclusion already reached at FMBRA and elsewhere that heat flux gives a much more useful measure of oven performance than temperature measurement alone.

During the tests with oven B, the nozzles were set at maximum heights about 230mm above the baking surface. Lower plenum pressures in the first half of the oven cause an irregular pattern of heat transfer. Subsequent tests in a number of full size commercial ovens, baking a variety of products, confirm that heat input is frequently irregular when the air circulation within the oven is uneven or indeterminate. In the second half of oven B, with higher plenum pressures, it is possible to see the effect of individual nozzles, and to see that heat flux increases when plenum pressures are increased, while the mean temperature at the baking surface remains constant.

Tests in both ovens have confirmed that faster baking can be achieved, and thermal efficiency improved approximately in proportion to the reduction in baking time, by increasing the air circulation at some or all stages of baking without changing the nominal temperature settings. This is confirmed in other work which shows that more than half the load on most baking ovens corresponds to the energy required to evaporate moisture from the product. Rates of moisture evaporation correlate closely with rates of heat transfer at the product surface.

CONCLUSION
A travelling heat flux sensor has been constructed following earlier work with fixed point sensors in collaboration with FMBRA. The new sensor has a rapid response, and can be used to reveal irregular patterns of heat transfer within baking ovens. The sensor output can be related to a fundamental calibration method based on calorimetry. Preliminary results from tests in baking ovens support the concept of heat flux measurement as a more useful indicator of baking oven performance than temperature measurement alone.

ACKNOWLEDGEMENT
The sensor has been used in a collaborative project 'baking oven improvement by performance modelling', led by FMBRA and supported by the Energy Efficiency Office, Energy Technical Support Unit (ETSU).

ILLUSTRATIONS
Fig 1   Outline of sensor for travelling probe
Fig 2   Results from oven A
Fig 3   Results from oven B

REFERENCES
Christensen A, Blomqvist I, Skjoldebrand C (1984)
'Optimization of the baking process with respect to quality
and energy' in 'Thermal processing and quality of foods'
Elsevier, London

McFarlane I (1989) 'Heat flux measurement for improved
control of baking ovens' Euro Fd & Drk Rev (1) 37-41

Sato H, Matsumura T, Shibukawa S (1987) 'Apparent heat
transfer in a forced convection oven' J Fd Sci 52(1)185-188

Shibukawa S, Sugiyama K, Yano T (1989) 'Effects of heat
transfer on browning of cookies' J Fd Sci 54(3)621-624, 699

Skjoldebrand C, Andersson C (1989) 'A comparison of infrared
bread baking and conventional baking' J Int Mwave Pwr & Emag
En 24(2) 91-100

Unklesbay K B, Unklesbay N F (1985) 'Effect of dough
temperature and infrared radiation on crust color of pizzas'
J Foodservice Sys 3 243-249

Wade P (1987) 'Biscuit baking by near infrared radiation'
J Fd Eng 6 165-175

Fig 1 - OUTLINE OF SENSOR FOR TRAVELLING PROBE

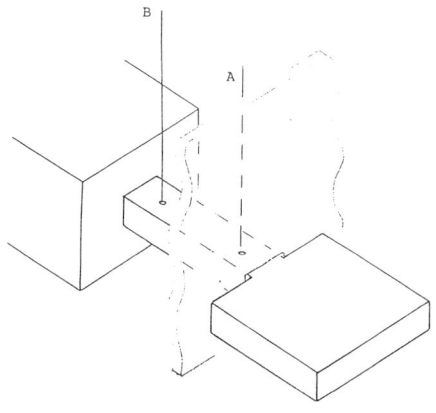

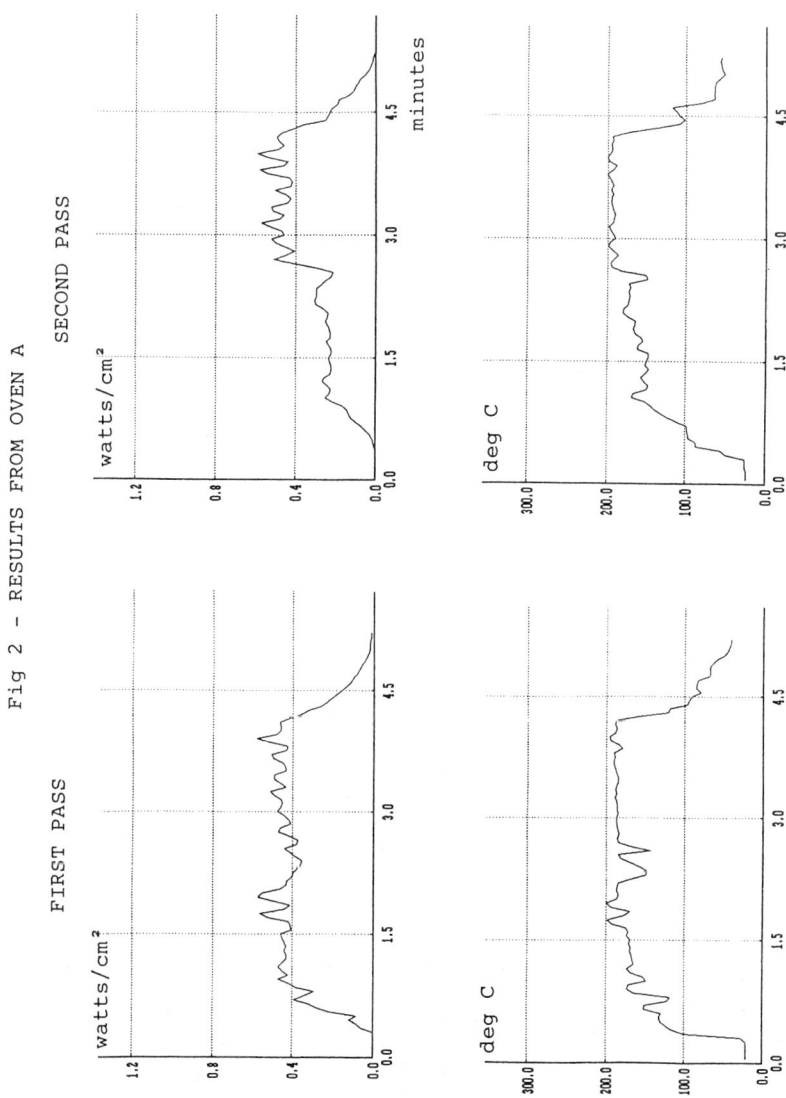

Fig 2 – RESULTS FROM OVEN A

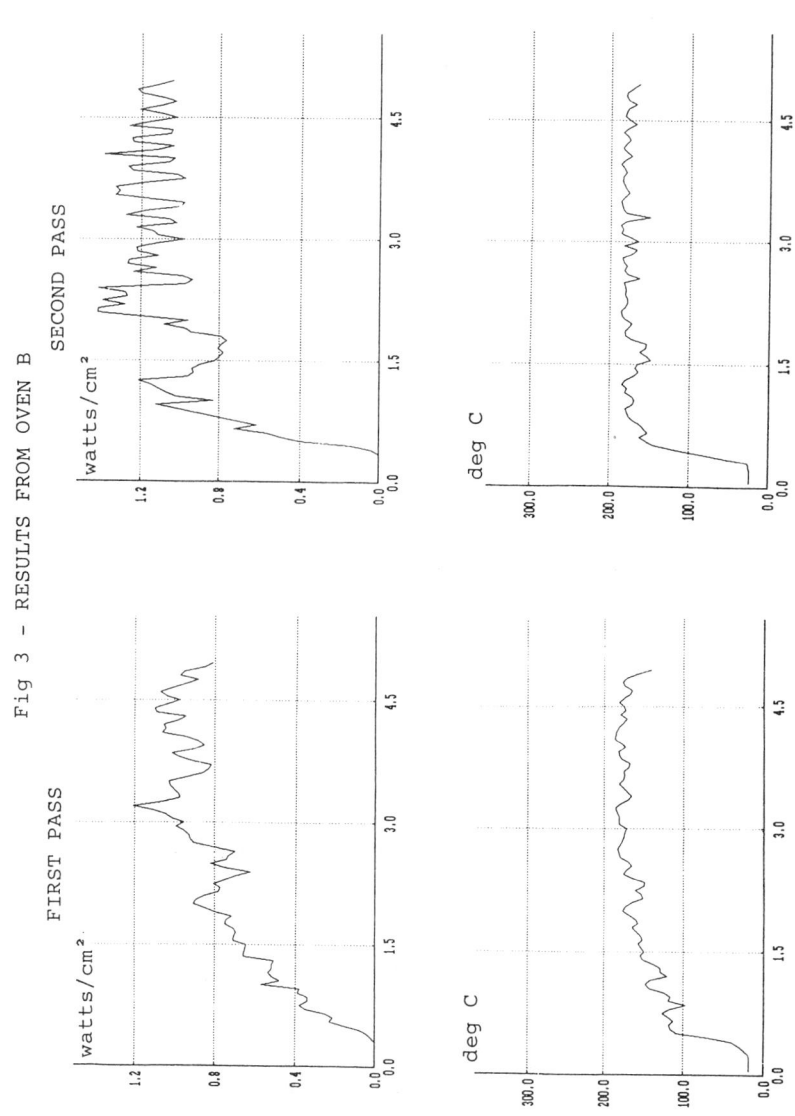

Fig 3 – RESULTS FROM OVEN B

A DYNAMIC SIMULATOR TO CONTROL HYGIENE IN FOOD PROCESSING INDUSTRIES.

E. Laporte*, P. Bourseau*, G. Muratet*, O. Cerf.**

Hygiene control on food processing plants is a complex problem involving knowledge of various kinds. Artificial intelligence techniques are well-suited to deal with such tasks. In this paper it is suggested to build an expert system in hygiene control around a plant dynamic simulator. The simulator structure and operation is explained in detail. As an example, the modelisation of a sandwich plant is presented. By the end, future developments are mentioned ; in particular it is briefly discussed how the simulator will be integrated into the expert system.

Keywords : hygienic control, food processing, expert system, dynamic simulation.

Introduction

Whatever the product diversity (milk products, ready-to-eat frozen meals, drinks, ...), food preservation techniques or presentation, food processing plants have a common challenge : to improve quality. Hygienic quality holds an important place in this approach, because it influences public health (outbreaks of food poisoning) and industry profits (rate of spoiled foodstuffs, shelf-life of manufactured products, etc). To control this quality, it is necessary to have great competence in varied fields, and to apply them at different stages of a plant life (conception, production, diagnosis, maintenance). The large number of implied disciplines explain the problems met by industry to devise a system of quality control and quality assurance.

For their part, experts have difficulties to evaluate the improvement proposition that they advocate after a food processing audit. The techniques HACCP and HAZOP (4, 6, 8) applied for a few years in the food processing world have the merit to give a general framework for the evaluation of hazards and the control of hygiene quality, but they stay qualitative.

Setting off from this statement, our approach consists in gathering the knowledge of several experts (engineering, microbiology research, ultra-clean techniques, rules and good manufacturing practices) using the knowledge and the techniques of process engineering.

A line of food production is a process of matter transformation that we split up into two different circuits : the main production is the one of foodstuff and the secondary production is the one of contaminants. This secondary production must be controlled, keeping in mind the necessity to preserve the technological and organoleptical qualities of the main production. To reach this target, our middle term objective is to develop a prototype expert system to aid decision-making. Little known in food processing units (1, 2, 10) beside production control, expert systems have proved their efficiency in chemical industries (7).

---

* ENSCP - Laboratoire de génie des procédés - 11 rue Pierre et Marie Curie - 75231 PARIS cedex 05.
** INRA - Laboratoire de génie de l'hygiène et des procédés alimentaires - 25 Avenue de la République - 91 300 MASSY - FRANCE.
This work is supported by the "Ministère de la Recherche et de la Technologie".

In particular our simulator is developed thanks to an object-oriented language. The kernel of the future expert system will be a dynamic simulator of process predicting the production of foodstuffs and contaminants. This approach presents numerous advantages. First of all, the simulator is of a modular type, every apparatus or operation (of transformation or transfer) being described as an autonomous entity. This structure is a good basis to organize the information related to the characteristics and the operation of the installation. On the other hand, it will constitute a tool to transfer knowledge (maieutic aspect). In this sense, building a plant model for simulation will direct the choice of the relevant parameters to describe every apparatus. Finally, the simulator will allow scenario tests to evaluate the impact of a control policy or the effects of an incidental situation. Another interesting point is the description of the history of a production line, as we demonstrate in the second paragraph. Thanks to the use of artificial intelligence techniques, this simulator offers a receiving frame to the more recent research results of microbiology. For example, it allows, without generating a deep restructuration, to receive predictive mathematical models of microbiological growth or survival, as well as the parameters to take into account in these models to establish the growth or destruction curves (3, 5). Furthermore, the techniques of microbiological analysis are regularly progressing : information on contamination is more easily available with shorter delays. One can hope that in the near future, this data will be registered by sensors and relayed in real time to a central computer in charge of supervision.

This paper deals with the struture and operation of the simulator, details an example and states the identified tracks for future works.

1. Simulator structure and operation

This simulator allows us to realise a dynamic simulation of discrete and continuous processes. It calculates the process state at regular intervals of time (synchronous simulation) taking into account the occurrence of events along time. An event can represent any action on the process or any modification on its environment. The list of events is stored in the simulation calendar. An event may be simple (e.g. updating the value of a property) or complex (e.g. a cleaning operation which involves the modification of several properties for one or several objects).

The modular aspect consists in representing a unit in terms of flows and box connections. Every box is a piece of equipment, an operation of transfer for instance or an interface (establishing a connection between the process and its environment). Each box contains its own working model. A box can also represent a specific zone in a plant. If the contamination by air is confirmed to be a preponderant mechanism then air flows across the plant can be taken into account. Different types of flows are listed. At present we have connected the boxes with mass flows (foodstuffs) and mass micro-organisms flows but later on we want to integrate the flows of people, foodstuffs, air and their contaminants.

The simulator allows us to calculate the state (mass and micro-organisms balance) of every box, in a sequential manner. The calculation of the unit state is done at regular intervals, thanks to the box models, the unit flowsheet and its initial state, taking into account the events happening on the installation or in its environment. For micro-organisms, we actually use simple models but nothing is against the fact that, when they are well-known, we will replace them by sophisticated ones.

The simulator is composed of three modules (see Fig N° 1).

• The first module, called supervisor, gathers the simulation algorithms. It controls a clock and, at every time signal, it reads in the calendar the actions to trigger. New actions may be introduced in calendar along the simulation and the supervisor may manage repetitive actions.

At each time signal, the supervisor establishes the input variables of each box and calculates its current state and its output variables using the box model (see point iii just below). An input variable can be either a command, the output of another box or an external disturbance. This general structure can be used for all types of food processing industries and allows the surveillance of the evolution of contaminants along the unit and the time.

• The second module holds the definition of the different kinds of apparatus, operations, namely their characteristics and their operation models. Some pieces of equipment are fairly common in all process industries, others are specific of a given production.

Every box is characterised by the following specifications.

  i) the parameters :

They recapitulate the characteristics of the apparatus (e.g. dimension, gross weight, ...)

  ii) the variables :

They describe the state of each box and properties of the connected flows ; a flow being used only to exchange information between two boxes.

  iii) the models :

A model defines a behaviour of a box and is used to calculate the production of foodstuffs and contaminants. Models are developed from mass balance equations describing foodstuffs transformation and kinetic laws for micro-organisms growth, survival and transfer. They must take into account the micro-organisms present in raw materials or semi-factured products that go into the transformation unit, and can multiply in or on the surface of the foodstuff components as well as in the biofilms adhering on apparatus surface. Those contaminants may be transferred to the food when they pass above but also may be carried by the airflows or human operators (sneeze, contact between hands or clothes and foodstuff). To know the appropriate level of description of these contamination processes is a central question for building the simulator. Development of micro-organisms inside the food is taken into account in two types of boxes only : storage boxes and delay boxes. To describe a real apparatus it is possible to add one of these boxes if micro-organisms development is expected (see Fig N° 2).

  iv) the constraints :

Simple constraints apply on a single variable (pH for example) and the complex constraints on several variables (e.g. couple time/temperature). They concern on the one hand the unit operation, and so the control policy (e.g. couple time/temperature, frequency of cleaning), and on the other hand the regulations (e.g. it is forbidden for a dusty circuit to cross a clean one), the know-how and the rules of usage.

• The third module describes the unit structure (the different apparatus and their connections) and fixes the parameters of every apparatus. Furthermore, the initial state (at t = 0) of the unit is defined.

2. The sandwich example

The knowledge of the process has been obtained from an interview of the quality engineer of a catering unit and from a detailed observation of the work achieved by the operators.

The sandwich story includes the sub-histories of bread, butter, salad and ham as presented in the following flowsheet (Fig N° 2). As an example we can follow how the ham is processed through the unit. Firstly it goes into the unit as a wrapped ham. Then it is stored and chilled to near + 2 °C. When needed, an operator takes it out and puts it near the unwrapping place : we call this place a delay zone, where micro-organisms can multiply if residence time is long or temperature warm enough. Unwrapped ham is then transported onto the cutting table, cut into slices then associated to the other components of the sandwich, during the assemblage phase. The sandwich is stored before being delivered. We will see underneath how we can integrate this story in the simulator.

On the sandwich flowsheet, the inlet boxes and the delivery box are interfaces between the plant and its environment. All other boxes represent operations of storage, transport and transformation. Each piece of equipment can be operated either in a continuous or in a batch mode. In a continuous operation, both input and output flows parameters change continuously along the time without discontinuity. In a batch operation, the parameters, input and output flows have zero value during the process operation and non zero values during the loading and unloading periods. Storage is usually necessary in input and output lines. Batch operation is a common mode in a catering unit (ham unwrapping, for example) but its modelling is more complicated. Nevertheless, such an operation can also be described as a continuous one if the discrete nature of the foodstuff is not important.

As mentioned above, no contaminant growth is modelled in the food transformation boxes. For the sake of simplicity, we assume that these transformations are instantaneous. If necessary, we add in the line a delay box where growth can occur. Such delay boxes can be seen on each line before assemblage (Fig N° 2).

Sometimes foodstuffs removed from the chilling room are not processed and so are returned to the storage. The reintroduction of a recycled product that may be highly contaminated in the storage increases the risk of contamination of the other products.

3. Further work

Our simulator will be used as the kernel of an expert system for which the name of Mirfak® has been chosen. This simulator actually works with a simple representation of the structure and characteristics of the installation. This representation will be improved thanks to the talks with the experts, on the basis of what already exists.

The second step is to validate the simulator. The simulator allows us to test various scenarios and to predict the consequences of control choices, or of environment disturbance on the final product and/or on the equipment itself. We will establish several scenarios allowing the validation of the simulator operation. Let's look at some examples! Running simulations with various levels of recycling in the ham line can modify the contamination level and thus indicate a possible cause of sandwich contamination. Modifications in the sequence and frequency of cleaning, in the surface state (hollows, crevices) will also be used to evaluate changes.

In order to obtain a realistic simulation of a contamination process, it is necessary to achieve an adequate description of the plant. The scenario tests will show rapidly the quality of our representation and will guide us in the search of complementary knowledge. It will appear as new flows and as new properties for flows and boxes. As an example, it is clear that we should integrate the organoleptic quality in our models because it is not worth destroying all the contaminants if the sandwich is not appetizing or has not a correct presentation.

In some apparatus, foodstuffs can be considered as homogeneous (for example, milk in a tank). In this case a simple set of variables can be used to describe the foodstuff state (water activity, pH, etc...). In other apparatus, foodstuffs take a discrete form like a loaf of bread or a wrapped sandwich. In this latter case, the mean value of each property over the whole population may give a totally misleading image of the real state of our system : a population with a low level of contaminants equally distributed is different from a population with a very low level of micro-organisms but containing one heavily contaminated individual. More elaborate descriptions, like property distributions, wil then be necessary.

The expert system will comprise, beyond the simulator, two principal knowledge bases :

    i) a first base of knowledge will help the user to build a simulation. If the circuit of main production (food products) is clearly defined by the list of operations, the circuit of secondary production will vary from a simulation to another. According to the objective of the simulation, it will be useful to check upon the contamination factors of each apparatus, or to take into account the transport of micro-organisms from ambient air. The matter is in fact to build automatically the model to simulate in function of the simulation objective. This knowledge base will equally hold an analysis of the installation structure and test some constraints (e.g. a dirty circuit does not cross a clean circuit).

    ii) a second knowledge base will be dedicated to scrutinize the results of the simulation. It will evaluate the bacteriological quality of manufactured foodstuff, testing constraints bearing on the micro-organisms number or the respect of operating procedures (e.g. couple time/temperature).

Both knowledge bases will use the same data base (especially the second and third modules of the simulator). This structure has been used with success in the chemical domain, for the preparation and exploitation of technical analysis for a cement kiln (9).

Conclusion

This paper describes a dynamic simulator for food processing plants. The simulator has been presented here through the example of a sandwich unit but its structure and operation is general enough to treat any food processing plant. It integrates models of food transport and transformation as well as models of transport, survival and growth of micro-organisms.

The simulator is developed and will be validated on a sandwich production unit. This example shows that with simple models of chemical engineering (mass balance with storage and generation of micro-organisms) food plant behaviour can be correctly forecast.

This simulator will constitute the core of an expert system to help hygiene control for food processing plants, which will be built in a project gathering partners of varied specialities. The next works will determine which improvements we could introduce into the simulator, to develop two knowledge bases to help simulation definition and to exploit the results of a simulation.

Acknowledgements

We thank the representatives of our industrial partners, Mr. Lelaidier, Mr. Fabre and Mr. Vergnaud of ONET group, Mr. Remond and Mr. Vialet of SERETE Industries.

We also want to thank Mr. Muller of SERVAIR and Mr. Sadoudi of INRA Massy.

References

1) Annales du colloque APRIA, 27 octobre 1987, Les systèmes experts et les IAA. Réalités et perspectives., Tec & Doc, 80 pp, Lavoisier, Paris.

2) ACoFoP II, 14/15 novembre 1990, Symposium on Automatic control of food processes. 250 pp. Food Working Party of the European Federation of Chemical Engineering, Paris.

3) Baird-Parker A.C., Kilsby D.C., 1987, Principles of predictive food microbiology, Journal of Applied Bacteriology Symposium Supplement, 43S-49S.

4) Bryan F.L., 1990, Application of HACCP to Ready-to-Eat Chilled Foods, Food technology, 7, pp 70-77.

5) Gibson A. M., Bratchell N., Roberts T.A., 1988, Predicting microbial growth : growth responses of salmonellae in a laboratory medium as affected by PH, sodium chloride and storage temperature. International Journal of Food Microbiology. 6, pp 155-178.

6) International Commission on Microbiological Specifications for foods, 1988, Micro-organisms in foods : Application of the hazard analysis critical control point system to ensure microbiological safety and quality, 357 pp, Blackwell Scientif. Public. Oxford.

7) Mavrovouniotis M., Ed, 1990, Artificial intelligence in process engineering, 367 pp, Academic Press Inc. San Diego.

8) Mayes T., Kilsby D.C., 1989, The use of HAZOP hazard analysis to identify critical control points for the microbiological safety of food. Food qual. and pref., 1 (2), pp 53-57.

9) Mizessyn F. 15 octobre 1990. Système expert pour audit cuisson de four à ciment. Thèse de doctorat de Paris VI. 150 pp.

10) Whitney L.F., May 1989, What expert systems can do for the food industry. Food technology, 43 (5), pp 135 - 138.

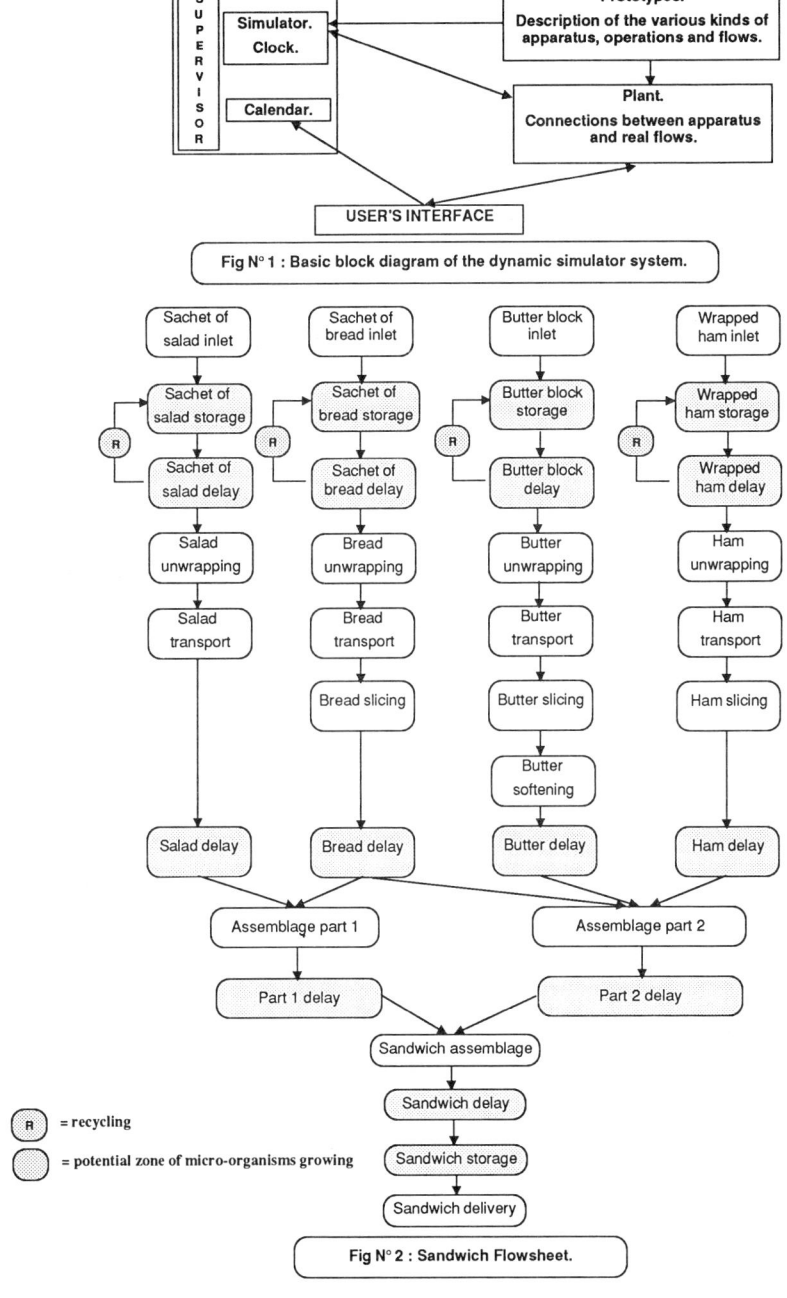

Fig N° 1 : Basic block diagram of the dynamic simulator system.

Fig N° 2 : Sandwich Flowsheet.

AUTOMATIC MOISTURE DETERMINATION OF RAW MATERIALS IN FEED INDUSTRY BY PULSED N.M.R.

A. DAVENEL

Feed industry needs rapid analytical informations from many raw materials to fit the mixture and the granulation of feedstuffs. A good determination of their moisture by low resolution pulse nuclear magnetic resonance (NMR) requires the use of a specific prediction equation for each type of raw materials. Classification functions to identify automatically nine-type membership were developed by discriminant analysis of five NMR parameters. For a test set of 207 samples, the correct classification results were 93,5% and the moisture contents were determined with standard deviations of 0,18-0,41%.

Keywords: Feed Industry, Moisture, NMR, Discriminant Analysis

INTRODUCTION

The technique of low-resolution pulse nuclear magnetic resonance is more and more used to the determination of fat and moisture in food products. As with near infrared spectrometry, the main advantages of the technique are the rapidity of the determination, the possibility of automation and the fact of being non-destructive.

The NMR signal is due to the magnetic moments of the protons present in the sample (Fukushima and al., 1981). Placed in a static magnetic field B_0, the sample acquires a macroscopic magnetization M_0, proportional to the total number of protons in the sample and aligned to this field. A short pulse of radiofrequence (RF) field B_1 of frequence f satisfying the Larmor resonance condition, as $f = \tau \, B_0 \, / \, \pi$, rotates M_0 in the plan perpendicular to B_0. At the end of the pulse the NMR signal is maximum and proportional of the total protons. After the RF pulse switched off, a relaxation signal, the free induction decay (FID), is recorded. The pulse NMR sequences allow to measure two distinct relaxation mechanisms: the transverse relaxation (FID, CPMG sequences) and the spin-lattice or longitudinal relaxation (inversion or saturation-recovery sequences). The shape of the relaxation signals can be roughly fitted by a sum of exponential or gaussian functions characterized by their relaxation times.

In the case of main raw materials of the feed industry, three T_2 transversal relaxation times roughly coexisted in the 7 to 15% moisture range: a very short time (from 9 to 15 µs) assigned to solid protons, an intermediate time (from 0.3 to 2 ms) to water protons and a long time (from 60 to 70 ms) to fat protons. Leung (1976) demonstrated that the longitudinal relaxation component could be fitted by a single-exponential function which the relaxation time T_1 decreases between 100 and 25 ms when moisture grows between 7 and 15 %.

For a given product, the liquid/solid ratio is related to the FID ratio between the FID signal measured in the 40-100 µs range and the FID signal sampled to 11 µs. (Hester and Quine, 1977; Brusewitz and Stone, 1987). Consequently Brosio and al.(1978) showed that the relation between the moisture and the FID ratio in foodstuffs rich in starch but very low in fat is dependent on products: to predict L/S ratio and moisture, he calculated extrapolation coefficients for several types of flours.

* C.E.M.A.G.R.E.F.- RENNES-France

In near infrared spectrometry, discriminant analysis were used to classify automatically wheat varieties according to their baking quality (Devaux and al.,1986). In this work, this statistical technique were used to try to identify automatically 9 types of raw materials with the aim to apply, after that, the equation of moisture determination specific for each type. Errors of moisture determination by this computerized technique or with a single equation common to all types were compared with ones obtained from specific equation after human identification.

MATERIALS AND METHODS

NMR equipement

The measurements were made with a pulse low-resolution NMR spectrometer operating at 20 MHz (0.47T), Model Minispec PC 120 Bruker. It was linked to a thermostatic bath, which allowed the thermoregulation of the probe 10 mm in diameter. The temperature was fixed to 30°C and the signal was recorded in diode detection mode. Two pulse sequences were programmed so as to digitize the FID at 11, 25, 42, 56 and 73 µs and the echo amplitude maxima of a CPMG formed by 50 echos 0.2 ms apart (Fig.1 and 2). 60 ms after the first 90° pulse of the first sequence, a second 90°pulse was produced and followed by a sampling at 11 µs to obtain an information dependent on T_1 (saturation-recovery sequence). The repetition rate between successive pulses was 0.5s; averages of 49 measurements were taken for all digital values. These ones were divided with the first 11 µs-value corresponding with the dead-time end of the apparatus. One obtained a set of 55 variables R_{25}, R_{42}, R_{56}, R_{73}, R_{200}...R_{7000},...,R_{10000} and R_{T1} independent on the size of samples. The variable R_{T1} is bound to the time constante T_1 by the equation:

$$+T_1 \text{ (en ms)} = -60 / \ln(1-R_{T1})$$

raw materials

A set of 54 raw materials and their chemical composition were provided from the chemical laboratory of a feed manufacturer. In order to screen the 7-15% moisture range, 8-10 samples per each raw materials were either slightly dried in a forced air oven at 50°C or humidified by placing them in a sealed container in the presence of free water at 30°C. Flour samples were poured as granular powders into the NMR tubes (approx.0.5g.). Tubes were sealed and placing in an environment chamber at 30°C for about 15 hours before NMR measuring. Reference moisture computed on a wet basis were obtained from drying of samples in the actual tubes placed into the forced oven at 103°C for 8 hours. A balance of precision 0.1 mg was used for weighing.

statistical analysis

At first, multiple regression relationship between reference percent moisture and NMR variables was fitted by least squares on a calibration subset of 277 samples (31 raw materials) for each of 9 types of raw materials: corn, wheat, cassava, peas, soft wheat brans, meals of alfalfa, sunflower-seed, rapeseed and soybean. Then these equations are tested with a subset of 207 samples (23 raw materials) in order to calculate a standard error of prediction (SEP) for each type of raw material. A single linear relation common to all types was calculated by minimizing the global standard error of calibration (SEC) of the calibration subset. Then this single relation was applied to the second subset to estimate a SEP for each types.

A multiple discriminant procedure was used to choose the best subset from the 55 variables which minimize the ratio within-group variation to between-group variation. Multiple discriminant analysis associates progressively to the most discriminant variable new variable until the discriminatory power does not improve significantly. The procedure generates 9 classication functions (Tomassone, 1988). Each samples of the prediction subset was classified by evaluating each function and assigning the sample to the group corresponding to the highest function value. Then, since each of the 9 groups were assimilated to a type of raw materials, the specific equations allowed to predict the moisture of these samples. After that each samples was assigned to a group and its moisture calculated, the correct classification results and moisture SEP were evaluated for each type of raw materials.

RESULTS AND DISCUSSION

Moisture determination by a single equation and by equations for each type of raw materials

In NMR spectrometry, moisture prediction equations of the low moisture samples are generally developed by fitting by the least squares method a multilinear model of a FID variable between 42 μs and 80 μs bounded to the L/S ratio and a spin-echo variable between 5 to 10 ms correlated to fat content. Variables sampled in these time windows are often strongly correlated between themselves: other variable combinaisons can give prediction very close to these ones set up in this work. FID variable R_{73} and CPMG variable R_{7000} were used for all specific relations (table 1). But the addition of R_{42} variable improved significatively the moisture prediction of alfalfa. Determination accuracy was often good (table 4): ESC and ESP fluctuated between 0.17% and 0.25% moisture range for peas, wheat, corn, meals of soybean and alfalfa. Though accuracy can be estimate barely enough for cassava and meal of sunflower-seed and rapeseed, and feeble for wheat brans. For raw materials poor in fat as cassava, peas, wheat, meals of soyabeans and alfalfa, it possible not to take into account the variable R7000 without affecting accuracy.

As with the determination by near infrared spectrometry, the use of a single equation common to all types, give a poor accuracy: the global moisture SEC and SEP were equal to about 0.9% (table 2). Cassava moisture content was estimated with strong standard deviation 1.75%!. It is absolutely necessary to identify the samples before moisture determining. The ability to identify automatically type membership was evaluated by a discriminant analysis taken into account additional NMR variables.

Automatic moisture determination after identification by discriminant analysis

The discriminatory power of different combinations of NMR variables were evaluated with the calibration subset. When the two variables R_{73} and R_{7000} generally used to fit the calibration equations were tested together, the correct classification results were only 44.4%. If the variable R_{42} or R_{T1} were associated with these two first ones, 78.5% and 71.5% of the samples were respectively identified correctly. The combinaison of these four variables raised the correct classification result to 91% (table 3). When the variable R_{200} were added, a slight improvement were obtained, since the percentage reached 93.5%. This last result was confirmed when the classification fonctions were applied to identify the samples of the prediction set. (table 4). If some samples of wheat and cassava were assigned to the "peas" group, it was between the"soybean" group and the "alfalfa" group that it the most difficult to allot samples. Discriminant analysis provides linear combinations of the NMR variables, called discriminant functions, which allows to graphically observe in a canonical space the relative distances between observations and group means. Though the discriminatory power of the third discriminant axis were still significative, the identification overlaps become apparent on the figure 3 which represents the observations of the calibration set in the plane formed by two first discriminant axis and accounting for 93% of the total variability.

The variable R_{7000} discriminate samples as a function of their fat content (corn, wheat cassava for example). But this content is enough heterogeneous inside some types of raw materials (meals of sunflower-seed and rapeseed). If the interpretation of the discriminatory power of the variable R_{T1} is more difficult to explain, the use of variables R_{42} and R_{200} allows to take into account differences appreciable of the transversal relaxation time constants of the water protons between the types of raw materials (fig.1). These two variables separate clearly the products rich in starch (cassava, wheat, corn, peas) from other products often richer in cellulose (meals alfalfa, sunflower-seed and rapeseed) or in protein (meals of soybeans, sunflower-seed, rapeseed). Wheat brans hold logically a intermediary position . Though, the close NMR behaviors of meals of soybeans and alfalfa cannot be explained by a likeness of their chemical compositions except these both types of raw materials are poor in starch.

The standard errors of moisture determination by the specific equations after automatical identification fluctuated in the same 0.18-0.41% range as this observed after human identification. For the groups where overlaps occurred, the accuracy slighly spoiled without moisture ESP were beyond 0.37% (table 2). In addition, discriminant analysis seems to show that the moisture determination accuracy is inversely bounded to the NMR variation of each group (fig.3).

CONCLUSION

The pulsed NMR moisture determination accuracy of raw materials for feed industry was very significatively improved when a specific prediction equation was applied for each type of raw materials. Discriminant Analysis of 5 NMR variables showed the ability to correctly classify 93,5% of the samples among 9 types of raw materials. Though some overlaps between groups occurred, errors in NMR based moisture measurements obtained after automatical classification were in the same 0.18-0.41% range as this one observed after human identification.

Times per sample for NMR measuring and calculating classification and moisture results were 110 seconds: low resolution pulse NMR provides an good computarized technique to determinate rapidly moisture content (and oil) of raw materials for processes in feed industry.

ACKNOWLEDGE

The authors gratefully acknowledge Mr Metra, Guyomard Compagny, for providing samples and analytical services.

REFERENCES

Brosio, E., F. Conti, C. Lintas and S.Sikova. 1978. J. Food Technology 13: 107-116.

Brusewitz, G.H. and M.L. Stone. 1987. Transactions of ASAE 30(3): 858-862.

Devaux, M.F., Bertrand D. and G. Martin. 1986. Cereal Chemistry 63(2): 151-154

Fukushima, E. and S.B.W. Roeder. 1981. Experimental pulse NMR: a nuts and bolts approach. Reading, MA: Addison-Wesley Publishing.

Hester, R.E. and D.E.C. Quine. 1977. J. Sci. Fd. Agric 28: 624-630.

Leung, H.K., M.P. Steinberg, L.S. Wei and A.I. Nelson. 1976. J. Food Science 41: 297-300.

Tomassone, R., M. Danzart, J.J. Daudin and J.P. Masson. 1988. Discrimination et classement. Paris, Edition Masson, Techniques stochastiques.

TABLE 1. regression relationship between reference moisture and NMR variables for 9 types of raw materials

type	prediction equations moisture % (wet basis)	R^2
corn	$49.095\,(R_{73} - 1.2\,R_{7000}) + 2.193$	0.99
wheat	$47.587\,(R_{73} - 1.2\,R_{7000}) + 1.893$	0.99
cassava	$40.502\,(R_{73} - 1.2\,R_{7000}) + 4.686$	0.98
wheat brans	$40.036\,(R_{73} - 1.2\,R_{7000}) + 2.284$	0.98
peas	$42.136\,(R_{73} - 1.2\,R_{7000}) + 2.761$	0.99
sunflower	$32.245\,(R_{73} - 1.2\,R_{7000}) + 4.755$	0.99
rapeseed	$30.885\,(R_{73} - 1.2\,R_{7000}) + 4.644$	0.97
soybeans	$32.101\,(R_{73} - 1.2\,R_{7000}) + 5.367$	0.98
alfalfa	$67.27\,R_{42} - 46.22\,R_{73} + 3.124$	0.98

TABLE 2. standard errors of calibration and prediction for moisture determination (% Wet Basis).

type	specific equations after human identification S.E.C.	specific equations after human identification S.E.P.	common equation S.E.C.	common equation S.E.P.	specific equations after automatic identification S.E.P.
corn	0.17	0.21		0.86	0.21
wheat	0.18	0.23		1.53	0.23
cassava	0.32	0.29		1.75	0.29
wheat brans	0.36	0.41		0.86	0.41
peas	0.18	0.18		0.50	0.18
sunflower-seed	0.26	0.29		0.4	0.37
rapeseed	0.30	0.30		0.44	0.31
soybean	0.25	0.23		0.37	0.31
alfalfa	0.25	0.24		0.61	0.37
TOTAL	0.25	0.26	0.91	0.90	0.31

TABLE 3. percent of correct classification in function of discriminant NMR variables choice

number of variables	NMR variable choice from NMR sequences FID	CPMG	T1	percent correct classification
2	R_{73}	R_{7000}		44.4
3	$R_{42}\ R_{73}$	R_{7000}		78.4
3	R_{73}	R_{7000}	R_{T1}	71.5
4	$R_{42}\ R_{73}$	R_{7000}	R_{T1}	90.9
5	$R_{42}\ R_{73}$	$R_{200}\ R_{7000}$	R_{T1}	93.5

TABLE 4. automatic classification results with the five-variable model (unit: number of samples)

type	calibration set discriminant analysis groups 1	2	3	4	5	6	7	8	9	prediction set discriminant analysis groups 1	2	3	4	5	6	7	8	9
corn	35									19								
wheat		35	3								24							
cassava			25	2								15						
wheat brans				24	1								15					
peas					46									27				
sunflower-seed						20								1	19			
rapeseed							30								2	35		
soybean								31	7								27	3
alfalfa							1	1	13							1	6	12
percent correct classification	93.5%									93.7%								

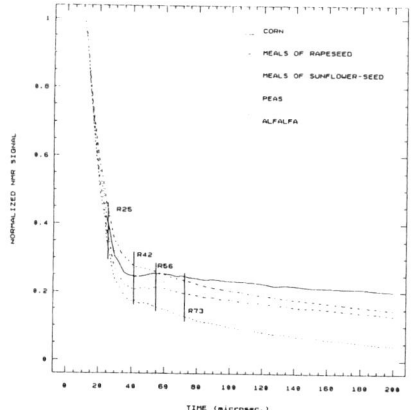

Figure 1: NMR FID signals from five raw materials
(moisture content between 10.5 and 11 %).
R25, R42, R56, R73: normalized NMR variables.

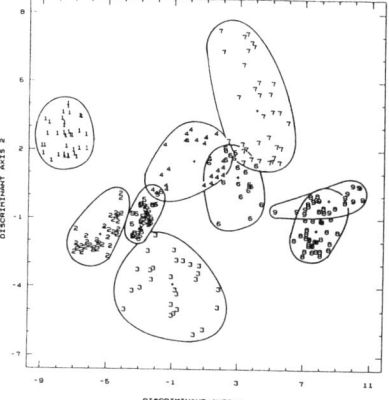

Figure 3: Plot of the 2 first discriminant axis
(1:corn, 2:wheat, 3:cassava, 4:wheat brans, 5:peas,
6:meal of sunflower-seed, 7:meal of rapeseed,
8:meal of soybean, 9:alfalfa)

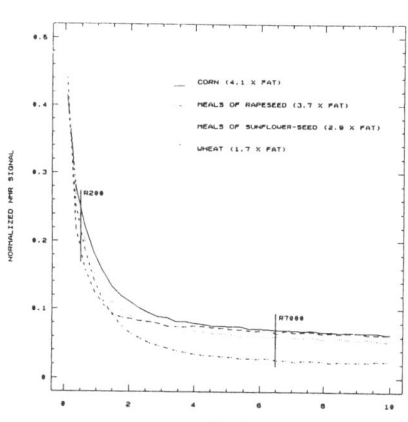

Figure 2: NMR CPMG signals from five raw
materials
(moisture content between 10.5 and 11 %).
R200, R7000: normalized NMR variables.

4TH GENERATION OF SW FOR FOOD PLANT CONTROL

LARS JARNEBRANT and JOHN EADIE

SYNOPSIS

This paper deals firstly with a definition and objective of plant control in the Food Industry, and then traces the historical background and future trends. It then defines the 4th Generation of SW as an object oriented method of programming, likened to a spreadsheet or wordprocessing package. It then describes in more detail what we mean by an object in object orientation. Finally the implementation of 4th Generation SW is looked at with regard to the structures, building blocks and plant adoption.

1.   DEFINITION AND OBJECTIVE OF PLANT CONTROL SW

In all food plants of today, automation plays an important role. The complexity of the processes, the quality and safety aspects for the products produced, an efficient use of the production facility, are all factors that each of them might necessitate the installation of an automation system. Depending on the required functionality the solutions might differ in each case.

There are two factors that will determine the automation functionality and these are:

-      the mechanical installation i.e. process sensors (temperature, flow, pressure etc) and actuators (valves, pumps etc).

-      the automation "logic".

With the technical stand-point of today, most automation installations are carried out with micro or mini-computer based systems.

The tendency is clear that the HW equipment is becoming more and more intelligent and relatively cheaper with time. While on the other hand, the SW also tends to become more and more sophisticated with a higher level of functionality, but also relatively more expensive to produce. It is quite obvious that this will lead to new methods of producing SW, also in the normal field of process control for food plants.

2. HISTORY BACKGROUND AND FUTURE TRENDS

The history of automation is not very old, but the development has nevertheless been very rapid in the past two decades.

A. Towards the end of the 60's and the beginning of the 70's, the relay technology was mostly used. Huge panels with up to 10,000 relays were built. The SW was achieved by wires and cables connecting the relay contacts with each other in complex patterns. This often called for smart engineering solutions, because the relays were very limited in logic capability and extremely space consuming.

B. During the 70's, hardwired electronics developed and were used. Theses systems had a higher functionality than the relays and were more space effective. But basically the SW was achieved in the same way as for relays: cables and wires. The disadvantages thus remained.

C. In the mid 70's computerised equipment was introduced, and has been further developed during the 80's. Now this meant a drastic change in SW engineering compared to what was done before. The SW was now easy to modify, it could be copied and reproduced, it could be tested in simulation modes and it offered much higher functionality than the relays or the electronics. In the beginning the SW was more or less a "translation" of the logic symbols and the relay symbols into computer executable equations. But since then the SW has gradually been developed into more normal computer-like languages.

We can therefore identify three earlier generations of SW-types:

1. Hardwired relay and electronics.

2. Computerised basic functions e.g."or" and "act" etc.

3. Higher level languages using "process-names", subroutines etc.

Today most process control systems use a mixture of second and third generation.

The future trends for the 90's are that there will not be any drastic changes in the HW technology, but a rapid development of the performance in the form of memory sizes, speed, buses etc.

The major changes will take place on the SW side. A new fourth generation will gradually come into use, made possible by the new available memory-sizes and speed, but necessitated by the demends of the SW functionality and the costs of producing it.

3.   FOURTH GENERATION OF SW

3.1   Comparison with other trends on SW

In all other areas of SW production for computer use, there has been a change in of methods for programming. The "old" languages like ASSEMBLER, BASIC, ALGOL, FORTRAN etc., are all languages that adopt to the way the machine works and are designed to do so, sometimes with a compilation as an intermediate step. If you required the machine to do something, you made a program for it. Now this might be a satisfactory way to work in smaller applications, but now, more effective ways to produce SW have been developed.

The programming methods should be more application orientated and utilising as much "configuration" as possible rather than programming. Let's for instance take the examples of calculations. Nowadays you buy a package with ready to use calculation functions like LOTUS, SYMPHONY or EXCEL. You don't program the functions any more, you simply configure with figures, texts, formulas etc., to achieve your own application and to make the program function in the way you want it to. You don't have to bother about the basic SW hidden behind anymore, all you have to do is add your own application configuration to the ready made package. The same goes for word-processing programs, and for data-base programs and for planning programs etc.

We can summarise by saying:

-    Basic SW has become more and more intelligent and is now packaged.

-    Programming becomes application and configuration of the basic SW packages.

This development has been very clear in the past five years but has so far not really been used when it comes to process control, but this will be a clear trend for the 90's.

3.2   Definition of fourth generation SW for process control

Now bearing in mind the development of other SW, you can recognise the following demands on SW for food processes:

-    Basic functionality will not have to be programmed, but should be contained in the "package".

-    Application will be made more by configuring rather than programming.

-    Flexibility will be required to suit different process requirements.

- Special demands are possible by add-on programming.

Now you could argue that this can be achieved already by today's control system SW by means of "standards", copying and multiplying. And that's partially true, but then you are also limited to today's level of functionality. In order to have the same benefits as are available on other SW i.e. higher functionality at lower cost with less time spent, the fourth generation SW thinking has to be implemented. The key functions for process control SW will be:

- Supervisory functionality

- Operator interaction with process

- Open system communication for horizontal integration with other systems.

3.3   Object orientation

It is quite obvious that large quantites of SW with a complex functionality must have a clear and well defined structure. Especially when you at the same time want to form a basic standardisation. The most recent method for achieving this is the object orientation. Object orientation means that you isolate and define the functionality in modules for each object which then, when combined together form the complete desired functionality.

Combining the modules in different ways will create individual plants with different functionality even though built up by using the same basic object orientated modules.

What then do we mean by an object, when we talk about object orientation ? Now that differs in different types of processes. It can be a mechanical machine like a conveyor, a valve, a pump, or a separator. Or it can be a process function like pasteurisation or cleaning.

Neither of these is the complete truth. The most optimal and efficient way of structuring objects is to use a combination of these two methods, individual for each type of process. Companies with integrated proess and automation know-how, will have the best possibilities of carrying it out.

For example in a dairy process:

- one object is a process valve with it's activations and feed-back surveillance.

- another object is the filling of a tank. This is a "soft" object communicating with other objects e.g. the valves or pumps to be operated during the filling.

4.   IMPLEMENTATION OF FOURTH GENERATION SW

4.1   General

Now the implementation of the fourth generation SW in process control has recently started and it will take a few years before it is completed. Of course the present suppliers of automation to the food industry have gathered experience over the past years that will be valuable. The change will not be abrupt but will take some time, also involving a change of thinking and attitude from both the suppliers and purchasers.

The benefits for the users are obvious:

-   clearly defined functions with a high functionality.

-   quality assured with accumulated experiences.

-   economical flexibility.

4.2   Structures and building blocks

As said before, the structuring is essential for the result and the object orientation is a tool for that. A library has to be built up for all objects in the application. The library must be complete with all types of objects :

-   mechanical : valves, pumps, conveyors etc.

-   soft ones : process-functions.

There must also be a complete functionality within the modules or in separate modules for:

-   process control

-   operator interaction

-   supervisory functions

The library functionality should be such that the modifications only have to be made in the library to show up in all the instances where the module is used. On the other hand it shall of course also be possible to create new library modules out of the modified ones and leave the original intact.

4.3   Plant adoption

Now we look more closely at how the fourth generation SW is used in practice. In fact, the engineering of a plant control will be more like configuring and adoption rather than programming. To create the proper plant function, the following steps will be made:

- analyse, define and structure the desired functionality of the plant.

- pick the proper modules from the library.

- add on special required functionality on the outside of the "standard" module.

- this will then be the new plant module.

- connect together all predefined and new signal communication between the modules.

- interlink with operator interaction modules, I/O control modules etc.

TYPICAL PLANT SPECIFIC MODULE

STANDARD LIBRARY MODULE	CONFIGURATION
	SPECIAL REQUIREMENTS
	CONNECTION TO OTHER MODULES

This way of working puts much more focus on the analysis and structuring of the required functionality rather than on the programming itself. The tool-box should make configuring as easy as possile but it is also vital that the SW structure and tools enable a complete plant-specific module to be created in case no existing ones have the proper functionality. In that case they will have to fit into the SW structure and interconnect with other modules, as easy as if they were part of the library.

In short, there is no doubt that the development on the SW side for process control will undergo a similar development as the SW for office use of computers have done during the past years. Some principals will be similar, but on the other hand, the nature of SW use is different. The goal is to have a SW with a large base of basic functionality that you don't have to bother about. Then can you configure it to your own plant specific performance by parameters. Then for some minor very special functions you progrm in the traditional way.

Both suppliers and customers will benefit from this development which will lead to higher functionality at lower cost.

Computer Integrated Manufacture - A Practical Approach

Roger Pilkington

Within the Food Industry the methods of providing automation at the plant level
are well developed. The industry typically using programmable logic controllers
or a distributed control system utilizing industrial computers.
In addition to these plant level control systems the industry uses computers at
corporate level to provide resource and production planning scheduling. The
integration of this system and the plant level system represent one area of
Computer Integrated Manufacture (CIM) which is vital for the effective
management of the production plant. This article describes a typical computer
based system that provides the integration between the systems.
The importance is stressed of planning the integration correctly, understanding
the eventual aim of the system, and producing effective specifications.
Finally the overall benefits of using system integration within the food
industry are postulated.

Introduction

The concept of Computer Integrated Manufacture (CIM) has been with us
for a number of years. Most people involved with the manufacture of
goods have various ideas as to what it means, and indeed many
manufacturing companies have successfully implemented schemes
incorporating the concepts of CIM. But what does it mean to the food
industry and how best can the industry apply CIM to benefit the
industry.

Firstly let us consider what CIM is. A manufacturing business can be
represented in the layered system approach as shown in Fig.1. Each of
the layers represent a single computer based system or a number of
systems interconnected together. The concept of CIM integrates, ie:
joins together, these individual or collection of systems, to form an
overall system. Various terminology is used to describe these
individual system for example "island of automation" and the
integration "bridges" these islands together. Each of the layers shown
has different attributes and can be identified as follows:

The first layer is called the information processing layer. This handles large, typically batch-orientated data processing tasks, running functions such as material control, order processing, financial control systems, production planning, CAD/CAM. The systems used at this layer can be characterised by such software packages as MRP II (Resource Planning) and J.I.T. (Just-in-Time).

The second layer of the architecture is termed the plant layer and is concerned with anything that is plant-wide in scope, including management of facilities, and local production scheduling.

The third layer is the area manager level. At this level, the concern is with things that might be specific to a given area of the plant, such as one complete production line.

The fourth level is the cell-controller. A cell is typically regarded as a group of machines, or process controller, which co-operate on a close basis. Such a cell could consist of a PLC (Programmable Logic Controller) supervising a number of discrete controllers. In many cases a cell could be configured to produce one particular product at any one particular time, and then, possible reconfigured for an alternative product.

The fifth layer covers the automation devices themselves, including instrumentation, actuators and sensors.

The process of integration links together the first and last layers of this structure, thereby providing a total solution to the transfer of information between these levels.

It is this integration and the method of achieving it we will consider next.

The Way Forward

The process of achieving this integration of the various systems described within the introduction has many facets. They concern hardware and software implication, the way the people within the organisation carry out their tasks, the management of the organisation. From all these the most important to ensure a successful outline relates to two main themes, firstly there must be will, at all levels within operation from the people involved, to achieve success and there must be clear goals stated for all showing the benefits of implementing the system integration.

Listed below are the major points that organisations should consider prior to implementing a CIM strategy:

-      Define what you want

-      Develop a team to do it

-      Give the team ownership

-      Take all people outside the team along with you, so that they understand the changes that will be taking place.

The first of these is concerned the mechanics by way of specification of what is required and how it can be realised in practice, and must include targets that are measurable to show that when the integration is analysed the benefits can be seen. The remaining three points relate to the people within the organisation and how they should be managed to ensure success.

The Specifications

The following sequence, each resulting in a written specification, is recommended to define what you want:

- Feasibility Study

- User Requirement Specification

- Functional Specification

In addition to the above further detailed specifications including hardware, software, and testing specifications will be required, but the above specification are essential and will ensure the original intent and aims of the integration are adhered to and met.

The above three areas represent the preparation required prior to the implementation of the integration and should always be completed before the organisation commits itself to any particular hardware/software solution.

Details relating to what should be included within each of the resulting specifications for the stages is given below. For further information the reader should refer to references 1 and 2.

Feasibility Study

The key elements that should be included within the feasibility study are to demonstrate the viability, costs and benefits of the computer system. In addition the question of change should be included, for example what will we have to do differently once we have the system and who will it effect? In establishing the changes to the organisation it will help later in being able to identify those people who need to be involved and whose commitment will be required to ensure a successful outcome.

The structure and content of the feasibility study will vary from project to project, guidelines on the contents of a feasibility study are given within reference 1.

Having completed the study and obtained general agreement within the organisation that it represents the way forward and the costs and benefits obtainable are acceptable the next stage is to produce a User Requirement Specification.

User Requirement Specification

At this stage have identified within the feasibility study the viability of the project, the User Requirement Specification defines what the system has to do. This User Requiment Specification forms the basis on which the eventual systems performance will be measured.

Implied within the title is of course that the users of the system should prepare this specification. Often though within organisations the identification of the user is not always straightforward. Is it the plant operator, his supervisor or the plant production manager? Additionally what is the role of the maintenance manager, what are the requirements of the financial department? It can be seen that assembling the team to prepare the URS can prove to be a difficult management task. Each of the people will require a different set of objectives from the system, some of these will be in conflict. Therefore a balanced team is required, but what is important is strong leadership to ensure the specification is a definite document, produced on time and has clear conclusions on the way forward. A typically core team could consist of a control/system engineer, production manager, process engineer and a data processing manager.

The specification should define that user requirements in terms of function, what the system must do and interfaces, how the system will connect to and interact with the outside world. Details of the structure of a specification are given in reference 1. The User Requirement Specification is a key specification and in its content will set the scene for the system and in particular in relation to the cost and timescale to implement the total integration.

Having established the URS and obtained agreement from all interested parties within the organisation the URS can be used to form the basis of obtaining tender proposals from suitable suppliers of software based systems. Additional consideration apart from the purely technical will have to be addressed at this stage, in particular, relating to cost, project timescale and condition of contract. Consideration should be given within the URS to the requirements of how the overall system is to be tested, and what are the performance parameters by which the system is to be judged, and how these can be demonstrated and tested by the prospective suppliers of the system.

The Functional Specification

The next stage of the process is to produce a Functional Specification. The first consideration should be who is going to produce the document. Experience has shown on successful implementation of computer based system a team consisting of the users and the suppliers is the best approach when preparing the functional specification. If a consultant or external design organisation is being employed then clearly this team should consist of the three participating members. Once again strong leadership is important in particular relating to any divergences that may occur between the Functional Specification and the User Requirement Specification. These should be identified and discussed fully before a change of intent from the User Requirement Specification is allowed to written within the Functional Specification.

Having prepared the Functional Specification the supplier or suppliers of the system will prepare additional documentation including software and testing specification. The user must check that these specifications are still adhering to the requirements of the Functional Specification.

The overall process described above from the feasibility study to final acceptance of the system is termed the project life cycle. For the further details of managing and implementing typical projects the reader should refer to reference 2.

Having described how we specify the integration next we shall consider a typical computer based system used to meet the requirements of the CIM implementation.

The Typical System

We have seen from above in order to integrate the various systems a "bridge" is required. The structure of a typical computer based system is shown in figure 2. The system consists of both hardware and software. The software element is further divided into standard fixed programme packages and application software. By way of example a standard spreadsheet package would form a fixed programme system, whilst the configuration of the spreadsheet package would form the application software. All of the computer based system proposed for CIM application have both these elements. The simple example quoted is the extreme case, when dealing with large computer based system for specific application it is highly unlikely to be able to select a system that will not require considerable application software to meet the User Requirement Specification.

The system illustrated in figure 2 consists of the following main elements:

-       A data processing unit (D.P.U.).

-       A local area network in this case "Ethernet" which links the D.P.U. to the operator interfaces.

-       A number of work stations. In this example the workstation, which provide the graphics and keyboard interface to the operators, are intelligent devices.

-       Serial communication to the plant controls.

The link upwards to level 1, the information processing layer, described earlier, is by means of "Ethernet" gateways to the computer systems at this level. The overall system is shown in the well known "pyramid" form of integration shown in figure 3.

Such a system has to be flexible and be able to be extended as the plant and information requirements of the business increase. A typical growth for the system is shown in figure 4. Commencing with a "single" station to a multiply D.P.U. based system.

At the core of the system is real-time database from which all other functions source their information. This structure allows other software based system to be easily integrated, and this "Open Structure" is a main feature of this system and essential for successful CIM projects. This structure and some of the features which result are shown in figure 5.

With the example shown it is possible to integrate other site based computer system, for example, the warehouse and distribution control system, so that the manufacturing computer system can ensure correct levels of stock are available and that customer orders are implemented effectively. Building management systems can be incorporated to ensure environmental conditions are correct to carry out the production.

Looking further than the specific production area, wide area networks can be used to integrated between various manufacturing sites. This will provide production management with data to enable production requirements on a national basis to be made.

Conclusion

The overall benefits that can accure from implementing a CIM scheme within our manufacture site are great. The following are just some of the benefits that food manufacturers will see:

-       Control of the process by authorised recipes, including best working practice.

-       Total batch recording

-       Repeatability

-       Efficient tuning of resources

-       Real time quality control

-       Realisation plant utilisation data.

In order to achieve such benefits careful planning is required. Aims for the integration have to be set and measured. Teams have to be formed to produce the correct specification at the right time within the project. Most of all people have to be committed to CIM and want to make it work and reap the benefits available to all within the organisation.

References

1.   IEE, 1990, "Guidelines for the Documentation of Computer Software for Real Time and Interactive System". 2nd Edition, The Institution of Electrical Engineers.

2.   DTI and NCC, 1989 "STARTS Purchaser's Handbook Procuring Software - based System", 2nd Edition, Natural Computing Centre.

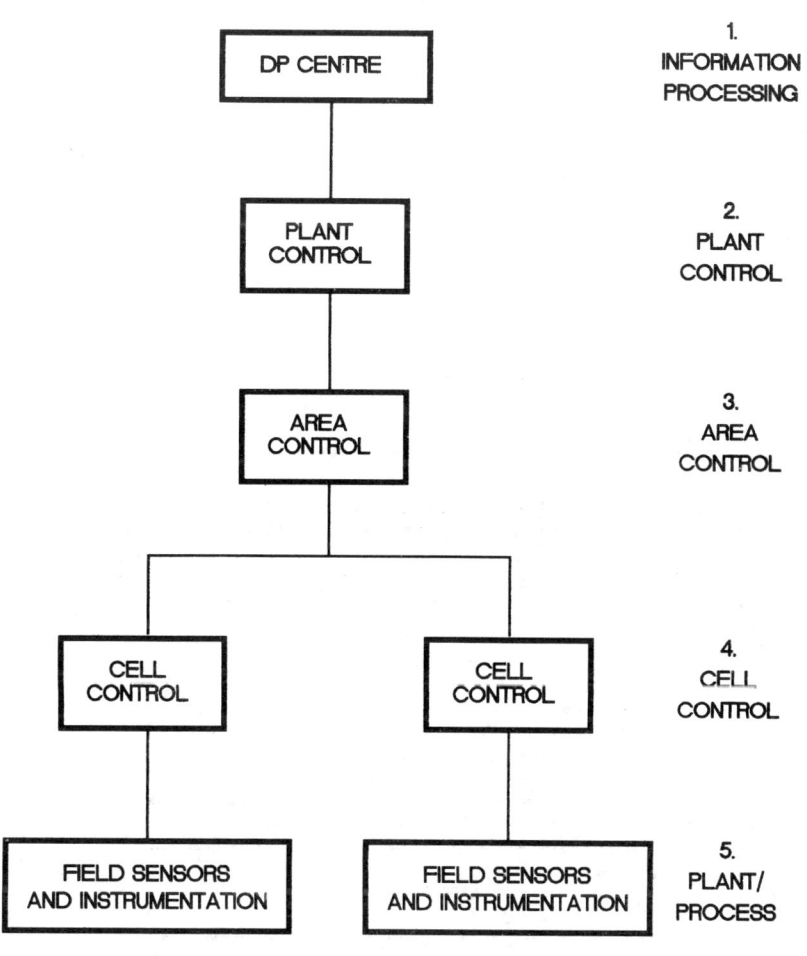

FIGURE 1

ARCHITECTURE

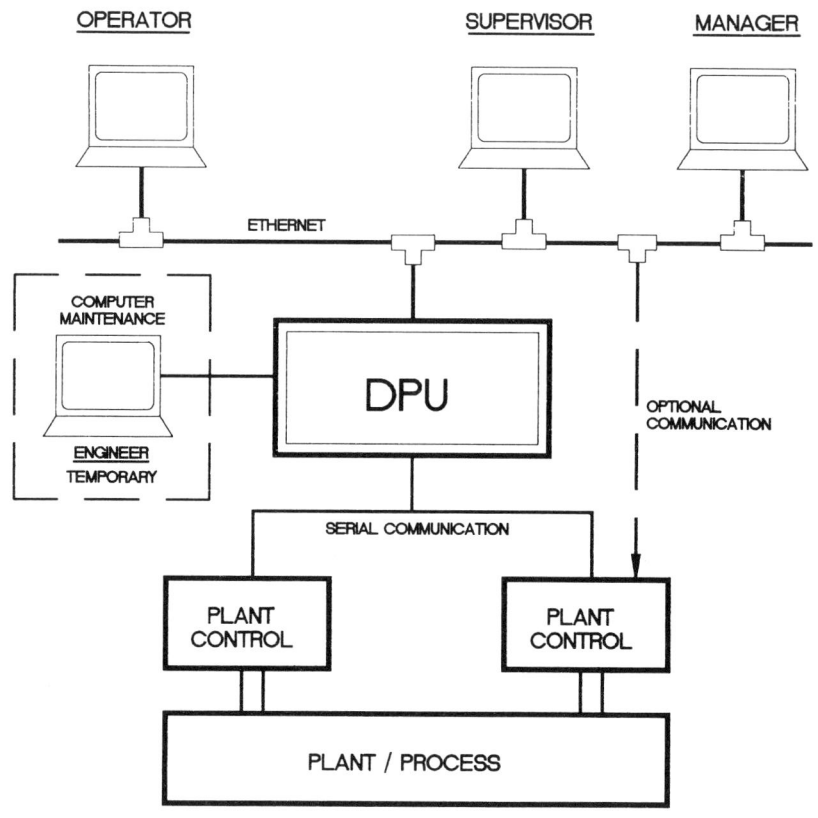

FIGURE 2

MEETING OF TWO WORLDS

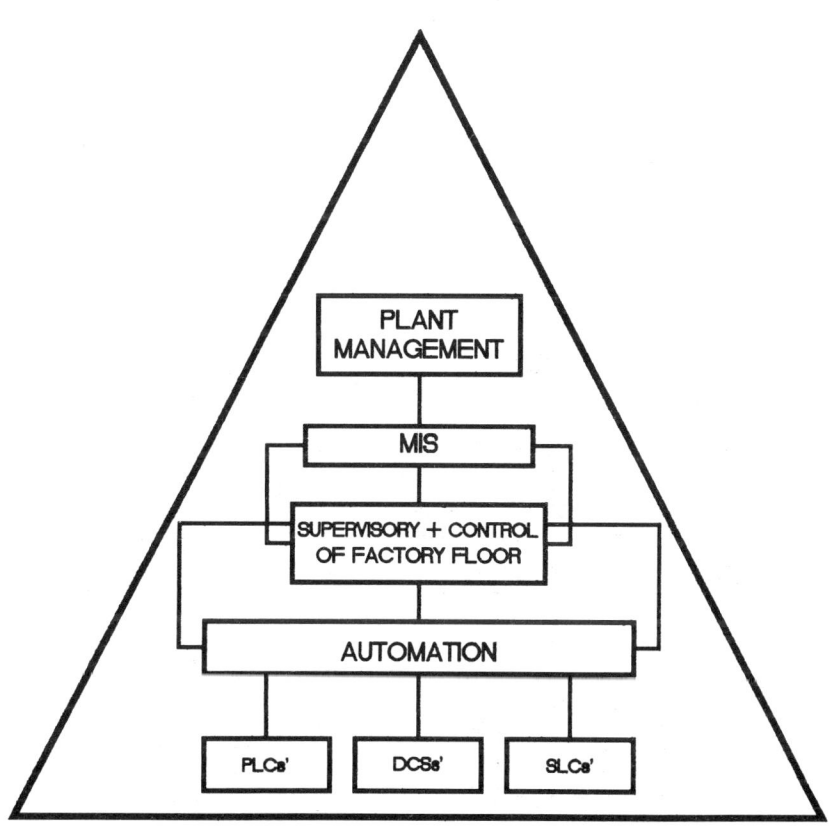

FIGURE 3

A SERIES OF USER-CONFIGURABLE PRODUCTS FOR INDUSTRIAL PROCESS CONTROL SUPERVISION

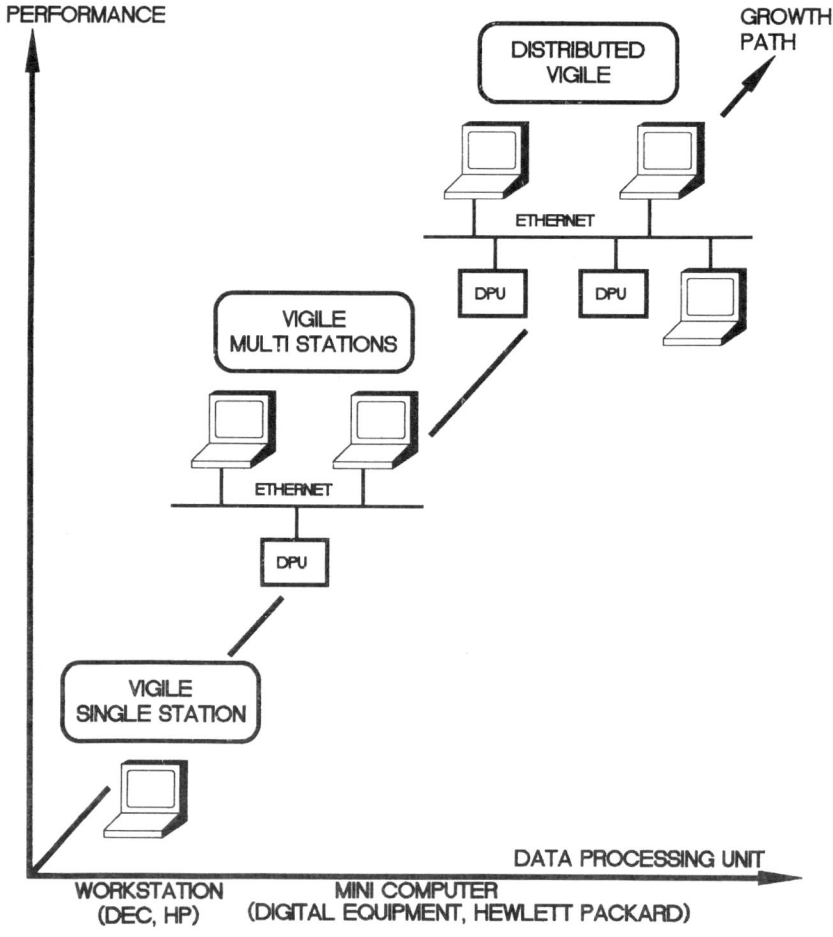

FIGURE 4

AN ADVANCED SYSTEM

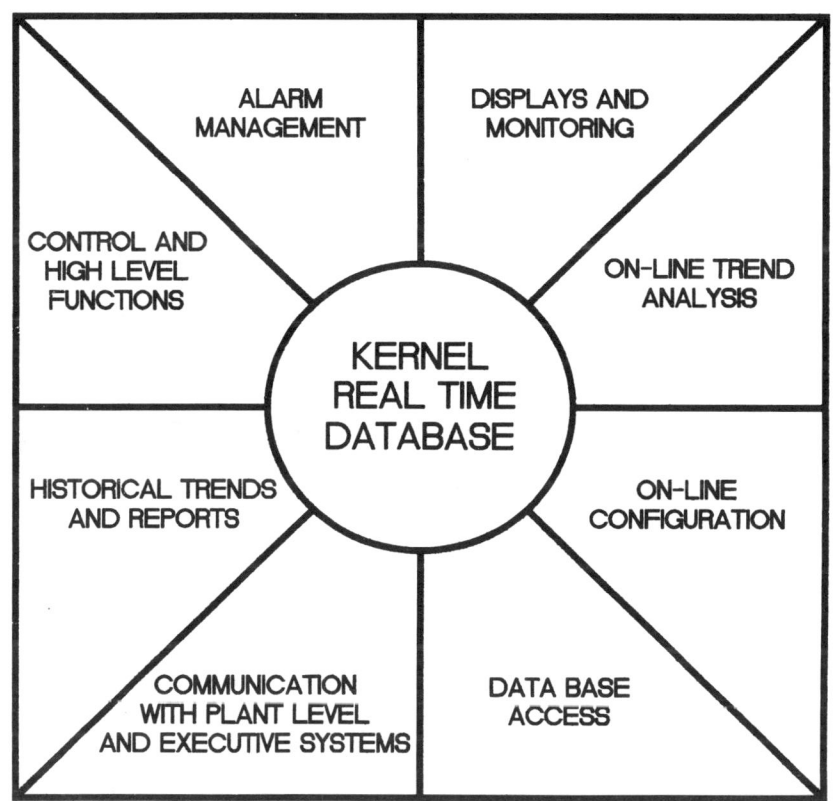

ADVANCED FUNCTIONS FOR A TOTAL
SUPERVISION OF THE PLANT

FIGURE 5

R.F. DIELECTRIC METHODS FOR MOISTURE MEASUREMENT IN

FOOD MATERIALS

W. PLEASS[*]

Not all the requirements of the food industry for on-line moisture measurement have been met by infra red technology. Radio-frequency dielectric techniques can overcome the main disadvantage of infra red reflectance, that bulk moisture content has to be inferred from a very shallow surface measurement. Prototype equipment is working at a bakery. There is scope for further development.

Continuous moisture measurement is a fundamental requirement for full computer control of a baking line. It allows a tightly controlled compromise to be maintained between consumer preference for a moist product and shelf-life considerations. Where the line has to cope with frequent recipe changes to meet market demands, such measurement is an invaluable guide to achieving correct process conditions. The optimum position for a single moisture sensor in a continuous process is considered to be ex-oven but there are advantages in having extra sensors at other locations. For example, a continuous oven may be fed by a preliminary batch mixing process and a sensor at this stage can give early warning of plant problems.

A radio-frequency dielectric method was chosen for moisture measurement on baked sponge ex-oven because it would not be affected too much by surface conditions. The same method was adopted for the aerated batter and in this case it offers a simultaneous measurement of density. Feasibility studies for some other food materials have also been carried out.

Most of the work has been based on probes which take the form of a truncated coaxial cable. When a radio-frequency wave is sent down such a cable which ends in free space, a small proportion is radiated from the cable end but the rest is reflected back again because of impedance mismatch. The reflected wave is approximately in phase with the incident wave at the cable end and the reflection coefficient is in this case: (magnitude almost 100%, angle approx. 0). An electric fringing field exists beyond the end of the probe. If a food sample is placed in this field, the reflection coefficient becomes a function of the complex permittivity of the material. Complex permittivity has a real or lossless component and an imaginary or lossy component. Figure 1 shows mapping of complex permittivity on to reflection coefficient for one of

[*] AFRC Institute of Food Research, Norwich

our probes. The polar diagram is labelled in terms of reflection coefficient with contours of permittivity on it. Figure 2 shows typical sensitivity versus distance from the probe face for the same probe (50 ohm characteristic impedance, dielectric i.d. 9.12 mm, dielectric o.d. 36.3 mm).

It can be shown that the sensitivity of the reflection coefficient phase angle to changes in permittivity is greatest in the region of 90° (1). It has not been possible to achieve this with food materials of low moisture and/or density. The phase angle for constant sample permittivity increases with frequency and probe diameter. For a given operating wavelength in the probe dielectric, the angle can be increased only by enlarging the diameter but there is a limit above which propagation modes of higher order than TEM cause problems. An intermeshing pattern of surface conductors on the face of the probe can increase the sensitivity (2) but at the same time will reduce the extent of the fringing field. For fluid samples including particulates, a hemispherical extension to the inner conductor can be used to good effect (3). Transformation to a higher impedance at the probe face using resonant-line techniques has been found capable of doubling sensitivity with coffee powder under practical conditions at IFRN.

The early food-compatible probes at Norwich were made with stainless steel conductors and ptfe dielectric. Problems arose because the ptfe had approximately seven times the linear thermal expansion of 316 stainless steel and was unstable under mechanical load. A styrene-based copolymer known as Lucentine proved to be better. It was used at the probe face as a slightly tapered disc with 50 ohm airline behind (figure 3). Three sizes of probe have been made in this way. These probes can endure usage at temperatures in the region of 100°C but not much higher. To cover the full range of food processing temperatures, the design had to be modified to use ceramic and stainless steel in a brazed construction. All the probes screw into stainless steel bosses which can be fitted into pipe walls or stationary plates for conveyor application.

As water has an exceptionally high permittivity, moisture content generally has a dominant effect on the dielectric properties of food materials. However, the moisture may have many different forms, ranging from free liquid to strongly adsorbed. As these forms can co-exist in proportions which depend on material characteristics and conditions, one would have difficulty in formulating a universal relationship between material permittivity and moisture content.

For a given material and moisture content, the principal conditions which affect permittivity are temperature and density, the latter varying as a function of air content for many food materials. Where the real and imaginary components of the permittivity may be taken as quasi-independent measurements, a dielectric probe working at a single frequency can be used to determine both moisture and density if the temperature is known. Figure 4 shows distinction between air content and moisture for aerated cake batter; figure 5 is a similar plot for a flaked biscuit product and the air content in this case includes any gaps between biscuit and probe.

Salt content can affect r.f. permittivity and interfere with this type of measurement. With tinned pet foods, which may have a moisture content exceeding 80%, the effect of conductivity variations needs either to be reduced by using a higher frequency in the microwave region or discriminated by making use of a supplementary measurement at another frequency. On the other hand, the common salt and raising agents in a cake mix of 35% moisture were found to be innocuous at 1 GHz, owing to the effect of the other ingredients.

As part of the DTI/MAFF Food Sciences LINK programme, a prototype moisture meter is undergoing plant trials for on-line measurements on baked sponge. A reflectometer, situated close to the probe, has two analog outputs corresponding in principle to 1 GHz reflection coefficient in Cartesian form. The computing unit, situated 35 metres away, operates on the ratio of these outputs combined with temperature readings and material thickness to produce a moisture reading which is strictly in terms of mass/volume. Other plant measurements (e.g. batter mass flow and batter moisture) can be added to the computer inputs to give density information and convert to mass/mass. Calibration is carried out daily using one measurement on air and one on a slab of a standard dielectric material. The calibration details are archived for future evaluation of long-term drift. A second prototype is nearly ready for trials on the batter. It will make use of a density signal from an existing Coriolis meter. The moisture meter could be independent of the density or even evaluate it if the modulus of the reflectometer outputs were brought into the calculations; this is shown clearly by figure 4. Such development could be the subject of a future project.

REFERENCES
(1) Athey, T., Stuchly, M. and Stuchly, S. IEEE Trans. Microwave Theory and Techniques, Vol. MTT-30, No. 1, 1982.
(2) Esselle, K. and Stuchly, S. IEEE Transactions on Instrumentation and Measurement Vol. 37, No. 1, 1988.
(3) Xu, Y. and Bosisio, R. Microwave and Optical Technology Letters Vol. 3, No. 2, 1990.

ACKNOWLEDGEMENT
The LINK work has been accomplished with co-operation from Lyons Bakeries, FMBRA, Beaconsfield Instrument Company and AT&T Istel.

Figure 1

Contours of permittivity for coaxial probe
Extrapolated Nevels' computation at 1.0 GHz

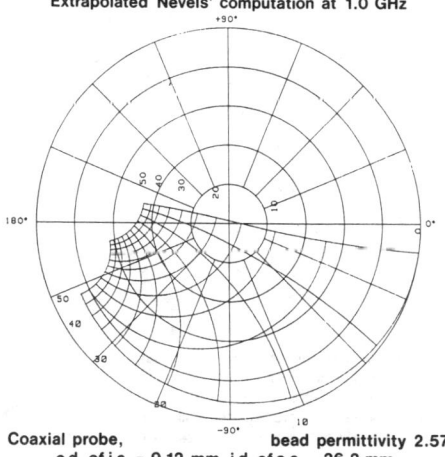

Coaxial probe,   bead permittivity 2.57
o.d. of i.c. = 9.12 mm, i.d. of o.c. = 36.3 mm

Figure 2

Sensitivity versus distance from probe face for a 50 Ω Probe
of dielectric o.d. = 36.3mm and i.d. = 9.12 mm (in cooking oil).

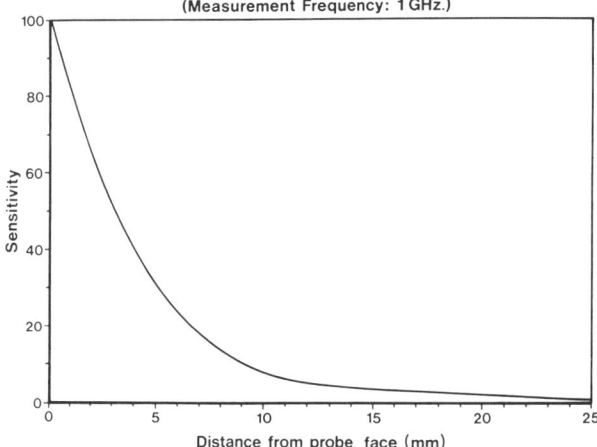

(Measurement Frequency: 1 GHz.)

Figure 3

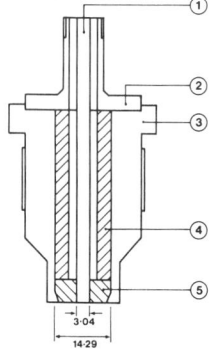

1. INNER CONDUCTOR 316 ST. ST. ∅ 3·17
2. CAP 316 ST. ST.
3. BODY 316 ST. ST. 1·25″ U.N.F.
4. INNER SLEEVE 316 ST. ST. SHRINK FIT
5. LUCENTINE INSERT ∅ 14·29 SHRINK FIT

14mm Lucentine Probe

Figure 4

Measurements on a flake biscuit product

(Measurement Frequency: 1 GHz., Temperature 20 Degrees Celsius)

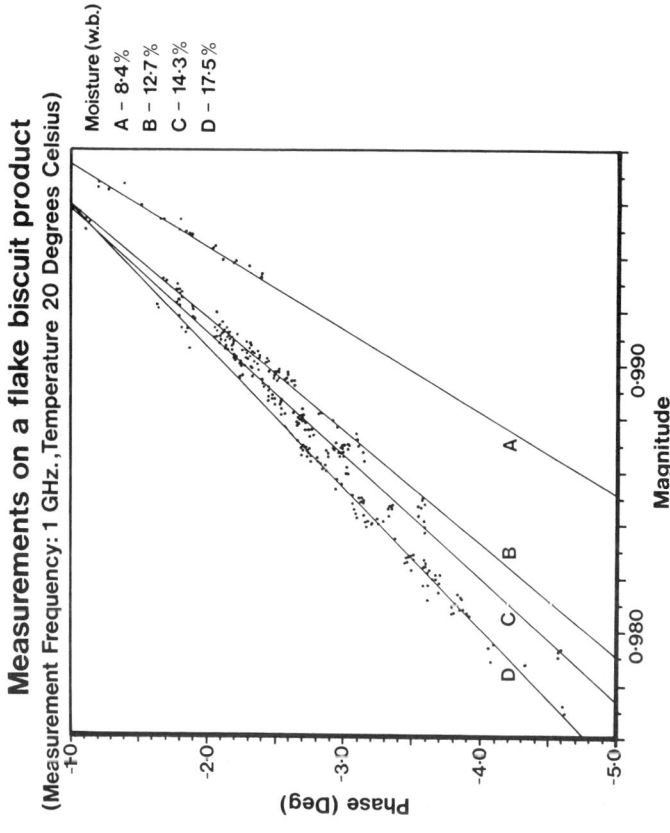

Moisture (w.b.)

A – 8·4%
B – 12·7%
C – 14·3%
D – 17·5%

Figure 5

Effect of Moisture and Bulk Density on Probe Response to an Aerated Food Dispersion

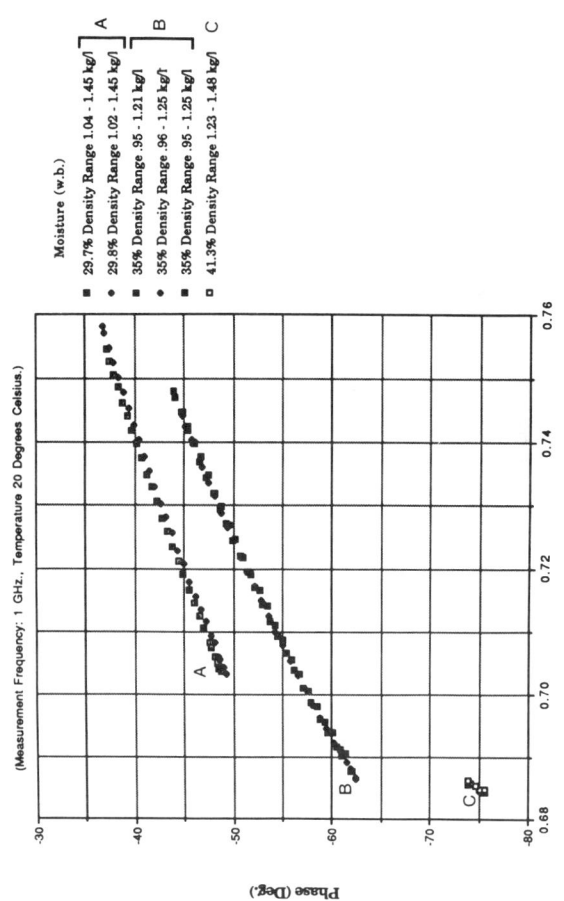

(Measurement Frequency: 1 GHz., Temperature 20 Degrees Celsius.)

Magnitude

Phase (Deg.)

Moisture (w.b.)

■ 29.7% Density Range 1.04 - 1.45 kg/l   ⎤ A
♦ 29.8% Density Range 1.02 - 1.45 kg/l   ⎦
■ 35% Density Range .95 - 1.21 kg/l   ⎤ B
♦ 35% Density Range .96 - 1.25 kg/f   ⎦
■ 35% Density Range .95 - 1.25 kg/l
□ 41.3% Density Range 1.23 - 1.48 kg/l   C

MAXIMISING THE OUTPUT OF A BATCH FOOD PLANT
- THE DESIGN ENGINEER'S ROLE

R.G.CADBURY[1]

The capacity of a batch food plant is determined by the size and configuration of the unit processes installed in it. Often the production capacity is unnecessarily limited because the user's requirements have not been fully stated and analysed at the conceptual design stage. The paper outlines the steps needed to optimise design capacity, with special reference to the demands of a multi-purpose batch food plant incorporating automation and CIP.

INTRODUCTION

Design of a batch plant for food processing begins with definition of the products and process techniques to be used, after which development of a flowsheet may begin. At this point the user's demands for product flexibility and clean in place (CIP) must be recognised. Choices to be made include:

Number and capacity of processing (eg heat treatment) lines?
Number and capacity of filling lines?
What tanks? Which tank can link with which line/filler?
What cleaning and sanitation strategy to adopt?

There seems no rational method of resolving these conflicting questions. Unlike continuous processes - which are rare in food manufacture - there is not the reassurance of preparing a plant-wide mass and heat balance. The design conditions which determine the capacity and duty of each process item occur at different times, under varying conditions, perhaps on different products.

Faced with this confusion, it is easy to abandon all pretence of orderly design, and launch into trying to create some sort of flowsheet, that meets part of the design needs. Expressed this way, it sounds a recipe for disaster, and indeed it is - but in many food processing projects the design does indeed evolve this way. Initial designs are created, engineered, costed - only to be discarded when the team reassesses the capability which the flowsheet offers. Their verdict might be: "Sure the flowsheet will make product X (custard). It can also make Y (rice pudding) - provided 12 hours' CIP per day is acceptable! But it will not make Z (blancmange), and X cannot be produced simultaneously with Y." A completely new scheme is required to meet these needs.

---

[1]John Brown Engineers and Constructors, Portsmouth

The approach described above is wasteful of time and money at the design stage. It may mean that the optimum design is never reached, and the bottlenecks only become evident when the plant is in production. This paper sets out what information must be obtained to form a clear design basis. It then shows how the plant's utilisation should be analysed to enable rapid convergence to the most effective conceptual design, before proceeding to initial engineering and costing.

PRODUCING THE BLOCK FLOWSHEET

There are two stages to producing the block flowsheet:
1. Prepare the design basis.
2. Draw the block flowsheet and test it against the design basis.

These actions are illustrated in Figure 1.

The design basis is really a series of answers to a questionnaire. Some will be matters of fact, such as (we hope!) the definitions of raw materials and products. Others are operational needs, on which a value can be placed: for example the user may wish to operate the plant on a five-day two-shift pattern, but can accept limited working of night shifts or weekends at premium cost. Below are some main headings for a design basis; the content of the sections is discussed further on in this paper.

TABLE 1
INFORMATION FOR DESIGN BASIS

CATEGORY	IMPORTANT INFORMATION
Raw materials	Form and packaging. How delivered.
Products	Definition. Form and packaging. Quantities: batch size, batches per day or week.
Manufacturing procedures	For each product - formulation, raw material usage, utility usage, manufacturing steps, time before CIP required.
Utilities, effluents, by-products	Quantities for each product. Further processing of by- or co-products.
Operating strategy and constraints	Campaign length: hours or days? Changes on the run? Optimum sequencing (eg light product followed by dark product). What speed of response to changes in production plan - 2 hours, 1 day, 1 week? Tolerance to breakdowns - how much slack time in schedule?
Clean/aseptic production: CIP and SIP	Cleaning/ sterilising demands and cycles. How many separate CIP units?
Level of automation	Choose between manual, semi-automatic, fully auto plant operation. Different level of automation may apply for sequencing as opposed to routing operations.

DESIGN BASIS - DEFINING RAW MATERIALS AND PRODUCTS

For raw materials the form and packaging must be defined. The range and formulation of products will be difficult to pin down and will usually change with time - but without product definitions the design basis has no meaning, so it is better to make some statement, at least as a point of reference against which to assess changes later. The packaging of the products, product instantaneous output and output per day and per week are also very important.

The production recipe must define both the sequence of operations in making each product, and also quantify usages of raw materials and utilities and production of effluents, by-products and co-products. To give an example on co-products: a dairy plant will produce various quantities of full cream milk, semi-skimmed milk and skimmed milk, with cream of several different fat contents (single, whipping, double, etc) produced from the cream arising. A number of output cases must be checked to ensure that the dairy has sufficient flexibility to handle variations in demand for the different products. This includes contingency planning for the co-product (cream) when the demand for this is significantly more or less than the supply.

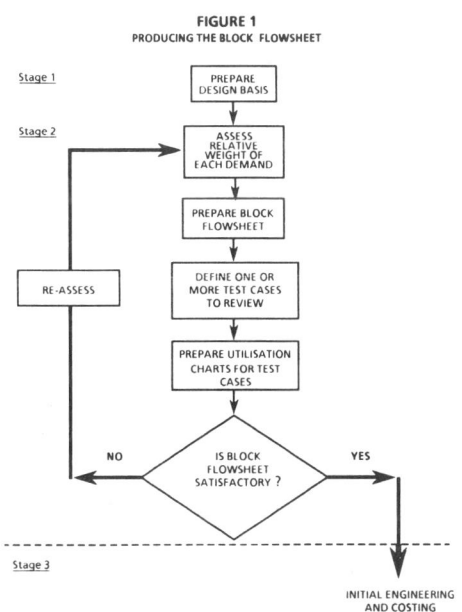

FIGURE 1
PRODUCING THE BLOCK FLOWSHEET

Production Strategy

The plant operator, on being asked to state the production strategy early in the design phase, may respond that the subject is too nebulous to define. In reality he will have strong views on a number of issues with regard to strategy and production flexibility, which are best revealed early on: otherwise much design effort will be negated by a comment such as "It's a nice design, but didn't you realise we wanted to make rice pudding and custard on a Thursday?" The designer must ask and obtain answers to such questions as:

For each product, what is the largest/smallest batch, or the longest/shortest campaign which will be run?

Where two or more products can be made on the same line, will there be a change "on the run"? Is this allowed in both directions, or only in one? (For example tomato sauce could follow white sauce, but not the other way round)

How many shifts, how many days per week?

What are the consequences of a stoppage or breakdown? How much slack is needed in the time schedule to allow for problems?

FIGURE 2
UTILISATION DIAGRAM

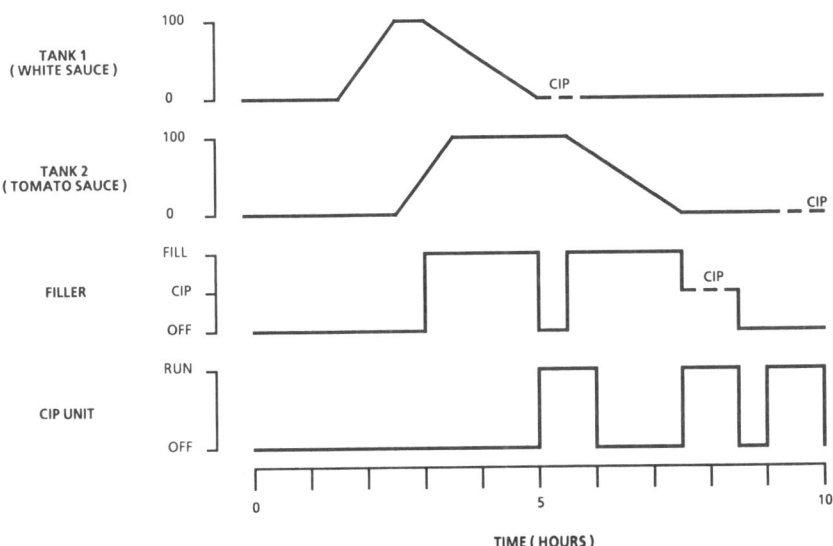

TIME (HOURS)

UTILISATION STUDIES

Having established a firm design basis, stage 2 is an iterative process to develop, test and improve the block flow scheme. This is done by developing one or more test cases, and studying the utilisation of the plant over a suitable period using a time chart. One test case might represent a normal product mix, another might reflect a peak seasonal case. For an example of the latter, consider the effect of the "strawberry season" on a plant making fresh dairy cream. The test criterion might be that normal production and CIP can be completed each day between 0600 and 2200. During the peak season 24 hours working is acceptable - but what if the utilisation diagram shows 28 hours are needed each day? Clearly there is a bottleneck. The decision then for the team is whether to increase peak capacity or reduce the peak demand imposed on the plant. This may require some cost estimation, to assess the extra capital spend and the revenue which it generates; but the costing exercise is limited and focussed, rather than a full cost estimate.

Figure 2 illustrates a simple utilisation diagram. The full value of such a diagram will be realised in more complex cases, where a number of process operations interact with one another.

Product Changes and Routing Problems
Product changes have a cost, in that there may be productive time lost in the changeover, and the utilisation study will again provide a useful insight. Take for example a cheese factory, mainly making cheddar cheese but with a limited demand for Red Leicester, which will produce coloured whey. The light-coloured whey from cheddar must not mix with the redder whey. Thus whey tankage which would be sufficient for continous cheddar production will not allow the changeover without a long shutdown. More but

smaller tanks are needed to speed up the changeover.

Utilisation studies may also show up routing problems. The production strategy may call for several products to be made in parallel. This not only calls for sufficient process units and tankage to allow the parallel operations, but also a check that the transfer piping and routes available do not lead to conflicts, either product-product conflicts or product-CIP fluid conflicts. This is often an issue in designing breweries, for example. Although it can be fairly straightforward to specify how many tanks, filters, pasteurisers and fillers are needed, the problem is that these units must be connected, and due allowance must be made for CIP of all connecting pipework. If the system is automated, the number of automatic valves in the pipework system will be 10-20 valves per process tank, eg 100-200 valves just for a battery of 10 beer tanks with full auto-routing and CIP. The supply, installation and control of these for a brewery with 100 or more tanks can represent a frightening cost. A review of the frequency with which the transfer mains are used may show that a manually operated hose transfer station offers adequate flexibility at lower capital cost.

Design for Cleaning
The plant must be maintained in a state of cleanliness consistent with product safety and shelf life. Although the following remarks refer to cleaning (CIP) and disinfection of plant, they apply equally to plants producing an aseptic product under commercially sterile conditions.

To arrive at a CIP strategy, the block diagram of the plant must be considered as a series of cleaning objects, generally defining each tank, processing unit and pipe section as a separate cleaning object. For each one identify:
        Level of cleanliness required
        Running time between cleans
        Soiling characteristics of plant
        CIP program and duration
Now it is possible to define the number of CIP units and what type of plant each unit is designed to clean.

Automation
The level of automation will determine whether sequences and route changes are executed manually or automatically. The decisions on level of automation should follow logically from the initial development of the block scheme already described. Studies of plant utilisation will identify which operations benefit from automation. These will be for example:

FIGURE 3
ROUTING OPTIONS

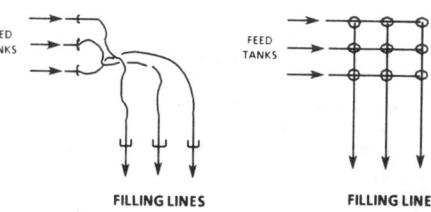

FILLING LINES   FILLING LINES

(a) MANUAL ROUTING USES HOSES TO ACHIEVE FULL FLEXIBILITY

(b) MATRIX WITH AUTO VALVE AT EACH NODE ALLOWS SELECTION OF ANY ROUTE

        Freqently run sequences - eg CIP cycles
        Situations where manual switching could be unsafe or
compromise plant sterility - eg on a tank holding aseptic product
before filling.

Routing systems where automation gives a useful increase in the range of routes available - see Figure 3. This contrasts the use of hoses and automatic valves to achieve any permutation of connecting a feed tank to a filling line. The hose system, although low in cost, will cause operational problems, in particular: product spillage, long changeover times and need for manual cleaning.

It is best to adopt a questioning attitude to automation: despite the relative decline in the cost of automation there are still many cases where the cost is not justified. One example would be a simple, infrequent operation - eg a syrup tank which is drained and cleaned at monthly intervals: a selector panel will be adequate for selecting the cleaning route. Another instance is a special item of plant (eg a filling machine) where some manual cleaning is obligatory: this will limit the overall value of automation.

REVIEW OF DESIGN METHODS

The preceding sections have outlined a systematic approach to define the user's requirements for the plant under consideration, followed by a modelling of the plant utilisation under operating conditions to verify the suitability of the design. As so much modelling of continuous processes is now carried out using computer-based methods, the application of computer simulation to the type of batch operation described needs to be considered. Benefits would include:

Automatic calculation of effect on common services to the facility such as CIP plant and utilities - the peak load on utilities is easily visualised.

Ability to rapidly display the answer to "what-if?" questions.

However it is not apparent that such computer-based modelling has yet been widely applied to the conceptual design of food plants. The logic required to build a utilisation chart and then modify it in response to "what-if?" questions may be quite complex. A successful modelling method should allow rapid preparation and redrawing of the utilisation chart, but should interact with the designer or user to maintain his control over the production plan as the chart is developed.

CONCLUSION

The expense of constructing a new plant for food or drink manufacture is such that obtaining maximum output and flexibility at minimum capital cost are clearly of the greatest importance. Achieving the optimum design is a task to be approached systematically. The design basis and the relative importance of the conflicting demands on the plant must be set out, and the initial flowsheet that is prepared must be tested by studying the plant's utilisation diagram under varying conditions. Any problems found are resolved by repeating the procedure, before allowing further development and costing of the design.

The method adopted relies on a blend of logic and calculation. While it is an area where development of computer-based simulation could be profitable, the computer method must not overlook the essential input of the end-user's qualitative needs and judgements in developing the design.

NEURAL NETWORKS IN FUZZY EXTRUSION CONTROL

P. Linko[1,2], K. Uemura[3] and T. Eerikäinen[1]

Neural network programming has during the last few years become one of the hottest research areas of artificial intelligence. Nevertheless, little information is available on the application of neural network models in food processing systems. Artificial neural networks differ from conventional programs in their ability to learn about the system to be modelled without a need of any *a priori* knowledge on the relationships of the process varaiables in question. A three-layered feed-forward neural network model of 3-10-4 topology was constructed in C-language for the simulation and control of flat bread extrusion process. Back-propagation learning algorithm was used in the training of the network. A reverse calculation procedure made it possible to simulate and control the extruder simultaneously.

INTRODUCTION

Extrusion cooking is one of the most versatile food processes owing to its capability to convey, homogenize, gelatinize, denature, and cook and/or cool food materials as applied in many conventional and novel food manufacturing operations, and more recently also in biotechnical and chemical processes (Linko et al., 1981; Linko, 1983; Mercier et al., 1989). Consequently, the optimization (Eerikäinen and Linko, 1989; Meuser et al., 1990), identification (Cayot et al., 1991), and automatic control (Olkku et al., 1980; Eerikäinen and Linko, 1989; Kulshreshtha et al., 1991) of food extrusion processes is of great interest. Nevertheless, unlike with polymer extruders (Parnaby et al., 1975; Costin et al., 1982) the automatic control of food extrusion cookers faces great difficulties because of the lack of on-line measurable quality variables and of the appropriate sensors, and because of the uncertainties involved in the behaviour of the biological materials and the complex and unclear interactions between the various process variables. Process identification employing mathematical models designed to describe the dynamic highly non-linear behaviour of such systems to be controlled and frequently based on a number of assumptions and approximations, may lead to problems when applied to real-life on-line control situations. Further, undesired process instabilities are typical of food extrusion cooking (Roberts and Guy, 1986).

[1]*Helsinki University of Technology, Laboratory of Biotechnology and Food Engineering, SF-02150 Espoo, Finland*

[2]*Author to whom correspondence should be addressed*

[3]*Visiting scientist at Helsinki University of Technology. Present address: National Food Research Institute, Ministry of Agriculture, Forestry and Fisheries, Tsukuba, Ibaraki, 305 Japan*

When in a single-screw synthetic polymer extrusion processes screw speed is typically the most important control variable, in food extrusion cooking mass feed rate, feed moisture (or water feed rate) and barrel temperature also have to be considered. The problems involved in employing one or more product quality characteristics such as crispness or degree of expansion as the primary controlled variables has led to the use of direct process outputs such as drive torque, drive motor current, mass temperature, pressure before the die plate, and energy consumption as dependent variables to be controlled. Thus the extrusion cooking is a typical multiple input, multiple output process (Olkku *et al.*, 1983) which is difficult to be reduced to a single output situation (Kulshrestha *et al.*, 1991).

Because of the complexity of the problem, extrusion cookers have been until recently controlled by relatively simple on-off controllers, and by expert's decisions relying on empirical knowledge of past experiences. One of the first attempts towards automatic control of a twin-screw extruder was that by Olkku *et al.* (1980), who employed adaptive feed-back control with recursive model parameter estimation and a low-pass filter to eliminate the existing pressure fluctuations. In wheat flour extrusion the pressure before the die was most effectively controlled by the mass feed rate. Antila (p. 189 in Eerikäinen and Linko, 1989) later demonstrated that the loading of the extruder drive motor often correlates better with the overall severity of material treatment during extrusion cooking than does pressure alone. When the main motor current was selected to act as a response to changes in mass feed rate and screw speed, the automatic control behaved like manual control with only a slight transient damping owing to the low-pass filtering of process parameters. Levine *et al.* (1986) emphasized the importance of moisture as the control variable and suggested that the initial rate of a pressure change would be an advance warning of moisture induced disturbances. Kondury *et al.* (1986) applied an optimal pole placement algorithm for feed-back control of mass temperature with the power input to the external heater as the control variable. Finally, Wiedman and Strecker (1988) demonstrated the advantages of employing several superimposed closed control loops in the microcomputer based PID-control of a twin-screw extruder. Both Ferdinand *et al.* (1987, 1988), and Wiedman and Strecker (1988) stressed the benefits of automatic start-up and shut-down of extrusion cooking.

Recently Linko and Linko (1987) suggested the application of fuzzy logic in the modelling and control of extrusion cooking. Fuzzy logic has been shown to provide a convenient tool for handling uncertainties in systems such as extrusion cooking (Linko, 1988). Unlike in the conventional theory of sets, a fuzzy set A on a universe of discourse X is characterized by a membership function $\mu_A(x_i)$, $\forall x_i \in X$ ($\mu_A : X \rightarrow [0,1]$) with a grade of membership of x_i in A, represented by a real number $\mu(x_i)$ within the interval of [0,1]. In fuzzy control both primary and dependent variables can be represented as sets of linguistic values such as 'high', 'very low', *etc.*, which in turn are related to numerical values by fuzzy sets. A fuzzy model is composed of a group of conditional *if-then* statements of the form: *if A then B*, where A and B are fuzzy sets and $\mu_{A \cap B}(x_i) = \min [\mu_A(x_i), \mu_B(x_i)]$, together with the corresponding membership functions of each linguistic value. Thus fuzzy models are based in part on subjective expert knowledge, and can be considered as a form of applied artificial intelligence (AI). Recently the potential of fuzzy modelling and control to extrusion cooking has been demonstrated (Eerikäinen *et al.*, 1988; Eerikäinen and Linko, 1989). More recently, Aarts *et al.* (1990) applied object oriented programming environment Smalltalk for the developing of a hierarchic rule- and frame-based on-line, real-time fuzzy control system for a twin-screw extrusion cooker.

Whereas the construction of conventional fuzzy and expert systems is based on subjective expert knowledge, artificial neural network models have the unique capability of learning from exemplar training data sets and an ability to adapt to a changing environment (Hertz *et al.*, 1991; Jansson *et al.*, 1991). Inasmuch as neural networks also are able to deal with uncertainties, and with noisy and approximate data, a neural network programming is rapidly becoming an interesting, novel method in the estimation, prediction, and control of dynamic bioprocesses (Linko and Zhu, 1991, 1992a,b,c). Miller *et al.* (1990) have discussed in detail the basic principles and application potential of neural networks in control.

Unlike with conventional expert systems, neural network models do not require any *a priory* knowledge on the relationships of the process variables in question. However, it has been shown that neural network models can be integrated to a knowledge based system (Rich, 1990). For example a neural network model can form an object in an object oriented program. Although the theory of artificial neural networks is not new, and neural network models have been applied for example in fault detection (Hoskins and Himmelblau, 1988), robot control (Handelman *et al.*, 1990), and bioprocess state estimation and prediction (Linko and Zhu, 1991), the application of neural network models to food processing systems is novel. The practical aim of the present work was to apply neural network programming in fuzzy control of a twin-screw extrusion cooker, and thus minimize problems associated with the construction of intelligent extrusion control systems.

THEORETICAL ANALYSIS

Artificial neural network models were initially developed to mimic the function of brain. Brain contains billions of nerve cells or neurons highly interconnected through synapses. An impulse to a neuron triggers the release of neurotransmitters which diffuse to bind to receptors at the adjacent neuron. It is believed that the synaptic strength of the junctions is modified when knowledge is stored in the brain. Consequently, a synapse can be considered as the basic memory unit of the brain. An artificial neural network is a computer program consisting of a number of parallel interconnected artificial neurons as processing units (Lippmann, 1987). The interconnected neurons process and propagate signals through the network. The architecture of an artificial neural network is chosen according to the type and the complexity of the problem to be solved. A feedforward multilayered network structure with interconnected neurons in three layers, an input layer, a hidden layer, and an output layer, as shown in Figure 1 is the structure of choise for bioprocess modelling.

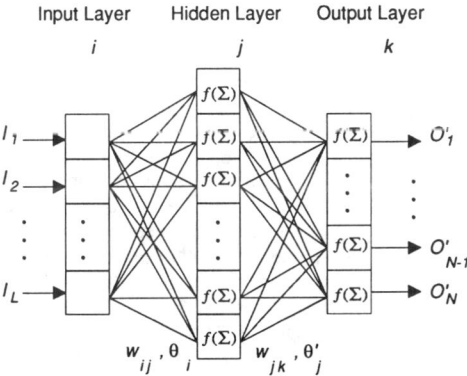

Figure 1. Structure of a three-layered, feed-forward neural network.

(Linko and Zhu, 1991). Each connection between two neurons in adjacent layers has a weight factor w, a real number which describes the strength of the connection. The number of neurons in the different layers describes the topology of the network. The number of neurons in the hidden layer(s) is related to the converging performance of the output error function during the training process of the network, and the optimal number is usually determined by trial and error. Too few hidden neurons limits the ability of the artificial neural network to model the process, and too many hidden elements can result in learning the noise present in the data base used in training.

The main function of an artificial neural network can be summarized as interpolation from known (teacher), often experimentally measured values to the requested (target) and/or simulated values. To acquire knowledge the neural network is trained by adjusting the weights of the neuronal interconnections through iteration on the basis of representative exemplar input/output data vector pair patterns. The weight coefficients are usually assigned random small initial values. The neurons in the input layer carry out no calculations. They only store the input values scaled to within the range of [1,0], and transfer them to the appropriate neurons in the hidden layer. The inputs to one processing unit from the neurons in the preceding layer are multiplied with the appropriate weight factors, the weighted values are summed up, and the output of the neuron is obtained by passing the weighted sum through a non-linear transfer function as shown for the hidden neuron in equation (1), and for the output neuron in equation (2):

$$O_j = f\left[\sum_{i=0}^{L-1} w_{ij} I_i - \theta_i\right] \qquad 0 \le j \le M-1 \qquad (1)$$

$$O'_k = f\left[\sum_{j=0}^{M-1} w_{jk} O_j - \theta'_j\right] \qquad 0 \le k \le N-1 \qquad (2)$$

where I_i is the scaled input vector, O_j and O'_k are the respective output vectors of the hidden and output layers, w is the appropriate weight of an interconnection between the neurons in adjacent layers, L, M and N are the respective numbers of neurons in the input, hidden and output layers, θ is the internal bias term which determines the coordinate space of non-linearity, and f is the non-linear transfer function, in the present work a sigmoid (min = 0, max = 1) of the type $f(x) = 1/[1 + \exp(-x)]$.

A useful and convenient training algorithm for feed-forward layered neural networks is back-propagation, which was also used in the present work (Rumelhart et al., 1986). In back-propagation the weights of the interconnections are modified via propagation of an error signal backwards from the outputs to the inputs. Back-propagation is a generalization of the least mean square procedure or delta rule, in which the gradient descent technique is employed to minimize a cost function equal to the mean square difference between the desired and actual neural network output. In adjusting the weights during each iteration cycle the training algorithm performs in principle by shifting each weight towards its own minimum along the error surface in the weight space, the height of which at any point is equal to the value of the error function. In other words, the neural network simulates the response between the input and the output.

PROGRAMMING ENVIRONMENT

The neural network program was written by using Microsoft C ver 6.0 and MS Windows soft-ware development kit. An IBM compatible computer with an Intel 80386/20 MHz processor with a math coprocessor, 40 MB hard disk, 4 MB memory on the main board, and a VGA display was used.

SIMULATED INTELLIGENT EXTRUDER CONTROL

Figure 2 represents a black-box approach to extruder control, with three input (control) ports and four output (sensing) ports. Figure 3 illustrates the same input/output set as the

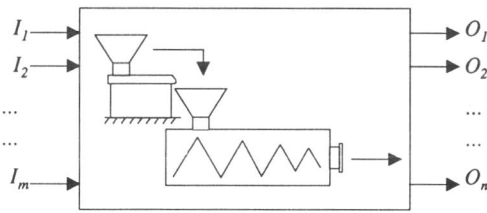

Figure 2. Black-box diagram of an extrusion process.

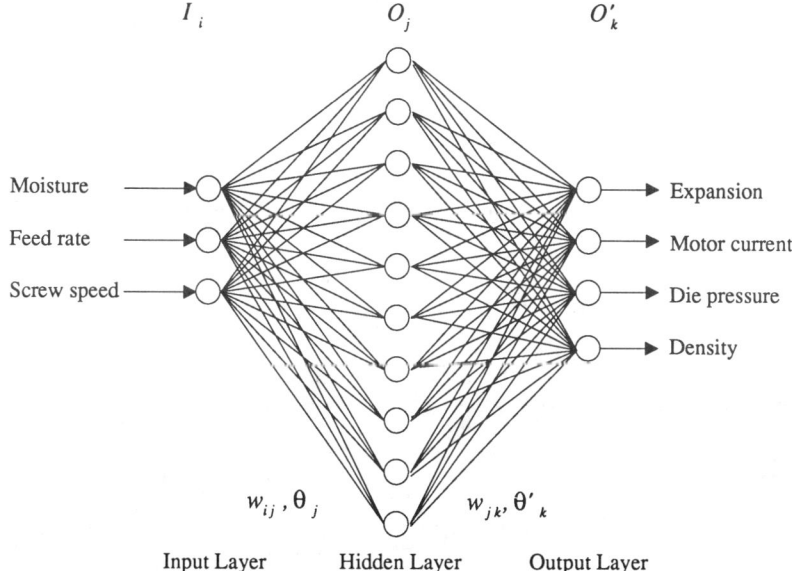

Figure 3. Neural network used in the simulation of flat bread extrusion.

neural network model used in the present work. Ten neurons were chosen for the hidden layer by experimentation, resulting in a 3-10-4 network topology.

The example product investigated was flat bread produced with a Clextral BC 21 twin-screw extruder. The selected input variables were mass moisture content, mass feed rate, and screw speed, and the output variables were product expansion rate, main motor current, pressure at the die plate, and product bulk density. The training data set for the neural network consisted of 15 experiments as shown in Table 1.

Table 1. Extruded flat bread data set for neural network training

Input			Output			
Moisture [%]	Feed [g/min]	Screw [rpm]	Expansion [%]	Current [A]	Pressure [bar]	Density [g/dm^3]
17.52	113	213	5.30	6.0	44	150.08
20.48	113	213	4.80	5.6	32	171.87
17.52	187	213	5.00	7.9	58	114.64
20.48	187	213	4.60	6.3	42	168.25
17.52	113	287	5.50	5.5	27	143.48
20.48	113	287	4.60	4.6	14	164.68
17.52	187	287	5.10	6.6	35	101.78
20.48	187	287	4.60	4.7	20	183.42
17.00	150	250	5.60	7.1	42	124.34
21.00	150	250	4.10	5.8	28	158.07
19.00	100	250	5.00	4.6	15	140.00
19.00	200	250	4.80	6.4	33	110.47
19.00	150	200	4.90	5.6	30	160.94
19.00	150	300	4.70	5.6	21	117.23
19.00	150	250	5.10	5.7	32	137.27

Both the input and output data were scaled to within the range of [0,1]. Each processing element in the neural network also transfered the values 0 and 1 as the minimum and maximum of the sigmoidal transfer function used to normalize the output of each neuron. The results of learning were illustrated as three dimensional contour graphs as shown as an example in Figure 4. In the example case in each graph the x-, y- and z-axes represent the mass feed rate, feed moisture, and product expansion ratio, respectively, when screw speed was kept constant at various levels.

The control action can be realized by applying reverse calculation. For simplicity the principle is demonstrated in Figure 5 for one variable input/output pair only. The x-axis gives the input (control) and the y-axis gives the output (sensing). If at a given time input is $x = a$ the neural network calculates for the output $y = b$. If one would like to increase the value of the output y to the level b', the step-wise reverse calculation would find a corresponding new control value for the input $x = a'$. A multiple input multiple output case is, in principle, analogical. The following example further illustrates the control calculation. If all of the input values were set to the center point of the preset range, the product expansion ratio was about 5.1% as shown in Figure 6. If a more expanded product was desired, the expansion 'paddle' in the 'N.N. Test'-window was moved to the desired position, changing the numerical display to show the new desired

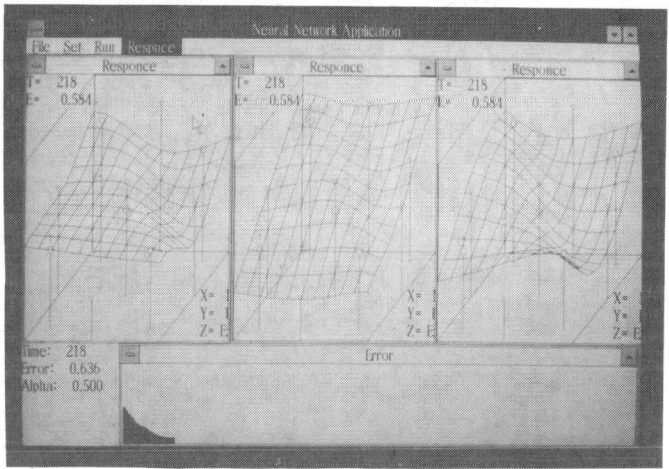

Figure 4. An example 3-dimensional representation of neural network learning. The three windows from left show 'high', 'middle' and 'low' screw speed, respectively. x-Axis is the mass feed rate, y- axis is the moisture content, and z-axis is the product expansion ratio.

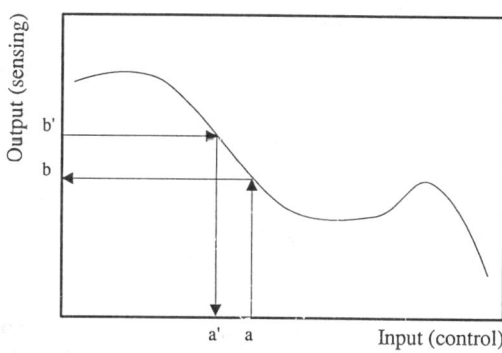

Figure 5. The reverse calculation control principle.

value. After the reverse calculation, the controller found out the respective revised input set, and the expansion ratio was in this case promoted to about 5.5% as shown in Figure 7. It should be emphasized, however, that changes in the input values have an effect on the other output values too.

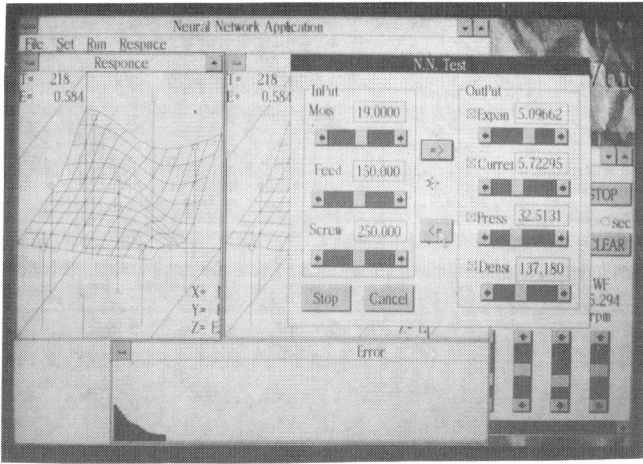

Figure 6. An illustration of the present datum of the neural network extrusion simulator and controller.

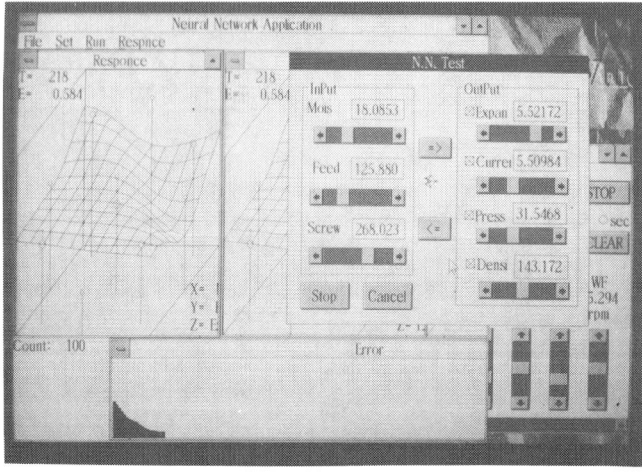

Figure 7. An illustration of an end datum after a control action of the neural network simulator and controller.

CONCLUSION

An artificial neural network model was constructed which could efficiently learn from prior extrusion cooking exemplar data sets. Reverse calculation of the neural network was found to be a suitable tool for extrusion cooker control. The use of reverse calculation procedure made it possible to simulate and control the extruder simultaneously. We are currently working on the translation of the neural network output signal into fuzzy sets in order to avoid problems associated with complex neural network responses. Further, a fuzzy user interface would be helpful in neural network control applications.

REFERENCES

Aarts, R. J., Seppä, L., Eerikäinen, T. and Linko, P. (1990) A real-time expert system in extrusion cooker control. In *Engineering and Food*, Vol. 1, *Physical Properties and Process Control* (W. E. L. Spiess and H. Schubert, eds.), Elsevier Applied Science, London, pp. 909-918.

Costin, M. H., Taylor, P. A. and Wright, J. D. (1982) A critical review of dynamic modeling and control of plasticating extruders. *Polymer Eng. Sci.* **24**: 626-632.

Cayot, N., Bounie, D. and Baussart, H. (1991) Model identification in extrusion cooking. *Food Control* **2**: 140-145.

Eerikäinen, T. and Linko, P. (1989) Extrusion cooking modeling, control and optimization. In *Extrusion Cooking* (C. Mercier, P. Linko and J. M. Harper, eds.), American Association of Cereal Chemists, St. Paul, Minnesota, pp. 157-204.

Eerikäinen, T., Linko, S. and Linko, P. (1988) The potential of fuzzy logic in optimization and control: fuzzy reasoning in extrusion cooker control. In *Automatic Control and Optimization of Food Processes* (M. Renard and J. J. Bimbenet, eds.), Elsevier Applied Science, London, pp. 183-200.

Handelman, D. A., Lane, S. H. and Gelfand, J. J. (1990) Integrating neural networks and knowledge-based system for intelligent robotic control. *IEEE Control Syst. Mag.* **10**(13): 77-87.

Hertz, J., Krogh, A. and Palmer, R. G, eds. (1991) *Introduction to the Theory of Neural Computation*. Addison-Wesley Publishing Company, Redwood City, California.

Hoskins, J. C. and Himmelblau, D. M. (1988) Artificial neural network models of knowledge representation in chemical engineering. *Comput. Chem. Eng.* **9**: 881-890.

Jansson, P. A. (1991) Neural networks: An overview. *Anal. Chem.* **63**: 357-362.

Kondury, K. P., Karim, M. N. and Harper, J. M. (1986) Optimal control of a food extruder. Paper presented at *AIChE Summer National Meeting,* Boston, Massachusetts.

Kulshreshta, M. K., Zaror, C. A. and Jukes, D. J. (1991) Automatic control of food extrusion: problems and perspectives. *Food Control* **2**: 80-86.

Levine, L. Symes, S. and Weimer, S. (1986) Automatic control of moisture in food extruders. *J. Food Eng.* **8**: 97-115.

Linko, P. (1983) Recent progress in the art of extrusion cooking. In *Progress in Food Engineering* (C. Cantarelli and C. Peri, eds.), Forster Publishing Company, Küsnacht, Switzerland, pp. 593-609.

Linko, P. (1988) Uncertainties, fuzzy reasoning and expert systems in bioengineering. *Ann. New York Acad. Sci.* **542**: 83-101.

Linko, P., Colonna, P. and Mercier, C. (1981) High-temperature, short-time extrusion cooking. *Adv. Cereal Sci. Technol.* **4**: 145-235.

Linko, P. and Zhu, Y.-H. (1991) Neural network programming in bioprocess variable estimation and state prediction. *J. Biotechnol.* **21**: 253-170.

Linko, P. and Zhu, Y.-H. (1992a) Neural networks in enzyme engineering. *Ann. New York Acad. Sci.* (in press).

Linko, P. and Zhu, Y.-H. (1992b) Neural network modelling for real-time variable estimation and prediction in the control of glucoamylase fermentation. *Process Biochem.* (in press).

Linko, P. and Zhu, Y.-H. (1992c) Neural network programming and on-line knowledge-based system in estimation and control. Paper presented at ICCAFT 5/IFAC-BIO 2 Conference, 30 March - 1 April, 1992, Keystone, Colorado.

Linko, S. and Linko, P. (1986) Fuzzy modelling and its potential. In *Data Collection and Analysis - Development of Mathematical Kinetic Models* (K. O. Paulus, ed.), *Berichte der Bundesforschungsanstalt für Ernährung* BFE-R-86-03, pp. 25-26.

Lippmann, R. P. (1987) An introduction to computing with neural nets. *IEEE AASP Mag.* **4**(2): 4-22.

Mercier, C., Linko, P. and Harper, J. M., eds. (1989) *Extrusion Cooking*. American Association of Cereal Chemists, St. Paul, Minnesota.

Meuser, F., van Lengerich, B. and Gimmler, N. (1990) Optimization in extrusion. In *Processing and Quality of Foods*, Vol. 1, *High Temperature Short Time (HTST) Processing: Guarantee for High Quality Food with Long Shelflife* (P. Zeuhten, J. C. Cheftel, C. Eriksson, T. R. Gormley, P. Linko and K. Paulus, eds.), Elsevier Applied Science, London, pp. 1.215-1.225.

Miller, W. T. III, Sutton, R. S. and Werbos, P. J. (1990) *Neural Networks for Control*, The MIT Press, Cambridge, Massachusetts.

Olkku, J. Hagqvist, A. and Linko, P. (1983) Steady-state modelling of extrusion cooking employing response surface methodology. *J. Food Eng.* **2**: 105-128.

Olkku, J., Hassinen, H., Antila, J., Pohjanpalo, H. and Linko, P. (1980) Automation of HTST-extrusion cooker. In *Food Process Engineering*, Vol. 1, *Food Processing Systems* (P. Linko, Y. Mälkki, J. Olkku and J. Larinkari, eds.), Applied Science Publishers (Elsevier Applied Science), London, pp. 777-790.

Parnaby, J., Kochar, A. K. and Wood, B. (1975) Development of computer control strategies for plastic extruders. *Polymer Eng. Sci.* **15**: 594-605.

Rich, E. (1990) Expert system and neural networks can work together. *IEEE Expert* **5**(5): 5-7.

Roberts, S. A. and Guy, R. C. E. (1986) Instabilities in a food extrusion cooker. *J. Food Eng.* **5**: 7-30.

Wiedmann, W. and Strecker, J. (1988) Process control of cooker-extruder. In *Automatic Control and Optimization of Food Processes* (M. Renard and J. J. Bimbenet, eds.), Elsevier Applied Science, London, pp. 201-214.

The Use of Biosensors to Achieve Feed-Back during Fermentation and Lagering in Breweries

U. Schrader, U. Hege, V. Denk

Working on the application of biosensors in food industry, we started with the automation of fermentation and lagering in breweries. We designed a flow-injection measurement-unit based on biosensors for on-line monitoring of product quality and compounds indicated by the concentrations of technological characterising substances. We used the data as feed-back to the process-logic control
To start we tested the parts (sampling, sample pretreatment, new flow-injections systems) and are building up a first measurement unit. This system will be tested in a german brewery (starting winter/spring 1991/92).

Introduction:

The automation of industrial food production is organized by sequence-step control systems and most of these are open-loop processes. This is true, even if every available sensor is used to measure on-line quantities and do any off-line analysis of chemical substances. Off-line analysis implies the results are coming too late. Up until now, there are mainly the physical parameters (T, p etc.) and only a few chemical parameters (pH-value, oxygen-pressure, wastegas analysis etc.) that are measured on-line to gain information about the actual situation of a process. The settings of the sequence-step control are very often time-temperature schemes caused by the lack of better opportunities.

It is known that the variation in the concentrations occurring in certain substances, can be used to monitor the actual biochemical situation during a food production step. These certain substances we call "technological characterising substances". The concentrations of many of these substances can be detected by biosensors. This provides an almost continuous feed-back signal and the control of this production step turns into closed-loop operation /1/.

The combined action of existing and additional equipment of the brewery is shown in fig. 1.

The methods we used for the specific determination of these concentrations are based on enzymatic reactions /2/. Since enzymes are very sensitive to changes in physiological conditions such as tempe-

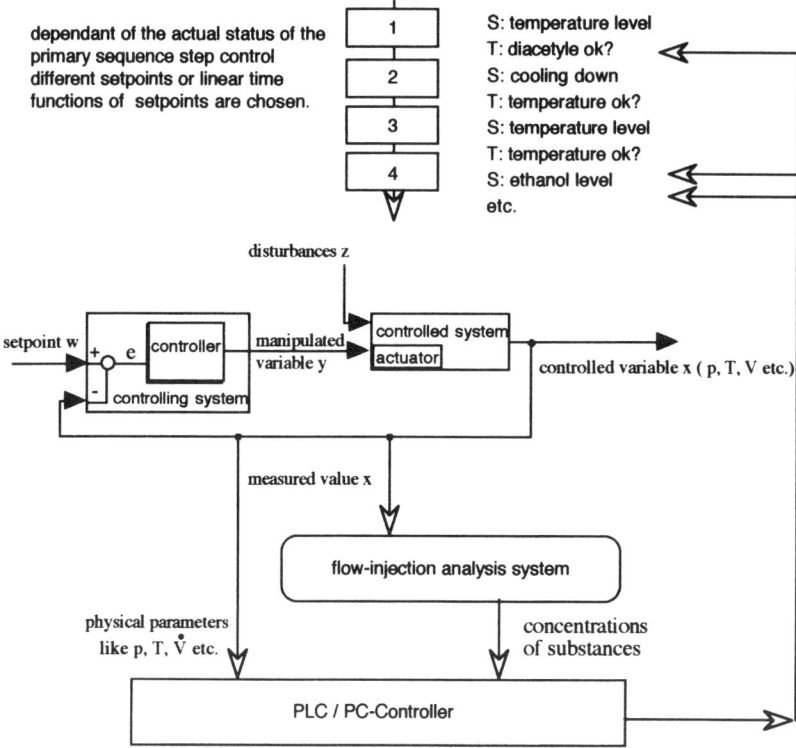

Fig. 1: Combined action of existing (upper part) and additional equipment replacing the temperature-time schemes by the concentration of technological characterising substances.

rature or pH-value, the direct and continuous monitoring with enzyme electrodes is very limited and has only been realized in a few cases so far (see /3, 4, 5/ e.g.). These problems could be avoided by the introduction of automatic sampling and sample pretreatment (cooling, adjusting the pH-value) without feeding the sample back into the food production process.

As a first step into this new technology a most simple process was chosen in which the results achieved by the biosensor could easily be checked by means of classical methods. Since we know brewing well at Weihenstephan, we use the alcohol-reduction in a brewery as a typical food production process and measured in a first step the concentration of ethanol.

Methods.

The normal range of ethanol concentration in beer is 0 to 1,2 M/l. According to german law in non-alcoholic beer the concentration must not exceed 0.5 w/V% (0.11 M/l). As the linearity range of our biosensors are between 0,05 and 0,5 mM/l, a dilution rate of about 2000 is necessary. To cope with this high dilution rate a special double dialysis cell was developed.

The results of the flow-injection analysis-system are peaks. The height of the peaks indicate the concentration of ethanol in the sample.

The measurement unit is controlled by a PLC-PC combination, connected by a simple SIMATIC®-L1 bus. The PLC is a small SIMATIC® S5 PLC, the PC industry standard (AT-bus). Using the L1-bus gives us the opportunity to connect the measurement unit to other PLCs, passing the calculated results.

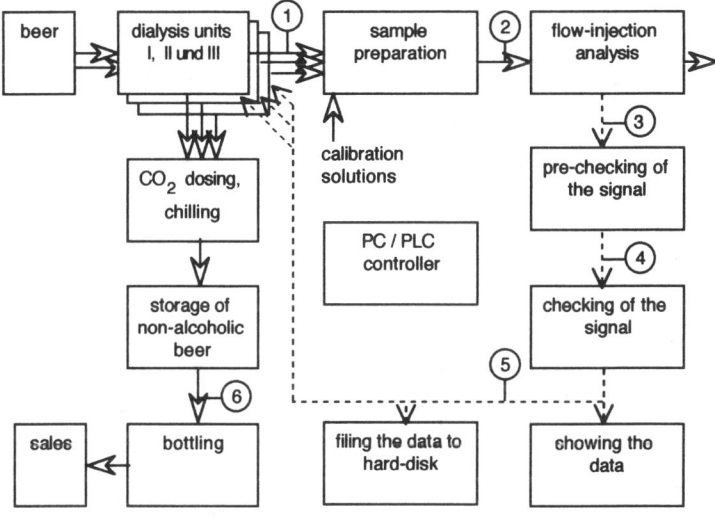

signal path ----------

Fig. 2:   schematic diagram of the measurement system
1: samples of alcohol-reduced beer
2: buffer stream with reduced concentration of ethanol
3. fluorimeter output 0 - 1 V
4: peak height in digital units
5: checked value
6: non-alcoholic beer

Results:

We want to present:

- the flow-injection analysis system and other parts of the measurement unit
- the installation in a german brewery
- first results.(not available before printing)

1   V. Denk, U. Schrader: Biosensoren als Istwertgeber lebensmittel- oder biotechnologischer Prozesse - dargestellt am Beispiel der Biergärung. Brauwelt, 130 (1990) 39, p.1679-1684.

2   I. Ogbomo, U. Prinzing, H.-L. Schmidt: Prerequisites for the on-line control of microbial processes by flow injection analysis. Journal of Biotechnology, 14 (1990) p.63-70.

3   S. L. Brooks, R. E. Ashby, A. P. F. Turner, M. R.Calder, D. J. Clark: Development of an on-line glucose sensor for fermentation monitoring. Biosensors, 3 p.45-56.

4   M. Mascini, A. Memoli, F. Olana: Microbial sensor for alcohol. Enzyme Microb. Technol. 11 (1989) p.297-301.

5   C. F. Mandenius, B. Danielsson: Enzyme thermistors for process monitoring and control. In: S.P. Colowick, N. O. Kaplan: Methods in Enzymology. 137 p. 307-318, Academic Press, San Diego, 1988

INTEGRATED PROCESS DESIGN: ISSUES AND OPPORTUNITIES

S. Bruin*

The impact that computer applications are having on
process design in the food industry is briefly
discussed. The opportunity for an integrated approach to
the product/process design cycle is indicated, leading
to a concurrent process engineering mode of operation
with short delivery times. Some bottlenecks in achieving
such integrated design environments are indicated.

Introduction

The theme of this conference is Food Engineering in a computer climate, with
its sub-sessions on modelling, process design, product safety, and finally
process control. Computers and computational methods have advanced to the
point where they have a significant impact on the way in which food process
engineers can approach problems in design, control and operations.

The effective speed of electronic computation by combined hardware and
software development roughly doubled every year over the past 30 years
(REF. 1). As far as I know this acceleration in computing power is expected
to continue over the coming decade, see FIC. 1. This fantastic rapid
increase in computational capabilities to handle more complex mathematics
which permits the exhaustive solution of detailed models will allow chemical
engineers and food process engineers to model process physics, process
(bio)chemistry and process microbiology from the molecular and cellular
scale to the full process plant scale. It will become increasingly feasible
to construct models that incorporate all relevant phenomena of a process and
to design, control and optimize more and more on the basis of computed
theoretical predictions and less and less on empiricism. In addition the
developments in expert systems and artificial intelligence will enable the
food process engineer to have empirical, qualitative information available
literally at her fingertips in a structured and easily accessible fashion.
Such developments in the computer climate will have a profound impact on the
way in which process design in any industry so also the food industry will
be carried out in the coming decade.

* Unilever Research Laboratory, Vlaardingen, The Netherlands

Also the speed of product innovation in the fast moving consumer goods business to which the majority of the foods business belongs is accelerating, FIG. 2. The half life of product development times has decreased from 10 years in 1970 to an estimated 2-3 years in the year 2000. This means that the high bonus on being first with a product innovation of substance is getting increasingly difficult to achieve. Speed up of the product/process development cycle is therefore of paramount importance.

In my presentation I will try and discuss the impact that such computer applications are having on process design in the food industry, identifying the advantages and limitations, issues and opportunities.

Process design

First a few remarks on process design and particularly food process design.

The primary goal of process design is to identify the optimal equipment units, the optimal connections between them and the optimal conditions for operating them to deliver the desired product at the optimum yields, at the lowest cost, with the highest production line efficiency and minimum waste generation. Design is a complex problem that involves not only quantitative computing but also the handling of often large amounts of information and of qualitative reasoning.

Process design is characterised by two complementary types of activity: process analysis and process synthesis.

In process analysis an existing process is broken apart, usually through mathematical and/or empirical models of its constituent elements. The aim of the exercise of course is the recombination of the sub system models into a total process model to predict the previously unknown performance or output of the processing system as a whole.

Process synthesis on the other hand implies the creation ab initio of the process itself, presumably from specification of the desired products, from the specification of desired inputs, such as raw materials and ingredients and from a basic notion of what sequence of treatments will be necessary in the process.

The key concept in chemical engineering linking process analysis and process synthesis activities is the concept of unit operations introduced by Arthur D. Little in 1915. His basic idea was that any chemical process can be resolved into a coordinate series of unit operations (e.g. pulverizing, drying, evaporating, crystallising). The number of these basic operations is not large and relatively few of them are involved in any particular process. This forceful concept has enabled chemical engineers to study processes independent from the particular branch of the chemical industry for which the process was intended. Of course this concept has also been extended from chemical processes to food processes. We will discuss this application now briefly.

The processes of the food industry can be divided into 4 broad categories (REF. 2):

- Separation processes e.g. diffusional extraction processes (isolation of fractions such as oil seed extraction, concentration of fruit juices, oils and fats fractionation), but also a host of mechanical separations where mixtures or slurries of particulates are separated into fractions (e.g. flour milling).

- Assembly or texturising processes e.g. emulsions processes (e.g. margarines, ice creams), foaming (e.g. whipped creams), extrusion processes, dough making, baking, etc. Here the end product is an often pretty complicated microstructure of dispersed phases held together by binding forces between the various phases and a continuous phase. This microstructure leads to desired product texture and the mouthfeel related to this texture and its destruction during mastication are usually absolute key to final product quality.

- (Bio)conversion processes where either chemical or biochemical conversions are applied to raw materials yielding ingredients, flavours, fermented products, roasted products and the like.

- Preservation processes where the main aim is to eliminate microbial, enzymatic or chemical spoilage of the raw materials which usually are food tissues (meat, vegetables) or liquids (milk, oils, juices).

Each of these broad categories of processes has a number of typical unit operations. Farkas (REF. 3) gave an overview of these typical unit operations for the food industry that is still relevant today, see FIG. 3.

As said above the unit operations approach to the analysis of food processes aims at simplification by breaking down the process into its components and applying generalised algorithms developed for each unit operation. Synthesis of food processes would likewise be simplified by reducing it to making an appropriate selection and sequencing of unit operations from the 'standard repertoire' and analyze the process created in this way using the process analysis mode.

A thing to keep in mind however is that there are more than 100 unit operations in food processing excluding packaging operations. This number is considerably larger than in chemical processes where the number is (say) about 30.

Another point of consideration is that the unit operations approach will only work when all thermodynamic properties, kinetic phenomena, transport coefficients, rheological parameters are known or sufficiently reliable estimation methods prevail and when sufficiently detailed models of the various unit operations have been developed in terms of balance equations at the right level of integration. I will come back on this point later.

The ideal product/process development cycle

The ideal development cycle of a product/process has a number of phases. The cycle usually starts with the development of product concepts and their potential positioning in the product mix. The next phases are: product development, process development, equipment design, pilot plant tests and scale up analyses, acquisition of equipment, factory tests, formulation of a total design package, construction of plant, commissioning, and finally production. This sequence of phases can take a long time to be completed if a strict step by step approach is taken, not starting the next phase before the previous phase is ready. It will be clear from what I said earlier on speed that this approach, if not outdated already, is certainly not feasible in the future. The way forward is of course to compress development time by having a number of phases in parallel execution. The development time needs to be compressed further than a normal network analysis would give as the minimum time needed to complete the project.

How can this be achieved?

In the product/process development cycle a number of enabling technologies are involved which are relevant in different stages of the cycle. A number of these technologies involve computers such as: mathematical modelling software packages, various types of simulation techniques (steady state and transient state, continuous and discrete event, lumped parameter and distributed parameter), data bases, computer aided design and computer aided engineering tools. They are essential design tools, providing knowledge, predictive capabilities, visualisation, etc.

In the ideal situation in the future, an integrated process design environment can be envisioned in which the various software packages for the techniques mentioned above are linked in such a way that they can directly be used in an interactive fashion. FIG. 4. is a schematic illustration of such an ideal system. The ideal integrated design environment would consist of an interlinked system of:

- a physical and biochemical properties data base system including property estimation correlations, phase equilibria models and the like.

- growth models of microorganisms, both for positive growth stimulation (fermentation) and for killing (pasteurisation, sterilisation).

- basic transport phenomena models of local processes in terms of constitutive equations, flux equations and rate equations for e.g. enzymatic reaction kinetics, crystallisation kinetics, cleaning kinetics for CIP operations etc.

- finite element simulation software packages for solving non-linear partial differential equations and integral equations of multiphase heat-, mass- and momentum transfer in complicated geometries including free boundaries.

- a library of most food process unit operations in terms of models linking inputs and outputs: heat-, mass- and momentum balances.

- static and dynamic flow sheet simulation software, including process control simulation capabilities.

- discrete event simulation software that enables the study of optimum integration of the designs of the process line producing the product and the packaging line that packs them. Here we touch the interface between process engineering and production engineering.

- a best proven practice equipment data base, hygienic design being one key factor.

- CAD plant engineering software packages.

This integrated software system would guide the product- and process developers through the design operation, bringing in relevant knowledge, identifying important gaps in the knowledge, and providing access to the necessary modelling and simulation tools. Final process and equipment specifications would be consolidated via computer aided design techniques.

In the operating mode of such an ideal process design environment a high degree of concurrent design and engineering could be realised, with minimisation of critical path times as a result. Because all the different disciplines involved in the design can interact very frequently using, always the most recent updates on the state of design information such an environment would enable a drastic reduction of the total design time needed. It would also minimise the risk of making errors due to lack of communication or to use of outdated information that have to be corrected too late in the development cycle at high costs and at the cost of precious time.

In the current environment of heavy competition being first with a new product carries a significant bonus: time is no longer negotiable. The product/process design environment just painted can become a very effective tool in the competitive struggle indeed. So the stakes to achieve it are high!

Current bottlenecks

However the ideal situation just sketched does not exist at this moment in time in the day to day practice of the food industry. So what are the bottlenecks?

There are some formidable barriers that have to be taken before this situation can even be approximated. Some of these are, and I take just a few examples:

- basic data on phase equilibria, transport properties and rheological parameters are usually quite incomplete and indeed not easy to determine experimentally due to the very complex composition and microstructure of many foods and food ingredients. The proverbial Daily Prayer of the Chemical Engineer: 'Oh Lord, let all solids be liquid and all liquids be gaseous' seems to be valid even more to the food process engineer! It takes a formidable effort for a food company to establish effective data banks etc. on such data for their key raw materials, ingredients and the 'process streams' they are handling. An example from my own company is the basic data for oils and fats and their crystallisation behaviour (equilibrium as well as kinetics) where we have made major progress over the last years but at considerable cost, see e.g. Wesdorp (REF. 4). Still the picture is far from complete however.

- knowledge on basic mechanisms of kinetic phenomena is quite often fragmentary. For instance in the unit operation of emulsification the real mechanisms of drop breakup and coalescence in various flow regimes and rheologies of dispersed and continuous phases and even semi-quantitative description are still not developed up to a state where they can be plugged into a model for an 'emulsifying unit' that in turn would be a standard 'book' in the software library of food process unit operations. Also here however progress has been made (De Bruijn, REF. 5).

- modelling of flow patterns in the often complex geometries of food processing equipment handling rheologically speaking extremely complex liquids, pastes, dispersions or doughs using advances CFD techniques has only relatively recently begun. This conference has shown us already some very interesting examples of what is possible in this area (Crilly, REF. 6). Results of such computations have to be summarised in characteristic yardsticks like spatial distributions of energy dissipation intensity, axial dispersion coefficients, total rate of strain histories of fluid elements that have passed through a piece of equipment.

- product quality characterisation of foods, in particular of the important category of assembled foods is far more difficult than for most chemical products. The quality is to a large extent determined by sensory properties and reliable models predicting the influence on process changes on taste panel results are very scarce indeed. Quantification changes in sensory attributes by process changes is necessary. A lot happens in this area but it is outside the scope of my paper to elaborate on these.

Most of the barriers just mentioned have little to do with the lack of computation power of modern computers, or lack of mathematical or computational techniques and tools. The rate limiting factors are more related to the painstakingly slow progress in the materials sciences of food products and changes in material properties during processing (either desired or undesired) and to the lack of basic insight into 'local' processes at the droplet-, liquid film-, crystal-, bubble-, fibre particle-, cell wall-, microorganism-scales.

Conclusions

What then is the influence of the computer climate on the growth and well being of food process design? What climate is it anyhow? Is it a sunny climate with mild rains that promotes growth? Is it a climate creating fata morganas interlaced with protracted periods of dense fogs that prevent us from seeing where the real obstacles are?

My conclusions are:

- achievement of integrated process design platforms for their core product areas as sketched above is a very important target for the major food industries. Partially complete platforms are already extremely useful in solving process design problems in many cases.

■ programmes in materials sciences that lead to better prediction methods of material properties and programmes that increase our understanding of micro-scale processes are rate limiting in achieving full fledged integrated process design platforms. The progress in these programmes will be considerably enhanced by imaginative use of computer based modelling techniques (e.g. CFD).

■ computer modelling of full scale unit operations (e.g. a spray drier to mention just an example) will be of great help in improving equipment designs, better control of processes and improved product functionality

References

1. Amundson, N.R. et al (1988), Frontiers in Chemical Engineering, Research needs and opportunities, National Research Council, U.S.A., page 135-175.

2. Bruin, S., Spaninks J.,(1976), Inleiding in de Proceskunde, Lecture notes Agricultural University of the Netherlands, page 1.12-1.30.

3. Farkas, D. (1977), Chem. Tech. 7, 428.

4. Wesdorp, L.H. (1990), Liquid-multiple solid phase equilibria in fats, theory and experiments, Ph. D. Thesis, Technical University Delft.

5. De Bruijn, R.A. (1989), Deformation and breakup of drops in simple shear flows, Ph. D. Thesis, Technical University Eindhoven.

6. Crilly, J.F., this conference.

TABLE 1

Ideal Product/Process Development Cycle				
phase	who	timescale	% of effort	design techniques
1. Discussion on concepts	Everyone	very short	< 1	■ CAD ■ Expert Systems
2. Basic material studies	Material Scientists Product Developers	3 months - 2 years	15	■ Mathematical Modelling ■ Expert Systems
3. Product Development	Product Developers Process Developers	6 months - 1 year	15	■ Mathematical Modelling ■ Expert Sytems
4. Process Development	Product Developers Process Developers Adv. manufacturing Group Transfer Group	6 months - 1 year	35	■ Numerical Simulation ■ Expert Systems ■ Flowsheeting ■ Dynamic Simulation ■ Control Simulation
5. Equipment Design	Adv. Manufacturing Group Process Developers Suppliers	6 months	15	■ CAD ■ Expert Systems ■ Control Simulation ■ Dynamic Simulation
6. Pilot plant tests	All	3 months	10	■ Expert Systems ■ Various Modelling
7. Acquisition of equipment	Transfer Group	3 months - 1 year	5	■ CAD
8. Factory tests	All	1 month	5	■ Expert Systems ■ Various Modelling ■ CAD

FIGURE 1

Acceleration Computing Speed
(rough estimates)

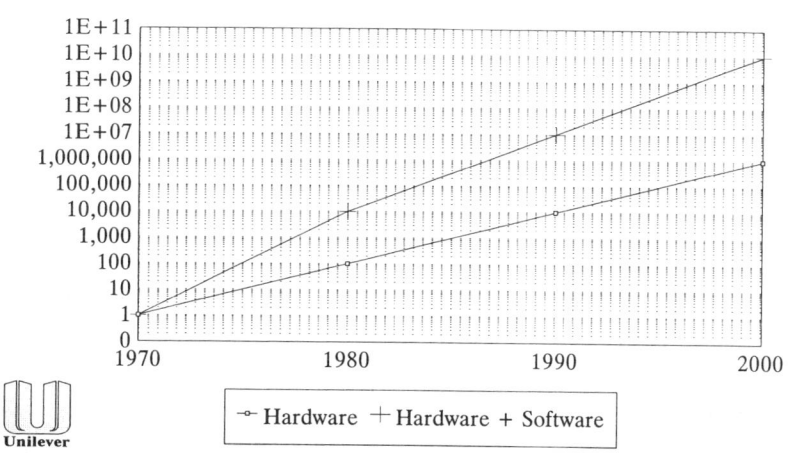

FIGURE 2

Acceleration of innovation time

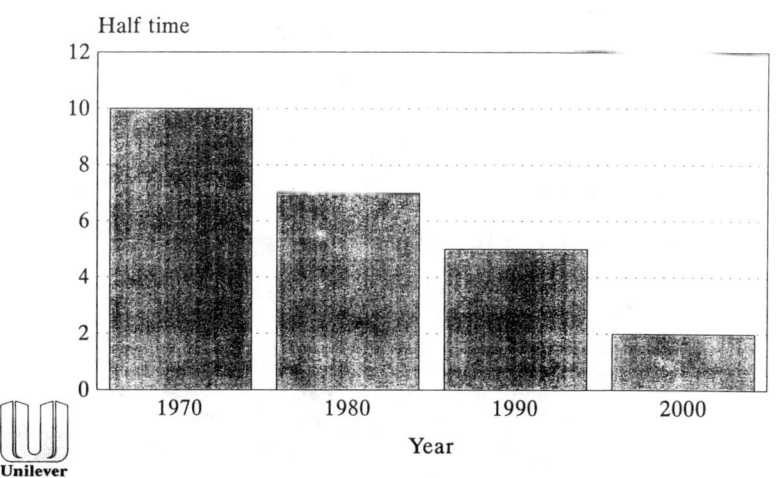

FIGURE 3

Unit Operations in Food Processing
(Farkas, loc.cit)

Category	Number of Unit Operations
Separation Processes	
- diffusional	15
- mechanical	45
Assembly Processes	38
Presevation Processes	24
TOTAL	122

FIGURE 4

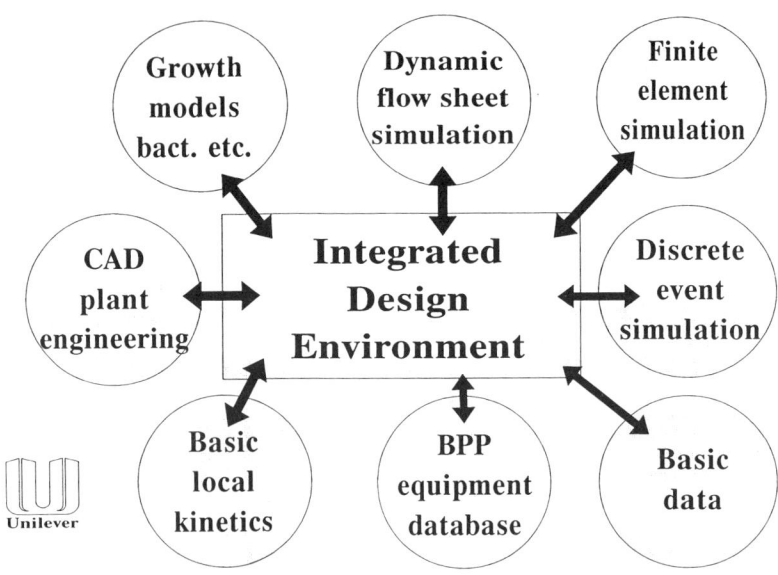

Computer Aided applications for Food Products Formulation

Gilles Trystram, Joseph Hossenlopp, Bertrand Heyd, Isabelle Bardot

Abstract

The paper describes the conception and several applications of the Automated Apparatus for Sensory Testing for food product optimal formulation. The apparatus is described. Different kinds of results were obtained. Optimal imitation ("me two"), is provide using two different ways. The Simplex sequential method gives better results as the Respons Surface Methodology classical method. Hedonic formulation were performed. Advantages of this approach based upon computer aided methods were discussed. and we establish that the validation is able to be performed on line.

I - INTRODUCTION

Sensory testing involves the interaction of a stimulus and one or several subjects and the recording of the resulting sensory perceptions. This type of methodology may be analytical (discrimination among stimuli, descriptive analysis) of affective (evaluation of acceptance and preference for the stimuli) (Figure 1).

These sensory experiments may have different purposes :

- to train subjects, to evaluate their ability to discriminate among different stimulus intensities or qualities (thresholds), etc ...

- to evaluate the sensory characteristics or various products or materials. This usually involves difference tests, descriptive tests (sensory profiling), search for defects, similarity or dissimilarity measurements (product imitation)

- to measure the hedonic value of a simple stimulus (sweet solution) or a complex one (aromatic mixture). Such measures evaluate the amount of pleasure given to the subject by the stimulus and the aesthetic value of the stimulus

- to create a product formula that meets a number of sensory criteria from a given set of ingredients. To achieve this goal, the experimenter may choose either of two approaches : (1) to match the formula by recollection of its characteristics (imitation or reproduction of a recipe for example), or (2) to combine the various stimuli until the optimum hedonic value of the formula is obtained (what sensory scientists refer to as "optimization of the hedonic value").

In this document we describe the design of an Automated Apparatus for Sensory Testing (ATS) and its applications using liquid solutions as the testing medium to achieve some of the objectives outlined above. We also present the results of the experiments conducted so far with the ATS.

The ATS is best suited for use with liquid food products and all solutions containing aromatic substances (seasonings, perfumes). The sensory modalities which may be tested with the ATS are the chemical senses (taste, smell, trigeminal nerve) and the senses of sight and touch, singly or in combination. This work is an application of Computer Aided in the field of Food Product Formulation.

II - METHODS

The main goal of this research project was to develop a feedback system between the response of a subject to a stimulus and the preparation of a new stimulus. The preparation of the new stimulus depends both on the objectives of the experimenter and on the responses of the subject to prior stimuli (Figure 1).

Combined efforts in two scientific disciplines - automation/computer science and sensory evaluation - allowed for the development of the backstep in the feedback system, i.e., calculations based on the response leading to the preparation of the new stimulus.

Contraints and factors affecting the design of the apparatus

By integrating computer science and automation techniques, the following objectives were achieved :

- integration of all the sample preparation steps (by defining and memorizing sample characteristics)

- automatic data collection, control of the test protocol and data processing

- improvement of the reproducibility of the sensory measurements

- monitoring of the conduct of the test without interfering with the tasting or biasing the subject's response

- reduction of the experimenter's involvement in the protocol leading to a self-service mode for the subject

The design of the feedback system and the constraints associated with a sensory experiment (especially the limited number of stimuli that may be presented to the subject in a given amount of time) demanded the conception of a quick and sure decision-making strategy to meet the objectives of the experimenter with a minimum number of feedback cycles.

III - RESULTS

We present the finished, patented apparatus (ATS) along with tree studies which illustrate the potential and applications of this feedback system.

III. 1 Presentation and description of the automated apparatus (Hossenlopp et al, 1989)

The apparatus allows for the preparation of mixtures containing liquid solutions or powders in predetermined amounts and their storage in a controlled environment. The resulting mixtures are evaluated by judges who record their answers directly with the ATS. The answers are collected and may be used to determine the characteristics of the next mixture.

The application of the ATS include sensory testing and formulation. The components of the ATS are (numbers refer to Figure 2) :

- a scale (1) interfaced with a microcomputer (2).

- a mixing apparatus which fills the cup placed on the scale according to a predetermined formula ; the mixing apparatus includes :

> - a series of reserve containers (3,1), (3,2) ...., (3,n) with the products to be included in the mix

> - a pair of all-or-none valves (4,1), (4, 2) controlled by the microcomputer (2) for each container (3). Valve (4,2) effects a flow rate that is 1/10 that effected by valve (4,1). These valves control the cup-filling process (6) by gravity flow (7) through tubes (8,1) or (8,2) according to the desired formula.

- a ramp for sample presentation (5) equipped with sensors (9) to check for the presence of cups on the ramp. The sensors are connected to the microcomputer (2) and signal the presence or absence of a cup.

The performance of this apparatus is detailed in Hossenlopp et al. (1989).

III.2. Examples of application of the ATS

Table 1 presents the different applications of the ATS as a combined function of type of sensory test and type of decision-making model.

Sensory tests are classified into analytical measurements (difference tests, scaling tests, descriptive tests) and affective measurements (preference, acceptance or palatability for food products) of the stimuli.

The decision-making models which are used to validate a sensory test are classified into three groups :

- direct methods which do not predefine any predictive or statistical model to account for the variations in the subject's responses. These variations simply are "registered" and eventually used to prepare the next stimulus based on the objectives of the experimenter.

- indirect methods which follow a model chosen by the experimenter. The responses are used to define and adjust the parameters of the model (i.e., the slope and the Y-axis intercept for a linear model).

- statistical methods which verify the validity of hypotheses (i.e, number of correct responses to achieve statistical significance for difference tests, comparison of means).

The five examples which are detailed below to illustrate the performance of the ATS are listed in Table 1.

Example I. Determination of the sweetening power for the development of a sweetened beverage

The measurement of a difference threshold is tedious and requires the preparation of many well-calibrated samples. Using the modified "up-and-down" method designed by Dixon and Massey (1960), we showed that the ATS allows for a quick determination of the threshold.

These measures are very useful in formulation, for example when sucrose is substituted with an artificial sweetener in the development of diet beverages. In the study conducted by Heyd (1991), we substituted a sucrose solution with a mixture of aspartame and sodium saccharin solutions.

Example II. Development of an imitation strawberry/apple syrup using an indirect method. Response surface Methodology (Figure 3)

We attempted to match a reference mixture of strawberry and apple syrups using two different approaches. Response Surface Methodology (RSM), (Figure 3) allowed us to determine the optimum composition of the match (corresponding to the smallest difference between the mixture produced by the ATS and the reference) and to validate the optimum using on-line difference tests with the reference. This experiment demonstrated the limitations of the RSM method which nevertheless is widely used in sensory formulation (Bardot et al., 1991). The mathematical validation of the model is always good, bud the validation on the sensorial basis is not easy. The optimal value, which is found, is not necessarily inside the range of variations of the ingrdients. A very discrimant test, like triangle test don't give good result for the optimal value predicted by RSM method.

Examples III and IV. Development of an imitation strawberry/apple syrup using a direct method (the simplex algorithm) and validation with a difference test (Figure 4).

The use of a simplex-type algorithm (stepwise search for the optimum by minimizing the difference between a reference product and the last mixture generated by the ATS based on the subject's response) resulted in the production of a reasonably close match of the reference. The quality of the match was assessed by and on-line difference test between the match and the reference (triangle test).

Example V. Optimization of a product based on hedonic value using a direct method - the simplex algorithm (Figure 5).

We used the simplex algorithm to optimize the hedonic value of a lemonade/cane sugar mixture. Figure 5 shows the hedonic optimum obtained for 8 subjects. Points with the same symbols represent replicates on different days for the same subject. This experiment emphasizes the difficulties associated with hedonic formulation : each individual has his own hedonic criteria and may not always maximize the pleasure brought about by the product if he/she is not familiar with it.

IV. CONCLUSIONS AND FUTURE PROSPECTS

The above-mentioned examples demonstrate the range of applications of the Automated Apparatus for Sensory Testing (ATS), and more generally, the interest of Computer Aids for Product Optimization. It can be used :

- to conduct reliable sensory tests on liquid products or mixtures of liquid products ; bias usually associated with these kinds of measurements are greatly reduced (no preparation errors) ; a great deal of time is saved in sample preparation, data collection and data analysis steps ; tasters do not have to be present all at once or at a fixed time (self-service); the ATS may be taken on location for consumer testing purposes.

- to familiarize subjects with testing procedures, to train them, to check their sensitivity (thresholds) and reproducibility. This particular set of applications is useful in the development of a trained panel in private companies or in academic institutions where sensory evaluation is taught and psychophysical experiments are conducted.

- to apply sensory formulation using the algorithms that we have already developed (i.e., various simplex methods). This apparatus lends itself to interesting prospects in the case of aromatic mixtures for which it is difficult to relate the stimuli space to the perceptual space. Artificial intelligence methods (particularly neural networks) could provide some insight on the relationships between these two spaces (a research project baptised "artificial chef" recently was launched along these lines in collaboration with an artificial intelligence laboratory and a private company).

Treatment of hedonic measurements with artificial intelligence methods eventually could lead to a better understanding of preference behavior.

Various industrial applications may be considered, among which the on-line sensory testing of products conducted by operators along the production line ; the automated apparatus could automatically collect samples and anonymously present them to the operators for testing ; based on the ensuing response, the appropriate software would propose or command the proper corrections of processing variables to adjust the sensory properties of the manufactured product.

The ability to automatically prepare samples based on the subject's response could also lead to the development of new types of sensory tests which require statistics not commonly used in sensory evaluation .

References

Bardot I., Heyd B, Trystram, G., Hossenlopp, J. 1991. Méthode automatisée de formulation sensorielle pour les produits alimentaires de type liquide. Sciences des Aliments, 12, 1992, 19-36

Dixon, W.J. & Massey, J. 1960. Introduction to statistical analysis. Mac Graw & Hill New York

Hossenlopp, J., Heyd, B., Trystram, G . 1989. Automate de tests sensoriels. Brevet n° FR/89 11231 du 23.08.89

Hossenlopp J., Trystram G.& Heyd B. 1989. Design and development of an apparatus for automated sensory testing of liquid products. Sciences des aliments. 9:613.

Heyd, B. 1991, Contributions de l'automatique en métrologie et formulation sensorielle, Thesis, ENSIA, Massy, France.

Models Type of sensory approach		Direct methods ("heuristic", without search for the sources of variation)	Indirect Methods (choice of a model; use in the search for the 'ideal" product)	Statistical Methods (Search for and use of probability models)
Sensory measurements	Difference tests	**Simplex Method** (imitation of a strawberry/apple beverage)	**RSM Method** (imitation of a strawberry/apple beverage)	**Triangle Test** (Validation of a match)
	Scaling tests			**Determination of a difference threshold** (Sweetening power of sweeteners)
	Descriptive tests (sensory profile)		research in progress	
Affective Tests Pleasure evaluation (acceptance; preference; palatability)		**Simplex Method** (preferred formula for a lemon juice/sugar cane syrup)		research in progress

Table 1. Relation between the type of sensory test and the model used in the search for the optimum product/stimulus depending on the objectives of the experimenter

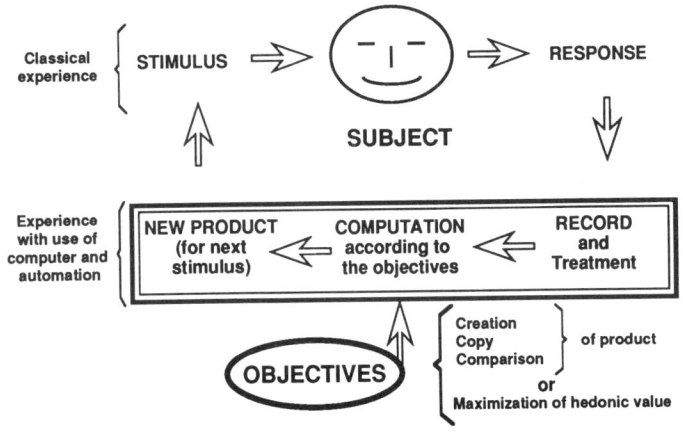

Figure I. Diagram of the feedback system used to design the ATS.

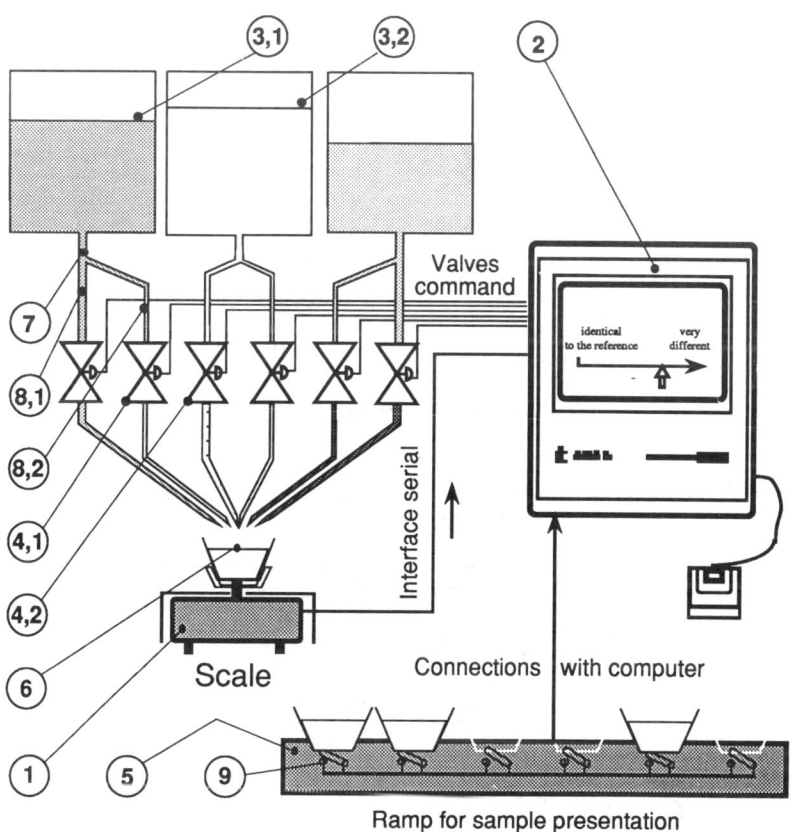

Figure 2. Diagram showing the operating principle of the ATS.

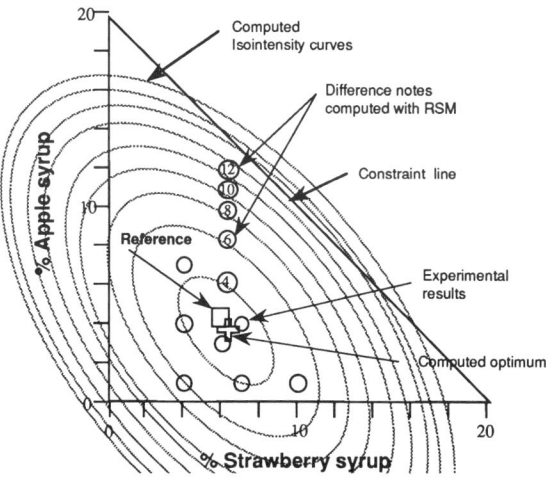

Figure 3. Illustration of the RSM method for the optimization of a strawberry/apple mixture based on the hedonic ratings of one subject

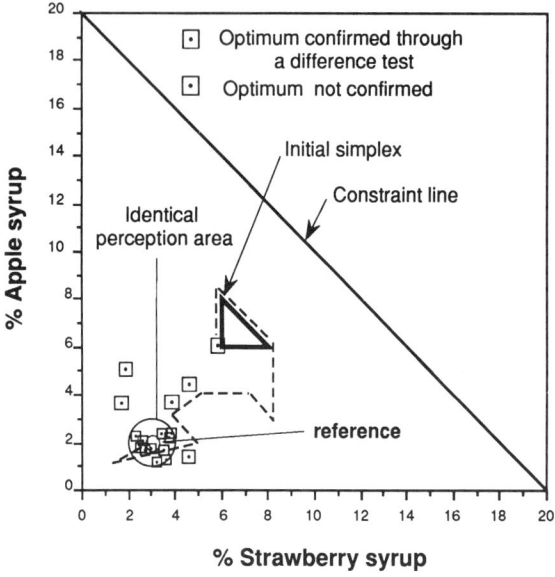

Figure 4. Application of the simplex method for the imitation of an existing product (reference). The point indicate the composition of the match for 17 judges). The line shows the pathway to the match for one judge.

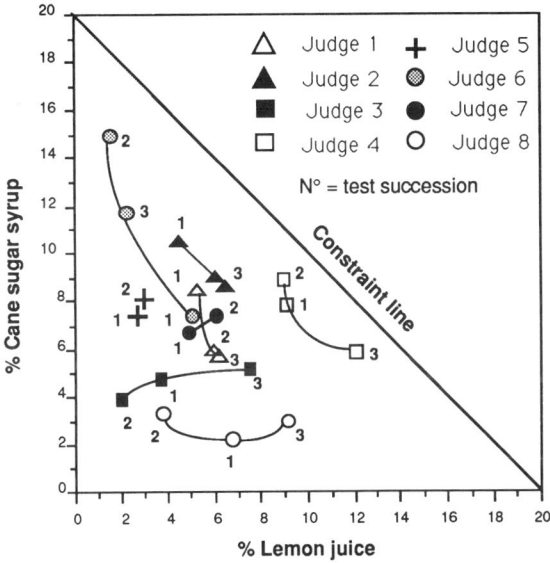

Figure 5. Application of the simplex method for the optimization of a product based on hedonic ratings (individual judges are shown). points sharing the same symbol represent the replications of a given judge obtained on different days.

HYGIENIC DESIGN OF MOVING PARTS OF MACHINES IN THE FOOD INDUSTRY

G.Hauser [*]

There is, at the present time, a demand for high-quality food products with a long shelf life, which means that the production environment has to be virtually germ free and antiseptic. To achieve this hygienically designed equipment and effective cleaning techniques are required. The equipment designer and user should have at his disposal CAD procedures, which will include data-bases containing information on hygienic requirements and regulatory standards. One of the most vulnerable areas where microbial ingress can occur are sealing spots of moving parts e.g. rotating or reciprocating shafts. Principles and examples of good hygienic design are presented which will ensure the highest standards of cleanliness are achieved.

INTRODUCTION

The production of high-quality long-life foodproducts demands virtually germ free or aseptic conditions, depending upon the nature of the product and the method of packaging. An important part of the production process is the automation of the operations, which involves computer control and the use of expert systems. The range of computer application is shown in Fig. 1, especially those operations involving the cleaning of the process equipment and its design. In order to achieve the goal of long shelf life it is necessary, on the one hand, to ensure that the food is correctly processed and, on the other hand, that the system handling the food is clean and contamination cannot arise through unsatisfactory design. The maintenance of hygienic conditions depends upon the development and use of satisfactory detergents and biocides, and automation of the cleaning system. It will also be necessary to use microbiological procedures to monitor and control the environment, to ensure that the highest standards of hygiene are being achieved.

The hygienic design of the equipment is one of the most important factors in the production of food products with the required quality and shelf life characteristics.

[*] Lehrstuhl für Maschinen- und Apparatekunde
TU München, Freising-Weihenstephan

It is necessary to avoid undue fouling and to ensure that there are no inaccessible places where cleaning is not possible. This includes crevices and dead areas in the piping system. In order to achieve satisfactory design the basic guidelines must be worked out and subsequently used in the computer control system, in the form of data-bases.

1 CONSTRUCTIONAL PRINCIPLES FOR SAFETY

For processing liquid foods and beverages, automated and computer controlled cleaning processes, in the form of CIP (clean in place) or SIP (sterilise in place), are state of the art. Liquid cleaning processes are also used in equipment for handling dry products, in the form of powders or granular materials. After cleaning by liquid sterilants in equipment of this type, it is necessary to use hot air to dry the surfaces which will come into contact with the food. If this is not carried out carefully remaining moisture and product agglomerations could lead to microbiological problems.

At an early stage in the design attention must be paid to the design of the piping layout so that the deposition of residues is prevented. This requires avoiding flow restrictions, flow shades, dead areas and guaranteeing automatic draining conditions so that the formation of coatings and incrustations are minimised. In relation to the cleaning operation it is important to avoid contaminating the food with the detergent or sanitizer. Today it is state of the art to clean one side of a closed valve without the risk of contaminating food product on the other side. Fig. 2 shows the various plant design features which affect the cleanability of the process plant. The designer of equipment as well as the user, should have available CAD procedures; these should embody standards for hygienic design in the form of computer data bases, and which can be used for selecting the most suitable types of equipment. In relation to surfaces it is necessary to keep the surface forces of adhesion as low as possible, whilst at the same time achieving good wetting properties. The compositions of the materials used for non-separable joints must be of comparable quality with regard to surface properties. In the case of jointing materials these must comply with guidelines, which are at present being established nationally and in Europe. In the case of detachable joints it is necessary to avoid crevices, gaps and dead spots which may not be accessible when cleaning. Microbiological danger points may today be avoided by welding the fittings into the pipeline. Means of choice for removing gaps at unavoidable screw joints are sealings carefully carried out. Especially, rotating or reciprocating shafts which are sealed off between product contacted spaces and the outside are vulnerable areas where microbiological ingress can occur.

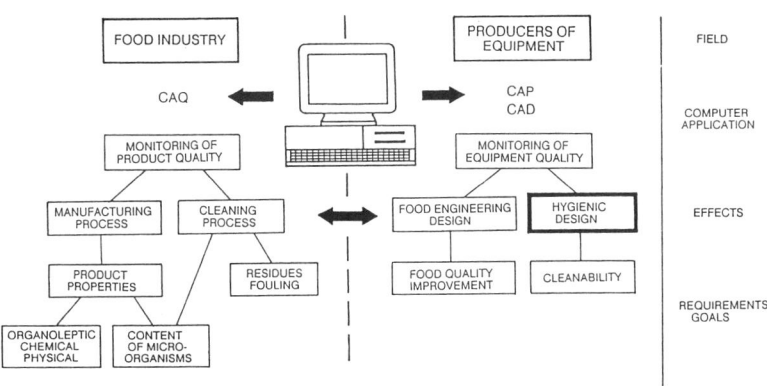

Fig. 1: Computer controlled processes in the food industry

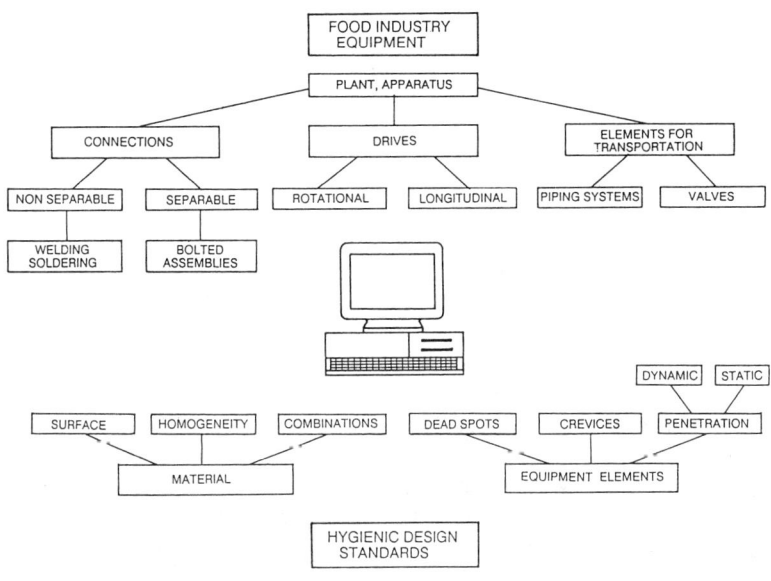

Fig. 2: Tentative systematic with respect to hygienic design for computerization

2 PROBLEMS WITH MOVING PARTS

One of the most difficult problems in the hygienic design of food processing equipment is the adequate sealing of rotating and reciprocating shafts. Fig. 3 shows some typicle examples of equipment which have rotating shafts i.e. cutters, mixers, centrifuges,

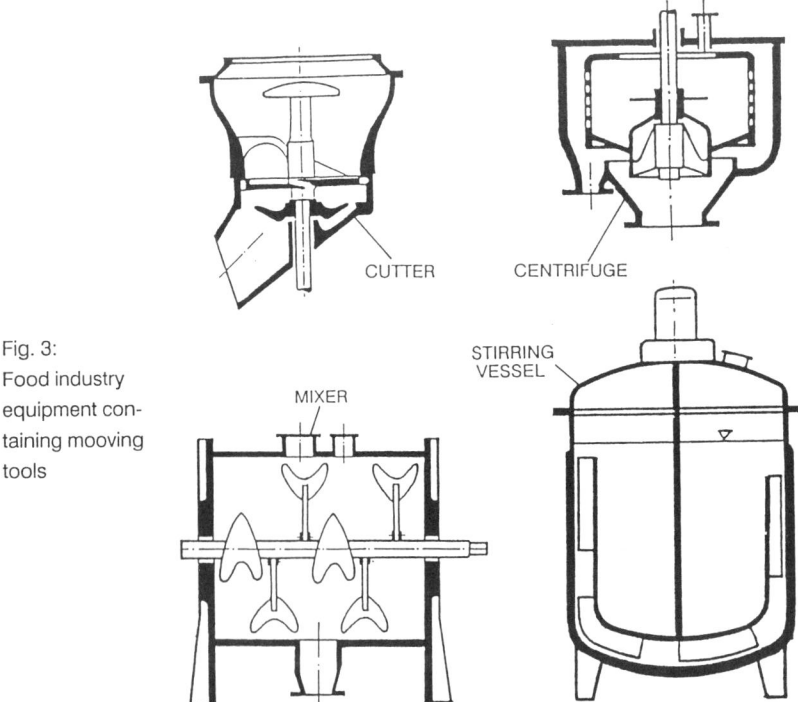

CUTTER   CENTRIFUGE

Fig. 3:
Food industry
equipment con-
taining mooving
tools

MIXER

STIRRING
VESSEL

stirrer and homogenisers. Equipment with rotating or reciprocating shafts i.e. screw feeders, rotary feeders, pumps, centrifuges, double seat valves and hinged valves can be seen following Fig. 4. The main problems causing contamination are the variability of the gaps created by the seals and the passage of thin films of food product adhering at the moving shafts. The mechanism of radial and axial penetration through sealings in different types of equipment are shown in Fig. 5. The product inclusions in narrow gaps and the coatings due to the motion behaviour do not permit a satisfying hygienic conditions by cleaning.

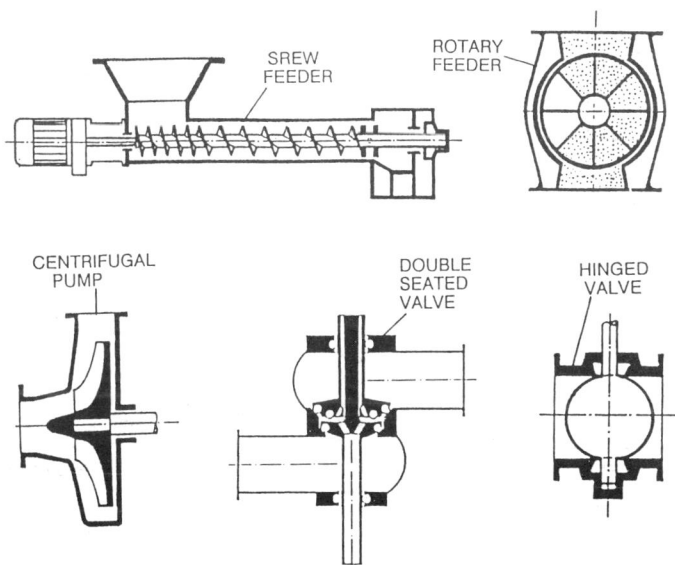

Fig. 4: Equipment with rotating or reciprocating mooving units

2.1 Conventional Dynamic Seals

Sealing elements or areas which seal moving parts against one another, are called dynamic seals. In order to avoid excessive wear it is necessary to lubricate the sealing area. This can be done either by the food product or a liquid e.g. water. The most common form of movement is rotary and several methods of sealing are known. One example (Fig. 6a) is the use of a packing box gland, but this has the disadvantage of causing relatively high shaft wear, especially in the presence of crystallizing fluids, such as sugars. Another example is the application of pre-shaped packings e.g. lip seals, having a stripping effect on coatings or residues, and O-rings fitted into grooves as shown in Fig. 6b. O-ring type seals can not prevent the ingress of product into the grooves which can not be cleaned. O-rings should be generally avoided in food contacted equipment. A final type is the slide ring packing (Fig. 6c). In this case the dynamic sealing gap is formed by one rotating and one non-rotating ring of different slide materials which are pressed against one another by

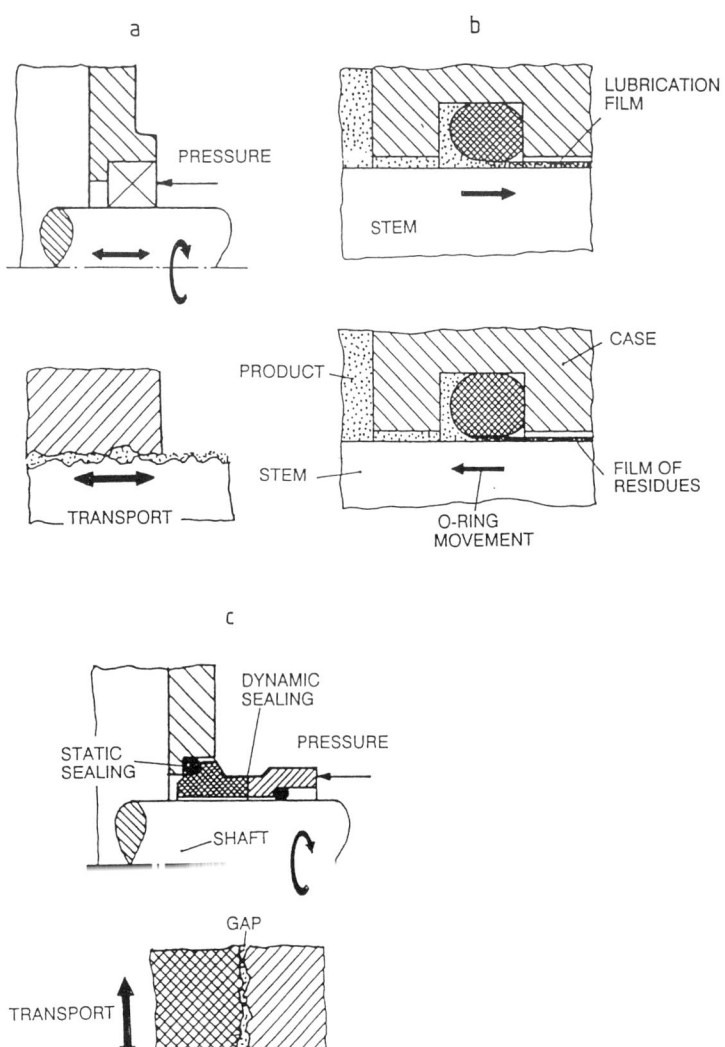

Fig. 5: Principles of dynamic sealings and ingress mechanisms:
a) Radial sealing for rotational and reciprocating movement causing axial penetration
b) ingress mechanism and residues caused by O-ring type sealings,
c) axial sealing for rotation with radial penetration

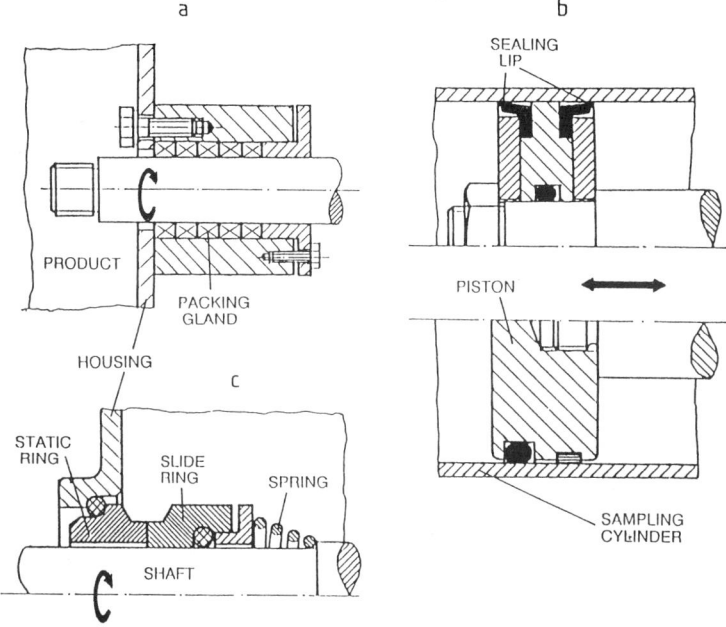

Fig. 6: Usual constructions of sealing spots
a) packing glands, b) shaped packings (lip respectively O-ring sealing), c) slide ring sealing

spring tension. Such seals cause frequently problems on dry run, although new materials have shown considerable improvement.

2.2 Improved Dynamic Seals

In respect to more severe hygienic requirements two points of important constructional improvements will have to be provided:

1. The ingress of germs from the outer environment into the product space due to the relative movement must be prevented.

2. The design of the sealing points must guarantee that they can effectively be cleaned or disinfected.

Trying to solve these problems systematically, there are two different design principles which are applicable both to rotary and to reciprocating movements. Fig. 7a shows a dual arrangement type of seal, which can be operated with a scavenging sterile fluid e.g. steam or condensate under pressure. It prevents the contamination of the product with microorganisms and scavenges coatings in areas which pass through the sealing. During the cleaning process, the scavenging chamber is included into the cleaning cycle. An essential condition of safe working is a careful design of the sealing spots and seal elements in order to avoid gaps in the sealing groove. Fig. 7b and 7c show systems in which the product is hermetically isolated from the actuating mechanism. Such hermetical seals are important for aseptic processing. In rotary movements they require a non-contact torque transfer e.g. a magnetic coupling. In the case of reciprocating movements the moved parts are separated by elastic or deformable elements e.g. a diaphragm.

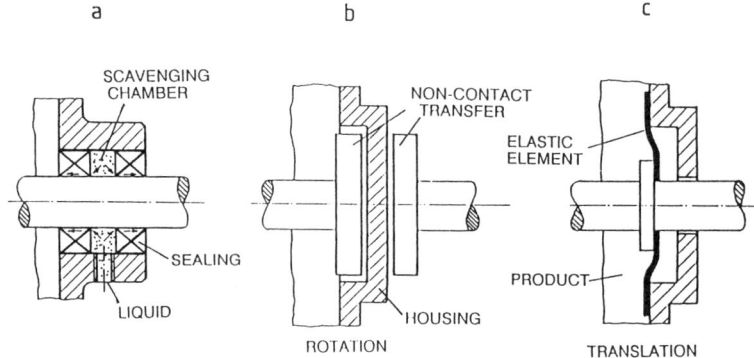

Fig. 7: Design principles for increasing hygienic requirements
a) Dual arrangement of sealings with scavenging chambers, b) Hermetic separation for torque transfer, c) Hermetic separation by elastic elements

2.3 Examples of Seal Design

Scavenged contact seals for rotary movements are mainly used for handling and processing dry products. Fig. 8a shows a gland sealing used e.g. in mixers, screw dosing plants or rotary vane feeders. Scavenging is carried out using virtually germfree air, although in principle, the introduction of steam with subsequent drying is a possibility. In the case of liquid processing equipment slide ring packings with scavenging chambers are being increasingly used. Fig. 8b shows a typical application in a centrifugal pump. It can be sterilised by using e.g. condensate. Similar designs will be met in ball mills, screw pumps and centrifuges.

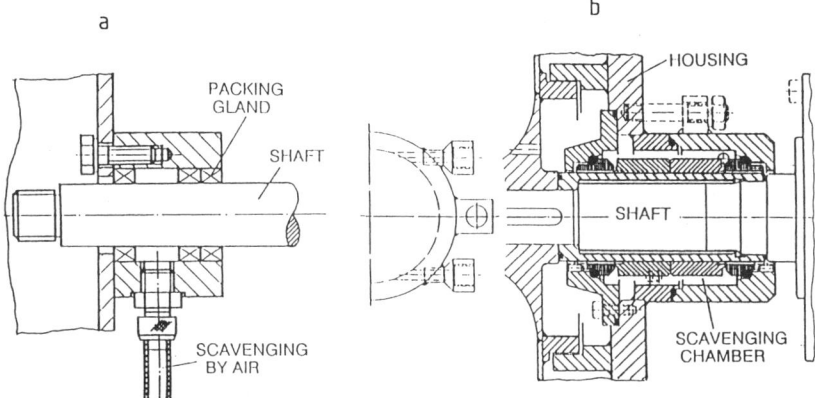

Fig 8: Examples of contact seals using scavenging chambers
a) Gland construction for dry products used in mixers, b) Dual arangment of slide ring sealings for ball mills or centrifugal pumps for sterile requirements (Fa. Hilge)

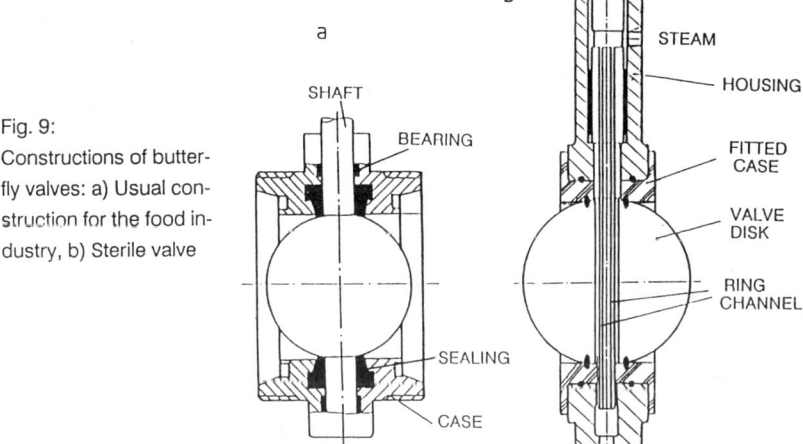

Fig. 9:
Constructions of butter-
fly valves: a) Usual con-
struction for the food industry, b) Sterile valve

In the case of butterfly valves the sealing ring is responsible for the sealing function of the disk and the sealing of the actuating shaft against the environment. The additional and perfect bearing of the shaft journals (Fig. 9a) is an important for virtually germfree conditions. Sterile embodiments of butterfly valves (Fig. 9b) may be sterilised by steam in the area between the shaft and the journal.For the purpose of maintaining a virtually germfree condition in case of reciprocating movements, either scavenged gland sealings are used as shown in Fig. 8a or scavenged and prestressed lip sealings reducing the danger of fouling by the stripping effect of the lips. The scavenging chamber filled with a sealing liquid during processing can be cleaned in regular intervals.

Two other examples of good design using hermetic seals are shownin Fig. 10: Magnetic drives avoid any contact with the outside allowing rotary movements e.g. for driving magnetic stirrers (Fig. 10a), pumps or turbine volume meters. In the case of reciprocating or translational movements, elastic bellows, diaphragms or plastic tubes may be used e.g. for aseptic dual seated valves (Fig. 10b), membrane valves, pinch valves or peristaltic pumps.

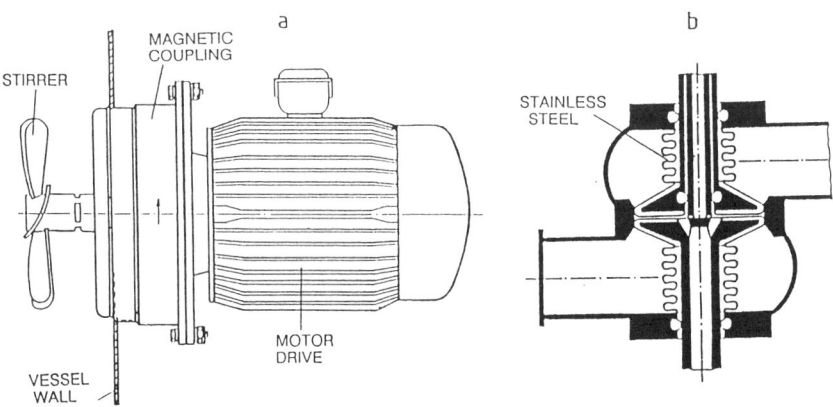

Fig. 10: Examples of hermetical seals
a) Non-contact torque drive for a stirrer, b) dual seated valve using a bellow

CONCLUSIONS

Improvements in the processing of food products can be achieved by carful design and selection of equipment under hygienic aspects. This has been made possible by systematic investigations of the vulnerable parts of the processing equipment. Particular problems are encountered with seals of rotating and reciprocating parts, and methods of designing these for use in virtually germfree or aseptic systems have been demonstrated. It is an important goal to have data-bases containing design principles and standards as well as examples of constructions to help designers of food processing equipment solving problems.

REFERENCES

/1/ Ball, A.: S. 118-127 in: PROCESS ENGINEERING in the FOOD IN-
DUSTRY - 2, (1990), Elsevier, London, ed Field, R. W. and
Howell, J. A.:

/2/ Hauser, G., Michel, R.: Chem.-Ing.-Tech. 56 (1984) Nr. 6,
Synopse S. 487

/3/ Hauser, G., Michel, R.: ZFL, 1 (1984), S. 40-45

/4/ Hauser, G., Michel, R.: Deutsche Milchwirtschaft 51/52 (1985),
S. 1733-1738

/5/ Grasshoff, A., Reuter, H.: Chem.-Ing.-Techn. 55 (1983)
Nr. 5,   S. 406-407

/6/ Hilge: Firmenschrift "Hilge-Reintechnik-Fibel", 2 (1989)
Philipp Hilge GmbH, Bodenheim/Rhein

/7/ Hauser, G., Michel, R.: VDI-Bericht Nr. 545 (1984) S. 1089-
1108

/8/ Hauser, G., Michel, R., Sommer, K.: S. 143-158 in: PROCESS
ENGINEERING in the FOOD INDUSTRY, (1989), Elsevier, London,
ed Field, R. W. and Howell, J. A.

/9/ Hauser, G. Michel, R.: 3R international, 24 Jhrg. (1985) Heft
4, S. 195-204

PROCESS CONTROL in the FOOD INDUSTRY

J.J.Bimbenet, G.Trystram

ENSIA (Ecole Nationale Supérieure des Industries Agricoles et Alimentaires), F-91305 Massy

SUMMARY

The biological nature of raw materials, the destination of products and the very special way they are evaluated (in the mouth) mean that :
- few sensors are able to measure the qualities of products, unless very indirectly
- many processes combine batch and continuous operations
- the knowledge of these processes is generally poor.

The Process control consists in
- controlling unit operations
- controlling the processes, i.e. several unit operations, towards optimal operation of them.

Trends in process control are many, like for example :
- computers are more and more used
- smart sensors
- intelligent control
- model based control
- artificial intelligence.

Different ways are used for different kinds of processes. The methods tools and difficulties are specific.

Three types of operations are considered:
- sequential operations: information is in logic form. Products fluxes are discontinuous. This type of operation is generally well controlled. Tools (graph theory, Petri nets, Grafcet) in automatic control science are successfully used because implantation on computer is easy

- other batch operations: information is essentially analogic but product fluxes are discontinuous. The right control depends on good real time information about the product, which is often difficult to obtain. New control applications based on modelling approaches are performed (adaptive control, batch optimization through maximum principle implantation)

- continuous processes ; this type of operation is the most studied. Many control laws using computer-based strategies are performed. Because of progress with numerical real time treatment there are new possibilities with "advanced control".

Furthermore, in many food processes several of these types of operations are combined, which adds to the difficulty of the control. The CIM model (Computer Integrated Manufacturing) is presented. Examples are given of supervision and optimization systems.

1. INTRODUCTION

In all industrial sectors, **objectives** of process control are :

- to increase the **productivity per capita** by reduction of the labour time. In fact, this objective is also met by mechanization, which is replacement of human (or animal) force by machines, when process control is replacement of man's perception and decision by mechanisms. In fact, mechanization and automatization are closely linked.

- to increase the **productivity of equipment and the yield on raw material** by a better control of all process parameters. An illustration of this is on fig.1.

- the good control of process parameters leads to the control of **product quality**. The curves of fig.1 may also be interpreted in terms of better control of "over-quality". This objective has become specially important in the last years with the outbreak of concepts of "total quality" and "quality management".

- process automatization also improves the **flexibility** of operations by a better and faster control of the phases of start-up, stops, flow-rate modification and product changes. The flexibility is a necessary requirement to perform the new production rules like "just in time".

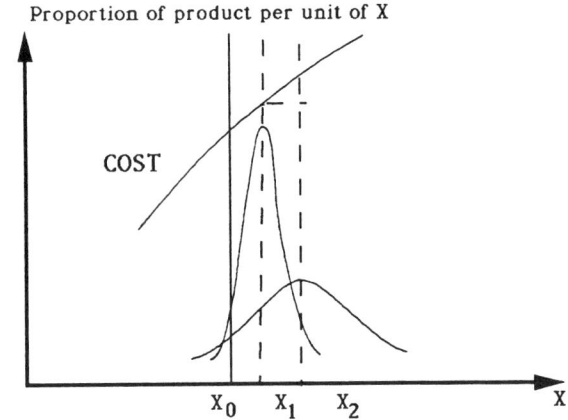

Fig.1.Influence of process control on productivity.
The constraint is to have less of, e.g. 5% , of product units under the weight limit of X_0 .With a poor control, the target must be X_2 , and with a better control X_1. The saving of product corresponds to the reduction of the overweight from X_2 to X_1 .

In **food industry**, process control also has specific objectives:

- **hygiene** requirements are important. In fact, they become more and more severe. The main way to improve the performance of many processes is reduction of human presence, which is attained by mechanization and automatization. Pushing this evolution to its extreme point probably leads to the food plant with nobody in it.

- the **perishability** and sometimes the **seasonal nature of production** of biological products also obliges, in view of quality objectives (including hygiene), to a better control of product fluxes in the plant. This means for example control of waiting lines of unit products or of residence times of liquids in buffer tanks.

These objectives are best met if the control **integrates the whole line**, not only individual unit operations.

2. TYPES OF PROCESSES FROM THE POINT OF VIEW OF CONTROL

Control has different features according to:
- the nature of product fluxes
- the nature of information exchanged with the process.

2.1. Nature of product fluxes

These fluxes are:

- **discontinuous**, e.g. batch operations like sterilization, fermentation, or preparation of a batch of powders from definite weights of various components. In these cases, upstream and downstream product fluxes, schematically only take two values (0-100%)

- **continuous**, like in an evaporator, a continuous can sterilizer or a bottle filler. In such operations, up- and downstream fluxes are maintained as constant as possible during operation.

In both types of operations, the products may be:

- **bulk** products, which means that no individual particle of the product is considered (gases, liquids, powders)

- **discrete** products (pieces) when product units receive individual treatment (e.g. cans, bottles, cartons).

2.2. Nature of information exchanged with the process

This information may be:

- **logic**, for example of the type: open/closed, working/stopped, yes/no

- or **analogic**: a flow rate or a voltage, i.e. parameters able to take a whole continuum of values.

This classification is independant of the fact that analogic as well as logic information may be translated in a digital form for computer treatment.

This information

- comes from the process via automatic sensors

- goes to the process as instructions (open/close a valve) from control-command systems

- flows in both directions **through a man** who, for example, gives to the system the result of a laboratory measurement or decides to stop a machine.

2.3. Types of processes

Combining the previous categories leads to three types of processes from the point of view of control, fig. 2:

		Products fluxes	
		discontinuous	continuous
Nature	logic	1. sequential operations: batch mixing, CIP, etc.	
of information	analogic	2. batch operations: sterilization, fermentation, etc.	3. continuous operations: concentration, drying, etc.

Fig. 2. Types of processes in the food industry in the perspective of control.

3. PROCESS CONTROL OF UNIT OPERATIONS

We now successively present the three types of unit operations and the state of process control in these operations in the food industry.

3.1. Type 1: sequential processes

Examples are found in liquids or powders mixing, in certain packaging operations or in cleaning-in-place processes.

3.1.1. Historical approach

Around the beginning of the 20th century, it became necessary to control industrial operations. Solutions were then developed, on the basis of logic information, using the electromechanical relay. Logic functions could easily be realized using this element. After the last world war, the transistor was discovered and electronic made very fast progress. Programmable tools were then available, the most important of which being the Programmable Logic Controller (PLC). From a model of the control law, a program is developed and implemented into the PLC.

There exist different levels of PLC. The higher one is able to control both analog control loops, sequences and a great number of inputs-outputs. Numerical treatments are possible. The language of PLC is specific to logic problems: boolean equations, ladder diagram, "Grafcet", etc.

3.1.2. Technical and economical motivations

The robustness and the flexibility of the PLC are reasons for the success of this apparatus. But there are also economical reasons: logic sensors and actuators are cheaper than analog ones. This reason is important for the understanding of process control motivations: process control is used to realize objectives. Why would you use sophisticated strategies when cheaper ones are able to reach the same objectives?

3.1.3. Modelling tools

Any type of process control requires the building of a **model.** First, logic functions have been used, but they gave complex models. More recently, new graphical models based upon graph theory have been developped

Grafcet (Sequential Function Chart)
The method Grafcet [CEI, 1988] is illustrated on the figure 3. The first part represents a mixing operation, which is very classical in food industry. The model describes the **sequences,** the operations in each sequence phase and the **events** which pilot the evolution of the operations. It is a step by step description. Each state is described by a square. The operation stays in this state until the event (called receptivity) is realized. The model can be very complex or very simple. An advantage of this method is the hierarchical approach of the complexity of the operation.

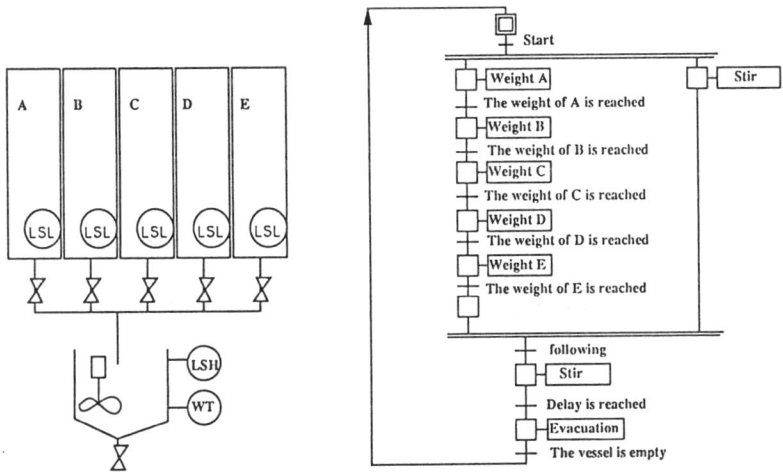

Fig. 3. Example of modelling a step sequence process control function

Petri nets
An other method, based upon the same kind of approaches, is the "Petri nets" [Petri, 1962]. Because of the performances of computers, the method of this german researcher today finds more and more applications. The graphical representation is shown on figure 4. The example is a representation of a Cleaning-in-Place process serving several unit operations. This type of model is able to describe and realize the synchronization of different operations. A mathematical method is able to give the optimal description of the model based upon this approach.

Using these methodologies and their implementation into PLC, food industry made very important progresses for the process and products regularity. These multivariable control systems are certainly **the most widely used** in food industry.

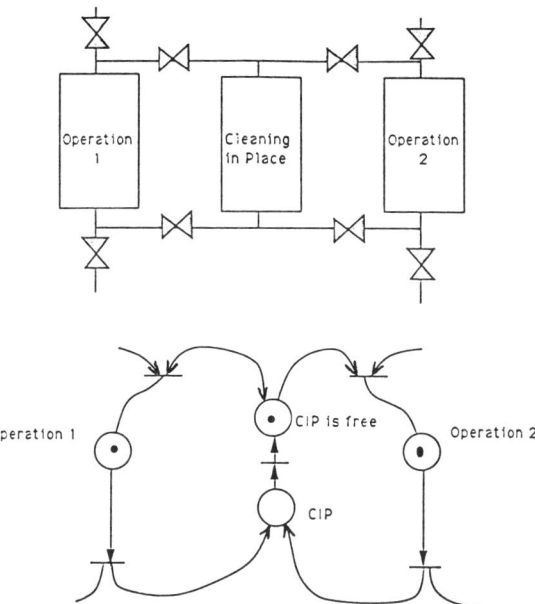

Fig. 4. Example of Petri nets modelling applied to CIP coordination

3.2. Type 2: batch processes

3.2.1. Importance of this type of unit operation

There are many batch operations in food industry: fermenters, retorts, cookers, evaporators, ovens, dryers, cristallyzers, etc. This is due to the small-scale origin of food preparation.

3.2.2. Three strategies for control

A batch control consists in the control of several analog variables, like temperature, pressure, flow rate or product characteristics, vs time. The objectives being not constant during the time, this is **more difficult** than a regulation problem.

There are two specific reasons for studying the control of batch processes. The first one is that often batch operations are unstable (example: fermentations): control is then indispensable. The second reason is that product characteristics are higly dependent on the batch history.

The figure 5 illustrates three kinds of strategies.

3.2.2.1. Time based process control

This method is **the most used** in food industry. It consists in the indirect control of the process through the time: it may also be presented as "open loop" or "a priori" control. Knowledge of the process is necessary to establish a combination between:

    (i) process duration and operating parameters

    (ii) products characteristics.

Methods for modelling and implementing this kind of control are the same as for sequential problems. But in this case, the elements which are taken into account for the

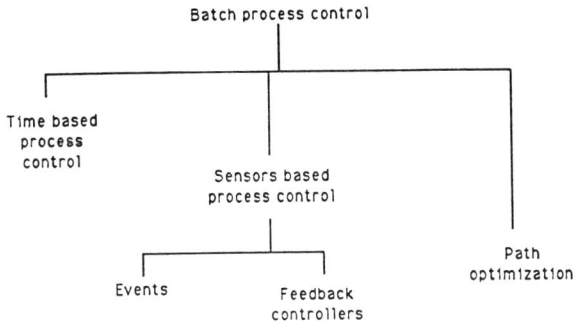

Fig. 5. Strategies for batch process control

command of the operation depend on both the sensor outputs and the time. No feedback is performed.

A typical example is the retort sterilization of canned products [Texeira and Mansion,1982].

Another one is illustrated on figure 6. This is a wine making process [Danzart and Trystram,1991]. A vessel is filled with grapes and grape juice. The operation consists of the fermentation of sugars in ethanol at a given temperature. But the quality of the wine also depends on its color and aroma, resulting from an extraction process. This extraction is performed using a pump and provoking a circulation inside the reactor. There are no sensors able to measure on line wine qualities. As described in the figure, time is the control parameter of the operation. Of course the knowledge of the wine making operator is here the most important element of the strategy.

3.2.2.2. Sensor based process control

One of the gaps between process control applications and food industry consists in the sensor problems. It appear that wherever sensors are available, it is possible to implement more efficient control laws.

Sensors in the Food Industry

It is classical to say [Corrieu and Picque,1988 and 1990], [Green, 1983], [Trystram, 1986; Trystram and Dumoulin, 1990] that sensors are the most difficult problems in food process control. It is well known that a sensor in that industry must comply with food process constraints: sensors have to be cleaned in place, sterilizable, and made of materials compatible with food. Furthermore, in some cases, modern production requires that sensors are available for several products processed on the same plant. The figure 7 is an illustration of the different possibilities of measurements used for control in food industry.

The best solution is **on-line direct measurement**. This is always difficult, because of food product specificities. A lot of progress was made with new materials development like glass fiber, ceramics, etc. [Kress Rogers,1985].

However, most food processes have no rapid dynamic characteristics, therefore the real time constraints are not so strong. That is why another possibility consists in **"at-line"** **measurements**, i.e. automatized analytical systems close to the line [Trystram et al., 1990]. At-line measures are integrated in the control system with an adapted control law. Many applications are realized in industry using classical laboratory equipment like chromatographs, spectroscopes or more recent analytical methods (NMR for example) [Dumoulin and Trystram, 1990], [Marc et al.,1990]. Another important avenue for progress involves **biosensors** [Turner et al.,1987], but these constraints (dilution, sterilization, etc.) mean that biosensors are used

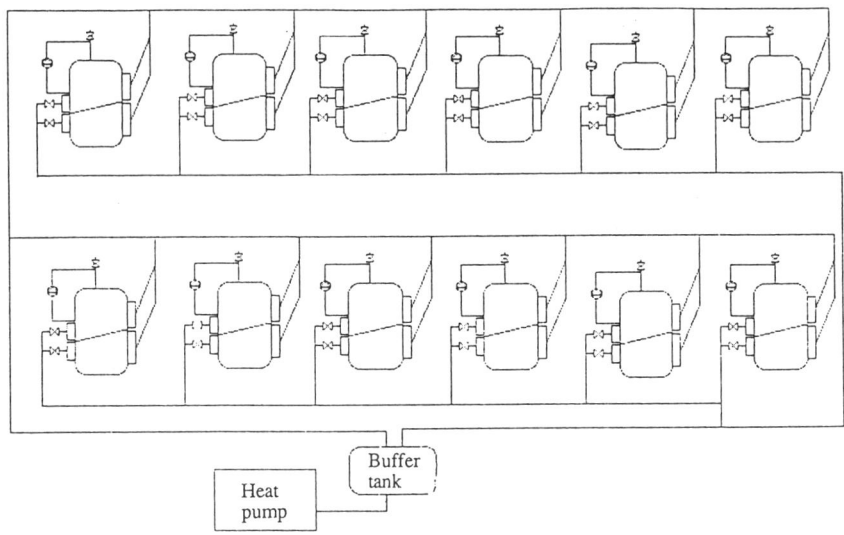

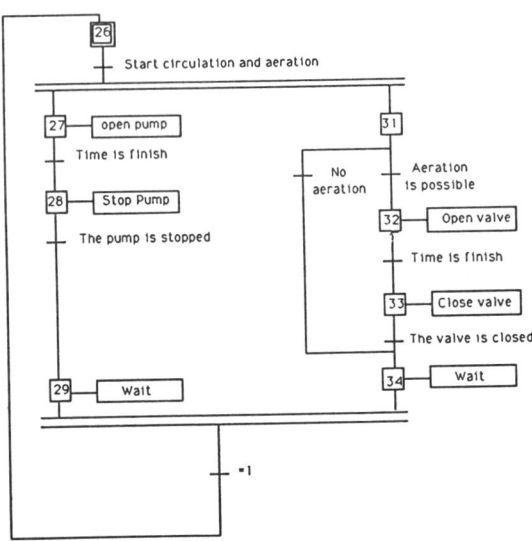

Fig. 6. Modelling the control of wine making process. Case of circulation and aeration.

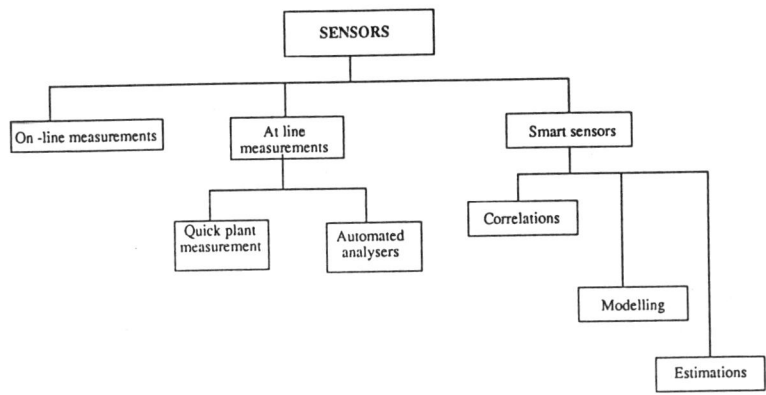

Fig. 7. Principles applicable for sensors and real time measurements

at-line [Scheller and Schubert, 1992]. Of course, sampling and automatic control of the analyser must be performed. Especially in the case of powders analyses, sampling and preparation of samples may integrate **robotics**. Others progresses are coming with FIA (Flow Injection Analysis), an other equipment close to the line [Lima and Rangel,1990].

Proposed applications of **smart sensors have increased** in recent years, involving the combination of classical measurement techniques and appropriate software. Progress has also been made with estimation techniques [Bastin and Dochain,1986], but implementation in industry has been rare. This is certainly a good opportunity for future research. Image processing is another way for sensor progress in the food industry.

Examples of sensors based strategies

Biomass production.
We take the example of a certain type of biomass production performed in batch fermenters. The problem here is to decide when the operation is over: this is realized when all the substrate is consumed.But the measurement of the substrate concentration is one of the most difficult problems for fermenter control. An indirect strategy is based upon the microbial activity measured through the NADH (nicotinamide adenine dinucleotide in its reduced form) fluorescence. Fluorosensors are used here, and figure 8 illustrates the relation between the substrate consumption and the sensor signal. A model, Grafcet type, is then built, using an event which is the decrease of the sensor signal. This strategy is better than that based upon time, because there is a closed loop between the phenomenon and the decision [Guenneugues, 1990].

Sterilization
The second example presented here is related to sterilization retort control. This is an important part of the process, because the productivity is directly related to the occupation time of the retort: the optimization of this duration is important. Many strategies are proposed and used in industry. Since several years, several methods based on the prediction of the lethal value have been used. A model gives this value from temperature measurements. An improvement is proposed with the prediction of the value in the future, taking into account the overshooting [Beyer et al.,1988].

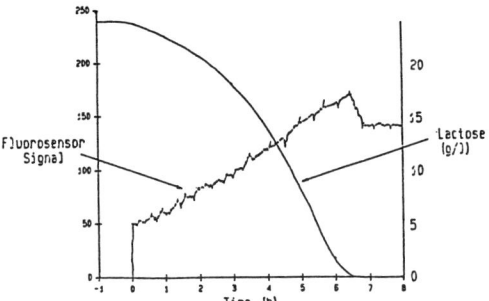

Fig. 8. Control of a batch fermentation with a fluorosensor (Guenneugues et al., 1990)

These two examples illustrate the efficiency of control strategies when the right sensors are available.

However, from sensors signals, more sophisticated strategies are possible. In the previous cases, the sensor signal gives an event which is used for decision. But it is also possible to use the analog signal to build a continuous strategy, even for batch operations. The specificity of batch is that the control is generally **non linear.** There are only few applications of non linear control problems. If some cases are studied in laboratories, the number of applications is very small. For example many works propose adaptive techniques for the controller design, like GPC controllers (Generalized Predictive Controller) [Clarke and Balsman,1990]. Today, it appears that industrial application of these regulators is not easy. New studies must be performed to take into account this kind of operations.

3.2.2.3. Path optimization

A way of looking at the batch operation control consists in considering the problem to find the better path for the product. From this point of view, the control appears to be an optimization problem: if I know the past of the process, which is the best path for the manipulated variable to perform the objective? Some strategies are proposed, but not yet implemented in industry. A number of possible mathematical methods for path optimization are available: Pontryaguin, dynamic programming, heuristics, etc. But their use requires good **dynamics models.**

All this shows that **batch operations,** which are considered as simpler, more rustic than continuous ones, **are more difficult to control.** This is one of the reasons which make that many efforts are done to change them for continuous operations.

3.3. Type 3: continuous unit operations

The problem for this kind of operation (heat exchangers, evaporators, fermenters, dryers, extruders, etc.) consists in maintaining an objective variable at a desired value (the setpoint).

3.3.1. Open loop

The review of the applications of process control in food industry must take into account the reality of these applications and not only the wish of the researchers: it appears that **the most used strategy in industry is the open loop control.** In other words, it means: no control. This is possible because many processes are stable and operators have a great knowledge of it. But with food products, many disturbances are encountered, especially coming from raw material variability: it appears that with tighter quality objectives a feedback control is necessary. Also, certain continuous operations are characterized by very short processing times (cooker-extruder, UHT treatments, falling-film evaporators, spray dryers,etc.) with the consequence that the human reaction is not fast enough to keep product flow rate and quality. All this makes the control necessary.

3.3.2. Closed loop strategies

Historical aspects

We all know the first published application of closed loop control, the James Watt speed regulator on steam engines But it is only around 1930 that the theory of feedback was developped (Nyquist, etc.): it is a recent progress. Analog regulators were then built and the PID (Proportional-Integral-Derivative) procedure found its application field. More recently, the computer allowed the development of new feedback strategies and the improvement of the performances of these regulators. It is the numerical control which makes possible the advanced control of processes.

The PID

In a recent conference presented at the World Congress on Chemical Engineering, Morari [Morari,1991] remarked that according to a Japanese study, **90% of the control loops used in industry were of the basic PID type.** This is certainly the same situation in all developped countries. PID is a very simple feedback procedure which is associated with a quite simple empirical tuning procedure [Ziegler and Nichols,1942]. Its success in industry is very large. But the simplicity of this controller must not mask the care needed for the implementation of such a control. There are two stages: the qualitative and the quantitative ones.

Qualitative aspect: structure of the control strategy

The first role of the process engineer is to define the manipulated and the measured variables and to establish the structure of the control strategy. This work requires **cooperation between the control engineer and the process engineer,** because there is a close relation between the technology, the performances and the process requirements. The best controller is not able to control an operation if the design is not the right one. Figure 9 illustrates the comparison between two control strategies, applied to a heated air dryer. In the two cases a closed loop between moisture and a manipulated variable is performed. The first case is simple: the relation is direct. In the second case, there are cascade controllers, feedforward control and dynamic interference compensation.

Using their "tool box", the engineers become architects who have to choose the best control structure. The choice is made on the basis of the required performances, of cost and evidently of the feasability of the strategy.

Quantitative aspect: the controller tuning

Once the control structure has been determined, the tuning functions have to be calculated. Researchers in process control have proposed a lot of methods, based on numerical information treatments: pole placement, state feedback, adaptive controllers [Aström and Wittenmark,1984] and Artificial Intelligence based controllers [Eerikainen et al.,1988]. The present trend is to integrate most of these controllers into Computer Aided Design tools. From experiments, the control engineer is able to choose the best controller and to evaluate the tuning parameters, which is not difficult. The real problem is to obtain **experiments** with sufficient information about the **process dynamics.**

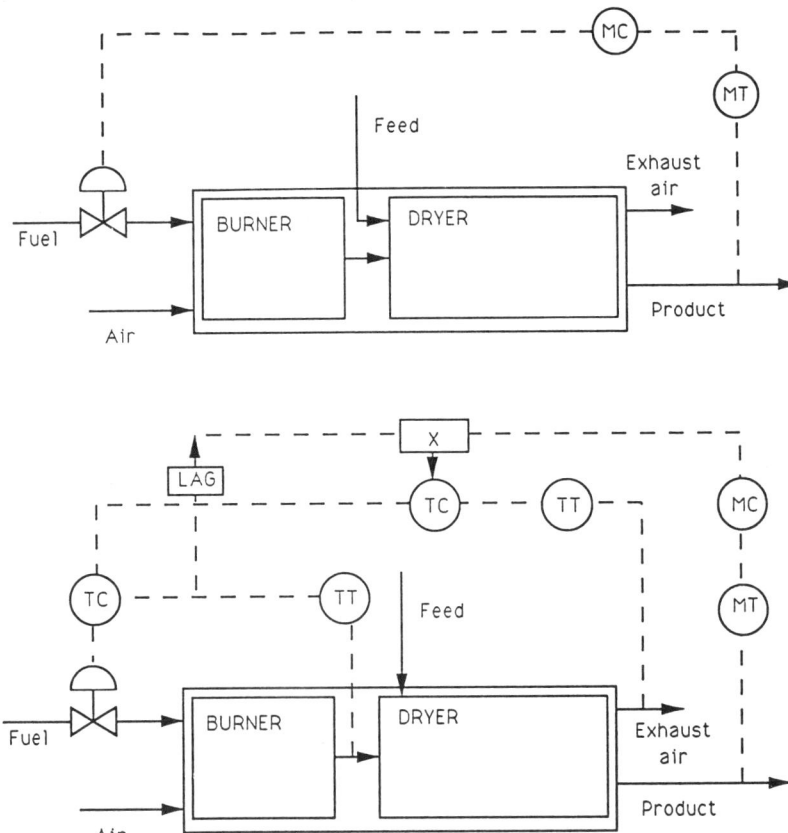

Fig. 9. Two control strategies of dryer control

Advanced process control strategies

We present two examples of such developments.

Multiple effects evaporators are principally used in sugar and dairy factories. Their control is difficult, specially when they are disturbed by variable input concentration and random steam extractions. Many tests have been realized with classical feedback, but recently some different strategies have been proposed. Figure 10 illustrates an example of a structure implemented on an existing plant [Rousset et al.,1989]. The feedback is realized through three cascade regulators. A feedforward is used to have an anticipation (feedforward effect) of the steam extractions. Figure 11 gives an illustration of the performances of this strategy. From the open loop situation to the closed loop one, we can see that the concentrations are more constant: the objectives are reached. In this example, the tuning of the controller was accomplished using a CAD (Computer Aided Design) software.

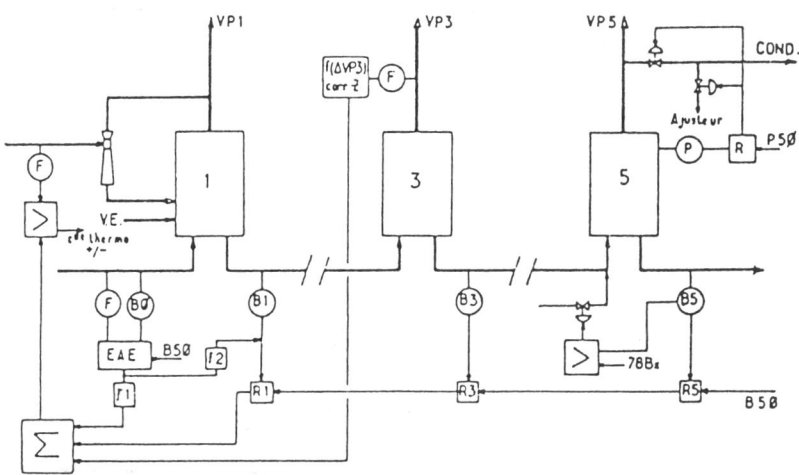

Fig. 10. Simplified scheme of the process control of a sugar factory evaporation station

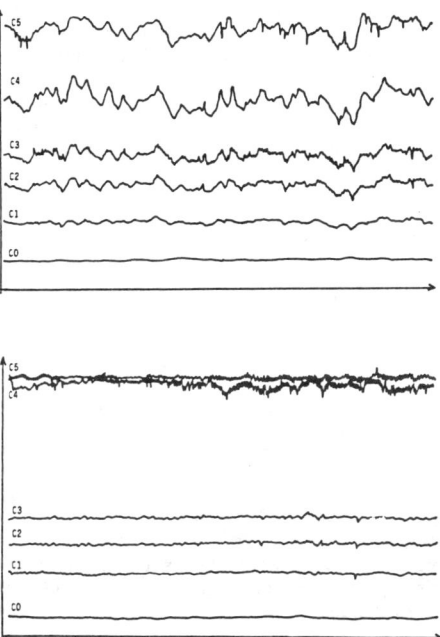

Fig 11. Performance of process control of the evaporation plant of Fig. 10: juices concentrations vs time. Top = manual control, bottom = automatic control (Rousset et al., 1989)

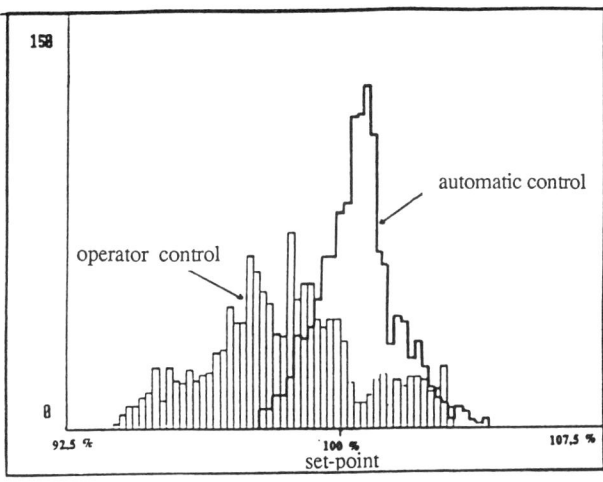

Fig. 12. Control of a spray dryer: comparison between manual and automatic control for product moisture control. (Desplans et al., 1991)

A second example illustrates the application of multivariable controllers. **Spray drying** is a very complex operation because of close interactions between parameters and of rapid dynamics. Some classical strategies are generally used, like output air temperature control. In the figure 13, the performance of an other control procedure is illustrated. A multivariable predictive control law using an internal model has been implemented [Desplans et al.,1991]. The figure presents the performance of the moisture control. It can be seen that product moisture is more constant than with manual control and refers to the discussion on fig.1.

As a conclusion of this chapter, it appears that many impovements have been made in the field of food process control. More progress requires better models, which supposes knowledge of process dynamics. Sensors have to be improved or developed.

4. SUPERVISION AND OPTIMIZATION LEVEL

4.1. The needs for optimization and coordination

The diversity of operations that are encountered in a classical process and the number of such operations in any production line is illustrated on many industrial plant, for example bread making process, dairy process, etc.... From this it follows that control of each operation is not sufficient: an efficient control requires the **coordination of the whole plant**: this is the optimization requirement.
Therefore, the control system must integrate:
- **horizontally,** the whole line
- which requires a more global view of the process, therefore a **vertical** integration of the various levels of decision, from the short term control of process parameters to the middle term objectives of the production staff.

This is what is now called : **"Computer Integrated Manufacturing",** or CIM model [Clark et al.,1987]. The figure 13 is a presentation of the CIM model.

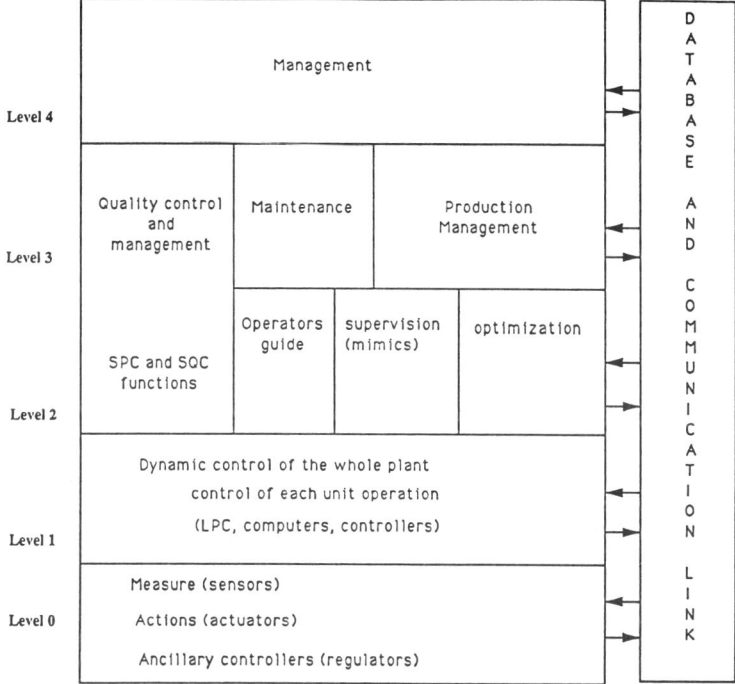

Fig. 13. The CIM model, a hierarchical approach for process control tasks

Five hierarchical levels can be defined:

- level 0 is dedicated to the process. We find there the measurement and the operating tasks, sensors, actuators and ancillary controllers,
- level 1 is related to the dynamic control of the plant. The real time characteristics of the process are taken into account here,
- level 2 represents the supervision: the operator is able here to modify the process parameters. This an important level, because the automatic control is today the combination between the really automatic control functions and the help, through specific tasks, of the operator,
- level 3 is the plant production management level,
- and level 4 is related to the management functions.

The model CIM is often represented as a pyramid to indicate that the quantity of data is gradually decreasing towards the upper levels.

If the model appears to be complex, it is important to note that the control tasks are built **from the process requirements.** Automatic control must be provided at the level of complexity just necessary for the process.

At this point it is possible to remark on the position of **robotics** in food industry. Only very few operations are controlled using robotic functions. Most of them are
-packaging
-transfer of product units from one line to an other,
i.e. operations **on pieces** like most of those on a bread-making line, for example.
As previously said, some laboratory tasks may also be robotised.

The most difficult task is to obtain a productivity higher than that of manual operations. Process industry appears here to be very different from manufacturing industry, where many robotised functions may now be found.

4.2. The food industry needs

We may consider that control at levels 0 and 1 have been presented in the previous chapter: we now concentrate on the levels 2 and 3.

What are the requirements of the food industry at these levels? This is a difficult question, because the food industry covers a wide variety of operations: continuous/discontinuous/ sequential operations, treatment of bulk/pieces. We recently completed a study to establish the needs of food industry [Danzart et al.,1992]. The results are presented in figure 14. We defined eight axes, subdivided into severals functions.

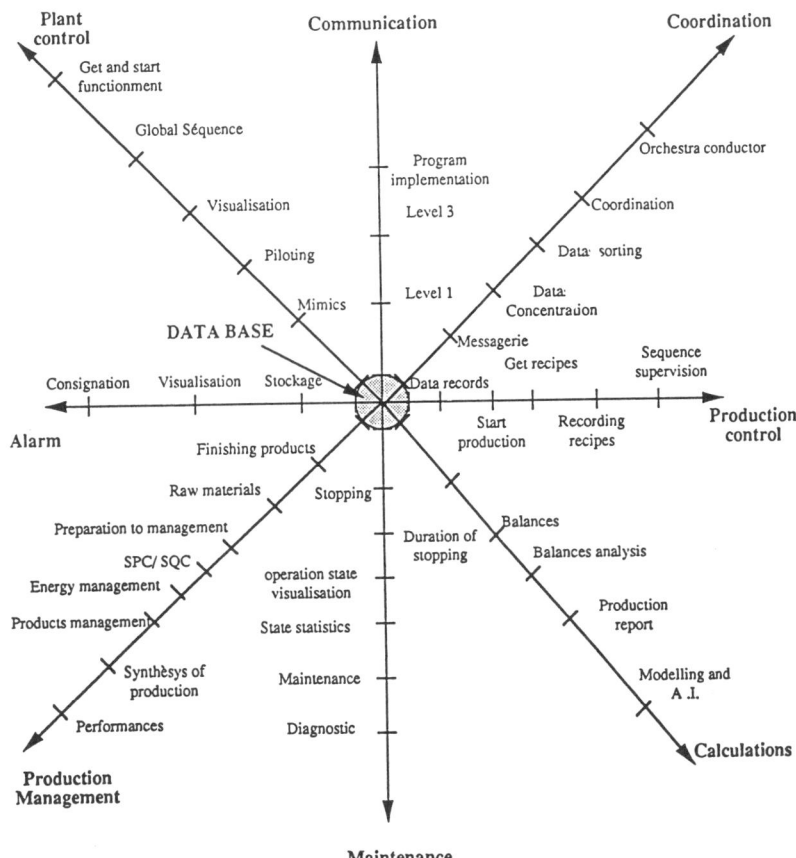

Fig. 14. Needs of food industry for supervision functions

This is the general picture. But every plant has its own needs: figure 15 presents the case of a dairy plant. Our study establishes that control systems must be **flexible** enough to handle the various situations.

Some functions are classical and they are performed for several industrial sectors. For these classical functions, it is now possible to find color high resolution on which mimics are realized, due to progress in peri-computer technology. The operator can see on the screen all the information from a part of the plant. Such **operator guide functions** are a significant part of process control systems today.

Because of the power of computer, there are **new functions** which are processed for helping the operator. For example, in management tasks it is important to have criteria about the variability of product quality: quality management appears to be one of the most important objectives of process control tasks. Softwares, for examples Statistical Quality (or Process) Control (SPC, SQC) can help [Yano,1986]. More and more **intelligent systems** are integrating real time data processing functions. Management specificities are taken into account at this level [Niyoyanka and MacKenna,1990], [Weisser et al.,1990], [Ohkubo,1990].

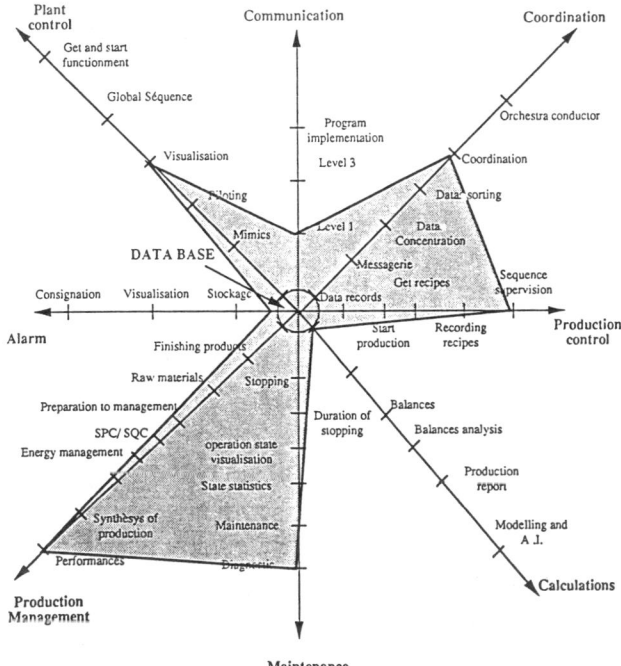

Fig. 15. Needs of a dairy factory in the field of process supervision

4.3. Communications and local industrial networks

The previous analysis gives a lot of functions which are necessary to perform the best process control. It can be seen that all these functions must be implemented on specific computers, Programmable Logic Controllers, scientific computers, analog regulators, etc. The engineer must establish the communications between all these computers, i.e. create the right architecture of the information system. The figure 16 gives an example in food industry: we can see the communication lines between the different apparatus used for the realization of the control functions. Many progresses in this field are possible with the local industrial networks. The information is vehiculed from the process to data bases. Then specific software is able to take into account this information to perform the various functions.

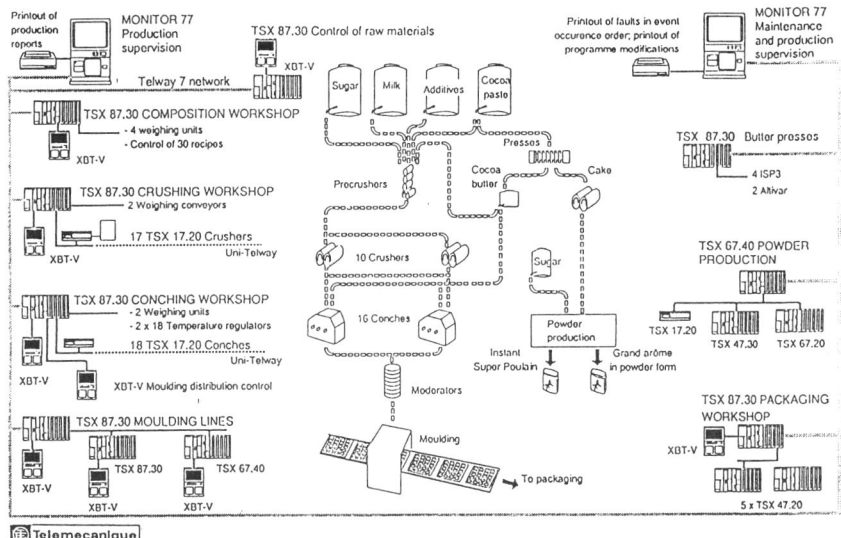

Fig. 16. Manufacturing organization of a chocolate factory (Télémécanique, 1992).

CONCLUSIONS

After this review of Food Process Control, it appears that we have been able to find many examples, which means that this industry is, in this domain, not as poor as is often suggested.

However, much progress is possible. From the hierarchical approach it is evident that the levels of the process (0 and 1) are important. Sensor development deserves more efforts and transfers from other industries where appropriate. The knowledge about the unit operation is not always sufficient. The dynamic behavior of the operations must be studied, through experiments and dynamic modelling. From this process knowledge, better strategies may be designed . The high level of sequence process control is due to good modelling methods for the control functions: similar progress is possible for the other kinds of unit operations.

Process control applications are developed to achieve specific objectives. The engineer must design the right information architecture to obtain the best performance in relation to these objectives.

Process control is a **multidisciplinary** approach. It is important to build teams with knowledge in Food, Control, Process, Computers, Engineeering.

In all the cases, the process control study is a methodological approach which is good to increase knowledge of the researcher and improve the performances of industry.

List of references

K.J. Aström, B. Wittenmark. Computer controlled systems. Prentice Hall, 1984, Englewoods Cliffs.

G. Bastin, D. Dochain. On line estimation of micobial specific growth rates. Automatica, 1986, 22, 705-709.

O. Beyer, A. Duquenoy, B. Couvrat-Desvergnes, A. Carrier. Vers l'ajustement automatique des barêmes de stérilisation. In: Automatic Control and Optimization of Food processes, Ed. Renard & Bimbenet, Elsevier Applied Science, London, 1988,223-240.

CEI, Preparation of sequential functions charts for control systems, 1988, n° 848.

J.P. Clark, W.F. Balsman. Computer Integrated Manufacturing in the food industry. In: Engineering and food, Ed. W. Spiess and H. Schubert, Elsevier Applied Science, London, 1990, vol I, 781-789.

D.W. Clarke, C. Mothadi, P.S. Tuffs. Generalized Predictive Control. Automatica, 23, 1987, 137-148 (part I) and 149-160 (part II).

G. Corrieu, D. Picque. Capteurs pour les industries alimentaires: situation actuelle et future. In: Automatic Control and Optimisation of Food processes, Ed. Renard & Bimbenet, Elsevier Applied Science, London, 1988,77-88.

G. Corrieu, D. Picque. Capteurs en biotechnologie. Symposium ACoFoP II, Paris, 12-13 November 1990.

M. Danzart, G. Trystram. Automatisation du procédé de vinification. ENSIA, Internal report, 1991.

M. Danzart, R. Treillon, G. Trystram. Supervision en industries alimentaires. ENSIA, Internal report, 1992.

J.M. Desplans, P.Lebois, M.Delouvrie. Commande prédictive multi-variable par modèle interne appliqué au cas d'une tour de séchage de lait en poudre. In: Proc. AGORAL, Dijon, France, avril 1991.

E. Dumoulin, G. Trystram. Method for the conception of at-line measurement: study of ethanol in complex liquid. In: Engineering and food, Ed. W. Spiess and H. Schubert, Elsevier Applied Science, London, 1990, vol I, 719-726.

T. Eerikainen, S. Linko, P. Linko. The potential of fuzzy logic in optimisation and control. In: Automatic Control and Optimisation of Food processes, Ed. Renard & Bimbenet, Elsevier Applied Science, London, 1988, 183-200.

D.A. Green. The use of microprocessors for control and instrumentation in the food industry. In: Engineering and food, Ed. B. Mackenna, Elsevier Applied Science, London, 1983, 757-771.

P. Guenneugues. Contribution à l'optimisation d'un fermenteur industriel, Thesis, ENSIA, France, 1990.

P. Guenneugues, S. Chibois, G. Trystram. Applications of NADH fluorosensor for on-line measurements in yeast fermentation on whey substrates, Food control, 1990, 1, 4, 236-241.

E. Kress-Rogers. Instrumentation in the food industry. J. of Phys. E. Sci. Instrumentation, 9, 13-21 and 105-109, 1985.

J.F.C. Lima, A.O.S.S. Rangel. The usefulness of the application of a stream splitting in FIA-systems to deal with pretreatment requirements in wine analysis. Symposium ACoFoP II, Paris, France, 12-13 November 1990.

I. Marc, F. Blanchart, E. Ronat, S. Taha, J.N. Rabaud. New in situ automatic and sterile liquid sampling systems for fermentors. Symposium ACoFoP II, Paris, France, 12-13 November 1990.

M. Morari, Process control and operations: current trends and a look at the future. World Congress on Chemical Engineering, Karlsruhe, June, 1991.

B. Niyoyanka, B.M. MacKenna. Scheduling in the food industry. In: Engineering and food, Ed. W. Spiess and H. Schubert, Elsevier Applied Science, London, 1990, vol I, 929-936.

Y. Ohkubo. Factory automation for multi-products and small lot. In: Engineering and food, Ed. W. Spiess and H. Schubert, Elsevier Applied Science, London, 1990, vol I, 937-942.

C. A. Petri. Kommunicazion mit automaten. Bonn University Thesis, 1962.

F. Rousset, Y. Saintcir, M. Daclin. Automatic process control of miltiple effect evaporation part II: practical realization and results .Zuckerindustrie, 1989, 114, 6, 470-476.

F. Scheller, F. Schubert. Biosensors, Ed. Elsevier, New York, 1992.

A.A. Texeira, J.E. Mansion. Computer control of batch retort operation with on line corrections of process deviations. Food Technology, 1982, 36, 85-90.

G. Trystram. State of the art of computer control of food processes. In: Engineering and food, Ed. Le Maguer & Jelen, Elsevier Applied Science, London,1986, vol II, p 459-474.

G. Trystram, E. Dumoulin. Process control in the food industry. Engineering and food, Eds W. Spiess and H. Schubert, Elsevier applied science, London, 1990, vol I, 705-718.

A. P. F. Turner, I. Karube, G.S. Wilson. Biosensors: Fundamentals and applications. Oxford University Press, Oxford, 1987.

H. Weisser, H. Kehl, F. Bechmann. Use of computer aided mangment information systems in the food and beverage industry. Symposium ACoFoP II, Paris, France, 12-13 November 1990.

T. Yano. Engineering control of food quality. In: Food engineering and process applications, Ed. M. Le Maguer, P. Jelen, Elsevier Applied Science, 1986, London, 475-490.

J.G. Ziegler, N.B. Nichols. Optimum setting of automatic controllers. Trans ASME, 1942, 64, 759-768.

OptiMod Software:
Mathematical Modelling, Computer Simulation, and Optimisation of Biotechnological Process.

A. A. Amelkin*

OptiMod is a complex of programs destined for investigation and optimisation of biotechnological processes. OptiMod fulfils a number of functions: investigation of the process dynamics (or statics) curves, the state coefficients identification, the creation of polynomial regression static models, and the optimal control problems solution.

OptiMod is a complex of programs realized on Turbo C (a registered trademark of Borland Groupe International) software on the IBM PC XT/AT (a registered trademark of International Business Machines Corporation) compatible personal computers and destined for investigation and optimisation of biotechnological processes. OptiMod fulfils a number of functions:
- investigation of the process dynamics (or statics) curves by changing initial values of state variables, values of state coefficients, control variable (feed or dilution rate) with adjustible increment/decrement step;
- the state coefficients identification with respect to the function of deviation of experimontal and calculated state variables values;
- the feed program optimisation in the fed-batch process with respect to profit, yield or another perfomance index by the steepest ascent method;
- the creation of polynomial regression static models with the aid of the least squares method (in this mode the diagram scales are adjusted automatically with respect to experimental data);
- the ivestigation of the image of bioreactor with pipes, sensors, operator's panel, and rotating impeller mixing the cultural liquid, which level and colour change with respect to feed rate and biomass (or product) concentration, respectively;
- the optimal control problems solution using continuous maximum principle.

During dynamics investigation, identification and optimisation modes the curves on the diagram change like an

* *Moscow Yeast Plant, Moscow 113114, Russia*

animated cartoon. The identification and optimisation history is stored in file. OptiMod is invariant to monitor (Hercules, CGA, EGA, VGA) and processor types and can be easily transformed by the author to the ivestigation tool for any technological process. The simplified version of OptiMod is used as a training tool for students during studying disciplines "Process Modelling and Simulation" and "Process Optimisation". There exist OptiMod versions for *Candida utilis* fed-batch and continuous cultivation, paraffins utilizing bacteria continuous cultivation and wheaten dough fermentation.

The results of this work are being applied as a computer working place of a technologist at Moscow Yeast Plant in Russia. On Fig.1 process dynamics curves acquired with the aid of OptiMod Software for fed-batch *Saccharomyces cerevisiae* cultivation process are shown.

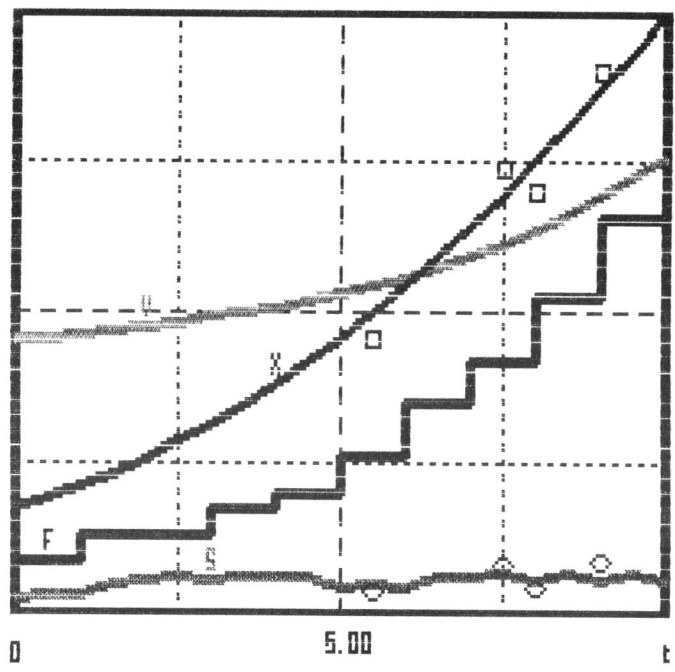

Figure 1. Process dynamics curves.

CONTINUOUS MAXIMUM PRINCIPLE IN OPTIMAL CONTROL OF FED-BATCH
FERMENTATION PROCESSES: THE CASE OF SWITCHING STRUCTURE OF
STATE EQUATIONS AND PERFORMANCE INDEX

A. A. Amelkin[*]

The switching nature of microbial
metabolism leads to ordinary
discontinuities of the right parts of
differential state equations with
respect to state variables. The using
of continuous approximations of
piecewise continuous functions
broadens the application of some
methods of fermentation processes
optimal control problems solution.

INTRODUCTION

In recent years there has been permanently increasing
interest in applying continuous maximum principle of
Pontryagin to fed-batch fermentation optimisation [1,2,3].
Fed-batch operation has been optimized to maximize the
productivity, the final outcome or the profit of amino acid,
organic acid, antibiotic, yeast, bacterial cell mass, enzyme
and ethanol production. In fed-batch fermentation nutrients
are continuously or intermittently fed into the reactor
(fermentor) over the fermentation period without withdrawing
any fermentation broth. Optimisation of fed-batch fermentation
has been traditionally sought with respect to the substrate
feed rate, which is natural control variable in such
operation. The optimal feeding policy, i.e. inlet flow rate,
can be determined by applying Pontryagin's maximum principle
[1,2,4]. Formulating the problem with the feed rate as the
control variable yields a singular control problem. Depending
upon the nature of the state equations describing the dynamic
behavior of the reactor and performance index (objective
function or functional) to be maximized or minimized, various
options can be used [1,2,5].

In practice the mathematical model equations and
performance indices often contain piecewise continuous or
logical algebra functions. The existence of such models is
conditioned by the switching nature of the microbial
metabolism. Therefore, in this article a method [6] is
developed, which allows to transfer the model equations and
the performance index containing points of ordinary
discontinuity by using the continuous approximation so, that
the continuous maximum principle can be applied to the optimal

[*] *Moscow Yeast Plant, Moscow 113114, Russia*

control problem solution. A specific example given in this paper is the fed-batch baker's yeast cultivation process optimal control problem solution.

OPTIMAL CONTROL PROBLEM FORMULATION

The basic sturucture of the fermentation process mathematical model consists of differentional material balances for the main state variables: cell mass concentration, x_1, substrate concentration, x_2, the volume of cultural medium in the fermentor, x_3, and product concentration, x_4.

Mathematical model of fermentation process can be written in general form:

$$\dot{x}_j = f_j(X, A, U, t); \qquad j = \overline{1, n} \qquad (1)$$

with the initial conditions

$$x_j(0) = x_{oj}, \qquad (2)$$

where **X** - vector of state variables; **A** - vector of model coefficients; **U** - vector of control or manipulative variables; t - time (independent variable); n - number of state variables.

In the common case the problem of optimal operation, subject to conditions in the form of differentional equations (1), may be written as:

$$I = \int_0^T f_o(X, A, U, t)dt + F_o(X(T)) \longrightarrow \max_{U(t)}, \qquad (3)$$

where T - fixed final time (terminal time); fo - integrand; Fo - terminal term.

The control is restricted

$$U \in D \qquad (4)$$

and must be found in the class of piecewise continuous functions (D - region of admissible values).

The problem (1)-(4) is called the problem of optimal control and it can be solved through application of Pontryagin's maximum principle, while functions fo, fj, Fo must be continuous with respect to all arguments and continuously differentiable with respect to **X** [4]. Nevertheless, as it will be mentioned below, these conditions get broken sometimes.

DISCONTINUITY CASES REVIEW

In practice the expressions fo, f_j, and Fo often contain ordinary discontinuities or they are not continuously differentiable functions with respect to **X**. This makes application of continuous maximum principle to the solution of problem (1)-(4) impossible. The review of typical representatives of such methods is considered below.

Case 1. The partial derivatives of kinetic dependences (the specific growth rate μ or the specific metabolia product evolution rate v) with respect to state variables contain one or two points of ordinary discontinuity [6,7].

Case 2. The specific rate of substrate consumption q contains the ordinary discontinuity [7].

Case 3. The kinetic dependences μ and v contain points of

discontinuity [6].
    Case 4. The partial derivative of the oxygen consumption
specific rate with respect to state variable x contains point
of ordinary discontinuity [8].
    Case 5. Function fo and its partial derivatives with
respect to state variables contain points of ordinary
discontinuity.
    Case 6. Function Fo and its partial derivatives with
respect to state variables contain points of ordinary
discontinuity.

DISCONTINUITIES APPROXIMATION

    It is necessary to approximate the dependences which
contain ordinary discontinuities or which are not continuously
differentiable (contain breakings) with functions which don't
suffer these shortcomings with the aim of transformation of
the model (1) in Cases 1-4 and of criterion (3) in Cases 5,6
to the form allowing to apply the Pontryagin's maximum
principle. In Cases 1,3,4 for this aim it is possible to use
one of the following dependences [6,9]:

$$H(a,b) = arctg((a-b)/\delta)/\pi + 0.5; \qquad (5)$$

$$H(a,b) = 2^{-exp((b-a)/\delta)}, \qquad (6)$$

where a,b - parameters, one of which is a constant as a rule;
    δ - small constant.
    The expressions (5) and (6) are the continuous
approximations of unit step function

$$h(a,b) = \lim_{\delta \to 0} H(a,b),$$

where

$$h(a,b) = \begin{cases} 0 & \text{if} \quad a \leqslant b; \\ 1 & \text{if} \quad a > b. \end{cases} \qquad (7)$$

    The expression of the type

$$H = a^+ / (\delta + a) \qquad (8)$$

is applicable in case of non-negativity of parameter a only
(Case 2), i.e. for the approximation of dependence

$$h^+(a) = \begin{cases} 0 & \text{if} \quad a = 0; \\ 1 & \text{if} \quad a > 0. \end{cases} \qquad (9)$$

    The δ value is chosen from the demands laid claim to the
problem solution precision. When choosing the dependence
approximating the step (7) it is necessary to take into
account the complexity of computational operations connected
with using this dependence and its derivatives in computer
calculations. That is why from two dependences (5) and (6)
preference should be given to (5).

INTEGRATION METHOD CHOICE

    As it has been stated above, the smaller the value of δ,
the higher the approximation precision. On the other hand
lessening the value of δ results in increasing the stiffness
of adjoint system containing in the right parts of equations
the functions $W(a,a^*) = dH(a,a^*)/da$ and $W^+(a) = dH^+(a)/da$.
This increases demands laid claim to the integration method to
be used. There exists the experience of elaboration of stable
numerical integration methods of stiff nonlinear differential

equations [10]. When choosing the integration method it is useful to use the test function *

$$dH/dt = W(t,t^*),$$ (10)

where $W(t,t^*)$ - the expression for the derivative of the approximation dependence with respect to the argument t. For example, for for the approximation function (5) the test function (10) can be written in the form:

$$dH/dt = 1 /\{ (1 + ((t - t^*) / \delta)) \pi \}.$$

During the testing of the numerical integration method the differential equation (10) is integrated for the value corresponding to the demanded precision with specified initiad conditions *

$$Ho = H(to,t^*); \quad to = 0 \qquad *$$

and the terminal integration time $T > t^*$. The aquired numerical solution is to be compared with precise (analytical) one by the value of the statistical estimation of the deviation dispersion. The comparison is accomplished on the concrete computer type by the precision and speed of solution.

PROBLEM FORMULATION FOR FED-BATCH YEAST FERMENTATION

In this and the following sections the described earlier approximation method is applied to the fed-batch baker's yeast fermentation optimal control problem treatment. The optimisation problem is to determine for a fed-batch yeast fermentation described by a set of unsteady state mass balance equations, the optimal feed rate profile (feeding policy) u(t) which will maximize a given profit functional:

$$I = \int_0^T f_o \, dt = \int_0^T (P_1 \, d(x_1 x_3)/dt - P_2 \, dx_3/dt) \, dt \longrightarrow \max_{u(t)}$$ (11)

where P_1 and P_2 are the unit costs for cell mass and feed, respectively.

Constraints are imposed on the substrate (sugar and salts solution) feed rate:

$$0 = u_{min} \leq u(t) \leq u_{max}.$$ (12)

Assuming that a single substrate (sugar) which is fed continuously into the fermentor during the course of fermentation is limiting for cell growth, the conditions in form of differential mass balance equations are

$$\dot{X} = d/dt \begin{bmatrix} X_1 \\ X_2 \\ X_3 \end{bmatrix} = \begin{bmatrix} f_1 \\ f_2 \\ f_3 \end{bmatrix} = \begin{bmatrix} \mu \, X_1 \\ -q \, X_1 \\ 0 \end{bmatrix} + \begin{bmatrix} - X_1/X_3 \\ (s - X_2)/X_3 \\ 1 \end{bmatrix} u,$$ (13)

where μ, q and s are specific rates of growth and substrate uptake, and the feed substrate concentration, respectively.

The initial conditions are specified:

$$x_1(0) = x_{o1} ; \quad x_2(0) = x_{o2} ; \quad x_3(0) = x_{o3} .$$ (14)

According to eqs. (13) the performance index (11) can be rewritten in the form:

$$I = \int_0^T (P_1 \mu \, x_1 x_3 - P_2 u) \, dt.$$ (15)

Thus the system to be optimized is described by eqs. (13) and (14) subject to constraints (12) and the optimal control problem is to determine the control variable u(t) which maximizes the performance index given by eq. (15).

The structure of kinetic model is chosen to describe the dependence of the effective yield $Y = \mu/q$ upon the substrate concentration typical for baker's yeast [6,8]. The critical substrate concentration x_2^{cr} exists, which corresponds to the maximum value of the effective biomass yield Y. In the point $x_2 = x_2^{cr}$ the derivative dY/dx_2 suffers ordinary discontinuity. So the function $q(x_2)$ is not continuously differentiable with respect to the substrate concentration x_2. Thus the kinetic dependences are written in the form:

$$\mu = a_1 x_2 / (a_2 + x_2) ;$$

$$q = \{a_3 + a_4 h(x_2, x_2^{cr}) (1-\exp(-a_5 (x_2 - x_2^{cr})))\}\mu + a_6 h^+(x_2). \quad (16)$$

The continuous approximation of the kinetic dependence (16) by the expression:

$$Q = \{a_3 + a_4 H(x_2, x_2^{cr}) (1-\exp(-a_5 (x_2 - x_2^{cr})))\}\mu + a_6 H^+(x_2) \quad (17)$$

allows to fulfil the condition of continuous differentiability of the function f_2 (the right part of the mass balance on the substrate) with respect to x_2 and to use the Pontryagin's maximum principle for the problem (12)-(15) solution.

The Hamiltonian for this problem can be written as

$$R = f_0 + l_1 f_1 + l_2 f_2 + l_3 f_3 = P_1 \mu x_1 x_2 - P_2 u +$$

$$+ l_1 (\mu x_1 - x_1 u / x_3) + l_2 (- q x_1 + (s - x_2) u / x_3) +$$

$$+ l_3 u = C_1 (\mathbf{X}, \mathbf{L}, \mathbf{A}) + C_2 (\mathbf{X}, \mathbf{L}, \mathbf{A}) u, \quad (18)$$

where the adjoint variables satisfy the conditions:

$$\dot{l}_i = - \partial R/\partial x_i ; \quad l_i (T) = 0, \quad i = \overline{1,3}. \quad (19)$$

COMPUTATIONAL ALGORITHMS AND RESULTS

The formulated optimal control problem (11)-(14) is solved through the numerical method of I. A. Krylov and F. L. Chernousko [5] application for the particular case $x(0) = x_2^{cr}$. The results analysis showed that optimal control consists of two parts: the singular arc on the time section $[t_1 =0; t_2]$, and zero control ($u° = u_{min}$) on the semisection $(t_2 ; T]$. During the singular control period $[t_1, t_2]$, which takes up to 99% of the whole control interval $[0,T]$, the substrate concentration is maintained on the critical level $x_2 = x_2^{cr}$. This is properly sequences with the experimental results, aquired under the circumstances of the commercial yeast production, where sugar solution is fed into the reactor over the growth period at an exponentially increasing rate so that the sugar concentration in the growth medium is maintained close to the critical level.

DISCUSSION AND CONCLUSIONS

The switching nature of microbial metabolism and the presence of stiff constraints imposed on state variables lead to ordinary (jump) discontinuities of the right parts of differential state equations, performance indexes or their partial derivatives with respect to state variables. This makes impossible the usage of some methods of fermentation processes optimal control problems solution, in particular, the continuous maximum principle of Pontryagin. The using of continuous approximations of piecewise continuous functions broadens the application of above mentioned methods. Nevertheless this approach leads to stiff differential equations system appearance, for which rapidly damping preturbations exist during slowly changing solution. That is why the technique of integration method choice is elaborated. The suggested approach is tested when solving the baker's yeast fed-batch cultivation process optimal control problem.

Thus the generalised algorithm of the similar problems solution is elaborated:

1. The choice of approximation dependence H from the minimum of labour consuming character of computing operations.

2. Approximation of discontinuous functions present in model and in performance index.

3. The choice of the approximation dependence parameter δ, which affects the unit step function approximation accuracy, proceeding from demands laid claim to the optimal problem solution precision.

4. Writing down of the expressions for Hamiltonian, adjoint equations and singular control.

5. The choice of the integration method according to the test function (10) with respect to demands laid claim to precision and speed of solution if the adjoint equations contain unit impulse function continuous approximation expressions W or W^+.

6. The choice of the boundary value problem solution method [1,2,5].

REFERENCES

1. J. M. Modak, H. C. Lim, and Y. J. Tayeb, 1986, Biotecnol. Bioeng., 28, 1396
2. J. Hong, 1986, Biotecnol. Bioeng., 28, 1421
3. K. -Y. San and G. Stephanopoulos, 1989, Biotecnol. Bioeng., 34, 72
4. L. S. Pontryagin, 1989, The Maximum Principle in Optimal Control. - Science, Moscow (in Russian)
5. N. N. Moiseyev, 1975, Optimal Systems Theory Elements, Science, Moscow (in Russian)
6. A. A. Amelkin and S. A. Amelkin, 1988, Biotechnology, Moscow, 4, No 5, 654 (in Russian)
7. V. V. Biryukov and V. M. Kantere, 1985, Batch Fermentation Processes Optimisation, Science, Moscow (in Russian)
8. B. Sonnleitner and O. Kappeli, 1986, Biotecnol. Bioeng., 28, 927
9. G. A. Korn and T. M. Korn, 1968, Mathematical Handbook for Scientists and Engineers, McGraw-Hill Book Company, the USA
10. K. Dekker and J. G. Verwer, 1984, Stability of Runge-Kutta Methods for Stiff Nonlinear Differential Equations, North-Holland, Amsterdam

MATHEMATICAL MODEL OF BAKER'S YEAST CULTIVATION PROCESS

A. A. Amelkin[*]

A novel mathematical model for the growth of baker's yeast on glucose is elaborated. The model allows to describe all basic metabolic ways of baker's yeast. The dependence of the optimal glucose concentration in feed upon volumetric oxygen transfer coefficient is obtained.

Success in microbial systems optimisation and automation depends upon progress in microbial growth modelling. In this work a novel mathematical model for the growth of baker's yeast on glucose is presented which was developed on experimentally easily accessible parameters only.

The mathematical model of baker's yeast cultivation process is based on the following observations and conceptual ideas [1,2]:

1. The hydrodynamical mode of ideal mixing is realized in bioreactor.

2. Batch growth on glucose and on ethanol follows ideal Monod kinetics.

3. The yeast growth on glucose under continuous aeration conditions proceeds with the same rate during glucose effect (aerobic ethanol fermentation) and during respiration (purely oxidative metabolic way).

4. Glucose inhibits the uptake of ethanol as a substrate for growth.

5. Ethanol can be utilized aerobically only.

6. The ethanol concentration level is not sufficient to inhibit the growth.

7. The growth on ethanol occurs only when glucose concentration is lower than critical value $Sc = 0.1$ g/L.

8. Glucose can be consumed either aerobically or anaerobically but with different rates and efficiencies.

9. The specific oxygen uptake rate is linearly correlated with the biomass specific growth rate on glucose and ethanol when glucose concentration is lower than the critical value. If glucose concentration exceeds the critical value Sc under aerobic conditions, i.e. when the so called glucose effect

[*] Moscow Yeast Plant, Moscow 113114, Russia

occurs, the specific oxygen uptake rate remains nearly constant.

10. Under the excess aeration conditions the value of the effective yield Y gets higher with the growth of glucose concentration if $x_2 <$ Sc and gets lower during glucose effect.

11. Ethanol is consumed with different rates and efficiencies in presence and absence of residual glucose in the cultural medium.

12. The ethanol evolution by baker's yeast takes place when at least one of the following conditions is fulfilled: the lowering of the dissolved oxygen concentration below the threshold value; the exceeding by the residual sugars concentration of the critical level. In this case the mechanism of ethanol fermentation, springing up in dependence of two factors, corresponds to the logical addition law.

13. During biomass growth on ethanol in absence of residual glucose in the cultural liquid the respiratory quotient RQ is practically constant and equal to the value RQ=0.5. This allows to make an assumption that in this case the carbon dioxide evolution and oxygen consumption occur due to the yeast growth only.

14. During respiration on glucose the RQ value is higher than in the case of respiration on glucose and ethanol if the glucose concentration is the same in the both cases.

With the aim of effective description of the baker's yeast features formulated in the items 8 - 12 the quantity of fermentation predominance degree e was introduced into the model equations. This quantity varies within the range 0<e<1 and depends upon glucose and dissolved oxygen concentration in the cultural medium.

Unaerobic fermentation almost spasmodically replaces respiration or aerobic fermentation when the dissolved oxygen concentracion falls below the critical value Cc. But aerobic fermentation gradually replaces respiration when the glucose concentration exceeds the critical value Sc. The diauxic lag phase, which occurs during batch biphasic growth, is not formulated in this model. This case is typical for the final stages of the industrial baker's yeast cultivation, when the culture is already adapted to ethanol consumption.

Taking into account the above mentioned assumptions the model can be formulated as following:

$$d(x_1 x_3)/dt = (\mu + \mu_p) x_1 x_3 - G x_1;$$

$$d(x_2 x_3)/dt = -q x_1 x_3 + F s - G x_2;$$

$$d(x_4 x_3)/dt = (v - q_1 - q_2) x_1 x_3 - G x_4;$$

$$d(x_5 x_3)/dt = K_L a (Ce - x_5) x_3 -$$

$$- OUR m x_1 x_1 x_3 /N - G x_5;$$

$$dx_3 / dt = F - G ;$$

$$\mu = a_1 x_2 / (a_2 + x_2) ;$$

$$q = (a_3 + a_4 e) \mu + a_6 h^+(x_2) ;$$

$$e = e_1 h(e_1, e_2) + e_2 h(e_2, e_1);$$

$$e_1 = h(x_2, Sc)(1 - \exp(-a_5(x_2 - Sc)));$$

$$e_2 = h(Cc, x_5)(1 - \exp((x_5 - Cc)/ å));$$

$$\mu_p = \{ a_7 x_4 /(a_8 + x_4) \} (1 -$$

$$- x_2 / Sc) h(Sc, x_2)(1 - e_2) ;$$

$$v = a_9 q ;$$

$$q_1 = (a_{10} \mu_p + a_{11} h(x_4)(1 - e_2)) h(x_2, å);$$

$$q_2 = (a_{12} \mu_p + a_{13} h(x_4)(1 - e_2)) h(0, x_2) ;$$

$$OUR = [(a_{14} - a_{15} e) \mu + a_{16} h^+(x_2) + a_{17} \mu_p] N / m_1 ;$$

$$CER = [(a_{18} + a_{19} e) \mu + a_{20} h(x_2) +$$

$$+ a_{17} RQ \mu_p m_p / m_2] N/ m_2 ;$$

$$RQ = CER / (OUR + å_1) ;$$

$$Y = (\mu + \mu_p) / (q + å_2);$$

$$h(a,b) = \begin{cases} 0 & \text{if} \quad a \leqslant b; \\ 1 & \text{if} \quad a > b; \end{cases}$$

$$h^+(a) = \begin{cases} 0 & \text{if } a = 0; \\ 1 & \text{if } a > 0, \end{cases}$$

where

a, b - parameters of unit step function, one of which is a constant as a rule;

h - unit step function;

h^+ - non-negatively defined unit step function;

q - specific substrate consumption rate, 1/h;

q_1 - specific ethanol consumption rate in presence of residual glucose in the cultural liquid, 1/h;

q_2 - specific ethanol consumption rate in absence of residual glucose in the cultural liquid, 1/h;

μ - specific growth rate on glucose, 1/h;

μ_p - specific growth rate on ethanol, 1/h;

v - specific rate of ethanol evolution, 1/h;

t - time, h;

x_1 - biomass concentration, g/L;

x_2 - substrate (glucose) concentration, g/L;

x_3 - liquid volume, L;

x_4 - product (ethanol) concentration, g/L;

x_5 - dissolved oxygen concentration, g/L;

$a_1 - a_{20}$ - state coefficients;

s - glucose concentration in a fresh feed, g/L;

$å$ - small constant, g/L;

$å_1, å_2$ - small constants, introduced with the aim of "zerodivide" situation escape;

e - ethanol fermentation predominance degree;

e_1 - ethanol fermentation predominance degree under condition of glucose effect;

e_2 - ethanol fermentation predominance degree under condition of dissolved oxygen lack;

OUR - oxygen uptake rate, mmol/(g h);

CER - carbon dioxide evolution rate, mmol/(g h);

RQ - respiratory quotient, mol CO_2 /mol O_2 ;

RQ_p - respiratory quotient value corresponding to biomass growth on ethanol under condition of glucose effect ($= .5$);

Y - the effective yield of biomass, g/g;

F - feed rate of fresh glucose medium, L/h;

G - the flow rate of the cultural medium on going out of bioreactor, L/h;

N - the conversion coefficient (- 1000 mmol/mol);

m_1 - oxygen molecular weight ($= 32$ g/mol);

m_2 - carbon dioxide molecular weight ($= 44$ g/mol);

Sc - critical glucose concentration ($= .1$ g/L);

Cc - critical dissolved oxygen concentration ($= .0011$ g/L);

Ce - the equilibrium dissolved oxygen concentration corresponding to saturation ($= .007$ g/L);

$K_L a$ - volumetric oxygen mass transfer coefficient, 1/h.

The mathematical model parameters identification was fulfilled with the aid of OptiMod Software [3] with respect to experimental data published in the work [1]. The results are presented in the Table 1.

The simplified version of this model ($x_2 >> 0$ and $x_5 > Cc$ assumptions are accepted) is used in the work [4] for the optimal control problem solution.

One of the possible applications of the model is the solution of static optimisation problem of the baker's yeast chemostat cultivation. The dependence of the optimal glucose concentration in feed s upon volumetric mass transfer coefficient is obtained:

$$s^o = .046 K_L a + .1,$$

which provides the continuous cultivation on the border of the mass transfer opportunities of bioreactor with the optimal dilution rate D = .3 1/h.

Table 1.   State coefficients values.

No	Value	Dimension
1	0.44	1/h
2	0.047	g/L
3	1.9	g/g
4	4.5	g/g
5	7.0	L/g
6	0.03	g/(g h)
7	0.14	1/h
8	0.05	g/L
9	0.4	g/g
10	0.07	g/g
11	0.24	g/(g h)
12	1.1	g/g
13	0.04	g/(g h)
14	0.64	g/g
15	0.2	g/g
16	0.064	g/(g h)
17	0.4	g/g
18	1.1	g/g
19	2.0	g/g
20	0.044	g/(g h)

Thus the developed mathematical model is a useful instrument for various optimisation problems solution because it describes all basic metabolic ways of baker's yeast:
a) respiration on glucose;
b) respiration on ethanol (undernutrition);
c) respiration on glucose and ethanol;
d) anaerobic ethanol fermentation (unsufficient aeration);
e) aerobic ethanol fermentation (glucose effect, feed overdosage);
f) unsufficient aeration plus feed overdosage;
g) ethanol consumption and the growth in the second diauxie phase stopping under insufficient aeration condition.

REFERENCES

1. B. Sonnleitner and O. Kappeli, 1986, Biotecnol. Bioeng., 28, 927
2. A. A. Amelkin and S. A. Amelkin, 1988, Biotechnology, Moscow, 4, No 5, 654 (in Russian, reprinted in the USA)
3. A. A. Amelkin, 1992, CONTINUOUS MAXIMUM PRINCIPLE IN OPTIMAL CONTROL OF FED-BATCH FERMENTATION PROCESSES: THE CASE OF SWITCHING STRUCTURE OF STATE EQUATIONS AND PERFORMANCE INDEX, Inst. Chem. Eng. Symp. Ser. No. 126
4. A. A. Amelkin, 1992, OptiMod Software: Mathematical Modelling, Computer Simulation, and Optimisation of Biotechnological Process, Inst. Chem. Eng. Symp. Ser. No. 126

A REVIEW OF PREDICTIONS OF HEAT AND MASS TRANSFER IN MEAT REFRIGERATION

S. J. JAMES[1]

A clear understanding of the factors that influence and control the rate of heat and mass transfer both within and from meat is required before the design of a process in the cold chain for meat can be optimised. This short review shows that predictive methods are having a growing influence on the understanding of these factors. More development is required in the area of mass transfer

Introduction

Refrigeration has been the predominant method of meat preservation in the 20th century. Research has shown that rates of reducing and subsequently maintaining the temperature of meat has important consequences in terms of microbiological safety, eating quality, appearance, weight loss and overall economics of the processing chain. However, there have been no legislative requirements, for internal trade within the United Kingdom, that defined specific meat temperatures.

On 1 April 1991 the new Food Hygiene (Amendment) Regulations 1990 first started to be implemented. The regulations divide the majority of chilled foods into two groups, one group consisting of the most *Listeria* sensitive foods will ultimately have a maximum temperature during storage, transport and display of 5°C. Other foods considered less sensitive will have to be maintained below 8°C. Unprocessed meat is not included in this legislation but many processed meats and products containing meat are covered.

As part of process to harmonise legislation throughout the European Community, regulations, that currently only cover export or intervention purchase of foods, are being modified and most will apply to internal trade in 1993. Among these regulations are some that specify the maximum internal temperature that carcass meat must be chilled to before cutting and transportation, maximum internal temperatures after freezing processes and maximum surface temperatures during thawing. Others specifically define chilling rates for minced meat and poultry, temperatures during storage of offals and display temperatures for 'Quick' frozen meat. The legal requirements to attain and maintain specific temperature criteria will create an increased demand for data on the relationship between environmental conditions and the temperature history of meat in carcass, joints and many other shapes. The low profit margins of the meat industry is also applying pressure to maximise meat yield and minimise weight loss during refrigeration processes. At the same time eating quality and microbiological safety need to be maintained.

Problems caused by biological variability make it very time consuming and expensive to produce all the data required by practical experimentation. Increasingly predictive modelling techniques, usually in combination with limited experimentation, are being used to generate the

[1] Food Refrigeration and Process Engineering Research Centre, University of Bristol

data and optimise refrigeration processes. Initially analytical solution based techniques were used but as the speed of computers increased and prices have dropped then numerical methods have taken over. Some of the work carried out and the problems encountered are sketched out in the following sections. Andrew Cleland's book (1) provides a good general mathematical description of the numerical methods that have been employed in prediction of food refrigeration processes.

The Refrigerated Cold Chain

Immediately after slaughter the warm (approximately 40°C) wet surface of a carcass presents an optimum media for bacterial growth. Without refrigeration the shelf life of the meat will be completely dependent on the ambient conditions and in mid summer could be measured in hours rather than days. Cooling is required to increase shelf life and minimise weight loss. However, too rapid cooling can cause toughening. After cooling, for chilled distribution, the temperature needs to be maintained as close to, but not below, the initial freezing point (approximately -1.5°C) during storage, transportation and display.

If a longer shelf life than that that can be realised by chilling is required then the meat can be frozen. All microorganisms on meat are inactive at temperatures below -12°C but enzymic activity which produces rancid flavours continues, albeit slowly at temperatures of -30°C and below. Most frozen meat is thawed or tempered before further processing or retail sale.

Chilling

Chilling is the first and probably the most important process in the cold chain for red meat. New United Kingdom legislation will require a maximum meat temperature of 7°C before carcasses can be cut or transported. There are economic pressures to maximise throughput by achieving this temperature in as short a time as possible and also minimise weight loss. Biochemical constraints lead to toughening if the lean tissue of beef or lamb is reduced to 10°C or below within 10 hours of slaughter, 3 hours for pork. Consequently the optimum modelling process would provide data on (1) the rate of cooling at the thermal centre of the carcass, (2) the temperature at the surface of lean tissue, and (3) the rate of weight loss from the carcass.

Meat carcasses are very irregular in shape and consist of layers of fat and lean tissue over a bone skeleton. The thermal and mass transfer properties of fat, lean and bone differ markedly from each other. Over the temperature range encountered in chilling (40 to 0°C) the properties of lean and bone are substantially constant but fat solidifies producing large changes in its thermal properties at different temperatures. The properties of a point within a carcass are therefore a function of its position and its temperature. Since the carcass shape and structure is so complicated the author knows of no attempt to try to directly model heat and mass transfer in a meat carcass.

Large experimental programmes have been carried out in the U.K. (2) and South Africa (3) to investigate the effect of air temperature, air velocity and relative humidity on cooling rates and weight loss from beef sides. Mathematical methods have been used to extend the range of cooling data outside of that covered experimentally. The methods are based on the recognition that, after an initial lag, the temperature at a set depth within the carcass decreases in an exponential fashion.

Plotting the log of $(T_p - T_a)/(T_i - T_a)$ against time, where T_p, T_i, T_a are the temperatures at a point, the initial and the ambient respectively, results in a straight line. Predictions of the time temperature history for different ambient conditions can be obtained by a simple transform of the y axis. Plots are available for the deep and surface of the leg, the slowest cooling section, and the loin. The data cover a wide range of side weights (100 to 220kg) and air velocities (0.5 to 3m/s). Similar but less comprehensive charts are available for pork (4), lamb (5) and goat (6) carcasses.

The effect of air temperature and velocity on evaporative weight loss during chilling is dependent upon the end point of the chilling process (Figure 1(a) and (b)). When chilling for a set time weight loss increases as temperature decreases and velocity increases. The opposite effect is found when chilling to a set temperature.

Freezing

To convert the free water in lean meat into ice a large amount of heat (300 Kj/kg) has to be extracted. However, the freezing process is aided by a three fold increase in the thermal conductivity of the frozen meat.

A number of equations (1), most based on the initial work of Plank (7), have been developed for the prediction of freezing times of slabs and cylinders. With experience they can be used to estimate the freezing time of 'homogeneous' under constant conditions with a high degree of accuracy. They are also very quick methods of indicating the sensitivity of freezing time to small changes in product thickness, media temperature, etc. Complex cases in which the ambient temperature, the heat transfer coefficient and the physical properties of the sold may vary can be handled using finite difference techniques described by Dusinberre (8).

Figure 2 shows the predicted relationship between freezing time and air temperature for meat blocks at low (0.5m/s) and high (5m/s) air velocities for different packaging configurations (9). The relationships were obtained using a modification to Dusinberre's method. Increasing the air velocity from 0.5 to 5m/s reduces the freezing time by an average of 29%. The freezing times of blocks in cardboard cartons with lids are between 25 and 82% longer than in metal trays for any given air temperature and velocity.

Table 1. Change in freezing time sustained by 15cm thick blocks in increasing or decreasing thickness. () % changes.

Heat Transfer coefficient (W/m²°C)	Air temperature (°C)	Change in block thickness			
		-1.0	-0.5	+0.5	+1.0
4	-30	-3.6 (-8.2)	-1.8 (-4.1)	1.8 (4.1)	3.7 (8.4)
	-10	-10.7 (-7.9)	-5.3 (-3.9)	5.4 (4.0)	11.0 (8.1)
20	-30	-1.3 (-9.3)	-0.6 (-4.6)	0.7 (4.8)	1.5 (9.6)
	-10	-4.4 (-9.6)	-2.2 (-4.8)	2.3 (4.9)	4.6 (9.7)

The power of the predicative method is that the effect of changes, for example in block thickness (Table 1), of the magnitude encountered in commercial practice on processing times can be easily evaluated.

Thawing

Thawing is the reversal of the freezing process, but the three-fold difference in thermal conductivity between frozen and unfrozen material increasingly restricts the rate of heat penetration during thawing. If bacterial numbers are to be maintained at an acceptable level then limitations must also be applied to the maximum surface temperature that can be tolerated. Thawing is a more difficult operation than freezing and research has been directed to methods of increasing the surface heat transfer coefficient without attaining high surface temperatures.

In chilling and freezing convective heat exchange between the surrounding medium and the food has been the sole method of heat transfer. However, in vacuum thawing very high h values are produced by the condensation of steam under vacuum on the surface of the meat being thawed (10). It has also been shown that in conventional air based thawing systems the contribution to h resulting from the condensation of water vapour is substantial (11). At 30°C and a dew point of 28°C, which would be considered to be saturated air in a practical thawing system, h at 3 m/s varies from 70 to a peak value of 115 W/m²°C over the surface temperature range -20 to +26°C (Figure 3).

The curves of h against surface temperature can be divided into specific sections, which are related to the dew point of the air and the orientation of the surface of the meat. At surface temperatures below 0°C water sublimes to ice on the surface of the meat enhancing the heat transfer coefficient as a result of the phase change. At 0°C this ice layer melts, and a temporary heat requirement causes the inflection in the curve. From 0°C to the dew point, water condenses as liquid on the surface of the meat, further enhancing the surface heat transfer coefficient by the heat of condensation. Above the dew point conditions are reversed; the layer of condensate evaporates and the heat transfer coefficient falls because of the evaporative requirement. When evaporation is complete h has a substantially constant value dependent on convection and radiation. The duration of the evaporative section is clearly affected by the orientation of the surface since a much larger amount of condensate will remain on a horizontal than an inclined surface.

Storage and Display

To achieve the temperature requirements of the Food Hygiene (Amendment) Regulations 1990 retailers are installing more powerful refrigeration systems and increasing the air flow over the food. With unwrapped delicatessen products and fresh meat, the latter not covered by act but often displayed in similar cases, this leads to increased desiccation and loss of display life.

Experimental investigations have clearly demonstrated the substantial effect of changes in in the relative humidity of the air on weight losses from chilled meat under retail display conditions (Figure 4) (12). The same investigations resulted in recommended combinations of conditions (Table 2) that would produce a 6 hour display life.

Table 2. Conditions required to achieve a 6 hour display life for fresh corned beef.

Velocity (m/s)	Relative humidity (%)	Temperature (°C)
<0.1	>50	<2
<0.1	>65	<8
<0.3	>75	<8
<0.5	>80	<8

Previous to these investigations it has been thought that poor temperature and relative humidity control in retail display cabinets produced increased weight loss and reduced display life. These investigations indicated that mean conditions around the product were more important that their degree of control. Computer predictions have since substantiated this view (13). However, substantial problems were encountered in the latter work in obtaining a relationship between heat (h) and mass (k) transfer coefficients that would allow predictions to be made of heat and mass transfer from the meat. A series of experimental investigations are being carried out to simultaneously measure h and k (14,15).

Conclusions

A clear understanding of the factors that influence and control the rate of heat and mass transfer both within and from meat is required before the design of a meat refrigeration system can be optimised. In many cases the thermophysical properties of the meat combined with quality considerations, such as the need to avoid freezing, provide practical limitations to the rate processes can be carried out.

The use of numerical techniques and the availability of fast, low cost, computing has had a large impact on the development of predictive models for heat transfer during freezing and thawing in particular. The development of models that accurately predict the rates of heat and mass transfer that occur simultaneously in processes such as the chilling of meat carcasses and the display of unwrapped food is still in its infancy.

References

1. Cleland, A.C., Food Refrigeration Processes, 1990, Elsevier Applied Science.
2. Bailey, C. & Cox, R.P. 1975. Proc. Inst. Refrig. 72. 76-90.
3. Kerens, G. & Visser, C.J. 1978. CSIR Report ME 1597, Pretoria, SA.
4. Brown, T. & James, S.J. 1988. IFR-BL Subject day "Meat Chilling".
5. Earle, R.L. & Fleming, A.K. 1967. Fd Technol. 21. 79-84.
6. Gigiel, A.J. & Creed, P.G. 1987. Int. J. Refrig. 10. 862-867.
7. Plank, R. 1913. ges Kalte-Ind., 20-5, 109.
8. Dusinberre, G.M. Numerical Analysis of Heat Flow, 1949, McGraw-Hill, New York.
9. James, S.J., Creed, P.G. & Bailey, C. 1979. Proc. Inst. Refrig. 75. 74-83.
10. Bailey, C., James, S.J., Kitchell, A.G. & Hudson, W.R., 1974, J.Sci. Fd Agric., 25, 81-97
11. James, S.J. & Bailey, C. 1983. XVIth Int. Cong. Refrig. Paris.
12. James, S.J. & Swain, M.V.L. 1986. Proc. Inst. Refrig. 3.1-7.
13. James, S.J., Fulton, G.S., Swain, M.V.L. & Burfoot, D. 1988. I.I.R. Commissions C2, D1, D2/3, E1 - Brisbane (Australia).
14. Daudin, J.D. & Swain, M.V.L. 1990. J. of Food Engineering.
15. Kondjoyan, A. & Daudin, J.D. 1990. I.I.R. Commissions B2, C2, D1, D2/3 - Dresden.

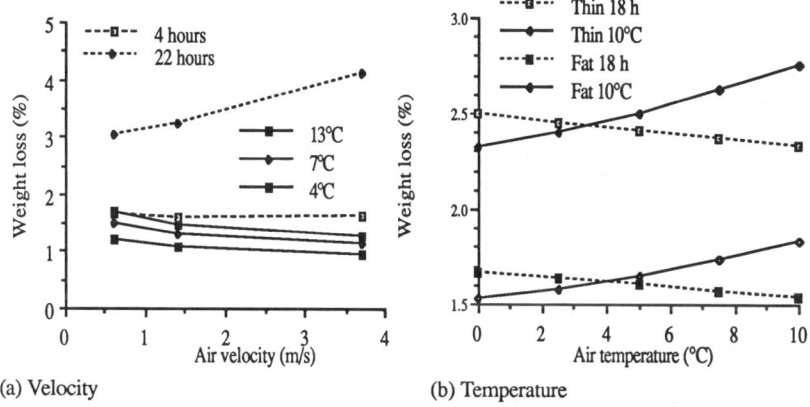

(a) Velocity   (b) Temperature

Figure 1. Relationship between weight loss and (a) air velocity and (b) air temperature when chilling for either a set time or to a final temperature.

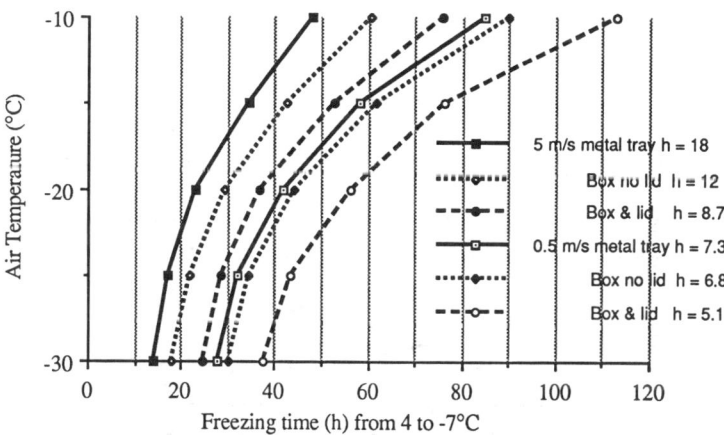

Figure 2. Predicted freezing times of 15 cm thick meat blocks wrapped in polyethylene (h = surface heat transfer coefficient in W/m²°C)

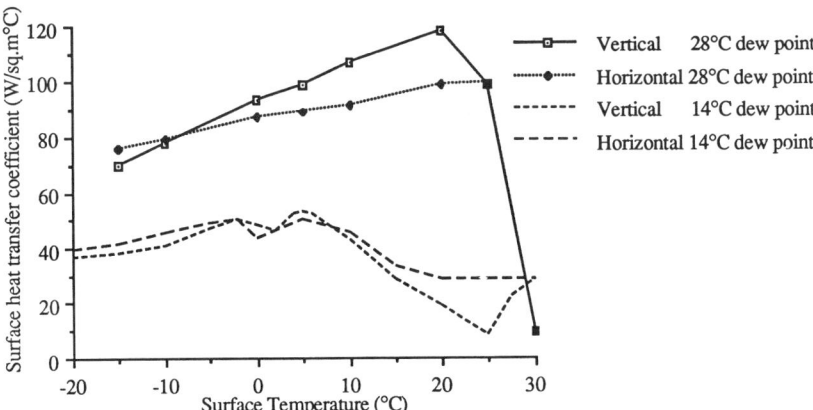

Figure 3 . Surface heat transfer (h) on vertical and horizontal surfaces in air at 30°C, 3m/s and dew points of 28 and 14°C.

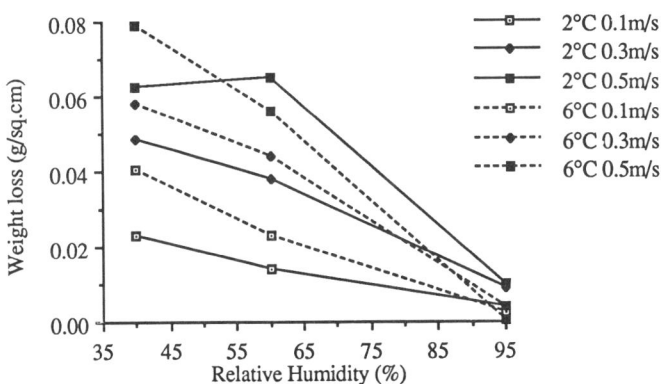

Figure 4. Weight loss from samples of beef steak under simulated display conditions.

MODELLING THE BUSINESS

V S STRATTON# & A M SUTTON#

The development of a computer model of a UK based food and drink manufacturer is described. The way in which the model works is briefly considered and conclusions drawn concerning the use of computer models in business planning in times of competition.

Introduction

This paper describes the development of a computer based planning model for a UK based International Food and Drink manufacturer. Since the model and more especially the results of the consultancy work are confidential the client will not be named and will be referred to throughout the paper as the Company.

The Company manufacture a wide range of similar food and drink products at a number of sites throughout the UK. Each of the fast moving product ranges could be made at a number of factories. Each of the factories has some storage capacity but prior to periods of high seasonal demand, outside storage might be used. If extremely high sales were predicted then outside contractors might be used. The finished product is either trunked direct to the customer or to Company depots.

The Company had identified the need for a planning model which could be used to examine strategic business options such as:

*   the impact of a new factory

*   the location of new product lines

*   the long term allocation of products to lines

#WS Atkins Management Consultants, Epsom, Surrey.

There was an existing computer model which ran on a large mainframe computer, was difficult to use and most importantly took a long time to analyse different business scenarios. The Company decided to use Management Consultants to act as the core of a team to develop the model.

The new model would represent the business in terms of products, product groups, production lines, factories, external contractors, own depots, and external storage. The model would cover the physical, cost and financial elements of the business. Thus an analysis that started with the recipe for a new product could end with a revised cash flow and set of product costs. The model was explicitly designed to be used for strategic planning, looking forward for a number of years, four weeks at a time. It was **not** designed to undertake day to day product scheduling.

Business Modelling

The current recession, and increases in Europe-wide competition, lead manufacturers to a need for a thorough understanding of their business, its current and future costs. With the advent of low cost, high performance computing power, such analysis can be readily undertaken on a desktop microcomputer using a computer model of the business. Our experience leads us to believe that a good business model needs to have a number of characteristics, namely:

* represents reality, containing sufficient detail to provide accurate forecasts but not so much detail that it is complex to use and difficult to maintain and keep up to date

* be easy to use, requiring few computer skills, so that modelling process does not dominate the planning process

* be easy to change in order that it can easily analyse a wide range of options

There is no doubt that a well structured strategic planning model can contribute significantly to a company's competitiveness in that it will assist the managers of the business to understand the sensitivity of the enterprise to change.

Model Development

The scope of the model development was to:

* form a joint team including both consultants and representatives from the Company to undertake the computer modelling exercise

* obtain an understanding of the business, its data sources and planning options

* develop a strategic planning model using the prototyping technique

* validate the model using past performance

* document the model and provide user training

In order to meet the Company's need for the model to be available for use as soon as possible it was proposed that the method of prototyping should be used during the development. Adopting this technique meant that:

* the model was available for use much earlier than if other development techniques had been used

* review of the model was undertaken using a live prototype of the model rather than a written specification

* the client was much more directly involved in the final form of the model since he reviewed the model by using the prototype, viewing the screens, producing graphs, undertaking analysis etc

* software and hardware constraints were understood much earlier and could be more easily taken into account

* a fourth generation computer language was used for the development of the model so that modifications could be made to the model quickly and easily

In essence after the consultancy team felt that they had understood the requirements for a model they produced in a matter of days, a prototype of that model. The review process then focused on that prototype, examining it, suggesting amendments and additions to bring it into line with the clients needs. This prototype was then refined as it passed through at least three formal reviews. The final review, at which stage the model was 90-95% complete, was undertaken with Senior Management from the Company, using real data, to ensure that the model completely fulfils the requirements.

The model development process was undertaken in a number of stages:

* initial presentation and discussion with management in order to ensure that there is an understanding of the objectives of the work, the deliverable, and the timescales

* structured interviews and data collection, which was aimed at understanding the business, its planning processes, and lastly the available data and related analyses which might be used to test the new model

* development of an initial prototype model which would only handle a limited quantity of data, its main purpose being to establish that it correctly reflected the requirement and that the client felt comfortable with the way in which it interfaced with the user

* iterative process of formal review, amendment and enhancement, followed by further review

* full model testing and validation using carefully designed test data to ensure that all aspects of the model are rigorously checked in a structured manner:the model was also validated using the latest real performance data for the business, in order to ensure that it correctly modelled reality

* final review with Senior Managers

* install model and provide both user and technical documentation

* train staff and handover the model to the Company

* ongoing support by means of a telephone hotline

The work was undertaken by a team of two computer modelling consultants working under the direction of a Project Manager. This team worked very closely with two managers from the Company who would be using the final product and who were very familiar with the requirement.

The Final Model

The model was designed to be able to estimate the costs of production, storage and trunking for a given projection of future demand. Typically such projections were for a number of years ahead so that capital investment programs could be developed to ensure that the company had the right facilities both to meet the anticipated growth in the market and to reduce total manufacturing costs.

As with all strategic models, the amount of detail included aimed to be sufficient for the purposes of accuracy and realism, but at the same time limited to those areas that have an impact on the long term decisions which needed to be made regarding production capability.

The model consisted of three modules (as shown in Figure 1):

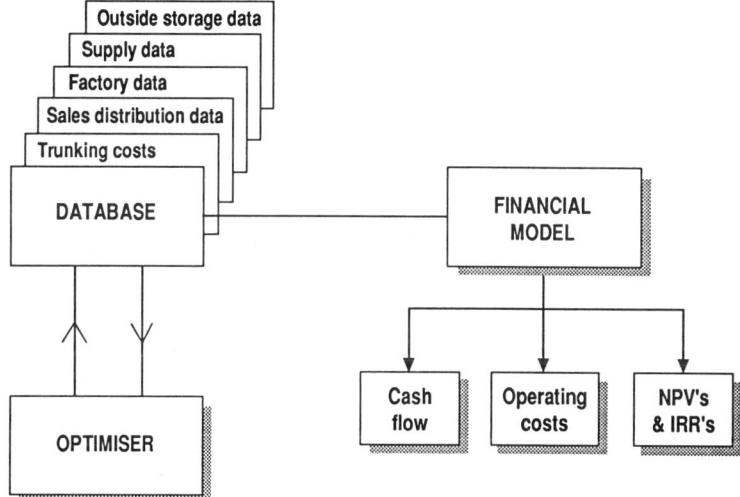

Figure 1 - **Business Model**

* a database which covered a number of areas. It included information about the production capacity and costs associated with both existing and proposed factories. It recorded sales projections in terms of annual volumes and the way this was distributed geographically throughout the country and by period throughout the year. It held the costs involved in trunking finished products to depots or directly to customers.

* an optimising model which calculated for every product group, the optimal supply areas for each factory in each period of time. (Periods of time can either be 4-week periods or quarters). The optimisation was carried out with a linear programming package which minimised the sum of the variable manufacturing and trunking costs, subject to the production constraints of the lines. It chose the appropriate mix of shift patterns on each line so that the requirements of each demand point were met.

* a financial summary model where the total operating costs were displayed together with the investments needed to implement the strategy. A cash-flow stream was assembled which could be compared with that obtained by other strategies. Pay-back periods and rates of return could then be computed concerning particular investment decisions.

The model used two software packages, "Lotus Symphony" and "Whats Best". The latter is a linear programming routine that extracts data from Symphony files, calculates an optimal solution, and returns the results to another Symphony file. This combination of packages was chosen as together they provide a wide range of facilities.

"Lotus Symphony" could be used as a user-friendly input medium and has considerable computational power. It can display results in a graphical form and it has a limited data base facility which was used to generate specific reports. All worksheets were driven by menus and there were "help screens" to show the user exactly what was expected at each stage.

"Whats Best" is a fast linear programming package and was able to accommodate the size of problems to be solved in this application. It is designed specifically to work in conjunction with either Lotus Symphony or 123.

The model was run on a Compaq 386 with a Weitek coprocessor, which speeded up the linear programming calculation by a factor of ten.

Conclusions

One test of the success of a computer model is how much it is subsequently used by the client. Has he adopted the model? Has it become part of his regular planning process? Or, has it been abandoned on the top of a dusty shelf? On the basis of this criteria the model described in this paper has been a great success. It has been used intensively ever since its development and has been used to plan the two major greenfield site developments that the Company has undertaken since the model was developed.

The development and use of a computer based strategic planning model in the food and drink industry has a number of benefits:

* it enables more options to be explored than would be the case otherwise

* it acts as a focus for the business planning function

* it brings together in one place all of the company data relating to the business strategy

* the use of modern software development techniques and close interaction between the developer and final user should ensure that the model is produced quickly and meets the requirements

When companies are under pressure to significantly reduce costs, computer based business models are the most appropriate way to determine the total impact of such reductions on the business strategy.

AUTOMATIC CONTROL OF RESPIRATION RATE DURING FRUIT STORAGE

G. Andrich(*), A.Zinnai(**), A.Tuci(*), R.Fiorentini(*)

Summary - In order to have an effectively automatic control of a cell for fruit storage, considerable information regarding the fruit physiology must be collected. In this paper, a preliminary mathematical model describing the respiration rate of stored apples is presented and discussed.

Introduction. - The efficient automatic control of a cell for fruit storage in refrigerated and controlled atmosphere should be ensured by a suitably programmed computer. This automated system requires that the information coming from the different sensors of the apparatus connected to the computer, should be elaborated by a specific program based on mathematical algorithms able to relate the main phisyco-chemical parameters of fruits with time and storage conditions (temperature, R.H., PO_2, PCO_2, etc.).

In order to determine these fundamental mathematical functions, considerable informations regarding the fruit must be collected. As the respiration produces the energy necessary for all the other metabolic processes of a fruit, it plays a fundamental role in determining its quality and storability.

In this paper, a simplified kinetic model describing the evolution of the respiration rate of a fruit as a function of storage time, temperature and the composition of the surrounding atmosphere has been hypothesized. The processes connected with the absorption and consumption of O_2 and the subsequent emission of CO_2 represent the three basic steps of the kinetic model.

V_1)　　$O_2 \rightleftharpoons O_2^*$　　oxygen mass-transfer between the atmosphere and the cellular solution of the fruit;

V_2) $O_2^* + C^* \longrightarrow CO_2^*$　　oxygen consumption and carbon dioxide production inside the fruit cell;

V_3)　　$CO_2^* \rightleftharpoons CO_2$　　mass-transfer of carbon dioxide from the cellular solution to the atmosphere.

(*) Istituto Industrie Agrarie, Via S. Michele 4, 56124 Pisa;
(**) S.S.S.U.P. S. Anna, Via Carducci 24, 56126 Pisa, Italy.

V_1, V_2, V_3 are the rates related to the three hypothesized steps, while the chemical species present inside the fruit are designated by an asterisk; C^* represents the sum of all the carbonic units which can be utilized as oxidation substrate. While the steps connected with the mass-transfer of the two respiratory gases are taken to be reversible, the cellular oxidation is assumed as an irreversible process.

The mass-transfer of the two "respiratory gases". - The gas (G = O_2; CO_2) exchange between a fruit and its surrounding atmosphere was hypothesized to be a mass-transfer occurring between two heterogeneous phases and the resistance to gas diffusion was assumed to be mainly located on fruit skin (Burton, 1974). The mass-transfer rates V_1 and V_3 ($mol \cdot kg^{-1} \cdot s^{-1}$) were calculated by taking the difference between the two partial diffusion rates $V_{n,i}$ (environment $\longrightarrow$ fruit) and $V_{n,-i}$ (fruit $\longrightarrow$ environment), where n = 1,3:

$$V_n = V_{n,i} - V_{n,-i}$$

$$V_{n,i} = k_{n,i} \cdot A \cdot PG \quad ; \quad V_{n,-i} = k_{n,-i} \cdot A \cdot [G^*]$$

where: $k_{n,i}$ ($mol \cdot m^{-2} \cdot s^{-1} \cdot Pa^{-1}$) and $k_{n,-i}$ ($kg \cdot m^{-2} \cdot s^{-1}$) are the kinetic constants associated with the direct and inverse partial diffusion rates, respectively; A ($m^2 \cdot kg^{-1}$) is the surface area of the fruit per unit of weight; PG (Pa) represents the partial pressure of the analyzed gas in the environment; $[G^*]$ ($mol \cdot kg^{-1}$) is the concentration of gas present inside the fruit.

When a condition of equilibrium between the environment and the fruit is reached, we have:

$$V_n = V_{n,i} - V_{n,-i} = 0$$

$$k_{n,i} \cdot A \cdot PG = k_{n,-i} \cdot A \cdot [G^*]$$

$$k_{n,i}/k_{n,-i} = [G^*]/PG = H_n \ (mol \cdot kg^{-1} \cdot Pa^{-1})$$

where H_n is the Henry's constant related to the saturation equilibrium.

If the system is far from the equilibrium:

$$V_n = d[G^*]/dt = V_{n,i} - V_{n,-i} = 0$$

$$= k_{n,i}/H_n \cdot A \cdot ([G^*]_{eq} - [G^*]) = k_{n,-i} \cdot A \cdot ([G^*]_{eq} - [G^*]) \ [Eq. 1]$$

In order to calculate the values of the constants involved, the initial rate method was applied. This approach is based on an evaluation of the initial rate of gas diffusion between the storage environment and the fruit, when the concentration of this gas inside the fruit is so low that the inverse diffusion rate can be disregarded. When these conditions are obtained experimentally, Eq. [1] calculated at the initial point (*t=o*) becomes:

$$V_n \ _{(t=o)} = d[G^*]/dt \ _{(t=o)} = k_{n,-i} \cdot A \cdot [G^*]_{eq} \ _{(t=o)} \qquad [Eq. 2]$$

Applying the ideal gas law ($P \cdot V = n \cdot R \cdot T$), if one knows the free volume of the storage cell (V) and the weight of the stored

fruits (w), Eq.[1] can be integrated and the following
logarithmic equation obtained (Andrich et al., 1989b):

$$\ln (H \cdot PG_{(t=o)})/(H \cdot PG_{(t=o)} - (H \cdot R \cdot T \cdot w/V + 1) \cdot [G^*]_{(t=t)})) = \ln Y =$$

$$= k_{n,i}/H \cdot A \cdot (H \cdot R \cdot T \cdot w/V + 1) \cdot t \qquad [Eq. 3]$$

In the plane $t, \ln Y$, Eq.[3] represents a straight line from whose
slope the ki can be calculated directly (fig. 1B).
    The experimental points relating to the amount of G which
has permeated into the fruit approach an asymptotic value which
represents an equilibrium point between the fruit and the
surrounding atmosphere, thus allowing the H constant to be
calculated (fig. 1C).
    In the first phase of this study, the two steps connected
with the mass-transfer of the respiratory gases were
investigated at room temperature for two different cultivars of
apples (Golden Delicious and Starking). The experimental protocol
and the apparatus used have been reported in previous papers
together with the data elaboration applied (Andrich et al,
1989a,b, 1990).
    When, for uniformly handled fruit, the obtained values of
the V_n $_{(t=o)}/A$ ratio were plotted as a function of the
corresponding PG, a straight line is obtained which agreed with
the theoretical Eq. 3:

$$V_n \ _{(t=o)} = d[G^*]/dt \ _{(t=o)} = k_{n,i} \cdot A \cdot PG \qquad [Eq.4]$$

Moreover, according to Eq.4 the best correlation coefficients
were obtained for straight lines passing near the origin of the
axes (fig.2).

The O_2 consumption inside the fruit cell. - More recently, the
rate of oxygen uptake inside the apple (Golden Delicious) was
studied and correlated with the partial pressure of oxygen (PO_2)
present in the atmosphere when PCO_2 was maintained close to zero
(Andrich et al., 1991).
    When an apple-environment system reaches the steady state,
the respiration rate (V_{res}) is equal to that of the O_2 mass-
transfer (V_{mt}) and, if one knows the values for the respiration
rate and for the parameters k_{1-i} and H_1 involved in the mass-
transfer equation, it is possible to calculate the amount of O_2
present inside the apple:

$$[O_2] = H_1 \cdot PO_2 - V_{res}/(k_{1,-i} \cdot A)$$

    In order to correlate V_{res} with the O_2 concentration in the
cellular solution ($[O_2]_{c.s.}$), the existence of an instantaneous
equilibrium between the intercellular O_2 ($[O_2]_{i.s.}$) and $[O_2]_{c.s.}$
was assumed, in accordance with the hypothesis of our kinetic
model. The value of the equilibrium constant K_1 between
$[O_2]_{c.s.}$ and the corresponding partial pressure of O_2 in the
intercellular space ($PO_{2(i.s.)}$) could therefore be calculated
assuming, according to Burton (1974), the cellular solution to be
a 0.4M sucrose solution:

$$K_1 = [O_2]_{c.s.}/PO_{2(i.s.)} = 1.35 \cdot 10^{-8} \ (mol \cdot kg^{-1} \cdot Pa^{-1})$$

    If one knows, the total amount of O_2 present inside 1 kg of apples and the value of the constant K_1 at different environmental PO_2, it was possible to calculate the corresponding amount of O_2 dissolved in the cellular solution. Assuming the intercellular space ($V_{i.s.}$) to be 21% of the total fruit volume, it was possible to express $[O_2]_{i.s.}$ as a function of $PO_{2(i.s.)}$:

$$[O_2]_{i.s.} = PO_{2(i.s.)} \cdot V_{i.s.}/(w \cdot R \cdot T) = PO_{2(i.s.)} \cdot 0.21/(d \cdot R \cdot T) =$$
$$= 1.02 \cdot 10^{-7} \cdot PO_{2(i.s.)}$$

Combining the two last equations, we could then correlate $[O_2]_{c.s.}$ with $[O_2]_{i.s.}$ and obtain the adimensional constant K_2:

$$K_2 = [O_2]_{c.s.}/[O_2]_{i.s.} = 1.35 \cdot 10^{-8}/1.02 \cdot 10^{-7} = 0.132$$

since $[O_2] = [O_2]_{i.s.} + [O_2]_{c.s.}$, the following equation, giving the amount of O_2 dissolved in the cellular solution as a function of the O_2 which had permeated into the fruit, was obtained:

$$[O_2]_{c.s.} = 0.117 \cdot [O_2]$$

Moreover, knowing the related value of V_{res}, it was then possible to evaluate directly the amount of $[O_2]_{c.s.}$ as a function of the environmental PO_2:

$$[O_2]_{c.s.} = 0.117 \cdot (H_1 \cdot PO_2 - V_{res}/(k_{1,-i} \cdot A)) \qquad \text{[Eq. 5]}$$

If the concentrations of the apple's main constituents (glucose, fructose, sucrose, glucitol and malic acid) do not vary in such a way as to change the total amount of respiratory substrate and therefore the respiration rate, the following equation can be adopted (Michaelis-Menten):

$$V_{res} = k_{res} \cdot [O_2]_{c.s.}/(K_m + [O_2]_{c.s.}) \qquad \text{[Eq. 6]}$$

where k_{res} = product of the kinetic constant and the enzymatic concentration corresponding to the maximum respiration rate ($mol \cdot kg^{-1} \cdot hr^{-1}$); K_m = Michaelis-Menten constant ($mol \cdot kg^{-1}$).

In order to determine k_{res} and K_m, the inverse of the respiration rates ($1/V_{res}$) was plotted as a function of the inverse of the related amounts of O_2 dissolved in the cellular solution ($1/[O_2]_{c.s.}$) (fig. 3):

$$1/V_{res} = K_m/k_{res} \cdot 1/[O_2]_{c.s.} + 1/k_{res}$$

The slope of the straight line obtained by applying the least squares method to these points gives the K_m/k_{res} ratio, while the intercept with the y-axis gives $1/k_{res}$.

The basic equations, variables and values of the constants involved in the hypothesized kinetic model are summarized in Table 1.

When the mass transfer rate is equal to the respiration rate (steady state condition), the following expression is obtained:

$$k_{1,-i} \cdot A \ (H_1 \cdot PO_2 - ([O_2]_{c.s.} + 1/K_2 \cdot [O_2]_{c.s.})) =$$
$$= k_{res} \cdot [O_2]_{c.s.}/(K_m + [O_2]_{c.s.}) \qquad \text{[Eq. 7]}$$

Thus, when one knows the values of the constants involved in this expression, it is possible to calculate the amount of O_2 dissolved in the cellular solution and of other species involved in the model as a function of the adopted PO_2 (fig. 4).

Table 1 - Equations, variables and constants involved in the hypothesized kinetic model.

Basic equations

1) $V_{mt} = V_{res}$ [at steady state]
2) $V_{mt} = k_{-i} \cdot A \cdot (H \cdot PO_2 - [O_2])$
3) $[O_2] = [O_2]_{c.s.} + [O_2]_{i.s.}$
4) $K_2 = [O_2]_{c.s.} / [O_2]_{i.s.}$
5) $V_{res} = k_{res} \cdot [O_2]_{c.s.} / (K_m + [O_2]_{c.s.})$

Variables	Constants
1) V_{mt}	$k_{-i} = 18.7 \pm 1.9 \ [kg \cdot h^{-1} \cdot m^{-2}]$
2) V_{res}	$A = 0.110 \pm 0.003 \ [m^2 \cdot kg^{-1}]$
3) PO_2	$H = 0.14 \pm 0.02 \ [mmol \cdot kg^{-1} \cdot kPa^{-1}]$
4) $[O_2]$	$K_2 = 0.132$
5) $[O_2]_{c.s.}$	$k_{res} = 0.75 \pm 0.06 \ [mmol \cdot kg^{-1} \cdot h^{-1}]$
6) $[O_2]_{i.s.}$	$K_m = 0.021 \pm 0.005 \ [mmol \cdot kg^{-1}]$

This model represents only the first phase of our research project. The relationship of the introduced constants to the temperature, as well as the effect of CO_2 on the respiration rate, are topics which need to be investigated further in order to increase the range of applicability of the model.

Acknowledgement

Research supported by National Research Council of Italy, Special Project RAISA, Sub-project 4, Paper N. 306.

References

Andrich, G., R. Fiorentini, A. Tuci, and C. Galoppini, 1989a, J. Am. Soc. Hort. Sci., 114, 5, 770-775.
Andrich, G., R. Fiorentini, A. Tuci, and A. Zinnai, 1989b, Ital. J. Food Sci., 1, 2, 35-43.
Andrich, G., R. Fiorentini, C. Galoppini, A. Tuci, G. Sommovigo, and A. Zinnai, 1990, Lebensm. Wiss. u. Technol., 23, 162-164.
Andrich, G., R. Fiorentini, A. Tuci, A. Zinnai, and G. Sommovigo, 1991, J. Am. Soc. Hort. Sci., 116, 3, 478-481.
Burton, W.G., 1974, Ann. Appl. Biol., 78, 149-168.

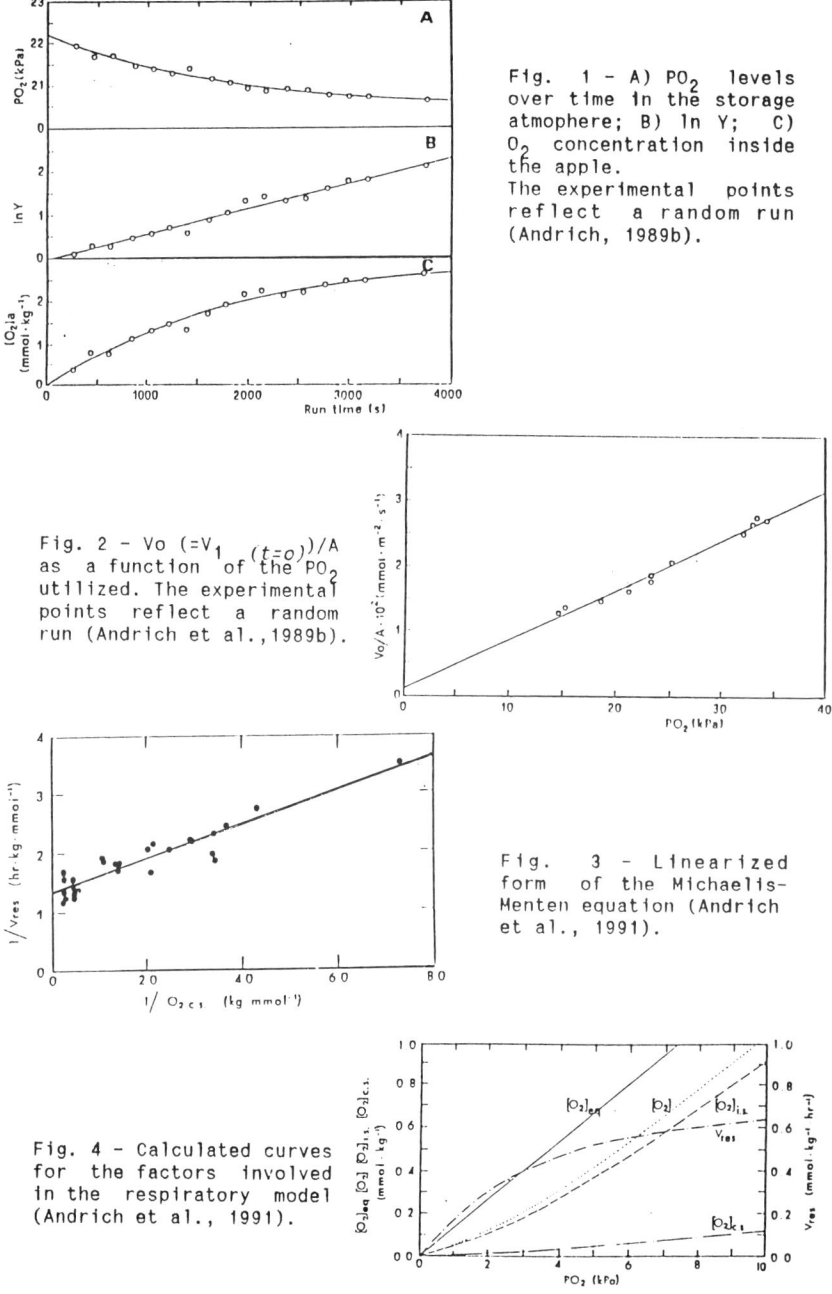

Fig. 1 - A) PO_2 levels over time in the storage atmophere; B) ln Y; C) O_2 concentration inside the apple.
The experimental points reflect a random run (Andrich, 1989b).

Fig. 2 - Vo (=V_1 $(t=0)$)/A as a function of the PO_2 utilized. The experimental points reflect a random run (Andrich et al.,1989b).

Fig. 3 - Linearized form of the Michaelis-Menten equation (Andrich et al., 1991).

Fig. 4 - Calculated curves for the factors involved in the respiratory model (Andrich et al., 1991).

COMPUTER INTEGRATION AND PROGRAMMABLE AUTOMATION IN THE U.K. MILLING AND BAKING
INDUSTRIES

W. A. Livesley and P. I. Maris

The objective of the paper is to examine the findings of a six month study into
the use of Computer Integrated Manufacturing (CIM) and Programmable
Automation (PA) in the Milling and Baking Industries. This was carried out by
the Flour Milling and Baking Research Association, in conjunction with the
Cranfield Institute of Technology,

To provide a common understanding of the terms used within the paper, a
background introduction to CIM and PA is first presented. The survey results
are then presented, sector by sector. Details include the number and type of
companies visited but only general conclusions are drawn, using the common
format provided by the methodologies outlined above, concerning the
current state of CIM and PA for each of the sectors. The general conclusion
of the paper is that the use of CIM and PA within the industry is likely to
increase, although slowly.

1. INTRODUCTION

1.1 Scope

The objective of this paper is to discuss the current state, and potential, of Computer Integrated
Manufacturing (CIM) and Programmable Automation (PA) in the Milling and Baking industries. The
current state of CIM and PA has been investigated during the course of a six month study carried out
by the Flour Milling and Baking Research Association (FMBRA), in conjunction with Cranfield
Institute of Technology (CIT), on behalf of the Ministry of Agriculture, Fisheries and Food.

Prior to the examining the findings of this report a common understanding of the terms CIM and PA
must be established. Whilst many definitions of CIM and PA exist most are sector specific;
concerned principally with the Engineering industries. More generic definitions are, therefore,
required. These can only describe the scope of the survey and suitable models, which can be used
as the standards for the description and comparison of CIM and PA installations, must also be
developed.

The findings of the survey are reported, sector by sector, using the developed models and
definitions.

General conclusions are reached concerning the current and future use of the technologies in the
milling and baking sectors.

1.2 A Definition of CIM

One method of analysing a manufacturing organisation is to attempt to classify different views of the
organisation. At its most fundamental, CIM is the attempt to relate such views through the
organisation of data, information technology and management. A more prosaic definition of CIM can
be provided by a slight alteration to the definition proposed by Conway[1]. The result is that CIM may
be defined as:-

· The integration and automation of a manufacturing enterprise through the use of Information
Technology

This interpretation suggests that the fundamental concepts of integrated manufacturing are integration and automation and that the fundamental technology of integrated manufacturing is Information Technology.

Integration is concerned with giving members of an enterprise the tools to make necessary and appropriate decisions. Such decisions should be made in line with the strategy of the enterprise; benefiting the whole rather than a single part. Information must, therefore, be presented in such a way that not only its contents but also its context, and thus, implications, can be assessed. A suitable definition of integration is, therefore:-

- The promotion of organisational synergy through the provision of a pervasive information system supporting recognisable information models

Automation initiates and controls the necessary operations to allow user decisions' to be implemented. A suitable definition of automation is, therefore:-

- The appropriate control of resources so that the right resource is in the right state at the right time

Automation may be further sub-divided into two processes. The first process identifies the type, states and dependencies of the resources needed to implement a decision. This process is essentially an off-line decision support process which includes the element of design. The second process uses the specifications provided by the first process to implement on-line decisions. This is essentially a logistics process.

Figure 1 shows a CIM model with automation and integration forming the two of the ordinates of the CIM structure. Automation is presented in the form of the decision support and logistics processes described above. Integration is also presented in its component parts. The first is the technology used to pass information between resources, including people, within the enterprise. Management, the second part is the process used to give the context, and thus meaning, to the information supplied to members of the enterprise.

Within the two automation strands described above it is useful to be able to relate the component to their support of organisational activities. This may be achieved by defining the following vertical integration layers:-

- Layer 1: Embedded Systems

- Layer 2: Machine Monitoring and Interfacing Systems

- Layer 3: Line Management Systems

- Layer 4: Site Systems

- Layer 5: Corporate Systems

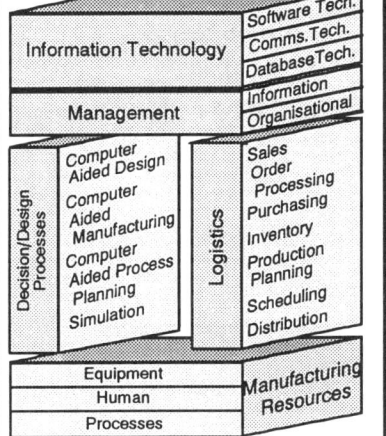

Figure 1: A CIM Model

2. SURVEY DETAILS

2.1 Introduction

The objective of the survey was to establish the level of use of PA and CIM techniques in the milling and baking industries. The survey was intended to provide the following:-

- An assessment of the current level of CIM and PA

- An assessment of the current interest in, and awareness of, CIM and PA

- Suggestions concerning the further application of CIM and PA to the industry, particularly where such techniques exist in other industries

- An assessment of the likely impact on the competitiveness of the industry; in improvements to production efficiency, hygiene, manufacturing flexibility, and product consistency; where relevant

2.2   Biscuits

2.2.1 Survey Scope

Six companies were visited - two from major groups, three medium sized companies and one small company.

2.2.2 Survey Findings

The survey showed that, in general, the industry was aware of the principles, and potential benefits, of CIM. However, the general level of CIM implementation was low and few companies had a policy of investment in CIM. Most of the current systems exist as stand-alone packages concentrating on isolated areas of production management or control. One of the companies visited, however, had a biscuit line controlled by an integrated computer system and is pursuing an active policy of implementing a comprehensive, vertically-integrated, computer management system.

Most of the companies visited were using equipment controlled by Programmable Logic Controllers; as most modern equipment is fitted with PLC control. The level of PA varied from simple sequencing to complex, multi-function control and the two major areas of PA were the computerised weighing of main ingredients and the wrapping and palletising operations. None of the companies interviewed expressed dissatisfaction with the introduction of PA in the form of PLC's.

In general most companies had sporadic implementation of Layer 1. A small number of companies had implemented Layers 1 and 2, and some had implemented systems conforming to Layers 4 and 5. None of the manufacturing lines visited had linked any of the Layers, except 1 and 2. One of the companies visited claimed to have linked a number of Layers, and a number of companies visited were investigating the possibility of further vertical integration.

2.2.3 Survey Conclusions

The industry is currently undergoing a shift in its market requirements. Previously, the market required a small number of low value, high volume, product lines; such items as cram cracker, rich tea and digestive biscuits. The market is now shifting to higher value products, often with coatings and fillings. The shift in the market means that biscuit manufacturers' are producing a greater variety of higher value products with high cost ingredients. Whilst products have a long shelf life, reducing the procure on scheduling lines, there are still problems with tracking products to maintain stock levels. The major pressure will, however, be to introduce product flexibility into manufacturing lines whilst tightening process control; increasing product quality and controlling product cost. It is unlikely that this will be possible with current operating practices which give operators little information concerning plant operation.

It was concluded that the introduction of complete CIM systems is unlikely in the near future. Much of the present plant is unsuited for integration and most integration projects are concerned with new lines. Many companies are investing in the integration of management functions (Layers 4 and 5) and this trend is likely to increase as the benefits become more widely understood. It is suggested that within 5 years several biscuit lines will be integrated with management systems. It is thought that a much longer time scale, between 10 and 20 years, will be required for the industry to be integrated as a whole.

It is unlikely that any investment will occur in flexible automation. However, it is suggested that PA will increase as the understanding of the manufacturing processes allows comprehensive control of the manufacturing operation.

2.3 Bread

2.3.1 Survey Scope

Twelve sites were visited - four of major groups, six of medium size companies and two of small companies.

2.3.2 Survey Findings

It was found that small bakeries consider that CIM would be unsuitable for their requirements. Larger companies, with experience of CIM and PA, expressed satisfaction with their current systems and, in general, were considering further investment. Larger companies with little CIM experience were less enthusiastic. Whilst many of the companies visited used a main-frame computer to perform financial, and sales tasks none of these was integrated with production tasks. In general, the level of CIM implementation among the companies visited was low.

As in the biscuit sector, the principle use of PA was in the PLC control of individual equipment. Although a number of integrated lines exist, most of the PLC controlled equipment operates as isolated islands. Two areas where PLC's are in widest use include the supply, handling and mixing of major ingredients and the wrapping and palletising of products. No flexible automation was used.

It can be concluded that little integration exists in the industry. There was sporadic implementation of Layer 1 technology, and a small number of examples of linking to Layer 2. One example exists of a Layer 1 through 3 implementation. Most of the larger groups had Layer 5 and 6 technology, although this tended to be more useful as a group, rather than an individual site, resource.

2.3.3 Survey Conclusions

In general the bread manufacturing plants are highly mechanised and operate smoothly. The market is reasonably static with minor fluctuations. Lines operate large batch manufacture with little physical change between batches. Whilst the cost of many of the ingredients is low, the ingredient cost represents a large part of the overall product cost. However, many of the companies visited had little direct control of the manufacturing process; relying on operator skill to optimise plant performance. This problem is accentuated by the compressed time schedule imposed by the product retailer. The introduction of process control would, therefore, provide quality and ingredient usage benefits but would also assist in the fulfilment of the daily production schedule.

The introduction of CIM would require some change to existing plant. It is thought unlikely, therefore, that CIM will be introduced in the short term as most plant has an extended life span. Similarly, many areas would also benefit from the introduction of PA; demonstrated by the success of the small number of plants using PA.

2.4 Confectionery

2.4.1 Survey Scope

Seven sites were visited - four of major groups, and three of single site bakeries. The companies involved in the survey account for 60% of the total production of flour confectionery.

2.4.2 Survey Findings

In general, little interest was expressed in CIM and PA in this sector. The companies expressing interest were those operating multiple sites who had more experience with CIM and PA technology. Most of the companies visited used main-frames to implement finance and sales functions. A small number of sites also had extensive line control facilities, implemented using either PLC's or specially developed controllers. Whilst none of these systems was fully integrated with the management information systems, one company was in the process of investing in a comprehensive vertically-integrated CIM system.

The use of PA was more extensive in this sector, particularly where expensive ingredients required careful process control. Little flexible automation was used.

This sector had a number of examples of Layer 1 and 2 technology and some companies also used Layer 6 technology. A small number of companies were investigating a comprehensive system integrating all of the Layers.

2.4.3 Survey Conclusions

The flour confectionery industry is, generally, based on small batch, high value, low persistence products manufactured with a high proportion of manual labour. Whilst the industry has many staple products, other products are being continually introduced. The high level of manual labour reflects both the complexity and the high mix of products and the low value of any one product line. However, the nature of the ingredients imposes particular hygienic manufacturing constraints.

A proportion of the industry's products; the longer life, lower value products; are suitable for export; demonstrated by the recent penetration of German, French and Italian products into this country. These are the product areas where the introduction of CIM and PA is most likely. However, it is accepted that many of the product lines are unsuited for automation. These areas demonstrate many of the classic "Job Shop" behaviours where other industries have found CIM to be of considerable assistance. Whilst the value of each product line is low, the value of the products manufactured is high and it is suggested that potential exists for further investigation of these problems.

In general, it was concluded that, although a number of CIM systems would shortly be installed, most of the industry is unlikely to introduce CIM in the near future. This reflects the widespread lack of interest within the industry.

2.5 Milling

2.5.1 Survey Scope

The following companies were visited:-

Major Groups	2
Independents	3

2.5.2 Survey Findings

All of the companies visited showed a well developed awareness of the principals and potential benefits of CIM and PA; present in all sites. Each site, or mill, had a controller performing tasks in Layers 1 through 4; taking the form of a PLC in the most recent mills although many of the original dedicated computer controllers are still in use. All of the milling companies use computers to perform financial and sales functions, and a number of companies also have a computerised quality monitoring function.

None of the companies visited had integrated the site controller with the higher level control functions. However, although not visited in the survey, it is known that there a four mills within the U.K. able to operate for prolonged periods without human attendance. It is understood that these directly interface into corporate computer systems, providing examples of comprehensive layer 1 through 5 systems.

The milling sector had a number of examples of flexible automation.

2.5.3 Survey Conclusions

Most of the problems caused within mills are process, not market, derived. In general, these are caused by variation in the ingredient characteristics and the slow response of quality monitoring systems. The use of CIM and PA has reduced the manning levels in the mills and allowed mill operators to optimise other, less profitable, aspects of their business. The milling sector exhibits a high level of CIM and PA usage. However, only the most modern implementations exhibit the necessary level of flexibility required for by a successful control system. The current level of PA within mills is limited by the available on-line sensors. In general, the milling industry is satisfied with its current CIM and automation products. It is likely that within the next five years, most of the U. K. mills will be fully automated.

3. COMMENTS AND CONCLUSIONS

3.1 Comments

When examining the milling and baking industries, it is possible to identify some of the features upon which the success of a particular plant, or line, depend. These can be directly related to some of the strategic benefits of CIM.

Such benefits can be defined as:-

- Quality: Quality within the industry would appear to mean that each product must be of the highest quality obtainable from a defined recipe. This requirement can be fulfilled by the implementation of process control. Unfortunately, many of the processes used within the industry are not well understood, and many processes that are understood lack suitable sensors to provide the necessary control information. A CIM system would at least provide the infrastructure necessary to collect and store line data, and later to process the data to allow informed decisions to be made concerning process failure. This would act as the basis of any future process control system.

- Production Control: In most of the industry sectors, production control is currently implemented at a plant level using a long term plan. This is because the market demand is predictable and because the goods produced have a long shelf life. In some sectors, however, the demand, whilst generally predictable, fluctuates daily. In addition, some of the sectors have a daily delivery schedule which can become quite complex. A CIM system would provide the data necessary to schedule the production requirements and to update the schedule in real time when required. Such a scheduling system would increase the efficiency of the manufacturing plant as well as relieving the plant managers of a complex task.

- Data Compression: One of the major complaints of those companies with existing computerised systems was that too much data was supplied and it was often the wrong type of data. Given the IM definition of providing the right information to the right person at the right time, a CIM system should streamline the reports to providing sufficient, but not excessive data.

- Traceability: The industry will shortly be required to provide product traceabilty. The data collection, storage and retrieval required to implement traceability would be implemented automatically using a CIM system.

- Hygienic Manufacturing: All food manufacturers wish to remove human operators from direct contact with the food. Without control of the automation required to manufacture food products, human operators will still be needed to adjust and control machines. A CIM system should allow the automation of most of these tasks; leaving humans only in a supervisory rôle.

The above describes some of the strategic benefits which could be achieved in the food industry by implementing CIM. Further benefits, such as the isolation of poor suppliers, would also be possible.

3.2   Conclusions

The above discussion on CIM and PA identifies one major theme, that CIM implementation is an organic process whose objective is to spur company growth through the promotion of organisational and operational synergy. Therefore, to support CIM systems must be flexible and extensible. Many of the systems seen within the industry have been developed with a specific requirement and are difficult to change. It is only recent systems, and particularly those implemented in the milling sector, that have the necessary flexibility. The industry must, therefore, learn to identify, and value, design flexibility.

The other general conclusion that can be reached is that investors in CIM are more likely to re-invest than are those with little or no CIM investment. It was particularly noticeable that those with current CIM systems had a high level of interest and enthusiasm in the subject.

The specific conclusions that can be reached are:-

- · The milling and baking industries have a small number of examples of mature CIM developments

- · The number of such developments is likely to increase, although slowly

- · Much of the industry remains unconvinced about the benefits of CIM and PA

- · It is possible to demonstrate some specific benefits that CIM and PA will bring to the industry

ACKNOWLEDGEMENTS

This paper has been prepared with the assistance of the Ministry of Agriculture, Fisheries and Food under the Grant Number. The authors would also like to thank the participating companies for their hospitality during the survey.

---

1   Conway J.; 'What's in a Name: Plain Talk about CIM'; CIME, Vol. 4, No. 3, pp. 23 - 31;1985

Computer Modelling/Simulation in the Food Industry

Richard V. Hardwick - Technical Manager
AMEC Design and Management Limited

The simulation of a single process or a complete food
plant activity - existing or proposed - is an essential
tool for the designer; a must for the user; a bonus for
the Board.

Computer Modelling/Simulation in the Food Industry

As manufacturing and distribution equipment becomes more technically
sophisticated, and the financing of capital projects more restricting, the
demands placed on the system designer are increased. No more can the
designer add factors for 'just-in-case' events. No more will company
directors and shareholders tolerate equipment being under-utilised in terms
of its optimum capabilities.

Simulation provides a tool for the designer to:

a) Develop a system design
b) 'Prove' a system's capabilities
c) Give the client(s) an unprecedented level of confidence and understanding

What is Modelling/Simulation

The Oxford Dictionary defines simulation as:

"an imitation of the conditions of a situation".

Today almost all models/simulations are computer based. We may re-define
simulation as:

"a representation of a series of inter-related activities each of which can
be expressed as mathematical algorithms and computed in a defined
sequence".

Computer based simulation programs generally fall into one of two categories:

    i)   Time based – in which the algorithms are computed at pre-determined intervals of time. In simpler terms, the status of every element in the system is re-established at fixed time intervals.

   ii)   Event based – in which each event duration is continuously monitored and the status of the system re-established when an event ends or re-starts.

What can Simulation Do

As experience in the use of simulation models grows so does the range of applications. Some examples are given below:

+ Batch production plants
+ Continuous manufacturing processes
+ Materials handling
+ Storage and warehousing systems
+ Customer services
+ Vehicle throughput and traffic movement

In fact, any situation where entities (products, customers, containers, fluids, etc.) have a time related dependency on finite resources (machinery, labour, facilities) can be modelled.

What You Need

In order to simulate a system the designer must undertake the following steps:

    i)   Understand the system – the simulation designer must gain a detailed knowledge of the system, and in particular what events trigger other events. In short, WHAT happens? WHEN does it happen? and WHY does it happen?

   ii)   Construct a logic diagram – an essential, and often arduous task. The logic diagram incorporates all activities in a system and their inter-relationships. The preparation of this chart in itself leads to a greater understanding of the systems operation.

  iii)   Obtain perforamnce data – the acronym GIGO (garbage in, garbage out) is particularly relevant. Accurate information is essential if the simulation is to represent the 'real' situation.

   iv)   A simulation program – an obvious requirement. Care should be taken to select a program that meets your requirements. Generally, a program that allows you to represent a system in detail will require a greater knowledge of programming and be more expensive than a simpler 'block' simulation program requiring fewer skills but providing less detailed results.

        The cost of employing more sophisticated simulation programs and the necessary expertise to programme and operate them, as well as the knowledge to interpret the results accurately and in a satisfactory way, is financially prohibitive to many companies.

After all, once the project is complete the company may have no
further need of these resources. Consequently, the use of
consultants, such as AMEC Design and Management Ltd. Engineering
Division is more productive and cost effective.

What are the Benefits

'Real' benefits gained by using simulation are illustrated in the
following examples:

1. To provide working models of manufacturing, warehousing and
   distribution systems at an early stage of their design in order to
   predict their manner of operation and behaviour under a variety of
   conditions.

2. To assist in the evaluation of alternative options or equipment
   solutions.

3. The process of developing the logic for a simulation can also provide
   a sound structure for the design of the control system.

4. To identify and find means of relieving system limitations such as
   bottlenecks and critical throughput capacities.

5. To generate statistical perforamnce data such as resource
   utilisation and path time through the system.

6. To identify buffer stock capacities as an aid to specifying space
   requirements and to assist in layout design.

7. To define production rates and customer service times under varying
   resource availabilities and labour levels.

8. Predicting and managing inventories and work in progress levels under
   varying production schedule strategies and batch sizes.

9. Allow "what if" tests to be run to determine the effect on the system,
   and the counter-measures recommended in the event of a machine
   breakdown, or labour shortage.

10. Animated displays generate more interest and add much more confidence
    to a proposed scheme. A simulation model therefore has great value
    as a sales tool or at management meetings, seminars or exhibitions.

11. Bringing vital understanding to larger projects where complex
    interactions have to be encountered by the flow of the items.

12. Testing new proposals without interrupting current production.

What Does Simulation Cost

There are few benefits to owning a simulation package unless a company is
large enough, or its operations so complex, to use it repeatedly. The
simulation package is a small proportion of the total cost of a
simulation resource which must incorporate continuous staff training,
software upgrading and programming experience.

It is generally more cost effective for a company to employ consultancy services, either of the company supplying the simulation, or a company which provides design engineering services and uses simulation for the reasons given previously.

A Cautionary Tale

The attraction of a high definition, animiated graphic simulation of his, or her, manufacturing process may lead the purchaser into a number of pitfalls. Issues to be considered include the following:

+ Simulation packages are NOT design tools. As a minimum a preliminary design must exist.

+ All logical interactions between all elements of a system must be incorporated into the simulation for it to be truly representative.

+ Output data must provide useful information.

+ Writing a simulation program can take a considerable amount of time and cannot be rushed.

+ Animated graphics may be superfluous to the simulation programmer, but of immeasurable value to the user. Graphics should be realistic and informative.

THE EFFECTS OF SAMPLING ON THE CALIBRATION OF ON-LINE GAUGES

Michael J Scott   Infrared Engineering Limited

Introduction

The food industry is late in embracing advanced automation and it has immediate access to powerful data processing and control techniques already routinely used in the Hydrocarbons industry.

The limiting factor in process control is the quality and appropriateness of the process measurement and this is particularly true in the food industry with the natural variability of the feed material and the long time constants of the process.

Most of the food industry is comfortable with measurements being made on infrequent samples with an interval of several hours between taking the sample and the result being available. With the need to tighten product quality, change recipes and products quickly and to minimise waste high specification, on line measurements are a vital input to the management and control computer systems. The ingredients and final product streams being measured are often difficult to handle, sticky, powdery, multi-phase, non-homogeneous stratified, unstable materials and yet we need to make analytical measurements such as protein, fat or moisture content in real time and to make multi-variable control decisions.

The purpose of this paper is to suggest that even when an analytical technique has been turned into a successful industrial on-line measurement considerable difficulties still exist in calibrating and validating the measurement. It is suggested that the pacing function for the development of advanced control for food production is the ability to determine the performance of the on-line analysers and that sampling is the major contributing factor. On line moisture measurement will be used to explore some of the issues involved and then the measurement and control of protein in a flour mill will be used as a practical example of the validation of an on-line analyser.

Sampling

To validate an on-line moisture gauge we must sample what the sensor is measuring and there is more to this than just synchronising the sensor reading with the sample taking:-

1.   Most product streams are not equilibrated and the matrix problem must be understood if a meaningful sample is to be collected. This is frequently made more difficult because samples cannot be obtained from under gauges. Flour may be measured via a window in a chute or potato chips may be measured immediately at the exit of an oven where it is difficult to safely take a sample.

2.   The gauge will have a 'viewing time' and it will integrate readings over this period and, since the process will almost certainly vary over the integration period, the sample must be organised to reflect the material the gauge viewed when its reading was taken.

     These considerations will, in the case of a Near Infrared gauge (NIR), need to include patch size and depth of product that the particular gauge measures and together with line speed, a calculation of product volume measured can be made. Ideally the sample will actually be the same material that the gauge saw but in a practical production environment this is rarely possible.

3.   It is essential that the dynamics of the process are understood and that, as far as possible, samples are only taken while the process is steady.

4.   Having obtained the samples, great care must be taken to preserve them in the on-line state. Products such as biscuits or paper can absorb moisture at several percent per minute. Fig 1 shows how fast a piece of paper changes if its moisture level is different to the ambient moisture level. Notice also the hysteresis of the stable moisture level. It is therefore vital that the samples are placed in dry air-tight plastic bags as quickly as possible.

Process plant managers and operators are frequently surprised at the short-term variability of their production process and having got used to controlling the process with infrequent samples that take several hours to be analysed, often initially reject an on-line analyser when it shows surprising process variations.

5. To partially separate the on-line analyser performance from the sampling and reference technique performance, each sample should be split into three or more parts and the spread on the replicates determined by separate analysis. It is also advisable to retain samples and submit them blind at a later stage of the calibration work.

If we assume a sample patch of 25mm diameter and an effective penetration depth of a few tenths of a millimetre, the instantaneous sample measured is only a few hundred micrograms for a conventional laboratory NIR analyser. A gravimetric oven drying reference method uses a few grammes and the user hopes that either or both of these represents perhaps a few tonnes passing on the production line.

The on-line analyser with the above patch size and penetration depth makes many instantaneous measurements as the product passes; it can very from a few samples per second up to many hundreds per second. The on-line analyser can be set to a short response time and show the short term variation or it may be set to average over a longer period; say ten seconds.

Calibration

The on-line gauge reading will obviously be significantly more representative of the product being produced than an infrequent sample taken for a laboratory analyser. However, conventional wisdom is that the laboratory analyser is the reference measurement and it is frequently judged to have no inaccuracy. Fig 2 and 3 are a summary of several months of work evaluating an NIR on-line analyser, used in an at-line mode, against a conventional gravimetric oven drying technique. Fig 2 shows cumulative data of the NIR analyser against an oven and Fig 3 shows the same data but with two ovens plotted against each other. It seems reasonable to claim that up to about 18% moisture the two graphs are extremely similar. In fact the difference at the top end is due to a particular product in the broad range of products being tested. These results were produced by skilled people over a period of months with a broad range of types of product under test. The appearance of a single set of short term tests as shown in Fig 4 is more familiar and although the narrow band of results makes them appear to be superior the absolute accuracy may be no better.

A simple understanding of statistics shows that to perform a credible calibration a number of samples must be taken at each point over a reasonable span and all passed through an identical reference calibration procedure.

A real set of results collected by a User is shown in Fig 5. The results were taken so as to compare the results of two on-line gauges and since the tests were all done in a short period by one group of people using common resources we can ignore the 'operator variability' part of the picture. The plots include both short-term variations in the process and the combined effects of on-line analyser performance and sampling and reference technique errors. It is immediately obvious that one of the analysers makes a significant contribution to the spread of results and a judgement could be made on that basis, but it is also obvious that both analysers read about 1% high and presumably the User investigated the implications of the piece of information.

It would be expected that the analysers would read low because the oven reference techniques used measures volatiles as well as moisture and would give a falsely high result. The fact that the User plotted only these results, is also interesting, because the spread of results is too narrow to make any judgement at all about the analysers' ability to respond to changes in process moisture.

As already noted above, to calibrate an on-line analyser it is necessary to obtain results over a reasonable part of the calibrated range yet production management is, quite reasonably, dedicated to running the process at an optimal value and does not take kindly to running out of specification and producing scrap.

Removing material from the process line and treating it to achieve a suitable range of moistures is an interesting way of achieving a preliminary calibration for the analyser, but rarely replicates the actual process conditions and can be misleading.

Having thoroughly analysed the relationship between the samples and the on-line analyser reading, it is essential that the significance of the reference techniques results are carefully considered before the calibration of the on-line analyser is changed. Failure to do this may lead to calibration hunting since the apparent need for change may be inside the random variations caused by the overall calibration circumstances because On-line moisture gauges have now reached the stage where their inherent accuracy is at least equal to the reference methods available to validate their accuracy.

Protein measurement

To validate the effectiveness of an on-line analyser and to demonstrate some of the techniques required, Infrared Engineering, the Flour Milling and Baking Research Association (FMBRA) and Greens Flour Mill in Maldon, Essex co-operated in the evaluation of an on-line analyser measuring the protein of the Mill's final flour output and the control of the gluten to achieve target protein levels.

Figure 6 shows a schematic representation of a protein measurement and gluten control system.

To evaluate the performance objectively data was collected during a number of routine production runs. These assessment runs included the system working the gluten addition in automatic operation and with the gluten addition switched off.

While the data was being collected production runs were fully monitored by a member of the FMBRAobserving the system in operation. The system was monitored over a period of at least 4 hours on each of three days and at least three grist changeovers were included on each day. Data was collected every 30 seconds by selecting the 'print' facility in the control unit thereby enabling a printout of gauge data (calculated over a 10s period). A chart recorder was used to record the 'gluten required' and the 'gluten actually added' signals. At the start of the production run or grist changeover, the time and target protein value were recorded.

Flour samples were collected at intervals throughout each assessment run and the protein content determined (in duplicate) by Kjeldahl analysis (Flour Testing Panel Method No. FTP 0009) at the FMBRA. Removal of the slide covering a port located immediately below the glass window in the main product chute enabled 500g samples to feed by gravity to a hand-held plastic sample receiver. These samples were taken over a 10s duration to coincide with a MM55 protein content reading over the same period. The close physical location of the port to the glass window, ensured that the sample collected for Kjeldahl analysis was representative of that passing the sensing head.

Because each production run included changeover periods it was necessary to identify the start and finish of individual grists. This process was complicated by the complex nature of the Millflow and the time delay before new grist flour reached the sensing head. It was necessary, therefore, to consult Millstaff to establish the length of production runs and the time at which each new wheat grist was fed to the Mill. At the beginning of each new grist recording commenced when the protein measurements were within 0.1% of the target protein value.

The duration of the runs varied from 11 min to just under 3 hours. Each run produced a single flour type at a single target protein content. Seven flour types (including two brown flours) with a range of protein contents and a range of gluten additions were used.

The results of the assessment runs are given in Tables 1 and 2. Table 1 gives the means and standard deviations of the individual 10 second measurements for each of the unsupplemented (no gluten) flour runs and therefore shows the natural variability of the protein content in the flour. The standard deviation of the differences between the recorded values and the target varied between 0.04% and 0.33% with an average value of 0.2%.

Table 2 gives the corresponding data for the supplemented flour. With the gluten addition in automatic operation (Table 2), the standard deviation of differences were much reduced, having an average value for the nine runs of 0.07%. The means were very close to the target values on all occasions, and within the natural variation of the grist. The mean deviation averaged over the nine runs is -0.027%.

Fig 7 shows a plot of the Kjeldahl and MM55 protein contents for thirty five flour samples. A listing of the individual readings together with their target values is given in the appendix.

Fig 7 also shows the calibration line fitted to the data by the method of least squares, and given by the equation:

Kjeldahl protein = -0.59 + 1.08 x IREprotein
(Correlation coefficient (r) = 0.989;
Standard deviation of IREreading = 0.13%

and, for comparison, the ideal 45 degree line on which all the data points would lie in the absence of error. A comparison of the slopes of these two lines indicates that the calibration is skewed, i.e. the points are becoming increasingly further away from the ideal line with increasing MM55 protein content. The skewness does not affect the usefulness of the measurement, as shown by the results, but it does demonstrate the point being made in this paper. The residual standard deviation from the regression corrected for skewness was 0.15%.

The control function of the MM55 gluten control system can be assessed by comparing the mean protein content achieved with the target protein value (Table 2). The average difference between achieved and target protein content was 0.02%, and the maximum difference was -0.15%.

Analysis of the flour samples for Kjeldahl in blind duplicate (data not shown) enabled an estimation of the repeatability of the technique to be made. This was calculated to be 0.13% protein. The accuracy of the on-line gauge and the reference technique are therefore of the same order of magnitude.

Without such a gluten control system the extent of variation in the final flour, shown in Table 1, would typically be found in the results for gluten addition production runs based on the principle of adding a fixed amount of gluten. To be sure of achieving the minimum acceptable protein content at all times the average amount of gluten added would be unnecessarily high. The function of such a control system is to save the expensive component by only adding the minimum as dictated by the constantly changing operational circumstances.

Conclusions

It can be seen that calibrating an on-line analyser is not a simple exercise and will frequently require off-site resources or skills. Both the moisture and the protein measurements discussed above indicate that the on-line analyser has an accuracy which is similar to the reference calibration and the controlling factor on the on-line measurement validation is the quality of the sampling technique and of the sample handling.

Acknowledgements

Acknowledgements are due to FMBRAfor permission to use a significant part of the report published in the January issue of their Digest. Greens Flour Millhave been very supportive in the evaluation work and thanks are also due to Infrared Engineering management for permission to publish this paper.

Figure 1

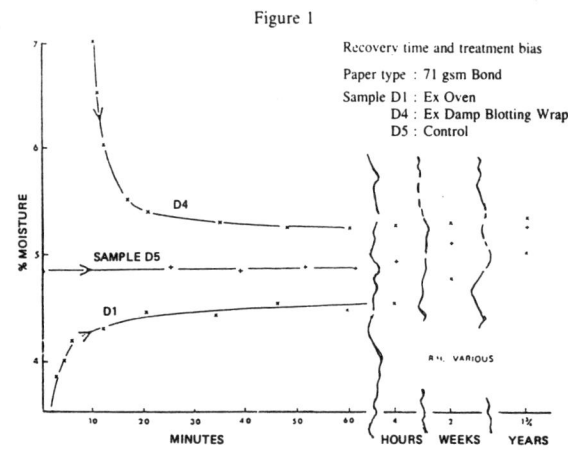

Recovery time and treatment bias

Paper type : 71 gsm Bond

Sample D1 : Ex Oven
D4 : Ex Damp Blotting Wrap
D5 : Control

Figure 2

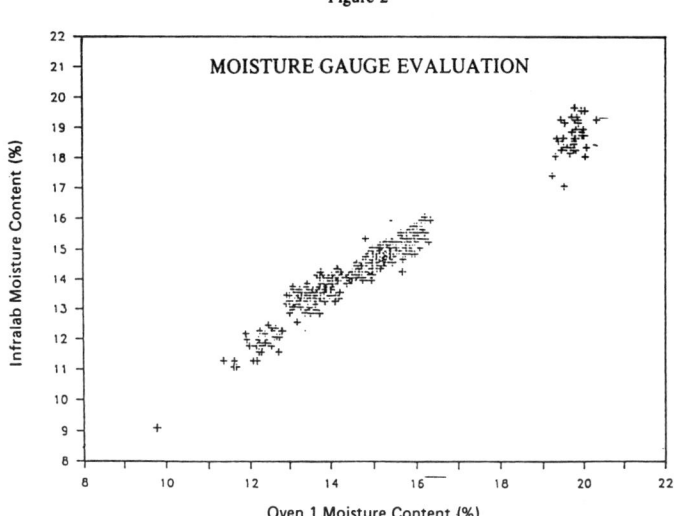

Figure 3

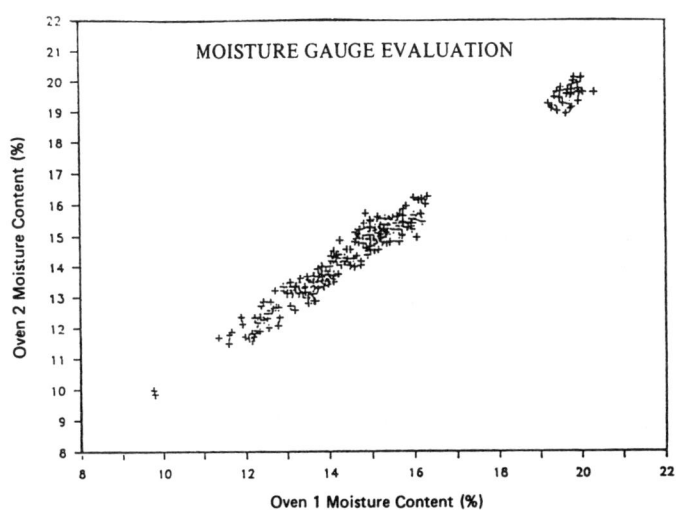

MOISTURE GAUGE EVALUATION

Figure 4

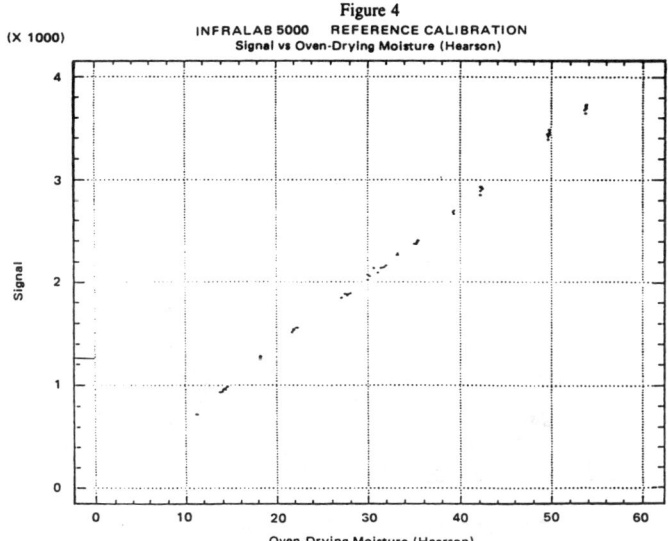

Figure 5

Sample Average

· Analyser 'A'
+ Infrared TM55

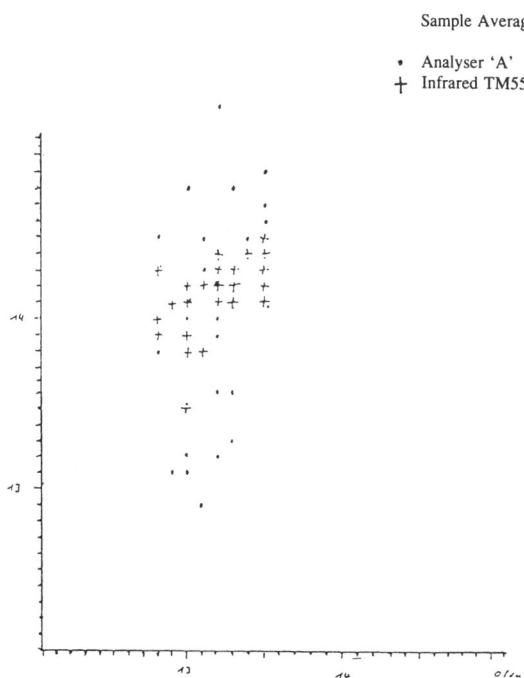

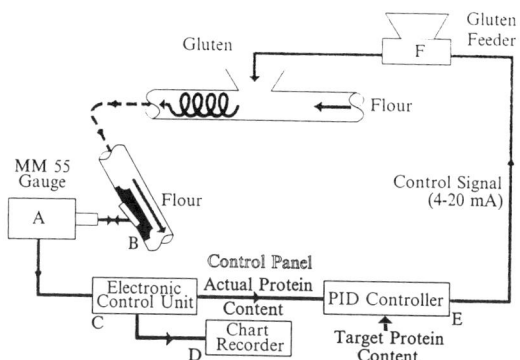

Fig. 6 Schematic diagram of gluten control system

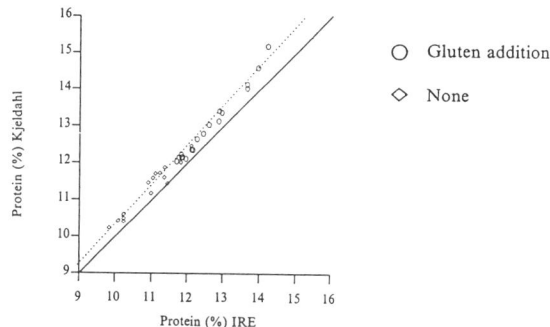

Fig. 7 Plot of Kjeldahl versus IRE protein contents for thirty-five samples of flour
_____ ideal 45° line   .... fitted calibration line

Sample No.	MM55 protein (%) as is	Kjeldahl protein (%) as is*	Difference**
1	9.79	10.05	-0.26
2	10.17	10.35	-0.18
3	10.22	10.40	-0.18
4	10.23	10.35	-0.12
5	10.25	10.55	-0.30
6	10.82	11.30	-0.48
7	10.93	11.40	-0.47
8	10.95	11.05	-0.10
9	11.03	11.55	-0.52
10	11.18	11.55	-0.37
11	11.25	11.45	-0.20
12	11.30	11.30	0.00
13	11.32	11.75	-0.43
14	11.68	12.05	-0.37
15	11.69	12.15	-0.46
16	11.73	12.20	-0.48
17	11.75	12.15	-0.40
18	11.75	12.15	-0.40
19	11.78	12.05	-0.27
20	11.80	12.15	-0.35
21	11.91	12.10	-0.19
22	12.07	12.35	-0.28
23	12.08	12.20	-0.12
24	12.09	12.20	-0.11
25	12.22	12.55	-0.33
26	12.41	12.75	-0.34
27	12.50	12.95	-0.45
28	12.81	13.05	-0.24
29	12.82	13.25	-0.43
30	12.88	13.20	-0.32
31	12.88	13.20	-0.32
32	13.53	14.00	-0.42
33	13.59	14.10	-0.51
34	13.89	14.50	-0.61
35	14.07	14.95	-0.88

Comparison of Kjeldahl and MM55 protein content

* mean of two blind duplicates
** IRE - (minus) Kjeldahl.

TABLE 1: Inherent variability of wheat grists

Run No.	Duration (min)	Target (%)	MM55 Protein Measurements	
			Mean difference from target, %	St. dev, %
1	19	10.9	0.01	0.04
2	62	11.9	−0.07	0.14
3	86	10.5	−0.28	0.28
4	11	10.5	0.39	0.33

TABLE 2: Performance of MM55 gluten control system

Run No.	Duration (min)	Target (%)	MM55 Protein Measurements	
			Mean difference from target, %	St. dev, %
1	110	12.8	0.02	0.05
2	11	14.1	−0.11	0.13
3	44	13.5	−0.03	0.06
4	44	12.3	−0.02	0.05
5	41	12.1	−0.02	0.04
6	73	11.7	0.03	0.06
7	48	11.7	0.0	0.05
8	53	11.7	0.01	0.04
*9	172	12.3	−0.15	0.16

* Observer not present during this run

AUTHOR/TITLE/KEYWORD